Founding the Far West

Founding the Far West

California, Oregon, and Nevada,
1840–1890

David Alan Johnson

UNIVERSITY OF CALIFORNIA PRESS
Berkeley   Los Angeles   Oxford

University of California Press
Berkeley and Los Angeles, California

University of California Press, Ltd.
Oxford, England

© 1992 by
The Regents of the University of California

Library of Congress Cataloging-in-Publication Data

Johnson, David Alan, 1950–
    Founding the Far West : California, Oregon, and Nevada, 1840–1890/David Alan
Johnson.
      p.   cm.
    Includes bibliographical references and index.
    ISBN 0-520-07348-7 (alk. paper)
    1. West (U.S.)—Politics and government. 2. West (U.S.)—Economic
conditions. 3. California—Politics and government—1846–1950. 4. California—
Economic conditions. 5. Oregon—Politics and government—To 1859.
6. Oregon—Politics and government—1859–1950. 7. Oregon—Economic
conditions. 8. Nevada—Politics and government. 9. Nevada—Economic
conditions.
    I. Title.
    F593.J59 1992
    979'.02—dc20   91-30434
                                                     CIP

Printed in the United States of America

9 8 7 6 5 4 3 2 1

The paper used in this publication meets the minimum requirements of American
National Standard for Information Sciences—Permanence of Paper for Printed Library
Materials, ANSI Z39.48-1984. ⊗

For My Parents
Margaret E. Johnson
and
Carl B. Johnson
sine qua non

CONTENTS

III • HISTORY AND MEMORY

PREFACE

The writing of this book has followed a circuitous path, and a brief description of that path, I think, will help to clarify my purposes. In 1987 I
put this manuscript aside to work on an intellectual biography of Charles
and Mary Beard. To evaluate the Beards' interpretation of eighteenth-
century politics, I spent a summer reading—and teaching about—the
books and articles that have appeared since World War II on the revolutionary and founding periods of the United States. Faced with presenting this material to inquisitive students, I read widely and closely. I was
somewhat astonished at the sheer volume of books and articles (which
still grows), but more impressive were the substantive and exciting controversies I found. What caught my attention in particular was the emphasis that postwar (especially post-1960) writers have placed on ideology and political culture, the countervailing influences of "classical
republican," "liberal," and other forms of political discourse among the
Americans who mobilized in revolution and then created the United
States. Reading the work of Joyce Appleby, Bernard Bailyn, Isaac Kramnick, Drew McCoy, J.G.A. Pocock, Robert Shalhope, Gordon Wood (to
mention but a few), I was struck by the language of politics—republican,
liberal, and otherwise—that has become the touchstone of scholarly debate. Ironically, these and other scholars' close delineation of the way
eighteenth-century figures reasoned carried my attention away from the
Beards and back to the nineteenth-century men whose lives and thought,
whose societies and political cultures, are the subject of this book.

My encounter with eighteenth-century politics carried me back to the
nineteenth-century Far West because it brought to mind, and then shed
new light on, words and ideas I had encountered in the letters, speeches,
and writings of political figures in California, Oregon, and Nevada. In
the case of the Oregonians, it did so in unanticipated ways. A peculiar

political vocabulary that I had found in both their private communications and public utterances, and that I had dismissed earlier as rhetorical flourishes, took on new meaning (and raised new questions), in that it repeated continually the lexicon of classical republicanism reconstructed by early Americanists. The more I looked, the more I found nineteenth-century Oregonians thinking in a republican "idiom" that had ostensibly dissolved with the "end of classical politics" at the close of the eighteenth century, as Gordon Wood has put it.[1] Loaded concepts such as corruption and virtue, fearful discussions of republican decline and degradation, invidious distinctions between agriculture and commerce, and an ironic critique of parties as instruments of self-interest (ironic because expressed by devoted party men) led me to pay new, and closer, attention to the language and systems of ideas, more generally the intellectual context of debate, around which Oregon politics swirled throughout the territorial and early statehood years. My attention was then drawn to the political ideas that predominated among the Oregonians' nineteenth-century contemporaries in California and Nevada. There I found variations on the different (if not absolutely contradictory) liberal individualist discourse more conventionally associated with the time, the antebellum years of Jacksonian democracy.

In what follows I have attempted to draw out the meaning of my subjects' language, as it shaped not only the writing of state constitutions but also, more broadly, the founding of American societies in California, Oregon, and Nevada. Inasmuch as I propose that distinctive ideologies and political cultures prevailed among neighboring peoples at roughly the same time, I have also tried to explain why Oregonians spoke—and thus conceived—of politics through the anachronistic filter of classical republicanism, whereas in California and Nevada variations on more characteristically nineteenth-century themes prevailed.

This distinction in the political language of men who otherwise shared nationality and a place in time turned my attention outward from politics per se to the social orders established by the first American settlers in the three states. Commonplaces—for example, differences among the California gold rush of 1849, the migration of farming families to Oregon's Willamette Valley in the 1840s and 1850s, and the rush of experienced California miners to the Comstock Lode of Nevada after 1859—took on fresh significance when I considered whether something about these pioneers had stimulated the political vocabularies and, more broadly, political cultures that I found in the three places. My conclusion is yes, and in presenting it in this book I have tried to go beyond ascribing talismanic powers to mining rushes and farming migrations, to draw out the ways migration and environment, culture and resources, intermixed in the founding of the first three American states on the Pacific.

This study focuses on ideology and political culture, and more specifically on the constitution writers of California, Oregon, and Nevada. It therefore goes without saying that I have slighted some important topics, as well as relied on the work of other scholars—in discussions of native American culture and society, the environment, women, racial minorities, and the family, for example. I expect that the lacunae in this book, on these topics and others, will be taken up and rectified by subsequent scholarship; indeed, I hope that I have raised questions that will encourage that wider inquiry.

In approaching my topic I have been particularly mindful of the extensive literature on western territorial history. While I have drawn on this body of scholarship and the example of finely detailed narrative it offers, I see *Founding the Far West* as complementary to rather than a part of it. As Kenneth Owens, among others, has noted, California and Nevada (though not Oregon) existed at the borders of the territorial regime as we know it.[2] Moreover, as I explain more fully in the Introduction, my choice of places originates in my interest in the larger context of nineteenth-century U.S. history—as it was idiosyncratically played out in the Far West—rather than in a desire to present a model of peculiarly western, or "frontier," politics. Bluntly put, I am writing about American history as it took place in the Far West. My premise is that it is as possible to find American (as opposed to strictly "local") history in a place like Nevada as it is in Massachusetts, New York, Pennsylvania, Virginia, or Georgia. To make a play on the well-known phrase of Sam Bass Warner, I am writing as if "all the world *weren't* Philadelphia."

In this enterprise I have accumulated extraordinary intellectual debts, which are evident, partially and inadequately, in the notes. In addition, scores of teachers, friends, and colleagues have assisted me directly. It is a great pleasure to thank them here, and to absolve them of responsibility for the use I have made of the ideas and suggestions they have offered so generously. My greatest intellectual debt is to four people—Joyce Appleby, Bruce Kuklick, Frederick Nunn, and the late Rodman Paul—who with the right measure of enthusiasm and skepticism pushed me to tell the story contained in this book. Their friendship, guidance, and honest criticism have been the richest reward of my career as a historian.

Other friends and colleagues helped me with this book in many ways. Bob Zemsky guided my first attempt to make sense of these materials while I was a graduate student at the University of Pennsylvania. My other teachers at Penn—Drew Faust, Murray Murphey, Rikki Kuklick, Charles Rosenberg, and the late John Shover—provided examples that continue to inspire. In writing the book I benefited from, and came to depend on, the counsel of many colleagues and friends: Cynthia Shelton, Gary Nash, Peter Clecak, Vivian Clecak, Linda Walton, Arthur Barrett, Cheryl Lommatsch, Sharon Lewis, Robert Lewis, Scott Bottles, Scott Cline, George Cotkin, Debbie Forczek, Christine Laws, Dean Laws, John Reesman, Rosalie Schwartz, Larry Schwartz, Ann Topjon, Dorothy Ueland, and Leila Zenderland.

I have benefited from the comments of a number of scholars who read earlier versions of the manuscript. Richard Maxwell Brown, whose vast knowledge of western American history—and whose republican generosity—I came to know while writing this book, wrote a lengthy critique that helped me to improve the book significantly. Robert Rydell's astute comments saved me from a multitude of errors and stylistic gaffes and, most importantly, helped me to clarify my terms and draw out the interpretive implications of my argument. Robert Chandler not only gave the manuscript a close reading, but he also generously shared with me his wide knowledge of California and of the men I treat. My Portland State University colleague Gordon Dodds contributed to the manuscript his unmatched knowledge of Oregon history; Russell Elliott of the University of Nevada, Reno, did the same for the Nevada chapters. Both Gordon and Russ, in addition to saving me from numerous errors, helped me to see the forest a bit more clearly than the trees. Susan Karant-Nunn sharpened my sense of western American mining society by giving me the perspective of a scholar of a very different age of mining rushes. Finally, the anonymous referees for the University of California Press offered stimulating insights and excellent guidance for revising the manuscript.

I am further indebted to colleagues and friends on whom I tried out parts of the book in conference papers and informal conversations, and who listened patiently and offered sage advice: Gary Topjon, Dennis Berge, Edward Bingham, John Porter Bloom, Malcolm Clark, David Duniway, Jim Heath, David Horowitz, Norris Hundley, Robert Johnston, Maureen Jung, Howard Lamar, Kimbark MacColl, Michael Malone, Ruth Barnes Moynihan, Spencer Olin, Kenneth N. Owens, Earl Pomeroy, Richard Reutten, Alexander Saxton, Sarah Sharp, Harry Stein, and Kathleen Underwood.

Although *Founding the Far West* is not precisely either a constitutional or a legal history, I have benefited greatly from the counsel of legal scholars and practicing attorneys who patiently answered my questions, corrected my misconceptions, and sharpened my appreciation of the intricacies of their field. In particular I want to thank Gordon Bakken, Lawrence Friedman, the Hon. W. Michael Gillette, Susan Leeson, John Philip Reid, Steven Rosen, Harry Scheiber, David Urman, Phillip Wolman, Anita Wolman, John Wunder, and my Portland State University colleagues Thomas Morris and Caroline Stoel.

At crucial points in the writing of this book I received vital assistance, financial and otherwise, from a number of sources. A Summer Stipend and Travel-to-Collections grant from the National Endowment for the Humanities, a grant from the Albert Beveridge Fund of the American Historical Association, and a summer fellowship from the Oregon Committee for the Humanities made possible essential research trips and, just as important, time to write and reflect. Similarly, my university has offered generous assistance. Funds from the Committee on Research and Publications assisted me early on. A 1988 grant from the Faculty Development Fund provided a term free of teaching responsibilities, during which time I finished the manuscript. I am grateful to former Provost Frank Martino, Vice-Provost Michael Reardon, Dean William Paudler, and my department chair, Bernard Burke, for supporting my application to the fund. The Portland State University Foundation provided funds for the reproduction of maps and illustrations. Finally, three staff members have been unfailingly helpful: Donna Kiykioglu made sure that I had a readable copy of the manuscript and, in the history department, Diane Gould and Lee Ellington helped in innumerable ways.

My students at San Diego State University, UCLA, and Portland State University have over the years listened politely and commented astutely on the ideas that appear here. Above all I want to thank Stan Beyer, Bruce Broderson, Rett Delia, Andra Forstner, Anna Hawley, Jan Kurtz, James Long, Carolyn Lundstrom, Ann Mussey, Gloria Myers, Paul Newton, Jill Riebesehl, Kenneth Van Vechten, and Jon Walker. An array of talented research assistants—Anna Borland, Susan Dubay, Diane Gould, Kenneth Hawkins, Richard Matthews, Athena Pogue, Joseph Prude, Dorothy Rackley, Steven Taylor, John Witherow, and Karla Zamiska—took my passions as their own and unearthed materials I had no idea existed.

Much of my research was carried out at the Huntington Library in San Marino, California. I am grateful to Virginia Renner, Mary Wright, Leona Schoenfeld, and other members of the Huntington staff for their constant help, and to Martin Ridge for making the library such a congenial place for scholarly work. The staff of the Bancroft Library at the University of California, Berkeley, cordially photocopied letters and other materials for my use. At the Beinecke Library at Yale, the Van Pelt Library at the University of Pennsylvania, the Powell Undergraduate and University Research Libraries at UCLA, the Houghton Library at Harvard University, New York Public Library, San Francisco Public Library, University of Washington Library, University of Oregon Library, Reed College Library, Multnomah County Library, and Lewis and Clark College Library my requests for assistance were met with professional efficiency. Last but not least, Marilyn Bateman, Mary Byrd, Joan Carey, Evelyn Crowell, Jerome DeGraaf, John Fraley, Kathleen Greey, Bruce

McKinney, and others at the Millar Library of Portland State University went out of their way to locate books and expedite interlibrary loan transactions.

In Oregon I used the collection of the Oregon Historical Society extensively and benefited greatly from the help of Rick Harmon, Peggy Haines, Steven Hallberg, Lane Sawyer, and Susan Seyl. My efforts to reconstruct the lives of historically obscure, ordinary politicians brought me into contact with dozens of other libraries and archives as well. I could not have written the book without the help of their staffs, and I was regularly astounded by the generosity of the people whom I met or with whom I corresponded. Donna Penwell of the Colton Hall Museum in Monterey, California, allowed me full access to that institution's fine collection of materials related to the 1849 California constitutional convention. Gary Kurutz helped me both at the California Historical Society Library and California State Library. More than once Judy Sheldon of the California Historical Society Library responded to my mail inquiries with unanticipated treasures. I am similarly indebted to the staff of the Nevada Historical Society in Reno, particularly Librarian Lee Mortenson, who, in introducing me to their collection and suggesting materials I would not otherwise have thought of, made my stay there so productive and enjoyable. Guy Louis Rocha, Nevada state archivist, guided me to numerous sources I otherwise would not have found. The staffs of the Oregon and California State Archives and the National Archives in Seattle and Washington, D.C., were similarly most helpful, as were the staffs of numerous institutions throughout the country who helped me find materials: the Searls Historical Library in Nevada City, California; the Illinois State Historical Library; Ontario County (New York) Historical Society; New York Historical Society; Bishop Museum; Mississippi Department of Archives and History; Chicago Historical Society; Utah State Historical Society; Florida State Library; and Arizona Historical Library.

It has been my great fortune to have Lynne Withey as my editor at the University of California Press. Lynne has brought to the manuscript the wisdom of a gifted historian and the skills of an accomplished editor. From the beginning she has guided me and the book along with insight and seemingly infinite patience. I am grateful as well to Pamela MacFarland Holway, who ushered the book through production with discernment, and to Anne Geissman Canright, who edited the manuscript brilliantly.

The book is dedicated lovingly to my parents. Words cannot convey my appreciation for them, and for my family: Nicholas, who rightly questioned the value of a book with no pictures to color; Benjamin, who brought his smile into this world just in time for the final flurry of revisions; and Joni, who inspires me in every way, and without whom I could not have finished.

INTRODUCTION

In 1840 the far western reaches of North America remained thousands of miles beyond the physical and cultural boundaries of the United States. California was an isolated and sparsely populated province of Mexico, dominated by a small class of landholders who controlled the trade in cattle hides with English and Anglo-American merchants. In the "Oregon Country" to the north were found an outpost of the British Hudson's Bay Company and a scattering of small, isolated settlements composed of former Hudson's Bay employees, retired trappers, and Protestant missionaries. To the east of California, across the Sierra Nevada in the Great Basin desert, no white settlements existed.

Before the end of the Civil War, however, three states had been carved out of this region and incorporated into the United States. In 1850 California entered the union, followed by Oregon in 1859 and Nevada in 1864. Statehood in each instance occurred quickly, alongside the arrival of thousands of immigrants. In 1847 the United States seized California in the Mexican War, and shortly thereafter gold in the Sierra Nevada initiated a rush of settlers that numbered in the hundreds of thousands. At the same time, though less dramatically, overland immigration to Oregon—encouraged by the end of joint British-U.S. possession in 1846 and the proximate effects of the gold rush—brought hundreds of farming families from the Ohio and Mississippi River valleys to the Pacific Northwest. Shortly thereafter the discovery of the Comstock Lode, conjuring up memories of the California gold rush ten years before, enticed thousands to (and in the process created) the territory of Nevada in the western reaches of the Great Basin.

Coming at midcentury, the political incorporation of the Far West was the work of Americans allegiant to antebellum political institutions, customs, and beliefs. Democrats or Whigs, localists or nationalists, advocates

1

of free soil or slavery, they carried westward political convictions that had been given American definition in the eighteenth century, later to be recombined in new forms according to the currents of the times: the symbiosis of European immigration, metropolitan industrialization, and commercial agriculture; the democratization of politics associated with Jacksonian Democracy; the evangelism of the Second Great Awakening; and new strictures of Victorian rectitude.[1] Their view of the world, of course, hinged most directly on the sheer effect of pioneering, of participating in what Patricia Limerick calls the U.S. "conquest" of western North America. The immediate subjects of this book—the constitution writers of California, Oregon, and Nevada—played a central role in this conquest. In constructing states they were involved, as Limerick puts it, in "the drawing of lines on a map, the definition and allocation of ownership, . . . and the evolution of land from matter to property."[2]

Given the youth of these men when they moved to the continent's edge, more than a few lived to see a vast transformation in the places they had, as it were, conquered. By the 1880s the "incorporation" of the Pacific slope into the United States, in the larger sense identified by Alan Trachtenberg, was well under way. An elaborate transportation and communication network now linked far westerners to national and international markets; more broadly, it undermined their physical isolation and initiated their integration into "a changed, more tightly structured [national] society with new hierarchies of control . . . and . . . [new] conceptions of that society, of America, itself."[3] As such, living at the geographic margins of the continent, the region's first settlers participated as fully as their eastern counterparts in what Robert Wiebe has called the American "search for order," the integration and synchronization of "island communities" into the nation we describe with that problematic term *modern*.[4]

In what follows I examine the incorporation of the Far West into the United States in both meanings of the term. The narrative is organized around the writing of state constitutions in California (1849), Oregon (1857), and Nevada (1864)—around, this is to say, the central event of political incorporation. I am equally concerned, however, with placing the construction of new states into a comparative framework related to the "incorporation," broadly defined, of the Far West into the national society apparent at the close of the nineteenth century. To this end I have explored in two ways the lives of the men who wrote the first far western constitutions. Most directly, I present them as the authors of formal charters of government who adapted familiar political practices to the local conditions they encountered. In addition, and less prosaically, I approach them as members of what T. H. Breen, writing about early America, calls a "charter group," those who, as the first "effective possessors" of a new region, "established rules for interaction, decided what customs would be carried to the New World, and determined the terms under which newcomers would be incorporated into these societies."[5]

California, Oregon, and Nevada are well suited to this analysis—though not because they constitute a geographic region. The environmental distinctions among the three are immense and as significant to my examination as the fact of their contiguity. Nor do they make up a cultural region in which a single "frontier" process, in Turnerian (or post-Turnerian) terms, took place. Rather, my starting point is the intriguing mixture of difference and commonality that marked the U.S. conquest of California, Oregon, and Nevada and these places' incorporation—broadly understood—into the United States.[6]

Specifically, three considerations underlie the larger purpose of this study and my focus on California, Oregon, and Nevada. First, the writing and ratification of each state's constitution took place before the end of the Civil War, a full generation before the next wave of state making in the Far West.[7] Thus, the early charter societies and the political charters of California, Oregon, and Nevada were the creation of antebellum Americans—people born in the first two decades of the nineteenth century who reached maturity in the 1830s and 1840s. Sharing a space in time, then, the settlers of these three areas carried to the Far West similar cultural baggage: a common national identity, institutional memory, recollection of exemplary public events, party symbols and allegiances, and, apropos the writing of state constitutions, understanding of the legal precedents available to them.

Second, the "first effective possessors" of California, Oregon, and Nevada, in addition to their commonalities, are distinguished by significant contrasts. Migration to the Pacific Coast, given its timing and the distances involved, entailed an act of separation qualitatively different from previous experience. Unlike the patterns of westward migration most familiar to Americans in 1840—the incremental migration westward from the Appalachians to the Mississippi—going to the Pacific involved a geographic leap from the "States" and a conscious (and, to many, seemingly permanent) separation from kin and community.[8] In so separating themselves, migrants to California, Oregon, and Nevada acted for different reasons, reasons grounded in their social and psychological backgrounds as well as in their knowledge of (and desires about) what awaited in the California goldfields, the farming valleys of Oregon, and the silver mines of Nevada. The outcome was not the imprinting of a singular version of American society, economy, and politics but, rather, significant variations on common cultural themes. To illuminate these variations (though at the risk of magnifying them disproportionately), I present those I call "charter settlers" as representatives of distinct, self-selected "fragments" of antebellum American culture and society. The environments and resources of California, Oregon, and Nevada—as these were advertised to and understood by prospective immigrants—drew distinctive groups to the Far West. The difficulties involved in migrating to the Pacific in the antebellum period heightened these distinctions, shaping in turn constitution writing and the longer-term incorporation of these places into the United States.[9]

Finally, the demographic makeup of my subjects bears directly on the above points. Born for the most part in the first two decades of the nineteenth century, the constitution writers of California, Oregon, and Nevada were part of the generational cohort whose adulthood encompassed the years 1840–1880. Their lives fit poorly into the standard historical chronology of the century, which possesses a generational cadence of its own, one in which the Civil War stands as a fundamental boundary. In both textbooks and specialized studies, the cast of characters that dominated the antebellum period (sliced into "ages" of Jackson, Manifest Destiny, and Sectional Crisis) disappears between 1860 and 1865, giving way to Gilded Age figures and their successors. While sharpening the contours of historical change in the nation as a whole, these categories screen from view the continuities that tied ante- to postbellum thought and fail to take adequate account of, or learn from, those whose lives encompassed both periods.[10] The constitution writers of the Far West, whose adult lives were divided, not ended, by the Civil War era, therefore merit close attention. In writing constitutions they left detailed records of their individual ideologies and common political culture at the threshold of the Civil War. Because their lives extended into the 1880s and even beyond, they confronted the long-term consequences of both war and industrial revolution. While some disappeared from the public eye, others remained prominent as local and state officeholders, congressmen and senators, and private citizens whose activities shaped the course of local events. Their individual journeys from the 1830s and 1840s through the 1880s were varied, displaying a range of the ways in which individuals born into preindustrial society made sense of and helped to create the new age that dawned in the late nineteenth century. Equally important, their lives after statehood also demonstrated—and reinforced—the persistence of customs, habits, and institutions they had helped to establish as charter settlers of the Far West.

I have divided my examination of politics, ideology, and society into three parts, each with single chapters devoted to California, Oregon, or Nevada. One purpose of this organization is to encourage different approaches to the book. For example, readers interested in only one state can read the relevant chapters and find a connected narrative. The same applies to those interested in only a particular aspect of far western or U.S. history—prestatehood society and politics (Part One), the writing of state constitutions (Part Two), or the later nineteenth century (Part Three).

This said, the book also has a larger, comparative, purpose, one embodied in the definition and juxtaposition of the three parts. Part One, "Politics and Society" (chapters 1–3), examines how each state's "charter group" gave shape to the society, economy, and politics of their territory before statehood. To this end I cover the arrival of immigrants from the United States and the ways they drew lines on the land—and around people—in building territorial polities and campaigning for statehood. To stress the local texture of politics in the three territories, I close these chapters with historical tours of the capital towns that hosted the constitutional conventions: Monterey, California; Salem, Oregon; and Carson City, Nevada. None was the foremost city of its region, each being eclipsed by better-known places—San Francisco, Portland, and Virginia City, respectively. Nonetheless, the public and private order of the convention towns captured features of the three charter societies—features essential to constitution writing—that the larger, more famous metropolises did not: Monterey as a meeting place of Hispanic- and Anglo-American cultures in the generation preceding the American conquest of California; Salem as the foremost rural crossroads of this agrarian society and as the literal embodiment of the intimate politics of the Oregon Country; and Carson City as the effective point of entry and exit for Californians making the trip to and from the Comstock Lode and as a staging point that linked, as well as divided, two Nevadas—the sparse ranching and farming areas and the raucous male world of Virginia City.

Part Two, "Personality, Ideology, and Political Culture" (chapters 4–6), is concerned with the constitution writing that took place in Monterey, Salem, and Carson City. Each chapter opens with a collective biography of the delegates to the three states' constitutional conventions, in an attempt to illumine the central features of these charter groups through both prosopography and detailed biographical treatment.[11] With few exceptions the subjects of these biographies fall far outside that troublesome category of "great men." I have not chosen these individuals in order to resurrect reputations or claim greatness; rather, I have reconstructed the lives of ordinary men in politics because one finds in the details, where experience, personality, and ideology intersect, a key to political culture.

The chapters of Part Two then move inside the convention halls of California, Oregon, and Nevada, to the far westerners' literal act of constituting governments. Here the book examines how these representatives of far western charter societies, through their debates and deliberations, attempted to resolve dilemmas they inherited from their times and carried to their adopted homes. Each body of constitution writers borrowed freely from existing charters of government.[12] However, the models they chose and the emendations they made differed by state, displaying idiosyncratic attempts to resolve perduring questions about race and citizenship, the proper role of banks and corporations in American life, the relationship between religion and the state, the balance of governmental power, and so forth. The constitution writers' debates thus not only reflected the prevailing legal and political discourse (and the incompleteness and contradictions thereby entailed); they also accented central features of the charter groups of which they were a part.

Part Three, "History and Memory" (chapters 7–9), carries the story forward from statehood. These chapters describe the transformation of the three states through the closing years of the century, the common as well as peculiar ways in which California, Oregon, and Nevada were incorporated into the United States. Within this context I close by tracing the lives of the constitution writers (and the charter group more generally) after statehood and the roles they played—as ally, antagonist, or onlooker—in the changes that transpired in the states they had made.

Central to my discussion of politics and constitution writing is the proposition that the charter groups that became the effective possessors of the Far West reflected different strains, or fragments, of nineteenth-century American "ideology" and "political culture." Although I do not adhere to precise definitions for these last two terms (trusting that context and common sense will make my meaning clear), in general I use them to distinguish between the system of political ideas that individuals hold (ideology) and the ways in which individuals, as ideological beings, together devise a common political ground (political culture). Ideology, then, refers to a socially constructed, interconnected, and purposive set of ideas—though a "set," or "paradigm," more often inchoate than precise—through which individuals make sense of experience. Political culture, in turn, refers to the ways in which ideology becomes a social force, articulated, organized, and embraced as a group, rather than individual, means of political action. The elements of political culture are myriad, including but not limited to institutions such as political parties and their nominating conventions, political rituals such as Fourth of July celebrations, and the writings and speeches of recognized leaders.[13] I see the relationship between ideology and political culture as neither fixed nor logically finished but, rather, as dissonant and dialectical. Ideology and political culture exist in tension, both with each other and with the unpredictable effects of experience, be it in the form of events (such as war and depression) or trends (demographic, economic, and the like), which contemporaries understand dimly, if at all.

A number of factors illustrate the fragmentary character of the political cultures that charter groups established in the Far West. The California constitution writers who met in 1849 did so in the midst of the gold rush, which completed the American conquest of an older, Hispanic California planted by Spanish missionaries in the eighteenth century and then recast, in the early nineteenth century, by native born Californians (known as "Californios"). The young, male gold rush participants who came west in search of treasure and fame were not the first immigrants from the United States; they were preceded in the 1820s and 1830s by New England traders, in the 1840s by overland settlers, and in 1845 and 1846 by soldiers of conquest. However, the sheer number of forty-niners made them the effective possessors—the charter group—of this land.

These gold rush migrants magnified a particular fragment of Anglo-American society, for they carried to the Far West an exaggerated sampling of social and political characteristics that students of American culture since Tocqueville have identified with the antebellum period: democratic individualism, an idealization of self-seeking within a market society, and a belief that government existed, in the words of J. Willard Hurst, to encourage and protect the "release of private energy and the increase of private options." [14] Their legal views were instrumental and their political economy, in nineteenth-century terms, individualist and liberal. Although they never used the term, *laissez-faire* captures a central conviction among them. Here the tenets generally subsumed in the term *Lockean liberalism*—the position that men who maximize their private satisfactions serve the common good—found fertile soil. [15]

The Lockean distinction between a state of nature and civil society resonated from the movement for statehood in California. Declaring the military government established after the American conquest of California illegitimate and "anarchical," the agitators for a constitutional convention insisted that California lacked a system of government necessary for the protection of property and person. In the mines and the instant city of San Francisco, the new arrivals governed themselves informally and spontaneously. They established a minimalist social contract through miners' assemblies, which regulated individual access to the goldfields, and vigilance committees, which punished perceived threats to public order. In both the statehood movement and the forty-niners' informal institutions of government, a narrow view was taken of public affairs, constrained by the conviction that the gold rush was at bottom about equality, opportunity, and individual liberty; that California provided enough room for all; and that the widest range of freedom that could be afforded the individual in pursuit of self-interest was indistinguishable from the common good. That this discourse encompassed only white males goes without saying. Indeed, the very preponderance of young white American males in gold rush California and the narrowness of purpose that carried them west gave special force to these ideas, helping to make California a place where conflict and violence between whites and nonwhites, "Americans" and "foreigners," was endemic.

The Oregonians who met in convention eight years later were contemporaries of the Californians in terms of the timing of their migration but in important ways distinguished from them. In contrast to the male tenor of gold rush California, the American conquest of the Oregon Country in the 1840s and 1850s was the work of midwestern farming families. Drawn largely from the ranks of rural people whose social and political world Allan Bogue, John Faragher, and Malcolm Rohrbough have reconstructed so effectively, they gave this territory a homogeneity that contrasted starkly with the individualist and cosmopolitan cast of gold rush California.[16]

The implications of this contrast Dorothy Johansen has pinpointed in a nineteenth-century Oregon yarn about how overland migrants chose between California and the Pacific Northwest. "At Pacific Springs," she recounts, ". . . a pile of gold-bearing quartz marked the road to California; the other road had a sign bearing the words 'to Oregon.' Those who could read took the trail to Oregon."[17] This apocryphal tale, which has always delighted Oregonians and perplexed Californians, underlines the fact that those who chose Oregon did so consciously, avoiding— in some fashion refusing—the lure of California gold and the values for which that gold stood. To no small degree, the Willamette Valley of Oregon drew settlers who sought a "middle landscape," a rural place somewhere between the isolated and self-sufficient (and thereby materially coarse and emotionally deprived) household order of yeoman myth and a world of commercialized agriculture dependent on uncertain markets and subject—so experience taught—to manipulation by corrupt men.[18] To people from the Ohio and Mississippi River valleys the perils of both alternatives were clear, learned on the one hand in the daily routines of rural life, on the other in the economic panics of the 1830s and 1840s.[19]

Oregon, advertised widely as a place with a mild and healthful climate, soil productivity without parallel, and free farmsteads a square mile in extent, lured thousands. By 1855 all but the least desirable lands of its Willamette Valley (which held the vast majority of Oregon's population) had been taken by settlers under the generous provisions of the Oregon Donation Land Law.[20] The fragment population that made up this charter group differed accordingly from the Californians. Rural folk chastened by economic panic in the countryside, they saw danger in the liberal logic of a market society where Californians saw freedom and opportunity. The Oregonians thus distinguished themselves in the private and public lives they constructed, the customs they planted, the precedents they honored, and, subtly, the charter they wrote.

At first glance, politics in the Oregon Country seems a replica of the second-party system. The conventional symbols of antebellum party combat were everywhere. Although rural Democrats were by far the predominant force in Oregon before the Civil War, the loyalties of Whigs, despite their smaller numbers, also ran deep. Yet the Democracy that midwestern farmers carried to Oregon did not represent the party of

Jackson so much as a particular radical agrarian strain within it. This agrarianism, which John Ashworth has delineated brilliantly on the national level, mixed a producer ethic with antipathy toward the financial, mercantile, and manufacturing imperatives of the emerging capitalist system.[21] Indeed, Jacksonian agrarianism was much more than a reactionary response on the part of anxious provincials to the liberal ideology of mainstream Democrats; in its time it was a major, though far from uncontested, strain within the Democratic electorate. In the Oregon Country, this agrarianism dominated politics in the 1850s. Reinforced by the residential and political persistence of the charter generation, it remained a defining feature of state politics long thereafter.

Significantly, Oregonians articulated Jacksonian agrarianism—in the process molding it in idiosyncratic, local ways—through the language of "classical republicanism," which scholars of the revolutionary and founding periods have recently placed at the center of early American politics.[22] In its eighteenth-century American incarnation, republican discourse drew on classical, Renaissance, and Enlightenment ideas and mixed them with the thought of eighteenth-century English opposition writers known as "commonwealthmen." Neither liberal nor individualist, this older republicanism defined citizenship in terms of "independence" and "civic virtue." It held that the foundation of a republican order depended on citizens who were independent of the will of others (by possessing land or skills that guaranteed familial self-sufficiency) and imbued with a disinterested, self-abnegating commitment to the common good. Where liberalism conflated politics and economics, holding that the pursuit of self-interest in the marketplace produced the common good, classical republicanism studiously separated the two, stressing the primacy of the political (as a binding undertaking addressed to the common wealth) over the economic (a socially divisive undertaking stemming from self-interest). Classical republican thinkers located the corruption and downfall of republics—in theory and in history—in precisely the activity that the liberal individualist ethos idealized: the pursuit of self-interest. According to the republican view, self-seeking corrupts civic virtue, because individuals, obsessed with luxury and display, seek power over others; in the process, citizen is divided from citizen, and the situation degrades inexorably to dependence, desperation, and anarchy.

Although classical republican thought (drawn as it was from the views of that part of the English landed class known as the "country party") was aristocratic in principle and pretension, the anticommercial, antifinancial, and antiurban strains within it spoke to antebellum rural Americans who had lost, or almost lost, their land—and thus their independence—in the collapse of rural commerce during the late 1830s. The first major overland trains to Oregon, in the early 1840s, moved out shortly after waves of panic and collapse swept the Midwest. Few if any markets in Oregon awaited these migrants. Even though the migrants anticipated eventual commercial opportunities, their anticipation was constrained by a persistent suspicion of monied, "nonproductive" classes and a correlative desire to control development and maintain, across time, the familial order of the first settlers.[23] That the charter settlers of Oregon sought neither to escape to some Eden nor to abstain from market enterprise goes without saying. By the same token, the very size of the midwestern immigration to the Oregon Country in the 1840s and 1850s, the command of the land these settlers gained through the Donation Land Law, and their tendency to stay put meant that their suspicions and desires shaped Oregon long after statehood.

The Nevadans present a third variant of the antebellum chartering of society and politics in the Far West, one linked directly to the California experience of 1849, yet in its own way as distinctive from it as was the Oregonians' experience. Those who first settled Nevada, and who wrote its constitution, were with but a few exceptions "old Californians": veterans of the gold rush who had remained in the Far West after the surface placer deposits of gold were exhausted, and in turn the promise of personal independence and individual mobility that had drawn tens of thousands to California between 1849 and the mid-1850s. By the end of the 1850s and beginning of the 1860s, when the rush to "Washoe" (as Nevada was known) began, a new—and to these men disheartening—California was ever more apparent. Mining had become less an individual endeavor and more an industrial undertaking marked by significant capital demands, complex machinery, and, above all, wage labor.[24]

In reality, by the end of the 1860s the mining centers of Nevada had become stark, one-dimensional examples of industrial capitalist society. However, the gold rush veterans who crossed the Sierra Nevada between 1859 and 1863 to the newly discovered Comstock Lode carried precisely the opposite expectation. What drew men to Washoe, as one migrant put it, was the hope of finding "another edition of the California gold rush, with a thousand per cent added thereto."[25] The charter group of Nevada looked back to the liberal individualist vision of 1849, although, given their experience in California, with eyes less fresh with wonder than their forty-niner counterparts'. Unlike the California case, moreover, constitution writing in Nevada occurred after, not before, the unraveling of the individualist hopes that had drawn migrants there in the first place. These "old Californians" convened in the midst not of boom times reminiscent of 1849 but, rather, during a sudden depression that forced them to confront the emerging industrial character of their society and, perforce, revise the liberal vision they had hoped to redeem. The coalescence of constitution writing and industrial crisis gave the Nevadans' meeting great immediacy. In forging a charter for their state, these men joined the logic of liberal individualism to corporate capitalism.

In writing constitutions, the charter group of each state used a common political vocabulary, drawn from the variety of ideological materials available in the larger national setting. Each constitutional convention therefore expressed a distinct version of antebellum American political culture. In turn, constitution writing served as a prologue to the later nineteenth century, an age of remarkable changes in the Far West—of incorporation in the broadest sense into the United States. In each state, the years of the Civil War and Reconstruction, the Gilded Age, and the industrial revolution altered the landscape and cityscape in ways unimaginable in 1840 or 1850. Yet even at the threshold of the "American century," a century heralded for the promised uniformity to be effected by modernity, these states were marked by local peculiarities that displayed the continuing influence, if no longer the presence, of the charter settlers—and not least the constitution writers—who carried out the United States' conquest of the Far West.

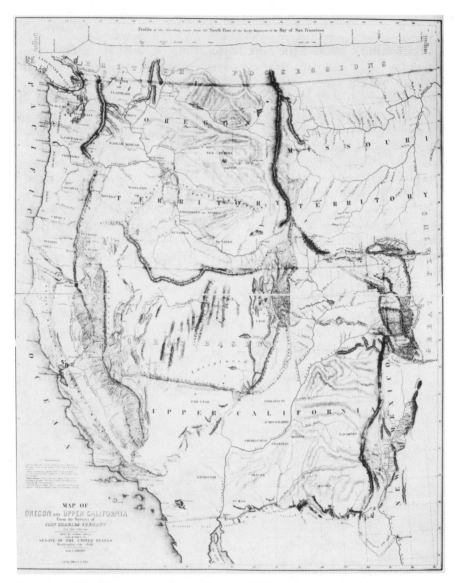

Above: 1848 Charles Preuss Map of Upper California and Oregon, prepared from the surveys of John Charles Fremont. This map, which was used as the basis for the California state boundary, illustrates the conceptions of the Far West prevailing in the 1840s. The region is divided into the lands of Native American peoples and vaguely defined territories of the United States ("Oregon Territory" and "Missouri Territory") in the north and of Mexico ("Upper California" and "New Mexico") in the south. Note also that the map shows no cities. (Courtesy Library of Congress.) *Right:* 1900 Map of the Union Pacific Railroad and Steamship Lines. This map of the Union Pacific empire depicts the transformation that occurred in the Far West during the latter half of the nineteenth century. In place of the vague "territories" shown on the 1848 Preuss map are cities and clearly defined states linked by an elaborate railroad and ocean transportation-communication system. (Courtesy Geography and Maps Division, Library of Congress.)

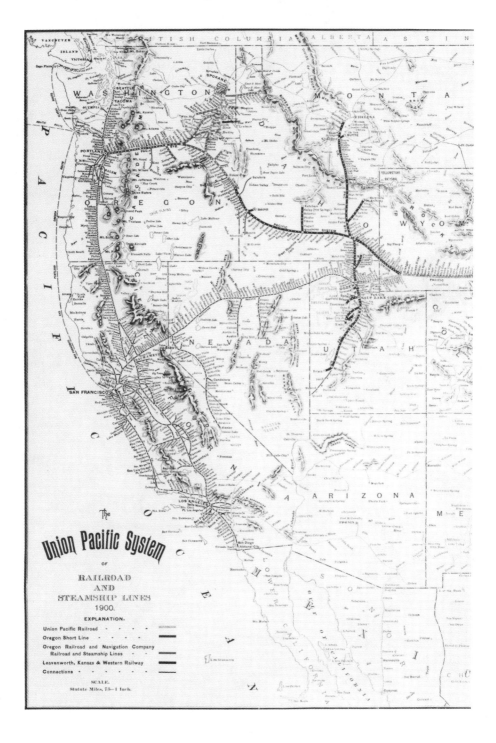

The
Union Pacific System
OF
RAILROAD
AND
STEAMSHIP LINES
1900.

EXPLANATION.

Union Pacific Railroad . . . . .
Oregon Short Line . . . . .
Oregon Railroad and Navigation Company
  Railroad and Steamship Lines . .
Leavenworth, Kansas & Western Railway
Connections . . . . .

SCALE.
Statute Miles, 75=1 Inch.

PART ONE

Politics and Society

ONE

Politics in a Divided World:
California, 1769–1849

During the fall of 1849, while thousands found fortune or failure in the canyon streams of the Sierra Nevada, forty-eight men met in the old California town of Monterey to create a state government. They met under unusual circumstances. None of the delegates was well known in the territory, and the bulk of the population, which was a hundred or so miles away, searching for gold, showed little interest in their gathering. Few of the delegates knew more than a handful of their colleagues, for California was a land of isolated regions, imposing geography, and poor communications. Nevertheless, this group of men was peculiarly representative of the place and time. Among them were Californio ranchers, wealthy in land and cattle, who had dominated the Mexican province in the 1830s and 1840s; New England merchants who had arrived in the 1830s and carved a comfortable and profitable niche in provincial Mexican society; settlers whose arrival via the overland trail antedated the American conquest of 1846; soldiers who had come in 1846 and 1847; and, finally, gold rush newcomers in search of the main chance. Gathered in one room, they represented California's past, present, and future: its Hispanic heritage, the aspirations of the pre–gold rush overland immigrants, the legacy of war and conquest, and the transformative effect of the discovery of gold.

The province these men represented was marked by profound social and cultural divisions, and these divisions were at the center of California's creation as an American state. The American conquest and gold rush immigration transformed—visibly and wondrously, arriving Yankees thought—a broad triangular region that began in San Francisco; passed through the central-valley trading towns of Sacramento, to the north, and Stockton, to the south; and then radiated outward into the mining regions of the Sierra Nevada foothills. Elsewhere, however, the Hispanic character of an older, Californio, society was still strong. In the settlements that stretched along the coast from Monterey to San Diego, "Americanization" had just begun.

During the summer of 1849 these two Californias confronted each other in the Monterey convention. Constitution writing put a final stamp on the United States' conquest of California. Yet the chartering of the state was shaped at every point by the Californio rancheros who, though defeated in war, held on to a measure of their former authority in districts bypassed by American immigrants. In the Monterey convention the nine representatives of the old regime were determined to protect, as well as they could, prerogatives hard won since the arrival, late in the eighteenth century, of Franciscan missionaries and Spanish soldiers in service to church and crown.

The Hispanic delegates in the constitutional convention were the heirs, even if through force and intrigue, of riches accumulated across two generations of mission settlement. Between 1769 and 1823 the Franciscans had established twenty-one missions to prepare California's Indian population for Christian conversion and citizenship in an expanding Spanish empire. Alongside the missions these colonizers built four presidios (San Diego, Santa Barbara, Monterey, and San Francisco) and three towns, or pueblos (Los Angeles, San Jose, and Villa de Branciforte, or Santa Cruz).[1] The new world created by Spain's missionaries and soldiers eventually attained a tragic magnificence, having been built with the labor and lives of California's native population.[2] Devised as impermanent settlements, the Franciscan missions were expected to exist for approximately ten years, during which time "gentile" Indians were to be converted into "neophytes" enjoying citizenship; with the secularization of the missions, a modicum of independence was to be granted them under the guidance of Mexican settlers and colonial officials.[3] Led by Junípero Serra, the first missionaries acted on these assumptions, working assiduously—despite resistance, even revolts—to bring Indians into the austere mission settlements. Upon Serra's death in 1784, however, Spanish California entered a new era in which the missions became something far different from the temporary shelters originally intended.

Serra's successor was Father Fermín Francisco Lasuén, and during his eighteen-year tenure the missions became impressive monuments to a new conception of the missionary enterprise. Under Lasuén, the number of missions along the coast grew from ten to eighteen, separated from one another by a day's travel on horseback. The Spanish completed an extensive building program at each establishment, giving the missions an air of permanence that was lacking under Serra and bequeathing to California the "Mission Style" of architecture.[4] Concurrently, the Franciscans transformed the mission economy. Agriculture and stock raising flourished, and rudimentary manufacturing, performed by neophytes under the direction of artisans recruited from Mexico, diversified mission production and brought about a self-sufficiency previously absent. Finally—and outwardly the most impressive sign of Lasuén's regime—the Indian population in the missions increased 400 percent from five thousand at the close of Serra's presidency to more than twenty thousand at the turn of the century.[5]

The years from 1785 to 1804 thus saw the florescence of California's mission society. Accompanying the physical elaboration of the mission system, however, was a fundamental shift in the nature of the mission enterprise. By the time of Lasuén's death in 1803, prospects for the missions' secularization—the transfer of control to secular officials, the bestowal of citizenship on Indian neophytes, and the transfer of the missionaries to other frontiers—had grown remote. Despite constant proclamations of fealty to the principle of secularization, the mission fathers insisted that the work of conversion in the existing missions was incomplete. To their minds, more time was necessary—and would always remain necessary until, in the 1830s, government officials imposed secularization upon them.[6]

This shift in the nature of the California mission enterprise, from temporary settlements to permanent institutions, stemmed from a variety of causes. In part it was a response to the native population's failure to embrace Catholicism and Spanish culture as quickly or completely as the fathers expected. By the 1810s it was the settled opinion among many missionaries that the California Indian was by nature a childlike brute incapable of "civilization."[7] Reinforcing this view was the growing comfort and wealth enjoyed by second- and third-generation missionaries at the expense of a subservient neophyte population. As the nineteenth century proceeded, the mission fathers confronted a paradox: as their mission settlements grew ever more elaborate and wealthy, secularization grew ever more remote. Seeing themselves more as fathers of settled communities than as transient missionaries, they put off the day of reckoning.[8]

There were, it must be noted, good reasons why the fathers saw their work of conversion as unfinished, for after 1805 they confronted a continuing demographic crisis that decimated the native population.[9] The twenty thousand Indians living in California's missions in 1805 marked a plateau population that the missionaries could not maintain, much less increase. In the missions, the neophyte birth rate suffered a dramatic decline during the first quarter of the nineteenth century, falling from a precontact level of approximately 45–50 births per 1,000 population to, in 1830, approximately 30 per 1,000 population. This 33 percent decline in the birth rate, exacerbated by epidemics of European diseases and a rising tide of desertions from the missions, foreclosed the possibility of increasing the neophyte population by natural means.[10] Thus for second- and third-generation missionaries, simply maintaining the mission population required that they continuously import more gentile Indians into the missions. Bringing more gentiles into the missions, however, was a perilous task, for in the face of demographic disaster the resistance of the nonmissionized native population increased. Contact between missionaries and potential converts occurred farther from the sanctuary of the missions, resulting in ever-increasing violence between missionary and Indian. As the sources of converts grew more distant, as they declined in number owing to disease, and as they continued to resist the fathers' entreaties, the Franciscans relied increasingly on military expeditions and forced marches to maintain the mission population base.[11]

With a growing sense of desperation, and in the face of constant inquiries about their progress toward secularization, the mission fathers held on, hoping, it seems, against hope. Secularization, delayed time and again, finally came in the 1830s, and then only because a new class of native-born Californians seized power and imposed secularization on the Franciscans. This new class of Californians, proclaiming themselves adherents of the liberalism and republicanism of the anticolonial movements that swept through Spanish America in the 1810s and 1820s (and that underlined Mexican independence in 1821) championed secularization as a humanitarian and political imperative.

In practice, secularization of the California missions turned less on the principles of the broader independence movement than on a tangle of local conflicts that Mexican independence in 1821 instigated.[12] For the mission Indian, in the end, secularization exchanged one set of masters for another. Mexico's independence removed Spain's restrictions on international commerce, initiating the California trade in hides and tallow that, first under the control of the mission fathers and then of private ranchers, provided a consistent source of foreign exchange and imported goods. Between 1828 and 1848 more than 1.25 million hides were shipped from California. The lowering of commercial restrictions also brought to California a group of English and American merchants— middlemen in the hide and tallow trade—many of whom became naturalized Mexican citizens and prominent landowners.[13] Above all, however, Mexican independence inaugurated a three-sided power struggle among local, native-born Californians, the mission fathers, and appointed Mexican officials. The outcome was a new social order—the very social order subdued by the U.S. military in 1847.

At the center of the conflicts unleashed by the end of Spanish dominion was a new, native-born class composed of the sons of Mexican soldiers, artisans, and colonists who first populated the presidios and pueblos during the mission period. Throughout the period 1821–1845 these Californios competed for control of the provincial government with a constant stream of officials sent by the Mexican government. Intertwined with the conflict between ambitious locals and the Mexican officials was the Californios' challenge to the mission fathers (who allied themselves with the appointed governors) over control of land, cattle, and Indian labor.[14] In both contests the Californians ultimately prevailed, although their rise to power had the effect of splitting them internally into family-based factions associated with specific locales, in particular Monterey and, to the south, Santa Barbara, Los Angeles, and San Diego. The result was political turmoil.[15] During the twenty-four years of Mexican rule (1822–1846), fourteen different men held the title of governor. Four of them—Manuel Victoria (in 1831), Mariano Chico and Nicolás Gutiérrez (both in 1836), and Manuel Micheltorena (in 1846)— the Californians drove from the province by force of arms. (All together, these four men held office a total of thirty-four months.) With the exception of California's first Mexican governor, José María Echeandía (1825–1831), the longest administration was that of Juan Alvarado, a native-born Californian who came to power in the 1836 uprising against Gutiérrez and remained governor until 1842.

During Alvarado's governorship, despite constant factionalism between northern and southern ranchero families, the Californios affirmed their command of the province's government, landed wealth, and former-mission Indian population.[16] Alvarado completed the secularization of the missions, and in the process changed the face of the province. Theoretically, secularization was to place control of the missions with civilian administrators who would see to it that half the land, equipment, and resources passed into the hands of the mission Indians living in newly created pueblos, with the remainder sold to meet pueblo expenses, including schools and "other requirements for civil peace and prosperity."[17] In practice, however, the land and cattle went to those with connections to the government.

Furthermore, coinciding with the shift of mission property into private hands, Alvarado instituted an ambitious program whereby government land grants would be made to private parties. By the time of the American conquest, these land grants encompassed a broad swath of land running from San Diego in the south to Sonoma in the north. More than eight hundred such grants, of which 75 percent were dispensed between 1836 and the U.S. conquest, transferred over eleven million acres of land into the hands of local rancheros, some of whom possessed in excess of three hundred thousand acres.[18] The land grants, along with the widening of California's hide and tallow trade with the United States and England, the downfall of the mission padres, and the Californians' virtual autonomy from Mexico, formed the basis of the short-lived Californio regime from which the United States wrested California in the 1840s.

Though a far cry from the Spanish Arcadia described by its romantic admirers, the Californios' world offered wealth, ease, and comfort to those who owned the land and controlled the trade. Owning vast herds of cattle that multiplied with minimal attention, being well placed in a trading system that exchanged hides and tallow for crude manufactured goods and luxury items imported from England and the United States, participating in constant intrigue against Mexican interlopers and their cousins in other parts of the province, the Californio rancheros and merchants—both native and foreign born—became a proud and imperious ruling class. Below them, in a social hierarchy that quickly grew more rigid, were the pueblo artisans who serviced the pastoral economy: saddlers, blacksmiths, muleteers, shoemakers, tailors, sawyers, scribes, and the like. At the bottom were the former mission Indians and other *pobladores,* a floating population that survived on casual employment as servants and day laborers.[19]

During the 1820s and 1830s, while the Californios were laying claim to larger and larger ranchos and widening their trade contacts with foreigners, the seeds of their eventual conquest were planted. Expanding contacts with foreign traders turned the attention of American and European imperialists to the distant province, with its good harbors, location facing Asia, impressive resources, and, above all, lack of stable government and effective defense.[20] In the aftermath of the panic of 1837, American overland immigration began in earnest from the Ohio River valley to the Pacific Coast, as farmers beset by the collapse and intrigued by descriptions of the fertile valleys of Oregon and California set out with their families. Before the gold rush, most overland immigrants had Oregon's Willamette Valley as their destination. A few hardy souls, however, responded to the writings of visitors to California such as Richard Henry Dana, John Frémont, and Lansford Hastings, as well as the invitations extended by colonizers John Marsh and John Sutter, and initiated the California trail to the Mexican province.[21]

By 1845 approximately seven hundred of California's four thousand non-Indian residents were American or English.[22] About half of these lived in or near the pueblos along the coast, and many were integrated into the Californio regime. They Hispanicized their names, becoming, for example, Don Guillermo Dana, Don Juan Warner, Don Benito Wilson, and the like. They converted to Catholicism, married daughters of Californio rancheros, became Mexican citizens, and took possession of substantial land grants in their own right. By the time of the American conquest one in five land grants was held by a nonnative.[23]

Beyond the coastal settlements, however, the presence of a very different foreign population became increasingly clear. The size of the over-

TABLE 1   Geographical Distribution (Hispanic vs. non-Hispanic) of the "Principal Men" of California (by residence in 1845)

	Hispanic	Non-Hispanic	Total (both groups)
San Diego	9 (50%)[a]	9 (50%)[a]	18 (100%)
Los Angeles	20%[b]	27%	23%
San Jose			
Santa Barbara			
Monterey	34 (82%)	7 (18%)	41 (100%)
Santa Cruz	76%[b]	21%	53%
San Francisco Bay			
Yerba Buena			
San Luis Obispo	2 (10%)	17 (90%)	19 (100%)
Sacramento	4%[b]	52%	24%
Bodega			
On Board Ship			
Total	45 (58%)	33 (42%)	78 (100%)
(all locations)	100%	100%	

[a] Top percentage refers to the ethnic group: here, 50% of the principal men identified by Larkin in San Diego, Los Angeles, and San Jose are Hispanic, 50% non-Hispanic.
[b] Bottom percentage refers to the locale: here, 20% of the Hispanic principal men reside in San Diego, etc., 76% in Santa Barbara, etc., and 4% in Yerba Buena, etc.
SOURCE: Thomas Larkin, *The Larkin Papers*, ed. George P. Hammond, 11 vols. (Berkeley and Los Angeles: University of California Press, 1951–1968), 4:322–334.

land immigration grew each year in the early 1840s, as did the number of American trading posts at San Francisco Bay. These Yankees found little to like in the Californio regime. They disparaged the charge that they were squatting illegally on land open only to citizens of Mexico and answered the demand that they depart by announcing that California was manifestly destined for annexation by the United States. Their potential as filibusterers was lost on neither Californio officials nor the U.S. government.[24] When, for example, Thomas Larkin, American merchant, U.S. consul, and secret agent for the Polk administration, surveyed the "principal men" of California in a private report to Secretary of State Buchanan, he reported not only that a significant number of the province's prominent figures were foreign born, but that many of them lived outside the confines of Californio society—socially and economically as well as geographically (table 1).[25]

Larkin's 1845 report revealed a circle of men who were alien to the world of the Californios. In San Diego, Los Angeles, and San Jose, the "principal men" he identified were divided equally between prominent

Californios, on the one hand, and Anglos connected to Hispanic families on the other; and in Santa Barbara, Monterey, Santa Cruz, Sonoma, and San Francisco, the preeminence of the native-born population was overwhelming. But at the periphery—in the Sacramento Valley, aboard the regular trading ships that plied San Francisco Bay, at the trading post of Yerba Buena, and to the north at Bodega—non-Hispanics held sway. This division was magnified by the fact that most of the Anglos Larkin identified as prominent in the older settlements were, as Leonard Pitt has remarked, "Mexicanized gringos."[26] The same could not be said about the traders in San Francisco or the settlers in the interior. At best, they were indifferent to the Californios. Most, however, were downright hostile, anxious for an opportunity to assist in their downfall.[27]

Shortly after Larkin submitted his report, the outsiders had their chance. In 1845 the Californios drove out another Mexican governor, Manuel Micheltorena, and with his departure competition for political control broke out between rival family factions in the northern and southern districts. In an uneasy truce between the two sides, the capital went to Los Angeles and the governorship to that city's favorite son, Pío Pico, while Monterey became the military headquarters under José Castro. This geographic division of authority, though politically expedient, was in the long run militarily disastrous.[28] In early 1846 the imperial-minded and already famous young army explorer John Charles Frémont arrived on his third expedition to the West. Frémont claimed that he was engaged in a survey of overland routes to the Pacific, but Military Commandant Castro (wondering at the artillery corps that accompanied Frémont) ordered the American to leave the province. Ostensibly marching to Oregon, Frémont and his company ultimately reappeared at the American settlements in the Sacramento Valley near Sutter's Fort.

When Castro learned of Frémont's return, he sent a force to expel him. American settlers in the Sacramento Valley, convinced that Castro also meant to remove them, and goaded by Frémont (who later insisted that he was acting on secret orders from the secretary of war), organized a military unit, descended on the Hispanic settlement in Sonoma, and, after taking the prominent Californio Mariano Vallejo prisoner, announced the formation of an independent "Bear Flag Republic."[29] Following this declaration, the filibusterers combined their forces with Frémont's dragoons and turned their attention to extending their revolution to the whole of California. Soon, however, they learned that war between Mexico and the United States was under way and that Commodore John D. Sloat had taken Monterey. On July 9, 1846, the American flag was raised at San Francisco and Sonoma, and two days later at Sutter's settlement of New Helvetia (present-day Sacramento).

In the north, from Monterey to Sonoma, the U.S. forces confronted little opposition. But in the south, from Santa Barbara to San Diego, the Californio resisters held the invaders at bay for six months. They defeated Stephen Watts Kearny in the Battle of San Pascual, though otherwise they avoided direct confrontation. Finally, after many embarrassments, the American forces caught the Californians in a pincer movement near Los Angeles. On January 13, 1847, the native regime surrendered.[30]

♪

The Capitulation of Cahuenga closed the California theater of the Mexican War, but in its wake came a host of problems for the conquering forces. Over the next two and a half years Congress, divided over how to organize the lands wrested from Mexico, failed to establish civil government in the territory, and so a succession of military commanders was sent to rule California's native, Anglo-American, and European population.[31] To the growing number of overland immigrants, in particular, military rule appeared, at best, a temporary necessity, and, at worst, a threat to liberty. By the spring of 1847 opposition to military rule had become a political movement—a movement that militated against the organization of Democratic and Whig parties in California (which did not appear until after the constitutional convention). From the capitulation at Cahuenga to the constitutional convention, public affairs focused narrowly on the legitimacy of military rule.

Colonel Richard Mason, who held the governorship for most of this time, was a particularly unlucky man. A career soldier, he neither wanted nor sought appointment as governor of California. It was natural that he should be reticent, for he was not convinced that a military commander could legitimately administer a civil government in time of peace. During his governorship he sought to assuage the concerns of recent settlers from the United States, only to find that his attention increased their hostility. Ironically, his relative neglect of the conquered Californios, whom he left to their own devices in the coastal settlements, resulted in their loyalty to the military regime. Concerned above all with the challenge of the American settlers, and encouraged by his second in command, Military Secretary of State Henry Wager Halleck, Mason acquiesced in granting standing authority to the Pico, Carrillo, Yorba, Bandini, de la Guerra, and Vallejo patriarchs and their Hispanicized Anglo cousins such as Abel Stearns and Juan Benito Wilson. The military rulers retained the forms of local government known to the Californio elite, conceded their control of pueblo affairs, appointed them to provincial offices, and attended to their requests for assistance.[32]

In contrast, relations between the military government and Anglo-American settlers in California were strained from the start. Critics never relaxed their attacks on Mason, from the time of the conquest to his resignation shortly after the discovery of gold in 1848. Over these two years approximately two thousand immigrants arrived via the overland trail, in addition to the thousand or so soldiers and sailors who were mustered out of the service after the conquest without any provision for their return to the United States.[33] Unlike the long-resident merchants who lived in the Californio pueblos and were tied by family and interest to the old regime, the new arrivals, along with the earlier settlers in the interior, disparaged the continuation of Mexican-Californio institutions under military rule. Although the overland immigrants (much like their counterparts in Oregon) likely brought with them to California an iden-tification with antebellum parties—above all the Democratic—their op-position to military rule stemmed less from partisan attachments than from residual hostility toward the Californio regime, which to their eyes had governed California arbitrarily and arrogantly.

Within six weeks of the Californio surrender, the *California Star,* pub-lished by Bear Flag filibusterer Robert Semple near the military gover-nor's headquarters in Monterey, became the mouthpiece of settlers de-manding the election of a provisional legislature to frame "a code of laws suitable to the present and prospective condition of the territory."[34] The proposal received no response from the military authorities, who themselves were unsure of their power or of the plans Congress and the president had for the conquered province. The military's temporizing only fired the settlers' attack, which continued for two years as "old settlers" like Semple ("old" because of their arrival prior to the gold rush), joined by former soldiers and newly arrived immigrants, condemned the "mongrel military rule" that Congress's inaction had forced on them.[35]

To the growing Anglo-American population, military rule smacked of despotism. Established and continued on the orders of military gover-nors, it retained the structure of the provincial Mexican government, subject to the military commander's arbitrary veto power. In practice, this arrangement had two important features. First, it vested legislative, judicial, and executive powers in the hands of local officials, the alcaldes. Second, it reserved to the governor the right of review and removal over alcaldes.[36] The result was awkward and confusing. In the absence of a written code, alcaldes were left to their own devices. As executive, legislature, and judiciary all in one, they had to define crimes, deter-mine guilt, decide on punishment, establish a basis for contractual agree-ments, and rule on the validity of titles to property—the last a particular point of conflict where American immigrants' appetite for land bumped up against the massive, unimproved, and vacant land grants issued dur-ing the Mexican era. The results varied widely from district to district, and everywhere Anglo-American immigrants looked on alcalde rule as despotism. "We had always thought," declared a correspondent to the *Californian* in July 1847, "that the inferior magistrates were responsible to some higher power, having jurisdiction over their acts, to remedy evils occasioned by their want of knowledge, or hasty decisions. But it seems the Alcalde here seems to be *the law,* THE WHOLE LAW, and NOTHING BUT THE LAW." [37]

In Sonoma, observed merchant Samuel Brannan in 1847, "the *alcalde* adopted the whole volume of Missouri Statutes, as the law for the government of the people in his jurisdiction. If this is allowed we will have as many legislatures in California as we have Alcaldes or Justices of the peace." [38] Like his counterpart in Sonoma, the first alcalde of San Francisco relied on published codes available to him—only in this case they were New York's. And so it went throughout the northern portions of the territory where American immigrants applied the test of their own common sense to the civil and criminal complaints brought before them. The office of alcalde, observed Monterey's Walter Colton, "involves every breach of the peace, every crime, every business obligation, and every disputed land title within a space of three hundred miles. . . . Such an absolute disposal of questions affecting property and personal liberty, never ought to be confided in one man. There is not a judge of any bench in New England or the United States, whose power is as absolute as that of the alcalde of Monterey." [39]

Although the authority of the alcalde appeared unlimited, the powers of the office were continuously revised in an ad hoc manner by the various military governors. Despite an 1846 proclamation by Commodore Robert Stockton making the office of alcalde elective, subsequent military governors appointed and removed alcaldes as they saw fit. [40]

Colonel Mason, who made 80 percent of all U.S. military appointments to civil offices, disliked the uncertain and arbitrary nature of his authority in the province. At best, military rule was justified during war; but during peacetime he could find no grounds to continue it. [41] In his reports to the War and State Departments, Mason implored his superiors to establish civil government and to recognize the legitimacy of the settlers' complaints. His entreaties were of no avail. The Treaty of Guadalupe-Hidalgo only worsened Mason's position in California. Sectional divisions in Congress over the status of slavery in the conquered territory defeated all attempts to resolve the status of California. Mason, despairing and asking, "What right or authority have I, to exercise civil control in time of peace in a territory of the United States?" submitted his resignation in November 1848. [42]

Mason resigned not only because he was convinced that continued military rule was not warranted, but also, and more importantly, because of the consequences of the gold discovery near Sutter's Fort in early 1848—a discovery that was as unanticipated as it was electric in effect. By the summer of 1848 gold mania had engulfed the entire province. Towns, north and south, were abandoned. Agriculture and commerce came to a halt. The territory's newspapers ceased publication. The ranks of government—soldiers, alcaldes, and officers alike—disappeared. "The discovery of these vast deposits of gold," Mason reported, "has entirely changed the character of Upper California. Its people, before engaged in cultivating their small patches of ground and guarding their herds of cattle and horses, have all gone to the mines, or are on their way thither; laborers of every trade have left their work benches, and tradesmen their shops; sailors desert their ships as fast as they arrive on the coast. . . . Many desertions," he added, "have taken place from the garrison within the influence of the mines."[43] With the abandonment of his men, the last remnants of Mason's resolve evaporated.

The gold rush altered the terms of politics fundamentally. North of Monterey, in particular, the stream of fortune seekers in 1848 and 1849 brought immense changes to the physical landscape and social order. From a small trading post and presidio populated in 1846 by four or five hundred hardy souls, San Francisco was transformed by mid-1849 into an instant city with a floating population of ten to thirty thousand.[44] Its harbor, choked with ships, appeared as a spectacular "forest of masts." Foreigners in native costume and miners wearing plaid shirts and heavy boots jammed the streets. Paths wound though the city's hills, which were covered with "tents of every color."[45] This manmade spectacle was summed up in one word by arriving Americans: *Progress*. As John Freaner wrote to the *New Orleans Daily Picayune* in October 1849:

> No pen can describe the progress of improvement in this country. The first we hear in the morning and the last we hear at night is the noise of the hammer and the saw. It is utterly impossible for any person to keep pace with the onward march of general melioration in all things. Walk the town of San Francisco today and make a memorandum of all the new houses, and some one will follow right after and report the erection of a new building. I came thither about three months ago, and since that time the town has more than quadrupled in size. Commerce and trade of every kind keep pace with the increase of buildings. The streets are filled with merchandise, while the beach is daily covered with goods, arriving and shipping for the coast and rivers. Real estate is cash in hand and sixty days, but still it has continued steadily to advance.[46]

Entrepôt for men and material bound for the mines, headquarters for merchants and shippers, and winter home to miners, San Francisco quickly became gold rush California's population and commercial center.[47] The city also became a center of renewed agitation against the military government, agitation not by old settlers but by newly arrived fortune seekers. According to the merchants and lawyers who dominated San Francisco's public life, military rule could neither assure the public's protection nor provide the necessary basis for the new city's commercial interests. Throughout the winter, spring, and early summer of 1849, these concerned citizens pressed their case against military rule before public grievance meetings and on the pages of San Francisco newspapers.

Large as San Francisco was, most of the eighty thousand immigrants in 1849 had as their destination the goldfields a hundred miles inland. Along the tributaries of the Sacramento and San Joaquin rivers, transitory mining camps appeared and disappeared throughout the first year of the rush as surface deposits were exhausted and miners heard of new strikes. Driven by the search for wealth, and without thought of permanent settlement, most miners aimed simply to "make a pile" and return home. In the camps, therefore, few were troubled by military rule or, for that matter, provincial politics in general. Public concerns here focused on more immediate issues: the regulation of mining claims and punishment of crimes against person and property. These responsibilities fell to informal associations such as the "miner's assembly and vigilance committee."[48] Where time was of the essence and impermanence the mark of social life, there was little interest in the questions that so vexed San Franciscans.

More substantial than the transitory mining camps were the towns of Stockton and Sacramento, which served as inland supply centers for the southern and northern mines. The commercial needs of miners drew merchants, shippers, businessmen, teamsters, and tradesmen by the score, and so gave these towns the mark of permanence. Stockton, remarked Bayard Taylor in 1849, was "bustling and prosperous. . . . The crowd on the levee would not disgrace a much larger place at home. Launches were arriving and departing daily for and from San Francisco, and the number of mule-teams, wagons, *etc.*, on their way to the various mines with freight and supplies kept up a life of activity truly amazing."[49] According to Louisianan John Freaner, "It is and will continue to be the depot for all the mines from the Macalemia [*sic*] River south. There is an average of $10,000 of goods disembarked there per day."[50] Sacramento, wrote Alonzo Delano, was

a city indeed. . . . An immense business was doing with the mines in furnishing supplies, the river was lined with ships, the streets were thronged with drays, teams, and busy pedestrians; the stores were large and well filled with merchandise, and even Aladdin could not have been more surprised at the powers of his wonderful lamp, than I was at the mighty changes which less than twelve months had wrought, since the first cloth tent had now grown into a large and flourishing city.[51]

Here, as in San Francisco, gold rush city builders raised the cry for civil government. To the ambitious new arrivals, public order and commercial opportunity demanded the certainty of American law. "Business was remarkably brisk, and continually increasing," observed Sacramentan Peter Burnett. "Lots were selling rapidly, and who should take the acknowledgements and record the deeds?"[52] Mexican law was alien and could not provide the desired framework to order the complexities of an instantly created market economy. For the "protection of their lives and property" and "some regular form of government," residents of Stockton and Sacramento joined their San Francisco counterparts in agitating for a constitutional convention.[53]

Governor Mason's decision to resign implicitly confirmed what events would show: the gold discovery had placed the situation beyond the control of any individual. During the winter of 1848–1849, questions of law, government, and military rule received renewed attention, particularly in the instant cites of gold rush California. The population of San Francisco was swollen by the arrival of newcomers and wintering miners, who voiced concern over public order and the lack of familiar rules and procedures to guide the city's commerce. The military government and alcaldes, formerly nuisances, created a situation, according to the recently merged *California Star and Californian* of San Francisco, that was "anarchical and anomalous."[54] San Francisco's alcalde, Thaddeus Leavenworth, was widely believed to have parceled out valuable town lots to friends. A certain sense of terror, moreover, descended on the city when an organization composed of former soldiers, alleged Australian convicts, and others, calling itself the "Hounds," rose to prominence. From headquarters referred to as "Tammany Hall," the Hounds paraded forth on Sundays to the Peruvian and Chilean quarters of the city, where they drank, harassed residents, extorted protection money, and visited the area's brothels. Matters came to a head in July, when the Hounds went on a rampage, raping a woman and murdering her mother, burning and plundering tents and shops, and beating anyone who resisted. The following day the alcalde appointed a city guard, which rounded up seventeen suspects. An informal trial, conducted by judges and attorneys selected by the alcalde from among the men who had raised the hue and cry, convicted nine of the suspects and banished them from the city.[55]

In the face of alleged alcalde corruption and such threats to public order as the Hounds, San Franciscans called for a "revolution." What was needed, insurgents proclaimed in the press and before public meetings, was a new "system." As the state's first delegation to Congress later observed in a memorial describing the events that led to California's constitutional convention, "the increased wants which were daily growing from a rapidly rising and extended commerce, and the growing demands of an enterprising and progressive people, all required a new and compatible system of government."[56] Declared Edward Gilbert, editor of the San Francisco *Alta California:* "A system that is without controlling power—without a steadfast guide, is as likely to turn its destroying hands against the good as the bad."[57]

What the immigrants meant by a "compatible system" was demonstrated in a series of local revolts against appointed alcaldes and a concurrent movement for a settlers' convention to frame a provisional government. In the winter and spring of 1849, public meetings abolished the office of alcalde in San Francisco, Sacramento, and Sonoma and transferred power to elected district legislatures.[58] The specific sequence of events varied from place to place, but central to each movement was a concern for public order and the demand that the structure of commercial life be regularized. Lawyers involved in real estate speculation; businessmen jockeying for control of new harbor wharfage; and merchants demanding a say in the allocation of public monies for roads and other public improvements, police and fire protection, and the creation of courts—these men played the central role.

In Sonoma and Sacramento, the alcaldes acceded to the new assemblies without delay, but in San Francisco the alcalde refused to comply. The ensuing conflict, which lasted into the summer of 1849, expressed the dissidents' concerns clearly: "No one can, or will deny," declared San Francisco's legislative assembly,

> that the country has been in a deplorable state since the news of the peace,—no one will pretend for a moment that the town of San Francisco has not been the most seriously afflicted of any in the territory. Her public funds have been squandered in unaccountable ways,—her public records have been mutilated and destroyed—her public domain has been disposed of without reserving lots for public squares or public buildings, and much of it has recently been sold by the *alcalde,* in defiance of the law, and without being accounted for. She is without police regulation, without public improvement, without the laws or machinery for raising a revenue, without a dollar in the treasury, and when her citizens rise up as one man and resolve that these evils shall be remedied, that there shall be an end to the system of peculation, fraud, and wrong by which they have so long suffered, a military government enters the arena and prostitutes its giant strength to perpetuate abuses such as no other community ever permitted.[59]

Complementing these revolts against alcalde rule was a more general movement—also concentrated in the northern districts—against de facto military government. During the first winter of the gold rush, public meetings in San Francisco, Sacramento, Sonoma, San Jose, and Monterey appointed "committees of correspondence" to arrange a settlers' convention to establish a provisional state government. These committees repeated on the provincial level the positions taken locally by the district assemblies. De facto military rule was arbitrary by its very nature. Based as it was on fiat rather than the consent of the governed, it was not a government at all but, rather, the absence of such: "anarchy." As the editor of the *California Star and Californian* put it, in a revealing if not felicitous passage, the peculiar conditions of the gold rush and the character of the gold rush immigrant gave great immediacy to the need for a regular system of civil government. Military rule, according to this "old settler," involved the perils of a state of nature:

> we are now virtually *without* law, and if ever its absence threatened serious evils to the country, it is at the present time. . . . Ours is a great-growing community. . . . Each and all are immersed in speculations whereby self-interest may be promoted—self-interest is paramount, and means [i.e., methods] for the most immediate attainment of fortunes [are] unscrupulously resorted to. By a rapidly increasing class law and order would be entirely set aside, that they might soonest become rich—such characters flourish only in anarchy. By another, perhaps, any system of government [they] would be set at defiance.[60]

Calling their movement a "revolution," the Anglo-American immigrants pressed their call for a settlers' convention throughout the winter and spring of 1849.[61] But no such convention was ever held. Owing to poor communications and the province's geographic, social, and cultural divisions, it proved impossible to agree on a date (originally scheduled for January, the convention was first postponed to March, then May, and finally to August) or, more importantly, to guarantee the participation of the districts south of Monterey.[62]

Ironically, it was through the offices of the military governor that the rebellious immigrants ultimately realized their larger aim. In April 1849 Mason's successor, Brevet General Bennett C. Riley, arrived. Quickly convinced by Secretary of State Halleck that the military government was incapable of controlling the district legislatures, impressed by the momentum of support for a settlers' convention, and discouraged by another congressional adjournment without a bill making California a territory, Riley moved to end the impasse.[63] "As Congress has failed to organize a new territorial government," he proclaimed on June 3,

> it becomes our imperative duty to take some active means to provide for the existing wants of the country. This, it is thought, may be best accomplished by putting into full vigor the administration of the laws as they now exist, and completing the organization of the civil government by the election and appointment of all officers recognized by law; while at the same time a convention, in which all parts of the territory are represented, shall meet and frame a State Constitution, or a territorial organization, to be submitted to the people for their ratification and then proposed to Congress for their approval.[64]

Riley's proclamation essentially legitimized the settlers' movement, but it also contained a bitter pill, for in return he demanded that the insurgents disband their district legislatures and, until the new government was ratified, recognize the military government's legitimacy—a position contrary to the charge that the military government was unwarranted.

In San Jose, Sonoma, and Sacramento, the military's critics accepted the conditions, but in San Francisco, where the movement was strongest, the district assembly balked. Two days after Riley's proclamation, a "mass meeting of the citizens of San Francisco" assembled at Portsmouth Square: "an enthusiastic and united demonstration," as the *Alta California* proclaimed. The meeting pronounced Riley's call for a convention as lacking force and declared that it was up to the "people of California . . . to assemble in their sovereign capacity, and elect delegates to a convention to form a constitution for a State Government." On the same day, the city's legislative assembly issued an "address to the People of California," thus defying the governor's declaration of their illegality. The *Alta California* characterized the day's busy proceedings as a "Revolution" and sympathetically reviewed its "Progress." "The great principles which are involved," asserted editor Gilbert, "can never wear away":

> Truth crushed to earth shall rise again,
> The eternal years of God are hers,
> But Error wounded, writhes in pain,
> And dies amid her worshipers.[65]

In a corner of the same issue, Gilbert made a less florid but more important observation. The necessity of a constitutional convention, he remarked, was undeniable, and although the arguments against cooperation with the governor were convincing and correct, "it is still hoped that some amicable arrangement can be made by which a harmonious and able convention may be brought together."[66] Gilbert's little-noticed comments were prescient. A week later, the rebellion against Riley ended quickly when the San Francisco district legislature and committee of correspondence agreed to accept "the time and place mentioned by General Riley in his Proclamation, and acceded to by the people of the other districts."[67]

Grudgingly, the military's most vehement critics thus submitted to a rapprochement, and preparations for the convention, which would meet in the old Mexican capital of Monterey, began. With the bickering at an end, a new set of questions arose. Who would be elected as delegates? What issues demanded the convention's attention? Which men, or groups of men, would dominate the writing of the constitution? What sort of "system" would they establish? When Riley announced the convention, these questions had no ready answer. Indeed, the election of delegates foreshadowed the diversity that would mark the state-making assembly.

Of the nine Californios who served in the convention, all but one represented the coastal settlements south of San Jose that were being bypassed by arriving forty-niners. With the exception of San Diego, where the military garrison dominated the voting, the elections in these southern districts were held under the auspices of the Hispanic gentry and their Anglo cousins.[68] In the vast Los Angeles district, recalled Stephen Foster, "so little interest was felt that the only election was held [in the pueblo itself]. . . . Only forty eight votes were polled and there was only one ticket in the field."[69] The elected delegates agreed to push for a north-south division of California; this would allow the northern districts to form a state and the southern ones to establish a territorial government, thus insulating the old regime from Anglo dominance. Otherwise the election, which was held during a feast and fandango at the home of a prominent Angeleno, proceeded without electioneering, party nominations, or dissent.

Reporting on the elections in San Jose and Sonoma, the *Alta California* regretted "that the people . . . [there] have not, in their primary assemblages, adopted resolutions expressing the sentiments of the public. The important political questions which are likely to arise in the convention [will therefore] be discussed and decided without any definite information as to the wishes and views of the constituency."[70] Nonetheless, both the elections and the delegates chosen in these districts displayed key features of their locale. Relatively isolated from the coastal settlements of Mexican California, San Jose and Sonoma had substantial Hispanic populations that had felt the effect of overland Anglo-American immigration in the early 1840s. The elected delegates aptly represented the uneasy accord that had emerged out of earlier conflict and conquest. "Old settlers"—Anglo-Americans who had arrived before both the war with Mexico and the gold rush—dominated both delegations. But each included a prominent Californio as well: Antonio Pico in San Jose and Mariano Vallejo in Sonoma. Both Pico and Vallejo had been involved in the movement for a provisional government, and both had long before made their peace with the earlier American settlers, if not yet with the gold rush Yankees.[71]

By contrast, in the instant gold rush metropolis of San Francisco, which had the largest delegation, the election was "one of the most animated and spirited contests . . . ever witnessed. . . . There were a great many tickets in the field and the canvassing by the friends of each was ardent, yet proper and orderly."[72] The tickets were not connected to parties; rather, they represented instant alliances of recently acquainted men who had captured central roles in San Francisco politics during the previous six months: opponents of the alcalde and the military government, participants in the chase and trial of the Hounds, members of the city's legislative assembly, and public speakers at the mass demonstrations for a settlers' convention.[73] Nowhere else were issues as clearly enunciated or the gold rush immigrants' conception of a proper governmental system as explicitly exposed. As editor Gilbert of the *Alta California* put it, "We desire to see [California] take that rank which her commercial position on the coast of the Pacific, her untold mineral wealth, and her great agricultural resources, point out as her destiny."[74]

To do so, the convention had to address pressing needs created by the anarchy of military rule. The constitution, according to the *Alta California*, should establish a legal basis for incorporation, insure universal (white male) suffrage, stipulate that public lands be distributed only to actual settlers, regulate access to mineral regions and define the method of their taxation, provide for the allocation of public funds for internal improvements, and memorialize Congress to build a branch mint in San Francisco.[75] Equally, if not more importantly, the constitution must outlaw slavery—in the interest of free white labor. Noted the *Alta*, echoing an argument pressed at antislavery meetings throughout the previous six months, "The interests of the mass, those who dig and delve, and earn their bread, and learn self respect and enterprise from the necessities of labor, render it [the prohibition of slavery] imperative."[76]

In the mining districts, the election was yet another matter. Few miners saw their residence in the camps, not to mention California, as permanent. Fewer still were interested in stopping work and participating in the state-making project. The conflict with the military government that so vexed California's city dwellers held little interest for miners in the flush summer season of 1849, and they left the politicking to others. Of the fourteen men who represented the Sacramento and San Joaquin districts, none was a miner. Instead these delegations were divided among old settlers, whose original agricultural vision of California had been rudely upset by the invasion of the forty-niners; recently arrived merchants, lawyers, and speculators from Sacramento and Stockton; and, finally, gold rush adventurers who saw in state making an avenue to position and prominence in this new land. These men gained the public's attention, and hence their election as delegates, in a variety of ways: by virtue of long residence; their prominence as town builders, merchants, and lawyers; their participation in the municipal revolt against alcalde rule and the military government; or simply their talents as political showmen before hastily gathered mining camp assemblies.

James McHall Jones, a self-proclaimed "citizen of nine days," exemplified this last type. With only a week to canvass the camps of the southern mines, this twenty-four-year-old Louisianan departed from San Francisco. "Picture me then," he wrote his mother,

> seven days before the election, mounted upon a staid and sober-going mule, wending my way to the Diggin's mumified [*sic*] with a blanket, provision bag, and letter of introduction, and armed with a brandy bottle and an enormous pair of Mexican spurs. Thus armed and equipped I made my grand entree into "Woods Diggin's," a great huddle of miner's tents in a wide ravine or "gulch," and opened the ball. I soon ascertained that a ticket of "old and respectable" citizens had been some time before formed and

sent through the mines. What a damper upon my prospects as a future
legislator. But "*nil desperandum*,"

I CALLED A MEETING

I MADE A SPEECH

I preached all sorts of patriotic sentiments and broached innumerable ex-
tempore theories of ameliorating the condition of mines and miners. And
I not only got on their ticket in the place of some unfortunate gentleman,
but they gave me letters to their friends at other places.[77]

By making his way through the southern camps, stopping miners on the
trail, and escorting them to the polls, Jones gained a seat in the convention—one of many who saw greater opportunity in politics and the law
than in digging gold.

In late August, the elected delegates departed for Monterey from all
corners of California. Some almost didn't make it; coastal transportation
was irregular and unreliable, and travel by land (there were neither
stages nor well-traveled highways) demanded stamina and weeks of
preparation. Governor Riley, recognizing the predicament he would
face should the delegates fail to arrive, sent the steamer *Edith* to transport the delegates from the south, and the brig *Fremont* for those to the
north. Fortunately, the southerners declined the favor, for the *Edith*
sank off Santa Barbara, with all on board killed. The northern delegates
on the *Fremont* were more fortunate, but their voyage was not free from
peril. Observed Jones:

> We were five days coming a little more than ninety miles, with a drunken
> captain and an inefficient crew, and continually surrounded by fogs, so
> that, from the time we started till we stopped, we never found where we
> were. On the fifth day, however, about 6 O'clock, there was a cry of break-
> ers, and we suddenly ran into shallow waters with the breakers running
> about 100 yards ahead. Our only salvation was to drop anchor. The sun
> broke out clearly for the first time the morning after, and wonderful to
> betell! we had run right into Monterey Harbor, when a mistake of half a
> mile would have wrecked us beyond a hope. Of course the captain, who
> had been awfully scared the night before, declared that he knew all the
> time exactly where he was going.[78]

Once on shore, the delegates got their first look at the convention
town, which few had visited before. The view, whether from land or sea,
was impressive. "The town of Monterey," reported convention observer
John Durivage, "is one of the most ancient . . . and to my mind it is the
pleasantest on the coast."[79] To Anglo visitors, Monterey presented a
stark contrast to the popular image of gold rush California. It seemed

almost medieval, a place where an older, and very un-American, way of life persisted. As forty-niner E. Gould Buffum put it:

> It retains its old Spanish peculiarities, and Yankee innovations have as yet made but little progress there. The Spanish don, clothed in his *serape* and *calcineros*, still walks through the streets with his lordly air, and the pretty *señorita*, her dark eyes peering through the folds of her *reboso*, skips lightly along the footpath. The ancient customs are still continued here, and the sound of the guitar and the light shuffling of feet are heard nightly in the *casas*. . . . There are several American residents in Monterey at the present time, engaged in mercantile pursuits, but very little building is in progress, and the town bids fair to remain for a long time a representative of California as she was before the indomitable Yankee introduced his "notions" into her territory.[80]

The American's exotic description, however, obscured more than it revealed about Monterey. The town's history, invisible to the arriving Yankees, contained in microcosm the sociology of Hispanic California and the consequences that "Americanization"—under way even before the conquest—would have on the old regime. An old town by California standards, Monterey had served as the province's capital for eighty years, under the flags of Spain, Mexico, and the United States. In the 1830s—following Mexican independence, the opening of the hide and tallow trade, and mission secularization—the town had been transformed from a moribund administrative headquarters into a prominent governmental and trading center. By 1836, Monterey's population of traders and merchants, prominent landholding families and their retainers, artisans, casual laborers, and visibly desperate Indians stood almost exactly at seven hundred.

Thirteen years later when the convention delegates arrived, Monterey had grown again by half, to almost eleven hundred inhabitants. But numbers alone do not begin to describe the new order of things in the town. Following the American conquest the Yankee alcalde, Walter Colton, a Congregational minister trained at Yale, did his best to impose an American sense of administrative efficiency and New England morality. Using the broad powers at his command he introduced trial by jury, enacted restrictions on grog shops and gambling, codified the town's laws, and established statutory penalties for crime.[81] Less formally, the conquest unleashed the Anglo-Americans' penchant for remaking the land in their own image. The signs of their presence were soon apparent everywhere. "El Cuartel," the former headquarters of the Mexican army, became the home of the American military governor. The Customs House became a warehouse, hospital, and office for the U.S. quartermaster. On the hill behind the town Yankee troops quickly put up barracks, and in a ravine near the harbor they built a dam and cistern to provide the town with a ready supply of water. Colton himself added the most visible sign of the American presence: a two-story schoolhouse cum public hall in the New England style.[82]

In addition to the official activities of the army, other Americans, both military and civilian, pursued their private advantage. In the months following the war's end, speculation in town lots increased the price of land 500 to 1,000 percent over its preconquest level. Where there had been only footpaths—"as each person has built on the spot and in the form he thought proper"—the newcomers laid out streets.[83] The Yankees' buildings, constructed of logs and planks, were easily distinguished from the adobes of the Californians and gave the town, to the eyes of American observers, a "more substantial, but rougher appearance."[84] On all sides, so it seemed, Americans were busy rationalizing the informal habits of the old town. "Improvements," reported the English trader William Garner, "are daily increasing in this town; the country has been for such a length of time under the Spanish government, and little or no improvements of note ever being made, either by the old Spanish or Mexican government, every step advanced by the Americans for the benefit of the country at large . . . excites the most pleasant feelings."[85]

Such "improvements" underscored the changes that American occupation had brought to Monterey's economic and social order. In 1836, when Juan Alvarado's revolutionary government conducted a census of the town, 90 percent of Monterey's residents were natives of either California or Mexico; of the remaining foreign population, only ten were from the United States: three prominent merchants, two young clerks, three craftsmen, a cook, and a soldier.[86] The town contained 24 percent more males than females, primarily because of an excess of males between the ages of twenty-five and forty: single male servants, laborers who boarded with pueblo families, and, above all, soldiers. Monterey's occupational structure was simple, reflecting the town's administrative and military role and its place as a port of call in the hide and tallow trade. The largest occupational group in the town was represented by the ninety-six soldiers—40 percent of Monterey's employed population—who resided in barracks. Of the remainder, two out of ten were unskilled, working when needed on neighboring ranchos and in town households. Fifty-seven Montereyans were skilled craftsmen, representing but fifteen different trades, above all blacksmithing, various building trades, and tailoring. A handful of clerks, scribes, secretaries, and cashiers provided services to town merchants and government officials. At the top of this foreshortened pyramid stood twenty-one men, fifteen of whom were merchants, who dominated the influential positions in government and trade.

Despite the presence of the military garrison, Monterey in 1836 was notable for the network of families that linked pueblo society and economy. Hispanics headed the vast majority (86 percent) of the town's households, which on the whole consisted of either a husband and wife and their children (16 percent of families) or, more commonly, a nuclear family augmented by kinfolk or boarders (59 percent). An additional 13 percent of the town's residents lived in single-parent households (accounted for largely by widows with children), a quarter of which had additional kin in residence. The remaining inhabitants (12 percent) lived beyond the town's family order in single-person households; these Montereyans, for the most part, resided in the town's three military barracks.

By the time of the constitutional convention, this older Monterey was gone. Between 1836 and 1849 Anglos—Americans above all—overtook the Hispanic population both numerically and economically.[87] During these years, as we have seen, Monterey's population increased by more than half, from 702 to 1,092, most of the increase accounted for by the arrival of Americans and Europeans. In 1836, Hispanics represented 90 percent of the town's population, but by 1849 their number, which had increased in absolute terms by only 5 percent, had declined by a third as a proportion of the total population. The non-Hispanic population, by contrast, grew significantly in the 1840s, increasing almost sixfold; thus in the year of the constitutional convention, four of ten Montereyans were non-Hispanic. A major portion of the newcomers were males between the ages of twenty and forty, which gave the town's population a youthful, male, Yankee cast. These newcomers wasted no time in entering business and speculating in town property, and they did so on a new, bigger scale. Between 1842 and 1848, for example, they patented over half of the house lots added to Monterey—in parcels ten times larger, on average, than those of their Hispanic counterparts.[88]

In terms of work and economy, the newcomers introduced a relatively diversified occupational structure, in the process initiating the historical segregation of Monterey's Hispanic population into lower-status occupations.[89] By 1849 the newcomers dominated the upper mercantile, professional, and official occupations and had doubled the number of skilled trades from fifteen to thirty. In addition, and predictably, American soldiers made their presence known in the Monterey garrison. Hispanics (surprisingly, given their domination of the town's mercantile and trading system in 1836) were by 1849 concentrated in small proprietorships (store-, hotel-, and saloon-keeping), farm work, and, most notably, casual labor: fully 60 percent of adult Hispanic males listed no occupation in the census of 1850.

The town's household order had likewise changed. The number of discrete residences in the town doubled between 1836 and 1849, from 93 to 188, with non-Hispanics heading almost all of the new ones. As a result, the newcomers, who in the 1830s had headed only 14 percent of the town's households, headed more than half in 1849, altering not only the makeup of the town's residences, but also the substance of its family life. Most noticeable was the increase in single-person households, which at the time of the convention accounted for over four out of every ten households in Monterey. Overall, the number of nuclear households (including those augmented by kin and boarders) declined by 20 percent, although pure nuclear families increased in number. Thus we see a dual effect of non-Hispanic immigration: first was the arrival of single males, mainly soldiers but also young, transient immigrants whose stay in Monterey would be short; second, and more important, was the settling in the town of a new American- and European-born class that intended, according to one report, "to make a permanent settlement, and engage in mercantile pursuits."[90] These newcomers had arrived with their families, had no parents or relatives in need of housing, and—expressive of a privatism that contrasted with the extensive familial life of the older Hispanic town—neither needed nor desired to take in boarders.

To no small degree, by 1849 these newcomers had made Monterey their own. Its old-world appearance to the convention delegates and onlookers stemmed from the visual effect of adobe buildings and the absence of the rectangular street system that physically defined most U.S. towns and cities. Particularly striking, however, was the want of institutions that Anglo-Americans intuitively expected to find in any capital city, but that simply did not exist in Monterey: hotels, restaurants, saloons, and public entertainments. In Spanish and Mexican California, such services had been unnecessary. Travelers, private as well as official, were expected to stay with family or friends. Social life centered on kin ties and the family circle.

Even before the constitutional convention ended, the establishments and entertainments expected by the Yankees had appeared. But when the convention delegates and observers descended on Monterey in September 1849, the California correspondent for the *New Orleans Daily Picayune,* John Durivage, commented that "where in the world the worthy delegates are going to sleep and feed is a case of *quien sabe*—there is scarcely a vacant room in town, and but one *fonda,* or restaurant."[91] Travel journalist Bayard Taylor searched half an hour for a hotel until discovering that there was none.[92] The rush of visitors to the town created a market for accommodations, and by the time the convention had been in session a month four makeshift hotels had opened, along with a handful of restaurants, which, Alcalde Colton's best efforts notwithstanding, doubled as billiard halls and "gambling dens."[93] In the meantime, the delegates had to make do. For the Californios this posed no problem: they stayed with relatives. Yankee delegates rented cots in various homes or else elected to sleep in the loft of El Quartel, the military headquarters, which Governor Riley made available to them. The latter quarters, however, were so infested with fleas that many opted to camp in the pine forest behind the town.[94]

Over the course of the convention, Monterey's first Californio families opened their homes to the delegates. That of Augusta Jimeno, sister of Santa Barbara delegate Pablo de la Guerra, was a favorite meeting place, despite the hostess's outspoken animosity to the 1846 American invasion (she had once declared her desire for a necklace made of the ears of American officers). Feliciano Soberanes, who had fought the Americans in 1846, also held receptions and dances during the convention, as did José Abrego, whose parlor contained one of the few pianos on the Pacific Coast.[95] Delegate Thomas Larkin, an American fixture in Monterey since the early 1830s, entertained one or more of his colleagues every day "at a regular set dinner, Boston cooking."[96] John and Jessie Frémont reportedly held "many informal star-chamber meetings" in lavishly decked out rooms located in the adobe of Frémont's 1846 nemesis, José Castro.[97] And in the convention's second week, the residents of the town as a whole put on a grand ball in honor of the delegates. After a lavish meal, the convention hall was cleared of tables to make way for dancing. Then, following a full evening, the *baile* closed with the early-morning wedding of the convention's chaplain to a recently arrived woman from the United States. All in all, Durivage reported, "it was quite a brilliant affair."[98]

In the midst of the search for lodging and meals and the round of festivities that the convention brought forth, the delegates began their business. The first three days were given over to debate on who was entitled to a seat. The governor's proclamation had provided for thirty-six delegates, but a dozen or so others demanded a seat, some claiming that the military officials and their "lackeys" in the convention had altered the election returns to deny them their rights.[99] After much testimony and debate, the delegates opened membership, for all intents and purposes, to anyone with a reasonable claim. A special committee arrived at a list of eligible delegates that, had all been in attendance, would have doubled the convention's size. Only twelve of these additional delegates were present in Monterey, however, and thus the convention proceeded with forty-eight members.

The delegates then turned to the election of a president. San Francisco delegate William McKendree Gwin, a headstrong former Mississippi congressman who made the most of his personal friendship with both Andrew Jackson and John Calhoun, had announced to his fellow delegates during the frightening voyage to Monterey that he was the obvious choice. According to Elisha Crosby, he "affected that air of superiority that to the average American is offensive. . . . We all supposed that one was about as good as another."[100] When selection of a president came on the agenda, Gwin's presumptuousness was mocked by delegate Jacob Snyder, an old settler renowned for his role in the ill-fated Bear Flag revolt in 1846. Noting that Gwin had come to Monterey not only expecting to be named president but also bearing a constitution that "he expected to have adopted at his dictation . . . [while] the rest of the delegates were to be merely dummies to represent numbers and sections and sanction whatever he proposed," Snyder nominated a fellow old settler, Robert Semple.[101] Semple, a somewhat legendary figure among pre–gold rush American settlers for his opposition to the military government, and before that for his role in the Bear Flag revolt, was easily elected to the post. The men appointed to escort him to the president's chair were similarly representative of California's pre–gold rush history: John Sutter and Mariano Vallejo—the latter being Juan Alvarado's uncle and ally in 1836 as well as the well-known captive of Semple, Snyder, and the other Bear Flaggers during their short-lived revolution.[102]

The convention's opening scenes suggested the course that the proceedings would take. The confusion over the seating of delegates underscored the disorder that had marked the territory's postconquest "interregnum." The selection of Semple, a man disparaged by some as an uneducated backwoodsman, demonstrated the distinction that California's pre–gold rush overland immigrants made between themselves and the new arrivals. Mariano Vallejo's self-conscious dignity testified to both his and the other Californio delegates' determination to insulate their people from the affects of Yankee domination. The animosity toward the military foreshadowed a key division among the delegates. And the effrontery of William Gwin, which ruined his chances of becoming the convention's president, illustrated the ambition and confidence, if not the political cunning, that made him and other gold rush immigrants the central figures in the writing of the constitution. The diversity, lack of familiarity with one another, and unpredictability that marked the opening of the meeting were stunning. On each point, the contrast with the constitutional convention that met in neighboring Oregon eight years later could not have been greater.

TWO

Farming and Politics:
Oregon, 1835–1857

Eight years after Californians held the Pacific Coast's first state constitutional convention, their Oregon neighbors followed suit. Despite the
proximity of the two states, their people, histories, and politics contrasted
sharply. At the time of statehood, Oregonians looked back on a generation of relatively slow, incremental American settlement, initiated by
Methodist missionaries in the 1830s and then recast in the 1840s by succeeding waves of farming families from the Ohio and Mississippi River
valleys. In contrast to California, the people of the Oregon Country were
a homogeneous lot. Tied to the land and arriving in familial groups,
they saw in the Willamette Valley an opportunity to remake a kin-based,
mixed subsistence-market agriculture on better terms than they had
known in their midwestern homes.[1]

The public life and political institutions they fashioned were closely
related to their rural ways. At the time of the constitutional convention
Oregonians had known and literally enjoyed local government for fifteen years, from 1843 to 1849 under a provisional government of their
own making, after 1849 under territorial institutions. Marked by face-to-
face relationships, conducted by well-known friends and neighbors, politics here expressed the settlers' common culture and provided the focus
of a community life otherwise attenuated by rural isolation. By 1857 territorial politics featured a familiar cast of local characters, old settlers
themselves, who stood at the head of organizations to which the men of
Oregon devoted their spirited allegiance. The constitutional convention
thus had a definite air of familiarity. Composed of old allies and adversaries, it was notable only for the number of luminaries in attendance.
Included in it was the entire territorial supreme court, seventeen past or
present members of the legislature, half-a-dozen federal appointees,
and a score of prominent party men and community leaders.[2] Passion-

ately devoted to various causes—personal, party, and ideological—these individuals aptly represented this rural society where, it was often said, "there are but two occupations . . . farming and politics."[3]

Oregon at midcentury differed markedly from California. But in crucial respects its history, like its neighbor's, turned on events that transpired between 1846 and 1849. To the south, conquest and the gold rush led to the rechartering of an older Hispanic society. During these same years in Oregon a very different society appeared, one dominated by immigrants who eschewed the lure of California gold, whose horizons were bounded by the experience and expectations of family farmers. Even as the Mexican-American War raged in the southwest, the Anglo-American Treaty of 1846 ended joint British-U.S. occupation of the Oregon Country and resolved the longstanding "Oregon question." Two years later, Congress established Oregon as a territory of the United States. Simultaneously, the California gold discovery drew men from Oregon and magnified the choice that immigrants had to make between the two Pacific Coast destinations.

Not all chose California (table 2). Although the vast majority headed for the goldfields, migration to Oregon after 1849 also accelerated. Between 1850 and 1855 more than thirty-three thousand overland settlers arrived, most of them from the rural regions of the Ohio and Mississippi River valleys.[4] Their arrival gave an enduring stamp to this territory. Indeed, their sheer numbers reinforced the social and cultural authority of kindred settlers who had come in the 1840s, thus bringing to an end the initial phase of the Pacific Northwest's history, which had been dominated by international rivalry and internal conflict between small groups of British subjects, American missionaries, and overland immigrants.

The midwestern immigrants who composed the charter group of the Oregon Country chose this place because of the prospect it held for landownership on a scale inconceivable in their former homes. In 1843, before the United States possessed Oregon, the province's provisional government passed an act that allowed any white male settler to claim at no cost a full section of land (640 acres, a square mile). The scale of landownership made possible by this act went far beyond the current United States law regulating possession of the public domain—the preemption act of 1841—which limited a settler to purchasing 160 acres at a cost of $1.25 per acre.[5] Added to widely advertised reports extolling the Oregon Country's healthy environment, mild climate, and wondrously productive soil, the provisional land law pulled upward of ten thousand people from the midwest between 1844 and 1849—even despite the absence of American dominion before 1846 and, until 1850, uncertainty of claims made under the measure.[6] Although the federal act creating the Oregon Territory in 1848 failed to mention, much less endorse, the provisional land legislation, two years later, in the Oregon Donation Land Law,

TABLE 2   Overland Immigration to Oregon and California,
1840–1860

	Oregon	California	Total
1840	13 (100%)	0 (0%)	13
1841	24 (41%)	34 (59%)	58
1842	125 (100%)	0 (0%)	125
1843	875 (96%)	38 (4%)	913
1844	1,475 (97%)	53 (3%)	1,528
1845	2,500 (91%)	260 (9%)	2,760
1846	1,200 (44%)	1,500 (56%)	2,700
1847	4,000 (90%)	450 (10%)	4,450
1848	1,300 (77%)	400 (23%)	1,700
Total 1840–1848	11,512 (81%)	2,735 (19%)	14,247
1849	450 (2%)	25,000 (98%)	25,450
1850	6,000 (12%)	44,000 (88%)	50,000
1851	3,600 (77%)	1,100 (23%)	4,700
1852	10,000 (17%)	50,000 (83%)	60,000
1853	7,500 (27%)	20,000 (73%)	27,500
1854	6,000 (33%)	12,000 (67%)	18,000
1855	500 (25%)	1,500 (75%)	2,000
1856	1,000 (11%)	8,000 (89%)	9,000
1857	1,500 (27%)	4,000 (73%)	5,500
1858	1,500 (20%)	6,000 (80%)	7,500
1859	2,000 (11%)	17,000 (89%)	1,900
1860	1,500 (14%)	9,000 (86%)	10,500
Total 1849–1860	41,550 (17%)	197,600 (83%)	239,150
Total 1840–1860	53,062 (21%)	200,335 (79%)	253,397
Percentage of Immigrants Arriving 1840–1848	22%	1%	6%
Average Annual Immigration, 1840–1848	1,279	303	1,583
Percentage of Immigrants Arriving 1849–1860	78%	99%	94%
Average Annual Immigration, 1849–1860	3,463	16,467	19,929

SOURCE: John D. Unruh, *The Plains Across: The Overland Emigrants and the Trans-Mississippi West, 1840–1860* (Urbana: University of Illinois Press, 1979), 119–120.

Congress placed its imprimatur on the claims of the early arrivals and continued the provisions of the provisional law through 1853 (later extended to 1855). The effects of the Oregon land laws were profound: they gave settlers the prospect of owning, simply through possession, magnificent family domains in the fertile Willamette Valley, and in so doing defined what settlers would come to Oregon. By 1856, when the donation law expired, settlers had entered approximately 7,500 claims, encompassing more than 2.5 million acres, mostly in the Willamette Valley (map 1). As early as 1851, observers noted with alternating wonder and concern that little land remained in the territory's heartland valley, a conclusion affirmed in 1857 when the surveyor-general of the territory reported that "there is but little vacant good land west of the Cascade mountains."[7]

❧

Both before and after the discovery of gold in California, commercial considerations played a decidedly secondary role in the decision of midwestern farmers to make Oregon their home. The 1840s saw a dearth of markets for the area's producers and no realistic prospect that they would quickly appear. Even after the gold rush created an instant outlet for agricultural goods, the behavior of Oregon farmers displayed, if not outright disinterest, a nonchalance and indifference toward the logic and opportunity of commercial agriculture that local merchants and outside observers found perplexing.

The effect of California gold on Oregon was more complex (and, by virtue of its complexity, more revealing) than generally believed. Oregon's settlers were well placed to take advantage of the gold discovery, and when word of the strike arrived in Oregon in August 1848, hundreds left. Those who stayed behind, along with new arrivals, worried about the consequences of an exodus to the goldfields. As the Reverend George Atkinson put it,

> Most of our men, mechanics, loafers, farmers, merchants, etc., have been preparing to leave for California to make their fortunes digging gold this winter. It is astonishing. Men from the sanctifying influence of the camp meeting, from the common table, from the comforts of home, from the bosom of their families are leaving every comfort to camp in the woods or on the plains in snow or rain for months with no provision but flour to obtain gold. They go in thousands and leave good business, sacrifice property, pay high for goods, venture health, all for gold. Boys go. Morals will suffer with industry, minds, bodies, friends. . . . The elder of our chln. [*sic*] goes, also all our physicians, 4 in no., 3 or 4 ministers go, 2 merchants . . .[8]

Atkinson's anxiety, while characteristic, overstated the extent and misjudged the consequences of the departures. In the final analysis, the gold rush affected Oregon not simply because it carried people away, but

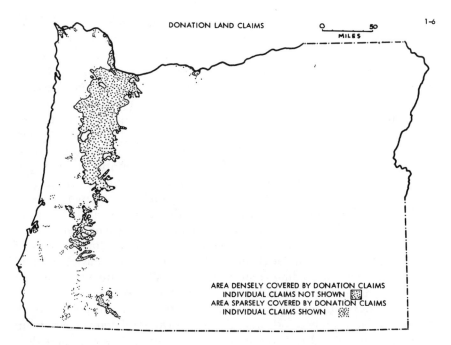

Map 1. Concentration of Oregon donation land claims. (Map courtesy of William Loy.)

because it had a filtering effect that magnified the social and cultural homogeneity of the region's population. Many left Oregon in 1848 never to return, pulled permanently by gold and related market opportunities in California. Others came back to the "comfort of home" and "bosom of their families."[9] And they did so quickly. By the fall of 1849 hundreds of Oregonian argonauts reappeared. By all accounts, they had done well during their brief sojourn in California. Arriving before the onslaught of forty-niners, they mined in relative isolation and brought home an estimated five million dollars in gold.[10] The swiftness of their return, as well as the satisfaction they felt from a single foray to the mines, was striking. Leaving the goldfields even as new rich placer deposits were being discovered, and well before mining and commercial opportunities had peaked, these Oregonians testified to the limited scope of their material ambitions.

The gold carried back by the miners of 1848 and 1849, together with the California market for timber, wheat, and other agricultural goods that grew out of the gold rush, inaugurated a period of growth and prosperity in Oregon, though along lines shaped at every point by the American fragment that made up the territorial population. Money and markets encouraged expansion of wheat growing, flour milling, lumber production, and, somewhat later, vegetable, dairy, and fruit production in the Willamette Valley. They also drew to Oregon a small group of merchants from the northeastern states, men who chose consciously to pursue the comparatively modest promises of Oregon's rural economy over the more dazzling, perilous, and competitive opportunities present in San Francisco and other instant cities of the gold rush.[11] Cautious and conservative, preferring "cash on delivery" as "our way of doing business," they fit in well with the rural settlers and were quick to settle down and make Oregon their permanent home.[12] Arranging for the transportation and sale of staples for the California trade, they helped lessen the economic isolation that had marked the Oregon Country in the 1840s. They set in motion regular transportation and communication connecting the Columbia and Willamette rivers first with San Francisco and then with the Panama and Cape Horn routes to the eastern seaboard and Europe. In this way they encouraged the expansion of agricultural production throughout the Willamette Valley. This widening of the area of cultivation in turn stimulated the development of river navigation and the rise of interior trading centers along the Willamette River, linking Oregon's hinterland with the head of navigation at Portland.[13]

Yet the development of the Oregon Country during the gold rush era had a peculiar cadence and character of its own, inhibited at every point by three interrelated factors whose combined effects were greater than the sum of their parts. First, the provisional and federal land laws were very generous, and the rapid appropriation of land under them created an agricultural economy dominated by large, relatively isolated, family landholdings (table 3). The large size of these holdings, along with the constraints of family labor and rudimentary technology, circumscribed the actual area under cultivation and limited the aggregate expansion of agricultural production.[14] Second, throughout the 1850s a dearth of labor restricted the growth of both agricultural production and manufacturing as potential workers, already limited in number by the isolation of the territory, more often than not chose the California goldfields over Oregon. Third—and this factor was both cause and consequence of the above—Oregon farmers showed themselves to be relatively indifferent to the ethos of capital accumulation. Their response to the California market—their enterprise—was motivated as much by a modest desire to improve their landholdings, assure their households' self-sufficiency, and enhance their families' material comfort as by a drive to command greater market share or increase production as an end in itself.

Faced with subsistence needs, and to some extent content with meeting them, Oregon farmers, according to one of their number, were not

yet prepared to cultivate the earth in such a way as to ensure the highest results which the land is susceptible of being made to Yield [sic]. Our emigrants often hurry in a crop after they arrive, with as little preparation as

TABLE 3   Average Farm Size, Oregon and the Midwest, 1850 and
1860 (with ratio of Oregon farm size to other states)

State	1850	1860
Oregon	372 (1.00)	355 (1.00)
Ohio	125 (2.98)	114 (3.11)
Indiana	136 (2.74)	124 (2.86)
Illinois	158 (2.35)	143 (2.48)
Michigan	129 (2.88)	113 (3.14)
Wisconsin	148 (2.51)	114 (3.11)
Minnesota	184 (2.02)	149 (2.38)
Iowa	185 (2.01)	164 (2.16)
Missouri	179 (2.08)	215 (1.65)
Kansas	—	171 (2.08)
Nebraska	—	226 (1.57)

SOURCE: *Historical Statistics of the United States, Colonial Times to 1970* (Washington, D.C.: Government Printing Office, 1975), 461.

possible, in order to bread them the following year; others attempt nothing more than to raise a sufficiency for their own use—and the very facility with which grain is produced leads to habits of careless cultivation.[15]

More modern-minded observers remarked often on the seeming disregard of Oregon farmers to the opportunities before them. When local producers failed to meet local demand for flour and other foodstuffs or allowed eastern and South American producers to gain shares of the California market that easily could have been theirs, critics were quick to find the cause in their "want of industry" and "carelessness." "During the last ten years," a Portland paper scolded at the end of the 1850s, "Oregon has produced and shipped to California wheat, flour, pork, potatoes, onions, butter, cheese, &c., to the amount of several million dollars. Now California speculators are shipping here, from San Francisco, butter, which costs there 42 cents, and selling it for $1 per pound."[16]

Such complaints most often expressed the sentiments of outsiders. In Oregon, farmers and merchants alike displayed a certain contentment with modest commercial attainments. Samuel Thurston, the first territorial delegate to Congress and author of the Donation Land Law, captured the prevailing opinion when, in describing Oregon to potential immigrants, he defined it as "the true *El Dorado of the West.*" The portrait of El Dorado that he drew, however, neither compared Oregon to California nor described it as a place where ambitious, self-seeking young men could make their fortune. Rather, in terms contrived for farming folk, he depicted Oregon as a rural place of comfort, health, and ease, where "aristocracy finds . . . a poor dwelling place, and a republican equality is the presiding genius of the land." In detail he described Oregon's terrain and climate, its "rich valleys," "water . . . no where surpassed, *no where equaled*," "timber of a mammoth race," and "temperate [climate], alike in summer and winter." In Oregon, he "desire[d] it to be distinctly understood,"

> with the same amount of labour, [a farmer] can raise produce of more value than he can any where in the states. I care not what he inquires after, whether corn . . . , wheat, oats, rye, barley, buckwheat, peas, beans, potatoes, turnips, cabbages, onions, parsnips, carrots, beets, currants, gooseberries, strawberries, apples, peaches, pears, or *fat and healthy babies;* in the production of all of them *we ask no favours.*

Pointing out that "whenever a man comes into the territory, he lays himself off 640 acres," Thurston urged his readers to "bring all your guns to bear and reach Oregon, for if you land there without staff or scrip, and having but one coat, or *none at all,* you have nothing to fear. Money is plenty, the highest wages are paid for men's and women's labour, and we have a generous and free people, who know how to sympathize with another's woes, toils, and hardships." [17]

Delegate Thurston keenly understood the character and desires of Oregon's farming people. As such, he was the first in a long series of local men who possessed the insight and instincts essential to political success in this territory. He died unexpectedly in Panama in 1851, however, while hurrying home to a hero's welcome for having ushered the Donation Land Law through Congress. Consequently, Oregon politics, which he had hoped to dominate (and to which end he made elaborate preparations), became the creation of others. Most important among them was a group of Thurston protégés, young men he recruited through friends in both Iowa (where he lived before coming to Oregon) and New England (where he was born). Others typified a prominent western type well represented in the Oregon Country: the farmer-lawyer. Still others were what Earl Pomeroy has termed "western carpet-baggers," party men who arrived with federal appointments to the territorial government. [18]

When news of Thurston's death reached the territory in early 1851, there was no lack of men eager to seek his congressional seat and claim his place as Oregon's leading public figure. Foremost among them was Joseph Lane, who had come to Oregon in 1849 as the territory's first governor. Lane was not a Thurston man (a fact of eventual consequence), but he was cut from the same midwestern cloth as the Oregon population. A prominent Indiana Democrat and Mexican War hero, he brought with him a heroic reputation that was captured in a number of sobriquets. Known as the "Marion of the Mexican War," "Cincinnatus of Indiana," "Young Hickory," he embodied symbols with immediate appeal to the rural people of the Oregon Country: the legacy of the revolutionary struggle, the republican virtues of the citizen-soldier, and the Jacksonian principles of local sovereignty and rural democracy.[19] Personally, Lane felt a genuine attraction to Oregon. As governor he demonstrated a capacity for dramatic action as well as a knack for well-placed flattery. In his first public address, he endeared himself to Oregonians with paeans to the territory's agricultural promise and "future greatness," its people's "virtue [and] intelligence," and their vital role in extending the benefits of civilization to the Pacific Coast. Even more appealing was the retribution he secured for the murders of Presbyterian missionaries Narcissa and Marcus Whitman.[20]

Despite Oregon's embrace, Lane's governorship was short-lived. The election of a Whig president in 1848 brought the appointment of a Whig governor in 1850. Out of a job, Lane left on an extended political tour through the territory's scattered southern settlements. After a short season of mining in California he made his way back north, preceded by news (surprising to all but his close associates) that he intended to challenge Thurston for the delegateship. The announcement upset many, particularly the growing circle of Thurston protégés, but the delegate's serendipitous death averted a division over Lane's candidacy, and in the campaign for delegate Lane faced only token opposition. He won in a landslide, defeating Willam H. Willson, the nominee of a hastily assembled anti-Lane meeting in Marion County.[21]

This election testified to Young Hickory's popular appeal in the territory, but more importantly, it opened a new era in Oregon politics, marking the point at which the overland migrants of the 1840s confirmed their effective possession of Oregon and their status as the charter group of the territory. Willson, Lane's opponent, was an "old Oregonian" by the standards of 1851, having arrived fourteen years earlier in the first reinforcement of settlers for the Methodist mission of Jason Lee.[22] By 1851 Willson and the world he represented had become an anachronism in Oregon affairs, a relic of the first years of American settlement, the passions and controversies of which the growing midwestern immigration had in the meantime overwhelmed. Willson embodied an era of isolation and ethnic-religious bitterness in the Oregon Country, when Methodist and Catholic missionaries, American mountain men, retired French-Canadian trappers, and pioneer farming families from the Ohio River valley settled the Willamette Valley under the watchful—sometimes solicitous, sometimes suspicious—gaze of the Hudson's Bay Company, the English trading company that from 1825 to 1845 was the Northwest's premier Anglo-American institution. Willson's candidacy marked the last time a figure closely associated with the Methodist mission sought elective office. His defeat signaled the close of this

tumultuous period—if not the disappearance of the politics of morality
to which it gave voice.

Oregon, like California, was beset in the 1830s by conflict between
missionaries and civilians. Here the antagonists were not Franciscan fathers and ambitious Californios but the followers of Methodist missionary Jason Lee, on the one side, and the Hudson's Bay Company and its
chief factor, John McLoughlin, on the other. The missionary era of
Oregon history is, locally, as romanticized as the Spanish Arcadia of Hispanic California. But if not of mythic proportions in fact, the conflicts
between Lee and McLoughlin did leave a lasting impression on politics
and society, contributing to strains of anti-Catholicism as well as anti-
(Protestant)-clericalism, magnifying ideological distinctions, and affecting the development of the local political culture long after the demise of
its American-Protestant and English-Catholic antagonists.

Jason Lee arrived in the Oregon Country in the mid-1830s with more
on his mind than the Christian conversion of the local Indian population: driven by moral earnestness and a commitment to the Methodist
gospel of free will, free grace, and individual responsibility, he set out to
create a perfectionist social order in this secluded corner of the North
American continent.[23] Shortly after his arrival, however, Lee concluded
that his program for regeneration was stymied by a powerful religious
and economic adversary, the Hudson's Bay Company (H.B.C.). Before
the mid-1840s, the English trading and trapping company was without
question the dominant institution in the lives of settlers and those Indians amenable to Anglo-American "civilization." Its fort at Vancouver
was the region's only regular source of defense, and the company's links
by sea to the wider world provided, for all intents and purposes, the
settlers' only access to supplies or outlet for agricultural products. In
this respect, Lee saw the H.B.C. as a barrier to the aims of his mission.
Events taught him that effectively, because of the company's economic
might, its head, Chief Factor John McLoughlin, was the region's dominant
moral authority as well.[24]

Thus Lee and his mission moved in 1841 to escape from the reality of
economic dependence and the prospect of religious defeat. At the falls
of the Willamette River, the most strategic mill and trading site south of
the H.B.C.'s fort on the Columbia River, mission steward George Abernethy established a store and a mill to serve local farmers and provide a
material mechanism for bringing them within the Methodist circle of
moral influence. In a direct offensive against McLoughlin, moreover,
mission agent Alvin Waller challenged the chief factor's twelve-year-old
claim to strategically located property at the falls.[25] Insisting that the
1841 preemption act would eventually be extended to Oregon along

with American sovereignty, Waller took possession and began to improve the claim. He held that since McLoughlin had neither lived on nor improved the property there was no warrant to his possession of it. Moreover, the Methodist missionary argued, no American court would take seriously the claim of a foreign citizen—indeed, the agent of a foreign "monopoly." [26]

These challenges to McLoughlin, conceived by Lee and his allies as a necessary part of the missionary enterprise, quickly assumed a life of their own, for they brought the enmity between the Methodists and McLoughlin into the open, squaring American Protestants off against the Catholic Englishman. By connecting the prospect of English sovereignty and Catholic dominance to the latent hostility American settlers felt toward the H.B.C., the Methodists helped open numerous fissures— ethnic, religious, and national—between the various groups in the Oregon Country. One result was a series of meetings in the spring of 1843 at which the region's settlers, after months of wrangling, established an independent civil authority in the form of a provisional government consisting of a legislature, three-man executive committee, and rudimentary court system. Among its first acts was the generous land law ultimately confirmed in the Donation Land Act.

Although the Methodist offensives of the early 1840s contributed to the events that led to the provisional government, in the founding meetings the missionaries played a limited role, sufficient only to insure the new government's endorsement of their land claim at the falls of the Willamette River. [27] Overall, their role was limited for a very good reason: at the time of the provisional government's founding the mission's existence was being threatened by an unexpected source—the mission board of the Methodist Episcopal Church.

Both within and outside the Methodist ranks were individuals who found Superintendent Lee's policies distasteful. Over time, as the mission's economic conflict with the Hudson's Bay Company intensified, missionary efforts among the Willamette Valley Indians—a population that, owing to imported disease, was dwindling all the while—came to a virtual halt. The mission's growing emphasis on its economic enterprises, in particular, led many to ask just what Lee was about. In 1843, responding to growing criticism, the mission board of the Methodist Episcopal Church ordered an investigation. The findings—which detailed the extent of the mission's secular activities, its conflict with the Hudson's Bay Company, and its abject failure to convert more than a handful of Indians—shocked the board. It removed Lee as superintendent, closed the mission, and ordered the liquidation of its assets. [28] The mission board's agent to Oregon, George Gary, arrived from New York in the summer of 1844 to carry out these directives. At auction he sold the mission's land claims, including the disputed one at Willamette Falls; its farms, parsonage, and Indian Manual Labor School building; and its grist and saw mills, stores, cattle, horses, and equipment.

Ironically, the vast majority of these assets (the most substantial properties in Oregon south of Fort Vancouver) went to various ministers and lay members of the defunct mission.[29] Thus, despite the mission's closing, the concentration of its property—its land, mills, and stores—transformed missionaries into a political and economic interest, a "Mission party," that remained a major force in Oregon until Lane, and territorial government, arrived in 1849.[30] Until that year, mission men wielded power out of proportion to their numbers and influenced mightily the political milieu that arriving immigrants had to confront in becoming the effective possessors of Oregon. They did so through a polemic drawn from long-standing elements of Methodism—temperance and hostility to Catholicism—mixed with animosity toward the H.B.C. George Gary's phrase, "Alcohol, Romanism, and Doctor McLoughlin," captured well the Methodists' definition of the imperative issues facing Americans in Oregon.[31]

Although there was no merit to the charge that McLoughlin, the Hudson's Bay Company, or the Catholic missionaries were involved in plots or encouraging alcohol consumption, this conflation of temperance, anti-Catholic, antimonopoly, and anti-British sentiments struck a chord among arriving settlers and served partisans of the mission party well. Longtime mission steward George Abernethy, who was personally interested in the outcome of the conflict with McLoughlin, served continuously as provisional governor from 1845 to 1849. Similarly, Samuel Thurston, when he ran for congressional delegate in 1849, embraced as his own the cry of "Alcohol, Romanism, and Doctor McLoughlin," and proclaimed that he would see to congressional confirmation the Methodist claim at the Willamette Falls as well as the donation law.[32]

Given the importance of the Mission party through the 1840s, it is surprising how quickly the power of its partisans dissolved. Although their emphasis on a politics of morality and ethnic-religious exclusion was later taken up by others, in the 1850s more secular political customs and habits came to dominate Oregon affairs. After 1849 the sheer number of new arrivals, American sovereignty, and, most importantly, the withdrawal of the Hudson's Bay Company to Vancouver Island dissolved the specter of "foreign monopoly."[33] The confirmation of the Methodist claim at Oregon City in the Donation Land Law gave the lie to the notion that McLoughlin was part of a conspiratorial triumvirate.

Lane's election as congressional delegate made it clear that matters had turned. His opponent, Willson, whom Marion County Methodists nominated after the death of Thurston, was handicapped by his identification with the Methodist causes of the 1840s.[34] An avid prohibitionist, founding member of the Oregon auxiliary of the nativist American

Bible Society, and well-known land speculator, Willson represented material interests and a moral agenda that, to a rural electorate soon to become the backbone of a Democratic majority, smacked of special privilege and antirepublican coercion.[35] Lane suffered no such disabilities, and his election marked the beginning of an effort to establish a Democratic party organization. Indeed, in the very issue that announced his election, the editor of the *Oregon Statesman,* a modest newspaper recently begun at Oregon City, sounded the call for a "thorough and permanent [Democratic] organization . . . ranking young Oregon with the party of the People, of Progress, and Popular Rights."[36]

The editor's name was Asahel Bush. Recruited to Oregon by Samuel Thurston, he had arrived from Massachusetts nine months before the election with a press that Thurston had purchased—privately—to further his own political career.[37] Thurston's death removed whatever restraints patronage placed on Bush's editorial activities, and the young editor made the most of the situation. Although unknown to Oregonians in 1850, he soon became the foremost political kingmaker in the territory, a position he retained until retiring from journalism and politics in the early 1860s. As the first chosen member of Thurston's circle of political allies, Bush came to Oregon with the express purpose of establishing a political paper that was to serve as the mouthpiece of a local Democratic party headed by his patron. The delegate election between Lane and Willson presented an opportunity to carry out this project, and soon thereafter a controversy over the location of the territorial capital provided the pretense to begin.[38]

Under the provisional government, Oregon's capital had been in Oregon City. During the second session of the territorial legislature (1850–1851), however, a majority of each house voted to move the capital to Salem, then a small crossroads settlement centrally located among the farming settlements of the Willamette Valley. Exactly why the measure was introduced is not known; nonetheless, the location act soon became a party measure extraordinaire, indeed, the crucible in which Oregon's Democracy was created.

Newly appointed Whig governor John Gaines, sensing that the bill was an act of defiance on the part of Democratically minded legislators, declared it "utterly" null and void on the grounds that it was illegally drawn—containing as it did more than a single provision, contrary to the organic act that had created the territory.[39] The showdown came at the next session of the territorial legislature, which, inopportunely for the governor, occurred directly after Lane's election as congressional delegate and Bush's call for Democratic organization. Twenty-six of the legislature's thirty-one members assembled at Salem, in defiance of the governor. In a memorial to Congress they declared that the territorial Whig administration, "from mental perverseness . . . sought by indirect

and extra official acts to usurp the powers placed in the hands of the representatives of the people alone."[40] Bush supported the legislators' defiance and in the *Statesman* declared the conflict one that set local sovereignty, defended by Democrats, against foreign interlopers, the Whig
appointees.[41]

The actual division over the location controversy was not as clear-cut
as Bush and other party men would have liked. Some Democrats, particularly those residing near Oregon City, opposed the move.[42] Nonetheless, the tactic was successful: presented as a party issue, it drew into the
open those who sympathized with the Whig governor. Chief among
these was Thomas Dryer, another newly arrived political journalist, who
in 1850 inaugurated the *Oregonian* in Portland, a small town recently established at the northern end of the territory near the confluence of the
Willamette and Columbia rivers. When he began the *Oregonian*, Dryer
announced that he would "recommend all the fundamental principles of
the Whig Party."[43] Soon thereafter, however, he denied any interest in
party politics and called for nonpartisanship in territorial affairs. When
Bush and others tried to turn the capital question to Democratic advantage, the *Oregonian*'s editor quickly labeled them "party hacks and political demagogues." "What are the people to gain by drawing party lines?"
Dryer asked.

> If the object is to secure the election of such men as have already disgraced
> the Territory by the party votes and regard for local interests, the people
> are not to be benefitted thereby. If it is to support the rickety and sinking
> prospects of the *Statesman* press, or to endorse and justify the deplorable
> course pursued by the Chicopee stripling who conducts it [i.e., Bush], who
> has undertaken to teach the people their duty to his party, the country will
> not surely be benefitted by it.[44]

Dryer's antiparty rhetoric was to no small degree a product of political
realities in territorial Oregon, for he realized that a call for Whig organization would little appeal to arriving settlers, a majority of whom carried
with them Democratic allegiances. Of equal importance was the *Oregonian* editor's own political sensibility, for, like Whigs elsewhere, he was
suspicious of a politics that turned on institutional loyalties and organizational concerns. For Dryer, the capital controversy presented a dilemma.
The legislature had attacked a governor with whom he was sympathetic
politically. Given the makeup of the immigrant population, a Whig
counteroffensive had little prospect of success. However, Bush's claim
that the controversy was at bottom a party issue threatened to make it
exactly that and, if it went unanswered, hasten the organization of a
Democratic party. Thus in the *Oregonian* Dryer denied that the location
question was a partisan one, instead painting defiance of the government as unconstitutional and factious. "Why," he asked, in phrases

meant to expose Democratic arguments as the illegitimate (and anti-Jacksonian) work of a small band of designing men, "are these men so suddenly and so earnestly enlisted in this nullification effort? What matters it if the seat of government is located at Salem or elsewhere? What public interests are to be injured or subserved if, by chance the seat of government would, or should not be fixed at Salem?"[45]

Dryer's attempt to portray Bush and the defiant legislators as "nullifiers" of the Constitution did not succeed, for his defense of nonpartisanship only drew him deeper into the controversy. In the end he assisted (against his better instincts) in creating an Oregon variant of the antebellum party system. His foremost contribution in this regard came in the form of a brilliant satire, *Treason, Stratagems, and Spoils,* which he published in the *Oregonian* in early 1852.[46] Written by William Lysander Adams, *Treason, Stratagems, and Spoils* was an "original 'melodramatic poem' in five acts." It offered a biting look at the location controversy, presenting it as the scheme of a corrupt, drunken crowd of place-men intent on deceiving the electorate in service to a dangerous, conspiratorial purpose: reducing Oregonians to subjects of a dangerous Mormon empire.[47] Adams's thinly disguised cast of characters was taken from life. His foremost target was a group in which Thurston recruits figured prominently; soon known as the "Salem Clique," these men formed the territorial Democracy's inner circle throughout the 1850s. First among equals in this group was editor Bush, and to the delight of his enemies everywhere, *Treason, Stratagems, and Spoils* painted him and his Democratic allies as craven rogues. In a characteristic passage, a Democratic conspirator praises his leader's

> . . . talents rare, for double tongued deceit,
> And foul disguise, for a feigning truest love,
> And harboring rankest, deadliest hate;
> Your conscience, of an indian rubber kind,
> And your political, chameleon skin;
> Your Cossack onslaught, bluffing impudence;
> Your swaggering, bullying, lying tone;
> Your restless chaffing, scorning, envying,
> Broil-loving temper, have recommended
> You to me, as one whom I safely
> Might commit the arguing of my cause
> Before the people, whom I wish to gull.[48]

As frontier art, *Treason, Stratagems, and Spoils* was unparalleled. As political journalism, it was the consummate example of the bitter, paranoid rhetoric—the "Oregon style"—that dominated territorial sheets.[49] It exemplified the extraordinary passion that marked Oregon politics in the 1850s and underscored the fact that for Democrats and anti-Democrats alike politics *was* public life, one of few activities that regularly drew men

from the isolation of the family farm. Similar emotions infected the political press and ceremonial gatherings of the party faithful on every
side, testifying, quite explicitly, to the denial by both Democrats and anti-
Democrats of the legitimacy of their opponents.

The brilliance of *Treason, Stratagems, and Spoils* rested in Adams's
artful synthesis of political metaphors that were employed on all sides in
Oregon: the corrupt self-interest of the opposition, its devotion to conspiracies against liberty, and its adherents' ill-restrained violence. Yet
despite the author's art, the melodrama was unsuccessful in stemming
the Democratic tide. In the 1852 territorial election, which followed the
standoff between Whig governor and Democratic legislature (and the
play's publication), the command of the newly anointed Salem Clique
was put to a test. When the results were in, the preeminence of the Bush
organization was apparent.[50] Although Dryer as well as Bush claimed
victory, with Lane in Washington, D.C., and a majority assured in the
legislature, the Salem Democracy had realized its goal.

Shortly thereafter, Lane underlined the clique's ability to have things
its way, announcing to readers of the *Statesman* that he favored Democratic organization in Oregon and, furthermore, that he had succeeded
in obtaining passage of a congressional resolution validating the capital's
removal to Salem. As if to reinforce the town's status as the territorial
place of power, Bush moved the *Statesman* press and editorial offices to
the new capital. For the rest of the decade, an admiring contemporary
observed, the young editor "wield[ed] the power of his party as the
leader of a band wields his baton of masterly direction."[51]

Although Thomas Dryer coined the term *Salem Clique* to portray a
ruthless set of power brokers gulling an otherwise virtuous population
for their own purposes, the epithet contained a more important truth
about the source of Bush's continuing supremacy.[52] Located in the center
of the Willamette Valley, Salem well represented the geography of electoral power in the territory. During the 1850s, the midvalley counties
surrounding Salem—Marion, Polk, Linn, Benton, and Lane—contained
well over half of Oregon's population, four-fifths of the improved acreage, and two-thirds of the recorded value of farm land, equipment, machinery, and stock (though a decidedly smaller share of the territory's
workshops and mills). The voters in these valley counties originated in
the border states and southern regions of the Old Northwest: Tennessee, Kentucky, Missouri, and southern Ohio, Indiana, and Illinois. Farmers predominated, farmers representative of the self-selected fragment
that formed the charter group of this far western society.[53]

The Willamette Valley electorate had carried to Oregon an allegiance
to the antebellum Democracy, with its emphasis on local sovereignty and

grass-roots organization, an independent producer ethic, and what Michael Holt has called the "doctrine of the negative state."⁵⁴ But while Oregon Democrats considered themselves part of the national party, they represented a particular strain within the Jacksonian "persuasion," a strain identified by their reasons for leaving the Midwest and their relative favor of landholding and familial self-sufficiency over commercial pursuits. In their local party, and in their political culture more generally, the discourse of eighteenth-century classical republicanism had an unusually prominent place, particularly with regard to the distrust of power and expectation of conspiracy and a complementary emphasis on civic virtue and a politics of disinterest. By the same token, Oregon Democrats were extremely wary, if not downright suspicious, of the liberal, market-oriented, economic individualism identified with Jacksonian Democracy elsewhere.⁵⁵

Bush, as a political editor and party leader, reinforced these predilections at every turn. He never tired, for instance, of denouncing Whig officials and their local spokesmen as "Federalists" and antirepublican promoters of "monopolies, tariffs, and Bank Charters [which] fertilize the rich man's soil with the sweat of the poor man's brow."⁵⁶ In Oregon these attacks were more than the conventional Democratic fare they appear at first glance. Although drawn from a discourse that turned on different conceptions of how government might best assist the "release of private energies" in a market economy, the more immediate symbolic effect was in reinforcing the gulf between the way of life of rural donation law farmsteaders and that of the few urban entrepreneurs found among Oregon's small band of Whigs. In the Democratic (and anti-Democratic) political cultures of territorial Oregon, in other words, precise matters of policy, particularly economic policy, did not loom large. Although few Oregonians, Democratic or otherwise, denied the public benefits that internal improvements might someday bring to their isolated country, and although Democrats themselves called for a liberal program of such improvements (while their opponents pointed out the contradiction in so doing), conflicts over roads, bridges, harbors, and transcontinental telegraphs and railroads affected the daily business of politics less than other, less material, concerns.⁵⁷ The most salient distinction between Oregon's Democrats and their adversaries, be they Whigs, independents, temperance advocates, or remnants of the Mission party, stemmed from alternative conceptions of party (and thus of politics) as a way of life.

Antebellum Democrats in Oregon understood their party as a social fact that had its roots in local communities. Organized from bottom to top in a system of precinct caucuses and county, territorial (or state), and national conventions, men became a part of "the Democracy" through participation in the winter-to-spring round of party ceremonies that punctuated the seasonal cadence of their productive lives as farmers. The calendar of antebellum politics, marked by Jackson jubilees, Jefferson-Jackson dinners, Fourth of July bonfires, precinct caucuses, county conventions, elections, and legislative sessions, made up the public life of individuals otherwise isolated one from another. In political terms, the Democracy thus constituted a system that projected local desires (and men) from secluded precincts into the state (or territorial) and national political arenas. On another, more pervasive level, these rituals, so rich in historical allusion, expressed a conception of the party as embodying an undivided public mind that extended geographically from the local community to the nation's capital, and temporally from the revolutionary era through the age of Jackson to the present.[58] "The Democracy," in this respect, was both a parochial and a cosmopolitan institution. Its national policies and universal principles were understood as the consequence of waves of convictions radiating upward from the nation's grass roots. Membership in the party involved subsuming oneself into a like-minded political community through ceremonies that, as Jean Baker has written, "were encrusted with republican symbols and expressions" and served as "civic classrooms . . . [that] offered symbolic representations of republicanism that moved beyond the written word into behavior." Party membership taught that only "through disinterested participation in public affairs . . . could [the] community survive."[59]

Anti-Democrats in Oregon shared—and fought over possession of— the classical republican idiom of their adversaries, but they understood the party concept quite differently. First principles of conscience, in particular temperance, Sabbatarianism, anti-Catholicism, and immigration restriction, constituted the foundation of their politics. Their partisan allegiances arose from a voluntary embrace of moral standards and a national ideal, be it the standard of native-born Americanism, the ideal of a (Protestant) Christian nation, temperance, or, more prosaically, an "American system" of centrally defined and implemented internal improvements. Politics, to the anti-Democrat, was properly about policies directed to the common good, carried out by men who virtuously placed common wealth above self-interest. Democrats, in contrast, stood for nothing; they had, as Adams charged in *Treason, Stratagems, and Spoils*, "conscience[s] . . . of an indian rubber kind" and "political, chameleon skins."[60]

In Oregon, anti-Democratic sentiments found their most persistent expression in temperance and nativist movements, two issues that, mixed with personal enmity toward the imperious Asahel Bush, predictably provided an incomplete foundation for party politics. Whereas the territorial Democratic party organized quickly and thoroughly at the precinct, county, and territorial levels, its adversaries remained divided, incapable of compromise, and thus isolated in a few locales. Alternately composed of Whigs, nativists, temperance advocates, and, at the close of the territorial period, sui generis Republicans, anti-Democrats nonetheless could depend on relatively stable (if insufficient) sources of electoral support. In the three-territory-wide congressional delegate elections of 1853, 1855, and 1857, Lane's opponents ran on different "party" tickets each time: the "People's" in 1853; Whig and American in 1855; and Republican, Independent, and Maine Law in 1857. Despite this diversity of party banners, however, the allegiances of territorial voters persisted from election to election: Lane supporters remained Lane supporters three-quarters of the time, and in about the same proportion his critics remained his critics.[61]

The political careers of prominent anti-Democrats illustrate this electoral stability. A number of former partisans of the Mission party, for example, migrated first into Whiggery, then into the various temperance, Maine Law, and nativist American (or Know-Nothing) party organizations, and finally into the Republican organization that ran tickets in legislative races during the 1850s. This progression is apparent in the editorial course of the *Oregon Spectator*, which from 1846 to 1855 was edited in Oregon City by former mission steward, provisional governor, and merchant George Abernethy. A well-known temperance sheet throughout its ten-year life, the *Spectator* hewed a nonpartisan, antiparty line until the early 1850s when, in response to the relocation of the capital, its editor called for organization of a Whig party. After two years of allegiance to the moribund Whig cause, however, the editors embraced "the American colors."[62] The paper closed down in 1855, but its patron, together with other Methodist ministers associated with the nativist American Bible Society, was soon back in business with another journal, the *Pacific Christian Advocate*, published in Salem. In the *Advocate*, assaults on Democrats mixed with attacks on the "humbug doctrine of the Romish Church," crusades against liquor and tobacco, and the promotion of a new political party: an Oregon temperance party.[63]

While former partisans of the Mission party like Abernethy drew on long-standing animosities in promoting alternatives to Democratic supremacy, more recent arrivals, unaware of the local conflicts of the 1840s, imported a complementary strain of anti-Democratic thought. The *Oregonian*'s Thomas Dryer arrived in 1850 intent on providing a platform for a territorial Whig party. Although he retreated to an antiparty stance during the location controversy of 1851–1852, after the capital's removal to Salem Dryer joined for a time with the *Spectator* in calling for a "partisan course" under "the Whig Banner."[64] Throughout the 1850s, however, Dryer proved incapable of maintaining an organizational allegiance. In him the antipartyism and lack of "organizational malleability" endemic to Whiggery from the 1830s on was manifest.[65] Dryer spent the 1850s embracing various political stances—political independence, Whiggery, temperance, Know-Nothingism, and, after three years of vacillation, Republicanism—without ever being able to place himself under the authority of a formal political organization. In his proudest self-description, Dryer declared that he, like the founding fathers, was "independent of all parties, factions, cabals, cliques, or combinations of men."[66]

In William Lysander Adams, the antipathy between devotional principles and the compromises imperative to party organization was even more starkly displayed. A lay leader in Disciples of Christ circles, Adams carried to Oregon a commitment to Whiggery, but his party identity was always secondary to his dedication to moral reform.[67] Remembered best for *Treason, Stratagems, and Spoils,* Adams's prominence in the 1850s stemmed from his editorship of the *Oregon Argus,* which he began in 1855 with the printing plant of the recently defunct *Oregon Spectator.* Through his paper he issued forth constant abuse of Bush and the Democratic Salem Clique. Bush, he declared, was the political equivalent of the medical crackpot Dr. L. J. Czapkay, director of the San Francisco Medical and Surgical Institute, whose advertisements for cures of "Spermatorrhoea" and "other infirmities in man" ran regularly in territorial papers.[68] His point in drawing the analogy was not simply to poke fun at Bush's expense but, rather, to expose the fraudulence of Democratic politics, a politics that to his mind existed solely to advance the interests of corrupt men. Instead he offered the alternative of a Christian politics devoted to preserving the republic through the prohibition of alcohol and the destruction of Catholic plots to debase republican institutions. These—not Whiggery, Know-Nothingism, or other forms of "mere" political organization—provided Adams with his political raison d'être.

The convergence of Whiggery, temperance, and nativism in remnants of the Mission party, Dryer, and Adams, and illustrated by the editorial courses of the *Spectator, Pacific Christian Advocate, Oregonian,* and *Argus,* displayed the diverse tendencies that mobilized Oregon's anti-Democratic electorate.[69] Never during the territorial period did these strains coalesce into a formidable opposition to Bush and the Democracy. Whiggery, initiated in Oregon at the very moment it was collapsing nationally, was stillborn; temperance, significant among remnants of the Mission party, did not appeal to secular-minded Whigs; and nativism, organized in the form of the American party, was suppressed easily by Democratic legislators with a viva voce voting bill in 1855.

Oregon Democrats advertised the viva voce law (a prominent eighteenth-century voting system, which required voters to declare their preference publicly at the polling place) as a republican remedy for dangerous conspiracy. As Bush noted proudly, the law proved an effective "Know-Nothing antidote. . . . There is not a man of prominence or influence belonging to the damning conspiracy in Oregon whose connection with it will not be known in less than six months. They are doomed men."[70] He was correct. The American Know-Nothing party withered into little more than a refuge for true believers.

The weakness of the anti-Democratic forces, however, had significant—and unexpected—consequences for the dominant Democratic organization. As the sources of opposition evaporated, Bush and his clique confronted the problem of holding their ranks together without the stimulus of a threatening adversary.[71] A tendency toward internal division, which beset state Democratic parties across the United States in the 1850s, was all the more troublesome in Oregon owing to the very nature of the territorial system. By withholding from territorial residents a substantive role in national politics—that is, by insulating them from the divisiveness of national campaigns—the territorial system encouraged a politics that focused on what remained: control over federal appropriations and patronage appointments to local office.

Here, Bush was a master strategist. From men recruited by Samuel Thurston and friends he made in Oregon, he gathered together a group of savvy farmer-lawyers whom he promoted privately for appointive office and publicly for elective posts. In return they provided Bush with a continuous stream of political intelligence from all corners of the territory—who is loyal and who is not; who would make a good (trustworthy) candidate for the legislature, who would not—which the editor used to knit local friends and neighbors into a territorywide political community.[72] Bush became the kingpin of Oregon's Democracy precisely because he stood at the center of this elaborate political-intelligence network.[73] Without the favor of the Bush circle, Democrats anxious for a federal appointment, personal promotion, or legislative honors had little chance for success. As long as anti-Democratic opposition appeared significant—whether in the form of a Whig governor and Whig "tyranny," as in 1851–1852, or in the form of the conspiratorial Know-Nothing "wigwams" of 1854–1855—party ranks closed around Bush and his circle. Yet the defeat of such threats, rather than ushering in an era of Democratic consensus, only let loose forces of intraparty conflict. After 1855 in particular, three distinctive fault lines appeared in Democratic ranks, each, ironically, arising from the party's very success in thwarting its adversaries.

The first rift was seen in the problematic relationship between congressional delegate Lane and local party leaders. Lane's ambitions extended well beyond Oregon, but he realized that his larger political aspirations depended on his political base within the territory. This base, however, required the cooperation of Asahel Bush and the Salem Clique. While in Washington Lane was out of sight and potentially, if access to the columns of the *Statesman* should be withdrawn, out of mind. Delegate elections, furthermore, recurred with maddening frequency, sometimes in the incumbent's absence. Without the clique's assistance— promoting him in the *Statesman,* fighting off challenges in precinct, county, and territorial conventions, and arranging demonstrations of grass-roots support—the possibility of defeat could not be dismissed. By the same token, Bush and his allies recognized that they were dependent on Lane. As the capital location controversy of 1851–1852 demonstrated, the popular delegate was a rallying point in these men's efforts to strengthen party loyalty and fend off anti-Democratic challenges. As importantly, Lane was indispensable to the distribution of contracts and patronage appointments, appointments that formed the ligaments of Democratic loyalty.

Throughout the 1850s, both Lane and Bush loyalists were aware of, and rankled by, their mutual dependence. As a result, relations between the man and the machine always displayed jealousy and suspicion mixed with admiration and support. Predictably, both sides sought ways to limit the other's influence without unleashing internecine struggle; by the mid-1850s, however, Lane's efforts to use his patronage powers to build a following independent of the clique became more pronounced.[74] As the delegate increasingly ignored the recommendations of Bush and his inner circle, Democrats in Oregon grew ever more wary. Territorial supreme court justice Matthew Deady fumed in 1855 when delegate Lane short-circuited the Democratic system—the mechanism for divining the undivided Democratic mind—by naming his friends to patronage positions in the place of men recommended by the Salem Clique. Deady found Lane's independent course unacceptable because it contravened proper party practice, without which the Democracy, according to the judge, sank "into a mere *personal* party, where the soulless Flunkey who sings old Jo's praise loudest and longest, is alone to be elevated and honored[.] I think the institution had better be abolished, to make room for the divine right of Kings."[75]

In the mid-1850s, when relations with Lane began to sour, the clique faced a second, even more nettlesome, challenge from within the party. Designated "softs" by Bush, a self-styled group of "National Democrats" emerged in Clackamas and Multnomah counties, north of the clique's Willamette Valley stronghold.[76] This insurgence made itself evident first (though vaguely) during the capital controversy, when Oregon City and Portland Democrats opposed Bush and others who wanted to make Salem the symbol of party regularity. By 1855, however, there was no mistaking the "National" challenge to Bush and his clique. In that year the "softs" found a journalistic patron in Alonzo Leland, editor of the (Portland) *Democratic Standard,* and they also had the temerity to promote a rival congressional candidate in the territorial party convention. A year later, the National Democrats emerged as a separate party organization in a number of counties.[77] In the 1856–1857 legislative session, they demonstrated their political ability by successfully defeating the clique's choice for presiding officer in the territorial council, manipulating the party caucus so that one of their own gained the post.[78] To this affront Bush reacted fiercely. At the Jackson jubilee dinner in January 1857, Leland and the *Standard,* along with "softs" who had defied the "regular organization," were read out of the party and denounced in conspiratorial terms as a "wolf in sheep's clothing . . . engaged in efforts to misrepresent, malign, and create discord among Democrats . . . unworthy [of] the confidence, respect, or patronage of any portion of our fellow citizens."[79] Two weeks later a legislative caucus affirmed the proscription, and in April the party's territorial convention similarly condemned them as "hypocritical foe[s]."[80]

By the middle of the 1850s these divisions within the Oregon Democratic ranks—clique versus Lane, hards versus softs—became all the more serious when a national issue arose that threatened to tear the entire party apart. Proximately, the issue was slavery; precisely, it was the Kansas-Nebraska Act of 1854, which, by negating the Missouri Compromise, opened the question of whether there were legal limits to the territorial expansion of slavery. From 1856 to the opening of the Civil War, slavery plagued the residents of this remote and virtually slaveless province. Particularly vulnerable were Bush and his inner circle. Territorial status provided no insulation from the slavery question; in fact, it made it all the more immediate, for after the passage of the Kansas-Nebraska Act the slavery issue came to be defined in terms of whether the institution was constitutionally protected in *western territories.* Since 1852 Bush had made adherence to the party position the prerequisite for political promotion and achieving a voice in patronage decisions. But on slavery his closest allies were divided between adherents to Stephen Douglas's principle of "popular sovereignty" and advocates of federal protection for slavery in all western territories. Because Bush realized that the clique could not enforce a party position, his organization composed a slavery plank that proved to be a tissue of contradictions, a pathetic attempt to maintain consensus where solidarity was impossible. Declared the Democratic platform of 1857:

> Each member of the Democratic Party in Oregon may freely speak and act according to his individual conviction of right and policy upon the question of slavery in Oregon, without in any measure impairing their standing in the Democratic Party on that account. Provided, that nothing in these resolutions shall be construed as toleration of Black Republicanism, Abolitionism, or any other faction or organization arrayed in opposition to the Democratic Party.[81]

This resolution testified to the general crisis of the Democracy in the 1850s. Conceived as the institutional embodiment of public virtue, the party could not withstand a sharp divergence of opinion within its ranks. To say (as Bush Democrats did in the resolution) that an individual's party standing would not be harmed by his position on slavery begged the issue: in the 1850s it was increasingly the case that one's political allegiances proceeded from one's position on slavery. Thus the sharp divisions on slavery that cut across the Democratic party paralyzed the organization. A party position on slavery would certainly have been de-structive; but avoidance of the issue only delayed the party's dissolution. Bush and his circle, perhaps understandably, chose the second course. In an effort to avoid the central question, they emphasized the weak common ground that Democrats shared: opposition to abolition and "black Republicanism." This course, however, was sorely insufficient for encouraging party unity. Confusion reigned.

Democratic attacks on anti-Democrats as "abolitionists" and "black Republicans," partisans of the "ebony, freedom shrieking, psalm sing-ing, God hating, Union destroying . . . [etc.] party," could not serve as a rallying point for the Democracy simply because Oregon's anti-Democrats were not abolitionists.[82] On the question of extending full civil equality to nonwhites they were quiet, declaring instead that talk of abolitionism was merely an attempt to divert attention from the main issue. Bush, averred Adams, Dryer, and other prominent anti-Demo-crats, was engaging in "niggerism" when he attacked others as aboli-tionists; his paper was the "nigger organ"; and the candidates of his "black Democratic" party were "nigger candidates."[83]

Far from being abolitionists, anti-Democrats opposed slavery, though for a different reason: slavery degraded white labor. It reduced white farmers, mechanics, artisans, and workingmen—indeed, everyone ex-cept the slave owner—to the debased status of the slave.[84] In the face of such a fate, freedom's survival depended on the protection of free soil—that is, on slaveless western territories. Free soil, unencumbered by slav-ery, was the foundation of free labor and, perforce, the guarantor of free men.[85] According to independent Whigs such as Dryer and ad-herents to the new Republican banner such as Adams, Democrats could not be trusted to protect the soil against slavery, for prominent men among them openly favored the extension of slavery to Oregon. Fur-thermore, they insisted, even Democratic supporters of Douglas's popu-lar sovereignty (the principle of letting local voters decide the question) did the Slave Power's bidding by denying the constitutional limits to the expansion of slavery, affirmed and reaffirmed ever since the nation's founding.[86]

By 1857 Bush and his clique realized that matters were slipping out of control. Assailed from within by the "softs," suspicious of Lane's dependability, and fearful of growing anti-Democratic exploitation of the slavery question, the Salem machine searched for a way to negate the emotional power of the slavery issue and at the same time secure their hold over the government. Statehood promised to do both.[87] Indeed, by the winter of 1857 statehood seemed to offer something to every political persuasion in the territory. From 1854 Bush had supported a call for a constitutional convention, but until 1857 only his closest associates in the party agreed with him. Three times the voters had turned such proposals down, fearing above all the increased costs that statehood would bring.[88] In 1857, however, opinion—both Democratic and anti-Democratic—shifted in favor of a state government. To partisans of the clique, statehood seemed to offer a way of settling the slavery issue, the main issue exploited by the resurgent anti-Democrats. Moreover, it provided an opportunity to send loyal members of the Bush circle to Washington, D.C., thus ending dependence on Lane.

For Lane, who looked forward to a seat in the U.S. Senate, the idea of statehood similarly meant an opportunity to build a local following independent of the jealous party leaders in Salem and, above all, a place on the national stage from which to pursue presidential ambitions. For insurgents within the Democratic party, statehood offered a hope of challenging the clique's control of the patronage system. "Heaven knows," blared Leland in the *Democratic Standard,* "we have had enough of this anti-Democratic dictatorship from the few. We have had men who acknowledged and conformed to the principles and measures of the [national] party abused and vilified, forsooth, because they did not bend the pliant hinges of the knee."[89]

Anti-Democratic leaders, moreover, had reached similar conclusions. Dryer, who previously opposed statehood, worried that the effects of "bleeding Kansas" and the recent Dred Scott decision might lead the Buchanan administration to impose slavery on western territories. For Dryer, statehood was a means of forestalling such federal action: "Let us have a state government and make the issue at once. If we are to have slavery forced upon us let it be by the people here and not by the slavery propagandists at Washington City."[90]

By the spring of 1857 opposition to statehood had evaporated, and in June Oregonians endorsed a call for a summer convention by a better than four-to-one margin;[91] they also chose sixty delegates to sit as constitution writers. In a hard-fought campaign, the clique's assorted adversaries attacked from all sides. Six different organizations fielded tickets in one or more counties: Regular (or "hard") Democrats, National (or "soft") Democrats, Whigs, Know-Nothings, Maine Law Prohibitionists, and Republicans.[92] Although opponents of the Bush Democracy constituted one-third of the elected delegates, the *Statesman's* editor viewed the election as a victory. With their adversaries clearly identified, he believed, regular Democrats could close ranks in confidence. "Our party," he declared in announcing the election returns, "is now purged of its corruption and is in better condition than ever before to assume the responsibilities incident to independent state organization."[93]

For the short term, Bush was certainly correct. The babel of opposition tongues made a concentrated attack on the dominant party at its weakest point—the question of slavery—impossible. Party lines and individual positions on slavery simply did not coincide, and few, if any, of the delegates went to Salem intent on raising the issue. Bush's proposal that the convention submit the question of slavery—as well as a proposal to outlaw the immigration of free Negroes—to the voters appealed to every political persuasion in the body.[94]

During the first week of August 1857 the delegates to the constitutional convention made their way to Salem. The trip held few surprises. Located near the center of the territorial population, the capital was well connected to the interior by roads and stage lines, and regular steamship service linked it with other towns along the Willamette River to the north and south.[95] Virtually every delegate, moreover, knew the town well. A good number of them spent much of the year there, sitting in the legislature, attending court, or visiting officers of the territorial government. Salem was Oregon's premier place of power, and the convention a veritable hall of political fame. To first-time visitors it was this aspect of the town that was most arresting. Californian Patrick Malone, who covered the constitutional convention for the *Sacramento Daily Union,* found the town "inconsiderable in point of numbers . . . but territorially omnipotent in point of political power. It is to Oregon what Rome is to Christendom—the point from which emanate mandates that are felt to the outward rim of its jurisdiction."[96]

Salem, while not an incorporated city in 1857, was the territory's oldest town after Astoria and Oregon City. Its past embodied the early Oregon Country struggles between missionaries and the Hudson's Bay Company, for it was the site in the early 1840s of Jason Lee's headquarters and a number of related mission enterprises: flour mills, an Indian training school, and the Oregon Institute (a school for missionary children). With the dissolution of the mission in 1844, most of these properties went to former missionaries organized as the Trustees of the Oregon Institute, who two years later created the town on the former mission lands, appointing future political candidate W. H. Willson to plat it. Willson's plan was visionary. The townsite, on the east bank of the Willamette River, encompassed an area one and a half miles square. On paper he defined it with broad avenues, ninety-nine feet in width. In the town's center Willson placed a large public square surrounded by streets named "State," "Court," and "Capitol"—in anticipation of a new state's public buildings.[97]

Until the end of that decade the streets and public squares of the Salem townsite stood as little more than a reminder of its founder's vision. But with the arrival of overland immigrants in the late 1840s and early 1850s and the relocation of the territorial capital, the importance of the place took a turn. By the winter of 1849–1850, where there had been mostly empty space and but a few modest houses, merchants, craftsmen, and traders were opening exchanges, shops, and general stores to serve valley farmers. Encouraged by the California market, individuals were constructing flour and saw mills along the riverfront. Steamships from Oregon City carrying finished goods to exchange for local produce began regular spring and fall service.[98] By the mid-1850s the town was the Willamette Valley's business and trading center, presenting a prosperous appearance to visitors.

At the time of the convention Salem's population was approaching one thousand, was predominately male (59 percent), and fell largely between the ages of twenty-one and forty.[99] Unlike Monterey, where the abundance of young men was attached to the town's military garrison, Salem's unattached males lived as boarders in a town of nuclear-family households (replicating a prominent feature of the overland trains that had brought settlers there):[100] fully 86 percent of Salem's inhabitants lived in nuclear households, one-third of which were augmented by boarders. Here the presence of unattached males followed from a paucity of eligible females; given the provisions of the Donation Land Law, which allowed married couples to claim 640 acres and single men only 320 acres, eligible women were at a premium in the Oregon Country— a premium testified to as well by the low average age at marriage of Salem's women, eighteen years.[101]

Work life in Salem revolved around the business of government and the products of the town's agricultural hinterland. A relatively small proportion of the town's working population (15 percent) was unskilled; these were primarily young men who had yet to leave home and begin families of their own and who, in the meantime, provided casual labor to town artisans, mechanics, and neighboring farmers. Otherwise Salem's working population was closely divided between skilled craftsmen (43 percent) and various proprietary, commercial, professional, and service workers (42 percent). The town's craftsmen, who directed a thriving apprentice program, offered to the region a somewhat larger number of crafts than Monterey: forty, as opposed to thirty. Their concentration in the building trades (41 percent) testified to the physical growth of Salem in the 1850s, while the services provided by the remaining crafts— bakers, blacksmiths, bootmakers, wagonmakers, coopers, tanners, and the like—demonstrated the presence of town and country markets.

Salem's proprietary and professional classes reflected the town's role in rural trade and, more importantly, its place in the territory's political life. This class consisted of an upper level of forwarding merchants, lawyers, physicians, ministers, and high government officials (16 percent of the work force), who dominated the town's commercial life and the major territorial offices. The remainder carried out the details of business and politics: these were Salem's small proprietors, petty government officers, clerks, and bookkeepers (26 percent).

While preparing for the arrival of the convention delegates Salem residents awaited completion of a local manufacturing enterprise, the first of significant size in the territory. Capitalized at twenty-five thousand dollars, the Willamette Woolen Mill was intended to take advantage of the potential supply of locally produced wool, new machinery designed in New England, and novel "industrial" methods of organizing work and managing labor. Construction of the mill began in early 1857, with machinery arriving that November; shortly after the constitutional convention adjourned, a grand ball heralded the beginning of production.[102]

Although Salem's material lifeblood revolved around financial, marketing, supply, milling, and mechanical services provided to valley farmers, its status as the territory's capital left a palpable mark on the town as well. To any visitor in the 1850s, Salem's political function was apparent in the work force and in the town's physical appearance. In the center of town, on lots set aside by Willson a decade earlier, were found the new courthouse (on, appropriately, Court Street) and statehouse (on the corner of State and Capitol streets). Bush's *Statesman*—which he moved to Salem so that it might be "located at that point which will . . . tend to make it a kind of head-quarters for political information"—was situated a few blocks away from the public buildings, in the center of a business district that boasted numerous hotels and saloons to serve visiting legislators, ambitious party men, and ever-vigilant journalists.[103]

Political Salem was concentrated in an area no larger than six square blocks. Here were found the town's hotels, Bush's offices, and the saloons and dining houses frequented by Oregon's wet politicos. Facing this district across High Street was the courthouse—which served as the constitutional convention's meeting hall as well as Salem's civic auditorium. By 1857 the affiliation of Salem's eight hotels (or "houses") was well established: the delegates probably preferred the Bennett, Union, or Marion houses, each of which was a known haunt of territorial officials. After hours, the Plamondon Saloon (housed in a building with "Headquarters" festooned above the door) was a likely place for Democratic strategy meetings, for the saloon was a favorite of Bush and his Salem Clique cronies.[104]

In this walking town, public entertainment was widely available. Traveling theatrical troupes, presenters of dramatic readings, and religious lecturers, as well as a circus, all passed through Salem during the convention summer. The "talented Chapman Family" arrived during the convention's last week and presented such dramas as Kotzebue's *The Stranger* and the thrilling moral play *Rosina Meadows, or the Roue of Boston* to respectable crowds. Campbell's Theatrical Troupe offered nightly entertainment at the pavilion in front of the Marion House Hotel, across the street from the courthouse. Mrs. Emily P. Lesdernier, the famous New England poetess, offered Shakespearean readings at the courthouse, which was also the venue for lectures by the Reverend Dr. John G. Bellows, Universalist of New York, who spoke throughout July and early August on "The Religion That Never Laughs" and "Six Reasons Why the Doctrine of Endless Misery in Another Existence Is Not of God." Bellows's audiences were well behaved; in contrast, a visiting Mormon speaker was quickly driven off by a barrage of rotten eggs. Most exciting of the summer's entertainments, however, was the "Mammoth Circus, direct from California," which boasted the "largest pavilion ever in this territory" and included in its cast such luminaries as Miss Celina Long, "The Daring Equestrienne"; Mr. N. M. Hinckley, "The Great Slack Rope Performer"; Mr. J. L. Hinckley, "Juggler, La Perche Performer and Equilibrist"; Master J. Armstrong and his "Incredible Act of Throwing a Double Somersault"; and Dave Long, "The Clown of Clowns." [105]

In these surroundings, the convention began its work. Predictably, before the constitution writers formally convened, the "regular" Democrats assembled. The evening before the convention was to begin, party loyalists met at the courthouse and, as their first order of business, decided who would be allowed a seat in the policy-making caucus. Forty of the sixty delegates were eventually seated, a number of them only after convincing a suspicious audience of their loyalty to the Salem organization. Three others sent messages that they did not seek seats in the caucus but intended to abide by its decisions. Seventeen delegates were thus left in the cold: they composed the hard-core anti-Democratic opposition.[106] Once the caucus decided on its membership it nominated convention officers, most importantly the president. Without discussion it selected Matthew P. Deady, a justice of the territorial supreme court and longtime member of Bush's inner circle. Deady's selection was a matter of some note, for he had been one of only two candidates for convention delegate who had run openly on a proslavery platform.[107] To free-soilers such as Thomas Dryer, this choice confirmed the Democratic capitulation to slavery. Yet as delegate George Williams later recalled, neither Deady nor any other delegate was interested in having the question come before the convention:

> The fact was that those democrats who figured in politics were looking forward to official positions under the state government, and were afraid to

say anything against slavery fearing that they would thereby injure their chances for success, for in those days to be a sound Democrat, if it was not necessary to openly advocate Slavery it was necessary to keep still upon the subject. . . . When the convention assembled in 1857, the same timidity . . . characterized a majority of the members of that body, and in order to avoid any personal responsibility upon the subject the convention decided to submit to the people at the time the vote was taken upon the constitution the question as to whether or not slavery should exist in the state.[108]

Williams correctly described the reticence with which Oregon Democrats—and, for that matter, anti-Democrats—approached the question of slavery. As the delegates began their work, most observers inside and outside the convention hall believed that the proceedings would be tightly orchestrated. Although this expectation was belied on a number of points, for the most part the Oregonians' convention proceeded according to the ingrained habits and customs of long-standing allies and adversaries. The certainty and familiarity that surrounded this meeting reflected in microcosm the culture and society of the Oregon Country. It testified to a place secluded—politically and culturally, if not geographically and temporally—not only from the mining settlements and gold rush politics of California, but also from the new society of the Comstock Lode, which appeared just across the southeastern border of the Oregon Country shortly after the Oregon constitution writers finished their work.

THREE

"The Land for the Old Californian": Nevada, 1849–1864

In the Far West as in the nation, a great deal transpired in the seven years that separated the Oregon and Nevada constitutional conventions. The Civil War, although a distant phenomenon, had far-reaching consequences. It severely damaged the secession-tainted Democratic party and for the duration of the war kept the Far West solidly Union-Republican. After the South's withdrawal from Congress, Lincoln's party passed the Pacific Railroad Bill, an act that affected the Pacific slope from the moment of its signing. The war's disruption of eastern industry, furthermore, provided a spur to far western manufacturing, creating new national markets and enhancing local demand for finished goods no longer available from traditional sources of supply. Finally, and fortuitously, mineral discoveries provided vast accumulations of capital with which nascent Pacific slope financiers and industrialists opened a new era of industrial growth. For these reasons the 1860s marked the point in time when a modern industrializing society began to emerge in the Far West. Nowhere was this new order realized as quickly or starkly as in the Nevada Territory. Sparsely settled before the 1859 discovery of the Comstock Lode, by 1870 Nevada had become an exemplar of industrial society, replete with clear class divisions, capital-intensive mining, corporate monopoly, and continuous labor-management conflict.

It is, however, incorrect to assume that Nevadans looked forward to an industrial destiny from the beginning of settlement. The charter group of this far western territory, those who joined the rush to "Washoe" in the early sixties, came not as an industrial army but as ambitious entrepreneurs in search of marketplace opportunities. The thirty-five constitution writers who convened in Carson City during the summer of 1864 exemplified these hopes, hopes redoubled by their own experience in California after the gold rush, when mining became less an individual, and more an industrial, undertaking.[1] All but one of the delegates had migrated to Nevada from California; all but six were veterans of the gold rush. Like thousands of others, they had journeyed to Nevada in the hope that the Comstock Lode would recreate California's halcyon days of 1849. Until the middle of the 1860s the territory sufficiently fulfilled this promise, drawing from California a steady stream of prospectors, miners, merchants, mechanics, and other small producers. Then, in the year of statehood, matters suddenly changed.

For Nevada, 1864 was a turning point. Politically, the year was marked by a continuing controversy over whether the territory would become a state, a question that its voters twice addressed in emotional and symbolically charged campaigns. The first occurred in January, at a time when it seemed like Nevada's silver-mining boom would never end, and the result was negative: convinced that statehood had been contrived to serve the interests of San Francisco capitalists, an aroused electorate roundly rejected the proposed constitution. Its defeat was hailed as a setback for "improper combinations" and a boost for the territory's virtuous "little interests"—its prospectors, small mine owners, merchants, workingmen, farmers, and ranchers. Six months later, however, when statehood again came before the population, circumstances challenged these convictions. In the interim, a depression had struck the territory. When the voters selected men to write a state constitution, opinion, shaped by the deepening crisis, set them the task of creating a legal and political framework that would aid recovery and nurture prosperity. This challenge took Nevada's constitution writers—and with them, the territory's inhabitants—onto ideological ground largely unforeseen six months earlier, and marked their convention as a turning point in Nevada's history.

As in the cases of California and Oregon, the charter group that became the effective possessors of Nevada, and who made it a state, were not the first comers to the region. Until 1850 and the arrival of the first overland gold rush immigrants, this bleak western corner of the Great Basin desert was devoid of white settlement. The gold rush, however, brought thousands of California-bound immigrants through the area, thus creating an instant market for trail supplies. Mormon traders from the Salt Lake colony responded, establishing a trading station in Carson Valley, at the base of the Sierra Nevada's eastern slope, to outfit immigrants for the perilous mountain crossing into California. Fifteen traders established this "Mormon station" in spring of 1850, packing in supplies from the Salt Lake.[2] So successful was their enterprise that after selling the original store of goods, half the party remained in the valley, ferrying supplies from Sacramento to trade with immigrant parties.

In 1850, Brigham Young's secret "gold mission" arrived; this influx increased the trading station's size, as did the arrival a year later of Salt Lake City merchant John Reese and an accompanying colony of Mormon settlers. More followed, and by 1856 the 450 Latter-Day Saints in what was now called "Western Utah" became an official outpost of the Mormons' Great Basin kingdom.[3]

The purpose of the Mormon colony in the Carson Valley was twofold. First, it had an economic purpose: to enrich the church treasury through trade with overland parties. Second, the settlement figured in the larger diplomatic designs of church leader Brigham Young. Beginning in 1849, Young initiated a series of settlements radiating outward from Salt Lake City. An inner cordon was founded in valleys neighboring the Mormon capital; a wider ring, located at strategic points along well-traveled emigrant trails, was created by colonies in the Carson Valley, Forts Supply and Bridger (Wyoming), Lemhi (Idaho), Moab (southeastern Utah), and Las Vegas (Nevada).[4] The Mormons' Carson Valley colony grew each year in the early 1850s, augmented by neighboring settlements of "gentile" (non-Mormon) traders, farmers, stock raisers, and gold prospectors working in the valleys that trailed out of the Sierra Nevada's eastern slope. In 1855 Utah's territorial government established formal control over the area, creating Carson County and appointing a territorial judge to oversee local courts. The Mormons, numerically predominant and motivated by a religious sense of mission, quickly—and unapologetically—took control of the county courts and offices, alienating non-Mormon settlers. These "gentiles"—sensitive to the connotation of the term and offended by the Latter-Day Saints' clannish ways—petitioned the California legislature in 1853, and again in 1855, for annexation. Quick action by the Utah government canceled the first attempt, and Congress denied the second, feeding controversy in Western Utah. Two years later, still grating at Mormon rule, the gentiles of Western Utah again petitioned Congress, this time to create a new territory (to be called Columbus) independent of the Mormons in Utah.[5]

In their demands for congressional relief the Great Basin insurgents appealed openly to anti-Mormon prejudice, rampant in the nation's capital in the aftermath of the church's 1852 proclamation making polygamy a formal article of faith.[6] In the same year that the gentile settlers submitted their petition, newly inaugurated president James Buchanan removed Brigham Young as governor of the Utah Territory and replaced him with a Democratic loyalist. In addition, Buchanan dispatched to Utah Colonel Albert Sidney Johnston and twenty-five hundred troops. Church leaders responded by raising a general alarm. As Johnston's "Mormon expedition" approached Salt Lake City, Apostle Young ordered those holding the "outposts of Zion" to abandon their colonies and "come home to Zion."[7] Carson County was suspended and its judicial offices transferred back to Salt Lake. The Western Utah Saints, in September 1857, obeyed the order to return. Selling their property at discount, they packed their belongings and set out to defend their endangered capital.[8] After the Mormon departure, about two hundred white inhabitants remained in the scattered settlements. The exodus marked the end of Mormon political and economic interest in the area and left behind an ambiguous state of affairs. Formally, the area remained subject to Utah's authority; practically, however, it was without government.

The gentiles' 1857 petition for relief from Mormon rule failed because of the small number of settlers in the area, the confusion surrounding Buchanan's "Utah war," and, equally, the sectional deadlock in Congress that followed the Kansas-Nebraska Act and the Dred Scott decision. Consequently, the settlers stewed—all the more when Utah's new governor, Alfred Cummings, decided to reestablish jurisdiction over them by restoring Carson County and appointing a judge to its court. The residents of Carson Valley interpreted Cummings's initiative as the first stage in the reinstatement of Mormon despotism, and in response held another series of grievance meetings to plot territorial independence.

Held in the summer of 1859 in the ambitiously named village of Carson "City," the meetings resulted in elections in each of Western Utah's scattered settlements.[9] The purpose was twofold: to select a Congressional representative to plead their case in Washington, D.C.; and to name fifty delegates to a convention charged with preparing a provisional constitution for the "Territory of Nevada." As the insurgents announced in a circular to the citizens:

> A long train of abuses and usurpation on the part of the Mormons . . . evinces a desire on their part to reduce us under an absolute spiritual despotism. Such has been our patient sufferings, and such is now the necessity for dissolving all political relations which may have connected us together, and we deem it not only our right, but also our duty, to disown such a government, and such a people, and to form new guards for our future security.[10]

Six weeks after the election, a provisional convention met and prepared a constitution.[11] Soon thereafter, Nevadans elected a governor, legislature, and representative to carry their case to Congress. The provisional government, however, was stillborn, for at the legislature's appointed hour of convening, only a handful of its members showed up. Left with no alternative, the governor proclaimed the nonexistent legislature adjourned.[12]

The collapse of Nevada's provisional government is easily explained. Between the time of the constitution's ratification and the legislature's scheduled meeting, reports in California newspapers and word-of-mouth rumors revealed a major mineral discovery in Six-Mile Canyon, fifteen miles northeast of Carson City near Sun Peak. Beginning in the late summer of 1859 and continuing until winter snows closed the mountain passes from California, politics and anti-Mormonism were forgotten as a small-scale mining rush began. With the spring thaw four months later the immigration began in earnest, as thousands of Californians hurried to unearth the bullion locked inside the newly named Comstock Lode.

The Comstock Lode created a new society in the sagebrush desert, a society that no one had foreseen before the strike. By the end of 1859 perhaps five hundred silver seekers had arrived, doubling Nevada's population. These first arrivals, after passing through Carson City, arrived at a hastily constructed mining camp called Virginia in honor of James "Old Virginny" Finney, one of the first locators of the underground ledge.[13] By the end of 1860 the crude camp had become a metropolis, "Virginia City," and Nevada's population—figured in the hundreds in 1859—approached seven thousand. Two years later the territory's population exceeded fifteen thousand, and before economic depression struck in 1864 even modest men were speaking of a state with fifty or one hundred thousand inhabitants by the decade's end.[14]

Such grand visions were premature. Throughout the 1860s (in fact, until well into the twentieth century), Nevada's population was marked by rapid in- and out-migration affected by the state of mining. Demographically there was always an imbalance in terms of age and gender. In the early 1860s, over nine-tenths of the immigrants were male; three-quarters were males between the ages of twenty and forty. The bulk of the population, moreover, was concentrated in Storey County, the location of the Comstock Lode's great cities, Virginia City and Gold Hill.[15] Populated in response to the discovery of the Comstock Lode; land-locked, surrounded by desert and mountains; and—with the significant exception of gold and silver—devoid of resources easily exploited with nineteenth-century technology, Nevada inevitably faced abandonment when the bullion ran out. As California senator John Conness observed at the time, "Nevada is a mining community exclusively, and can never be anything else. It must always be *fed from adjacent countries.*"[16]

Powers of hindsight, however, were not available to those who rushed to Washoe in 1860 and 1861. For the Californians who made the trek, the discovery of the Comstock Lode had a special meaning: behind their immigration was a powerful myth born of the California gold rush, one magnified by the passage of time and the disappearance of the conditions of 1849. According to the popular imagination of the 1850s, during the first years of California's gold rush the ethos of liberal economic

individualism had found—if only briefly—a basis of genuine equal opportunity. In the mines, the size of a claim was limited by convention to
what one person could work. Mining required little in the way of capital
investment, and profit fell directly to the laborer who exploited the public domain as his individual means of production. In the face of energy,
fortitude, and no small measure of luck, ascribed attributes such as
wealth, education, and former station in life counted for little.[17]

Although the equality of the first years of the gold rush disappeared
quickly with the exhaustion of surface placer deposits and the replacement of the individual miner by increasingly capital-intensive mining,
memories of 1849 lingered, creating a mythological golden age that was
almost perfectly congruent with nineteenth-century ideals of economic
freedom, social mobility, and male self-reliance. The discovery of the
Comstock Lode suggested a renewal of that age and awakened the "old
Californians'" hopes. By then, as the nineteenth-century political econo-
mist John Hittell observed, California's miners were "ready to go anywhere, if there was a reasonable hope of such diggings, rather than submit to life without the high pay and excitement which they had enjoyed
for years in the Sacramento placers."[18] Among the thousands of Californians who rushed to Nevada in 1859 and 1860 was the journalist J. Ross
Browne. With a sharp eye, Browne captured the hopes and aspirations
of the charter settlers of Washoe:

> Who would be a slave when all nature calls upon him in trumpet tones to
> be free? Who would sell his birthright for a mess of pottage when he could
> lead the life of an honest miner?—earn his bread by the sweat of his
> brow—breathe the fresh air of heaven without stint or limit? And of all the
> miners in the world, who would not be a Washoe miner? . . . The life of the
> miner is one of labor, peril, and exposure; but it possesses the fascinating
> element of liberty, and the promise of unlimited reward. In the midst of
> privation, amounting, at times, to the verge of starvation, what glowing vi-
> sions fill the minds of adventurers?[19]

In the longer view, Browne's vision of Nevada's promise was mistaken.
The birthright of individual economic freedom and opportunity for unlimited rewards, so central to the producer ethic of the immigrants, dissolved over the 1860s under the pressure of industrialization, concentrated ownership, and the emergence of a permanent working class in
the mines.[20] In the first years of the Comstock rush, however, the situation appeared otherwise. In 1863, as Grant Smith has pointed out, thousands of claims dotted the hills and valleys surrounding Virginia City.
More than four hundred companies—some genuine, many imaginary—
offered stock on local exchanges. Similarly, dozens of men, using the
oddest assortment of machinery, operated the crushing mills that reduced Comstock bullion to gold and, more importantly, silver. As early
as 1861, more than seventy-five mills were operating (and twenty more

were under construction) in the canyons and rivers near the mines. Most of these were crude hand mills operated by individuals, and even the larger ones were secondhand affairs brought over from California.[21] In retrospect, there was a certain absurdity to the imaginary mines and marginal mills that covered the countryside. But as Eliot Lord, the Comstock Lode's late-nineteenth-century chronicler, observed: "It was different at the time. In the unknown there is an almost infinite range of possibility, and who would oppose the confident faith of the optimists except with unsupported doubts. . . . The nabobs in fancy might yet be nabobs in fact."[22]

Such "nabobs in fancy" dominated the charter society of early Nevada, giving it the mark of a relatively undifferentiated socioeconomic order in which an individualist producer ethic had wide play. Lines between miner, merchant, prospector, speculator, entrepreneur, and manager were sufficiently blurred to keep class-based sensibilities to a minimum. Workers who prospected and speculated in mining stocks drifted in and out of the labor force; small merchants and teamsters vied for a corner on growing markets; businessmen invested their savings in new leads discovered by itinerant prospectors; "briefless lawyers" traded their services for shares in disputed claims. Nevada, declared the *Gold Hill Evening News* in 1863, is, after all, the land for the old Californian: "The constant excitement, the fortunes, made and lost, the bright hopes of all—for "no man knoweth what a day or an hour may bring forth"— all, all go to make up what once constituted the hey-day of the glory of California. And to-day, Washoe is only another edition of the early gold seeker's experience, with a thousand percent added thereto."[23]

Politics imitated life in Nevada. For almost two years following the Comstock Lode's discovery, the area's political status remained confused. It was every man for himself. Because of the mining excitement, political activity came to a halt. Nevertheless, the provisional government's forlorn emissary to Congress continued his efforts. In 1859 and 1860, these were to no avail. But in 1861, the major barrier to congressional action was removed when the senators and representatives of seceding southern states abandoned the Union. California's senators introduced a bill establishing the Territory of Nevada. The Republican-dominated Congress, cognizant of the importance of the Comstock Lode treasure in the impending conflict with the South, quickly affirmed it. Nevada became a territory in the spring of 1861, and the new government arrived in Carson City, the capital town, that July.

Lincoln's appointee to the governorship was New Yorker James Nye, a "political henchman and bosom friend of William Seward." Nye was an ardent organization man who had gone to Washington, D.C., after Lincoln's inauguration and applied for every patronage post available in New York City. According to the *New York Herald*, "he . . . applied for Collector, Postmaster, Surveyor, Naval Officer, Sub-Treasurer, and Superintendent of the Assay Office, on the principle, probably, that by making a grab for all he will be likely to secure one."[24] Nevada was a bit distant from the city in which he wished to serve, but Nye accepted the offer with alacrity.

As territorial secretary, Lincoln named Missourian Orion Clemens. With him came his brother, Samuel, with his own appointment as personal secretary to the territorial secretary. Writing as Mark Twain in *Roughing It* eleven years hence, he recalled the arrival of Nevada's government:

> The new government was received with considerable coolness. It was not only a foreign intruder, but a poor one. It was not even worth plucking— except by the smallest of small fry office seekers and sich. . . . The Organic Act and the "Instructions" from the State Department commanded that a legislature should be elected at such and such a time, and its sittings inaugurated at such and such a date. It was easy to get legislators, even at three dollars a day, although board was four dollars and fifty cents, for distinction has its charm in Nevada as elsewhere, and there were plenty of patriotic souls out of employment; but to get a legislative hall for them to meet in was another matter all together. Carson blandly refused to give a room rent free, or to let one to the government on credit.[25]

Three years later, when Nevada entered the Union, the government could afford executive offices and a legislative hall convenient to Carson City saloons, but in other respects Nevada politics lacked the marks of an established system.[26] Organized parties were unknown; in their stead one found a version of the "chaotic factionalism" identified by Kenneth Owens.[27] To no small degree this was because politics had little to do with why people immigrated to the territory. Particularly during its first boom years, Nevada had a transitory quality. Its population came and went, concerned, it seemed, only with extracting as much bullion as possible, as quickly as possible. Few considered their residence as anything other than a short-term adventure. But more than irrelevance mitigated against party politics. Even as time went on and it became apparent that Comstock Lode mining demanded a commitment of both time and capital—matters that do invest politics with social and economic significance—formal political organizations failed to emerge. The Civil War made them impossible.

With the South's secession, "old Nevada residents" as well as recently arrived Californians proclaimed their allegiance to the wartime Union party. While talk of "secesh" conspiracies in Nevada was common during the war, actual southern sympathizers were, practically speaking, difficult to find.[28] Rather, the political divisions in the territory cut across the Union party's ranks. These involved, first, a division between Nevada's farmers, ranchers, and traders, whose settlement antedated the Comstock discovery, and the transitory denizens of the new mining towns. Second, they reflected animosities between the territory's prospectors and small miners, on the one hand, and, on the other, the agents of San Francisco mining corporations, whose interest and involvement in Washoe's resources grew with each reported mineral discovery.

Until 1863 the agricultural/mining division in territorial Nevada simmered below the surface, but conflict between individual and corporate interests in the mines was evident from the start. During the first and second sessions of the territorial legislature the division surfaced in the form of a controversial bill to regulate corporations. The bill required that corporations holding property in Nevada but headquartered elsewhere "remove their places of business, principal offices, books, and other papers necessary for the transaction of such business, to some point . . . within the limits of this Territory."[29] According to its supporters, the act was necessary because of the growing number of San Francisco corporations doing business in the territory. "Lasting wrongs," they declared,

> may be done by the passage of laws tending to the detriment and injury of the Territory, such as the building up of foreign monopolies with no direct interest in the Territory, but whose sole object is to extract the precious metals from the mines and convey it to foreign countries, thereby tending greatly to retard the progress, cripple the enterprise, and otherwise hinder the development of the resources of the Territory by its own citizens.[30]

In the first legislative session, opponents managed to postpone the measure indefinitely, but the following year public pressure demanded action.[31] For six weeks territorial Nevada's lawmakers argued over the provision. Five days before adjournment, matters came to a head. As the legislature discussed the issue in a special evening session, a large crowd assembled outside the hall. The racket they created made it impossible for the lawmakers to continue, so they adjourned. The bill's supporters joined the assemblage while opponents fled—and then the fun began.

Known as the "Third House of the Territorial Legislature," the crowd outside the lawmakers' chambers was a fixture in territorial Nevada politics. Properly, the term referred to a local nickelodeon that included among its acts a burlesque of the territorial legislature.[32] More generally, however, it was attached to crowds that, in rituals combining politics with merrymaking, pressed various demands on the legislature. In this instance, the "Third House," backed by a brass band, fueled with alcohol, and illuminated by a bonfire, voiced the opinion that opponents of the corporation bill were the conscious, well-bribed tools of San Francisco monopolists.[33] Their demonstration, at this and other times, was effective. The next day, in the absence of a number of the bill's opponents (intimidated by the Third House, some said), the corporation bill passed.

A grand celebration applauding the legislature followed. According to reporter Andrew Marsh, the town was taken by a "general drunk. . . . Vast quantities of barrels and boxes, gunpowder, fire crackers, champagne, brandy, whisky and other combustibles are consumed," he wrote, "and the brass band is out adding to the universal din." [34]

Overshadowed by the bonfires and general drunkenness that attended passage of the corporation bill was another piece of legislation. On the evening before final adjournment, Nevada's lawmakers quietly passed "An Act to Frame a Constitution and State Government for the State of Washoe." The measure took everyone by surprise, including the legislature's reporter, who declared for the record that "the important measure comes up with startling suddenness. . . . The general impression of members with whom I have conversed on the subject heretofore has been that 'Washoe' has not sufficiently developed as a Territorial Chrysalis to think at present of emerging into a butterfly state!" [35] Despite any misgivings that may have existed, the bill passed without discussion. The closing of the territorial legislature, which many thought would be Nevada's last, was accompanied by a nightlong revel. "A brilliant bonfire blazed in the street," reported Marsh, "and the whole town proposed to go on a grand and universal bender. The brass band speedily took up a position in the vicinity of the bonfire, and played a few pieces. . . . After the adjournment a procession was formed, headed by the band and the presiding officers, which marched to Governor Nye's house, and called the Governor out." [36] They were, a teetotaling resident noted, "all foolishly drunk. The band was out and after adjourning they serenaded Governor Nye. He was foolishly drunk, I understand, and sang Dixie to the crowd." [37]

The origins of the first statehood act are not revealed by the historical record.[38] But during the flush times of 1863 there was little opposition to the idea. Nevada's voters ratified the call for a constitutional convention by a four-to-one margin. A month later, thirty-nine delegates assembled in Carson City to write a state constitution. Using California's charter as their guide, they accomplished this task in thirty-two days. The session, particularly in light of what lay ahead, was calm and sober. Only one controversy upset the convention, a controversy that appeared, incorrectly, to be amicably resolved. This concerned the taxing of Nevada's mines.

The controversy over taxation of the mines surfaced two and a half weeks after the convention began its work, when the delegates turned to the Article on Taxation. The first section of the article, as reported from committee, stated simply:

> The Legislature shall provide by law for a uniform and equal rate of assessment and taxation, and shall prescribe such regulations as shall secure a just valuation for taxation of all property, both real and personal, *includ-*

ing mines and mining property; excepting such only as may be exempted by law for municipal, educational, literary, scientific, religious or charitable purposes.[39] (emphasis added)

For three days the delegates debated this provision. Its most outspoken opponent was delegate William M. Stewart, who argued that the voters would repudiate the constitution if mines were not treated differently from other types of property. Instead of the above provision, Stewart proposed an exemption from taxation for "nonproductive" mines and, otherwise, a tax only on a mine's "net proceeds."

William M. Stewart was a resourceful attorney and, in politics, a dangerous antagonist.[40] During Nevada's early years, he was known (unaffectionately) as the "great lawyer" because of his work for San Francisco mining corporations operating on the Comstock Lode. Stewart was notorious not only for the income this activity brought him (estimated as high as two hundred thousand dollars per year), but also for the less-than-scrupulous tactics he employed in his clients' behalf. This notoriety followed him to the constitutional convention. A majority of the delegates, unsympathetic toward the large corporations that Stewart represented, suspected his every word. Thus, when he opposed the mining tax few were convinced by his insistence that he spoke for the "honest prospector" and the "poor miner." His intent, it was widely assumed, was to exempt his corporate clients from paying a fair share of the new state's expenses.[41]

In his arguments against the tax, however, Stewart gave no indication that his concern was for anyone but the "poor miner" who prospected in "bed-rock tunnels" in the sanguine, and usually forlorn, hope of finding a bonanza. These hardy souls, he insisted, were the foundation of Nevada's future prosperity, and they simply could not afford to pay taxes on mining claims whose value was based not on fact but on hopes and expectations. "Take any of your mining districts," Stewart argued to his colleagues:

> Men go there without money and prospect. They manage to live by working by the day for their "grub," for a little pork and a little flour, and then they work alone upon their claims. They spend only so much time as is absolutely necessary to buy provisions and clothing; they live in huts; they have got no money, and if you call upon them for fifty or a hundred dollars or so, for taxes, it would be impossible for them to raise it and you would have to take the claim. What would you do with it when you got it? Are you going to sell it to somebody else and let them run the tunnels? You don't want it. The government does not want these wild, extravagant prospecting claims. They are worth nothing to anybody but the man that is full of sanguine hope.[42]

During one evening session Stewart assaulted the proposed tax for three hours. So labored was his disquisition on the "poor miner" and his "bed-rock tunnels" that he became the object of mild ridicule. One delegate responded with his own amendment, exempting from taxation "unproductive town property and unproductive farms" to go along with Stewart's exemption of unproductive mines. Another remarked that he had "heard so much [from Stewart] that 'bed-rock tunnels' has been running in my ears for days."[43] Stewart's grandiloquence inspired even Samuel Clemens, who convened the Third House. Meeting "in the Hall of the Convention at eleven p.m.," President Clemens's rump convention roasted their daytime counterparts—above all William Stewart. When "Bill's" alter ego rose to address the Third House on the mining tax, Clemens denied him the floor:

> Take your seat Bill Stewart! I am not going to sit here and listen to that same old song again. . . . When I want it, I will repeat it myself—I know it by heart anyhow. You and your bed-rock tunnels, and blighted miners, and blasted hopes, have gotten to be a sort of nightmare to me, and I won't put up with it any longer. I don't wish to be too hard on your speech, but if you can't add something fresh to it, or say it backwards, or sing it to a new tune, you simply have got to simmer down for awhile.[44]

While Clemens and his friends had their fun, others responded seriously to Stewart's proposed tax exemption for the mines. The most considered and effective speaker in this regard was John Wesley North, the convention's president and a Lincoln appointee to the territorial supreme court. North agreed with Stewart that mining was the "great interest of the State" and that the constitution should not discriminate against it. However, he insisted, this consideration in and of itself gave "no reason for compelling the other interests to bear the whole burden of government."[45] Shifting attention away from Stewart's lament for the "poor miner," North pointed out that a tax limited to the net proceeds of mines would allow the largest mining companies to escape taxation altogether. Accounting sleight-of-hand, he pointed out, was the stock in trade of the Comstock's large corporations. Recently, the judge reminded the delegates, some of the territory's biggest mining enterprises had accomplished the impossible—distributing dividends to stockholders in excess of the company's reported *gross* proceeds. His conclusion was obvious: a tax on only the net proceeds of mines opened the door to fraud; in effect, it released the largest companies from any responsibility for supporting the government. "In framing our organic law," North ended, "we should seek to make it so fair and so just, and clear, that if a man is disposed to do wrong he cannot do it without great difficulty."[46]

North's arguments carried the day. Farmers, merchants, and mechanics were not going to bear the entire burden of taxation so that Bill Stewart's clients could escape responsibility. When it came time to vote, three-quarters of the convention held firm and sustained the original language of the taxation article. Although a few mining-county delegates grumbled that the provision would turn the voters against the constitution, they did not press the matter. Two weeks later the convention adjourned *sine die* amid what its reporter called "An Era of Good Feeling." Stewart, among others, gave short speeches "expressing kindly feelings," and then President North closed by referring to "the beautiful association we have had, the happy time which we have spent together while performing the task of framing a Constitution for our new state."[47] All the delegates proclaimed their support for the constitution, with observers predicting quick and unanimous ratification. Clemens and the Third House then inaugurated an evening of celebration with their own adjournment: "Gentlemen," President Clemens announced,

> you have considered a subject which you knew nothing about; spoken on every subject but the one before the House, and voted, without knowing what you were voting for, or having any idea what would be the general result of your action. I will adjourn the convention for an hour, on account of my cold, to the end that I may apply the remedy ascribed for it by Dr. Tjader—the same being gin and molasses. The Chief Page is hereby instructed to provide a spoonful of molasses, and a gallon of gin for the use of the President.[48]

Unexpectedly—and notwithstanding the "good feelings" that marked the convention's close—within two weeks Nevadan statehood was facing certain defeat. An election campaign that most thought would be quiet and uneventful suddenly exploded into a monthlong round of charges and countercharges that split Nevadan society into its elemental parts. Statehood itself came to be of secondary importance, a proxy for other concerns, concerns that went back to the original reasons for the rush of Californians to the territory: What kind of a society was Nevada to be? Was it "another edition of the early gold seeker's experience," or, rather, falling under the control of concentrated capital? Such questions had been at the heart of the previous year's legislative controversy over the regulation of corporations, but then the uproar had been limited to the legislative chambers in Carson City. This time it enveloped the entire territory.

The storm of controversy over ratification was raised, though without the effect intended, by the man who most ardently supported statehood: none other than William Stewart. Despite his defeat on the mining tax, Stewart had left the convention fully intending to work for the constitution's ratification. To his mind, the tax article did not constitute a fatal constitutional flaw; rather, he considered it (as he announced to audiences across the territory) open to a variety of interpretations—including his own, that a tax be laid only on the net proceeds of mines. Just what construction the legislature would eventually arrive at, he admitted, was unknown. But a carefully selected set of lawmakers, he asserted, could undo any damage done by the constitutional convention.[49]

This interpretation of the taxation article became known as "Stewart's construction." The great lawyer apparently adopted it because he believed that statehood would resolve another, larger issue in his favor. Since 1862 Stewart had unsuccessfully argued in the territorial courts for what Nevadans knew as the "one-ledge" theory of the Comstock Lode. Simply put, this theory held that the lode consisted of one ledge of ore that ran, on a north-south line, the length of Sun Peak's eastern slope. Opposed to it was the "many-ledge" theory, which insisted that the lode was made up of a series of parallel quartz ledges (running north and south), divided by silver-free clay and porphyry. At stake were millions of dollars, indeed control of Nevada's bullion: for if the Comstock Lode actually was one ledge, those mines operating to the east and west of the original Comstock locations were trespassing on drifts legally the property of the original claimants.[50]

The geological structure of the Comstock Lode was not determined until the fall of 1864, when an expert hired by the territorial supreme court established that it was in fact a fissure vein composed of a single ledge.[51] In the meantime, however, both the evidence and overwhelming popular sentiment supported the contrary interpretation, the "many-ledge" theory. Stewart's "one-ledge" interpretation had little to recommend itself to the bulk of the population, which saw it as a stratagem on the part of corporations who had purchased a controlling interest in the original locations to drive out the smaller concerns that claimed the parallel ledges. To those who prospected and speculated in the stock of new, "wildcat" leads, the "odious one-ledge theory" was nothing more than a bald attempt by San Francisco capitalists to monopolize the Comstock Lode at the expense of the "little man."[52]

In 1862 and 1863, Stewart pressed his client's "one-ledge" claims numerous times in the court of Judge John North. Yet he consistently met defeat. To Stewart's chagrin, the judge personally examined the disputed ground and declared that Stewart's allegation was without merit. The evidence in favor of a single ledge, North declared, was "the most vague conjecture." He thus ruled time and again in favor of claim holders—small operators—to ridges parallel to the large corporate mines. Consequently, North (without intending to) became the champion of "the people." In applauding the judge's actions, the *Gold Hill Evening News* pronounced that the

one ledge theory meets with almost universal condemnation. . . . Its adherents have no basis for their idea save the mere opinion of self styled "experts," and [it] cannot by any possibility be established by actual demonstration. One thing is morally certain, and that is that its endorsement by the courts would have the most disastrous effect upon the interests and prosperity of the Territory.[53]

Stewart, however, had other interests in mind; having been blocked by the courts, he therefore turned to the politics of statehood. Under the constitution proposed in 1863, the judiciary would become elective— and the "great lawyer" had the resources necessary to insure a court without John North. In the weeks before the ratification vote, Stewart mobilized the funds at his command and promises of political prefer- ment to capture Nevada's Union party and its candidates for state office. Given that the election of state offices was to be held concurrently with the vote on the constitution, success in controlling the nominations seemed to assure a governor, legislature, and, especially, a judiciary that would do his bidding.

Stewart began by packing the Union party convention in Storey County with his supporters. As chairman of the committee on nomina- tions at the county convention, Stewart then single-handedly selected Storey's delegates to the territorial meeting in Carson City (these men formed the largest delegation to that convention), as well as the local candidates for state senator, assemblyman, and district judge. He also pushed two resolutions through the county convention that set the stage for the coming election. The first restated his contention that "the power to control the taxing of mines is conferred upon the Legislature" and that the legislature should "only subject to the burdens of Government such claims as yield net profits to their owners." The second instructed Storey's delegates to the territorial convention "to oppose by all honor- able means the nomination of . . . John W. North to office by said State Convention."[54]

To many, Stewart's control over the county meeting, his hold on local nominees and delegates to the state convention, and his resolutions denying the constitutional convention's tax measure and denouncing the people's champion, North, were oriented toward but one purpose: con- trol of the state government by San Francisco financiers. As a result, sup- port for statehood evaporated. Nine Storey County men, incensed at what they called Stewart's "high-handed" domination of the county con- vention, challenged the credentials of Storey's delegation to the territo- rial Union party convention. When their appeals failed, they left Carson City and announced their opposition to statehood on the grounds that Nevada's Union party had come under "a base and unparalleled submis- sion of imposter leaders . . . whose effrontery and heartlessness impel them to infer that *their* rights are the first rights to be known and guaran- teed in all this part of Nevada."[55]

Although Stewart's supporters dismissed the charges as the ravings of "sore headed and disappointed office seekers," opposition to statehood spread to every corner of the territory.[56] In the weeks leading to the vote on the constitution, statehood's opponents, defining themselves as the "little interests," made a variety of charges against Stewart. Because these charges represented the perspective of miners, businessmen, mechanics, and farmers, they gave the movement electoral strength; in the long run, however, the very diversity of the alliance meant that it would be shortlived.

All of statehood's opponents agreed that Stewart had hand-selected the Union party candidates to state office and that, if the constitution was ratified, control of the government would fall on men beholden to him and the mining corporations he represented. All similarly came to the defense of North, arguing that Stewart desired his removal "because the Judge is too honest to be bribed; too intelligent to be hoodwinked, and too firm to be driven."[57] "Stewart and Company," the *Virginia Daily Union* proclaimed,

> want a state government because they have come to the conclusion that our present judiciary care more for the people and for justice than they do for the influence of improper combinations; and there are several legal gentlemen who would like to have an opportunity to try the "one ledge" theory before new and different judges. All the representatives of these private interests would like a State Government, and if they can obtain one, and thereby achieve their personal ends and advancement, it matters but little to them how immeasurable the disaster which would be inflicted on this Territory.[58]

Yet on the constitution's mining tax provision—in the longer view a more crucial question—statehood's opponents achieved only tenuous agreement that masked essential differences among them. Universally, they denounced Stewart's position that the legislature, if carefully selected by the voters, could "leave free from taxation undeveloped mining claims of a mere speculative value; and only subject to the burden of Government such claims as yield net profits to their owners."[59] But in rushing to denounce Stewart's deception on the tax question, his adversaries failed to recognize that they themselves were deeply divided over the same issue.

On the one hand, merchants and farmers throughout the territory believed that Stewart intended to have "his" legislators violate a provision they considered equitable and essential. His scheme, charged the *Virginia Daily Union*, would "destroy our only means of raising a sufficient revenue" and thereby "ruin the public credit and inflict a ruinous tax on the little interests outside the mines."[60] Siding with the merchants, the farmers and ranchers of Carson and Washoe valleys agreed that Stewart's ambiguous reading of the constitution meant the "surrender of ourselves and our rights to the possession of capitalists of San Francisco and to William M. Stewart, who is their agent."[61] They charged that "his" nominee for governor, Miles N. Mitchell, had taken one position on the question in the mining counties and another in the agricultural counties, and declared that "if a clause is to be construed to suit the interest of a certain class, and millions of dollars of property released from taxation, then it [the constitution] is not worth the paper it is written upon."[62]

On the other hand, prospectors, mining speculators, and small mine and mill owners attacked Stewart because they found duplicitous his contention that the legislature could, under the new constitution, exempt mines from taxation. These parties opposed the constitution's tax article, believing that Stewart's argument was but a cover for his true intentions: the removal of Judge North and the election of judges under Stewart's own control who would invalidate the many-ledge theory and thus deliver the Comstock Lode into the hands of San Francisco capitalists. The "Stewart constructionists," they argued, were

> slippery, wiry fellows, lacking the straightforward manliness to meet the issue and oppose the constitution. [They] have discovered a mean, roundabout, under-handed way to circumvent and defeat the plain intent and meaning of the taxation clause, by a far fetched and false construction; which if likely to be carried into effect, is the most potent reason why we should reject the constitution.[63]

Workingmen, many of whom prospected and speculated in mining stocks in addition to working as wage laborers, also opposed taxing the mines. Recognizing a common interest with the small mine owner on this question, they repudiated the "Stewart constructionists" as well. "How dare they now turn around," asked a laborer from Como, "and vote for that which they condemned as unjust and declared to be wrong. Can they conscientiously do it? *Will* they do it?? Brother miners, watch each one of those . . . who in the convention stood up for your rights, and if they now repudiate you and your rights, mark them well, and remember them."[64]

In the weeks before the vote, as the charges against Stewart intensified, he tried to deflect his critics by discrediting North. Charging that the judge had bought his seat on the bench, that he had received loans from companies who appeared before his court, and that he had been continually bribed by litigants for favorable decisions, Stewart pled with Nevadans to vote for statehood as a way of purifying government.[65] The strategy of discrediting his adversary failed; indeed, it backfired. North answered the charges in the press and demanded that Stewart make a public retraction. Popular opinion was with the judge, the declared champion of the "little interests" against "improper combinations." At a public meeting held at Maguire's Virginia City Opera House three days before the election, North and Stewart met in a public debate. Before a packed auditorium, Stewart repeated his attack in a two-hour diatribe. But to no avail: Stewart, reported the *Virginia Daily Union,* "made an ass of himself. . . . North then came forward, and in about three minutes so completely used up Stewart that he commenced to froth and foam at the mouth like a mad man—which he certainly was—and while he was trying to say something, which he could not, the meeting adjourned, with three rousing cheers for Judge North."[66]

The repudiation of Stewart—and, by implication, of statehood—was complete. "The defeat of the constitution is a foregone conclusion," announced the *Reese River Reveille* two days after the North-Stewart confrontation; "no other mode of safety is left. The ticket belongs body and soul to the Comstock interest, and if elected, the odious 'one ledge' theory will be triumphant."[67] On election day, the voters rejected the constitution, four to one. In defense of individual enterprise, the open marketplace, and the right of the "little man" to join in the race for wealth and prominence, the territory's residents vanquished the monopolistic enemy. "Bill Stewart & Co. are busted out," rejoiced Washoe City's *Old Piute,* "and some of the balance of us are busted in."[68] The outcome, according to the *Virginia Daily Union,* vindicated North: "The Judge showed, the 'Hon. Bill' blowed, the people voted and the case ended by rendering of the following verdict: 'The Judge is not a rotten magistrate and thief, as charged; but somebody else is a rascally liar as everybody knows.'"[69]

In the aftermath of this campaign, interest in statehood evaporated. Those who suggested a reconsideration of the defeated constitution were roundly denounced. Most agreed with the *Virginia Daily Union,* which argued that the question should be postponed at least a year, to allow passions to cool and, more importantly, to recognize the Union party so that it "is said no longer that we are controlled by Stewart and his minions, and that the Central Committee is subservient to him and his clique."[70]

Those who counted statehood out, however, failed to foresee Nevada's importance to Republican party strategists inside Congress and the Lincoln administration. As the 1864 presidential campaign approached, party leaders in Washington, D.C., predicted a close race that might end up in the House of Representatives—in which event Nevada's representative could make a difference.[71] "Her votes are wanted here," declared California senator John Conness in an open letter to Nevadans; "every loyal man awaits her admission."[72] Radical Republicans, furthermore, saw in Nevadan statehood an opportunity to establish a stern precedent for reconstruction. As Ohio congressman James Ashley recalled, Nevada statehood offered a means "to establish a new principle of admission of states . . . negativing so far as I could in the enabling acts, the old idea of State Rights." With this Conness concurred. Nevada, he stated, would have the "great honor of being the first to rebuke the pretense that states are merely partners, as well as having set National over state sovereignty."[73]

Thus, when notice of the Nevada constitution's rejection reached Washington over the new transcontinental telegraph line, the reaction was immediate. Three weeks after the vosters refused statehood, Wisconsin senator James Doolittle resurrected it by introducing another enabling act. On February 24, the Senate unanimously passed the bill, without discussion. Three weeks later the House followed suit.[74] News of the reprieve evoked little enthusiasm in the territory. "We don't want any constitution," proclaimed the *Humboldt Register,* "and we don't propose adopting one just because it is good, and handy to have around the house."[75] Governor Nye, however, had little choice in the matter. In early spring he announced a June election of delegates to a new convention.

If interest in statehood was low at the time of Nye's announcement, by the time of the June 6 election it had all but disappeared. In the interim, a sudden and devastating depression struck the territory. Actually, a few insiders had known of the coming collapse since the beginning of 1864, for the surface deposits were approaching exhaustion and the output of the richest mines of the Comstock Lode had begun to fall off precipitously. Speculators and insiders thus quietly began to unload their stock. By spring, the news could no longer be contained. A general panic began in the San Francisco and Virginia City stock exchanges. Between April and September countless speculative empires collapsed. The value of shares in the largest mines plummeted 70 to 80 percent. Stock in small mines, prospecting claims, and wildcats became worthless. Investors were ruined, and small mine owners had to abandon their claims. As the large companies reduced operations, unemployment soared. With the contraction of capital, commerce of every type approached a halt.[76] "All branches of business are depressed," reported the *Virginia Daily Union,* "and even the largest mercantile houses feel the pressure. Fear is entertained that many small dealers will be obliged to yield to the severity of the times. Many mechanics and laborers have been thrown out of employment, mills and mines have reduced the number of their hands, and few mines, except those of the first class, are being vigorously worked."[77]

By summer, depression hung like a pall over the territory. The old issues—improper combinations, William Stewart's perfidy, the one-ledge versus many-ledge theories—were overwhelmed by a single question: What had caused the "dull times," and what could be done about it? As the depression went on, and as Nevadans prepared for the second constitutional convention, answers began to emerge. Slowly but surely, newspaper editors, ruined speculators, hard-pressed businessmen, mechanics, and unemployed miners converged on a common explanation of the territory's plight. The source of the evil, they held, was speculation: Nevadans' frenzied quest for the wildcat.[78]

With more truth than they realized, Nevadans from all walks of life began to point at economic cunning and unscrupulous promotion as the cause of the panic. The San Francisco and Virginia City exchanges were in fact flooded with stock in worthless or nonexistent mines. Overgullible investors had been victimized by schemes, and once the panic began, victims did not stop to discriminate between wildcat promotions and legitimate enterprises. "That the people have fought the wild-cat to their sorrow and damage . . . we are forced to admit," the *Gold Hill Evening News* declared in early May, but this

> does not mend the matter as regards them, nor is the fact that "mining sharps" from Washoe have succeeded in duping and swindling an over credulous people, any credit to the Territory. On the contrary, that very fact has damaged the reputation of our mines, and in the revulsion of feeling towards silver-mining speculations, the real and permanent interests of the territory have been made to suffer from the temporary success of wild cat swindlers.[79]

While correct in its essentials, this argument was a delusion in one respect: the speculative mania that collapsed with the crash of 1864 was not simply the work of a handful of swindlers. On the contrary, Nevada's population as a whole had shared a preference for promoting rather than working undeveloped and questionable claims. Indeed, such promotions had been at the heart of the promise of quick wealth, immediate independence, and socioeconomic mobility that had made Nevada "another edition of the early gold seeker's experience."[80] That Nevadans failed to face the fact that collapse had originated in the combined actions of a population on the make, however, had little effect on the conclusions they would ultimately reach. Once having found the source of their travail in the unchecked ambitions of individual speculators, they embarked on a path that necessarily forced them to reconsider their understanding of political economy—in short, to question and revise the commitment to economic individualism that had provided the critical perspective in the previous winter's statehood campaign.

The outlines of this redefinition came slowly into focus in the weeks preceding the second convention. It consisted of three broad propositions, one concerning the past and two the future. First was the "lesson" of wildcat speculation: its baleful influence on social stability and continued prosperity. "The experience of the past," proclaimed the *Humboldt Register*, "has taught us that these feverish speculative manias of to-day leave business prostrate to-morrow."[81] Second, and a corollary to the first lesson, was the conviction that recovery, prosperity, and progress could come only from one source: the systematic development of paying mines. The *Register* admonished: "We want no water spout stream of prosperity, whose turbid muddy waters bear all before it for a season, and then leave our business field ruined and fruitless."[82] From these premises Nevadans concluded that, third, the development necessary for genuine recovery and lasting prosperity could not come from small mining enterprises: capital was required, "capital to the extent of millions."[83] Observed a survivor in the Reese River district, "Experience has taught us that it required much more capital to develope [*sic*] the mines than was anticipated a year ago. We then thought it was necessary only to find a vein and fortune awaited us; in this how many were most grievously disappointed?"[84] The answer was obvious. All around them, Nevadans saw "hardworking, industrious men . . . reduced to the last extremity." As a writer from Virginia City argued, "Men of small means can not, or will not, develop and work silver mines. . . . We have yet many rich cropping ledges that have never been prospected at all. . . . Let capitalists get possession of these, and . . . bring to light their true value. . . . Thus there will be an avenue open for employment of hundreds of laborers, and our country will receive an impetus which will be lasting."[85]

At the same time that this prescription for Nevada's recovery was gaining adherents, the election of delegates to the second constitutional convention took place. Given the depression and the conviction that voters would likely reject any proposed constitution, little interest was shown in the election. In each county the Union party nominated an unopposed slate. Little if any campaigning preceded the vote, and on election day the turnout was poor, with perhaps a quarter of the eligible voters participating. As the *Esmeralda Star* observed, "The people generally felt no interest in the matter. They care but little who goes to the convention since they are determined to vote down the constitution anyway."[86]

The men selected as delegates composed a group of intimates and strangers. More than a third of them were newcomers to local politics. Ten, however, had been delegates to the 1863 convention, among them the most ardent supporters of the mining tax provision.[87] In addition, several had risen to prominence by virtue of their opposition to Stewart and statehood in the campaign of the previous winter, including five of the "bolters" who had made a public issue of Stewart's domination of the Storey County Union party convention.[88] The great lawyer himself, on business in San Francisco, did not participate in the election, and in the campaign his name was neither mentioned as a candidate nor taken in vain. Another figure conspicuous for his absence was John North. By the beginning of summer the public standing of this former champion of the people had fallen dramatically. In an odd twist of fate, the search for explanations of the depression had focused attention on the territorial courts. When Nevadans asked why the capital needed to develop their mines was not forthcoming, they pointed to the tangle of lawsuits over

the one-ledge theory. "The Cause of Dull Times—The Ghoul of Litigation," declared the *Virginia Daily Union:*

> From the Ophir to the latest development of the Comstock . . . there is not
> a mining claim of proved or presumptive richness in this county but is in-
> volved in an apparently interminable network of litigation. Quartz veins
> from which pay rock could even now be extracted, as well as quartz veins
> which give promise of return after a few weeks more of labor, are left lying
> idle and unproductive until it can be ascertained as to which one of half a
> dozen conflicting claims have a right of ownership and possession.[89]

Thus, when the delegates set out for the convention, it was difficult to
predict the direction their deliberations would take. The previous six
months had seen territorial affairs turned upside down. The convention
was made up of men new to territorial affairs as well as veterans of the
previous statehood campaign, veterans famous for their defense of Nevada's "little interests" against "improper combinations." Just what this
disparate group would accomplish was anyone's guess.

With no fanfare and few expectations, the delegates made their way
to Carson City, where the convention began on July 4. The town was
easily accessible, for most of the territory's population was found within
a day's journey, either in the Comstock Lode to the north, the Reese
River mining camps to the east, or the farming and cattle-raising region
(the "cow counties") along the base of the Sierra Nevada to the west. Regular freight and passenger service, a consequence of mining boom commerce and market demand for food and supplies, connected Nevada's
compact settlements to one another in a comprehensive system of roads
and turnpikes.[90] Although Carson was not a mining town, its location at
the hub of the territorial and overland road system, its proximity to the
area's few ranches and farms, its access to Sierra Nevada timber, and its
selection as territorial capital had made it a substantial center of trade,
merchandising, lumber production, and services.[91]

Founded before the discovery of the Comstock Lode—in 1858, out of
a moribund cattle ranch bought by partisans of the area's anti-Mormon
movement—Carson City was nevertheless as much a product of the
Comstock Lode as any mining town in the territory. Even though it was
declared the capital of the insurgent (and provisional) Territory of Nevada, the town had languished until 1860. Its site on an alkali plain four
thousand feet above sea level certainly had little to recommend itself; a
surveyor whom Abram Curry, Carson City's proprietor, tried to hire recommended against the townsite and refused to accept lots in lieu of cash
payment for his work.[92] Curry thus surveyed the town himself, creating a
characteristic western town in which wide avenues at right angles formed
one hundred square blocks, which were "regularly laid out" and broken

up by a central plaza.[93] As in the original plan of Salem, Oregon, Curry expected that Carson's central plaza would be the site for the capitol building of a future state, "the hope of which," a pre–Comstock Lode immigrant remembered, "[Curry's] own mind alone seemed to grasp."[94]

Despite its unpromising site and less-than-auspicious beginning, Carson City grew rapidly in the 1860s. It was the logical stopping place for immigrants and goods traveling between California and the Comstock Lode, and so it grew as a center of trade, lumber production, merchandising, and services. In 1861 Congress formally designated it the territorial capital, an industry in and of itself.[95] Consequently, the town's population increased steadily. By the middle of 1860 some three to four hundred people had settled there, and seventy-five buildings were complete or under construction. The town doubled in size by the end of the year, and again by July 1861, when the number of inhabitants exceeded fourteen hundred.[96] At the close of 1863 observers estimated Carson City's population at between two and three thousand.[97]

Early visitors had mixed responses to the place. Susan Mitchell Hall, who passed through during the first months of the mining rush, found it "lively" but remote, "so far removed from other towns."[98] Dr. Charles Anderson, a settler of 1862, considered it "decidedly the most pleasant place in Nevada," an impression corroborated by boosters in the *First Directory of Nevada Territory* (1862), who gilded the lily by describing the town as "beautifully situated . . . in the midst of a fertile and well-watered plain, and immediately under the wooded heights of the Sierra Nevada . . . surrounded by grand and picturesque scenery, easily approached from every quarter, located near the geographical center of the territory, with wood, stone, and other building material convenient."[99] J. Ross Browne, in contrast, was

> much impressed with the marked difference between the country on this side of the Sierra Nevada range and the California side. [Near Carson City] the mountains were but sparsely timbered; the soil was poor and sandy, producing little else than stunted sage bushes; and the few scattering farms had a thriftless and poverty-stricken look, as if the task of cultivation had proved entirely hopeless, and had long since been given up.[100]

Carson City's origin in the mining rush and its major economic functions—service, merchandising, and the processing of raw materials—gave the town a particular cast from the beginning. The first buildings aimed squarely at the incoming immigration. As the *Territorial Enterprise* announced in the midst of the town's initial boom, "all is life, bustle, and activity at this growing place. There is a hotel in progress of construction by Sears and Co., 100 × 50 feet. Rice and Co. have a large saloon adjoining their hotel, nearly complete. Mr. Curry has commenced a building also intended for a saloon. There are also many other buildings in course of construction intended for stores and private dwellings."[101]

Along with a water company, telegraph office, newspaper, and projected gas works, by 1862 Carson City boasted twelve hotels and seven boarding houses, most of them concentrated near the plaza on Carson Street, the road from California to Virginia City.[102] The hotels included "first class houses" which were "well lighted and ventilated," such as the White House on the plaza and the St. Charles, "new and elegant . . . conducted in the best of style." Others were less commodious establishments such as the Phoenix Hotel and Baths or the Orleans House, located at some distance from the town's center.[103] Complementing the hotels were Carson City's saloons, nineteen of them in 1863—one for every seventy-seven inhabitants. These, too, were found in the center of town along Carson Street; packed closely together with the hotels near the plaza, their number made it possible for one to take a drink at the Young America, Deer Lick, and What Cheer saloons, or any of a dozen others, and still not miss the entertainments that took place daily at the plaza and nearby theaters: prize fights, wrestling matches, horse races, cock fights, bonfires, band concerts, and even an occasional dance.[104]

The centrality of hotels, boarding houses, and saloons, and the prevalence of male entertainments, underscored a central feature of the town in the 1860s. As the Placerville (California) *Observer* remarked, it was "a rough and ready town" inhabited by a largely male population and "infected with rough characters."[105] In Carson, the *Gold Hill Evening News* observed, "men live in restaurants and sleep in bunks. They feed on whiskey, and that diet causes rowdyism as naturally as turtle soup lays fat on an alderman's ribs."[106] According to another critic, Sundays in Carson were like "any other day . . . hammers and teams and stores and rum shops all going [the] same." Dr. Charles Anderson, although taken with the town when he arrived in late fall of 1862, was quickly disillusioned. "There is wisdom in sagebrush," he wrote his wife in early 1863;

> when I landed in Carson I was struck . . . with the immense numbers of well dressed and leisurely looking individuals. Cloth satin and silk flowed past me in profusion. I thought to myself where there are so many gentlemen and ladies so elegantly dressed and apparently so rich, I might stand a good chance to be one of them. Everybody in fact seemd "flush." Clerks would pass every minute tossing carelessly in their hands great yellow 20$ and the stores appeared to be crowded with goods and customers, and great bars of precious metals were thrown carelessly into the coaches to send to the mint. . . . I have become somewhat sage[;] too large a majority of those well dressed men are gamblers and rum sellers. They can afford to dress richly and appear leisurely. The women—but I will not offend that purity of thought, inspired by the word women to call them such. Those forms in the garments of women are found to be on a par with the men—dissipated and worse than dissipated.[107]

Yet Anderson, along with a handful of others who lamented the absence of a sober population and domestic institutions, was in the decided minority.[108] In 1864 and long after, Carson City was a male domain. Over three-quarters of the town was male; in fact, more than half of the population (54 percent) comprised men between the ages of twenty and forty.[109] With such a preponderance of single males, Carson City's households were small, averaging a little over three persons. More than half of all residents lived either alone or as boarders in hotels and houses; another quarter rented a room from one of the town's families. Such domestic surroundings, however, were hard to find: nuclear families accounted for only one in five households.

Carson City's work force reflected the town's position in Nevada's mining economy. In the year before the convention, 14 percent of the working population was employed in a service occupation—as waiters, barkeeps, cooks, hotel clerks, and the like. An additional 11 percent provided transportation services, working as draymen, porters, teamsters, stage drivers, and job wagon operators. Mechanics and craftsmen made up the largest sector, accounting for approximately 33 percent of the town's workers. Reflecting Carson's larger size than Monterey and Salem and its place in the mining economy, the number and variety of its tradesmen exceeded those found in the California and Oregon capital towns. The forty-five different crafts represented in Carson ranged from the expected to the exotic. A demanding consumer could find a "french hair dresser," daguerreotype artist, brewer, furrier, lithographer, and upholsterer.[110] The bulk of Carson's workingmen, however, followed conventional urban trades. Half were in the building trades, above all carpentry and masonry. The remainder, serving Carson and the neighboring rural population, worked as wheelwrights, blacksmiths, shoemakers, barbers, tailors, watchmakers, and so on.

More than 40 percent of Carson City workers did not work with their hands. This was a service, merchandising, and government town, and its white-collar side was as prominent as its blue. A quarter of the work force was in the lower-white-collar category: mining agents, clerks in the town's merchant exchanges, ranchmen, auctioneers, and minor civil officials. At the top of Carson's occupational pyramid were the major officials in the territorial government (7 percent of the town's workers) and the town's large merchants (9 percent), among them operators of the lucrative timber trade with the mines as well as dealers in dry goods, furniture, groceries, and hardware.

The most striking feature of Carson City was the instability of the population—to be expected given the town's other notable features: the boom mentality of the mining rush; its hotel and saloon culture; the predominance of young, unattached males; and the prevalence of (relatively) well-paid craftsmen and white-collar workers. The increase of Carson's population between 1859 and 1864 actually understates the extent to which the town changed, for turnover was always high (the change, that is, involved not only the arrival, but also the *departure*, of residents). Significant population gains occurred in the space of four years despite continuing outmigration from the town.

For example, of the 650 Carson City residents listed in the 1862 *Territorial Directory,* only 133 (20 percent) had lived there two years earlier, when the first federal census was taken. Similarly, in 1863, when another directory was compiled, only 40 percent of the entries from the previous year's directory remained.[111] Carson City thus had a substantial "floating population" in the 1860s, men (primarily) whose residence in the town is best measured in days, weeks, or months rather than years. Surprisingly, approximately half of this floating population consisted of individuals— small proprietors, traders, and workingmen—who stayed in Carson long enough to establish property and business interests. The other half were propertyless.

Outmigration from the town, predictably, rose noticeably after the 1864 depression struck.[112] Before its full effect was felt, over 1,200 Carsonites were included in the county assessment rolls. A year later, however, hundreds had departed Carson, abandoning property and in the process paring the town tax list significantly. In 1865, the tax list included barely 500 individuals, of whom 252 were newcomers. In short, significantly more than 700 residents had left the town within the year. More than half of these had owned taxable property in 1864, 100 of them substantial parcels assessed above the town average. With these people went a number of the town's largest businesses.

In Carson City as in the entire territory, the summer of 1864 was not the best of times. Arriving convention delegates were sure to have seen the territory's dull times reflected in the street scenes of the capital town: departing tradesmen and laborers, closed businesses, half-finished buildings and abandoned property, and a forced quality to city life, even in the boisterous saloons and hotels on the town's midway, Carson Street. A foremost sign of change was the demise of the Third House, occasioned by the loss of its leader, Samuel Clemens, who had fled Nevada in fear of his life the previous spring. Clemens's trouble had occurred when he lampooned a Carson City ball to raise money for the Union "sanitary fund." When he characterized it in the *Territorial Enterprise* as a fund raiser for "a Miscegenation Society somewhere in the East," three men challenged him to a duel. As Kenneth Lynn remarks, Clemens met their challenge "unflinchingly . . . he ran away."[113]

No matter how bad the times, however, the day of the constitutional convention's first meeting, July 4, saw festivities in Carson City's plaza, and the "fantastics" of the day proved too great a diversion for the delegates. After thirty minutes they adjourned, without having selected a president or settled on a permanent organization. As delegate Lloyd

Frizell later put it, the office of delegate was one "of some dignity," and he deserved the "opportunity to take a cocktail and smoke a cigar, and get my feet up as high as my head, so as to show that I am a free American citizen."[114] On July 5, the convention finally began its business. Unanimously, they elected as president J. Neely Johnson—a member of the previous year's constitutional convention as well as a former governor of California.[115] The veterans of the previous winter's statehood campaign seemed well in control of the convention, and they promised a brief meeting so that the people's vote on the constitution could be taken quickly. The delegates discovered, however, that the politics of the previous year, a year full of hope appropriate to "old Californians," would be of little help in the task before them.

PART TWO

Personality, Ideology, and Political Culture

FOUR

A New Regime: California, 1849

The constitution writers who assembled in Monterey, Salem, and Carson City were not in any statistical sense representative of their territories' peoples. But in less tangible ways—not the least being the very *un*representativeness of these middle-aged men of property—they exemplified central features of the three far western territories. The common antebellum political inheritance of the delegates was a powerful force in each convention, providing a framework of precedents and ideas that shaped state making at every turn. Equally important were the differences that marked the three conventions. The background of the delegates, the distribution of power and authority within the convention halls, the alliances and conflicts that characterized each meeting, the issues emphasized (and ignored) in debate, and the ideas and strategies applied to resolve disputes—all these differed widely, in ways sharply resonant of the charter societies these founders of the Far West constituted, literally, as states of the Union.

When, in September 1849, the California constitution writers assembled in Monterey, no one could be sure of the outcome of their meeting. Voters everywhere had selected their representatives on the basis of local, parochial concerns. Thus, in the absence of parties or issues around which territorywide constituencies might otherwise have coalesced, the delegates lacked the usual cement of American legislative politics. In its stead a diverse collection of influences pushed and pulled throughout the proceedings: ethnic divisions; the personalities of individual men; family, town, and district allegiances; the timing and reasons behind different men's coming to California. Over the course of the convention these factors mixed together in ever-changing ways, creating

transitory alliances that came and went as the delegates addressed different pieces of the constitutional puzzle before them. Nevertheless, the
Anglo-American majority in the convention did bring to Monterey a
common understanding of their task and of the precedents available to
guide them. Their lifetime, they believed, had witnessed the resolution
of political and constitutional dilemmas bedeviling to previous generations. They also largely shared the view that the gold rush exemplified
this resolution, for it had created in experience a genuine democracy of
free individuals that, elsewhere, the weight of history constrained.

As a result, when the convention got under way, both the delegates'
unfamiliarity with one another and the myriad divisions between them
seemed less important than this broad area of agreement. From Monterey, delegate Morton Matthew McCarver testified to his sense of an un-
derlying consensus in a letter to an Illinois friend:

> In about one week more we shal hav given California a Constitution that I
> have no doubt will be acceptable to the people. . . . It is thoroly Demo-
> cratic[,] prohibiting Banking [or] Granting exclusive monopolys[,] issuing
> lottery tickets &c[.] Corporations under general Laws for municiple &
> other purpises may be passed but with out Banking privaleges[,] but the
> stock holders are ameneable to the full amount of all the indebtedness of
> the corporation[.] [S]lavery is prohibited by unanimous vote.[1]

As it turned out, McCarver's confidence was mistaken, but in the opening days of the convention there was no sign of the disagreements that
eventually unfolded. Approaching constitution writing as a clerical task,
a matter of fitting available materials to the circumstances of California,
the delegates looked forward to completing their work quickly. Because
they felt there was no need to assign separate committees the tasks of
writing a bill of rights, defining the responsibilities of executive, legislative, and judicial departments, and so forth, they agreed eagerly to
William Gwin's call for appointing a select committee to assemble a constitution in its entirety for the consideration of the delegates. The weight
of opinion had it that other, recently composed state constitutions were
suited perfectly to California, requiring only minor emendation. Gwin
favored the (1846) Iowa constitution, copies of which he carried to Monterey and distributed to each delegate to serve as a "standard or plan"
for the convention's work.[2] Most found this document acceptable, although some preferred other models, most importantly the recently revised charter of New York.[3]

Together, the Iowa and New York constitutions lay behind virtually
every section of the Californians' document. Iowa's constitution was
known in its day as a "loco-foco" document because of its stringent regulation of corporations and its prohibition of banks of issue (that is, banks
that distributed paper notes that served as money). New York's constitu-

tion Marvin Meyers has described as an "epilogue to Jacksonian Democracy," exemplifying the dissolution of partisan energies in the 1840s as both Democrats and Whigs approached a common ideological ground, one that emphasized each side's devotion to the extension of popular rights and opposition to corporations, banks, and paper money.[4] Michael Holt has similarly emphasized this coalescence of political discourse in his study of the 1850s, tracing to it the collapse of the Democratic-Whig system as party men compromised over previously divisive questions. In his telling, the political crisis of American politics in the 1850s stemmed to no small degree from the common (and thus all the more problematic) Whig-Democratic embrace of a vision of democratic government committed to the "release of individual creative energies" and the notion that progress—moral and social as well as economic—was tied to the individual pursuit of personal advantage.[5]

In the California convention, where there were no parties and where the gold rush screwed to a new pitch men's devotion to liberal democratic principles, the dilemmas that led to what Roy Nichols has called the "disruption of the American Democracy" were not resolved but rehearsed.[6] Despite—in part because of—the delegates' programmatic approach to constitution writing, their convention proved much less tidy in the end than McCarver and others expected. There were clear limits to the ideological consensus the delegates carried to Monterey, and these the Californians were ultimately forced to confront. Contrary to expectation, they discovered that their democratic consensus was riven with contradictions on economic questions. Furthermore, their inherited understandings skirted the issue that, in the 1850s, struck the nation with a vengeance: the conflict between slavery and the democratic principles of freedom and equality.

DIVERSITY AND GOLD RUSH DEMOCRACY

Ironically, the absence of well-established divisions in the California convention contributed to a full, if inconclusive, discussion of these political and economic questions. Driven not by organizational imperatives but by proposals that individual delegates devised, the convention proceeded through the interplay of personalities. This gave the proceedings an elusive quality that cannot be reduced to the effect of party, ethnicity, prior residence, occupation, or religion. These variables operated at one remove, informing but not determining the transitory alliances that shaped the outcome of debate.[7] Such a state of affairs is not surprising, for in this respect the convention captured the general amorphousness of gold rush society, where the relationship between an individual's prior and current station in life—one's "ascribed" as opposed to "achieved" status—often counted for less than intangible qualities such as perseverance, native intelligence, and luck. Individual qualities, in other words, had an importance in the California convention that elsewhere, where party or long-standing factional divisions held sway, they did not.

The human materials of the California convention, within and among which the play of personalities swirled, were diverse.[8] Party affiliations, which can be established at the time of the convention in only thirty-three cases (69 percent of the convention), indicate a Democratic plurality by a margin of twenty-two Democrats to eleven Whigs. In an age where one's work was central to one's identity, moreover, the delegates carried with them the perspectives of a score of occupations. Proportionately, the greatest number of delegates called themselves lawyers, farmers, or merchants; others said printer, editor, surveyor, soldier, physician, dentist, and rancher (see Appendix 1A). One man demonstrated the jackpot mentality of the gold rush by declaring his calling "elegant leisure."

Such a tally of the delegates' stated occupations, however, misrepresents the character of the convention. Work for these men was not necessarily tied to the modern notion of a career within a profession. Rather, their lives were full of different employments, reflecting a constant search for advantage, an ongoing quest in which various skills—of the lawyer, trader, printer, surveyor, and so forth—held value. The convention's lawyers, for example, were also merchants, editors, trail guides, soldiers, and, in one case, a physician. Likewise the farmers, among whom were merchants, town promoters, teachers, a physician, and, for that matter, a lawyer. The same held true for the convention's merchants, printers, and surveyors. These men, to recall a phrase of Richard Hofstadter, were "Jacksonian men" who collected rather than mastered skills applicable to the demands and opportunities of a preindustrial society.[9]

The variety of skills the delegates could claim to possess must be seen in the context of their migratory habits. On arrival in California they looked back on lives spent not only in different occupations but also in constant movement across space. Many of the non-Hispanic delegates had become independent (or "semi-independent") of their parents while in their teens—a fact that reinforces gold rush California's status as a land of mobile and youthful males.[10] As a whole the constitution writers averaged thirty-six years in age; their birthplaces included five different European nations and fifteen American states, as well as California, where six (13 percent) had been born. Seventeen (35 percent of the total convention) had moved to California as young men directly from their places of birth; for the most part these were traders who had arrived during the heyday of the hide and tallow trade or soldiers who came with the U.S. Army in 1846 and 1847.[11] For more than half the convention, however, California was but the most recent stop in an ongoing series of moves. On average, these men had resettled across regional or national borders twice before setting out for the Pacific Coast; for thirteen of them, migration to California marked a third, fourth, or even fifth move.[12]

The delegates' movements were of some importance to the convention proceedings. Among the Anglo-Americans, three regional cohorts were represented, each of which reflected distinct migratory motives as well as conceptions of California's promise. The largest such group, comprising thirteen delegates (27 percent of the convention), was made up of men from the Middle Atlantic states of New York and New Jersey. Eleven others (23 percent) came from the Midwest-border region (above all, Missouri); and nine (19 percent) had set out for California from the South.[13]

The midwesterners in the convention had arrived in California with the overland parties of the early and middle 1840s, before both the conquest and the discovery of gold. As of 1849 these "old settlers" had been in California an average of four and a half years. Included among them were the oldest Americans in the convention: two were over fifty, and as a whole they averaged forty years of age. Within the convention these men composed a group that Josiah Royce described as the "Americans of the interregnum . . . [who] had a concern in California that was prior in origin to the gold discovery, and that seemed apt to outlast any immediate good fortunes or reverses that might come to them in consequence of this discovery."[14] Among them were the best known of the old settlers who had vied with Mexican authorities and later with the American military: Bear Flaggers Robert Semple and Jacob Snyder; trail guide and filibusterer Lansford Hastings; and Central Valley impresario John Sutter.[15] In the convention they represented rural districts that surrounded San Francisco: San Jose, Sonoma, Sacramento. They followed a range of occupations, with a plurality calling themselves farmers. Although political parties had not yet been organized in the territory, these men carried to the convention the baggage of the western Democracy.

In contrast to the old settlers from the Midwest-border states, the Middle Atlantic delegates were recent arrivals and the convention's youngest men. Averaging less than thirty-two years of age, they had been in California, on the whole, about two years, most having arrived as soldiers during the conquest. More than half had come with Colonel J. D. Stevenson's New York Volunteers, a regiment largely from rural, northerly areas of the Empire State.[16] These volunteers shared an adventurous spirit, for the battalion had been raised with an eye to providing not only military might, but also a group of willing settlers for the nation's new possession on the Pacific Coast. Following the gold discovery, the New Yorkers made their way to the mines (usually for only a short while), then drifted to Sacramento, Stockton, or, most likely, San Francisco. In the instant cities of the gold rush they quickly attained

prominence as lawyers and merchants, land speculators, insurgents protesting alcalde rule, participants in the San Francisco vigilance committee that prosecuted the Hounds, and partisans of a settlers' constitutional convention. New Yorkers Alfred Ellis, Rodman Price, and Francis
Lippitt were well known in San Francisco as merchants and landowners;
they also had participated in the revolt against alcalde rule, as had Myron Norton in San Francisco, Elisha Crosby and Winfield Sherwood in
Sacramento, and Kimball Dimmick in San Jose. In addition, Ellis, Norton, and Lippitt had been members of San Francisco's vigilance committee. And at one time or another, all of these men had played a part in the
constitutional convention movement.

The best-known New Yorkers in the convention were Edward Gilbert,
editor of the San Francisco newspaper *Alta California,* and Henry Wager
Halleck, military secretary of state under governors Mason and Riley.
From his desk at the *Alta,* Gilbert had been at the center of San
Francisco's political insurgency since the fall of 1848.[17] Halleck was re-
sponsible for most of the policies of the military government after 1848.
Ironically, he was a constant target of disgruntled settlers, although he as
much as anyone was responsible for Governor Riley calling the constitu-
tional convention. Halleck and Gilbert—and with them a majority of the
Middle Atlantic delegates—were Democrats like the border men, albeit
Democrats of a different kind, northern and urban.

The most recently arrived delegates were the nine men who migrated
to California from the South upon hearing news of the conquest and,
particularly, the gold discovery. Only one of them had arrived before
1849, and four had been in California less than six months at the time
of the election of convention delegates. The southerners' motives for
migrating did not involve mining per se, for they settled not in the
gold regions but (given the preponderance of lawyers among them) in
the territory's two places of political power: San Francisco, center of opposition to the established order; and Monterey, the provincial capital.
Despite their brief residence they had gained wide notice for their activities in the settlers' movement against military rule. Three in particular—
Montereyan Charles Tyler Botts, former Mississippi congressman William McKendree Gwin, and San Francisco merchant William Steuart—
were closely associated with the antimilitary insurgence that filled the
early summer of 1849. Two others, James McHall Jones and Oliver
Wozencraft, had arrived in California only a few weeks before the election, but decided immediately (on the advice of William Gwin, it seems)
to campaign in the southern mines for seats in the convention.[18] Such
confidence was common to the southerners, but otherwise they shared
little. Their ages varied widely—they averaged thirty-six years of age,
which placed them between the young New Yorkers and the older
border men—and they hailed from every corner of the South, from

Maryland to Florida and Virginia to Texas. Their partisan allegiances reflected this diversity, as they divided evenly between Democrats and Whigs.

Finally, there were thirteen men who comprised a Californio bloc (27 percent of the convention). They were the only group of delegates who brought to the proceedings a common interest, informed by a shared sense of vulnerability. United by language, history, and culture, they participated in the convention in order to protect what few prerogatives remained to them. In addition to the convention's six native-born Californios, their ranks included four European-born delegates who were naturalized Mexican citizens and three Anglo-Americans tied to the old regime by marriage.[19] With the exception of Stephen Foster and Henry Tefft, two young Anglos who allied with the old regime, they were as a group the oldest members of the convention, averaging forty-two years.

The Californios' individual histories reflect the contours of society and politics during the province's Mexican era. In contrast to their fathers, most of whom arrived early in the century with the Spanish army and led lives of near poverty, these second-generation Californians had reaped the benefits of the social revolution that accompanied the missions' secularization and government land grants of the 1830s and 1840s.[20] Their livelihood was directly related both to their control of land and to the cattle and tallow trade. At the time of the conquest they were among the wealthiest of their class, controlling vast estates—all together, 647,000 acres.[21] Furthermore, they could boast of having played central roles in the turbulent affairs of the 1830s and 1840s. José Antonio Carrillo of Los Angeles, for instance, had been known as the "Mirabeau of California" for his agitation in favor of secularization. Abel Stearns, a Massachusetts-born Mexicanized gringo, had been a conspicuous partisan of Los Angeles interests in the revolts against Mexican rule in the 1830s and 1840s. Pablo Noriega y de la Guerra, the "king of Santa Barbara," came from a Californio family long dominant in the affairs of that southern district. Mariano Guadalupe Vallejo, the "duke of Sonoma," was the uncle of Juan Alvarado as well as his military ally in the 1837 movement that resulted in effective independence for the Californians.

The Californios had responded to the 1846 American invasion in unpredictable ways. Pablo de la Guerra, for example, had thrown himself into the movement of resistance against the United States, as had Abel Stearns. Sonoma's Mariano Vallejo, in contrast, had acquiesced in the conquest—even despite imprisonment by the Bear Flag filibusters— for he preferred American rule to what he considered the inevitable alternative, British dominion. Spanish trader Miguel Pedrorena reacted in a third way, collaborating with the invaders, enlisting in the American forces under Stockton, and gaining the brevet rank of captain.[22] No matter what their attitude toward the Americans, however, after the conquest all the Californios became American citizens by the Treaty of Guadalupe Hidalgo. At the time of the convention their views on American political parties are difficult to decipher. Indeed, the political affiliations of only half are known for the post-statehood period; these divided evenly between Democrats and Whigs.

Within the convention two factors ordered the delegates' behavior. First was their embrace of the Iowa and New York constitutions as models, which provided them a framework for deliberations and the starting point of debate. Second—a crucial if much less tangible factor— was the role of a handful of individuals (six of the forty-eight delegates) who, in the absence of an institutionalized party system, competed for supremacy. These men established the terms of debate, shaped the activities of committees, and, by the very force of their presence, drew forth the support—as well as enmity—of their colleagues.[23] These individuals were leading men rather than "leaders" per se, for they did not stand at the head of parties or well defined groups, and their influence on constitution writing was both positive and negative.

The lives of these leading delegates not only suggest the convictions that ordered their actions in the convention, but also show them to be representative political men of their time and place in American history. Democrats predominated, although party loyalty did not necessarily indicate likemindedness. Collectively they represented a wide range of occupations, having followed numerous formal and informal callings in California and elsewhere. Three of the six were southerners, though southerners of very different kinds: former Mississippi congressman (and Andrew Jackson intimate) William McKendree Gwin; twenty-five-year-old Louisiana lawyer James McHall Jones; and the one-time Virginia agricultural reformer Charles Tyler Botts. In addition there was the New York soldier Henry Wager Halleck, military secretary of state under Mason and Riley; the Missouri trail guide Lansford Hastings; and Kentucky-born Morton Matthew McCarver, a peripatetic pioneer who had spent half his life settling different spots in the Mississippi Valley before migrating to Oregon in 1843 and, five years later, gold rush California.

The last of these men, McCarver, was known to the convention as the "delegate from Oregon" because of the times he spoke against measures on the grounds that they would be unacceptable to "the people of Oregon."[24] Such slips of the tongue exposed McCarver as a marginal far westerner, whose adulthood was spent in an unending quest for wealth, distinction, and the public's embrace. California for him was but the most recent stop in his search after the main chance, and it was not his last. As he wrote from Monterey to a friend, "I came to California about twelve months since and commenced mining and after making a few thousand I commenced merchandising at Sacramento City and shall continue that business until next spring when I shall retire to my farm in Oregon."[25]

At the convention, McCarver was best known for his proposal to include in the constitution a provision prohibiting the immigration of free Negroes to California. In this he articulated a view he had held throughout his life and promoted everywhere he settled.[26] Born in Kentucky, McCarver spent the first thirty-six years of his life in the states that bordered the Mississippi and Ohio rivers. Upon joining the first major overland immigration to Oregon in 1843, he therefore carried with him a combination of Negro-phobic and antislavery sentiments common to those states.[27]

McCarver's antipathy toward slavery had been instilled during his teens, when, alienated from his widowed mother's Shaker faith, he fled Lexington on an Ohio River flatboat, ultimately landing in New Orleans. For four years he lived in Louisiana and, briefly, Texas, where, without family resources, he felt fully the power of the slave-owning class and developed an undying hatred for white masters, black slaves, and the institution that linked them together.[28] By the mid-1820s McCarver was back in Lexington, but, failing either to reconcile with his mother or complete a medical apprenticeship, he again left, this time for Illinois, where he married and spent four years moving his wife and a growing family from Galena, to Rock Island, to Monmouth. McCarver prospered in Illinois through the Indian trade, which took him into the Sauk and Fox territory that, in the early 1830s, became the object of the Black Hawk War. When war broke out he enlisted as a foot soldier in the Illinois militia, and a year after the peace he moved across the Mississippi to what would become the Iowa Territory, where with two in-laws he founded a new town, Burlington. In the 1830s McCarver profited from the sale of town lots and surrounding farmland, as well as from speculations in Iowa lead mines, Chicago town lots, and another attempt at town building in Iowa, "McCarverstown."[29]

Despite McCarver's economic success in the thirties, the first years of the following decade brought financial desperation. In 1837 depression struck, and for the next seven years its effects radiated across the nation. By the early 1840s hard times had enveloped the Iowa Territory, ruining hundreds, among them town builder McCarver, the unlucky possessor of thousands in worthless notes and ten thousand dollars' worth of debts.[30] For McCarver and other hard-pressed Mississippi Valley residents, escape from debt and depression was achievable only through departure to new lands. Concurrent with the panic's onset came a wave of reports about the virtues of the Oregon Country. The timing could not have been better: in 1843, one thousand pioneering families set out in the "great migration" from Independence, Missouri, to the Willamette Valley.

Among the migrants was McCarver. Once in Oregon he looked for the same kinds of opportunities that had caught his eye in Illinois and Iowa. He joined a fellow overland immigrant, Peter Burnett, in promoting the town of Linnton at an unlikely Willamette River site north of Oregon City. The speculation failed, and McCarver then moved to a claim near Oregon City, capital of the newly created provisional government. There he farmed and opened a merchant house. In addition, he threw himself into Oregon politics. In 1844 and 1845 he was elected to the new government's legislative committee, which chose him as its presiding officer. In this capacity he oversaw the passage of two signal pieces of legislation: the provisional government's prohibition of "the introduction, distillation, or sale of ardent spirits" and a measure outlawing both slavery and the immigration of free Negroes.[31]

In the fall of 1848 news of the California gold discovery reached Oregon. Leaving his family behind, McCarver joined one of the first Oregon parties to set out for the Sierra goldfields. For a time he mined a claim on the Feather River, but soon his attention turned to the point of transit and trade growing up by Sutter's Fort. In December 1848 he approached Sutter, offering to promote a town on his land in return for a share of the profits. They agreed, and McCarver—in his third effort at town building—had the site surveyed and platted as Sacramento. His connection with Sutter soon ended, however, for after McCarver's survey was complete, and without his knowledge, Sutter accepted another man's offer to oversee the building of Sacramento. The other man, to McCarver's dismay, was his old friend Peter Burnett, with whom he had crossed the plains in 1843, built the town of Linnton, and allied in the Oregon provisional government.[32]

McCarver overcame his anger with his erstwhile friends and threw himself into the life of the new boomtown. He purchased lots, opened a merchandising exchange, and ran a schooner to and from San Francisco carrying goods and men. By the time the first forty-niners arrived he was established as one of Sacramento's leading men. Politically he allied himself with the older settlers of the Sacramento Valley who initiated the movement against military rule. In early 1849 he addressed a public meeting, called by Sacramento's mechants opposed to alcalde rule, to elect a district legislature. In the election that followed he was chosen as one of the eleven district legislators.[33] Later in the year, after Riley's proclamation announcing the constitutional convention, McCarver's long residence in the town and his record of opposition to military rule made him an obvious candidate for convention delegate.

McCarver brought to Monterey twenty-five years' worth of experience in the old north- and southwests, a lifetime of speculation in pioneer enterprises, bitterness at the financial forces that had ruined him after the panic of 1837, a deep hatred of slavery, and, finally, the conviction that contact between blacks and whites served only to "degrade" the latter race. Although he was a newcomer to California, as a Mississippi Valley emigrant drawn to the Pacific Coast before the conquest or gold rush he was naturally allied with the American settlers of the Sacramento Valley, and in the convention he promoted their views zealously.

With McCarver in the Sacramento delegation was another early emigrant from the Midwest, Lansford Hastings, whose first acquaintance with the Pacific Coast had also occurred in Oregon.[34] By 1849 thirty-year-old Hastings was already a far western legend. For almost a decade he had promoted Pacific settlement—for the purpose, according to his detractors, of creating an independent Pacific republic along Texan lines. He was known nationally as a trailblazer and guide for the earliest overland parties to the Pacific Coast (though less happily, his name was linked to the tragedy of the Donner party, whose decision to take his time-saving "cutoff" south of the Great Salt Lake led to disaster). And finally, as soldier, lawyer, and merchant, he had been a visible participant in the events that transformed the Sacramento Valley in the mid-1840s: the conquest, antimilitary insurgence, and gold rush mania.

Hastings was born in Mt. Vernon, Ohio, in 1819, but little is known of his life prior to his 1842 arrival, a year before McCarver, at the head of an overland party to the Oregon Country. Then began a remarkable life in the Far West. Hastings remained in Oregon less than nine months, but in that time he was busy. During the winter of 1842–1843 he surveyed Oregon City for John McLoughlin, chief factor of the Hudson's Bay Company, and served as McLoughlin's agent for the sale of town lots. In the growing conflict between McLoughlin and the Methodist missionaries over ownership of the Willamette Falls mill site, he supported and provided legal advice to the British company's representative.[35] Hastings also participated in the meetings that led to the creation of Oregon's provisional government. At one such meeting in March 1843 he called for the organization of a government independent of both the United States and England, an act that fed later charges that he was a filibusterer intent on creating an independent Pacific republic.[36]

Hastings's advocacy of independence was not heeded by the Willamette Valley settlers, and before they inaugurated their government he departed for California's Sacramento Valley. His destination was New Helvetia, the domain of the Swiss immigrant John Sutter. Hastings and Sutter hit it off immediately, and within weeks the young trail guide was on his way back to Missouri, committed to the cause of California as he and Sutter understood it. His plan, as he explained it to U.S. consular officials he encountered in Mexico on his way home, was to turn the tide of overland immigration from Oregon to California, whose "rich soil and attractive climate," he believed, put Oregon to shame. Mexico's control of California, he further declared, was about to end. Hastings intimated that there was a movement afoot to hasten the end of the Californio regime and that, in consultation with its leader, John Sutter, he intended to return with a party of one or two thousand American settlers whose presence would quickly make Mexican rule untenable.[37]

By early March 1844, Hastings was back in Missouri. There he began his promotion of emigration to California in a series of letters to the *St. Louis New Era.* These he followed with a book, *The Emigrants' Guide to Oregon and California,* the publication of which he financed by giving temperance lectures in Missouri.[38] His return to California in 1845, however, was a major disappointment. Instead of the thousands of settlers that he, Sutter, and other Sacramento Valley promoters hoped for, Hastings brought ten.[39] Consequently, four months later he was off again, this time to intercept emigrant parties and convince the Oregon-bound of California's superior features. He described his purpose in a letter to Sacramento Valley settler John Marsh: "Sir, you can rely upon an accession of six or seven thousand souls to our foreign population in California. . . . As to the natural—the inevitable[—]result of this unprecedented emigration to the western world, I will not trouble you with my own speculation, for the result must have been long since anticipated by yourself."[40]

On this trip Hastings discovered what he believed was a better route—a cutoff to the south of the Great Salt Lake—that could save overland emigrants weeks of travel time. East of Fort Bridger at Independence Rock, Hastings went to work on arriving parties. His efforts succeeded: in 1846, for the first time, more settlers arrived in California than in Oregon.[41] A number of these parties used Hastings's new cutoff. All but one made it to California without incident, though without saving time. The last, the famed Donner party, did not.

Although grieved by the fate of the Donners, Hastings did not miss a beat. By the time of his return to Sutter's Fort, the American invasion was well under way, and he hurried to join in. The capture of California from Mexico—an end he felt he had contributed to by guiding settlers—was fast approaching by force of arms. He enlisted in Frémont's volunteer battalion and, breveted as captain, set out for southern California, where he participated in the Californio's capitulation at Cahuenga. With the end of hostilities and, a year later, the gold discovery, it was no longer necessary to encourage emigrants to choose California over Oregon: by then it seemed that all of America was coming to California of its own accord. Hastings's life therefore took a turn, for he married and opened a law office in San Francisco, speculating in town lots on the side. Yet old habits did not disappear, and in the spring of 1848 he advertised for volunteers to join him in a filibustering expedition to Mazatlán, Mexico. For reasons that are unclear, the expedition did not come off. Most likely news of gold in the Sierra Nevada intervened.[42]

Hastings was one of the first to hear of the discovery. His interest, however, was not so much in mining for gold as in mining the miners. From a base he established in Sacramento in 1848 he began to trade throughout the northern mining camps. Traveling widely and offering liberal credit terms, he became a favorite among the arriving miners. This activity, in addition to the renown he enjoyed for his earlier exploits and his participation in the indignation meetings that attacked military rule, made him one of the leading men of the district.[43] He turned down election to the post of alcalde, but the constitutional convention was another matter, and in the Sacramento election he was one of the top vote-getters.

McCarver and Hastings went to Monterey in part because of their identification with the settlers' revolt against military rule. At the convention they not only encountered but on occasion locked horns with the man who embodied that military rule, Henry Wager Halleck. Halleck, a thirty-two-year-old West Point graduate, arrived just after the Californios' capitulation in January 1847. Denied battlefield laurels, his distinction in California was of a civil, not military, kind. For more than a year and a half the stern and humorless soldier, as secretary of state, was second in command to the military governor, but in reality the government was his. An admiring contemporary, the Reverend Samuel Willey, described him as the "ruling spirit of both the administrations of Governors Mason and Riley."[44]

In his youth Halleck was something of a prodigy. Born in Oneida County, New York, he despaired as a boy of following his father as a farmer and ran away from home. Adopted by his grandfather, he attended an upstate academy and Union College before gaining a place at West Point. Third in his graduating class, he was appointed assistant professor of chemistry and engineering at the academy the year after his graduation. Following this he was stationed in New York City, where he oversaw the design and construction of the harbor's fortifications. On the strength of this work Marshall Bertrand, the famed confidant to Napoleon, invited him to review French military installations. From this trip resulted Halleck's "Report on the Means of National Defense" (1844), which established his reputation as an expert on national defense and garnered for him an invitation to give the prestigious Lowell Institute lecture series. Published as *Elements of Military Art and Science* (1845), the lectures shortly became an authoritative treatise on military strategy and tactics and were widely used to train the Civil War generation of West Point officers.[45]

With the outbreak of the Mexican War, Halleck was dispatched to the Pacific Coast. During the seven-month voyage he pursued a lifelong fascination with Napoleon by translating Henri de Jomini's *Vie politique et militaire de Napoléon*, a project that he later published in four volumes. In California, Halleck's service as secretary of state under Governors Mason and Riley was decisive. He took it upon himself to maintain cordial relations with the first families in the Californio settlements to the south of Monterey.[46] He personally translated and compiled the Mexican laws in effect at the time of the conquest to give Mason the means for operating the military government until Congress acted. He oversaw the collection of port duties, which provided the military government with sufficient funds to carry on. Most importantly, after concluding that military rule was untenable, he pushed Governors Mason and Riley to act. It was his plan for a constitutional convention that, in the summer of 1849, Riley embraced.[47]

In the convention, Halleck later wrote, his intent was to "relieve Congress and General Taylor's administration from the difficulties which they were involved in by the free soil and pro slavery parties of 1849."[48] A nominal Democrat, he was a soldier, not a politician. Accustomed to the habits of military command rather than political maneuvering, he wielded influence at the convention on two fronts: first, among the handful of soldiers who sat as delegates; second, and more importantly, among the Californios. On the main points of deliberation, the latter group followed the lead of the soldier who, as the key officer in the conquering regime, had taken special care to recognize their authority in the southern districts. This odd combination proved to be a force to reckon with.

Among Halleck's colleagues from Monterey was an outspoken, eloquent, and hot-tempered Virginian, Charles Tyler Botts. The forty-year-old Botts had arrived with his wife in 1848 with an appointment as U.S. naval storekeeper at Monterey, a post he resigned in early 1849 to practice law and speculate in property.[49] For unknown reasons, Botts had departed Virginia and the distinction of his family's name for the uncertainties of California following the American conquest. His father, Benjamin Botts (who with his wife died tragically when his son was two years old), had been a well-known Richmond lawyer, distinguished for, among other things, his defense of Aaron Burr in the latter's 1807 trial for treason.[50] His brother, John Minor, was a well-known, if idiosyncratic, Virginia congressman, who as a Whig opposed all things Democratic, particularly the expansion of slavery. Charles Tyler Botts had gained his own small renown in Virginia, prior to departing for California, as a member of the reform-minded Henrico County Agricultural Society; inventor of numerous labor-saving farming devices aimed at the needs of small, non-slave-owning farmers; and, most importantly, editor of the *Southern Planter,* which he founded in 1841 and dedicated to the reform of southern agricultural practices.[51]

Charles Botts, like his brother, was a puzzle with regard to politics and society in Virginia. He was quick to defend his state and region against the charges of northerners, whom at times he saw as nothing but damnable abolitionists bent on revolutionizing the South. At the same time, however, he was clearly alienated from the South's planter class and the institution on which their world stood.[52] Botts's plan for the *Southern Planter* is a case in point. As he stated in its prospectus, the southern people were "peculiarly agricultural . . . the great producers of America . . . [yet] the fact is undeniable that, in economy and management, we are in many respects inferior to our northern brethren." He modeled the new journal on the great New York agricultural guides, intending to provide "plain, economical men" with a "medium for the promulgation, in condensed form, of the observations and deductions of practical men."[53]

To Botts's way of thinking, a reformed South, while not slaveless, would see small freehold farmers in the ascendancy, much as he believed was the case in the North. Yet his vision was not simply Jeffersonian, as his age understood the term, for although he considered himself a faithful Democrat, he shared his brother's admiration for Henry Clay and Daniel Webster. Botts's political views, in the end, were both clear and puzzling. He carried to the convention a commitment to a commercial republic consisting of market-minded farmers and dynamic city systems, made coherent by the fostering arm of government. Slavery he considered a blight but, as a southern institution, rightly beyond the authority of Congress.[54] Although he arrived with a military appointment, he had contempt for California's military authorities—particularly Henry Halleck. And despite the fact that he was a recent arrival with next to no connections with the pre–gold rush American settlers in the interior, he gravitated toward them and their spokesmen—McCarver and Hastings above all—in the debates.

A fellow southerner, with whom Botts had, as it turned out, nothing in common, was James McHall Jones, at twenty-five the convention's second-youngest member. Born in Kentucky, Jones spent his youth in rural Louisiana following his widowed mother's remarriage to a country doctor. A quick study, Jones was admitted to the bar after reading the law in Iberville Parish a short while; before he reached his twentieth birthday, he was practicing before the state supreme court. Yet neither he nor his mother, with whom he had an unusually intense relationship, could see him spending his life as a country lawyer, and in the fall of 1845 he was sent to Paris for study and exposure to refined society.[55]

While abroad, Jones spent a year and a half in Paris and another six months in Rome. There he mastered French, Italian, and Spanish; collected a large library of European law books; alternated the practice of law with dancing, fencing, boxing, and drawing lessons (the "accomplishment[s] of a gentleman," as he put it); and sought out the most advanced remedies for consumption. He had contracted the disease in his late teens, at the same time as his mother. Foremost among his treatments were daily doses of opium, taken to deaden both the pain and the depression the disease brought him.[56] Apparently, he remained an opium user until his death.

In letters home Jones was alternately obsessed by his disease and convinced of his cure; at the same time that he provided his mother with morbid reports of his descent toward death, he also delighted in recounting how he "cut quite a figure at the French court" because of his "extraordinary facility" at the manly arts. Similarly, Jones was both attracted to and repelled by the French nobility with whom he came into contact. In one breath he could declare that he "count[ed] a Prince (Spordze of Waldania) among my acquaintances" and exclaim that "my principle desire is to cut the acquaintance of my noble friends . . . , the small fry of counts, barons, etc. . . . I wish I did not know any of them."[57] Whether the emotional peaks and valleys that marked his correspondence from Paris were the result of opium addiction or simply reflected the alternating spirits of a sick and self-possessed young man cannot be said. Nonetheless, the qualities displayed in these letters were a persistent part of his personality, indeed, the very source of the influence he wielded in the constitutional convention.

The path that brought Jones to California from Paris was predictable. He returned to his mother's home in the fall of 1846 and joined the law practice of his former tutor in Plaquemine Township. Two years of country law, however, was all he could take, and in 1849 he left with his mother's blessings for the Pacific Coast, to test its salubrious climate as well seek his fortune. He made the voyage from New Orleans to Panama on the *Falcon,* among whose passengers was his future convention colleague William Gwin. Jones may well have continued on to San Francisco aboard the *Panama,* which carried Gwin and a collection of luminaries from Washington, D.C.: Georgia congressman T. Butler King, whom the president had dispatched as his personal emissary to the troubled military government; former Ohio congressman John B. Weller, en route to take up his duties on the commission setting the U.S.-Mexico boundary; John Frémont's wife, Jessie Benton; and a young Joseph Hooker.[58]

Regardless of how they met, before the convention Jones had made the acquaintance of each of these individuals. Without question he was drawn to William Gwin, whose advice likely encouraged him to undertake his bold, lightning-quick campaign for convention delegate.[59] After his arrival in Monterey, the self-possession (one might say the delusions of grandeur) that Jones displayed in Paris and the "Diggins" only grew. From there he wrote his mother that he had "made the warmest personal friends of those who command the convention, the government, and the trade," evidently referring to Gwin, Weller, and King. His friends, he was sure, would go to Congress, and once there, "there is nothing in the president's gift they would not insist on my having if I wanted it. . . . The pathway of fame seems open to me, that of fortune I know I can command."[60]

As ever, though, Jones was plagued by hidden devils. Despite his claim of being a favorite of those "who command the government," he was convinced that Henry Halleck was out to get him. Halleck, Jones declared, had tried with all his might to block him from his rightful seat in the convention; he was "a man of no calibre, an intriguer with no tact, void of ability and ridiculous from self-conceit." Similarly, Jones believed that convention president Semple "hates me as he does the devil," although in the same letter he had claimed credit for leading the movement to elect Semple in order to defeat the designs of "government officers and toadies" (read Halleck).[61]

Jones's politics cannot be separated from his personality. Contentious as well as brilliant in debate, he alternately alienated and won over his colleagues. At one point he responded so sharply to a fellow delegate that a duel seemed inevitable.[62] In contrast, at the convention's most tense moment it was Jones who devised the crucial compromise.[63] His party allegiances were likewise unclear. Although he proudly declared himself a Whig, his declarations bore little relationship to his behavior as a delegate. Above all Jones was drawn to men who held out the prospect of future patronage, and for the most part they were Democrats. Indeed, the man whose favor Jones valued most highly, William McKendree Gwin, was anything but a Whig.

William Gwin was the convention's most prominent member. Fiercely partisan, openly ambitious, and seasoned in national politics, he had set out for California in the spring of 1849 with the declared purpose of ushering California into the Union and returning to Washington, D.C., as the state's first senator.[64] At forty-four years of age, Gwin was a veritable graybeard among the delegates. He had been born in Tennessee in

the first years of the century. His father, a friend and neighbor of Andrew Jackson, had marched to New Orleans as chaplain to Jackson's
army in 1812, and the relationship that grew between general and minister bequeathed to the younger Gwin a "most precious passport to political favor and public status."[65]

William Gwin was trained in both law and medicine. Although he was
admitted to the Tennessee bar at the age of twenty-one, he was uncertain
of his abilities as an orator and switched his sights to medicine, enrolling
at Transylvania University, where he received an M.D. in 1828 on the
strength of a thesis entitled "Syphilis." Shortly thereafter he married
and, moving to Clinton, Mississippi, began his medical practice. In 1833
tragedy struck the young physician when his wife and three children
suddenly died. Gwin never discussed the deaths publicly, nor can they be
explained by the extant record, but following the loss of his family he
turned from medicine to Andrew Jackson.[66] The president offered him
escape, calling him to Washington, D.C., where Gwin served as the president's confidential secretary for six months. At the end of this period,
Jackson nominated him to a lucrative U.S. marshallship in Mississippi.
In the Senate the nomination was met with concerted opposition on the
part of Jackson nemesis George Poindexter, Mississippi's senior (Whig)
senator, but after a prolonged struggle the profitable appointment was
his.[67]

Gwin did not forgive Poindexter's affront. On his return to Mississippi
Gwin plunged into Democratic politics and openly encouraged a feud
with the powerful Whig senator. When Poindexter blocked another
Gwin appointment—this time that of William's elder brother, Samuel, to
the post of land registrar—a stalemate between president and Senate ensued. Jackson prevailed, and Samuel Gwin received his appointment,
but the Gwins' victory was ultimately an empty one. On their return to
Mississippi, the Gwin brothers gave vent to their hatred of Poindexter,
spearheading a movement to replace him with a young Natchez attorney, Robert J. Walker. In the midst of the campaign, William Gwin
wrote Jackson: "You need never fear [Poindexter's] return to the Senate.
If elected he will have to walk over the dead bodies of three persons before he takes his seat. Mr. Walker, my brother, and myself he has used
every effort to destroy. If we cannot disgrace him by beating him he shall
atone for his attacks upon us by his blood."[68] The letter was prophetic,
though not in the way Gwin intended. Walker won the seat, but still the
Gwins were not satisfied. Samuel dogged Poindexter and, for his abuse,
was challenged to a duel by an ally of the senator. On the appointed day,
the combatants squared off. Gwin killed his opponent on the spot, but
was himself mortally wounded and died after months of agony.[69]

In the space of two years Gwin had lost his wife, three children, and brother. He was not yet thirty. His response was to accelerate his political activities and to plunge recklessly into widespread land speculation. Through his ties to Jackson and his role in the Poindexter affair he had become a prominent man in Mississippi Democratic circles. In the mid-1830s he joined with other noted party men—Walker, Henry S. Foote, Joseph Davis (brother of Jefferson Davis), among others—in a syndicate that speculated in the Cocchuma Tract, some million acres of ceded Indian lands. Until the panic of 1837 the speculation was highly profitable, but suddenly in 1838 the bottom fell out. The value of Gwin's investments in that and dozens of other speculations collapsed. Bank notes he held became worthless; at the same time, claims against him in his capacity as U.S. marshall were ordered paid in gold. Debt—blame for which he laid to the perfidy of bankers—plagued him for years thereafter.[70]

As one avenue of relief from creditors (at least according to his friend Robert Walker), Gwin sought and in 1840 received the Democratic nomination to Congress from Mississippi. The election of Whig president William Henry Harrison insured his removal from the marshallship, and even though he lacked the rhetorical skills so essential to nineteenth-century public life, he gained the post. In Congress Gwin served a single, undistinguished term. While there, however, he met John Calhoun—they boarded in the same rooming house—and to his surprise found himself drawn to Jackson's old political enemy. It was Calhoun, Gwin later recalled, who brought California to his attention and impressed on him that the city to be built on San Francisco Bay "was destined to be the New York of the Pacific Coast, but more supreme, as it would have no . . . rivals." The effect of Calhoun's words, Gwin testified, "was never effaced."[71]

At the close of his term Gwin did not seek reelection. The congressional seat had not provided the escape from creditors he sought, nor did service in the lower house coincide with his own measure of his abilities.[72] He returned to Mississippi and, with Democratic friends, established a series of commission houses to service the great planters of Vicksburg. Two years later politics beckoned once again with the return of the Democracy to the White House and the appointment of Robert Walker as secretary of the treasury. Walker arranged another profitable patronage post for Gwin, commissioner of public works in New Orleans. From New Orleans he watched the progress of the Mexican War, ever mindful of Calhoun's predictions as the American conquest came to a close.[73]

Confirmation of the gold discovery pushed Gwin to act, all the more because it arrived at the same time as Washington, D.C., prepared for the arrival of a Whig president, Zachary Taylor, whose election Gwin realized meant removal from his post in New Orleans. Gwin resigned the position and returned to the nation's capital, arriving on March 4, 1849. "The following day," he recalled in his memoirs,

> General Taylor was inaugurated; and as the procession was passing Willard's Hotel, Mr. Gwin, returning from the Treasury Department, where [he] had been settling his accounts, met Stephen A. Douglas in front of the hotel, and while looking at the procession as it passed, remarked to the Senator that the next morning he intended to leave the city en route to California. He said that the failure of Congress to give that country a territorial government would force its inhabitants to create a state government, that he intended to advocate that policy and to advocate it with success, and announced himself then and there a candidate for United States senator from California, and [said] that within one year from that time he would ask him [Douglas] to present his credentials as a senator from the State of California.[74]

Three months later Gwin was in San Francisco. Within a week of his arrival he had joined the antimilitary insurgency, speaking to a mass meeting at Portsmouth Square and calling for independent citizen action to create a state government. On the Fourth of July he addressed crowds in Sacramento, and from there he took his message to Stockton and other, smaller, towns.[75] Similarly, when the crisis of the Hounds struck San Francisco, Gwin was able to turn the affair to his advantage. By chance, or so he recalled, he came upon the meeting called "to form . . . a committee of safety, to protect the city from the depredations of the Hounds." Out of the meeting came an informal trial over which—"most unexpectedly to himself"—Gwin was chosen to preside.[76]

Gwin's speeches for statehood, augmented by his part in the Hounds trial, had the hoped-for effect. In the San Francisco election of delegates his name appeared on most tickets, and he was easily voted in. Gwin then set out for Monterey with his copies of the Iowa constitution, confident that he would keep his date with Stephen Douglas. His haughty air alienated many of his colleagues from the moment they met, but he could not be ignored. As no one else could, he served as a living reminder of the political history of their age.

THE DILEMMAS OF DEMOCRATIC FREEDOM

For six weeks these men—a footloose pioneer, trail guide, West Point prodigy, agricultural reformer, self-possessed consumptive, and Jackson intimate—met with their colleagues in Monterey's hastily prepared Colton Hall. Until the final week the convention proceeded according to plan. The Select Committee on the Constitution drafted the constitution's different articles, which were then considered in committee of the whole and, finally, voted on by the convention. For the most part, consensus reigned as the delegates adopted sections of the Iowa constitution verbatim.[77]

There were, however, twists and turns along the way, and on four questions the delegates' equanimity dissolved. These concerned banking corporations, suffrage, the rights of free Negroes, and, above all, the state's boundary, in the context of which the delegates debated the expansion of slavery into the western lands won from Mexico. These controversies encompassed political-economic issues and the dilemma of race and citizenship that so bedeviled antebellum America. The Californians' stumbling path toward their resolution testified to the depth of their—and their countrymen's—passions and uncertainties.

While at first glance only a tenuous relationship may appear between economic controversies and racial questions, recent studies have shown that they were but different sides of a common concern with the shape of freedom. Central to antebellum America's rhetoric of popular democracy was a correlation between liberty and individual freedom in a market economy. Within this conception of the socioeconomic order the place of corporate enterprise was necessarily problematic. Until recently, the delegates knew, corporations had been based on special (royal or legislative) grants of monopoly power.[78] The 1830s had seen the institution's democratization, its opening as a mechanism of commerce to all parties that met a set of legal conditions; nevertheless, the specter of large, faceless combinations imposing their will on the individual laborer or, for that matter, the market could not be erased.[79]

Similarly, the presence of two million black Americans, overwhelmingly but not completely bound in slavery, posed troubling questions of the greatest magnitude. To white Americans outside of the South, slavery was anathema; its existence threatened the very ideal of a social order based on individual freedom. For this reason, northerners could not countenance the spread of slavery to new western territories (the "area of freedom," in the parlance of the times), but still they shied away from attacking it in the South. Consideration of emancipation and the place of liberated slaves in society thus led to a dilemma, one in which democratic equalitarianism bumped up against deeply held convictions about race.

During the generation preceding the Civil War, Americans participated in an extended discussion of race: the propensities and capacities of different peoples; their origins; their fate. Religious, scientific, and political perspectives were all brought to bear, and by 1850 the weight of antislavery opinion—abolitionists notwithstanding—stemmed from a hardened, racial definition of American nationality. The findings of a new, "American school" of ethnology, theological treatises, and theories

of society converged, denying the Negro the inherent capacities required for membership in progressive society.[80] Politically, however,
such a view contradicted the basic terms of individual liberty, and in any
discussion of constitutional principle, basic terms could not be glossed
over. In California, as we shall see, a racial definition of American nationality contained unanticipated perils.

On each of these questions the California constitution writers talked
for days. With one exception—the Californios—no persistent alignment
of delegates emerged. The exception was an important one. From beginning to end representatives of the conquered regime voted together,
and at times they controlled the balance of voting power in the convention.[81] Their common front became apparent on the fourth day, even
before the convention had finished its initial organization. At their request, Henry Halleck introduced a resolution that, had it passed, would
have divided California in half, creating a territory in the southern,
largely Hispanic, settlements while the northern regions, where Yankees
dominated, organized as a state.[82] No one spelled out the reason for the
resolution, but it was apparent: separation would hold back the conquest
of Americans and their culture in southern California a bit longer. The
measure failed, but it did signal the Californios' like-mindedness as well
as their regard for Halleck, both of which remained intact when other
conflicts divided the convention.

Twelve days later, the convention's first bitter division occurred over
the extent to which the constitution needed to guard against corporations. Contrary to their prior (and subsequent) practice, on this point the
Committee on the Constitution turned to the constitution of New York,
not Iowa, adopting the former state's prohibition of special legislative
charters. In a notable departure from all constitutional precedent, the
convention embraced the principle of *individual* stockholder liability.
Through it they gave voice to the economic individualism of the gold
rush, projecting an image of California's future in which individual proprietors, not corporate combinations, would flourish. Individual stockholder liability, though known here and there in statutory law, placed
unusual restrictions on corporate enterprise, for by it individual stockholders were made liable for their proportionate share of a corporation's
entire indebtedness; the more usual legal structure of corporate charters
relied on the principle of *limited* liability, whereby a stockholder's liability
was limited to the value of his stock.[83]

On the provisions for organizing corporations, the Californians acted
in complete accord. But when they turned to the specific question of
banks and paper money, a long and acerbic exchange ensued. The de-

bate was an odd one, for on the surface everyone insisted that they sought the same end: an absolute prohibition of banks and paper money. As Robert Semple announced, "There is . . . no necessity of discussing this subject . . . or in reiterating arguments which have . . . become established truths in political economy."[84] These principles had been learned in the panic of 1837, which was immediate in the memory of unlucky speculators such as William Gwin and Morton McCarver. Among the delegates and their contemporaries, the panic was widely believed to have been caused by the unrestricted issue of bank notes by small, local, "wildcat" banks. "The banking era of 1834, '35, '36, and '37," Gwin reminded his colleagues, had brought "misery, ruin, and destruction to the citizens."[85]

In California, where a metallic currency was found literally resting on the ground, nature seemed to have provided a means of avoiding the evils of paper money. Nonetheless, the delegates were unable to agree on alternatives to banks and paper money. Gwin believed that an ironclad prohibition was necessary. Conversely, Charles Botts insisted that the only way to "crush this bank monster" was to have the state carry out the banking and currency functions that, otherwise, private individuals or associations would provide. Citing Daniel Webster ("the greatest genius of the age"), he held that paper currency was unavoidable: "In every great commercial community," he averred, "you must necessarily have a paper currency of some sort or other."[86] Against the positions of both Gwin and Botts, however, a majority of the delegates followed Henry Halleck's ambiguous line of reasoning, which held that the conditions of gold rush California necessitated certain kinds of paper securities—for example, certificates of deposit for gold and silver left in the care of third parties.

Gwin, no doubt recalling his ill fortune in the 1830s, described the evils of banks and paper money with great fervor. They created, he insisted, a "monopoly and the legalized association of wealth to appropriate the labor of the many for the benefit of the few."[87] He argued that the provisions Halleck endorsed, which were drawn from the New York constitution, were inappropriate to the unique conditions of California. The very novelty of the gold rush, he held, provided an opportunity for a new system that took advantage of the lessons of recent history. Gwin thus favored the language of the Iowa constitution, which gave no quarter to banks of issue:

> No corporate body shall hereafter be created, renewed, or extended with the privilege of making issuing or putting in circulation, any bill, check, ticket, certificate, promissory note, or other paper, or the paper of any bank, to circulate as money. The General Assembly of this state shall prohibit, by law, any person or persons, association, company, or corporation,

from exercising the privileges of banking, or creating paper to circulate as money.[88]

Although a few delegates followed Gwin in insisting on the necessity of this unsubtle language (including Morton McCarver and James McHall Jones), the convention as a whole rejected his position. Botts's proposal that the state treasurer serve as depositor for gold and silver mined in the state received the same response. Only one other delegate even responded to Botts's proposal, and then only to insist that it contravened the U.S. Constitution. On a voice vote, the convention repudiated his proposal.[89]

Between these two proposals—one outlawing anything that looked like a bank or paper money, the other making such currency a monopoly of the state—stood the majority of the convention. The provision finally placed in the constitution, for which Halleck served as spokesman, prohibited the legislature from passing acts that granted charters for banking purposes, but allowed the establishment of "associations . . . for the deposit of gold and silver."[90] It was this latter provision that so bothered Gwin and Botts, both of whom thought it made banks of issue an inevitability. Gwin, as well as James McHall Jones, railed against the provision as allowing "a banking system of the very worst character."[91]

When Gwin, Botts, and Jones asked how "associations for the deposit of gold and silver" differed from banks, they asked a question for which there was no good answer. Halleck could not explain how certificates of deposit could be prohibited from serving as a form of paper money. Nonetheless, neither Gwin's extremism nor Botts's reliance on the state was acceptable. Gold rush California was preeminently a commercial society. At its very heart was money: money circulating from miner to merchant, supplier, and workingman. Although gold made California commerce possible—indeed, wondrous—the metal was difficult to store or transport and thus not only a less than ideal currency but, ultimately, a brake on commerce. Paper was the obvious proxy for gold; yet the received wisdom of historical experience made it difficult for the delegates to embrace it.

Caught between their memory (and repugnance) of banks and paper money and a half-formed sense that such were necessary, the delegates acted in contradictory ways. On the one hand, they effectively legalized banks—as Gwin, Botts, and Jones charged. On the other hand, they issued forth a torrent of invective against them, filling the constitution with banking prohibitions. For example, in the very section that endorsed the controversial "associations for the deposit of gold and silver," Halleck successfully moved a proviso (which became the constitution's third prohibition of banks) assuring that "no such association shall make, issue, or put in circulation, any bill, check, ticket, certificate, promissory note, or other paper, or the paper of any bank to circulate as money."[92] In this multiplicity of constitutional prohibitions against banks and paper money the delegates protested too much. The measures, as Gwin, Botts, and Jones foresaw, ultimately had little effect. The measure championed by Henry Halleck and a majority of the delegates did in fact create a banking system that flourished after statehood.[93]

In their debate over banks and paper money the delegates reached a conclusion that cut two ways, testifying to mid-nineteenth-century uncertainties about the proper structure of economic life. While they deeply suspected the institutions of a complex world of corporate enterprise and faceless financial dealings, at the same time they were drawn to commercial growth and development, new visions of which the gold rush had created before their very eyes. A comparable uncertainty also marked their deliberations about race and citizenship, the question that occasioned the convention's most tense moments. Early in the proceedings the delegates outlawed slavery without discussion, adopting verbatim the prohibition contained in the Iowa constitution. But their action on slavery must be considered in relation to their resolution of ancillary questions concerning the voting rights of Indians, the status of free Negroes, and the boundary of the new state. Local conditions had much to do with the delegates' difficulties over these questions, for whereas the Anglo-American delegates were settled in the view that the boundaries of citizenship should be delimited by race, provisions in the Treaty of Guadalupe Hidalgo, as well as the ethnic makeup of California's population, forced a confrontation with exclusionary principles.

The question of race and citizenship first arose during discussion of the rights of suffrage. As in the case of the slavery prohibition, the delegates began with language from the Iowa constitution, which repeated the conventional terminology of antebellum state constitutions: "Every white male citizen of the United States, of the age of twenty-one years . . . shall be entitled to vote."[94] To the delegates these racial and sexual restrictions on the franchise were unexceptional. However, the very makeup of the convention and the conditions under which California fell to the United States made it impossible for them to leave the section at this.

Without intending to, San Francisco's Edward Gilbert first raised the question of race. Citing the Treaty of Guadalupe Hidalgo, he argued that the convention was explicitly required to extend suffrage to "every male citizen of Mexico" and moved to add this language to the suffrage section. Gilbert thus presented the convention with a conundrum, for as the Californio delegate Pablo de la Guerra pointed out, Mexican law did not necessarily deny citizenship to Indians or Negroes; consequently, language limiting the vote to *white* males threatened to disfranchise many Californians who "have received from nature a very dark skin . . . among them men who have heretofore been allowed to vote, and not only that, but to fill the highest public offices."[95]

In response Charles Botts insisted (disingenuously, it seems) that he did not wish to disfranchise the native Californians but that the convention had to limit the vote to "white males" in order to "exclude the African and Indian races . . . to exclude," as he put it, "those objectionable races."[96] According to Botts, these "objectionable races" were by their very nature incapable of fulfilling the obligations of citizenship; including them within the social contract would necessarily degrade popular government and lead to tyranny. Hastings and Gwin elaborated Botts's argument directly. According to Hastings, the necessity of denying the vote to Indians arose from the fact that "there are gentlemen who are very popular among the wild Indians, who could march hundreds up to the polls"; to this Gwin added, "they [the Indians] would vote just as they were directed."[97]

Understood in these terms, granting the vote to "objectionable races" undermined liberty. "Wild Indians" and Africans were, by reasons of race, dependent beings and, as such, open to manipulation by designing (white) men who by controlling their livelihood controlled their votes. Thus, once the franchise was extended to them, popular government devolved to tyranny. Sacramento's Winfield Sherwood made this argument with a pointed reference to his fellow delegate, John Sutter, whose Central Valley domain was home to many Indians who, for all intents and purposes, were bound laborers. "Mr. Sutter . . . ," Sherwood opined, "if he desired to become a politician, and wished office, could, by simply granting a small portion of land to each Indian, control a vote of ten thousand."[98]

Logically, such reasoning supported the exclusion of a wide variety of peoples: certainly Indians and blacks, but also, given the violence occurring in the mines, Mexicans and Californios. In the convention, however, no such proposal was made. The delegates were unwilling to challenge the provisions of the Treaty of Guadalupe Hidalgo, and in any case, such a move would have made a mockery of the participation of Hispanic delegates with visibly nonwhite complexions. Only one delegate was willing even to hint at excluding Mexicans; instead the discussion of suffrage restrictions focused strictly on Indians.[99] But as Henry Halleck reminded his colleagues, an outright denial of suffrage to Indians would prove embarrassing as well, for it, too, would disfranchise one of the convention's members, Los Angeles's Manuel Domínguez, a mestizo.[100]

Halleck's observation gave the convention pause but ultimately had little effect. In two close votes, the delegates defeated compromises proposed by Halleck that would have extended the franchise to Indians who owned property and paid taxes. Only when the suffrage section came to its final reading was a bit of leeway around the "white male" condition included, a proviso stating that "nothing herein contained shall be construed to prevent the Legislature, by a two-thirds concurrent vote, from admitting to the right of suffrage Indians, or the descendants of Indians, in such special cases as such a proportion of the legislative body may deem just and proper." [101] The proviso was ineffective: eight years later delegate Domínguez was prohibited, on the grounds of race, from testifying before a San Francisco court. [102]

The debate over the suffrage section turned on the question of whether or not Indians, particularly those who enjoyed citizenship under Mexican law, should be allowed to vote. In this discussion no delegate, Anglo or Hispanic, questioned the propriety of excluding free Negroes from voting. However, less than a week after the delegates first broached the question of race and citizenship in the context of the rights of suffrage, just how far they were—and were not—willing to go in the exclusion of blacks became apparent when Morton McCarver proposed a measure ordering "the Legislature . . . at its first session, [to] pass such laws as will effectually prohibit free persons of color from immigrating to and settling in this State." [103]

McCarver, who had ushered a similar proscription through Oregon's provisional legislature three years earlier, explained the proposal in terms that echoed racial doctrines voiced about "wild Indians." "I have no doubt," he began, ". . . that every member of this House is aware of the dangerous position in which this country is placed, owing to the inducements existing here for slave-holders to bring their slaves to California and set them free." [104] According to McCarver, in the absence of such a prohibition southerners would quickly bring slaves to California and then, in light of the constitution's antislavery provision, free them on the condition that they agree to work as indentured servants in the mines for six months or a year. This would allow the slave owner sufficient time to make a fortune in the mines and then leave—having in the bargain "freed" himself of the burden of supporting the ex-slaves he had imported to California.

In support of McCarver, a number of delegates observed that they had evidence proving that slave owners proposed to do exactly as McCarver charged. The result of such an immigration, convention president Robert Semple stated, would be "an immense and overwhelming population of negroes, who have never been freemen; who have never been accustomed to provide for themselves. What would be the state of

things in a few years? The whole country would be filled with emanci-
pated slaves—the worst species of population—prepared to do nothing
but steal, or live upon our means as paupers."[105] A population of free
blacks, Hastings offered, would necessarily degrade California society,
for "a free Negro is the freest human being in God's world." Henry Tefft
agreed: "They are free in morals, free in all the vices of a brutish and
depraved race. . . . Of all classes of population, the free negroes are the
most ignorant, wretched, and depraved."[106]

Such portrayals ascribed to Negroes qualities that were the antithesis
of civility as the delegates understood it. Blacks were incapable of independent thought or action. Inherently lacking in sobriety, self-sufficiency, and restraint, they were the natural tools of tyrants. This understanding of the Negro race the delegates and their age captured in one
word: *degraded*. The term was central to a theory of race mixture that
was analogous to Gresham's law of money; that is, the degraded condition of nonwhites, when brought into contact with whites, destroys the
virtues of the white populace, making them unfit for citizenship.

Use of the term *degraded* in regard to blacks antedated the convention
by a generation, when it had served those who sought to explain the
Negro's alleged inferiority by reference to environment. By this line of
reasoning, environmental change—above all, the end of slavery—would
eventually remove the causes of the race's inferiority and make possible
full citizenship. By 1849, however, this older environmentalism had
been inverted. To the delegates, the Negro's degradation was inherent; it
could not be affected by environmental conditions. Indeed, without restrictions on Negro citizenship, the social environment itself was put
at risk.

James McHall Jones, McCarver's foremost ally in the discussion of the
free Negro prohibition, applied this argument to materials close at hand.
He reminded his colleagues that the measure was "of vital importance to
the people of the mining districts," precisely because free Negroes would
undermine the equality of condition that made California's mining communities the epitome of free society. In the mines, Jones argued, the individual laborer enjoyed a "vast advantage . . . over capital." But once
southerners introduced their black indentured servants, an intention
"made manifest to members of this House by private letters, . . . they
will enter into competition with and degrade the white labor of the
miners." San Francisco's Francis Lippitt agreed: "The two races," he insisted, "cannot mix without degradation to the white race."[107]

Three delegates took exception to the free Negro prohibition. Yet despite a description of their arguments as "the most latitudinarian in character," even they did not repudiate the belief in blacks' inherent inferiority. William Shannon, for example, argued against McCarver on
the grounds that "free men of color have just as good a right . . . to emi-

grate here as white men"; nonetheless, Shannon's conception of the freedom to which blacks were fit was severely limited, for he considered their place in society restricted to providing domestic service to whites.[108] Similarly, while Kimball Dimmick called for the rejection of McCarver's measure in the hope that California's constitution would serve as "a model instrument of liberal and enlightened principles," he felt compelled to declare his opposition to Negro immigration, citing their "habits of life, their indolence, and deficiency in force of character."[109] Edward Gilbert's reasoning followed the same line: arguing that the measure perpetrated a "great injustice," he added that "my prejudices against negroes are as strong as any man's can be, for my whole education has tended to make them repugnant to me."[110]

The reasoning of Shannon, Dimmick, and Gilbert is important not because it swayed the convention, but because it betrayed the confusion that followed when the delegates tried to square exclusionary doctrines with the universal language of democratic equality. Until the final vote, however, no difficulty whatsoever seemed to exist. As McCarver observed to a friend midway through the convention, the measure's passage was virtually assured: "On today comes up a Resolution again which I offered & which I have but little doubt will pass the house making provisions similar to those contained in the new constitution of your state which makes it the duty of the first Legislature to pass laws to effectively prohibit free persons of colour from coming to this state." In a postscript he added, "We have just carried by a large majority the provision making it the duty of the first Legislature to prohibit the introduction of Free Negroes under any pretense whatever."[111]

Despite McCarver's confidence, when the Free Negro prohibition came before the convention for a final vote two weeks after its passage in the committee of the whole, the delegates voted it down.[112] No sudden embrace of "latitudinarianism" turned the convention against the measure, although the recognition, dim as it was, of the contradiction between Negro exclusion and the more general logic of equalitarianism cannot be dismissed. What proved decisive was a concern over the measure's effect on Congress. Some congressmen, the delegates recognized, would interpret the exclusion of Negroes as a denial of rights. The resulting debate would unleash sectional passions and jeopardize congressional ratification of the constitution.

Charles Botts outlined a rationale that allowed the convention to avoid not only problems with Congress but also confrontation of the conflict between their racial beliefs and the logic of their democratic ideology. He observed that the free Negro immigration to which McCarver and Jones alluded was anticipated, not actual. Whatever remedies might later become necessary could be left to legislative action. "To the Legislature and to the people," Botts argued, "I wish to leave it."[113] Others

agreed. Jacob Hoppe of San Jose declared that he had supported Mc-
Carver's measure in the committee of the whole but had since changed
his mind: "If the Constitution . . . be burdened with articles which
should not be there, it may be rejected." San Francisco's Alfred Ellis
stated that he had described the measure to public meetings in San
Francisco and that the resulting "excitement was general"; such a provision, he was convinced, would defeat the constitution.[114]

At the end only eight delegates stood with McCarver, and in vain
they tried to salvage something. Jones, for example, proposed submit-
ting the exclusion to the voters along with the constitution. Hastings argued for a provision that pointedly instructed the legislature to guard
against free Negro immigration. Neither motion, however, was seriously
considered. In the final analysis, the Californians proved neither more
nor less capable of articulating a consistent doctrine of race and citizenship than their contemporaries. Characteristically, they put off the
day of reckoning.

Within the convention, emotions ran high on banks and money, suffrage, and McCarver's free Negro measure, but nothing prepared the
delegates for the convention's closing week. At this time they turned to
the mundane task of setting the state's boundary, only to find themselves
embroiled in a debate over the expansion of slavery. The boundary first
became an issue halfway through the convention when William Gwin introduced a substitute to a proposal prepared by Lansford Hastings.
Hastings envisioned a state in the form of a triangle, with boundaries
that extended into the Great Basin in the north (so as to include the mining districts at the eastern base of the Sierra Nevada) and then ran directly south to the U.S.-Mexico border (map 2).[115] Against this Gwin proposed that California take in the entire Mexican cession except for New
Mexico, thus encompassing the current states of California, Nevada, and
Utah, as well as parts of Colorado, Wyoming, New Mexico, and Arizona.
Halleck, to everyone's surprise, sided with Gwin, though he added a proviso that would allow Congress, in consultation with the California legislature, to scale the boundary back to the Sierra Nevada summit (map 3).[116]

Gwin and Halleck's alliance (a "copartnership, coalition, corporation,
confederacy, or bank," according to an incensed Charles Botts) surprised many, for the two had differed on most other questions before
the convention.[117] Together, however, they were a powerful force and
produced a solid bloc in favor of their proposal. The division between
their supporters and opponents—the latter favoring a boundary that set
the state's eastern border somewhere near the summit of the Sierra Nevada—was narrow, separated by two or three votes. Complicating the
debate was the fact that behind this basic split were four distinct perspec-

Map 2. The boundary of California initially proposed by the Committee on the Boundary, chaired by Lansford Hastings. (Map by Robert Abrams.)

tives: namely, on each side was one group that saw the boundary question in relation to the national issue of slavery, and another for whom the question concerned local considerations of a quite different character.

Foremost in the minds of Gwin and Halleck was the national debate over the expansion of slavery, recently magnified by the conquest of Mexican territory. In 1846, before American victory was assured, Pennsylvania congressman David Wilmot had attached his controversial proviso to a war appropriations bill, which, had it been enacted, would

Map 3. Extended California boundary proposed by William Gwin and Henry Wager Halleck. (Map by Robert Abrams.)

have prohibited slavery in any territory taken from Mexico. Following the peace, conflict between advocates and opponents of the proviso paralyzed Congress, defeating every proposal to establish territorial or state governments in the ceded territory.[118] In 1849, however, newly inaugurated president Zachary Taylor moved to end the impasse: he sent emissaries to New Mexico, the Mormon colony in Utah, and California to push for the creation of two slave-free states—New Mexico and California, the latter to include the entire territory outside of New Mexico, from the Pacific coast to the Rockies.[119] Taylor's emissary to California was Whig congressman T. Butler King. Prior to the election of convention delegates, King consulted with Halleck and other military authorities; he also toured the mining districts and Sacramento Valley settlements, speaking to public meetings (at some stops, with Gwin) in favor of the convention and statehood.[120] Following the election, King went to Monterey where he allegedly watched the convention closely, "'log-rolling' . . . in the lobby," promoting as best he could President Taylor's plan.[121]

Halleck later insisted that as military secretary of state and as a delegate to the constitutional convention, he was concerned to relieve the difficulties that the president faced.[122] These he understood through King, who carried to California the very message that Halleck impressed upon the convention: the extended boundary would "close . . . forever this agitating question of slavery in all the territory this side of the Rocky mountains."[123] While Halleck fully favored the extended boundary, he offered his proviso in order to give Congress a safety valve. If it could more readily decide to admit California with its boundary extended to the Rockies, Halleck argued, so be it; if not, Congress could limit the state to the area west of the Sierra Nevada. The national legislature's foul temper, the young soldier said, dictated a flexible course of action.

Gwin agreed with Halleck that the convention should do whatever it could to resolve the slavery question. The boundary, he declared, was "the most important [question] that had to be settled in this Convention"; the Union's very survival, he argued, would be brought into question if the delegates turned down the extended boundary: "if we leave a portion of territory out, we would necessarily open a question which we here should not interfere with. . . . The time has arrived to settle the question that agitates the Union, or it is in danger."[124]

More than this, however, seems to have been on Gwin's mind. Neither the Whig president's difficulties nor King's entreaties meant much to him. Rather, personal considerations, along with his stated concern for the Union, underscored his behavior. Gwin was taken with the idea that in one stroke the convention could resolve a question that had paralyzed Congress for better than two years, and he believed he knew how to do it. His most likely inspiration was Illinois senator Stephen Douglas. During Gwin's stay in Washington, D.C., before his departure for California, Douglas was promoting a bill to admit California as a state, as a means of ending the congressional stalemate over the status of slavery in the ceded territory. During the winter and spring of 1849 Douglas's bill went through a number of incarnations, one of which was uncannily like the proposal Gwin later placed before the California convention: not only were the proposals alike, but the evidence, precedents, and arguments that the two men used were identical. In Washington, Douglas's bold stroke met defeat because, more timid senators declared, Congress had no authority to determine state boundaries. That prerogative belonged to the affected citizens.[125] Gwin's plan, however, obviated this objection, for the definition of the boundary would be by the people of California, not Congress.

Assuming that Gwin understood the territorial issue and the temper of Congress along the same lines as Douglas, the importance he attached to the extended boundary is comprehensible. By this reckoning, had the convention embraced the extended boundary and Congress admitted the state, the slavery question would have been resolved, with credit going to Gwin. He would have returned triumphantly to Washington, D.C., as California's first senator, his rank in Congress assured. Moreover, as he reminded the convention on numerous occasions, he did not believe that California as envisioned in his proposal would long remain a single state. Other states, perhaps a dozen or more, would be carved out of it.[126] Gwin, one can surmise, looked forward to a central role as U.S. senator in shaping this western empire.

To Gwin and Halleck fell the task of speaking for the extended boundary. Their support came from small groups of military men who followed Halleck; southerners, foremost among them James McHall Jones, who lined up behind Gwin; and, above all, the Californios.[127] Although the latter delegates did not state why they supported the Gwin-Halleck proposal, it is unlikely that they did so out of concern for the congressional deadlock over the expansion of slavery. Rather, the best explanation of the Californio position stems from Gwin's last-mentioned comment. His expectation that California would not long remain a single state clearly appealed to their desire for a southern, Hispanic territory separate from the area overrun by Yankees. The extended boundary thus offered another way of realizing an aim that, weeks before, the convention had defeated.[128]

During the convention's third week, the alliance behind Gwin and Halleck carried the extended boundary in the committee of the whole.[129] Opposition quickly crystallized, however, and three weeks later, when the measure came before the convention, lines were firmly drawn. Hastings moved a revised version of his original proposal, as a substitute for Gwin and Halleck's (map 4). He succeeded, but his measure was in turn quickly reconsidered. For the next two days the convention seesawed back and forth.

In the final confrontation all the "old settlers" and a majority of the New Yorkers stood against Gwin and Halleck. Two concerns, one local and one national, melded these delegates together. The first stemmed from the conviction, a matter of common sense to overland immigrants, that the Sierra Nevada formed a "great natural boundary" and that it was contrary to reason and representative government to include the

Map 4. Revised California boundary proposed by Lansford Hastings in response to the Gwin-Halleck proposal. (Map by Robert Abrams.)

Mormon colony on the Salt Lake within California's territory. The second arose from a very different reading of the consequences of the extended boundary on the slavery issue.[130] The foremost spokesmen for this group (one notable for the number of "old American settlers" in it) were Hastings, Botts, and McCarver. Although they did not originate any particular point in the debate, they best articulated the argument against Gwin and Halleck's proposal; in so doing, they steeled resistance to the extended boundary.

If Gwin and Halleck saw a resolution of the slavery question as best accomplished in one dramatic act by the convention, Botts, McCarver, and Hastings insisted that the issue could be resolved only in piecemeal fashion, through the actions of the affected citizens in each area of settlement. This view approximated the principle of "popular sovereignty," enunciated by Democratic presidential candidate Lewis Cass in the 1848 campaign.[131] Within the convention, it served as a bridge between two rather different reasons for opposing Gwin and Halleck: opposition to including the Mormon settlements within California's limits, and the conviction that the extended boundary, far from settling the slavery question, would only inflame debate and deny California statehood. Regarding the first point, Botts and Hastings argued time and again that the convention's inclusion of the Salt Lake settlements without Mormon consent and participation "avoided the first principle of republican liberty." As Botts put it, "To institute a government, directly or indirectly, over a people, without their consent, is a violation of every principle of republicanism and justice." Hastings agreed, and held that if the constitution contained the extended boundary, "the Mormons will insist, and justly too, that they had nothing to do with the formation of our government—that they had no representation in the Convention, and never gave their assent to the Constitution which we attempt to impose upon them."[132]

Reasoning similarly, Gwin and Halleck's adversaries repudiated the proposition that the extended boundary would resolve the slavery question. The convention, insisted McCarver, Botts, and Hastings, consisted of men drawn exclusively from settlements west of the Sierra Nevada. They could not legislate for other territories. The question of slavery elsewhere was properly decided by the affected residents. "I hold the doctrine," Botts explained, "that the people of the State have a great natural right to exclude slavery from their own limits; but sir, I deny that by an unnatural extension of their limits, they could, even with the consent of Congress, exclude slavery from territory that does not belong to them."[133] According to McCarver, the very idea that Congress "will stand by and allow a handful of citizens in California to settle the slave question . . . is preposterous. . . . It is a monstrous doctrine."[134] If the convention attempted to do so by means of the extended boundary, the resulting constitution would divide Congress exactly as the Wilmot proviso had. Warned Hastings: "We will never be admitted as a state in that way. . . . The South will readily see that the object is to force the settlement of this question. The South will never agree to it. It raises the question in all its bitterness and in its worst form."[135]

Despite their long and earnest arguments, Botts, Hastings, and McCarver lost when the extended boundary came before the convention for a final vote. The margin was but two votes, and the result unleashed a bitter exchange as "members rose to their feet under much excitement, and great confusion ensued." McCarver demanded that the delegates adjourn *sine die*, declaring that the "convention has done harm enough."[136] Cooler heads prevailed, however, and convinced their colleagues to recess until the following day. The next morning, the convention's last, saw the past week's alignments turned upside down: in a remarkable turn of events, the convention reconsidered the extended boundary and then established California's eastern border at the summit of the Sierra Nevada.

Behind the shift was the Californios' abandonment of Gwin and Halleck.[137] Their reasons for doing so, though unclear, are perhaps best accounted for by an argument against the Gwin-Halleck boundary that received little attention before the final day. James McHall Jones alluded to it, observing that during the recess that followed the extended boundary's passage "a gentleman—I don't know to what wing he belongs" had argued that Gwin contrived the extended boundary proposal in order to hamstring Congress and, in the ensuing delay, pave the way for the extension of slavery to the Pacific. As Jones paraphrased this argument, Congress's difficulties with the extended boundary "will prevent our admission by Congress as a State into the Union, for some two or three years to come, and thereby give to the south a chance, while we are a territory, to bring in their slaves."[138]

Jones, probably correctly, denounced the attribution of proslavery intentions to Gwin as "not worthy of consideration."[139] Nonetheless, the discussion led others to observe that if the boundary kept Congress from admitting California, the slavery issue would indeed explode, with unforeseeable consequences for California. Anything was possible, including the extension of the Missouri Compromise line to the Pacific, which would in effect impose slavery on the Hispanic settlements of southern California.[140]

It cannot be said that the prospect of being joined to the southern states (and slavery) turned the Californios against Gwin and Halleck. Nevertheless, it was at this point that they ceased to align themselves with the Gwin-Halleck coalition and fell in behind James McHall Jones's hastily contrived compromise proposal. After a round of amendments, the Jones compromise was rewritten to set the border at the summit of the Sierra Nevada.[141] The Californios' shift was decisive: they essentially set the new state's boundary.

᧸᧸

Thus the convention ended. The excitement over the boundary subsided, and shortly thereafter the delegates unanimously endorsed the constitution before adjourning for an evening feast and *baile*. The next morning they assembled in an outdoor ceremony at which the constitution was presented to Governor Riley while cannons roared from vessels in Monterey Harbor.

The delegates' resolution of the boundary question, like their approach to banks and paper money, voting, and free Negroes, testified to their ambivalence on main points. In their debates, they had opposed the powers associated with a system of banking and paper money, while at the same time effecting its creation. They had insisted on democratic ideals of equality, yet avoided addressing the contradiction between their equalitarianism and their racial definition of citizenship. Finally, they agreed that slavery was a curse, yet refused to consider the larger, racial, questions that slavery presented to advocates of democratic principle. They were men of strong convictions, and in following those convictions revealed that the dearest doctrines of antebellum politics were less than whole.

The document the Californians presented to Governor Riley spoke to the intersection of time and place in the history of both California and the United States. This mixture often forced the convention away from the predictable, and made the delegates engage in more than the clerical exercise they originally foresaw. In the final analysis their charter was unremarkable as constitutional doctrine; from beginning to end it merely repeated the received wisdom. The ways in which the delegates arrived at the conventional wisdom, however, was telling, for in the process they explored, though without resolving, the central dilemmas of their time as only contemporaries could. After Monterey they departed on widely different paths. Over the next twenty-five years, as they moved beyond middle age to gray-haired eminence, both they and the constitution they created would find the old ways of thinking challenged at every turn.

FIVE

A Liberal Commonwealth: Oregon, 1857

Eight years after the California convention adjourned, a very different group of men set about the task of constitution writing in Oregon. The distinctions between the two groups were striking. Those who sat in the Oregon convention had decided—as many as fifteen years before—to make this isolated country their families' home. They emigrated to Oregon knowing that they were in all likelihood separating themselves permanently from relatives, friends, and community. By the same token, their emigration had involved a conscious decision to leave behind, at least for a time, the growing national market system and the commercial prospects it entailed. Landownership and a familial competence, more than the profits of personal self-seeking, provided the critical incentive to the settling of this land. What resulted was a self-selected fragment society of family farmers who, if not eager to escape the emerging world of commerce, finance, and manufacturing, saw in Oregon a chance to engage (and control) this world on their own terms.

These features of the Oregon Country were refracted in the ideological perspective of Democrats and anti-Democrats alike. Here, in attenuated form, strains of eighteenth-century republicanism were as evident as the growing commitment of nineteenth-century men to a natural-rights liberalism defined in terms of individual self-seeking for economic advantage. The debates of the Oregon constitutional convention, like the political culture of the territory itself, were marked by this vestigial political vocabulary. This was evident in the nature of Oregon Democrats' allegiance to their party. To them, as Jean Baker has observed, the party was a veritable school for republican citizenship. Its "curriculum" taught that Democracy was more than the sum of its individual human parts; rather, membership involved the subsuming of self and individual interest to the undivided voice of the party, understood as the embodiment of the common good. Through an intricate structure of conventions and ceremonial rituals of patriotic renewal, party life in rural areas became (in the minds of Democrats, if not their adversaries) the ligature of a community of republicans.[1] For Whigs and other critics of Democracy, antipartyism served a similar purpose. Opposition to the party in power, they insisted at every opportunity, involved an act of disinterested service to the common wealth *against* the venal, "factious" actions of Democratic party men. Adherence to principle, they proclaimed, not parties for mere men, honored the republican heritage of the nation's founding. To this end, their prose was infected with the classical, exemplary image of Washington the Spartan Father.

The importance of the Oregon constitutional convention, in this respect, rested less in the charter the delegates wrote than in the manner in which they wrote it. As in California, the Oregonians embraced and in some cases slavishly copied existing state constitutions. However, attention solely to the document they fashioned misleads insofar as it suggests that the delegates reached characteristically nineteenth-century constitutional conclusions easily or on the basis of conventional "Jacksonian" doctrine. To the contrary, these men arrived at "modern" destinations circuitously, via the dimming passageways of eighteenth-century ideas. Writing fundamental law led these constitution framers to articulate first principles. In so doing they testified to the persistence of a political discourse that, although fast disappearing in the nation, found in the isolation of this fragment society a nurturing environment.

NINETEENTH-CENTURY COMMONWEALTHMEN

Horace Greely, editor of the *New York Tribune,* received startling news in the fall of 1857. According to an Oregon correspondent, the horror of "bleeding Kansas" was being played out once again. In the Oregon state constitutional convention

> Pro-Slavery desperadoes . . . [intend] to carry things at the point of a dagger. . . . The vexed subject of slavery was introduced before the Convention had been in session two hours, by the introduction of a resolution, the purport of which was to prohibit the discussion of that bloody question on the floor of the Convention.
>
> The resolution fell like a fire-brand! Members (Pro-Slavery) rose to their feet with flashing eyes and distended nostrils, and with frantic eagerness shouted, or rather yelled their disapprobation of the resolution; timid members left the hall in disgust, while those who remained, consisting of all the Pro-Slavery men and a few others who would be called in Kansas "freedom [fighters]," waxed warm, till the discussion rose to such a pitch that the cry of order, order, was called in vain. . . . Bowie knives, dirks, and pistols were drawn; the vilest personalities were indulged in; the most scurrilous attacks were made upon Free State men; the most bitter invec-

tive was hurled indiscriminately; the most infamous calumnies were ban-
died by reckless Border Ruffians. . . . Several shots were fired, and two
members were slightly wounded. One Free State Democrat, the [cham-
pion] of Umpqua County, received a severe wound in the abdomen.

The authorities were requested to suppress this disgraceful riot . . . ,
and the Mayor of the city . . . immediately called out the Salem Band, an
independent company, and marshalled them in front of the Court-House,
with loaded weapons, in time to prevent a general scene of bloodshed.
While those blood thirsty villains were thirsting for human Free State gore,
they were approached by the Marshall and Sheriff . . . , and were dis-
armed amid the [proclamations] of the populace, who, I assure you, felt
grateful to a retributive Providence for arresting this evil in the nick of
time.[2]

The story, of course, was apocryphal. As any Oregonian could attest,
the violence described by Greely's correspondent was simply not in character. "Philosopher Greely," *Oregon Statesman* editor Asahel Bush observed with some glee, had been "Sold." There had been no shots, no
melee, no untoward incidents of any sort. The Salem Band was, in reality, a brass ensemble, whose "arms" were never "loaded with anything
but wind."[3] In point of fact, the tenor of the Oregon convention was subdued and predictable. The debates, although full of partisan attack and
counterattack, proceeded formulaically, according to a script written
from the delegates' shared experience in territorial politics. Few unanticipated confrontations marked the proceedings, nor was there a decisive turning point comparable to that of the California convention.
Rather, the convention was marked by ingrained habits of party loyalty
and opposition, by the delegates' familiarity with one another, and, no
less, by their chosen models of constitutional doctrine.

Even more forcefully than the Californians, the Oregonians began
their work by asserting that their age had found answers to perennial
questions of principle. Democrat Cyrus Olney reminded his colleagues
that constitution writing was "clerical work."[4] David Logan, an old-line
Whig and longtime Democratic adversary, seconded the sentiment.
"The making of a constitution," he argued, "now is not such an interest-
ing proceeding as it may have been heretofore. What is said and done is
not of that character, and the constitution that we make, and every principle we can engraft into it, has been discussed and decided time and
again. It is no solution of new principles; it is no solution of new doctrine."[5] Of all the Oregonians, however, it was Frederick Waymire who
most vividly expressed the prevailing view. "We might as well take old
constitutions," he observed, "that the people are familiar with, as to try
to strike up into something new, that we know nothing about. If [I] was
sent here to form a new Bible, [I] would copy the old one, and if [I] was
employed to make a hymn book, [I] would report an old one—they are
better than any [I] could make."[6]

The scriptures to which these constitution writers turned for guidance were the charters of the midwestern states from which the bulk of the Oregon population had come. Patrick Malone, correspondent of the *Sacramento Daily Union,* observed that the Oregon constitution "will be more like the Constitutions of some of the western states . . . than of California." The Oregonians, he continued, "feel an interest in their country which your [California's] population . . . do not. They are mostly agriculturists, who have come here in search of homes, carrying with them the virtues incident to an agricultural people. . . . That is a sufficient guarantee that they will act differently, and choose a different class of rulers, from what your mining nomadic population do."[7]

Malone gauged the situation correctly. The Oregonians' constitutional guides came, above all, from Indiana, but also from Ohio, Michigan, Iowa, and Wisconsin—states that had been swept by a wave of constitutional reform in the late 1840s.[8] The choice, on demographic grounds alone, was unremarkable, for of the sixty delegates to the Oregon convention, forty-nine (82 percent) had lived in this older west before setting out for the Pacific Coast. Nineteen (33 percent) had migrated directly to Oregon from one of the states to which they turned for inspiration.

Politically, these western constitutions fit the Oregonians well. The Indiana constitution, Delazon Smith remarked, was "gold refined; it is up with the progress of the age."[9] It, as well as the others, was the work of rural reformers who saw in constitutional revision a way to deal with new political conditions that, in the second quarter of the nineteenth century, arose alongside a national market system. In response to the era's wildcat banking, speculative booms and crushing panics, and indiscriminate (legislative) grants of economic privilege, western constitutional reformers circumscribed the power of state government, particularly its legislative branch. To check legislative logrolling, they shortened legislative sessions and, more generally, required that election, rather than appointment, be used to fill the range of government posts.[10] Finally, in a paradoxical democratization of the franchise, they both extended and restricted the right to vote. Drawing on reforms initiated in the 1820s and 1830s, these midwestern constitutions removed property qualifications from voting and shortened the length of residence required of immigrants before they could vote. At the same time, they dealt harshly with those free blacks and women who, through property ownership, had voted from time to time in the late eighteenth and early nineteenth centuries. Without apology, these constitutions limited the franchise to "free white males."[11]

The Oregonians' embrace of these midwestern models testified to the framers' common mold. Indistinguishable in terms of origin, age, length of residence, or occupation, as a group they underlined the one-dimensional character of the charter society of Oregon. With few exceptions, the delegates were residents of long standing, having arrived around the time Oregon became a territory. The course they followed to the Pacific was much the same. In contrast to the diversity—regional and national—that marked the California convention, more than three-quarters of the Oregonians had migrated overland with their families from the farming regions of the Ohio and Missouri River valleys. They had left these older states as youthful patriarchs of small and growing families, and at the time of the convention were between the ages of thirty-five and forty. Their decision to make the long journey, as Patrick Malone observed, was not made lightly. Unlike gold rush Californians, but like the Oregon Country's settlers as a whole, the constitution writers came to the Pacific Coast to find a permanent home. A common vision of the future, one informed by their rural experience in the Old Northwest and border states, had drawn them westward. To them Oregon offered land, a healthy climate, and the prospect of reproducing, on more favorable terms, the rural society they left behind. By the time of the constitutional convention they evinced a certain self-satisfaction about their choice, for in migrating to Oregon they had become land rich. Forty-three (75 percent) of the delegates held donation land claims; thirty-eight of these possessed more than three hundred acres, and eighteen had more than six hundred.[12]

The material lives of the delegates displayed their homogeneity as well. Of the sixty men, at least forty-eight (80 percent) were either farmers (thirty-one) or lawyers (seventeen), and in many cases the distinction between the two occupations was a distinction without a difference, for no fewer (and perhaps more) than eight of the convention's legal men were farmers as well.[13] Whether farmers, lawyers, or farmer-lawyers, the delegates brought to the Salem convention a wealth of experience in territorial affairs. Oregon politics had been their joint creation. With a few exceptions,[14] the convention was made up of those who had dominated the territory's legislative halls, courts, and rounds of political ceremonies since the beginning of the decade. Thus, when the delegates looked across the convention hall they saw men they knew well, men with reputations etched sharply in the territorial press.

Given these similarities, it is difficult to explain just why some men were Democrats and others anti-Democrats. Three factors, however, illuminate (if not explain) the division. The first relates to the territory's political geography. The strength of the Salem Democracy came from those farming counties within the compass of the Willamette Valley capital: Jackson, Douglas, Lane, Linn, and Polk. In contrast, the anti-Democratic strongholds—Columbia, Washington, Yamhill, and Multnomah counties—were clustered to the north, within the urban shadow of Portland, which was then emerging as the territory's financial and commercial center.[15] Second (though suggestively rather than conclusively), the occupations of the Democratic and anti-Democratic delegates echoed this urban/rural division. Whereas all but a handful of the Willamette Valley Democratic delegates were farmer-lawyers, anti-Democratic delegates from the northern, more urban and commercial counties included men who followed a broader range of callings. This group contained farmers and lawyers, to be sure, but more than a third had other occupations: medicine, teaching, editing and publishing, surveying, and the mechanical arts. Finally, a major distinction marked the public lives of Democrats and anti-Democrats. While the former were inveterate political men, their adversaries, more often than not, expressed their energies in a different sphere: that of religious and secular voluntary associations concerned with education and the promotion of moral behavior. In part the distinction stemmed from control of local and territorial government, but it went beyond officeholding. By any measure, the Democratic delegates were more likely to have participated in precinct, county, and territorial conventions, to have served on the party's local and territorial executive committees, and to have been prominent figures—celebrities of a sort—at the party ceremonies that marked the calendar of this rural society. The public spirit of anti-Democrats, in contrast, focused on a different, but equally passionate, sphere of public life: temperance meetings, the advancement of educational seminaries, and individual exhortation about the necessity of voluntary regeneration.

Long experience in territorial politics had the effect of identifying certain men as leaders and others as followers. The contrast with California is again striking. Before the Oregon convention began, it was apparent who would play the central roles; by virtue of reputation and party standing, six men stood out. Four—La Fayette Grover, George Williams, Matthew Deady, and Delazon Smith—were Democrats associated in differing degrees with Asahel Bush and the Salem Clique. Two, Thomas Dryer and David Logan, were similarly expected to speak for what Democrats dismissingly referred to as the "opposition." Old-line Whigs, Know-Nothings, soldiers in the local armies of 100 percent Americanism and (in the case of Dryer) temperance—they were long-standing antagonists of the party in power.[16]

From beginning to end these six men had a disproportionate effect on the debates. Aptly, the four Democrats represented their party's rural constituency in Marion, Linn, and Douglas counties, while both of the anti-Democratic leaders came from Portland. The four Democrats had been in the political limelight since their arrival in Oregon: George Williams had brought a presidential appointment as chief justice of the territorial supreme court, to which Matthew Deady had also been appointed after two terms in the territorial legislature; Grover and Smith were prominent legislators and, along with Deady, close friends of Bush.

Anti-Democrats Dryer and Logan had also served in the territorial legislature, though for only a term apiece. Their renown, however, was ultimately not the same as that which majority party legislators and jurists enjoyed. It stemmed, rather, from their persistent belittling of the Democratic status quo.

Among the Democratic constitution writers, La Fayette Grover was perhaps the closest associate of Asahel Bush. The two shared a New England background, and both had come to Oregon on the urging of the territory's first congressional delegate, Samuel Thurston. Throughout the 1850s Grover and Bush were politically inseparable. The *Oregon Statesman,* to no small degree, reflected the political instincts and ambition of Grover as much as his historically more famous friend. When Bush was away from Oregon, he entrusted Grover with his editorial duties, and by extension with carrying on the business of the party. Similarly, when Bush tired of the paper, as he did from time to time, it was Grover whom he asked to take it over.[17] Grover, however, never accepted Bush's offer to buy the *Statesman,* for while Bush was always content to remain behind the scenes, Grover was drawn to public office. Prior to the constitutional convention, he held continuous appointive and elective positions that, combined with his place in Bush's circle, made him by 1857 one of the territory's foremost public figures.

Over the course of a long political career—for thirty years he was a man to reckon with in Oregon—Grover's reputation was that of an extreme, and to some vicious, Democratic partisan. His partisanship was likely that of a convert who, at an early age, chose to exile himself from a New England environment inimical to the Jeffersonian Republicanism of his family. Late in life he made much of his family's Puritan roots and historical ties to the American Revolution. In a privately published biography he noted that his ancestors had arrived on the *Arbella* with John Winthrop, associated with Miles Standish in the settlement of Massachusetts, and in the early eighteenth century helped carry the New England way to the Maine wilderness. His grandfather fought the British as a minuteman at Lexington. He and his brothers had been named (in a self-conscious slight of New England Federalism) La Fayette, Talleyrand, and Cuvier to recall and honor the family's dedication to the Enlightenment and republican revolution.

In 1846, after two years at Bowdoin College in Brunswick, Maine, Grover left New England never to return. His destination was Philadelphia. There he read the law, attended lectures at the Philadelphia Law Academy, and, in the spring of 1850, gained admittance to the Pennsylvania bar. Before the year was out, however, he had departed for Oregon on the urging of Samuel Thurston, a fellow Maine native and Bowdoin alumnus whom the young lawyer met in Philadelphia during one of the Oregon congressional delegate's recruiting trips north of Washington, D.C. There, as Grover reminded Thurston in a letter sent on the eve of his departure, the delegate made the young lawyer a "kind offer of admitting me to your office and advancing my interests by the association of your name with my own professionally." [18] Thurston's death foreclosed the promised partnership, but the brief association nonetheless served Grover well. He settled in Salem and there made the acquaintance of Thurston's first man on the scene, Asahel Bush. Through Bush he met Benjamin Franklin Harding, another young Democratic friend of the deceased delegate, with whom he established a "general and lucrative practice." [19]

Grover soon made clear that private practice of the law was to be an adjunct to his life as a public man. With other Thurston recruits, he participated in turning what Thurston had foreseen as a personal organization into the core of a territorial Democratic party. Temperamentally reserved, Grover quickly proved himself as a behind-the-scenes strategist and organizer. He quietly built ties with local leaders, rewarded rank-and-file loyalists, and punished those who departed from right.

For these purposes Grover was always well situated. Throughout the 1850s he held a string of appointive as well as elective offices that sent him throughout the territory, where he could collect local political intelligence and, when necessary, apply the lever of patronage. Shortly after arriving in Salem, for example, he became clerk of the territorial supreme court, in which post he made the acquaintance of other party men. In 1852, the insurgent Democratic legislature—then battling with the Whig governor over the location of the territory's capital—appointed him not only prosecuting attorney for a district that ran from Salem to the California border, but also auditor of territorial revenues and compiler of the provisional government's archives. The following year, Marion County's voters sent him to the territorial house of representatives, to which he returned in 1855 and was elected speaker.

Simultaneously reinforcing Grover's stature was his role in two highly politicized wars against Northwest Indians. During the Rogue River (1853) and Yakima (1856) Indian wars he commanded volunteer companies, Democratic as well as military, recruited in his home county of Marion. The volunteers in each "campaign" elected him to a command rank. In the aftermath of both, moreover, he put his military experience to political service through appointments to commissions that audited (and served as the political advocate for) the financial claims of Oregonians who had fought with and supplied the volunteers.

Closer to home, among the townspeople of Salem and farmers in the surrounding countryside, Grover affirmed his prominence through his role in organizing the territory's first substantial manufacturing enterprise, the Willamette Woolen Mills in Salem. Promising both a market for local sheep farmers and a source of woolen goods for local households, the manufactory was greeted enthusiastically in the town and its hinterland. Stock in it, payable in modest monthly installments, was subscribed quickly and widely. As it happened, preparation for the mill's construction and the recruitment of hands to run it coincided with the opening of the constitutional convention, composing one of many backdrops to the delegates' meetings.[20]

On the strength of his government service, place in Bush's circle, political and military exploits, and role in organizing the Willamette Woolen Mill, Grover was by 1857 as well known as any man in the heartland counties of the Oregon Country. The election of constitutional convention delegates attested to his standing: of the candidates on the Marion County ticket, he received the largest vote.[21] That he would have a crucial role in constitution writing was assumed by all who tried to predict the convention's course. The *Oregonian's* Thomas Dryer mused that Grover was one of "at least half a score of self-called Democrats in the house who are experienced political jockeys, and who are determined that no other man in the party shall get the start in the race for office, place and power, under the State organization."[22] Although Dryer's tone failed to capture Grover's self-image, the Portland editor correctly identified the Salem lawyer as a man to watch.

With Grover the voters of Marion County sent to the constitutional convention another man of territorial as well as local prominence: George Williams, chief justice of the territorial supreme court. Like Grover, Williams was closely identified with the Willamette Woolen Mill, in that he presided over the corporation's board of directors. Willams was also a prominent Democrat, though one who always remained, by choice it seems, outside the inner councils of the Salem organization in which La Fayette Grover figured so prominently. Williams's aloofness arose in part from the circumstances of his arrival, for his place in the territory originated in a presidential appointment, not the favor of local men. It was also embedded in his very sense of himself as a public man. Large and self-assured, Williams exuded an air of command and an expectation of deference. Although Democratic insiders often found him pompous, arrogant, and even stupid, they never said so publicly, partly because he had come into their midst with the imprimatur of the national party, partly because he never defied the local organization, and partly because the rank and file responded to him with the deference he expected. As a judge Williams was more confident in his authority than learned in the law, but when he spoke, in court or on the stump, his very manner commanded respect.[23]

Williams was the son of a Democratic shoemaker in the upstate New York town of Pompey Hill. When as an old man he looked back on his youth, however, he identified neither family nor the crafts tradition of his father as the greatest influence on his life; he pointed rather to the town academy, its rich lyceum tradition, and the man with whom he studied the law. From a young age his parents had prepared him to leave home and discover greatness. They saw to his completing an academy education and then placed him in the law offices of Pompey's most famous citizen, a Whig lawyer and future congressman, Daniel Gott. Gott, whom Williams revered, taught him the law and, through example and drill, instilled in him the desire to attain honor and acclaim in public service. The lawyer also, it seems, pushed his student to do so beyond the confines of Pompey Hill, for shortly after Williams completed his studies he set out for the West, equipped by Gott with a small library of law books.

In 1844, twenty-one-year-old Williams departed down the Ohio River, stopping finally in Fort Madison, Iowa. There, curiously, he joined the law practice of another Whig, Daniel Miller. While practicing law, Williams also became the proprietor of a newspaper, the *Lee County Democrat*, which—again curiously—he renamed in less partisan tones as the *Iowa Statesman*. In Iowa Williams lost little time in seeking out public position. Drawing on Democratic connections established through his newspaper (and with the expectation that his partner would send Whig support his way as well), in 1847 he won a seat on the bench of the state district court, where he remained until he left Iowa five years later. Traveling through his circuit, young Judge Williams displayed himself as an able practitioner of "friends-and-neighbors politics"—a side that had disappeared from his personality by the time he went to Oregon. Known as the "Old Bull Fiddler of Iowa," he made it his practice to end court days with a dance. "When court adjourned," recalled a contemporary, "the judge would have the store-boxes cleared out of the 'court room' . . . and the dance would be kept up till midnight—letting up only half an hour at a time to enable the Judge, the jury, the lawyers, the witnesses, and women folks, to refresh themselves with 'red eye,' or genuine 'Kentucky corn-juice' from a *tin coffee-pot*."[24] In addition to establishing himself as a democratic man of the people, Williams also nurtured an identity as a politician independent of sheer partisanship, and he became the friend of men in both parties, among them the ubiquitous Samuel Thurston. Many of them he would later join in Oregon, including Edward Dickinson Baker, a young Whig attorney from Illinois, and two men, Delazon Smith and Cyrus Olney, with whom he served in the Oregon constitutional convention.

The practical benefits of Williams's democratic and nonpartisan poses became evident in the role he played in a highly charged congressional election in 1850. In that year Congress removed from office the incumbent Iowa representative, Democrat William Thompson, on charges of electoral fraud brought by the Whig candidate he had defeated. His challenger, as it happened, was Williams's former partner, Miller. Thompson proclaimed his innocence and succeeded in obtaining his party's renomination before the special election, but in doing so left Iowa's Democracy in disarray. Some Democrats sat the election out, a small number rallied around an "independent" candidate (whom we will encounter below), and others—Williams prominent among them—supported the Whig nominee, Daniel Miller, who went on to win the election. Far from losing face among Democrats for what might have been seen as apostasy, Williams, insisting that he stood on principle when necessary to the dignity of the party, profited from his role in the race. In the 1852 presidential campaign, the state Democratic convention made him an elector for Franklin Pierce. Pierce carried Iowa, and some, including Illinois senator Stephen Douglas, gave Willams a portion of the credit. When the young judge traveled to Washington, D.C., to deliver his state's electoral votes, the new president, prompted by Douglas and the Iowa congressional delegation, offered him an appointment as chief justice of the Oregon territorial supreme court. Williams accepted readily. He returned to Iowa, collected his wife, and sold off his property. Within three months of his nomination he and his wife arrived in the territory. They settled in Salem, their home for the next five years.

Although there is little doubt that Williams's support for a Whig in the 1850 Iowa congressional campaign was known, and viewed suspiciously, by Oregon Democrats, Chief Justice Williams artfully (if never completely) allayed whatever fears Bush and others had. Through the territorial period he quietly abided the authority of the local organization and carried out the expected duties of a loyal party man. He affirmed the regular organization at party conventions, and he stood for it in the party ceremonies that bound Democrats together. Nonetheless, Williams always remained at the margins of the party's inner councils. Outwardly, party regulars accorded him the deference due his office and the national prominence his appointment bespoke. But a certain reticence always marked their treatment of him. From the perspective of jealous insiders, arm's-length treatment was justified. For although he never questioned the Democratic status quo, Williams displayed an independent streak that pressed suspiciously against the conventional practices of his party.

Williams displayed his independence shortly after he assumed his post on the territorial court, by taking on the untouchable issue of slavery. Upon his arrival, he found on the court docket a case his predecessor had avoided for better than a year. It concerned the children of a former Missouri slave, Robbin Holmes. In 1844, Holmes, with his wife and children, had moved to Oregon with his master, Nathaniel Ford, on the promise of freedom in exchange for his labor in establishing a farm. After five years of work and no freedom, Holmes threatened suit and received, along with his wife, release from bondage. Ford, however, refused to free the Holmes's three small childen. In fact, he prohibited the parents from seeing them, threatening to take the children to Missouri and sell them as slaves. Finally, in 1852 Holmes brought suit. The (Whig) judge who heard the case refused to act, as did his (Democratic) successor, who preferred to leave the matter to the new chief justice. Williams did not hesitate. He took the case from the court's docket and ordered the children's immediate release to their parents in a decision that was both principled and direct—and thus politically indiscreet. Slavery, he declared for the court, did not exist in Oregon: "As soon as the laws of Oregon touched the parties, the relation of master and slave was dissolved." In his written opinion, moreover, Williams implicitly rebuked Delegate Lane for testifying in behalf of Ford.[25]

The overall effect of Williams's decision was to establish in the minds of Democratic insiders the image—one never erased—of a man who harbored abolitionist sentiments and, more to the point, was capable of acting unilaterally. Shortly after his election as delegate to the constitutional convention, Williams reinforced the latter suspicion when he sent to Bush a lengthy essay outlining his views on slavery. Published in the *Statesman* under the title "Free State Letter," the piece, though hardly abolitionist (indeed, the letter struck directly at the equalitarian strain in his *Holmes v. Ford* decision), caused him no end of trouble.[26]

Williams began the letter by declaring his hatred of abolitionism and his belief that slavery was unobjectionable where it existed as a local institution. He then recited a familiar litany of arguments against its extension. Slavery, he asserted on the authority of Webster, had reached its natural limits in the Southwest, and in any case, Oregon's environment was unsuited to it: "it can only be profitable when employed in the production of a few favored articles confined by nature to special districts."[27] Its cost, too—the expense of purchase, transcontinental transportation, food, clothing, and shelter—made it unlikely that any but a handful of Oregon's farmers could ever afford property in man. Moreover, Oregon was surrounded by free territory, Washington to the north and California to the south, which would hold out a constant inducement to escape. Even worse, he argued, fugitive slaves would have every reason to join with hostile Indians and strike back at Oregon's isolated and ill-protected white settlements, placing the entire population at risk.

Having made these points, Williams turned to the heart of his brief: slavery's incompatibility with free labor. Although many Oregon Democrats denounced the free-labor argument as a Trojan horse of "black Republicanism," Williams firmly asserted that, "from the nature of the case," a necessary relationship existed between free labor, free men, and, generally, free institutions. With the confidence of the natural-law theorist, he asserted "that slavery would be a burden and not a blessing to Oregon." In a passage that suggested (despite his disclaimers) Republican free-soil reasoning, he declared:

> Slavery is involuntary servitude—labor forced by power from unwilling laborers. There is no ambition, no enterprise, no energy in such labor. Like the horse to the tread-mill, or the ox to the furrow, goes the slave to his task. Compare this with the labor of free white men. Take the young man without family or property—no bondage fills the little horizon of his life with its unchangeable destiny. Conscious of his equality, of his right to aspire to, and attain any position in society, he will desire the respect and confidence of his fellowmen. All the world is his for action, and all the future is his for hope. . . . Anxious to make his home comfortable, to educate his children, to provide a competency for old age, he will have strong inducements to be diligent and faithful in business. These motives energize free labor, but have little or no influence upon the slave. . . . Establish slavery here, and [y]ou will turn aside that tide of free white labor which has poured itself like a fertilizing flood across the great States of Ohio, Indiana, and Illinois.[28]

Williams's opposition to slavery countenanced neither abolition nor Negro equality under the law. Lest anyone charge him with abolitionism, he affirmed (in terms reminiscent of the debates in the California constitutional convention) that

> Negroes are naturally lazy. . . . [They] are an ignorant and degraded class of beings, and therefore they will vitiate to some extent those white men who are compelled to work or associate with them. Moral differences when they meet, like water, seek a common level, and therefore if white men and negroes are brought in contact without that perfect subjection and rigid discipline which prevail among the slaves of the South, the white men will go down and the negroes go up, till they come to resemble each other in the habits, tastes and actions of their lives.

Williams asked in closing: "Is not the true policy of Oregon to keep as clear as possible of negroes, and all the exciting questions of negro servitude?" His answer was obvious: "Situated here on the Pacific . . . we are not likely to be troubled much with free negroes or fugitive slaves, but as a slave State there would be a constant struggle . . . and there would be no peace."[29]

Overshadowing a few endorsements was an outpouring of criticism directed toward Williams by proslavery Democrats and, more important, the reticence of regular Democrats to say anything at all. Years later Williams insisted that opposing slavery had doomed forever his chances for office as a Democrat, but in so claiming he flattered himself. On slavery and free Negroes the vast majority of Oregonians, Democrat and otherwise, agreed with him. His free-state letter caused him political harm not because he spoke out for freedom (which he did not) but because he announced his position *after* his election to the constitutional convention and without prior warning or consultation with party men around the state. Slavery had stymied the institutions of Democratic doctrine making ever since the organization of the party in Oregon. Even so mild a departure as this from the deafening silence of the party conventions exposed the fears within the undivided Democratic mind.

Among the Democrats in the Oregon convention the greatest counterpoint to George Williams was his supreme court associate Matthew Deady. Whereas Williams carried to the convention a northern free-soil strain of Democratic ideology, Deady promoted Southern proslavery views. Whereas Williams advocated commerce and local manufacturing, though on a modest scale, Deady held to antagonistic country views that (correctly or not) he drew from Thomas Jefferson. Whereas, after statehood, Williams embraced the Republican party and went on to gain a measure of national prominence in it, Deady remained committed, to the end of his life, to a complex strain of eighteenth-century ideas. A cerebral and enigmatic figure, Deady's life turned on a personal quest to make himself over according to an eighteenth-century image of statesmanship. In his private reflections as well as public activities he attested to a desire for fame and honor gained through disinterested public service. Personal wealth he associated with infamy, and, although with misgivings, he consciously eschewed seeking it. What is remarkable about the man is the extent to which he succeeded in transforming himself, in erasing the conditions of his birth and denying the more usual measures of status in nineteenth-century America.

A youth spent *in,* but never *of,* the South had lasting effects on Deady. His father was an itinerant Irish-Catholic schoolmaster who moved the family constantly from place to place in search of employment. As a teacher the elder Deady was a Lancasterian who emphasized the role of emulation in a student's intellectual and moral development. As a father he was a man of iron will whose insistence that his son emulate *him* led to an early and irreconcilable break between them. To Matthew, it appears, his father's demand for emulation meant doom—doom as a self-conscious Irishman in a society dominated by cavaliers who celebrated their English ancestry, doom as a Catholic among Anglicans, and doom as a propertyless professional among a landed gentry. At seventeen, perhaps in response to his father's command that he prepare for the priesthood, Deady left his father's home for good.[30] Although his life recapitulated elements of his father's (he trained as a teacher and for a time taught, and the Lancasterian system of instruction marked his own children's upbringing), the most prominent features of this almost-famous man stemmed from a model of the southern gentleman-statesman that Deady embraced, it seems, in defiance of his father. Although Deady never owned a slave and was a farmer only by avocation, in Oregon during the 1850s he became the most prominent exponent of the country virtues of slave society, defender of the South, and advocate of a southern republicanism drawn from the preceding century. He similarly repudiated his father's Catholicism when he reached adulthood, embracing the Anglicanism he had first encountered as the faith of the southern upper class.

For five years after his break with his father, Deady's life was shaped by the necessity of surviving on his own and his indecision as to how to proceed. He first apprenticed himself to a blacksmith in Barnesville, Ohio. While training in this craft, he also attended a local academy. After completing both the apprenticeship and an academy education, he read the law in the office of Judge William Kennon, Sr., a former Democratic congressman and president judge of the state court of common pleas.[31] In 1846, at age twenty-two, this sometimes blacksmith, sometimes tutor, qualified as an attorney. Yet neither the life of the craftsman, nor of the schoolmaster, nor of the practicing attorney appealed to him. Rather, he sought honor and public place, as his very decision to migrate to Oregon attested.

As Deady later recalled, in 1849 he participated in a local lyceum called in light of the recent California gold discovery. The day's subject was "whether mines of the precious metals are an advantage to a country in which they exist," to which he noted: "I was on the negative side and cited the experience of Spain and her colonies as proof that mining for gold and silver was an injury to a country. Whatever I did with my hearers, I convinced myself that I was right. And this probably had as much to do with my casting my lot in Oregon, when all the world was going to California."[32] Shortly thereafter, he enlisted in an overland train for the Oregon Country, trading his blacksmith skills for a place in the company. He arrived in November 1849, settling in the Yamhill County town of La Fayette, where he got by tutoring and practicing law.[33] Deady's attention, however, soon fastened on gaining a place in the public life of the new territory. In the first election that followed his arrival he ran for and won a seat in the territorial assembly, largely on the strength of having organized a series of indignation meetings protesting the removal of Joseph Lane as territorial governor. As a freshman legislator, then, he went to Oregon City, where he made an alliance that carried him to the center of the new territory's political life. The alliance was with Asahel Bush, recently arrived with his printing press and letter of introduction from Delegate Thurston. Assemblyman Deady provided the young editor with a place to sleep, and in the legislature helped carry out Thurston's wish that the assembly make Bush chief clerk.[34] The two young newcomers became fast friends.

During this session, Chief Clerk Bush quietly encouraged the legislature's defiant removal of the capital fom Oregon City to Salem. Deady opposed the move, likely out of sensitivity to his Yamhill County constituents' proximity to, and favor of, Oregon City. Bush's reaction was revealing. Far from attacking his new acquaintance, he honored Deady by imploring him to reconsider. "I am very anxious," Bush wrote, "that your judgment shall approve [my] course, and I think it will. You cannot but see that capital for the future can be made against the [Whig] Governor and [Whig Attorney General] Holbrook."[35] Deady did not disappoint him. By the next session of the legislature the value of the capital question to party purposes had dissolved his misgivings. He joined the insurgent legislators in Salem, and there wrote the legislative memorial that asked Congress to affirm the move.

In doing so Deady became a central player in the growing Democratic movement. Although a resident of only two years, he had become a valued friend of both Lane and Bush, through the indignation meetings he organized in behalf of Lane and his legislative activities for Bush and the Democratic organization. Enjoying the trust of both men at the moment they began to make their sometimes coordinated, sometimes jealous moves for dominance, Deady was able to act as a broker between the two. Bush made him the Yamhill County agent for the *Statesman*, relied on his intelligence-gathering outside of Marion County, and published as Democratic doctrine the letters Deady wrote under the name "La Fayette."[36] Among the topics his letters emphasized (at least in the beginning) was the Democratic virtue of congressional delegate Lane. In 1852 Deady's place in territorial politics was affirmed. Yamhill's voters sent him to the territorial council, which promptly made him its presiding officer.

Deady's position in the upper house of the territorial legislature placed him in a particularly strategic position, for immediately after the 1852– 1853 session came the campaign for territorial delegate, which Lane held and desired to keep. Already, however, Bush and others were growing suspicious of Lane's ambition and looking for a more trustworthy man to take the post. Deady, as a leader of the legislature, participated in these maneuvers. Writing to Lane, he informed the delegate that "the Assembly is still in session. Among other things, we are doing a little at *delegate making.*"[37] Deady promised Lane his support, but only after informing him that "friends intended to put him [Deady] forward as a candidate."[38] Lane, reading between the lines, understood the letter for what it was: before the spring party convention he informed Deady that the president wished to appoint him to the territorial supreme court.

Before accepting, however, Deady allowed friends to nominate him for the delegateship, only to be dealt a humiliating and long-remembered defeat by Lane. Publicly chastened (and privately incensed), Deady then accepted the appointment to the territorial supreme court, an honor that appealed to him mightily, providing as it did a position of trust that did not require campaigning—to Deady a too often undignified exercise in demagoguery (a view reinforced by his failure to defeat Lane).[39] With his wife he moved to Douglas County and took up a donation land claim. Although he went into the fields from time to time and wrote often of the joy he found in the life of a gentleman farmer, in reality he was devoted more to the idea of farming than to its daily routine.[40] During his tenure on the territorial court he spent most of his time in the courtrooms of his circuit, the county seat saloons and Douglas County conventions where political talk went on, and periodic pilgrimages to Salem to attend the supreme court. In Douglas County, moreover, he continued to serve as a circulation agent for, and contributor to, the *Statesman,* his importance as a party counselor multiplied by his distance from the seat of power in Salem.

As a judge whose decisions touched the lives of scores of southern Oregonians who brought to his court disputes over land, debts, and contracts, Deady became a respected figure known for evenhandedness and spare, well-reasoned decisions. His earthy sense of humor and enthusiasm for the saloon culture of the West endeared him to those men with whom—often to the morning light—he tipped a glass. Already known in the Willamette Valley, his position on the court and his growing prominence in the southern reaches of the territory made him a figure of territorywide prominence. By the mid-1850s, when Bush's displeasure with Lane began to increase, Deady had become an obvious alternative for congressional delegate. In both 1855 and 1857 a Deady challenge almost came to pass in the territorial nominating convention; but in both instances he withdrew before matters reached a head. His retreats were made with republican pride—his honor upheld, his reputation reinforced, and the party preserved as an organization *of independent men,* not an organization *for a man.*

Deady might have added that avoiding a challenge to Lane spared him the pain of actively seeking voter approbation. Like his model, Jefferson, he abhorred the self-promotion that campaigning required as an indignity to his honor, yet he always awaited a call to serve. From the end of his third term in the territorial legislature to his death in 1893, although he made his living over the entire forty-year period as a public official, he stood for election in a contested race only once: in 1857, when he descended from the bench to run for delegate to the constitutional convention.[41]

In this race, Deady ran an odd campaign that seemed almost calculated to produce defeat. As the point man for slavery in the territory, he took it on himself as a candidate (unlike Williams, who expressed an opinion only after the campaign was over) to argue the case for slavery as an institution that would contribute to the preservation of the republican virtues of the Oregon Country. Deady's openness led Bush, despite his personal sympathy for Williams's position, to rally to Deady's defense. In reporting the returns for Douglas County, the editor defied the fact that Deady won his seat in the convention by a narrow margin: "Judge Deady," reported the *Statesman*, ". . . obtained the full vote of the Democratic party, but the freedom shriekers, softs, and disorganizers opposed him with all the bitterness of fanatics and renegades."[42]

Deady's campaign brief for slavery, like Williams's against it, began from the "nature of the case."[43] Drawing on natural-rights doctrines (doctrines against which Deady later argued in the constitutional convention) he insisted that the right to hold property in man could not be distinguished from the right to hold any other kind of property. From this premise he reasoned that the possible positions a person could take toward slavery were but two: one either defended the sanctity of property or joined the ranks of abolitionism and denied it. "Depend on it," he declared, "there is no middle ground between the . . . so-called Abolitionists and pro slavery men"—and only the latter position was tenable.

> There are some millions of Africans owned as property in the United States, and whatever shallow-brains or Smatter-much may say about "property in man," they are just as much property as horses cattle or land, because the law which creates all property makes them such. Governments like ours were instituted not to teach or compel me to own this or that kind of property, but to protect me in the possession and enjoyment of any kind of property which it may be my good or bad fortune to lawfully acquire.

According to Deady, government could not rightfully touch property in man, either by abolishing it or by subjecting it to popular opinion (the doctrine of popular sovereignty). Those who advocated expropriation of property in any form "assume a power for government which I deny that it should or can rightfully possess and which is at war with every principle of our constitutions." And yet, accompanying Deady's natural-rights defense was a broader argument *for* the extension of slavery to Oregon, which he expressed in the contrapuntal language of classical republicanism. This side of his campaign oratory involved a moral evaluation of slavery's opponents and a social estimate of the consequences of abolition. Regarding the first, Deady denounced abolitionists and "Blacks" (meaning Republicans) as the agents of a "tyrannical, arbitrary, fanatical, meddlesome, Super-Godly sentiment that now rises rank from that rotten hypocritical Society that applauds an adulterer so he be a Seditious Stump Pulpit declaimer, that prates about liberty equality and morality in its public prints, while in reality it is festering with the lust of dominion, with upstart-pride with griping avarice and debasing luxury."

The words are notable for their passion—passion loaded with eighteenth-century meanings: tyranny, arbitrary lust of dominion, avarice, and debasing luxury. These same republican symbols, used here to warn against threats to republican virtue, Deady also emphasized in arguing that, in Oregon, slavery would protect republican virtue. It would construct a "'high wall and deep ditch' . . . between us and the tide of New England fanaticism which has quite covered all the free states of the West." In addition, he insisted, it "will render independent and attractive agricultural pursuits and thus induce the bulk of our population to continue tillers of the soil, instead of swarming into over grown cities to strive to live by their wits—becoming in some instances purse proud millionaires, but more frequently sharpers, thieves, rowdys, bullies, and vagabonds."

As the convention approached, and in particular after Williams's free-state letter appeared, Deady's proslavery friends and correspondents urged him, as Benjamin Simpson put it, "to advocate all the ramifications of the Slavery question to the entire satisfaction of all unprejudiced minds."[44] Deady, in response, pledged (and called on his friends) to stand by "the white race, the Constitution, and the institutions of [the] country."[45] In the weeks preceding the convention, it appeared that a confrontation between slavery and free soil, Deady and Williams—both prominently mentioned as candidates for the U.S. Senate[46]—was unavoidable. Those who expected this outcome, however, failed to reckon with the force of party on the opinions of men. Discussion of slavery proved to be beyond the pale; still, differences between Democrats over the question did ramify on the proceedings in other ways—ways unanticipated and, in the end, imperfectly contained.

As renowned as Grover, Williams, and Deady were, the acknowledged spokesman of the Oregon Democracy in the constitutional convention was Delazon Smith, the "Lion of Linn County." As a party leader in the legislature, he was admired, almost revered, by Democrats throughout the territory. As an orator, Smith was unmatched. Recalled Republican John McBride: "He simply swept men by his force and intensity to coincide with him."[47] What McBride failed to note was that his effect came from the language of classical republicanism, from constant declamations that portrayed the Oregon Democracy as the voice and protector of the common wealth. In this regard his local reputation as a spellbinder, his status among Oregonians as one of the great American orators of the times, takes on added meaning. For while Smith was not unknown before he came to Oregon (he had spent the previous twenty years moving throughout an older American West, one that stretched from upstate New York to Iowa), it was not until he went to Oregon that he gained genuine fame and popular renown.

Born in 1816, the son of a "humble mechanic," Smith left home at age fifteen on an odyssey that continued until he brought his family to Oregon in the early 1850s.[48] First moving among the homes of relations (a pattern characteristic of the "semi-independence" prevalent in the lives of antebellum male youths),[49] Smith broke from his family in 1834, when he went to Ohio to train for the ministry at the newly established Oberlin Institute. There he got into trouble immediately. Denouncing the evangelical curriculum of the institute—particularly its joining of Christianity to abolition—and condemning institute leaders as corrupt operators, he was summarily dismissed from the college within a year of his arrival, excommunicated by the Oberlin church, and, briefly, jailed. Notoriety, however, only encouraged Smith. Moving to Cleveland, he published a "large edition of a small pamphlet," *Oberlin Unmasked*. In it and the columns of the free-thinking *Cleveland Liberalist* he exposed the college as a "hot-bed of abolitionism" where students and faculty—"ranters, desperadoes, and bloodsuckers"—engaged in "Negro worship [and] advocat[ed] miscegenation." Displaying a talent for sensationalist reportage, he informed readers that at the college "men and women students [engaged in] practices more erotic than matriculating in the same classes."[50] The exposé made him famous in the Western Reserve and started him on his long career as a party journalist, stump spokesman for the antebellum Democracy, and ever-eager, if seldom successful, candidate for office.

From 1837 to 1844 Smith moved back and forth between Ohio and upstate New York editing Democratic campaign journals. He might well have continued to do so had he not, in 1844, brought the scorn of Ohio Democrats on his head by calling, in the columns of the *Dayton Miamian*, for the Democratic party to readmit to its ranks the former Democrat—at the time, Whig president—John Tyler. Subscriptions to and advertising in the *Miamian* evaporated, and Smith became an outcast; in the end he was saved by Tyler, who, in the closing months of his administration, appointed Smith U.S. special commissioner to the Republic of Ecuador. Smith set out for South America but, for unknown reasons, stayed in Quito only a few weeks before disappearing for more than a year. According to legend, he wandered the Andes. To some he became known as "Tyler's lost minister," and to others, "Delusion," a sobriquet that stuck to the end of his life.[51]

In 1846 Smith reappeared, this time in Iowa. There he farmed, practiced law, edited another Democratic newspaper, and, finally fulfilling the call that had earlier taken him to Oberlin, worked the countryside as a Methodist exhorter. There he made the acquaintance of a number of future Oregonians, among them George Williams and Samuel Thurston. Although a presence in Democratic affairs, and regularly his county's champion for Congress or the governorship, Smith did not run for office until 1850. The occasion was the special congressional election in which George Williams supported his Whig law partner against the regular, if tainted, party nominee. Smith—having "lived on 'hope deferred' long enough"—"announced himself as an independent Democratic candidate."[52] His effort to save the party, however, failed miserably, with only a handful of voters taking his side. Shortly thereafter he left for Oregon, pushed by dim prospects in Iowa and pulled by the promise of land and health in Oregon that, he later recalled, Samuel Thurston had impressed upon him. Smith had good reasons for leaving. Iowa was disappointing politically. Farming had been a constant struggle. And the health of his family had been ruined by periodic waves of cholera: in five short years he had buried his wife and a number of his children.

In the late fall of 1852 Smith arrived in the Willamette Valley with his second wife and surviving children. In Linn County he entered a donation land claim, naming it "Grand Prairie Home." Oregon, he reported to his brother, was "the very best country for a *poor man* I have ever known. The wages of labor of all kinds are high. The climate is mild and healthy and the soil prolific."[53] Unlike Deady, whose celebration of country virtues was accompanied by a studied avoidance of farm labor, Smith lived the life he preached, mixing law with the duties of the farmer.[54] Politics, however, was never far from his thoughts. Shortly after his arrival he made the acquaintance of Asahel Bush, who, aware of Smith's ability on the stump and perhaps fearful that he would start a rival newspaper, courted the newcomer. Smith responded in kind. To the end of the territorial period he remained constant in his proclamations of personal loyalty to Bush, seeking out and taking on party assignments that the *Statesman's* editor devised.[55]

Smith served his party as an orator, legislator, strategist, and *Statesman* contributor. By coincidence, shortly after his arrival the remains of deceased delegate Thurston were returned to Oregon from Panama for reinterment. In a ceremony called to mark the occasion and pay homage to his life, Smith, touted as the "Rev. Delazon Smith," delivered the principal address.[56] For this sermon cum stump speech—his first in the territory—he became renowned. Listeners praised his eloquence, but of equal importance was the symbolic message of his speech. In Smith's hands Thurston became the embodiment of the civic virtue of the Oregon country. "He displayed," Smith told the assembled mourner-celebrants, "the highest and best qualities of man—self sacrifice, patriotism and an unflinching and unwavering devotion to the cause of republicanism and the best interests of the State and people." Thurston's genius was that of the Oregon Country distilled in the life of an individual. His life taught that

> riches cannot perpetuate our liberties. . . . Turning our eyes, then, from the mere acquisition and possession of gold, we are called upon to push our faculties into a higher and holier sphere, where vast stores of mental

and moral riches are thrown broad cast over limitless fields. If we would preserve the glorious heritage bequeathed to us, our young men must study Agriculture. Of all the occupations to which we can turn our attention, there is none more honorable or enviable than that of Farming. . . . To labor should not be thought vulgar, or to perform any species of useful manual labor, ungenteel. Here the jack-plane should be made as respectable as the lawyer's green bag, and the hoe handle as dignified as the yardstick.

Smith's mention of the "faculties" and a "higher and holier sphere," concepts unfamiliar to the twentieth century, provided cues instantly recognizable to his audience. He referred to the psychological theory of the faculties, an eighteenth-century construct, which posited an innate, hierarchically organized set of capacities that governed human behavior. Although faculty psychologists were divided over just what faculties constituted man's makeup, there was general agreement on two: reason (rational calculation) and conscience (a moral sense that, properly, balanced the reasoning faculty). It is to the latter, conscience, to which Smith referred, and he did so in republican (mixed with Methodist) ways, identifying it as the wellspring of virtuous behavior. His point, in context, is apparent: Oregonians, by following "Farming," nurtured the conscience and balanced the rational faculty; thus they preserved virtue, forestalling the fate of a people in whom the reason (rational calculation of interest and advantage) dominated—to wit, the fate of gold rush Californians, among whom "mere acquisition of gold" produced corruption, vice, and degradation. "If you would not see," he declared in closing, "the miasma of luxury, indolence, and sloth, poisoning the very fountains of political and moral life, and pouring its floods of distilled death and liquid corruption upon this fair land, you must uphold the rights of labor and the legitimate claims of the Union our fathers formed."

After this performance, Smith became a fixture on the Democratic circuit. Four months later, he proudly informed Bush that his Fourth of July address had drawn an audience of fifteen hundred people.[57] For the first time in his life, moreover, he won an election—to the territorial assembly. As a freshman during the 1854–1855 term, he cemented his place in the party by introducing and then shepherding through the legislature an act notable for both its practical political effect and its symbolic resonance of the classical republicanism enunciated in his eulogy of Thurston: the notorious viva voce voting law. Targeted at the secretive Know-Nothing movement, the measure was indeed, as Bush put it, a "Know Nothing antidote."[58] But there was more to this antidote than the party purposes for which it was—then and thereafter—renowned.

During the colonial period, viva voce voting was widespread. But by the mid-nineteenth century it had generally (particularly where party competition was intense) lost favor to printed ballots.[59] Hence, although viva voce voting served the Oregon Democracy by exposing Know-Nothings to ridicule, it also had the potential effect of cutting against the party, in that it required party voters laboriously to state their individual preferences for an array of offices, rather than simply deposit a prepared ballot in the box. In Oregon, as Smith and other advocates described it, viva voce voting required that voters be informed and that they be ready to have their choices inspected by their neighbors—that is, by the undivided mind of the party, assembled at the polling place and ready to proscribe men who departed from republican right. In this regard, viva voce voting was more than just a device to smoke out the errant Know-Nothing; it was, for Oregon Democrats, an antidote legitimated by its larger republican purpose.

Smith's act, then, served as a mechanism to reinforce, in the ceremony of voting, the civic virtue he had memorialized in his eulogy of Samuel Thurston. Smith's position on slavery followed a similar line of reasoning. An advocate of popular sovereignty, at first glance he seemed to follow the same logic as George Williams in his free-state letter. "In our opinion," Smith averred, "the laws of nature, climate, soil, production, immigration, interest, and the convictions and will of a large majority of the people of this Territory, and of all the other organized Territories of the Union, are *against* such an establishment [i.e., slavery], and will conspire to prevent its adoption."[60] There was, however, an important, if subtle, distinction between the two men's views. Smith differed from the chief justice not in the conclusion he reached but in the logic by which he reached it. To him the force and legitimacy of the natural-limits thesis of slavery followed not from reason alone, but from reason substantiated in an open vote by voice, carried out by a Democratic citizenry whose thinking was guided by conscience. Popular sovereignty, to Smith, could be relied on to reach political truth because it expressed a collective republicanism nurtured by regular participation in the ritual of viva voce elections.

Delazon Smith's debut before the people of Oregon in 1853 and 1854 was remarkably successful. He became renowned as an orator of the first rank; his viva voce act affirmed Democracy in practice and principle; and his explication of the logic of popular sovereignty became the settled opinion of both Democrats and more than a few of their partisan opponents. In the ensuing years, moreover, his place in the territorial Democracy grew ever more important. Like Deady and Grover, he became a presiding officer in the territorial legislature. He, too, was regularly touted as a rival to Delegate Lane—though, also like Deady, he always pulled back in the end from mounting an open challenge. His reticence in taking on the incumbent delegate stemmed, no doubt, from fear of defeat, but also from an ingrained suspicion of ambition, be it others' (for example Lane's) or his own. Smith often wrote to Bush about the dangers of ambition, noting his reluctance, even privately, to "write about myself—or [do] anything which [may] seem to assist or magnify my own importance either in my own or the estimation of others."[61] He awaited (and by waiting, encouraged) the call to service. Such sentiments, exchanged privately between friends, of course reinforced one's worth as a public servant, one's civic virtue and disinterestedness. But even when the voters of Linn County gave Smith a large majority of their votes for convention delegate, he carefully hedged his thoughts about what statehood would bring: "All I desire, or have desired to know for the government of my own action is, that certain judicious, well informed and influential friends were desirously disposed to favor my nomination, in their own way *at the proper time*. We shall be wiser at the adjournment of the Constitutional Convention than we are now. Anon 'we shall see what we shall see.'"[62]

Democrats Grover, Williams, Deady, and Smith carried to Salem habits of command and an expectation of deference gained through experience as party leaders during the territorial period. Yet they did not lack—and they knew it—capable adversaries, men who were well known, practiced in the art of political maneuver, and able to marshal opposition to the Democratic regime. Anti-Democrats in the convention included figures such as the "Sage of Yoncalla," Jesse Applegate, a local institution by virtue of his leadership in the "cow column" immigration of 1843 and role in the provisional government; and Yamhill County's John McBride, the only Republican and forthright opponent of slavery in the constitutional convention. Neither man, however, was of much effect. Early on, Applegate withdrew from the convention on an odd point of honor, and McBride, uncompromising on either slavery or temperance, was a lonely voice.[63] Leadership of the anti-Democratic side of the convention fell rather to two men, both of whom, even in 1857, held on to the banner of the Whig party: *Oregonian* editor Thomas Jefferson Dryer and Portland lawyer David Logan. Although both had carried to Oregon a deep antipartyism endemic to Whiggery, otherwise they were political men of very different kinds. Dryer was an ideologue who thrived on partisan combat. Logan was a troubled soul.

Details about the early life of Thomas Dryer are scarce, but he did share with the other Oregon constitution writers a youth spent in constant movement. Born in 1808 in Cananduiga County, New York, he moved west with his family at the age of ten, settling in Ohio near Cincinnati. At seventeen he left his family and returned to New York, where he remained for the next sixteen years, working, apparently, as a journeyman newspaperman. In 1841 he set out for the West again, reuniting with his family in Cincinnati, where he tried his hand at a number of occupations: shipping beef to New Orleans, running a mail contract, operating a steam laundry. In 1849 he escaped this mundane life, joining, together with his wife, the first American settlers in gold rush California. There, after spending a short time in the mines, he turned to political journalism in San Francisco.

Dryer served briefly as the city editor of the *California Courier*, an undistinguished sheet among the city's few Whig papers. In 1850, however, his stay in the gold rush city came to an end when the proprietors of Portland, Oregon, Stephen Coffin and W. W. Chapman, arrived in search of an editor for a newspaper to promote their new town. They preferred a Whig, and Dryer jumped at the chance. After arranging the purchase of an old press from the San Francisco newspaper *Alta California*, he followed his patrons north. In the summer of 1850, the *California Courier* announced the imminent departure of its city editor, informing Oregonians that Dryer was "a practical and forcible writer, and a Whig of the right stripe. . . . We cheerfully commend him to the Whigs of Oregon, and ask them to give to his journal a strong and substantial confidence and support." [64] In Oregon, the Whiggish *Spectator* looked forward to his arrival and the journalistic counterpoint it would present to another newcomer, Asahel Bush: "Mr. Dryer has been connected with the California Courier since its establishment . . . and has displayed ability as editor through its columns . . . —He looks as sharp as a steel trap. Some time towards the spring the 'Statesman' will probably be put in blast. We then expect to see the rocks fly." [65]

The *Oregonian*, the first issue of which appeared in December 1850, remained Dryer's mouthpiece for better than a decade. During his tenure the paper was outspoken in its denunciation of Democrats in general and Asahel Bush in particular. Yet it was equally suspicious of any attempt to organize formal opposition. Although Dryer styled himself an advocate of the "great Whig party" (which he defined as the lineal descendant of the Founders), to his mind Whigs composed a party only insofar as they, like George Washington, stood against party. Membership in its ranks, he insisted, stemmed not from the levers of patronage or the jockeying of interested men for office, but from the spontaneous mobilization of citizens who virtuously put aside self-seeking to defend the republic from cunning factions—factions exemplified by the Democratic spoils system. Dryer devoted the columns of the *Oregonian* to encouraging this kind of spontaneous, disinterested republicanism. He hammered away at a set of interrelated themes full of foreboding: the corruption of Democratic placemen; the declining moral tone of republican society (evidenced specifically by the consumption of alcohol and, more generally, by the absence of Spartan habits among the masses); and the danger posed by enfranchised immigrants unfamiliar with American institutions and easily corrupted (often by drink) by conniving Democrats. In the *Oregonian* these three themes formed a neat package and provided the basis for Dryer's decade-long tirade against the local Democratic regime. Over the course of the 1850s his views changed little, testifying both to the isolation of the Oregon Country from national political currents and to the fixing, in the early 1850s, of the local cast of political characters. Between 1850 and 1860, all that varied was the weight Dryer gave to each component of his anti-Democratic brief and the intensity with which he promoted the package as a whole, for his failure to spark an effective opposition lent his columns an increasingly desperate tone over time.

When Dryer inaugurated the *Oregonian,* he made temperance the foundation of his republican message. Although his concatenation of temperance and republicanism, articulated at public meetings shortly after his arrival, struck some observers as novel, within his scheme of thought they went hand in hand. For example, the editors of the *Spectator,* themselves at the forefront of the temperance movement in the territory, described Dryer as one who "dared to venture outside the usual boundaries, and present some of the more distant aspects of intemperance." What the *Spectator* found "distant," however, was to Dryer uppermost: the link between temperance and republican virtue. This connection he made through the symbolic figure of George Washington, whose imagery was at once historical, political, and moral. Updating this Founding Father for the times and bringing the example of Washington's life down to the level of his less exalted audiences, Dryer asked that his listeners consider—retrospectively in the case of Washington, and prospectively in their own case—the contrasting fates that followed from a life of "dissipation" versus one of "sobriety." "What if Washington," Dryer asked,

> when he had received his first rewards as a surveyor, had met his youthful companions and said, "Come boys, let us go to the grocery and have a frolic." . . . What would have become of the Father of the Country? It would have deprived him of the qualities necessary for greatness. . . . [How] many, for the pleasures of the cup, sacrifice the distinction of the scholar, the statesman, and the philanthropist, nay, more, deprive themselves of the dignity of the man![66]

Dryer's insistence on temperance as a necessary quality of the public man, while eminently consistent with his views of Democratic corruption (and, in turn, of the dangers of foreign immigration), was easily dismissed by his Democratic adversaries. Indeed, the very passion with which Dryer promoted temperance encouraged ridicule, for, as Bush

claimed with delight, Dryer's advocacy of temperance was patently hypocritical. According to the *Statesman's* editor, his counterpart at the *Oregonian* was a well-known drunk. In his native state of New York, Bush
wrote, as well as in California and the Ohio River valley towns where he
had resided prior to 1849, Dryer was known by a variety of names that
referred to his weakness for drink: to some he was "gimlet eye," to
others "toddy Jep," or "Mother Dryer," or even "slop basin." So notorious was he, Bush averred, that the Sons of Temperance had dismissed
him from their organization for repeated violations of the pure water
pledge.

In the early 1850s such charges appeared regularly in the pages of the
Statesman, and the private correspondence between Bush and his friends
contained frequent reports of the Portland editor's sprees around town.[67]
Although the notices were perhaps apocryphal (his attackers were, after
all, Democrats), they had the intended effect.[68] Other temperance advocates shied away from defending Dryer, and so by 1853–1854 he began
to emphasize other elements in his anti-Democratic brief. Above all he
gravitated to nativism, with which both temperance and his republican
denunciation of the Democracy were linked. Through him, the *Oregonian* became a foremost advocate of "native Americanism" and its institutional defenders such as the American Tract and American Bible
Societies. So taken was he with nativism that for a time in the 1850s he
appealed to Whigs to embrace the "one hundred percent Americanism"
of the Know-Nothing party. In 1855, the high point of nativism in the
territory, he proclaimed this support proudly on the masthead of the
Oregonian: "Put none but Americans on guard! Americans in sympathy,
feeling, and sentiment! Americans by the provisions of the Constitution
of the United States."[69]

Against Delazon Smith's viva voce antidote Dryer defended the secret
ballot and the Know-Nothing target of Democratic wrath in fulsome
phrases that tied nativism to the very founding of the United States. In
defaming the American party, he told his readers, Bush and the Democracy slandered true patriotism.

We should not forget that we are indebted for our Liberty now enjoyed,
not to foreign countries, foreign influences or foreign laws, but to Americans, Americans by birth or adoption, Americans in feeling, education,
and sentiments—Americans, who like the ancients, were proud of their
country, and ready always for its defense—Americans who would not surrender to King George, or any other prince, potentate or power, their
principles of Liberty. To perpetuate those principles, and transmit those
blessings to our children's children, we must not surrender the helm of our
government to the hands of inexperienced pilots. Amid all the political
revolutions which have swept over the country, entirely changing in the

phase of things, under the cognomen of all sorts of names and titles, there has been no political party more infamously belied, or more wilfully and grossly slandered, misrepresented and abused, than the present Republican or American party—called by way of reproach or derision, the Know Nothing party.[70]

Dryer's attraction to Know-Nothingism stemmed from more than his sympathy with its program to proscribe the civil rights of immigrants. It appealed to him because it captured his sense of Democratic corruption and decline from the rectitude of the Founders, who "like the ancients . . . would not surrender to King George, or any other prince, potentate, or power, their principles of Liberty."[71] In contrast to the party of spoilsmen, who anxiously courted foreigners ill suited—by background, education, religion, and personal habits—for republican citizenship, the men of Dryer's "true American" party defended the last remnants of the nation's revolutionary heritage. Know-Nothingism, by his lights, was both more and less than a "party." It did not attract adherents through promises of spoils and personal advantage; rather, it prompted the spirit of self-sacrifice that had made the Revolution and constituted the greatness of the Founders. It required a willingness to risk defamation and ridicule in order to protect their gifts for posterity. It required, furthermore, secrecy, for the danger was immediate and of apocalyptic dimensions.

Among his detractors, Dryer's pompous rhetoric in the *Oregonian* appeared alternately humorous, because of its inflated self-importance, and terrifying, in its vicious depictions of immigrants, especially Catholics and Jews. But as events (the national collapse of Whiggery, the repudiation of Know-Nothingism) displayed the practical bankruptcy of his views, Dryer's tone grew ever more extreme. Magnifying his desperation was the absence of any alternative. The Republican successor to Whiggery appealed to him not at all. Republicans, in his view, avoided the central issues of the day by making free soil the heart of their appeal. In trucking with abolitionists, they posed a threat to the racial and ethnic lines implicit in his Americanism; in emulating the corrupt partyism of Democrats and appealing to immigrants, they threatened to fasten yet another party sore on the founders' republic.[72]

In his campaign for a seat in the constitution convention, in which he ran as an "Independent" and an "American," Dryer returned to fundamentals as he understood them.[73] Declaring himself independent of all factions, he appealed directly to the "freemen" of Oregon, warning them that parties, historical and contemporary, were the preferred vehicles of tyrants. The Oregon Democracy, if not countered in the convention, would turn the creation of the state into a shameless episode in self-promotion. Unless restrained, that party would empower the enemies of the republic and do the bidding of Slave Power tyrants. With Machiavellian precision he reminded his readers that

> Hannibal, Nero, Robespierre, and a thousand other ancient and modern tyrants, have at different periods of the world's history attempted to control the public mind by hypocrisy and deception. Judas Iscariot and Benedict Arnold were but the *prototypes* of many of their latter day followers *incog.* of Christianity and patriotism, who would sell their religion and their country for gold and power, and barter their priceless heritage of "life, liberty, and the pursuit of happiness," if thereby they can wield the scepter of political sovereignty. But none of these have ever attempted a political tyranny equal to that of the Salem inquisitors, self-christened and self called, "the democracy of Oregon."[74]

Dryer was elected to the convention, but with no mandate from the electorate of Washington and Multnomah counties. His election, particularly in Portland, turned less on the details of his views than on his high profile as editor of the *Oregonian* and his advocacy of Portland against a Democracy dominated by the rural voters of the Willamette Valley. Despite the honor of election, he carried to Salem a sense of foreboding at what the constitutional convention, controlled by a powerful and dangerous faction, would do. Even so—and notwithstanding his denials—he had a greater effect on constitution writing than anyone expected. Seven years of partisan editorializing had sharpened his republican vocabulary, a vocabulary whose meanings were not lost on the other delegates, Democratic and otherwise. Delegate Dryer thus proved impossible to ignore and difficult to dismiss.

Although he matched, and perhaps exceeded, Thomas Dryer in his loathing of the Oregon Democracy, the other leading opposition man in the convention, David Logan, drew his anti-Democratic sentiments from different sources. Like Dryer, Logan remained a Whig long after it was practical to do so. But in contrast to his fellow Portlander, his allegiance endured for reasons that were more personal than ideological. Neither classical images of the Founders nor a commitment to temperance or nativism motivated Logan. His politics, rather, originated in a youth that was at once full of promise and scarred by failure. Logan's Whiggery had been instilled by a prominent father in a town—Springfield, Illinois—where a man's political affiliation was a primal element in his self-identity. Yet his coming of age had been painful, culminating in banishment—on the grounds, apparently, of his failure to meet the tests of Whig manhood. As a result, Logan's political career in Oregon bore the marks of a man seeking redemption in the eyes of an unforgiving father. These features, mixed together in a quirky personality marked by intelligence and oratorical genius, humor and a fierce temper, a weakness for drink and an un-Victorian sexual appetite, made Logan a man destined for disappointment.

Logan was born in Kentucky and came of age in Springfield in a family where Whiggery and scrupulous, "Spartan-like" personal habits were coincident with civilization.[75] In the 1830s and 1840s the capital of Illinois, home to Stephen Douglas and Abraham Lincoln, constituted a world in which political affiliation was reflected in the daily rounds of one's life—one's home, one's occupation, one's church. Politics had not been a matter of choice for David Logan but a matter of birth, magnified by the prominence of his father. The "undisputed leader of the Sangammon [County] bar," a member of the famous "Whig junto," and law partner of Abraham Lincoln, Stephen Logan taught his son with his every act that manhood and Whiggery were inseparable.[76] As a teenager David read the law with his father and Lincoln, preparing for a career in service to the great causes identified by Springfield's Whigs, foremost among them the elder Logan, Lincoln, Edward Dickinson Baker, and Simeon Francis. He was known as a naturally intelligent youth who, unlike his stern father, was charming and eloquent as well. In 1844 the Sangammon County bar admitted him to its ranks, and the expectation was that he would join his father's practice to carry on the family's tradition in the law and Whiggish public service.[77] As the elder Logan recalled, upon his son's admittance to the bar "I . . . told [Lincoln] that I wished to take in my son David with me who had meanwhile grown up. . . . Lincoln was perhaps by that time quite willing to begin on his own account. So we talked the matter over and dissolved the partnership amicably and in friendship."[78]

The partnership of father and son, however, never came about. Shortly after Logan and Lincoln dissolved their joint practice, the elder Logan forced David to join an Illinois company of volunteers heading for the Mexican War under the command of the prominent young Sangammon County Whig (and future Oregonian), Edward Dickinson Baker. Logan returned within the year, but neither celebration of his service nor a place in his father's practice followed. To all appearances son and father had had a falling out, one that wartime service did not resolve. After his stint in Colonel Baker's volunteer regiment, David hovered at the margins of Illinois politics and Springfield society. His father kept him at arm's length, encouraging his law practice but blocking entry into Whig circles. Whatever the reasons for this treatment, matters came to a head in 1849 when the elder Logan sent his son to Oregon, suddenly and without ceremony. David's departure closely followed his father's unexpected defeat in a bitter campaign to succeed Lincoln in Congress. Whether David's behavior in that election had anything to do with his subsequent departure is impossible to say, although the coincidence, in light of subsequent events, is suggestive. Outfitted by his father with livestock, equipment, and money—and perhaps a family reputation to redeem within the growing community of Illinoisans in the Oregon Country—Logan set out. Thereafter direct relations between son and father ended. His only surviving letters home mention friends and his mother but refer to his father only once, when he noted that he had drawn a draft on his father's credit, and that he had done so only because others—Whig others—depended on it.

Logan's emigration from Illinois, it seems clear, was not by choice, but the decision of a patriarch hoping for his son's reform and redemption.[79] David, for his part, filled his letters with the thoughts of a man wishing to reach a disapproving father, with news of imminent success of a kind that Stephen Logan could understand: political victories by a Whig swimming against a Democratic tide. For a decade, with growing pathos, David wrote home that he would soon return triumphantly to Illinois— en route to a seat in Congress. The success he foretold, however, was always prospective, not actual, and his return never came to pass. Why this man, whom even adversaries admired for intelligence, charm, and political wit, failed to gain what he sought so long and hard is suggested by another topic broached in his correspondence—poor health, bouts of "hysteria" and "neuralgia of the stomach and nerves" that forced him to bed for weeks on end.[80] Logan cloaked these fits in the neutral terms of medical science, but friends and enemies, political allies and adversaries, knew better: his sickness was alcoholism.

Although no sources confirm the supposition, Logan's alcoholism was likely the cause of his banishment from Illinois. It seems probable, as well, that the political environment he encountered in Oregon did him no good whatsoever. His arrival coincided with that of Asahel Bush and the successful organization of the territorial Democratic party. Against the Democratic juggernaut Logan labored mightily, but never with more than minor success. His initial impressions of the Oregon Country— "The time is fast approaching in fact is now here when with industry and economy almost any one can make a fortune. . . . I could easily make 1500 or 200 $ a year even now"—were soon replaced by an ongoing litany of complaints about the people he met, the prospects in Oregon for a young man, and, above all, the dearth of political opportunities for a Whig with talent: "This is," he wrote a year after his arrival, "no place for a *Whig*."[81] The appointment of a Whig territorial administration in 1850 proved a particular disappointment. "When I came to Oregon," he observed, "I had reason to expect an appointment from the government, but instead of that I have not even met with encouragement from the *Whigs* appointed to office in this territory until since [*sic*] I have been place[d] in a situation to be useful to them." Whether he was overlooked for reasons stemming from his Illinois years or because of his reputation in Oregon cannot be said. Whatever the cause, his response was defiant: "Those things are passed & I hope never to need their offices or their influence—certain I will never ask either."[82]

Although denied the patronage of his party and burdened with a very un-Whiggish reputation as a drunk, Logan remained a strong advocate of the party throughout the territorial period. His reasons, however, had little in common with those of his colleague Thomas Dryer. The crucial factors, it appears, were, first, a constitutional inability even to conceive of joining another party and, second, a need to prove himself according to the measure of manhood—that is, election to national office—that he internalized in Springfield. Although his personal demeanor never approached the Spartan-like moralism central to his father's Whiggery, he endured and, after a fashion, even prospered in Oregon. Democrats admitted his abilities as a lawyer and almost enjoyed his wry, wincing attacks. Anti-Democrats, it appears, recognized his talent for swaying audiences, appreciated his spirited combat with the Democracy, and stood by him even when his behavior made a mockery of their standards of rectitude. He prospered financially and benefited politically through partnerships with men prominent in both the business affairs of the seaport and the councils of anti-Democratic politics: W. W. Chapman, Mark Chinn, and Erasmus Shattuck.[83] Through his travels around the countryside with the circuit court he gained a reputation as a sharp and effective litigator. But Logan's prominence as a lawyer never translated into the political victory he sought as an avenue to redemption. As George Williams gently put it long after the partisan passions of the 1850s had passed, Logan was a man of "fine ability and good lawyer, but unfortunate habits blasted . . . [his] bright prospects for future usefulness and distinction."[84]

Logan's first political defeat came less than a year after he arrived, and its effect was lasting. In the spring of 1851 he ran for territorial representative of Yamhill County against none other than (the incumbent) Matthew Deady. Occurring directly after the insurgent legislature removed the capital from Oregon City to Salem, the campaign was charged with the party question. In a county with a large contingent of Illinoisans (and soon an anti-Democratic stronghold), organizing Democrats feared Logan as a formidable opponent. As Deady wrote to Bush, in Yamhill "the election of delegate or anything else is not much thought of, all the excitement is between logan and myself."[85] Deady's victory, in the end, depended on a tactic neither man ever forgot: he got Logan "drunk—a state in which Logan sustained himself without appreciable aid through much of the campaign."[86]

Logan took the defeat bitterly, and it marked the beginning of a feud that lasted more than a decade. In it, the Democrat easily bested the Whig. To Logan's aggravation, Deady's star shone all the more brightly as the 1850s progressed, while he remained at the margin of territorial affairs. Moreover, the Democratic judge seemed to seek out opportunities to humiliate Logan. The high (or low) point in their feud came in 1854, shortly after Logan finally gained a seat in the territorial assembly, when Deady (with malice aforethought, it appears) sent an unsigned letter to a Democratic paper reporting, in gruesome detail, a drunken Logan's rape of an Indian girl at high noon on the main street of Jacksonville. Logan, when he discovered that Deady was the author, threatened to sue for slander and (according to Deady) to kill him as well.[87] Deady did not take the threat lightly. As he wrote to Bush, "Logan has been beastly drunk and gambling since the first day [of the court session]. We meet every day. . . . Nothing has passed between us, but when I am not about he flourishes his revolver and says that he will shoot me on the bench."[88]

In the end Logan did not carry out his threats, nor (in striking testimony to the racial boundaries of Victorian morality) was he ever prosecuted, or even threatened with prosecution, for the assault—despite witnesses, according to Deady, willing to testify to the act. Rather, the rape became part of the political folklore that defined Logan to the end of his life. To the political men of the Oregon Country, his deed was neither extraordinary nor horrifying. Democrats thereafter knew Logan as the "Mingo Chief," a tag applied with a wink of the eye.[89] Anti-Democrats remained outwardly indifferent to the deed; indeed, but two months after the report surfaced Logan figured prominently in the only territorywide Whig party convention ever held. Two years later, when he stood for election to the constitutional convention, he garnered the largest number of votes in his county, more than Dryer and the two Democratic delegates that Portland voters sent to Salem.

Logan's election as a constitution writer was not the result of his commitment to the issues (or the republican vocabulary) featured in Dryer's *Oregonian*. Logan, as the Californian Patrick Malone correctly observed, "has no politics; he is only opposed to the Democratic Party."[90] While he never articulated a precise ideological stance, he was willing to employ whatever tactics and appeals came his way. Temperance was out of the question, and although Logan later admitted to having "been slightly burned with Know-Nothingism" in 1854–1855, he allied himself with the Americans only so far as to threaten the Democracy.[91] Similarly, on slavery Logan's views were evasive and confused. By 1857 his father and other (now ex-)Whigs in Springfield were moving toward the free-soil doctrines of the Republican party, but he refused to go along. Republicans he dismissed as "negro worshippers." "I cant go to the Loco focos," he remarked in describing his quandary, "and I'll see the Republicans to the Devil before I'll vote with them. I dont know what I am exactly, but any thing but an abolitionist." And later: "I intend so far as the 'negro' question is concerned to be identified hereafter, with that political party, that favors the submission of the question of slavery to the people of the organized Territories—and is opposed to any kind of Federal intervention therewith." [92]

Logan's embrace of popular sovereignty echoed the predominant view in Oregon and explains in part his election to the constitutional convention. Taking the popular (though Democratic) position, while maintaining his stance as an enemy of the majority party, he forestalled the usual attack against anti-Democratic "freedom shriekers" and abolitionists. But perhaps the key to his victory in Portland was his appeal to the commercial ambitions of voters in the port town. In attacking Democratic domination of Oregon politics he played up the rural roots of that party and consequent neglect of urban interests. In Portland in 1857, this line proved effective, mobilizing nascent antipathy toward the countryside within the territory's only pocket of urban voters.

VIRTUE AND INTEREST

The distinction politically between Thomas Dryer and David Logan captures the formlessness of opposition politics in territorial Oregon. It illuminates as well the despair that anti-Democrats felt when the constitutional convention delegates assembled. In contrast to the commanding majority enjoyed by delegates loyal to the Salem Clique, the loose-knit opposition was unorganized and without common purpose. Like Logan and Dryer, they were held together above all by a common jealousy of Democratic power. Jesse Applegate was mocked and John McBride ignored. Others—John S. White, John W. Watts, William Watkins—were unknown except for their Know-Nothing activities a few years before; their agenda was that of evangelicals devoted to temperance and nativist restrictions. What alienated Democrats like Portland's William Farrar and Yamhill's Martin Olds would do was anyone's guess.

On the other side of the partisan aisle, the apparent order within the Democratic ranks was striking. Not only was the majority set on avoiding the slavery issue by offering voters alternative sections regulating slavery and the immigration of free Negroes, they had agreed to use, per Delazon Smith's recommendation, the Indiana constitution as their guide. Moreover, some of them had already been hard at work on specific parts of the constitution. The judges of the territorial supreme court, for example, were all present as Democratic delegates and had brought with them the outlines of a plan for the state judiciary. To underscore Democratic unity, on the evening of the convention's first day the party held a caucus in the convention hall (thus symbolically claiming the building as theirs). There forty-five of the delegates— clique insiders, well-known loyalists, and even a handful of men viewed

with some suspicion—met, pronounced their solidarity, and chose Matthew Deady as their candidate for convention president.

The first week's proceedings gave every appearance that the delegates
would complete their work quickly, and for exactly the reasons that anti-
Democrats like Dryer and Logan charged: caucus dictation. Deady, as
expected, was elected president, as was the party's slate of candidates for
secretary, assistant secretary, sergeant-at-arms, doorkeeper, and printer.
Democrats similarly resolved a dispute over a contested seat from small
and isolated Coos County, giving it to an unknown Democrat who, as
things went, proved an unreliable party man. The convention also turned
back an effort, spearheaded by anti-Democrats from Washington, Multnomah, and Yamhill counties, to hire a chaplain for the purpose of
beginning each session with a prayer. To the key committees—Bill of
Rights, Judiciary, Suffrage and Elections, the Schedule, and Corporations
and Internal Improvements—Deady appointed healthy Democratic majorities and leading Democratic chairmen: Grover to Bill of Rights as
well as Schedule (which was to contain the slavery and free Negro referenda), Williams to Judiciary, Smith to Suffrage and Elections, and loyalist Charles Meigs (assisted by the sure-handed Williams) to Corporations and Internal Improvements. Organized, disciplined, and guided
by a model congenial to former residents of the Ohio and Mississippi
River valleys, the delegates began their work in earnest on the convention's fifth day.

Attesting to their preparation and the suitability of the Indiana constitution, the Democratic committees quickly sent draft articles to the floor.
As these reports appeared, however, the Oregon constitution writers
discovered that the tranquility of the opening week was misleading. The
appearance of Democratic unity and oppositional disarray, while generally correct, glossed over the blend of the expected and unexpected that
would mark this convention. In the debates over a number of topics—
the judiciary, the relationship between religion and government, immigrants and the rights of citizenship, and banks and corporations—the
anti-Democratic opposition proved larger in number and firmer in sentiment than anticipated. The evangelical agenda of diehard Whigs and
nativists was difficult to dispense with. Questions regarding the proper
relationship of church and state, pressed by the opposition, hovered
constantly. Calls for an Oregon version of the prohibitory Maine Law,
reinforced by a constant stream of petitions, proved difficult to contain.
Proposals to restrict immigrants' rights as citizens, promoted by Dryer
and others, enjoyed significant, if in the end insufficient, support. Moreover, despite the declarations made in the Democratic caucus, at many
points the majority was less solid than thought. The judiciary plan devised by Williams and his supreme court colleagues, once tagged by the
opposition as a plot to usurp local sovereignty, was finally unacceptable

to locally minded Democrats as well as anti-Democrats. The issue of race, despite preconvention agreement to leave slavery to the voters, intruded time and again, in the discussion of the schedule, bill of rights, rights of suffrage, and miscellaneous provisions. Finally, on the convention's most vexing issue, the organization and regulation of corporations, the Democrats were divided, and acrimoniously so.

At those points where anti-Democratic unity coincided with divisions in the majority party, Dryer, Logan, and other opposition men sensed the opportunity and encouraged confrontation with a rhetorical ploy that told a great deal about the political culture of the territory. First they granted that the Democratic leaders had the power to have things their way. They then added that the solidarity of the majority party rested only on shaky, and illegitimate, grounds of personal interest, embodied in a spoils system through which Democratic leaders assured personal control by dispensing and withholding patronage crumbs to the rank and file. Hence, they charged, the majority was in fact nothing but a "faction." Their use of this word, one full of powerful eighteenth-century republican meanings, was not by happenstance. Through it they portrayed the Democrats as self-interested men who, if not restrained, would turn the writing of the constitution to the purposes of personal power against the "common wealth." Using this code language, anti-Democrats, throughout the convention, called wavering men to principled defiance. Democrats responded in kind.

Debate over whether delegates were acting factiously or disinterestedly pervaded the proceedings. Anti-Democrats set the tone early on by charging that "the majority were disposed to 'gag' and 'cram measures down the throats' of the minority" so as to produce a party constitution that would serve Democratic aspirants to state and national office. Delazon Smith threw the charge back, insisting that "faction had begun to triumph here; frivolous and captious amendments not expected to carry had been proposed by gentlemen of the opposition merely to consume time and confuse and confound the convention. . . . This whole week had been consumed by such factious proceedings; and the majority had patiently borne and permitted this."[93] Dryer responded by mocking Smith's pose: "How generous, how magnanimous to treat the prisoners of war with that sort of humanity, and then talk about your democracy. . . . I have but little hope," he went on, "that we can get up a constitution here, with the present feeling to crush out the liberties of the people and their rights, for party interests." His ally from Yamhill County, Martin Olds (an anti-Bush Democrat), continued the attack, calling "upon the members of this convention to let no party faction bear them down, but to get up a good constitution, one that will mete out to freemen their rights. Let all these party talkers go away."[94]

Ironically, the very pervasiveness of this discussion of motives only

magnified the one-dimensional—party—division within the Oregon convention. In contrast with California, the passage of time in the Oregon
convention mattered little: the division of the convention on the first
order of business (the election of the convention president) was virtually
reproduced in its last roll call vote (to accept or reject the constitution).[95]
Between these two points almost every discussion turned on a ritual exchange of charges that one side or the other was acting as a faction.
These exchanges occurred not only in the debates over old issues such as
viva voce voting and the location of the seat of government in Salem;
they appeared throughout, drawing out and encouraging the use of a
republican vocabulary in other ways as well.

This aspect of constitution writing was most evident in the Oregonians' debate over the bill of rights and articles on the judiciary, rights of
suffrage, and corporations. Even though they did not reach novel constitutional conclusions on any of these topics, their debates followed revealing, sui generis lines, lines first drawn in the discussion of the judiciary,
to which the delegates turned four days after completing their organization. The discussion was long and intense, to no small degree because
the article reported by Judiciary Committee chairman, George Williams,
disregarded the Indiana precedent. When Williams made the report,
anti-Democrats, David Logan foremost among them, recoiled, for reasons partly reflexive (the characteristic opposition of men like Logan to
Democratic proposals) and partly substantive. The very getting up of the
article, Logan charged, displayed the tyrannical intent of the majority.
Although appointed to the Judiciary Committee, he had not seen the
final draft of the article before it went to the floor of the convention. "If
we are to be excluded from the committees," Logan insisted, "and if the
appointment of one of our number is but a mere complimentary appointment with a secret understanding that our suggestions shall all go
unheeded, then let us know it. . . . You have the numerical strength and
can force us to it—we will have to submit."[96]

There was, however, more to Logan's condemnation of the majority's
course than his charge of "party clap-trap."[97] Williams's proposal for the
state court system departed from both the territorial and Indiana precedent by substituting an enlarged county court for the usual probate
courts and county commissions. The reason for consolidating county institutions into a single court, the judge argued, was to promote efficiency
and end confusion over local legal authority by vesting the various powers of probate courts and county commissions in one elected figure, the
county judge. To anti-Democrats this granted too much authority to a
single man (most likely a Democrat), giving him broad and, as they saw
it, unchecked powers over private property and public rights. More directly, to Portland delegates Dryer, Logan, and (from the anti-Salem
Democratic side) William Farrar the measure seemed designed to fur-

ther the personal economic interests of Portland Democrats with ties to the Bush organization. They characterized it as patently self-interested, lacking any pretense of evenhanded justice. Indeed, Logan insisted, what was needed was not consolidation but expansion of the judicial system by the addition of a municipal court of record to the proposed system of supreme, circuit, and county courts.

Logan's amendment was quickly dismissed by the Democratic judges in the convention and, following their lead, by a firm (Democratic) majority in the convention, but not before Logan, Dryer, and Farrar made clear why they saw the proposed court system serving venal Democratic interests. In calling for a municipal court *of record*, Logan had a specific referent, and purpose, in mind. In the existing local courts ("justice's courts"), the presiding judge issued oral decisions, which, by virtue of being oral, could not be appealed. A court of record, in contrast, required a written record of both the proceedings and the judge's decision, and thus allowed for appeal to a higher court on the grounds of error in either procedure or the law. The Portlanders' desire for a municipal court of record in the constitution stemmed from a long-standing struggle in the port town over control of the Willamette River levee. "Buildings are being erected on the public levee in Portland," Dryer pointed out while defending Logan's amendment, "by the political friends of the officers in power there, and they (the officers) refuse to obey the city ordinance to enforce their removal." [98]

For Logan, Dryer, and Farrar, the controversy over the Portland levee was a manifest case of the public good against private interest—private interest allied to party. Neither the territorial judicial system nor that countenanced in Williams's plan promised to resolve the conflict in favor of the public. A municipal court of record, they thought, did, for it would be a *local* court with decisions "on the record" and thus enforceable. [99] Before the convention, however, their argument fell on deaf ears. Williams ridiculed it, charging that "on account of the city of Portland there must be something in our constitution that is not in any other constitution in the Union." Conferring general jurisdiction on municipal courts "would lead," he warned, "to a conflict of jurisdiction between the courts thus established, and the district courts." [100] The Democratic majority denied Logan's motion on a voice vote.

Similar wrangling pervaded the rest of the delegates' discussion of the court system, as anti-Democrats pointed to other features that served the creation of a "judicial monarchy." In the end, though, the result was the same as in the first skirmish: the Democratic report, with minor adjustments, was affirmed. This early debate over the judiciary set the tone for subsequent proceedings: opposition charges of factious intent met by Democratic denials and minor amendments. The pattern repeated itself when the legal system again came before the convention during debate over the bill of rights. The issue concerned a provision (taken directly from Indiana) that "in all criminal cases whatever, the jury shall have the right to determine the law and the facts."[101] Initially, the Democracy was divided, with judges Deady and Williams opposing lawyers Smith and Grover. The latter supported the Indiana language on the grounds, as Smith put it, that "the jury [was] the safest depository of the power of determination of the law. . . . To give that power to the court, was giving one man too much power, and making the trial by jury a farce."[102] To Grover, the principle at stake was imbedded in the history of liberty: "The juries were the judges of the law and the facts by virtue of the rights guaranteed them by the *Magna Charta*. . . . In Indiana the subject is incorporated in the constitution."[103] Without acknowledging any alliance with Democrats, Logan and Dryer supported this line of reasoning. Logan insisted that, should the constitution give "the judge the power of determining the law, . . . if he is biased he will warp those facts to fit any law, and extort a verdict in accordance with his bias. You might as well abolish the jury at once, if you do not give them the right to decide the law."[104] Dryer seconded the sentiment: "Every juryman," he averred, "could understand the law and judge of it just as well as any judge who ever sat upon the bench. . . . [Otherwise t]he judges could concentrate power in their own hands, that they might direct and control juries." Elaborating the argument he had introduced in the earlier debate over the judiciary, and drawing again on republican imagery (mixed with a salute to the popular will), he pointed out that the delegates had come to Salem "not to for[m] a judicial monarchy, but to frame a constitution. Popular prejudice has sprung up in consequence of the advocates of the judicial monarchy."[105]

To judges Deady and Williams, however, the section under discussion was preposterous. Deady tried to amend it by "making it the province of the court to decide the law."[106] After his motion failed, Williams proposed "to make the farce complete" by adding the phrase "nor shall a judge be allowed to instruct a jury or grant new trial!"[107] The wrangling ended only when Delazon Smith offered, in what must have been an attempt to defuse tension within Democratic ranks, an amendment that contradicted his original position. To the language of the Indiana constitution he proposed, successfully, an additional phrase: "The jury shall determine the law and the fact, *under the direction of the court as to the law*" (emphasis added).[108]

For the moment Smith's amendment affirmed Democratic solidarity in the convention. It also gave voice, quietly and unnoticed, to a transformation of the law that was occurring in the larger context of nineteenth-century American jurisprudence: the subtle yet fundamental shift in legal power from citizens and juries to judges and attorneys.[109] In the Oregon convention the longer-term implications of Smith's modest proposal went unremarked. The immediate significance of the amendment rested in the fact that it moved the convention forward—at the moment, a matter of some importance to Democratic leaders, given the conflicts over the bill of rights as a whole, particularly its sections on religion and the rights of immigrants.

❦

The bill of rights that Grover reported to the convention differed most from the Indiana model in its treatment of organized religion and immigrant rights. What the Oregonians deleted from, and what they added to, the corresponding sections of their model spoke loudly and elicited pointed responses from the anti-Democratic side of the convention. For example, the preamble to the Indiana bill of rights stated: "We, the people of the State of Indiana, grateful to Almighty God for the free exercise of the right to choose our own form of government, do ordain this Constitution." In contrast, the report of Grover's committee pointedly removed all references to Godly ordination; it held instead that "we, the people of the state of Oregon, to the end that justice be established, order maintained, and liberty be perpetuated, do ordain this constitution" and similarly excised the wording "[all men] are endowed by their Creator." The committee also amended the Indiana provision that "no money shall be drawn from the treasury for the benefit of any religious or theological institution" to include the phrase "for the compensation of any religious services, or for the benefit of any theological institution," and they amplified the provision that "no person shall be rendered incompetent as a witness, in consequence of his opinion on matters of religion," by adding "nor be questioned in any court of justice touching his religious belief, to affect the weight of his testimony."[110]

To anti-Democrats who carried evangelical commitments to the Salem convention, these alterations to the Indiana charter were heretical—in Dryer's words, "infidelity, and nothing else."[111] Few, however, agreed with them. Against Dryer's claim that the section's infidel authors wished to prohibit prayers in the legislative halls, Democrats lined up behind Williams's simple remark that "the people should not be taxed to give preference to one creed over another."[112] Deady seconded the point, allowing that while he had no problem with legislative sessions being opened by (voluntary) prayers, "a pious and good man would not be insulted by being asked to pray without pay. . . . If he was a holy man, a man of practical piety, and one who had at heart the good of his fellow men; if he possessed those qualifications I should vote to invite him. But if he were one of those stump pulpit orators and fanatical demagogues with which our generation is cursed, I should vote against him."[113]

Dryer's failure to affirm Christian fidelity was matched by his, and other anti-Democrats', failure to affirm ethnic homogeneity in the bill of rights or suffrage article. In a pointed affront to the Know-Nothing remnant in the constitutional convention, the report of Grover's Committee on the Bill of Rights affirmed that "foreigners who are, or who may hereafter become, residents of this state shall enjoy the same rights in respect to the possession, enjoyment, and descent of property as native-born citizens."[114] Dryer moved to substitute *citizens* for *residents,* but to no avail; the section passed with only one change from the committee report—Deady's proposed addition of *white* before *foreigners.*[115]

A similar exchange marked the delegates' consideration of the rights of suffrage article, which Delazon Smith carried to the floor immediately after the debate over the bill of rights. On this point the committee report was faithful to the language of the Indiana constitution, extending the vote to "every white male of foreign birth of the age 21 years and upwards, who shall have resided in the United States one year, and shall have resided in this state during the six months immediately preceding such election."[116] Even so, anti-Democrat nativists challenged it for encouraging the immigration of suspect aliens whose presence would threaten the homogeneity requisite to a republic. Dryer, charging that the proposed section was a party measure, painted it in antirepublican hues that to his mind offended memory of the Founding Fathers. "There was," he proclaimed, "a great disposition on the part of some members of the convention to court popularity by sympathizing with foreigners." In order to pack ballot boxes, he argued, Democrats stood ready to give "foreigners more liberty than those who were born on the soil. The great principles that influenced the patriot sires of the republic had been transmitted to the sons as an invaluable inheritance, and," he reminded the assembly, the patriot sires "thought that no foreign influence should ever control the liberties of this republic."[117] Smith dismissed this and other charges about "secret societies of foreigners to control the ballot boxes," noting that "in all the western states, as a matter of policy, citizens were admitted by liberal laws." Grover followed, pointing out (without irony) that the U.S. Supreme Court, in Dred Scott, had reserved to states the regulations of citizenship.[118]

The debate went back and forth along these lines for a morning, the Democrats decrying the nativist fears of those who argued for restrictions, Dryer and others warning of foreign—and thus antirepublican—intrigue. Once again, the debate ended with a compromise that upheld the Democratic position. On Deady's motion the section was revised by requiring foreigners to announce their intention to naturalize one year before the election at which they first intended to vote.

The Oregonians' debates over religion and immigrant rights, both terminated by the imposition of Democratic might, turned on anti-Democratic fears of heterogeneity and Democratic repudiation of their adversaries' conception of the religious and ethnic uniformity necessary

to a republic. But on one closely related point the two sides were in absolute agreement about the need to preserve a homogeneous population,
and that was race. After the Democratic side had its way on the citizenship rights of white immigrants, the deliberations devolved into a
venting of racial hatred marked by equal measures of vitriol and light-
heartedness. In contrast to the Californians, who were restrained, if
mildly, in their discussion of race by the presence of Hispanic delegates,
the Oregonians were uninhibited. No delegate argued against the notion
that nonwhites—Negroes, mulattoes, Indians, Chinese, Kanakas—were
by virtue of race properly prohibited from the full range of citizens'
rights. "All elections shall be free and equal," the first section of the suffrage article taken from Indiana proclaimed, but this, Delazon Smith retorted, "did not mean Chinese or niggers." His sentiment was seconded
by both sides, as Democrats and anti-Democrats competed to put themselves on record. In addition to prohibiting Negroes and mulattoes from
voting, Grover moved (successfully) to add "Chinamen." Deady, going
even further, proposed that the section require that "no person, other
than those of the white race, shall have the right of suffrage." Logan,
agreeing with the spirit of his nemesis's proposal, nonetheless feared
that the language was dangerously imprecise: it would, he argued, "admit quarter-blood Negroes"—for they had a predominance of white
blood, and would be entitled to vote under Mr. Deady's amendment."
No problem, Deady responded, and moved to add *pure* before *white*.
Heaping absurdity upon absurdity, William Bristow followed by suggesting (to laughter, according to the *Statesman*) the qualifier *Simon*. The discussion ended only when anti-Democrat Watkins observed that "he was
opposed to 'pure white'—it would exclude two men of doubtful white
color in his county who had voted for his opponent." [119]

The Oregonians treated race lightly because they could not conceive
of nonwhite suffrage ever coming to pass. (Women's suffrage was not
even broached in the convention.) So complete was their unanimity, so
self-evident their truth, that in the end they found sufficient the simple
language originally proposed, which identified the electorate as "every
white male citizen of the United States." In the closing days of the convention they affirmed this view when, at long last, they turned to the
wording of the slavery and free Negro referenda in the schedule. From a
slightly different angle delegates on both sides reemphasized the racial
boundaries to citizenship when the anti-Democratic delegate William
Watkins moved, unexpectedly, to include in the free Negro referendum
a measure to prohibit Chinese as well. Drawing on free-soil reasoning,
Watkins argued that "if Chinese emigration continued to come . . . in
five years no white man would inhabit [the mining counties of the state].
White men could not compete with them—they would work for $1.50 or

$2.00 per day." His Jackson County colleague, Paine Page Prim, added that "Chinamen were an evil in the mines, and were growing to be a greater one." Deady agreed, asserting that he would "vote to couple Chinamen with negroes, and should vote for submitting the question of excluding both. . . . He saw no reason for making a difference between Chinamen and negroes." Williams, in contrast to his decision in *Holmes v. Ford,* agreed, stating that "he was in favor of excluding both Chinamen and negroes. . . . He would consecrate Oregon to the use of the white man, and exclude the negro, Chinaman, and every race of that character." Dryer, in an unusual nonpartisan display, averred that "he would vote to exclude negroes, Chinamen, Kanakas, and even Indians. The association of those races with the white was the demoralization of the latter." [120] As it turned out, Chinese exclusion was less troubling for the constitution writers than that of free Negroes. Instead of leaving the question to the voters, they simply included in the article on miscellaneous provisions a clause prohibiting any "Chinaman, not a resident of the State at the adoption of this Constitution," from holding real estate or a mining claim, or working a mining claim. [121]

The delegates' unanimity on matters of race, though a departure from the partisan rituals that otherwise dominated this convention, testified both to the homogeneity of this charter society and to the Oregonians' common fear of losing it. Similar concerns informed the single moment in the convention when a significant division in Democratic ranks appeared; this occurred midway through the convention, when the delegates turned to the article on corporations and internal improvements. On this point there had been no preconvention discussion, and as a result the debate was unexpectedly frank and open, displaying as nowhere else in the convention the contours of ideology and political culture in the Oregon Country.

When the delegates first turned to the article on corporations and internal improvements the acrimony that eventually emerged, pitting Democrat against Democrat as well as majority against minority, was momentarily avoided. The first order of business had to do with banks, and on this point the assembled delegates were united. Following a ritualistic display of antibank sentiment, they placed in the constitution a prohibition of banks as strident in tone, and as impotent in effect, as the Californians'. "The Legislative Assembly," they commanded, ". . . shall not have the power to establish, *or* incorporate, any bank *or* banking company, *or* monied institution whatever, *nor* shall any bank company, *or* institution exist in the State, with the privilege of making, issuing, *or* putting in circulation, any bill, check, certificate, promissory note, *or* other paper, *or* the paper of any bank company, *or* person, to circulate as money" (emphasis added).[122]

Having dispensed with banks (or so they thought), the delegates moved to the more general question of how corporations were to be organized in the state, and on this point their consensus dissolved. For a day and a half they debated the liability of stockholders. George Williams acted as spokesman for the report of the Committee on Corporations and Internal Improvements, and again he found himself defending constitutional language that, by departing from familiar doctrine, encouraged debate. The proposed section differed from the Indiana constitution by providing for stockholder liability *without limit* for the claims of workingmen. The measure pleased almost no one, and in the ensuing debate three positions emerged.

At one extreme were most anti-Democrats in the convention, who followed (in the absence of Logan and Dryer) the lead of John McBride and William Watkins. McBride, the convention's lone Republican, and Watkins, a largely unknown man from the mines of Jackson County, denounced any barrier to corporate enterprise. Affirming that incorporation was "the genius of the age," these men evoked a cosmopolitan vision of corporate-capitalist development. Arrayed against this view at the opposite extreme was a group of Democrats led by Deady and another supreme court justice, Reuben Boise. Denouncing capitalist commerce and manufacturing in eighteenth-century republican terms, these delegates argued for, in effect, a prohibition of corporations. Finally, occupying a position midway between these two was a majority of the Democrats, led by Williams and Grover. In the end this group accepted limited liability, but they did so for reasons that differed fundamentally from those of McBride and Watkins. Uppermost in their minds was a conception of the corporation drawn from the experience of organizing the Willamette Woolen Mills—an institution local in origin, scope, and benefit; one that, to their minds, did not threaten the rural character of their charter society but promised, rather, to enhance it modestly.

In the debate over liability proponents of each view developed their arguments, and through them alternative conceptions of Oregon's future, in detail. Throughout, the Democratic divisiveness contrasted markedly with the unity of opposition speakers. Watkins put the latter case clearly:

> It is the genius of our age to incorporate—the genius of our institutions, and has laid the very foundation of the improvement and progress of the present time. It is the foundation of the religious and benevolent and natural progress of the United States and of the world. Why, the United States is nothing but a great corporation.
>
> Look at the old state of Massachusetts, what is her position? Why, her corporate wealth is sufficient to buy up a half dozen of the smaller states of

the Union. . . . And she has obtained it by acting according to the tendencies of the age.[123]

Alexander Campbell agreed: "It has been remarked . . . that society is one great corporation. I agree. . . . Everything is taking that direction. . . . We should pause before we put into our constitution a . . . preventive to the employment of capital here. . . . We should place no law in the way of forming corporations for manufacturing purposes." Logan's law partner, Erasmus Shattuck of Portland, added that the question was "whether the capital that shall come into the country shall receive such protection as will cause it to be productive." McBride attacked any hindrance to incorporation on the grounds that it was discriminatory, giving "to the person contracting with the corporation a stronger security than he would have contracting with an individual." This, he concluded,

> would result in entirely prohibiting corporations here. . . . We want capital here. Can we get it if we lay on this restriction? If a gentleman in New York or Boston has capital to invest in any enterprise that this country stands in need of, will he send his capital here and make all the property he has left behind liable? Certainly not while there are other states where the restrictions would not be such as to lay him liable for all that he is worth.[124]

The response to these anti-Democratic calls for constitutional encouragement of incorporation was immediate. Deady, in particular, saw McBride's visions of a society dominated by manufacturing, an integrated continental system of finance, and wide-ranging capitalist commerce as fraught with error. Counterattacking, he proposed a substitute section that would establish unlimited stockholder liability: "The stockholders of all corporations and joint stock companies," it read, "shall be individually liable for all the debts and liabilities of such corporations or joint stock company." The purpose behind his proposal differed dramatically from the Californians' aim in including a similar provision in their constitution. The latter provision enacted unlimited liability to protect individuals in the dynamic market economy created by the gold rush. Deady's proposal, conversely, was intended to forestall the corruption of Oregon's rural virtues. As he admitted:

> If this provision is adopted, it would have the effect of preventing the creation of any joint stock company in this country except where persons, having confidence in one another, would associate themselves as partners. . . . I am in favor of the individual stockholders being liable to the extent of every cent they possess, and the reason is that I do not want to encourage a fungous growth of speculators in this country.[125]

In a long and impassioned speech rife with classical republican terms, Deady recounted the evils that attend the rise of commerce and asked his fellow constitution writers to consider the consequences for Oregon if their charter were to encourage financial speculation, corporations, and manufacturing. "A great deal," he remarked, "has been said about bringing capital into the country and encouraging enterprise. [But] how much better off will we be then than now?" Countries where manufacturing corporations prevailed, although outwardly prosperous and wealthy, were rife with the corruption of "millions of poor human beings degraded into the condition of mere servants of machinery." In your mind's eye, he urged the convention, consider the factory scene—"that hive of human beings . . . and the mournful sense of servitude legible on every limb." Contrast, furthermore, the plight of these dependent beings with the present advantages Oregonians enjoyed: "individual independence" in an "agricultural community" possessed of "domestic virtues." Echoing phrases from Jefferson's *Notes on Virginia*, he reminded the delegates that "in manufacturing countries power, political and otherwise, is in the hands of capitalists; there are many people dependent on them, and dependence begets servility. . . . I am not," Deady reiterated, "in favor of encouraging a fungous growth of improvement in this country."[126]

Reuben Boise followed Deady with an attack on corporations that was equally full of republican references to the vices of a manufacturing society. The responsibility of the convention, Boise argued, was not to legislate for private interests, "the increase of wealth or of internal improvements"; rather, "it is for the purpose of carrying forward the race itself," and anything (meaning corporations) that "decreases the moral and intellectual power of the community . . . is but a curse upon that community."[127] Witness the people of New England, he asserted. There, the people "had fallen from the ancient dignity which they once had. . . . [They] have degenerated in physical, moral, and intellectual force." But, he added, the degradation so evident in the present had not always been the case. It was not evident, for example, in "the days of the Revolution when the tea was thrown overboard into Boston harbor." The Founders of the republic "were of a different stamp from the effeminacy to which [New England has] now degenerated." Why, he asked, had "the old commonwealth . . . indeed fallen from her high estate"? The answer to Boise was self-evident: "These manufacturing establishments have been a curse to her population which has degenerated them. . . . She is conscious of becoming sunken and sickly, but her public men can not prevent it."[128] Drawing on the cyclical view of history prevalent among eighteenth-century republican writers—the idea that republics inevitably collapsed when simple agricultural ways were undermined by commerce—Boise pleaded for a constitution that would, as far as possible, put off the fate displayed in the history of New England:

These manufacturing establishments will perhaps at some future time in Oregon grow up to suck out the wealth of the country from the vitals of the people. They can then by little steps advance until they are lords and govern with an arbitrary rule. . . . Preventions are always said to be better than cures; and it is for this reason that I now wish that this constitution should be so framed that those evils will not be likely to result to us.[129]

The views of Deady and Boise, put to the test in the former's substitute motion, failed. Only thirteen—a quarter of those present—favored it. But defeat of Deady's unlimited-liability proposal did not end the discussion, and for two more days the debate continued before the delegates passed the limited-liability provision favored by McBride, Watkins, and other anti-Democrats. No uproar followed the final vote; in fact, both Deady and Boise, without comment, opted for the measure.[130] Nonetheless, the outcome was not an affirmation of McBride's and Watkins's vision of a vital place for corporations in the state. Rather, the argument that carried the Democratic ranks (and in which Deady and Boise acquiesced) was that of Grover and Williams. In their remarks to the convention, these Democrats took a position that, although espousing limited liability, followed a logic that drew on the republican fears of Deady and Boise as much as on the liberal corporate dreams of men like Watkins and McBride.

In contrast to their anticorporate colleagues, Grover and Williams held that incorporated enterprise offered advantages that Oregonians could not ignore. Their conviction, however, rested on a particular conception of the manufacturing corporation, one shaped by their personal experience in organizing the Salem mill. Throughout the debate their remarks were peppered with references to the groundbreaking for this manufactory and the benefits it would bring to the rural people it served in the Oregon Country. Deady's and Boise's desire to prohibit incorporation outright, they reasoned, was in error, for without local enterprises like the Willamette Woolen Mills Oregonians "would be compelled to import for years." "Removed from manufacturing states," Williams averred, "we must continue to pay a heavy yearly tax. We must pay tribute to Massachusetts and New England." To underscore the point, he referred the delegates to local experience:

> Only through corporate enterprise—organized under liberal provisions in the constitution, [can] those little farmers throughout the country . . . put their capital together, as they have in the case of the woolen factory now in this city. Then a man can put in $250, one $500, and another a $1,000, and the prospect is that there will be a fine and flourishing manufactory established in the territory of Oregon.[131]

Williams's image of the manufacturing corporation was of an association of "men of moderate means"—friends, relations, and fellow churchgoers whose reputations were well known in a face-to-face world, neighbors joined together to meet local needs and wants and thereby able to rescue their community from dependence on foreign capitalists. Regulations, Williams granted, were necessary to protect workers from unscrupulous operators. To this end he praised the stipulation in the committee report holding stockholders liable without limit for claims of working men and women; this provision, he argued, would properly protect laborers from "these soulless and irresponsible bodies called corporations."[132] Witness, he directed his fellow delegates, the plight of the mill workers of New England—"the young girl . . . [who] has no means of knowing what the operations of the company are . . . [and who] may be cheated out of . . . [her] honest dues."[133] Consider, he continued, who was hurt when a corporation failed: "Is it not more equitable that the corporators, the men who conducted that business and brought about that result and perhaps return rich upon their profits, whether they ought to suffer the loss or the honest laborer who has expended his health and strength and time in the corporation? Which would you choose? I put it upon the equities of the case." For Williams the equities were self-evident. "If it is known that every individual corporator is liable for the labor performed, they will see that the laborers are paid."[134]

Although Grover shared Williams's conception of the corporation as a provincial complement to Oregon's agricultural society, he disagreed with his fellow corporator's proposal to protect working men and women. To the contrary, Grover argued that those in need of constitutional protection were the farmers who invested in the corporations. "Foreign capital," Grover informed the convention, will "not come here to any considerable extent to enter into the operations of incorporated companies"; rather, the companies "would be carried on mainly by the capital in the country. Who had that capital? In most cases the farmers, who by their small earnings had accumulated a few thousands—more than they needed to stock their farms or for their daily use."[135] This, he reminded the delegates, was the case in the building of the Willamette Woolen Mill, and would likely be the case in other instances as well. Although willing to accept a liability provision that made "the stockholder liable for twice the amount of his stock . . . [thus] requiring twice the responsibility of corporations than was required of individuals," Grover warned against a measure that would be of such "crushing weight" that "no man would take stock in any corporation." Remember, he reiterated, it is the "farmers here [who] own all the dormant capital of the country, and . . . we must legislate for the protection of the farmers, so that they may feel confidence in coming forward and supplying the business men."[136]

As the debate wore on, Williams drew back from his call for stockholder liability for the claims of workingmen, as did Grover from his proposal to hold stockholders liable to double the amount of their stock. Convinced in part by the argument that the legislature could protect laborers with a mechanics' lien law, in part by the very force of their localistic conception of the manufacturing corporation, and perhaps most of all by a desire to bring the debate to a close, the Democratic majority finally passed the section (through an amendment offered by Democrat Frederick Waymire) with exactly the language anti-Democrats desired: "The Stockholders of all corporations, and joint stock companies, shall be liable for the indebtedness of said corporation to the amount of their stock subscribed, and unpaid, and no more."[137]

The resolution of the debate over stockholder liability was doubly ironic. Most simply, it was ironic that the Democratic majority—including those who upheld the anticorporation views of Deady and Boise—in the end accepted constitutional language that the anti-Democratic minority favored. Still, it did not follow that in accepting the language of their opponents, Oregon Democrats also accepted their historical vision. The meaning of the liability provision rested ultimately in the actions that followed from it. Doubling the irony back on itself, then, experience affirmed, if not the views of Deady and Boise, the provincial perspective of Grover and Williams, more than the cosmopolitanism of McBride and Watkins. The same can be said generally about the other articles of the Oregon constitution. Although much of the language was taken from other states, once taken, this language took on meanings peculiar to the charter society of Oregon, and those meanings persisted.

A tension between republican ideals and liberal convictions thus distinguished the Oregon constitution, and its authors as well. At the time, however, what struck observers was the document's Democratic (with a capital *D*) stamp. In the round of speeches that preceded final adjournment, both sides of the convention gave ample testimony to this view. Smith spoke for the Democrats, and Dryer for the opposition. Their remarks contained neither startling admissions nor serious reflections, for over the course of the convention nothing had changed. Smith's long peroration reviewed the constitution article by article, declaring that it conformed to the "genius of republicanism." He gave particular weight to the delegates' virtuous conduct in sending the slavery and free Negro questions to the voters. In doing so, he asserted (unaware of a dramatic shift about to take place in his own views), they had "vindicat[ed] before the nation, the excellency of that elementary principle of republican government which constitutes the distinguishing feature of the 'Kansas-Nebraska bill'—the affirmation that the people of the territories are capable of deciding that vexed question of slavery for themselves, and they can do it better than can the congress of the United States."[138]

Dryer followed Smith and, predictably, declared his intent to oppose the constitution at the polls on the grounds that it served only the corrupt ambition of Democratic placemen. "When we came here," he observed,

I supposed . . . that we were to adopt a constitution, not for a party, but under which we could exercise all the rights that are granted by the constitution of the United States. That no man was to be proscribed or crushed for opinions' sake; that he should entertain his own views, and have a fair, at least a liberal opportunity to express those views. . . . Sir, when I see gentlemen take upon themselves authority which their numerical strength alone gives them, to crush out liberty of speech and the right of thought, I am opposed to them and to their schemes. . . . Sir, we have been choked off.

And why had he and his colleagues in the opposition been choked off? The answer to Dryer was obvious and emblematic of the dangers the constitution posed: "There are a large number of gentlemen seeking office. . . . They desire a state government for office sake and that office controls them to some extent in relation to . . . other political matters." [139]

After Smith's and Dryer's speeches the delegates voted on the constitution, their endorsement of it following the same lines that, four weeks earlier, had seen Deady become president of the convention. Their business complete, Deady declared adjournment *sine die*. Without fanfare or celebration, the Oregon constitution writers hastened home. They left as they had come, confirmed by the very experience of constitution writing in the views they had carried to Salem. These views would have remarkable staying power, despite the crisis of political faith that soon followed in the isolated and already ingrown Oregon Country.

SIX

Between Golden and Gilded Ages: Nevada, 1864

The 1864 constitutional convention in Nevada was as different as could be from the meeting that took place seven years earlier in Oregon. In the latter territory, statehood originated in the desire of political men to settle local disputes and insulate themselves from national solutions to the sectional crisis. Its constitution writers proceeded ritualistically, re-playing for the most part political customs ingrained in a parochial political culture. In Nevada, to the contrary, statehood came in the midst of the Civil War and an economic crisis in the mines that made the recent dreams of speculating individuals seem illusory. This territory's constitutional convention was, for all intents and purposes, a product of plots hatched in Washington, D.C.—plots fully apparent to the assembled delegates.

On the first full day of convention business, delegate E. F. Dunne turned his colleagues' attention to the fact that they had been called together not by their constituents but rather by Republican strategists in Congress and the White House. More to the point, he argued, the current economic depression in the territory made statehood a mistake. "Under the circumstances," he moved, "we deem it our duty to return to our constituents, leaving to them the right to call a Convention for the formation of their State Constitution, whenever they shall deem it advisable for their own interests to do so."[1] The times, he insisted, were simply not right to make a state, given the depression—economic and emotional—that stretched across the territory. If, as the doomsayers claimed, the mines were indeed depleted, the territorial population would soon wither away. At the very least the making of a new state was imprudent, no matter how urgent the national cause. The delegates would be well advised to end the charade.

Dunne's resolution failed, both on the first day of the convention and a week later when he raised it again.[2] Ironically, it failed for the very reasons that its author identified as cause for adjourning: pressure from Washington, D.C., and the depression within the territory. To Nevadans the Civil War—more broadly, the mission of a continental Union—required that they create a state to further the policies of the Lincoln administration. Even though a majority of the convention delegates had not voted for Lincoln in 1860, by 1864 they were (with a single exception) all administration men, committed to writing a constitution that would provide electoral support for the wartime leadership and a model for amendments to the federal Constitution.[3] As Benjamin Mason put it, in becoming a delegate "I enlisted for the war, and I am for fighting it through. . . . I have been opposed to adopting a State Government on a previous occasion, upon principle, because of our poverty, and because of our isolated position; but, sir, it is at this time a Federal call. [Good!] It has come to us from Washington—an appeal to our patriotism, an appeal to the loyalty of our hearts, and I responded to that appeal."[4] Complementing this view of constitution writing as wartime service in the delegates' minds was the view that statehood was necessary to revitalizing the mining economy and ending the "dull times" that burdened the territory. In a unanimous chorus local newspapers had pressed this argument throughout the spring and early summer of 1864, emphasizing in particular the need for new tax and judicial systems. In the convention, the delegate J. G. McClinton expressed the sentiment well, declaring:

> I am tired of this rat-trap of a Territorial Government, sir. I want a government of a more substantial character—one which will encourage the development of our rich mines and all our resources. I want to see the numerous valuable mines which are now locked up by litigation, unlocked, and developed as they should be, in order that their hidden stores of wealth may be brought forth and cast upon the commerce of the world. I want to see the two thousand men now idle in Storey County . . . and scarcely possessing the wherewithal to obtain a living, once more in constant employment, and to accomplish that end I desire to see the Judiciary so reformed that the numerous cases now in litigation may be promptly disposed of and the mining claims unlocked, and allowed to be developed. Then those strong men, now idle, can be put to work in the mines, earning their four dollars a day, and so obtaining an honest and honorable livelihood.[5]

In different ways, these two considerations—taken by Dunne as disqualifying the convention from legitimately carrying out its task, and by other delegates as the very grounds of its business—shaped the work of the Nevada constitution writers from beginning to end. This fact is evident in two contrasts between their meeting and those in California and Oregon. First was the predominance of narrow economic concerns at the Nevada convention. The language of personal and class interests pervaded those debates, highlighting the importance Nevadans gave to the proposition that the first responsibility of fundamental law was to shape the economic environment. Questions of national versus state sovereignty similarly marked their discussions, and as volunteers in a war against "disloyalty" the constitution writers spun out the broader implications of the Civil War. Allegiance to the Union, as matters turned out, had no small effect on the way the delegates linked economic interest to the writing of fundamental law.

This linking was most obvious in their discussion of the Pacific railroad, which they addressed through a proposal to subsidize the Central Pacific line then under construction from Sacramento to the Great Basin. But it intruded into other questions as well. As these two concerns—self-interest as inseparable from the common good and loyalty to the Union—intermixed, the Nevadans, without fully realizing it, were carried to the logical conclusion of their liberal views. Veterans of the California gold rush, they had carried to Nevada an individualist producer ethic. But, first in California and then in Nevada, they had witnessed the unraveling of this vision toward a corporate capitalist conclusion. In writing a state constitution they confronted the counterclaims of individualist and corporate convictions and took stands that pointed unmistakably toward a future at odds with what had drawn them to Nevada in the first place.

THE OLD CALIFORNIANS

The centrality of economic questions to constitution writing in Nevada was not surprising at the time, nor is it in hindsight, for in the 1860s the territory was a colony of California—a "fragment society" of gold rush veterans. Underlining the Nevadans' knowledge and memory of the gold rush mining frontier of 1849–1852 was the presence in this convention of a number of older men: twenty-four were over thirty-five years of age, and of these thirteen were over forty and four over fifty.[6] Of the thirty-five delegates, all but two had moved to Nevada from California. Two-thirds (twenty-two) of them had migrated to the Pacific Coast during the gold rush years. Ten had arrived with the first wave of miners in 1849, and sixteen more before the middle of the 1850s. Numerically preponderant were twenty-six men (three-quarters of the delegation) who had been born in the northeast; for seventeen of them, migrating to gold rush California had been a first departure from their place of birth. Fifteen delegates went to the Pacific Coast overland; the rest arrived by sea during the early 1850s. When they first came to California most had worked, if only briefly, in the placer fields; others had mined the miners as merchants. Their status as veterans of the gold rush was underscored by the fact that most had remained involved in mining after the early stages of industrial ("deep rock") mining replaced placer mining in the mid-1850s, moving into associated occupations—mining engineer or superintendent, for example. Others, such as lawyers, became pioneer practitioners of the increasingly complex mining law that accompanied the transformation of gold rush California.

The migration of these Californians to Nevada correlated directly with the early "wildcat" phase of the Comstock Lode mining economy. Only two of the delegates had settled in Nevada before the discovery of 1859; of the remaining thirty-three, twenty-two had arrived during the three-year rush that followed 1859, and the rest during the remarkable (though now feared by many to be illusory) speculative boom of 1863 and early 1864. To Nevada they carried memories of the early days of mining and the experience of having had to remake themselves "after the gold rush." Twelve—mine superintendents, engineers, mechanics, surveyors, or managers—were involved directly in mining as an industry. Eleven others worked the Comstock courtrooms, where disputants in the early 1860s fought over possession of feet and inches of the ledge. Seven others operated businesses that serviced the mining economy, lumber companies, merchant houses, and banks. As a reflection of the terrain and its unsuitability to farming, only two of the delegates called themselves "agriculturists": one operated a small truck farm in one of Nevada's few oases; the other owned a ranch. Two newspaper editors and a Virginia City physician rounded out the delegate ranks.

The predominance of mining-related occupations in this convention was key, in yet another way, to the distinction between the Nevadans and the California and Oregon constitution writers. For example, although lawyers had been a notable presence in the Oregon convention, their Nevada counterparts were lawyers of a different kind: law was their primary occupation. They were in this regard "professionals," in that their practice was not but one of a variety of occupations followed as opportunity waxed and waned; rather, it was the focus for most, if not all, of their working lives. To a lesser degree, the same was true for the merchants, mechanics, mine superintendents, and mill owners: they were workers in an increasingly capital-intensive economy, and their occupations required specialized training and experience. As a result, the Nevadans were more apt than their California and Oregon counterparts to see their lives through the prism of a precise economic interest.

At the outset, the Nevadans viewed the task before them narrowly, concerned with affirming loyalty to the Union and constructing a charter that would help resolve the economic crisis. Also contributing to their narrow view was the fact that, even more so than in California and Oregon, the Nevada constitution writers had a constitutional model ready at hand. By common consent they began with the charter defeated the prior winter, having agreed to limit their work to repairing those provisions that had led to its repudiation. Identifying what needed attention seemed, at least in the beginning, to involve only two or three matters: the taxation of the mines, reform of the judiciary, and an ironclad barrier to disloyalty. Success or failure, from this perspective, required changes to the earlier charter only in order to promote recovery of the mining economy and, in turn, root out disloyal elements in the territory.

And yet, contrary to the constitution writers' initial sense of ease, experience quickly proved otherwise. The narrow focus with which they began could not be maintained. The delegates knew one another well (or so they thought), for ten had participated in the prior season's convention and almost everyone carried to Carson City a reputation based on their opposition to statehood in the first campaign. In the aftermath of the spring depression, however, the conflicting reasons behind their earlier opposition to statehood, glossed over because of their common antipathy to William Stewart, could no longer be put aside. In July, as opposed to January, there was no longer a basis for an alliance between pro– and anti–mining tax men. Furthermore, the unalloyed danger of "foreign capitalists" and San Francisco financiers, so powerful a political force the winter before, had lost its salience. The depression complicated in a fundamental way the nature of the interests at stake in constitution writing, forcing the delegates to sort out, and in some cases discover anew, the interests they represented.

In this context, one could not say where different men stood at the outset, how the convention would divide on the questions before it, or who would play the pivotal roles. Over the course of the proceedings different men affected the pace and direction of the debates, but in the end four stood out: John Anderson Collins, Thomas Fitch, Charles De Long, and the convention's president, John Neely Johnson.[7] All had brought to Nevada reputations etched in California. Two, Collins and Johnson, had served in the prior convention, while Fitch and De Long were recent arrivals who had come to local attention during the winter campaign against statehood. Three of the four—Collins, Fitch, and De Long—resided in Virginia City and represented Storey County. They were not, however, of one mind as to how to repair the defeated constitution, in particular its tax provision. The diminutive De Long, a veteran California mining lawyer and politician known as "California's Bantam Cock," had been a major critic of the 1863 constitution; he opposed its provision on taxing the mines and could not buy the "Stewart construction." Nevada's prospects, he believed, were inseparable from the prosperity of its large mines. Johnson, in contrast, represented a very different view. He was committed to the tax measure in the defeated constitution and, more generally, to the necessity of taxing the mines on the grounds of equity to those who did not engage in mining directly.

Fitch and Collins carried to Carson City still different perspectives, though their position was closer to Johnson's than that of their Storey County colleague. Collins, a Virginia City hotel operator and small-time speculator, and Fitch, a lawyer and newspaper editor in Virginia City, identified their primary constituency as the "little interests" of the mining counties: merchants, small mine owners, and, at least in the case of Collins, laborers, whose relationship with the mining corporation the winter campaign over statehood had shown to be tense and problematic. Collins had served in the prior convention, and he supported the mining tax provision. Fitch, who had been a leading editorial opponent of William Stewart and the first constitution, had a more complicated agenda. Recently arrived from California, where he had gained equal measures of admiration and dislike as a tireless publicist for the Republican party, he brought to Nevada a close relationship with the California party's founding figures, above all former governor Leland Stanford and his Republican business associates, Mark Hopkins and Charles Crocker. In this regard Fitch was allegiant not merely to a Republican vision of the Union, but to one influenced by the wartime enterprise of his Republican friends in California: the Central Pacific Railroad, the building of which had just begun in the summer of 1864.

Together, these four men displayed the range of perspectives that the constitution writers carried to Carson City. Within the convention, they were at the center of the shifting alignments that shaped the writing of the Nevada charter. Although on the question of loyalty to the Lincoln administration they were of one mind, their political backgrounds were diverse. Johnson, born and raised a Whig, had played (to his misfortune) a key role in the California Know-Nothing movement in the mid-1850s and then moved into Republican ranks. Collins in his youth had been a radical abolitionist and utopian socialist. After migrating to California he had become a Whig and then, in 1860, a Republican. Fitch—among the youngest of all the far western constitution writers—had embraced Republicanism upon reaching adulthood. De Long was a self-styled Jacksonian who from the mid-1850s had figured prominently in the Douglas wing of the California party. With the outbreak of the Civil War he had moved into Union organization, and at the time of the convention was on the brink of becoming a Republican. But over and above the four men's basic Union-Republican affiliation and dedication to the Lincoln administration, their individual perspectives toward the dilemma that bedeviled the convention—the proper place of the individual vis-à-vis the corporate producer in society and economy—differed significantly. On this latter point these leading men, and like them the constitution writers as a whole, found little guidance in the Union doctrines of the Civil War years.

⚜

Eldest of these four leading men was fifty-year-old John Anderson Collins. At first glance (and for that matter second and third), the very presence of Collins in Nevada is surprising. The migration of this native northeasterner to California in 1849 had shocked his old friends, for his departure had marked a dramatic shift in his life. Born in Vermont in 1810, Collins had grown up in a Calvinist household that had more in common with eighteenth-century Puritanism than nineteenth-century capitalism. In his mid-twenties he entered Middlebury College, leaving before graduation to enroll in Andover Seminary to become a Congregational minister. "A man of tremendous energy" in whose presence "nothing could stagnate," Collins, while a seminary student in the late 1830s, was drawn to the abolitionist movement of William Lloyd Garrison.[8] His interest in Garrisonian immediatism, significantly, came at the same time that the New England Protestant establishment—among them the faculty at Andover—was organizing to deny Garrison a following. Incensed by the abolitionist's critique of them as acquiescent to (and thereby co-conspirators in) slavery, New England's churchmen closed their meeting houses to Garrison and his co-workers, attacked the prominence of women in his movement, and generally damned him for espousing doctrines that led "inevitably to disorganization and anarchy."[9]

In the midst of the controversy, Collins left Andover, joined Garrison, and uncovered to him the so-called clerical plot against his cause. Soon Collins gained a place in Garrison's inner circle. In 1839, he was chosen secretary of the annual meeting of the Massachusetts Anti-Slavery Society, and a year later became its general agent as well as editor and chief writer for the *Monthly Garland*. Impressed by Collins's success as a fundraiser in New England, Garrison sent him to England in 1841, recommending him to British allies as a man of "zeal, energy, tact, and indomitable perseverance."[10] All the descriptors were correct except tact, the absence of which English abolitionists found his most striking trait. Self-righteous and condescending, Collins lectured English abolitionists about perfectionism and the various sins of the Christian clergy, destroying in the process whatever effect he might otherwise have had. In the end Garrison was forced to recall him, indeed, to send money to pay his passage home.[11]

This trip to England, although a failure for the cause of abolition, marked another turning in Collins's life. While in England he saw for himself the working-class squalor of the industrial revolution. Shocked, he went to Chartist meetings and met Robert Owen, under whose spell he fell. Having left the United States a dedicated Garrisonian perfectionist, he returned a confirmed environmentalist and socialist, convinced by observation and his talks with Owen that slavery was but a symptom of larger evils. Although Collins remained in Garrison's movement for two more years, his energies now turned to building an American socialist movement. As Edmund Quincy informed Garrison, on the "'Property Question' . . . Collins is horsed just at present, and galloping away at a great rate." [12] Slavery had become for him but an aspect of a degrading profit system. "Upon deeper investigation," Collins wrote as he moved away from abolitionism, "we find that war, slavery, and intemperance, are but the effect of some cause lying further back. . . . May not then this question of the admitted right of individual ownership in the soil and its products be the great cause of all causes, which makes men practically an enemy to his species?" [13]

After his return from England, Collins turned the abolition meetings he organized into socialist gatherings. This led Garrison privately to despair; in the spring of 1843 he wrote: "Of his benevolent desire to aid and bless our suffering race I have no doubt, but I do not think his judgement so sufficiently solid, or his moral perceptions sufficiently clear, or his System of moral philosophy sufficiently christian, to render him a safe and successful leader." [14] Garrison, who in the mid-1830s had been drawn to "anti-governmentalism" himself, was no longer sympathetic. Collins, he confided with worry,

> seems to be an earnest convert to Robert Owen's absurd and dangerous dogma, that men are "the creatures of circumstances"—not sinful, but unfortunate—not inwardly corrupt, but outwardly trammelled—and that it is by association alone, in a distinctive community formed on the basis of equal rights and equal property, that the regeneration of the world is to be effected. His theory is, that it is as wrong, for principle, for one man to claim absolute ownership to his hat or his coat, as it is for another to claim a human being as his property. For human beings to buy and sell to and of each other, even on terms of exact reciprocity, he regards as wrong, and contends that every body should help himself, according to his necessities (he being the sole judge), wherever the means of subsistence and comfort exist. [15]

Garrison went on to predict, correctly (and with evident relief), that Collins would soon leave the antislavery movement to pursue his newfound socialist dream. And so he did. In the fall of 1843 Collins purchased (the source of his funds is not known) 350 acres near Skaneateles in upstate New York and there set up a socialist community. [16] Called Community Place, the experiment was part of what Arthur Bestor has called the "Owenite excitement" of the 1840s. [17] An odd mixture of socialism, anarchism, and perfectionism, its "Articles of Belief and Disbelief" emphasized the negative: a denial of direct revelation from God to man; a rejection of organized religion and the professional clergy, the

Bible, and miracles; a disbelief in the necessity of government; and a disavowal of property. Affirming only cold water and vegetarianism, Collins became known as "No-God, No-Government, No-Money, No-Meat, No–Salt and Pepper Collins."[18]

Contrary to expectation, Community Place struggled from the start. Because of dissension within the ranks of his fellow communitarians, Collins was forced, before a year had passed, to disavow the original charter and replace it with a credo "as broad as the universe, and as liberal as the elements that surround us. They forbid the adoption and maintenance of any creed, constitution, rules of faith, declarations of belief, touching on any or all subjects in which we estimate the man by his acts rather than by his peculiar belief. We say to him, 'Believe what you may, but act as well as you can.'"[19] Revising the settlement's cardinal rules, however, did little to remedy the conflicts that dogged Community Place. "The undirected goodness of men," learned a surprised Collins, led not to unanimity but to division and rancor.[20] The experiment, he lamented, was beset by "impostors and rogues," each of whom "seemed to be setting an example, and trying to bring others to it." Anarchy in practice, he concluded, was an invitation to free loaders and snipers. By 1846—two short years after the founding of his utopia—he had lost his faith. His perfectionist and socialist will broken, he reasoned that Community Place was "too heavily charged with an unpracticable, inexperienced, self sufficient, gaseous class of mind."[21] Cutting his losses, he sold his interest and left.

Shortly afterward, Collins's life took yet another turn, one more dramatic and unexpected than his movement from Garrisonian perfectionism to Owenite socialism. Through his experience at Community Place Collins concluded that socialist principles had been proved "false in theory and pernicious in their practical tendencies." They might have worked, he observed wryly, "if men were angels, and angels Gods; but human nature is too low, too selfish, and too ignorant for relations so exalted."[22] In a 180-degree turn, he proceeded to embrace the individual pursuit of self-interest as inevitable (if not, precisely put, perfect) and set out to "make as much money as possible." The quest for lucre, in 1849, carried him to California with the first wave of gold seekers. Shocked by his metamorphoses, those he left behind observed with dismay that he had become a "brazen-faced businessman" who denied "his earlier and better life."[23]

With the exception of seven years' residence in Nevada, California remained Collins's home to his death in 1890. Although he never realized the fortune or fame he sought there, during his forty years on the Pacific Coast he remained at the fringes of public life, in ways that highlighted both his departure from the zealous perfectionism of his early years and the persistence of these youthful passions. During the 1850s Collins speculated in mining in San Francisco property, engaged in a variety of mercantile endeavors, read the law, and joined the bar. According to scattered reports, he made and lost a number of fortunes and gained for himself a reputation as an unlucky if not completely scrupulous promoter.[24] In addition, "No-Government" Collins became in California a political partisan. For a time he edited a Whig newspaper; in the 1850s he served as a stump speaker for that party; he even sought, without success, election to the state legislature.

With the same self-importance that had marked his abolitionist and utopian past, he explained his electoral defeats as the consequence of orchestrated Democratic movements against him: "The Locos not only of this county but of the state," he wrote to a friend during his first legislative canvass, "are determined to defeat my election. Dr. Gwinn [*sic*] did what he could in this county. [Future governor] John B. Weller *et id omne genus* have done the same."[25] Of equal significance to his defeat was a widespread suspicion about his abolitionist past, harbored by Whigs as well as Democrats. These suspicions Collins and his friends went out of their way to answer. Against the charge that he was still an abolitionist, the *San Francisco Evening Press* insisted that "long ago Mr. Collins made a public recantation of the opinions to which [his critics] alluded."[26] Privately, Collins implored friends to spread the word that he had no current sympathy for abolition. "You know," he wrote with reference to a speech he had given in San Francisco,

> that all the southern men present—all the audience who heard me were satisfied in relation to my position. That has been my position since 1843. . . . I wish you would write on the subject to Judge Buckner and Col. Anderson of Nevada City. They both desire to vote for me but the statement of my being an abolitionist and that I have acknowledged that I was have been made with such assurance that they do not know what to think upon the subject.[27]

Although Collins's political forays failed, he survived as a mining entrepreneur, won a prize (from the New York City Mechanics Institute) for a quartz mill he designed, and gained a certain renown in the mining region near Nevada City and Grass Valley.[28] When news of the Comstock Lode strike reached California in 1859, he set out across the Sierra Nevada with the first wave of Californians. There, from 1859 to 1864, he engaged in an array of small enterprises: he practiced law, invested in silver mines, organized the Virginia City stock exchange, and operated a hotel–gambling hall (the "Collins House"). In between he dedicated himself to the cause of frontier education—a faint echo of his old reformer self, although an echo without much effect in this virtually childless territory.[29] In addition, in Washoe Collins did manage to claim a measure of the political prominence denied him in California. In 1862, the voters of Storey County elected him superintendent of the nonexistent schools, and the next year—largely on the strength of his visibility as a mining entrepreneur, popular hotel-saloon operator, and colonel in the territorial militia—he was elected a delegate to the first constitutional convention.

Although a friend nominated Collins for president of the convention, the delegates chose John North. Shortly thereafter, Collins took ill and left Carson City. In the statehood campaign, however, he left his Virginia City sickbed to fight William Stewart and the constitution, and six months later, in the second election of constitutional convention delegates, he was among the top vote-getters in Storey County and, according to press reports, the likely choice for convention president.[30] When the delegates assembled, however, Collins withdrew (without explanation) from consideration, deferring to former California governor J. Neely Johnson. Even so, "Colonel" Collins was expected by onlookers to be a central figure in constitution writing. No longer tainted by abolitionism, he was known to his colleagues and constituents as a gold rush entrepreneur, political operative, militia officer, outspoken Unionist, and, through his speeches against Stewart the winter before, champion of the small "wildcat" miner. The months since that campaign, however, had brought significant changes to the political as well as economic environment of Nevada. Just how Collins would respond, just what lessons he had learned from the local depression and Civil War, would be known only after the convention adjourned.

J. Neely Johnson, the man to whom John Collins deferred in the election of convention president, brought to Carson City a past that, although not marked by the vagaries of Collins's life, also moved along unexpected lines. Born in 1825 into the family of a prominent Indiana Whig (his father was an intimate of William Henry Harrison), Johnson, like so many antebellum youths, came to politics as a family inheritance.[31] When the panic of 1837 ruled out the college education planned for him, instead he was apprenticed to a printer. Before his training was complete, however, his father found him a place with an Evansville attorney, with whom he read the law. Soon after finishing there, he left Indiana for Iowa, where he first worked in a merchant house and then joined the bar and practiced law. Three years later, news of the California gold discovery arrived, and he left behind the settled prospects of a small-town lawyer for the dazzling promise of the gold fields. Arriving with the first forty-niners, Johnson tried his hand at placer mining only for a time; within two months, he returned to the law, opening a practice in Sacramento.

There Johnson's political ambitions became immediately apparent. In the first election after his arrival he ran, as a Whig, for city attorney of Sacramento and won. Over the next five years, despite the Democratic predominance in California politics, he became ever more prominent. After his Sacramento victory, he gained the imprimatur of the national Whig party with a patronage appointment from President Fillmore (as special agent to conduct the California census). That year and the next he joined with others in organizing California Whigs and played a prominent role in the party's state conventions. In 1853, Sacramentans elected him to the state legislature. Although the following year he tried unsuccessfully to gain a state office (attorney general), in 1855 his ambition was realized when, just short of thirty years of age, he won a two-year term as governor of the state of California.[32]

Born and raised a Whig, Johnson claimed the governorship as an "American," or "Know-Nothing." The California version of this movement had little in common with its namesake elsewhere. California Know-Nothings, with Johnson in the lead, downplayed nativism in favor of attacks on the corruption of the state Democratic party, particularly its southern wing led by the indomitable William Gwin. Also contrasting with Know-Nothings elsewhere, the party in California proved, if briefly, a political success: not only did Johnson defeat his Democratic opponent handily, but he took office with a Know-Nothing majority in the legislative assembly as well.[33]

Shortly after Johnson's inauguration, however, political disaster struck. In the spring of 1856 San Francisco was engulfed by a vigilance committee, eventually six thousand strong, that mobilized in response to the killing of U.S. Marshall William Richardson and a sensationalist newspaper editor, James King "of William."[34] With force of arms, three thousand vigilantes seized the two men's assailants—Charles Cora and James P. Casey—from the city jail. Shortly after the (appropriately) dramatic burial of King, the killers' hanged bodies were put on display at the committee's headquarters. The vigilance movement then took on a life of its own, commanding the city for months and defying every challenge raised against its ad hoc rule. According to adherents, it represented the spontaneous organization of citizens committed to the eradication of crime, vice, and corruption.

As recent scholars have shown, however, the committee's middle-class merchant leadership, and much of its rank and file, consisted of prominent Whigs and Know-Nothings. The sources of vice and corruption they targeted, moreover, were disproportionately Democratic, in particular Irish-Democratic: ward leaders who ruled the workingmen's sections of the city.[35] Johnson, as governor, had to take a stand toward the extralegal movement, one dominated by men who had supported his election yet defied the constituted authorities in the interest of a self-defined "higher good." As such, Johnson faced a no-win situation: he could either repudiate a movement composed of his political allies (and thereby accede to their repudiation of his authority) or, alternatively, denounce the movement and alienate his base of support in the gold rush metropolis.[36]

Johnson took the latter course and paid the consequences. When the vigilance committee first organized, he tried to negotiate with its leaders, offering, in return for their laying down arms, his personal guarantee that their immediate objective—the execution of Richardson's and King's murderers—be carried out quickly.[37] The deal fell through, however, and Johnson ordered the major-general of the city's militia, a prominent young banker, William Tecumseh Sherman, to call up his forces. Johnson declared San Francisco in a state of insurrection and ordered the imposition of martial law. Then things fell apart. General Wool, the commander of the federal armory who had promised Johnson that he would arm the militia as soon as the governor declared martial law, backpedaled and announced that he had no authority to act. Sherman, although opposed to the vigilante movement and supportive of Johnson, was beset by desertions to the vigilantes, lack of arms for those men who remained, and pressure from merchant vigilantes to desist or face a run on his bank. In a public broadside, he resigned his post.[38] Governor Johnson, isolated and abandoned, had no alternative but to acquiesce to the rule of the vigilance committee. As Sherman put it, "When . . . this storm burst upon him his old friends left him. . . . He is now powerless; for the militia, his reliance to coerce obedience to his orders, have deserted him in mass, leaving him [in] the naked, unsupported position of governor."[39] For the next six months, the committee governed the city according to its own reckoning, disbanding only after it had hanged four alleged criminals, banished thirty others, and ordered, on its own authority, new elections, which it then oversaw and, through hand-picked candidates, dominated.[40]

Johnson's futile confrontation with the San Francisco vigilance committee ended his political career in California. The uproar in San Francisco did not subside until the very end of his term, and Johnson's inability to master the situation—his impotence, essentially, in the face of the anti-Democratic seizure of power—made him a pathetic figure, a hapless lame duck. Before his term was out, he had to endure the impeachment of two members of his administration. By the time his governorship ended in early 1858, both he and the Know-Nothing cause had lost any semblance of authority. Johnson left politics and went into self-imposed exile in Trinity County. There he turned his attention to quartz mining, speculating heavily and unsuccessfully in various mining schemes. When news of the Comstock Lode crossed the mountains, nothing remained to keep him in California, and with thousands of others he set out to remake himself once again.

For Johnson, as for other "old Californians" of the gold rush, the prospect of personal renewal held out by the Nevada strike was irresist-

ible, and indeed, in Nevada he found success both economically and politically. There he chanced upon a "jackpot," not in a mine, but in the
person of Sandy Bowers, one of the early Comstock era's legendary, if
comical, figures, who by virtue of being at the right spot at the right time
came into possession of a rich section of the Comstock Lode. Johnson
met Bowers in Carson City and became his attorney. When nabob
Bowers left with his wife on an extended tour of Europe, Johnson took
over the management of their fortune. From the fees he assessed, as well
as his own stock investments, he acquired a modest fortune in his own
right, and on the strength of his new wealth, along with old associations
reaffirmed with the passage of time, Johnson turned his attention to
politics once again. Now a Republican, he joined in organizing the territorial Union party. Furthermore, he made ample use of his newfound
fortune, spreading it around to the end of helping the old Californians
in Nevada forget his streak of bad political luck in the 1850s.[41] By 1861,
Johnson's ignominy as Know-Nothing governor was largely forgotten.
His wealth, and no less the unity encouraged by the Civil War, transformed him into a senior statesman known respectfully, not sarcastically,
as "Governor" Johnson.

In 1863 the voters of Ormsby County elected Johnson as their delegate to the territory's first constitutional convention. There he was a firm
ally of John North and others who argued successfully in favor of a taxation article that treated mining claims as no different from any other
kind of property. In the first statehood election, Johnson, although like
North in favor of the constitution, joined the movement against the
"Stewart construction" of it. Six months later, when the second convention was called, no one questioned that Johnson would again serve. Described as "the truly representative man of what has in common parlance
been termed the 'cow counties,'" he went to the convention at the head
of a delegation elected without opposition.[42] Then, in the opening moments of the convention, he was chosen unanimously as presiding officer—a suggestive selection, in that he represented a nonmining county
and brought to the convention a well-known reputation as an advocate
of the nonmining interest in the territory. That he would in 1864, as he
had the previous year, advocate a mining tax, no one questioned. In this
regard, his selection as president of the convention testified to his new,
reborn stature as a Republican statesman and firm Union man. But just
as important, it showed, at the beginning of the convention, that positions on the tax question remained in much the same half-formed condition as the statehood election of the previous winter had left them.

There is a great misconception of the character of the Infinite, exhibited in
the familiar and often quoted saying, that "some men are born great, some

achieve greatness, and some have greatness thrust upon them." Men never achieve greatness who are not born great, and if fame be thrust upon a man of common nature, he contradicts the proverb, by being unequal to the occasion. Circumstances, accident, or industry, never made a great man. They often develop latent genius, but God Almighty enjoys a monopoly of the creation.[43]

In early 1862, the twenty-four-year-old editor of the *Placerville Republican*, Thomas Fitch, Jr., wrote these words as a tribute to the recently martyred Edward Dickinson Baker—Union Army colonel, Oregon Senator, Lincoln intimate. Although his ostensible subject was Baker, Fitch's sentiments as likely as not expressed a subconscious sense of his own destiny as well. At the time he wrote this passage, Fitch was widely known in California and Nevada as a man of great energy, strong will, and limitless ambition. For him, service in the Nevada constitutional convention was but a means to the larger end of national greatness.

Fitch stood out from among the delegates to the Nevada convention in many ways. A recent immigrant to the Pacific Coast, he was the second youngest man in attendance and one of a handful who were not veterans of the California gold rush. He had arrived in California from Wisconsin four years before, in 1860, for expressly political purposes. Born in New York City in 1838 to a merchant family, Fitch had left his parents' home at the age of sixteen, embarking on a transcontinental odyssey that continued long past 1864—indeed, into the twentieth century. Before he appeared in the Far West he had lived briefly in Chicago, Milwaukee, and St. Joseph, Missouri. In Chicago and Milwaukee he had worked as a clerk in merchant houses, and in St. Joseph he had operated his own exchange. According to his own testimony, however, the most important experience he gained in these early years was not in business but in a brief stint as a political writer for the *Milwaukee Free Democrat*. In the spring of 1860, the paper had sent him to the Republican national convention in Chicago as its special correspondent. There, he later recalled, sitting "only a few feet from . . . the white-haired abolition leader, Joshua R. Giddings," he took in the scenes and was converted to the Republican cause of Lincoln and, more generally, what became Fitch's lifelong calling: politics. Without a backward glance he set off at the close of the convention for California, and in Panama took passage on a ship that also carried that state's delegation home. "Political discussion ran high" during the voyage to San Francisco, Fitch recalled:

A glasseyed [*sic*] and wooden-legged schoolmaster en route for Oregon challenged me to discuss the political issues of the day. I probably knew as little about them as he did, but I accepted his challenge and made my first public speech on the forward deck of the steamer. One of my auditors chanced to be a member of the [California] state central committee of his party, and after we reached San Francisco the gentleman arranged a meeting at Platt's Hall, which I accepted his invitation to address.[44]

Fitch's San Francisco speech—his political inaugural—was a success, although, he admitted, his comments were "more pungent than parliamentary."[45] On the basis of it the central committee of the state Republican party recruited him to speak for Lincoln and other Republican candidates in the 1860 election, sending him to the northern regions of the state. That September and October he traveled almost two thousand miles and, by his own count, delivered speeches in more than sixty towns and hamlets.[46] Promoting what contemporaries called "straight-out republicanism," he was conciliatory toward Democrats but otherwise close to the radical edges of antebellum Republicanism. To free-soil Douglas men he extended a sympathetic hand, recognizing the dilemma they faced in abandoning the "old organization." "But," he went on, "the thing itself [is] not today what it was in the days of Jefferson, Madison, and Jackson. Then it was a vigorous mailed warrior; now it [is] a feeble, decrepit old man, with a black browed, blood stained harlot, whose name [is] 'slavery,' by his side." Lincoln and his Republican supporters, Fitch advised wavering Democrats, differed little on the essential points from Douglas and Bell: all favored popular sovereignty. As such, Fitch argued, the young, vigorous Republican party had become the appropriate home for the range of northern opinion, from those who believed slavery a crime against humanity, through those who found it simply inexpedient or opposed it as interfering with white labor, to those who cared nothing at all about it. This said, Fitch personally did not shy away from appealing as well to those with more radical egalitarian sympathies: "Men could not help feeling a sympathy," he argued along the campaign trail, "with freedom, and right, and justice everywhere [applause]. All systems of ethics were punctuated with the idea of a millennium—the idea that at some time or other slavery, injustice and oppression would perish from the earth."[47]

Traveling through the northern mining towns in the late summer of 1860, Fitch discovered his power to sway men, gaining a "reputation for eloquence unsurpassed by any public speaker in the state." (After emigrating to Nevada he was known as the "Silver-tongued Orator.") Above all—and despite being a "recent comer among us"—he became a friend of the youthful organizers of the California Republican movement. To them and their interests he remained tied through the 1860s.[48]

Fitch's service to the party as editor and speaker in 1860 quickly paid dividends. After Lincoln's narrow victory in California (for which Fitch immodestly claimed more than a little credit) he edited in quick succession Republican papers in San Francisco (the *Daily Evening Gazette* and *Times*) and Placerville (the *Republican*), broadcasting his name and talents across northern California. These were followed by an even more important opportunity sent his way by another Republican spellbinder (and friend of Lincoln), Edward Dickinson Baker. Although Baker departed California before the 1860 election, on the basis of his recommendation President Lincoln appointed Fitch to a profitable and influential position: cashier (manager) of the San Francisco mint. Fitch held the post for only a few weeks, but in that time he proved his partisan mettle: he removed all Democrats from positions in the mint and replaced them with loyal Republicans (who, according to Democratic reports, repaid him with bribes).[49]

Fitch's ambition, however, was not bureaucratic; he resigned from the mint to take on another political assignment from the central committee of the California Republican party: the election of Leland Stanford as governor.[50] In the summer and fall of 1861 he once again set off on an extended campaign tour. When Stanford won and Republicans (now Unionists) took the state legislature, Fitch's capital in the party grew all the more. Shortly after the election, his patron Baker reappeared in San Francisco with a commission to raise a regiment of Union volunteers. Fitch enlisted with a brevet appointment as major and followed Baker east. He thereafter wore the title Major Fitch proudly, even though his wartime service was short-lived. For upon his arrival in Washington, D.C., Fitch learned of Baker's recent death at the Battle of Ball's Bluff; he immediately resigned his commission to escort the body back to California and a martyr's burial.[51]

Fitch returned to California sanctified by his proximity to, if not participation in, combat. Now twenty-four, "Major" Fitch became a noted figure in the ranks of the Union's defenders in California. Despite the fact that he had no permanent residence in the state (between his arrival in 1859 and 1862 he had edited newspapers in San Francisco and Placerville but otherwise spent his time campaigning on the road), in 1862 he was sent, on a fusion Republican–Douglas Democrat ticket, to the state legislature as a representative from El Dorado County.[52] His term in the California assembly was uneventful; the stage, it seems, was too small and inconsequential for his ambition. Shortly after adjournment, in June 1863, he joined the immigration across the Sierra Nevada to booming Virginia City, where opportunity, political and financial, beckoned.

That Fitch's emigration to Nevada was connected to political ambitions of a specific sort, stemming from his association with Stanford (and in turn Stanford's great railroad enterprise), can neither be affirmed nor discounted. Yet it is certainly suggestive that his move to Virginia City coincided with both the first Nevada statehood movement and the beginning of construction of the Central Pacific Railroad, on a route that promised to connect Washoe's silver mining districts with California. In Nevada Fitch, as a well-known Republican and associate of Stanford, was soon involved in both the territorial Union party and promotion of the Central Pacific Railroad, and he quickly came to public attention as a speaker for Union causes and editor of the *Virginia Daily Union*. In every regard he proved himself an astute student of the local scene.

Shortly after Fitch's arrival, the first statehood campaign took place, and as editor of the *Daily Union* he set himself firmly against William Stewart and the alleged monopoly interests for which the "great lawyer" stood. On the mining tax, Fitch upheld Judge North and the principle of equal taxation of all property without discrimination, a position that appealed to many miners as well as the nonmining business men of Storey County.[53] In the controversy over Stewart's heavy-handed manipulation of the Storey County Union convention in late 1863—the meeting that denounced North and affirmed Stewart's construction of the first constitution's tax clause—Fitch joined the group that sought to unseat Stewart and his allies.[54] Although the insurgents failed to get their way at the territorial convention, they nonetheless gained the high ground in Nevada politics and, arraying themselves against Stewart and statehood, captured a major role in the campaign against the 1863 constitution. Fitch's reputation in this regard—gained in bolting from the county convention and through his persistent attacks on Stewart and statehood in the *Virginia Daily Union*—made him, virtually overnight, a leading political figure on the Comstock Lode. When the call for the second convention came from Washington, D.C., the Storey County Union convention nominated him, along with other insurgents from the prior winter, for the office of delegate. Unexpectedly, Fitch faced a fight in the balloting. At Union party meetings during the depression spring he had spoken in support of greenback currency as a necessary weapon of war—an unpopular position in this mineral-rich territory. As a consequence, a week before the election he was forced to meet the public in open debate and, in the race for delegate, a hastily named opponent. In the vote, Fitch placed tenth, receiving the fewest votes of the Storey County delegates (48 percent of the number of votes that went to the top candidate).[55] The close call, however, did not phase him. A month later he went to Carson City ready to play a central role. And that he did, displaying in the process the commitments he had carried to Nevada from California and, as well, his expectation of personal greatness.

Reflections on fame—its costs and rewards—which distinguished Thomas Fitch's life in the Far West, also marked the thoughts of Charles E. De Long, his Storey County colleague in the constitutional convention. Two years before the convention, while considering a move from California to Nevada, De Long made the following entry to his journal:

> Thou wilt choose the path of fame
> And barter peace to gain a name,

> But when honors most increase
> Thou wilt mourn departed peace.
>
> Sister tis true, such is my aim
> To wed for life the Goddess Fame.
> Till won; none other will I know
> Though all of life should be but woe.[56]

Although in background and interest De Long differed significantly
from the other leading men in the Nevada constitutional convention, on
the matter of fame he was, like them, a characteristic mining frontier
politician. Like Collins, Johnson, and so many other Nevada delegates,
he had come west in the early gold rush years in search of the main
chance. Typical of the group as well, De Long arrived in Carson City
with a reputation built during the 1850s and early 1860s in the rapidly
changing mining society of California. His experience in California after
the gold rush paralleled in important respects that of his colleagues, for
he had remained a resident of the northern mining regions and, in his
daily life, closely involved in the mining economy. In this respect, he well
represented the "old Californian" in whom the visions and hopes of the
gold rush persisted, visions and hopes informed and chastened by the
transformation of the mining economy during the 1850s.

De Long was born in rural New York in 1832 to a staunchly Democratic family. Uneducated except for a few months in a local common
school, he seemed bound, until his late teens, to carry on in the footsteps
of his farmer father. But when news of the California gold discovery
reached Dutchess County, De Long escaped with his brother and never
returned. Traveling by sea, the two arrived in California in mid-1850.
From San Francisco they set off for the northern mines to try their hand
in the placer fields. For the next thirteen years the mining towns near
Grass Valley and Nevada City, and the central-valley merchant centers
(Marysville, Sacramento, Stockton) composed his world. There he became a leading citizen, although neither wealth nor fame came his way
easily. As a miner he was a failure (his brother, dispirited, returned to
New York in 1853), and for better than five years he faced a constant
struggle simply to get by, moving from job to job as chance would have it.
After giving up on mining, he peddled in the camps, tended bars, and
kept hotels. At other times he lived by gambling; running stables, toll
roads, and bridges; and working the bounty system offered by the state
to men who "captured" Chinese for nonpayment of California's foreign
miner's tax. As a gold rush jack-of-all-trades he made little money, but
because he stayed behind when others left, he became a recognized old
citizen in the northern mining towns. Poor and without settled prospects, he gained a certain stature in the public life of the mining towns
through other means. Single and always around, he was a hale fellow

well met in drinking, dining, and gambling establishments, participant in mining town Masonic assemblies, and a ready performer in quickly got up entertainments. Through the 1850s his name appeared in broadsides featuring his appearance as a singer, boxer, and fencer. Above all he was known for his acting in local theatrical troupes, whose productions ranged from silly farces to austere classics.[57]

A turning point in De Long's life came in 1856. Wary of the struggle, in his words, to make "an honest living," following another failure "in a mercantile business I was engaged in at Young's Hill . . . I turned my attention to the study and practice of the law."[58] He proved a quick and natural learner. An avid reader of the classics, he mastered Blackstone, Kent, and other commentaries without tutoring. After admission to the bar he opened an office in Marysville, a river town above Sacramento that serviced the northern mining regions. Drawing on acquaintances from the early days, willing to take on any case he could get from San Francisco to Stockton to Placerville to Yuba County, he built an extensive (if small-scale) practice and, in common with other small lawyers in his time, accumulated substantial property holdings through payments made in lieu of cash. A gifted courtroom performer who won more often than not, lawyer De Long also accumulated stores of goodwill, which he drew upon when his attention turned to politics.[59]

Displaying a natural bent for the friends-and-neighbors politics of the northern mining towns, in 1857 De Long ran for a seat in the state assembly and won handily. Preparing to set off for his first session in the legislature, he expressed his pride and his progress as a gold rush pilgrim in the following "Memorandum" to his journal:

> Six long years have nearly flown
> Since first I trod this mountain's brow
> I came a stranger boy unknown;
> A Lawyer, Legislator, and a man I leave it now
> With empty purse and sorrowing heart
> I came, a toiling stranger, here
> Since then, with energy [I]'ve filled my part
> Until honor's and indep[en]dence now I bear.[60]

In the state legislature his inherited Democratic allegiance reasserted itself, although at an awkward moment, for between 1857 and 1861 the California (like the national) Democracy split apart and collapsed. De Long stood near the center of the political whirlwind in California. There the national conflict over the Lecompton constitution of Kansas, dividing northern Democratic followers of Stephen Douglas from southern Democratic adherents of President Buchanan, was played out in a contest between two local men: U.S. Senator William Gwin—Lecomptonite, Buchanan adherent, and spokesman for a self-styled, pro-southern "Chivalry"; and David Broderick—anti-Lecomptonite, Douglas ally, and head man of what its opponents referred to as the workingmen's "Shovelry" of San Francisco.[61]

In this local contest, De Long allied with fellow New Yorker Broderick. In public and behind the scenes he worked tirelessly to break the domination of Gwin Democrats over the state organization. In the short term, the effort proved disappointing. Although reelected to the assembly in 1858, in the following year, when De Long set his sights on the state senate, the candidate of the Gwin Chivalry beat him badly.[62] Between this defeat and his departure for Nevada two and a half years later, both De Long's political fortunes and his political identity were whipsawed by events local and national.

Shortly after the election of 1859 the stakes, and the depth of the conflict within the California Democracy, increased dramatically when Broderick died in a duel of honor with a Democratic adversary. This event—which Democrats like De Long saw as the "assassination" of their leader—quickly overrode all other political considerations and defined the local context in which the national travail of the Democracy was played out. For De Long, Broderick's death initiated a slow transition from Democrat to Republican that was completed only after the Civil War ended. In the short term, Broderick's martyrdom finalized De Long's repudiation of the Gwin wing of his party and led him to ally with old Whigs and new Republicans to the end of breaking the Chivalry— and, more personally, regaining office himself. Among those with whom De Long worked in this effort was Thomas Fitch's friend E. D. Baker (whose own standing increased dramatically after the Broderick-Terry duel through his eulogy of Broderick to an audience of thousands in San Francisco). Before Baker departed for Oregon he worked closely with Douglas Democrats to smash the Gwin organization—among them, De Long. Baker supported De Long's candidacy for the state legislature in 1860 and convinced other Republicans to refrain from nominating an opponent. De Long won, enjoying both Democratic and Republican support, including that of several men—James Nye, John Collins, and Thomas Fitch—he would meet again in Nevada.[63]

Shortly thereafter the Civil War broke out. Although De Long's ties to the Democracy began to dissolve, he became a Unionist and Republican more slowly than his constituents, and in 1862, when he ran for reelection, he met defeat along with the entire ticket in his county. The day after the returns were announced, he recorded in his journal that he had awakened "to find myself cleaned out by hundreds in the County and the whole state gone Republican in a thunder." Two days later he added that "bad news coming from the seat of war and discouragements of a political defeat all tend to make me feel much depressed," to which he added shortly after, "nothing doing in the shape of business . . . felt blue meditated selling out & leaving for Washoe or some other country."[64]

Although depressed by political defeat, worried by dull business, and intrigued by reports from the Comstock Lode, De Long did not leave California immediately. Holding him back was his recent marriage, after a stormy five-year courtship, to the daughter of a prominent California Democrat who he thought would prove a powerful ally. Within a year his wife gave birth to a daughter, which tied De Long (or so he said) all the more to Marysville. However, the lure of Washoe, impressed upon him by the rush of California miners (many of them clients) across the Sierra Nevada, never left his mind, and in the spring of 1863 he decided to make a preliminary reconnoiter. From Virginia City, he wrote his wife that business there was so good that he had no choice but to stay. Leaving wife and child in Marysville, he opened an office and plunged into the mining litigation that filled the Comstock courts. To his brother (then a soldier in the Union army) he described Virginia City as "a lawyer's paradise. . . . I have a good reputation and have in the short time that I have been here become engaged in some important cases. When these Silver mining companies get at law millions are often involved and of course their money flows freely. . . . Brother, this is a mining country, much more extravagant in its proportions than California ever was."[65]

In 1863 and early 1864 Nevada did not let De Long down. Surrounded by old friends and neighbors (though not yet his family), he quickly had more than enough clients, drawn from California acquaintances and (an important new feature in his professional and, as it turned out, political life) San Francisco syndicates vying in the courts for control of the Comstock Lode. The fees he gained as attorney for his new corporate clients had a major, almost magical, effect on his understanding of the nature of individual opportunity. In Nevada, as De Long's personal interests became increasingly tied to the fortunes of corporations, the lessons he drew carried him quickly, if not with full consciousness, across a biographical divide. By 1864 this former exemplar of antebellum individualism had become an agent of, and then spokesman for, corporate capitalism.[66]

For De Long, as for his Nevada colleagues, this shift was encouraged by the chance happening of the Civil War. Given his place in California politics in the late 1850s and early 1860s, and with so many Californians still around him, no one was surprised to find him taking part in local and territorial affairs. Shortly after his arrival in Virginia City he joined the Union party, reuniting there with old allies and adversaries in the sectional battles of California from 1859 to 1862. Although De Long was not yet a Nevadan at the time of the 1863 convention, he arrived soon after and jumped immediately into the campaign against ratification of the first constitution. In it he worked against statehood alongside Fitch, Collins, and Johnson, but his reasons for doing so differed significantly from theirs.[67]

In Nevada, De Long's profession of the law shifted from a general practice dealing with small personal actions (criminal as well as civil) to one increasingly specialized and dependent on large corporate clients. As such he saw the constitution in terms of its alleged effects on "miners and mining"—meaning the large Comstock companies. Stewart's sanguine construction of the mining provision as one that the legislature *could* interpret so as to release mine owners from tax obligations De Long found untenable. Unlike Johnson, who feared that Stewart's construction *would* work, he, to the contrary, feared it would *not*. Unlike Fitch and Collins, who argued that a tax on the mines was necessary, De Long insisted it would be ruinous.

In this respect, De Long represented but one side of the multifarious (and, as events would show, internally contradictory) alliance against statehood that coalesced in the campaign of the winter of 1863–1864. The opposition of men such as Collins, Johnson, Fitch, and De Long to statehood had but one common element: a general concern with the effect of the constitution on one interest or another. But the interests with which they were concerned differed—indeed, they conflicted with one another directly. Yet opposition galvanized by the figure of William Stewart allowed men to avoid these points of conflict. Even in the election of delegates to the second convention, the common cause against Stewart in the earlier dispute overshadowed the differences. Once the Carson City convention of 1864 was assembled, however, these divisions could no longer be avoided. Charles De Long, more than any other man, made them the first order of the convention's business.

THE CORPORATION AND THE INDIVIDUAL

When Collins, Johnson, Fitch, and De Long, with thirty-one others, assembled in Carson City in early July, they expected to a man that their convention would be brief. Although the weight of the economic depression hung over them (witness delegate Dunne's resolution to adjourn and go home), the majority of the constitution writers went along with Collins in his faith that "notwithstanding the fact that at present poverty seems to be staring us in the face, and many of our business men feel overwhelmed by its depressing influence, and disposed to look at the future only through a cloud of darkness, yet I have faith to believe that our Territory is only under a cloud for the time being." [68]

Collins and others expressed this view uneasily, evincing a complex of concerns that stemmed from worry over depressed conditions and, more subtly and importantly, over what the future had in store. Would Nevada remain, as writers had put it the year before, "another version of the gold rush"? Or did the future rest in the development of a different material environment, one dominated by industrial mining corporations? These alternatives, understood dimly in the first days of the convention, came increasingly to dominate the proceedings. At the outset, the Nevadans' views reflected a confusing mix of sentiments in which an individual producer ethic, drawn out of the mythology of 1849 and so central to the campaign over the first constitution, combined uncomfortably with a half-formed conviction, born in the depression of 1864, that individual self-interest was tied (paradoxically) to the fate of large combinations and "foreign" finance. By the close of the convention, however, the conflict between these two views had come to the fore with a crash.

Confusion over the individual producer versus corporate ethos, carried over from the campaign to elect delegates, beset the 1864 constitutional convention. Heightening it was the very manner in which the Nevada constitution writers went about their task. Instead of beginning from scratch, they adopted the defeated 1863 constitution as the basis for their work. Although Charles De Long argued in favor of starting over, with the New York constitution as a model, and others called for using the California constitution, these suggestions were quickly turned aside, for, as Johnson pointed out, the 1863 constitution was "section following section, without the substitution of a word, or change of a single clause, copied from the Constitution of California." Why, he asked, should "we go back and do this work over again?"[69] Only a few sections of the defeated constitution were marred, most believed, and it seemed clear just which sections were in need of repair: those that concerned taxation, the judiciary, and loyalty to the Union.[70]

From the perspective of July 1864, voter concern over these three areas, and these three areas alone, had led to the constitution's defeat the winter before. Opposition to the mining tax offended many, although here memory missed the complexity of the views that had marked the winter debate of the provision. Similarly, many asserted that secretive bands of disloyal "copperheads" had leagued against the constitution in order to damage the Union cause. Finally, without noticing the irony, the delegates embraced the very critique of the territorial courts that William Stewart had prosecuted, without success, the winter before. Testifying to the force of depression in changing men's minds, the delegates agreed that litigation over mining claims had contributed to, if not created, the dull times that beset the territory and that the sorry state of the territorial courts—incapable of resolving the single- versus many-ledge controversy, burdened by a growing backlog of suits, and, above all, infected with corruption—required construction of a new court system.

Otherwise the first constitution was acceptable to most delegates. On the convention's first day they quickly, and without apparent partisan strife, organized themselves. Despite reports that the delegates intended to make John Collins their presiding officer (and that he would then move the convention to Virginia City), Collins withdrew his name and urged election of Johnson by acclamation.[71] The action—given Collins's well-known ambition and Johnson's favor of the mining tax—was significant because it was so surprising. Johnson, a "cow county" delegate, was committed to retaining, indeed strengthening, the provision in the 1863 constitution that taxed the mines.[72] Collins's withdrawal thus suggests that he did not expect the convention to divide between mining and non-mining interests. That he (and others) so believed was corroborated by a minor vote shortly after the delegates made Johnson president: election of the convention secretary. Two men were nominated for the post, and, given the absence of discussion beforehand, the vote, seventeen to twelve, was remarkably close.[73] Curiously, the delegates chose a cow county man from Carson City—William Gillespie—over a Virginia City miner, thanks to a coalition of cow county delegates and a handful (a pivotal group, as it later turned out) of Virginia City men, prominent among them Thomas Fitch and John Collins. Although the vote went unremarked, it demonstrated the presence of a swing group of Comstock Lode delegates who later proved decisive.

The import of the election of cow county men as president and secretary of the convention became evident only later on, when the comity of the first days collapsed into bitter partisanship—a partisanship narrowly conceived but having wide-ranging effects. With the exception of four questions, the Nevadans repassed, for all intents and purposes, the same constitution the voters had rejected six months earlier. On the four points, however—a loyalty oath to the Union, a subsidy for the construction of the Pacific railroad, taxation of the mines, and the state court system—the debate was long, angry, and full of twists and turns. Although at first glance these issues appear unrelated, in writing the constitution they became multiple sides of a single complex discussion, a discussion that saw a shift in conceptions of self, economy, and society: from a society based on the local community to one centered on the nation-state, and from an economy of freely competing individuals to one dependent on an intricate balance of interrelated corporate enterprises.

In the convention, the Nevadans' discussion of the loyalty oath (part of the Article on the Rights of Suffrage), bonds for the Pacific railroad (Corporations and Internal Improvements), the mining tax (Taxation), and provisions for impeaching judges (Judiciary) did not proceed along neat chronological lines. Rather, the four debates—chronologically and contextually—intermixed. During the convention's first week the delegates shifted their attention back and forth between a measure requiring voters to take an oath of loyalty to the Union and Thomas Fitch's proposal to include in the constitution a provision allowing the state to subsidize construction of the Pacific railroad. Midway through the three-week convention this debate was interrupted by an angry confrontation over taxing the mines, which forced significant changes of mind among a good number of the constitution writers and, as such, marked the decisive turning point in the convention. At the conclusion of this debate, the delegates, divided now along new lines and allegiant to new ideas, returned to the railroad, the loyalty oath, and, finally, the constitution's provisions for impeaching judges. Covering old ground in new ways, the Nevadans concluded each matter according to lessons learned in the taxation debate, lessons no one had anticipated at the opening of the convention.

In their discussions of these questions, the Nevadans divided roughly into three groups. The most basic division was between those from the (nonmining) cow counties and those sent by mining constituencies, above all Storey County, site of the Comstock Lode. The cow county delegates, who represented ranchers and the traders in the settlements along the trails from California to the mines, had come to Carson City cognizant of their minority status and, above all, united on the necessity of reenacting the mining tax defeated with the 1863 constitution. More generally, these delegates brought a parochial perspective toward constitution writing, a wariness of grand schemes that appeared to serve the interests of "foreign monopolists."

In contrast, the mining county delegates were at the outset considerably less united. For much of the convention (beginning with the election of Johnson and Gillespie) they were divided between a group who saw the essential business of the convention as exempting the mines from taxation and a smaller group whose position on this issue was ambivalent. To further complicate matters, the mining county delegates who opposed a mining tax did so for various, in part contradictory, reasons. Those from smaller districts away from the Comstock Lode, where prospecting and "small-interest" individual proprietorships were more important than large, "foreign" combinations, tended to see a tax exemption as necessary to forestall disaster. Among the Storey County (Comstock Lode) delegates, however, above all Charles De Long, a different perspective prevailed: in their view, the future of Nevada depended on the encouragement, whatever the cost, of corporate-industrial mining.

Between these two sides, finally, was a small but pivotal group of mining county representatives—foremost among them Fitch and Collins—for whom the mining tax was not the paramount issue. Rather, they brought to Carson City a sympathy for the nonmining businessmen in their districts who rightly worried that exemption of the mines would increase their own tax burden. More importantly, this group possessed a broader, more modern view of the task before them. To Fitch (and, although less stridently, Collins as well), the tax question paled before the need to promote the grandest and most progressive achievement of the age: the Pacific railroad. Partly from partisan calculation, partly because they questioned the equity of a mining tax exemption, these delegates went to Carson City ready to support the cow county proponents of a mining tax in return for the latter group's support for more important objectives.

❧

Enveloping these primary—and precisely interested—lines between the Nevada constitution writers was the ever-present shadow of the Civil War. The war was the immediate referent in the Nevadans' debate over a loyalty oath, but it also shaped, symbolically and substantively, their approach to political economic issues as well. As Californians, these men were accustomed to think of self-interest as the engine of the common good. The war, by tying economic questions to the mission of the nation, led them to recast their discourse in ways that emphasized the virtues not of the free individual but, rather, of combination and centralization. In this respect, the war had the effect of legitimating a new, national and corporate, vision of the republic.

This "reenvisioning" did not come all at once, nor did the delegates at the time comprehend completely or consciously the broader implications of their commitment to the Union. Rather, the new conception existed as a subtle undercurrent that grew in force as time went on. During the first week of constitution writing its presence was made apparent, and reinforced, when the delegates turned to the paramount allegiance clause in the 1863 constitution.[74] The discussion turned on the contradiction between the section's first sentence, which articulated a contract theory of sovereignty (standard fare of antebellum constitutions), and the section's subsequent affirmation of the paramount authority of the national government. As such the section opened familiarly, stating that "all political power is inherent in the people. . . . But," it went on, "the paramount allegiance of every citizen is due to the Federal Government: and no power exists in the people of this or any other State of the Federal Union to dissolve their connection therewith."[75]

Thomas Fitch, among others, worried over the seeming contradiction between the two passages. In trying to sort it out, he and his colleagues expressed a range of views, though all were within the compass of a common devotion to the supreme authority of the nation-state. The emotional, and therefore political, force of the war, magnified no doubt by the Nevadans' own safety from combat, nurtured nationalistic fervor.[76] James Banks put the point strictly: "The philosophy of this [paramount allegiance] section," he argued, is that as a state

> we waive all claims to the following enumerated rights. However the Supreme Court may decide; however much they may be disposed to accede; we, as the State of Nevada, waive all our claims to any rights embraced in the following enumerated cases. No power, we say, exists in the people of

> this or any other state of the Federal Union to perform any act tending to
> impair, subvert, or resist the authority of the Government. Even if the
> Courts give that power, we disclaim it.[77]

Fitch, who favored striking the section on the grounds of expedience,
nonetheless couched his opposition to it in spread-eagled nationalism. "I
believe," he testified, "that above all the flames of war, of the groans of
the dying, the shrieks of the wounded in battle, and above all the turmoil
and strife of this wicked rebellion, the power and dignity of the Federal
Government will stand unmoved, unsubverted, undestroyed."[78] To him,
the fact of national supremacy was sufficiently apparent as to require no
special declaration in the constitution.

Fitch's colleagues, however, less sensitive to the paradox he identified,
retained the original language. The convention then took up what
seemed a more important part of the constitution, with regard to loyalty:
the Article on the Rights of Suffrage. Here, too, the debate focused on
questions raised, and lessons learned, through the war. Should the constitution disenfranchise rebels? What would be the force of such a prohibition if Congress were to establish a general amnesty? More generally,
should the constitution require a loyalty oath as a condition of voting?
To what extent—given the delegates' earlier affirmation of the sovereignty of the national government—could the state regulate voting? Was
it now a matter within the purview of the federal government alone?

Given the number of old Democrats in the convention, it is striking to
behold the unanimity with which the Nevadans affirmed the supremacy
of the Union over the states, glorifying the holy purpose of a distant war
they were not fighting. They defined this holy purpose, however, narrowly. Only one delegate, George Nourse, suggested that the convention
reconsider the provision (carried over from the prior constitution) re-
stricting the franchise to "white males." He remarked with obvious
unease:

> I wish to make one motion here, which I suppose will be voted down, but I
> will not occupy much time with it. I move to simply strike out the word
> "white" in the first line. I think it is pandering to an old and disgraceful
> prejudice—and none the less disgraceful, I will say, because I myself have
> partaken of it—against that race which is certainly doing grand work for
> the Union now.

Yet lest he find himself outside the limits of propriety, Nourse proceeded, almost apologetically, to undermine his motion to strike the
word:

> I suppose that here this [Negro suffrage] is not in reality a practical ques-
> tion, and while I would not be in favor of the proposition in a population
> where there would be a great many of those ignorant people to turn loose
> at the polls, still I think here it is a mere theoretical matter. I offer the

amendment, therefore, although I presume it will be voted down, simply because I think it is my duty to do so.[79]

Nourse misjudged his colleagues, for his amendment was not voted down: it failed for want of a second.

For these Nevadans the Civil War was not a war against slavery, despite the Emancipation Proclamation. Rather, it remained a war against treason of the "Union," a Union understood because of the war in a fundamentally new way. Speaker after speaker attested to this fact, describing how southern treachery had forced them to deny Democratic gospel learned in their youth, a gospel that, even if it stopped short of making states rights a first principle of the (U.S.) Constitution, nonetheless erred in upholding the political primacy of locale and community. For the Nevadans, war had magnified the majesty of the Union and the primacy of loyalty to it. Constitutional vigilance in upholding this loyalty was beyond question.[80] For some delegates, this topic was virtually the only matter that aroused comment inside the convention hall. Benjamin Mason, an otherwise quiet follower of more persuasive men, waxed eloquent in describing the effects of secession on his views:

I do not think that any traitor should be allowed to exercise that birthright of freemen, under the government which he has raised his impious hands to destroy. I do not think that men, after having banded themselves together as assassins, after having perpetrated every crime—for treason involves the commission of all crimes—should be allowed to come forward and insult the majesty of the Deity by calling upon his name, and taking an oath denouncing the very crimes which they have committed. . . . I have been for many years a pro-slavery democrat. . . . But when slavery itself became a traitor, and fired upon the flag of freedom; when armed treason raised its red right hand against the Government, then I, in common with other freemen of the North, "cried havoc, and let slip the dogs of war." We set wide open the doors of democracy, and let the day-light in. Why, sir, they said that poor, crazy, old John Brown must be hung; but this day old John Brown stands far higher in my estimation than that vile old Iscariot, James Buchanan. [Applause][81]

For others, the issue was more complicated. Lloyd Frizell, while "yield[ing] to no man in my devotion to this government," expressed himself with these words: "'If you are willing to repent of your folly, I will take you by the hand. You have heretofore been my brothers; in this matter you have been wrong, but if you repent you may be my brothers still.'" Southerners, he noted sympathetically, were fighting for

the principle of State Rights, as they term it, self-government. . . . I hope to God that this war, when it is fought out, will put an end to that principle—a principle for which, by the way, I have contended for years, in consequence of the prejudices of early education. I had always heard my father and my grandfather speak in contemptuous terms of Alexander Hamilton, Chief Justice Marshall, John Adams, and others of those statesmen who were endeavoring to make the Federal Government strong; and I had heard them advocating what they called the principle of democracy, or States Rights. . . . But in the past three or four years of my life I have seen my error. . . . I now see that I have been cherishing a heresy.[82]

J. Neely Johnson, taking a middle ground, proposed an amendment to the original provision requiring that any man take an oath if his loyalty was challenged, leaving the procedures of making the challenge to the legislature.[83] Collins, displaying unexpected sobriety for a man with his past, cautioned against the zealotry of Mason and questioned the propriety of Johnson's proposal. He advised, rather, that the convention leave the entire matter to the legislature, "bear[ing] in mind that we are legislating as unimpassioned men—that our judgment should be cool, calm, and clear, and that we should establish this Constitution under the influence alone of that calm and clear judgment."[84] Resolution of the question—albeit only for a time—followed the first of many impassioned speeches by Charles De Long. Speaking with characteristic urgency, this former Democrat, veteran of the late political wars of California, and brother of a soldier who had fought at Gettysburg, called on the convention to do their obvious duty for the Union by requiring an ironclad oath for *all* voters:

> I want every man who proposes to exercise the right of suffrage among us not only to record his name, but, in the presence of Almighty God, to swear that oath, and so to seal his everlasting and eternal damnation if he ever again raises his hand in rebellion. . . . I hope that this Convention will adopt this oath . . . as a guarantee that we will not hereafter be met at the polls, and in the exercise of our sacred right of suffrage, be counterbalanced and stultified by those in whose veins runs no blood save that which is black as hell with the taint of treason.[85]

Their passion spent, the delegates, in committee of the whole, quietly passed the measure for which De Long argued.

Before the suffrage article was taken up for final passage, however, seven days elapsed and a great deal of other business transpired, business that changed the context of debate over suffrage and loyalty substantially. The intervening debates—which involved, first, the proposal to have the state subsidize the Pacific railroad and, second, taxation of the mines—were marked with unanticipated acrimony and brought a realignment of the delegates. Although at first glance unrelated to voting rights and loyalty oaths, in practice they proved inseparable; in the end, their resolution forced a reconsideration of the demands of loyalty.

The proposal for a railroad subsidy and the reopening of the debate over taxing the mines occurred midway through the Nevada convention.

The latter, in particular, marked a crucial turning point in the writing of the constitution and, through it, the history of this region. The two issues, tactically and, as it turned out, ideologically, were closely related both to each other and, over the long run, to the composition of the constitution as a whole.

Setting the stage was the delegates' discussion of the railroad. In 1864 construction of the Central Pacific was just beginning to move eastward from Sacramento to its meeting place with the Union Pacific line. Allied with Republicans who took control of Congress after the withdrawal of southern representatives, the Central Pacific's officers proved adept at gaining vast public subsidies—local, state, and national—for their enterprise. The company's president, Leland Stanford, was at the time of the Nevada convention also a former (Republican) governor of California, a post to which he had been elected during the dramatic days of 1859–1861. In his quest to secure subsidies for the railroad, he hurried to Carson City in the summer of 1864 to lobby for a constitutional provision allowing the state to issue railroad subsidy bonds and also to convince the delegates to restrict any such bonds to one road: his. Stanford arrived in Carson City to find old acquaintances within the assembly. Foremost among them was Thomas Fitch.

In the convention, Fitch was point man for the railroad. His friendship with Stanford, going back four years, was (at least for Fitch) close and important. The two had campaigned together for Lincoln, and Fitch had taken to the field again when Stanford had run for governor in 1861. The two shared a common Republican vision, sharpened by the war, as to the need to recast the nation's institutions, public and private. Politically, they were dedicated to centralization and nationalism, as opposed to the localism embodied in the doctrines of the antebellum Democracy. Crucial to their politics was the vision of a continental union progressing through the creation and extension of institutions national, not regional or local, in scope. Their foremost, though not yet actual, exemplar was the transcontinental railroad.

In the Nevada constitutional convention, the building of the Pacific railroad elicited unanimous praise. Without dissent the delegates saw it, in the words of John Collins, as "one of the grandest and most sublime movements of this or any age."[86] For Collins, Fitch, and others, its construction was tied intimately to the preservation and progress of the Union. As J. H. Warwick of Lander County put it, through the railroad Nevada would become materially as well as politically "part of a great united free country. . . . The great railroad tie which shall bind our brethren of the east with our brethren of the west, shall remain as an enduring monument of the wisdom of the people who have called us together here."[87] Fitch connected its construction to the issue of loyalty explicitly, remarking that anyone who opposed the subsidy favored "the Pacific Railroad . . . in the same manner as the Democrats are in favor of the Union at the same time that they are opposed to all measures for its preservation."[88] Others linked the railroad to economic recovery. Collins, for example, argued that with the arrival of the railroad "the cupidity and avarice of capitalists will be stimulated, and, consequently, capital will rush to this country for investment and the rat-tat-tat of mills will be heard by thousands, where they are now heard only by scores."[89]

The discussion of the railroad occurred during the convention's consideration of corporations and internal improvements. Here, issues that had bedeviled the constitution writers of California and Oregon—banks and stockholder liability—caused little consternation. The combined effects of the national crisis and, most importantly, the local depression overwhelmed the distrust of corporations that had played so signal a role in Nevada politics just months before. No delegate proposed a personal liability provision, in striking contrast to the discussions in California and Oregon.[90] In addition, loyalty to the Union, along with a depression-bred desire to encourage capital investment from outside Nevada, reshaped the delegates' views on banks significantly. Although the constitutional language they ultimately agreed on held (like the 1863 constitution and, for that matter, those of California and Oregon) that "no bank notes or paper of any kind, shall ever be permitted to circulate as money in the state," to this clause Fitch proposed, and his colleagues agreed to add, "except the Federal currency and the notes of banks authorized under the laws of Congress."[91] Some delegates, compelled it seems by the hold of old doctrines, did vent characteristic antebellum anger toward banks. For example, Nourse (an old "states rights Democrat" lately become a proud Republican) warned his colleagues that if they

> set up a system of State banks, with the right to issue bank notes, and all that sort of trash—I tell you, if we do it, we shall be guilty before God and man. We shall have such a sin to answer for, that we shall not know where to hide our heads, because if we sin in that way now, we do it with our eyes open; we do it with the experience of the whole country before us, and with the full knowledge of all the ruin that has been brought about in other States by this miserable, wild-cat, paper trash.[92]

Yet Nourse's outcry was unusual; for the most part the discussion of banks was subdued and moderate, marked by a new sense (one absent in the 1863 convention) of the importance of banking to a corporate economy. As De Long put it:

> Why should we, at this stage in our country's history, say that for all time to come no bank notes shall ever circulate in this State as currency? . . . California has such a provision as this in her Constitution. . . . And what has been the consequence? . . . Why, sirs, California is dragged down . . . [its people's] material interests are greatly crippled and injured. Their com-

merce, their manufactures, and their business prospects of every character and description, [are] immediately blighted.[93]

In the end the banking provision reflected an odd balance of the old and new, an equilibrium of Jacksonian suspicions and a more modern financialism reached simply and without rancor. What, with regard to the article on corporations, engaged the Nevadans above all was Fitch's proposal to allow the state to issue bonds to subsidize construction of the Pacific railroad. Although no one opposed the railroad per se, Fitch's measure necessarily raised the question as to what state revenues (that is, taxes) would finance the subsidy. When it was connected to taxation, then, the railroad subsidy became problematic as well, particularly when cow county delegates asked how the state could afford to support the railroad without taxing the mines. On a number of occasions Fitch was asked point blank whether he would vote for or against taxing the mines. His response: for—quid pro quo.

At the convention's midpoint, after three days of discussion, Fitch rejoiced when the committee of the whole placed in the constitution a measure authorizing a state subsidy to the first railroad company to connect the state with either the Pacific Ocean or the Mississippi River.[94] Central to the passage of this measure was the support of the cow county delegates, who openly backed Fitch on the railroad in exchange for his pledge to support the mining tax. The bargain, however, did not hold. The delegates' confrontation with taxation, when it came, caused a realignment that forced major changes in the suffrage, railroad, and judiciary provisions of the constitution. More importantly, the taxation debate nurtured ideological changes of mind.

When the Nevadans initially approached the tax question, the division of opinion was complex. At one extreme were the nonmining, cow county delegates who insisted on retaining, if not the exact language of the 1863 constitution, at least the spirit of that problematic provision. At the other end was a majority of the mining county representatives, who just as insistently opposed any such measure. In between was a small but decisive bloc of mining county delegates, foremost among them Collins and Fitch, "the party of compromise," who had come to the convention committed to a constitution that taxed the mining corporations.

The initial division over taxation—and its transformation—illustrates the centrality, the legitimacy and importance, that the delegates placed on matters of self-interest in this convention. The long debate over this issue, marked as it was by complex calculations of the revenue the state would take in under different systems and of the correlative costs and benefits of various proposals to the taxed and untaxed, called forth a narrow, precise, and personal political calculus. But in addition, the confrontation over the mining tax brought to the surface contradictory visions of Nevada society, in a way that marked some men (above all, the cow county delegates) as backward-looking advocates of an ideology of individual self-interest and others (the mining county bloc) as receptive to a new corporate political economy of self-interest. Thus, while at one remove the protracted debate over the mining tax focused on just whose ox was being gored, it also forced delegates to proclaim their conception of Nevada as it presently stood *and* as they hoped it would be.

In brief, the taxation debate proceeded as follows. It began with the tax measure of the 1863 constitution, which provided for the "taxation of all property, both real and personal, including mines and mining property," and a motion to strike out the phrase referring to mines.[95] Despite De Long's hope "that this question might come to a vote without further discussion," debate could not be contained when Johnson, speaking for the cow counties, offered an additional amendment that substituted the phrase "possessory claims" for "mines and mining property," stating that the former would have the same effect but be less offensive to miners.[96] Over these alternatives—the first leaving out all references to mines in the taxation article, the second specifying the taxation of "possessory claims"—the convention was divided evenly, with a small but crucial bloc of delegates, led by Fitch and Collins, holding the balance of power. For better than two days the constitution writers carried on, with increasing acrimony, over the two proposals, before finally passing the De Long amendment in a voice vote. Then the Johnson proposal (as an amendment to the De Long amendment) became the order of business. The debate was protracted and angry, with mining county delegates attacking the proposal from all sides. Their offensive failed, however, and after yet another day the Johnson proposal passed—precisely because of the votes of Fitch, Collins, and other mining county men who defended their action as in the interest of "compromise."[97]

For a moment, at least, it appeared that the cow county delegates had gotten their way and that the new constitution, like its predecessor, would require taxation of mining claims. But De Long (after one unsuccessful attempt to get the convention to adjourn so that "consultations" might take place) convinced a majority to stop work on the tax section before voting on its final passage. The delegates adjourned for the evening, and through the night mining county representatives huddled in the public houses of Carson City to work out a new strategy. The next morning, the effect of the informal caucus was immediately apparent. Francis Kennedy—who previously had voted with Fitch, Collins, and other mining county men *for* a tax on "possessory rights"—moved to amend the Johnson amendment by adding to it the clause ". . . excepting mines and mining claims, the proceeds alone of which shall be subject to taxation."[98]

The effect of Kennedy's proposal could not be missed, despite his characterization of it as a compromise that allowed a tax on the mines but that would burden only profitable enterprises. Reasoning from experience, nonmining delegates denounced the proposal as a ruse that mining corporations would use to evade paying any tax whatsoever: it was, they insisted, virtually impossible to establish the valuation of "proceeds" of mines. A. J. Lockwood of Ormsby County made the point explicitly: "Last year, as we all know, under a law of a similar character only five hundred dollars was collected from the mines, and that was paid out for attorney's fees, in trying to collect more. I think I can safely venture to say that under the provision as it now stands not a single dollar will ever be collected from the mines."[99] Johnson, as presiding officer, tried to rule Kennedy's amendment out of order (on the grounds that it was the same as a previously defeated motion), but his ruling, on an appeal by De Long, was overruled by the convention.[100]

This last vote marked, in precise terms, the convention's turning point, for now those mining county delegates who had previously aligned with the cow counties suddenly switched sides and voted with the mining delegations. To the cow county delegates, their shift was unexpected, a signal not just of defeat but of treacherous capitulation to caucus dictation.[101] Angry recriminations and denials flew back and forth, but the die had been cast. In a series of roll calls that followed in quick succession, the delegates passed Kennedy's measure. A few efforts to amend it were thwarted easily, and De Long, in an extraordinary parliamentary move, called successfully for the previous question, cutting off debate.[102] The convention, now divided neatly between "cow" and "mining" counties, quickly passed the Article on Taxation.

On the level of parliamentary give-and-take, the protracted debate over the tax question required the delegates to pay close attention to the effects of different proposals on tangible interests, both theirs and their constituents': the burden a mining exemption would place on ranchers and businessmen, for example, or the effect on various mining interests should previously untaxed property be made subject to taxation. Yet interspersed through the debate were other points that placed the discussion within a broader context, one that transcended a mere calculus of interest. On this level the two interests in this convention—cow county and mining county—also represented two disparate conceptions of nineteenth-century political economy. Delegates from the cow counties placed themselves squarely against "foreign monopolies" (that is, capitalists) in defense of the individual proprietor. Spokesmen for the mining bloc, in a manner reminiscent of the previous winter's campaign over the first constitution, resorted in part to a narrow identification of mining, its symbol being the lone, struggling prospector. More importantly, though, when forced to detail the rationale for protecting mining, they emphasized a wholly different and, it turned out, decisive view, outlining, over the course of long and often passionate debates, a corporate vision of Nevada's mining economy. In this sense the taxation debate, over and above the partisan maneuvering between different blocs, brought to the fore striking testimony by these old Californians about their views of the past, their worries in the present, and their hopes for the future.

Crucial in this regard was a simple point that supporters of the mining tax emphasized throughout the debate: if the constitution exempted the mines from taxation (or allowed the legislature to do so), the state would effectively be delivered to foreign capitalists. "It is a principle in political economy," the appropriately named Andrew Jackson Lockwood argued early on, "that capital is sensitive, not to principles of patriotism, not to principles of State pride, but to the principles of loss and gain alone." The mine owners who were subject to any tax, he pointed out, were for the most part "foreigners—aliens, who wish us no good. . . . They send men here to take out the gold, or the bullion, and when it is taken out, it is sent to the city of London, and there is nothing left to show for it in this Territory. What other country in the world allows a thing of that kind to be done on its public domain?"[103] In the same key, George Nourse repudiated the notion that a mining tax posed an onerous burden on working miners:

> It [the tax issue] is not a question between the mining counties and the cow counties, but it is a question between the poor, honest miner, who digs with his pick in the mines, and those rich stockholders and shareholders—those wealthy men. . . . I take it the working-men constitute a majority of the voters in Storey County, and will they have to pay a cent of this tax on the mines? Is it not simply the owner, and not the working-man, who will be taxed?[104]

This stance the advocates of a mining exemption attacked from two angles. Appropriately enough, the convention's oldest representative, sixty-four-year-old Nelson Murdock, insisted that "all this valuable property in the Territory is, and has been made what it is, by the active energy of the prospector." Referring to himself as "one of the early miners of California," Murdock was willing to grant that "foreigners'" money did come to Nevada as investment in paying mines, but only after the individual prospector found the ore and proved that it would pay. Otherwise, he insisted, there was nothing; to keep his work going, the prospector had to sell investors on its future value. "Now," Murdock insisted, "will you go and assess them, and put a stop to their energy? If you put a tax on their enterprises, or if you assess their claims for what they imagine them to be worth, they will have to abandon those claims." In closing he noted, "Suppose when I go back home to my constituents, and they say, 'Well Murdock; have you got a mining clause?' I answer, 'Yes, we have.' They will say, 'Very well; away goes your Constitution'—and I would help them."[105]

The delegates in attendance during Murdock's speech found it amusing, in part because of the older man's talent for delivering well-aimed, homespun, sarcastic asides, but equally because the world Murdock described was almost fantasylike; certainly it was hard to square with the corporate-industrial combinations growing in Virginia City and Gold Hill. In contrast, when the foremost spokesman for the exemption, Charles De Long, rose to speak, the audience's light-heartedness dissolved. Not only was De Long a sharp antagonist in debate, but he was deadly serious—about a line of reasoning that differed substantively from Murdock's, despite the two men's common cause in opposing the mining tax.

Although De Long, like Murdock, placed great store in protecting miners from ruinous taxation, his miners were workingmen, wage laborers, not lonely prospectors or individual proprietors. To De Long, the agent of progress and development was not the individual prospector with his small speculations and grand visions but, rather, capital. De Long worked out this line of reasoning from a simple, and narrow, legal premise. Legally, he insisted, the mines could not be taxed because they were not *property*, but only usufructory rights granted to the miner by the federal government, which retained title to the ground. All the miner possessed was the right to remove minerals from the ground he "claimed," much like the fisherman who "prospected" in the sea.[106]

More importantly, De Long continued, even if a legal artifice could be constructed by which the state taxed a mine, to do so would strike at the heart of an indivisible collective interest crucial to every Nevadan, whether workingman, prospector, "cabbage plat" farmer, rancher, timberman, or merchant. For investment of foreign capital in the mines would be driven away, thus stopping development of the only resource Nevada possessed. "The gentleman from Washoe (Mr. Nourse)," De Long observed, "complains here of the capitalists of San Francisco, and of California, and the capitalists abroad, who do nothing, he says, to build up the Territory." But, he asked rhetorically, could one take Nourse's assertion seriously? No, he quickly retorted, for where did the dollars go that "foreign capitalists" invested in Nevada's mines?

What has become of that money of theirs? It has been paid out to the operatives here. It has been paid to the farmer for the products he has taken to the city of Virginia, to feed the laboring men working in the Chollar mine. It has been paid to the mill-owners for crushing quartz; it has been paid to the teamster for hauling lumber; it has been paid to the laboring-man and the mechanic; it has been paid for improving the streets, and for erecting buildings. That money has been dispersed throughout the community.

"That," he summed up, "is our answer to the complaint in regard to foreign capitalists." [107]

Here De Long painted a picture of Nevada—indeed, of modern political economy—that moved beyond the claims of his opponents and, for that matter, of allies such as Murdock, both of whom approached the mining tax question from the perspective of a society based on free competition among individual proprietors. In De Long, an environment of competing individuals receded from view; in its place one found a society of interdependence and incorporation: workingmen whose existence depended on a wage received from the mining company, farmers and merchants who fed and clothed these corporate employees and serviced the corporations themselves. As political men, De Long insisted, it was incumbent on the constitution writers to recognize that their and their constituents' self-interest was subsidiary to, even subsumed within, the interests of the supraindividual corporation.

De Long's was not the only view of the matter, but it was the view that won out in the end. It did so, however, only by carrying to its side the swing faction, which through the first half of the convention had lined up with the cow county advocates of the mining tax. Exactly why this group switched their allegiance (they did so suddenly and without forewarning) is a matter of speculation. What was said, offered, threatened, or otherwise discussed in the evening meetings outside the convention hall before they switched their votes is unknown. Yet there are hints. By their own testimony, both Collins and Fitch admitted that they supported the mining tax initially because of its link to the provision allowing the state to issue bonds for construction of the Pacific railroad from Sacramento to the Mississippi River. Without such a tax, the prospect that the state could afford, or even afford to consider, issuing bonds to the railroad was unlikely. "I had the honor," Collins remarked as the debate over the mining tax got under way,

> to address the convention the other day in favor of aiding the Pacific Railroad; and one of the strongest arguments I could urge in behalf of that great enterprise was that it would bring into play hundreds and millions of tons of quartz that are now worthless, and worse than dead on the hands of miners, because they are in the way—that it was going to open up new fields of productive mines to the mining class, and give employment to thousands and tens of thousands of laboring men. Now, do you say that it

would be unjust to tax the mining interest to pay the interest on those railroad bonds?[108]

Furthermore, support for the mining tax, in addition to being fiscally important, was strategically wise (or so it seemed early on), for in a quid pro quo it drew to the side of railroad supporters the votes of delegates for whom the mining tax was the uppermost issue before the convention. During the debate over the railroad measure, a cow county delegate asked Fitch: "If we will go for this railroad proviso, will the gentleman coincide with the views of the Washoe delegation in relation to Article X [the tax article]?" Fitch responded: "I think when that article comes up, the gentleman from Storey will be found not very far from the Washoe delegation."[109]

Initially, Fitch's estimate-cum-promise was correct. But when push came to shove he, Collins, and four others changed their minds—to cries of treachery from those who had earlier supported them on the railroad measure. Possibly, if not likely, Fitch, Collins, and those who took cues from them shifted their votes because they were reminded in no uncertain terms that if they did not, if the mining tax measure was not changed, the other mining county delegates would at the very least work against the constitution, and perhaps even walk out of the convention. Either step threatened to sink the constitution and render moot any role for Nevada in the cause of the Union, much less railroad building. Both Fitch and Collins, in explaining their switch, suggested that they were moved by considerations such as these, that the Kennedy measure was a valid "compromise" that would render the constitution palatable to the mining population and—of the utmost importance—assist in its ratification.[110]

One thing is certain: Fitch and Collins did not change their votes as a means to reviving the railroad subsidy provision. For in response to their action, cow county representatives quickly withdrew their support of it. James Sturtevant, for example, objected to any further consideration of the railroad proviso on the grounds that, as the taxation issue demonstrated, "[the mining counties] can beat us all back, if they hang together, and I have no doubt that in this matter they will. The gentlemen who represent Storey County here are all very influential, and no doubt they could carry this question in their county, but gentlemen will remember that the people of the rural districts, and the floating property, have got to pay all the taxes."[111] As if to give the lie to such fears of a mining county conspiracy, De Long taunted his "'cow county' friends" by announcing that despite his belief that benefits of state aid to the Pacific railroad would far outweigh the costs, he would "vote against it . . . if it is their wish, so as to show them that I have not got the words 'mines and mining claims' stricken out of the taxation clause in order to trick

them, or with any view of afterwards putting in a railroad appropriation."[112] Despite a weak effort by Fitch and others to revive the question,
in the aftermath of the tax debates the prospects for the railroad proviso
disappeared.[113]

With the resolution of the mining tax question in favor of exemption,
the framework of the remainder of the convention was set. Although a
week remained and much of the constitution had yet to be finished, the
taxation debate produced a division between the delegates that determined voting lines thereafter and quickly settled the remaining issues
before the house. Until the final adjournment of the convention, the
swing delegates from the mining counties sided with their district colleagues. United, this bloc enjoyed a substantial majority and was able to
dispense with the remaining business with little fanfare. On only two occasions did their adversaries mount a challenge. In neither case was the
opposition effective, but the challenges deserve notice, for they illustrate
how completely Collins and Fitch were converted.

The first question to arise after the settling of the tax issue had to do
with the unfinished business of the loyalty oath. Before the realignment
of forces during the tax debate, the delegates had agreed unanimously
to a constitutional requirement that all voters take an oath. In the aftermath of the taxation fight, however, De Long—shifting from his emotional demand for the oath—moved to reconsider the issue on the
grounds that the wording of the passed oath might effectively, if unintentionally, disenfranchise loyal citizens. His motion to reconsider
passed easily, but De Long's purpose turned out to be more complex
than it first appeared. The article was submitted to a special committee,
chaired by De Long. When his committee reported back, instead of
bringing an amended section, it proposed that the delegates strike the
loyalty oath altogether.[114] Instead, De Long recommended leaving the
question to the legislature—despite his previous insistence that the convention adopt an oath "as a guarantee that we will not hereafter be met
at the polls . . . and be counterbalanced and stultified by those in whose
veins runs no blood save that which is black as hell with the taint of
treason."[115]

Johnson, shocked, charged that striking anything at such a late date
would send forth a dangerous message, and hence "the legislature might
possibly be inhibited" from taking any action on its own.[116] De Long dismissed the argument, but others pressed it. The debate, turning alternately on legal and patriotic grounds, focused on a single question: why
had De Long changed his mind, and why was he insisting on a reconsideration? To cow county delegates, there was more to the matter than met
the eye. J. H. Haines voiced his suspicions directly, noting, undoubtedly

in reference to De Long, that earlier many men had "expressed themselves anxious to have the oath incorporated; they were not merely desirous, but strenuously anxious to have it incorporated. But there seems for some reason to have been a change in the minds of gentlemen." Why? Haines suggested an answer. When the convention had first discussed the oath, "the taxation clause had not been sprung upon the Convention. . . . When that question came up . . . we were told that certain members would withdraw from the Convention, unless a certain measure should pass—unless the taxation clause should be so modified as to exclude certain portions of the property of the State from taxation." Having accomplished this purpose, he continued, "Those gentlemen . . . so far from opposing the Constitution, as they had previously declared they would do . . . are now very anxious that the Constitution be ratified by the people."[117] How did this line of reasoning relate to the striking of the oath? To Washoe County's James Sturtevant, it looked like a "flank movement. Now the majority of the Convention having got things all their own way, it is policy for them to secure all the votes they can. . . . My understanding of this matter, and I think it is correct, and that the whole Convention will bear me out in it, is that whenever you strike this oath out it will suit the Copperheads. 'This is a pretty good Constitution,' says the Copperhead, 'now they have struck that oath out.'"[118]

Haines's and Sturtevant's charges rang sufficiently true to force a response. Storey County delegate Lloyd Frizell, in support of De Long's recommendation to strike the oath, argued that the convention, given the emotional dimension of the Civil War crisis, "should not get up, under such circumstances, in a deliberative body like this, and seek to inflame men's passions." In Nevada, he estimated, there resided between fifteen hundred and two thousand men who had come from states now in the Confederacy. "These men are in the main loyal men," Frizell asserted, "although they adhere to old names, old principles, and old tenets. . . . They think this oath should not appear in the Constitution, and nevertheless they are loyal men. Now if you call it a question of expediency, I will admit it to that extent."[119]

When the delegates finally voted on the oath, they struck it out. Whether they did so because they thought (as De Long argued) the oath was properly a legislative, not a constitutional, matter or because (as Frizell's remarks suggested) of expediency cannot be said. In a clear display of the parliamentary effects of the taxation debate, a firm majority of mining county delegates (John Collins among them; Fitch was absent) once again defeated the cow county coalition.[120]

Before adjourning the convention divided a final time, with similar results, over the judiciary article, in particular its provision for the impeachment of judges. The discussion was necessarily shaped by the recent history of the courts: the prevalence of bribery, the notorious court tampering of William Stewart and others, and the ongoing conflict between Stewart and John North. In the face of these issues George Nourse, aided by Johnson, moved to ease the constitutional procedures by which the legislature could impeach judges, on the rather cynical grounds that it was harder to bribe three or four senators and assemblymen than a handful of judges. Against them the mining county delegates, once again, were solidly opposed. It is not known whether the opposition stemmed, as De Long put it, from respect for the sanctity of an "independent judiciary" or from a cynical desire on the part of mining lawyers to retain a judiciary amenable to bribery and other forms of persuasion in major cases.[121] But one way or another, the small interests—the provincials in this convention—lost. Indeed, by this point the outcome was a foregone conclusion. On the courts, as on the loyalty oath and the railroad subsidy, the miners' newly defined interest carried the day.

So ended the Nevada convention, without fanfare, celebrations, or rousing speeches. Nerves were more dulled than raw, for after the resolution of the tax question the outcome of issues was apparent before the fact. Indeed, many of the delegates had already gone home: interests there beckoned, and for the most of the constitution writers these were more important than the increasingly tired debates in Carson City. Johnson closed the convention not with a proud review of the assembled representatives' work, as had Delazon Smith in Salem, or by arranging a grand ball and military display such as the Californians enjoyed. Rather, he simply extended to the remaining twenty-one delegates (barely a quorum) the simple wish that "the labors which have brought us together, and which are now happily ended, may culminate in the advantage of the people of the new state of Nevada." To this he added, pointedly: "And even should their judgment be adverse at this time . . . we shall have this upon which to congratulate ourselves, that although the result of our labors be not now adopted, it will nevertheless serve as the basis for the action of some future convention."[122] At midnight, July 27, 1864, Johnson declared the convention adjourned *sine die*. The remaining constitution writers hurriedly departed Carson, back to their businesses, their interests, to await the outcome of their labors. In ways not yet apparent, the vision of Nevada's future to which they had given voice soon became a force with which they, and their neighbors, had to deal.

MASS MEETING!

Of the

Citizens of San Francisco!

"The People — Must Rule!"

The undersigned would most respectfully invite their fellow citizens to hold a

PUBLIC MEETING,

In front of the Custom House, Ports-

mouth Square, on Tuesday next, June 12th, at 3 o'clock, P. M., to take into consideration the necessity of electing Delegates to a Convention to form a Government for Upper California. The late Congress of the United States having adjourned without doing anything for the neglected people of this country, *excepting to impose upon us the burdens of Government, without any of its benefits,* it becomes us to act for ourselves, and no longer await the uncertain and protracted action of Congress. We earnestly invite our fellow citizens to attend the proposed Meeting.

MELLUS, HOWARD & CO.,	WARD & SMITH,	THEODORE SHILLABER,	ALFRED ROBINSON,	WILLIAM H. DAVIS,
HENSLEY, READING & CO.,	HENRY D. COOKE,	PETER H BURNETT,	ROBERT WELLS & CO.,	SHERMAN & RUCKEL,
GEORGE HYDE,	R. SEMPLE,	WM. B. JONES,	NAGLEE & SINTON,	ROSS, BENTON & Co.
C. V. GILLESPIE,	PROBST, SMITH & Co.,	ANTONIO BARRENA.	E. H. HARRISON,	FINLEY, JOHNSON & Co.,
S. BRANNAN & Co.,	JOHN PATY,	G. B. POST,	J. WALSH,	JOHN SIMMS,
JAMES COOK,	DEWITT & HARRISON,	CROSS, HOBSON & CO.,	WM. A. BUFFUM,	STARKEY, JANION & Co.,
ROACH & WOODWORTH,	JOHN T. HALL,	T. R. PER LEE,	DAVID DRING,	JAMES J. JARVIS,
BRADY & SIBLEY,	THOMAS B. WINSTON,	C. R. V. LEE,	ROBERT A. PARKER,	EDW. GILBERT,
HIRAM GRIMES,	E. GOULD BUFFUM,	W. M. STEUART,	FRANCIS J. LIPPITT,	A. ROANE,
JAMES C. LEIGHTON,	ANTHONY L. BLEECKER	BOOKER & CONVERSE,	EDW. A. KING,	AGNEW, RODGERS & Co.
JOHN S. OWEN,	J. MEAD HUXLEY,	JOHN A. PATTERSON,	RODMAN M. PRICE,	A. M. VAN NOSTRAND,
WARD, MERSCH & Co.	MYRON NORTORN,	G. C. HUBBARD,	JOHN TOWNSEND.	

San Francisco, June 11, 1849.

1849 broadside calling for an independent citizens' movement to create a state government in California, in defiance of the military government. (Courtesy California State Library.)

Monterey, California, in the 1840s. (Courtesy California State Library; from J. W. Revere, *A Tour of Duty in California*.)

William McKendree Gwin of California. (Courtesy California State Library, Negative #11.)

Henry Wager Halleck of California. (Courtesy California State Library, Negative #6990.)

Lansford Hastings of California. (Courtesy California State Library; from Charles Kelly, *Salt Desert Trails* [Salt Lake City: Western Printing Co., 1930].)

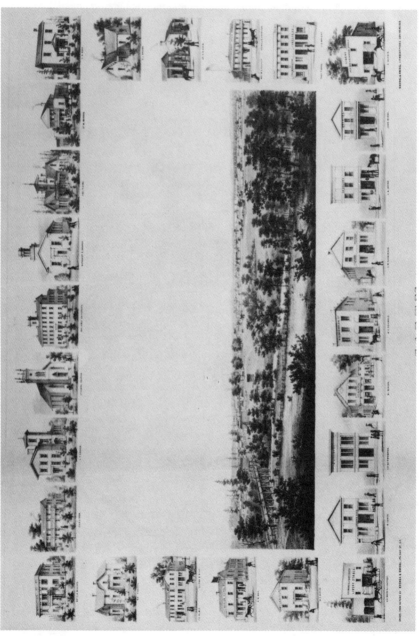

Salem, Oregon, in 1858. (Courtesy Oregon Historical Society, OrHi #59300.)

STOUGHTON RANCH, PROPERTY OF LOUIS PETTYJOHN
1058 ACRES 4 MILES S.W OF SALEM OR.

Oregon donation land claim farm of Louis Pettyjohn, 1878. (Courtesy Oregon Historical Society, OrHi #086183.)

Matthew Paul Deady of Oregon. (Courtesy Oregon Historical Society, OrHi #63119.)

La Fayette Grover of Oregon. (Courtesy Oregon Historical Society, OrHi #9173.)

Delazon Smith of Oregon. (Courtesy Oregon Historical Society, OrHi #086130.)

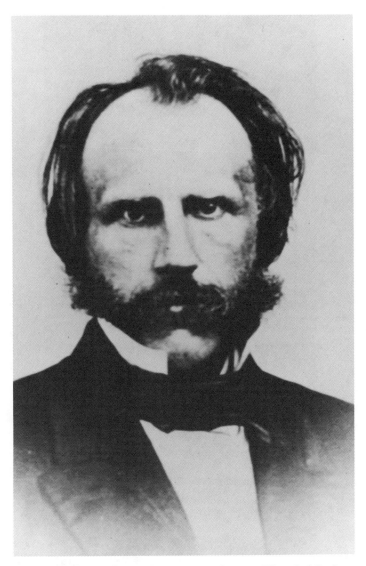

George Williams of Oregon (Courtesy Oregon Historical Society, OrHi #230.)

David Logan—the "Mingo Chief"—of Oregon. (Courtesy Oregon Historical Society, OrHi #86816.)

Asahel Bush, editor of the *Oregon Statesman.* (Courtesy Oregon Historical Society, OrHi #9157.)

Carson City, Nevada, circa 1870. (Courtesy Nevada State Library.)

The rush to Nevada in 1861. (*Harpers New Monthly Magazine*, 1861.)

Carson City in 1861. (*Harpers New Monthly Magazine*, 1861.)

Conflict over title to the Comstock Lode. (*Harpers New Monthly Magazine*, 1861.)

Virginia City in 1861. (*Harpers New Monthly Magazine*, 1861.)

Charles De Long of Nevada (third from right), U.S. minister to Japan, with the
Iwakura Mission, 1871. (Courtesy California State Library, Negative #22838.)

J. Neely Johnson of Nevada. (Courtesy California State Library, Negative #1282.)

Judge John Wesley North of Nevada. (By permission of The
Huntington Library, San Marino, California.)

Thomas Fitch of Nevada. (Courtesy Library of Congress, Negative LC-USZ62-27949.)

PART THREE

History and Memory

SEVEN

Progress and Poverty: California, 1849–1885

Over the generation that followed the California, Oregon, and Nevada constitutional conventions, each state changed dramatically. Population growth, railroad and telegraph systems, elaborate agricultural, manufacturing, and extractive economies, and metropolitan cultural institutions linked them to the wider world and displayed the extent of their incorporation into a national society. Yet the course and the consequences of the Far West's "progress" was far from the same in each place. To be sure, different geography, resources, and climate shaped local people's history and their consolidation into the nation in distinctive ways. But nature alone did not make California, Oregon, and Nevada. Although by century's end only a handful of these states' first settlers still lived, the force of their pioneering—their conquest of the Far West and construction of charter societies—if unacknowledged, persisted. In the aftermath of statehood one finds the final, perhaps most revealing, measure of the fragment societies of the 1840s and 1850s.

Thirty years after the Californians submitted their constitution to Congress in 1849, another constitutional convention took place in the state. It convened shortly before the visit of the famed Englishman (Lord) James Bryce, in whose classic study of American institutions and "national character," *The American Commonwealth*, California figured prominently. California in the gilded age dazzled Bryce. "What America is to Europe," he wrote, and "what western America is to eastern . . . California is to the other western states. . . . It is a State on which I dwell the more willingly because it is in many respects the most striking in the whole Union, and has more than any other the character of a great country, capable of standing alone in the world." [1] Bryce's description of the state, offered through English eyes and based, he admitted, on only random impressions of San Francisco, nevertheless illuminates the nineteenth-century history of California in significant ways. Trusting his instincts, this English aristocrat captured, without fully realizing it, both the vast changes that had taken place since 1849 and the link between those changes and the charter society created by the gold rush immigrants.

Bryce opened his discussion of "The Character of California" by noting that

> the chief occupation of the first generation of Californians was mining, an industry which is like gambling in its influence on the character, with its sudden alternations of wealth and poverty, its long hours of painful toil relieved by bouts of drinking and merriment, its life in a crowd of men who have come together from the four winds of heaven, and will scatter again as soon as some are enriched and others ruined, or the gold in the gulch is exhausted.

Bryce began with this portrait of "the first generation of Californians" because to his eyes in the 1880s the influence of the gold rush had endured long past the end of the mining era.

> Mining in this region means gambling, not only in camps among the miners, but among townsfolk in the shares of the mining companies. Californians of all classes have formed the habit of buying and selling in the mining exchanges, with effects on the popular temper both in business and in politics which every one can understand. Speculation becomes a passion, patient industry is distasteful; there is bred a recklessness and turbulence in the inner life of the man which does not fail to express itself in acts.[2]

As Bryce saw things, the persistence of traits planted in the "popular temper" by the argonauts of 1849—the "expression in acts" of the gambling "habits" of the gold rush miner—had carried the state far beyond the individualist order of the early camps and towns. The upshot was a place where divisions "between wealth and poverty" had not so much appeared out of whole cloth; rather, they had grown geometrically according to the habits and hopes of the early mining population.

The California Bryce described was not just a society divided by class; worse still, it was a place where class divisions were all the more visible and dangerous, more full of envy and irritation, because capitalists and laborers alike possessed a common "temper" and "character." To him this fact was evident in the very makeup of the men who dominated industry and agriculture in the state. The Central Pacific Railway, the most powerful corporation in the state (indeed, in the Far West), was "controlled by a small knot of men who had risen from insignificance to affluence." Arriviste aristocrats who had started out at the bottom, they ruled "an enormous number of clerks and workmen, and made the weight of their hand felt wherever their interest was involved." In the countryside, Bryce asserted, one found exactly the same. Rural California was marked by "great domains" and "enormous farms," owned by "speculators" who held "their lands for a rise" or rented them "on short leases to farmers, who thus came into a comparatively precarious and often necessitous condition." Other land barons cultivated their holdings with "hired laborers, many of whom are discharged after the harvest—a phenomenon rare in the United States, which, as everybody knows, is a country of moderately-sized farms, owned by persons who do most of their labour by their own and their children's hands." The "land system of California," he concluded, thus "presents features both peculiar and dangerous, a contrast between great properties, often appearing to conflict with the general weal, and the sometimes hard-pressed small farmer, together with a mass of unsettled labour thrown without work into the towns at certain times of the year."[3]

Bryce offered this portrait of California as a prelude to discussing the constitutional convention of 1879, which he presented as the spinning out of institutions and habits established in the era of the gold rush. To his mind the class hatred let loose in the 1879 excitement over constitutional revision stemmed from the fact that both the capitalist and the laboring classes of California were made up of the same kind of men— men imbued with the jackpot mentality of the gold rush, into whose "blood" had passed the "wildness of that time," making "them more tolerant of violent deeds, more prone to interferences with or supersessions of regular law, than are the people of most parts of the Union." Because of this universal expectation of wealth and success, there was nothing to mitigate the "envy" and "irritation" of small farmers, tradesmen, and laborers who failed to join the ranks of newborn "potentates." To make matters worse (particularly to this self-conscious aristocrat), the Californians who succeeded—more often because of luck, not ability— had no sense of stewardship, humility, or aristocratic service, not even in the small measure found among the nouveau riche of the Atlantic states. "As great fortunes have in America been usually won by unusual gifts," Bryce observed,

> any envy they can excite is tempered by admiration for the ability shown in acquiring them. . . . But there were . . . in California millionaires who had grown rich merely by lucky speculation. They displayed their wealth with a vulgar and unbecoming ostentation. They did not, as rich men nearly always do in the Atlantic States, bestow a large part of it on useful public objects. There was therefore nothing to break the wave of suspicious dislike.[4]

Bryce's portrait of the character of California, and his explanation of the passions that marked the second constitutional convention, have, of course, been revised time and again by scholars and commentators. But his impressions, offered through the wondering eyes of an outsider, captured an important truth about the transformation of California between 1849 and the 1880s, in a way observers wedded to the evidence could not. In calling a second constitutional convention, the voters of California testified explicitly to the belief that a new world had emerged since 1849, that a generation of political, economic, and social change demanded a rewriting of basic law. Time, according to radicals and conservatives alike, had made the original constitution obsolete. What Californians failed to recognize—in contrast to the English aristocrat who visited them but briefly—was the thread that tied the controversies of 1879 to the charter settlers of the gold rush.

In the 1870s and 1880s few stopped to consider the implications of Bryce's insight that the corporate and industrial regime dominating city and country marked the culmination, not antithesis, of the earlier individualist order of the gold rush; that change, paradoxically, involved the persistence of older habits and institutions. Californians failed in this, above all, because the scale and speed of the metamorphosis they experienced was so stunning. By 1879 "developments" usually associated with centuries had swept aside the visual signs of 1849, as well as many of the men who had possessed power, prominence, and wealth in the 1850s.[5] The "sudden alternations" in the fortunes of men that Bryce associated with the gold rush camps proved to be not a transitory phenomenon, but a persistent feature of California long after mining, for all intents and purposes, disappeared as a way of work and life in the state.

Thus it is not surprising to find that, in the debates preceding the 1879 convention, virtually no attention was given to the men who wrote the 1849 constitution. Only one article in one newspaper—the *Alta California,* pioneer journal of the gold rush era—referred to them at all. "Many of the framers of our first and present State Constitution are still alive, and citizens of the State of California," the editors of the *Alta* reminded Californians. "The Constitution which they created for a new country has served a very good purpose for nearly twenty eight years . . . [and] one cannot but form a quite favorable opinion of these men as lawmaking citizens. . . . Their experience in the first Convention, and since then, of its working," the editorial concluded, "might prove of immense benefit to the members of the Convention soon to assemble." Halfheartedly, it was suggested that veterans of the first convention might make good delegates to the second, and then the paper listed those who were still alive as well as those who had died. The *Alta's* tally, however, was off the mark in twelve of the forty-eight cases. Three who were counted as dead still lived at their homes in California, while nine men who the editors assured their readers were still alive (including two of the 1849 convention's most notable members, James McHall Jones and Morton Matthew McCarver) had died some time before.[6]

The inability of the *Alta California* to place the 1849 convention delegates testified, if unintentionally, to the transitory prominence of the state's founding fathers. In a manner reflecting the rapid pace of change that marked California in the thirty years after statehood, the authors of the first constitution quickly disappeared from view. Because of death and departure, more than a quarter were no longer in the state three years after the convention adjourned. By 1855 this figure had increased to a third, and by the end of the Civil War to half. Their departures and deaths (eight died within five years of statehood) undoubtedly limited their effect on the public life of the new state.[7] But even among those who remained behind, it is striking that their public lives seemed to reach a natural limit well before they passed beyond middle age. The Civil War—broadly conceived—constituted a barrier beyond which they could not pass.

With the exception of the first year of statehood, the number of surviving delegates elected (or appointed) to local, state, or national office, in California or elsewhere, was small indeed. Sixteen held office in 1850 (ten of them in the state legislature). That total declined to twelve the following year, eleven in 1852, and five in 1853; by the end of the decade only two were in office, and after 1865 none. Of those who had a political career of any significance after 1849, only two attained national prominence. One, Rodman Price, did so in New Jersey, to which he returned in 1850. A year later he was elected to Congress, and from 1854 to 1857 he served a term as governor. The other, William Gwin, represented California in the U.S. Senate from 1850 to 1861. Price and Gwin lived long lives, dying, respectively, in 1894 and 1885. Politically, however, their careers ended with the 1850s. For both men the Civil War brought early retirement.[8]

The 1860s proved to be a watershed in California history no less than in the delegates' lives. The political revolution that secession and war brought to the United States as a whole, along with the consequent economic and social change in the Far West, presented challenges the founding fathers of California could not meet. The Civil War decade brought to the fore, politically and economically, a new generation.[9] By the middle of the 1870s, a time when idealized memories of gold rush society seemed irrelevant to current realities, the state's founding fathers had become relics of a bygone age. Their experience and convictions, which together had reinforced a vision of a society of independent producers, were out of step with an age of industrialism, deepening class divisions, and growing social conflict—the new capitalist order that inspired Henry George's troubling vision of "the persistence of poverty amid advancing wealth" and moved him to write his striking analytical work *Progress and Poverty*.[10]

Over the thirty years that separated California's two constitutional conventions, the state changed in myriad ways. In 1880 its population approached a million, an eightfold increase since statehood. Its racial and ethnic composition, and furthermore, the very geographic distribution of the state population, testified to a worldwide immigration and a generation of economic development along lines unanticipated in 1849. Of first importance, California had become an urban state. More than a quarter of its residents (233,000) lived in San Francisco, which had grown from a collection of tents and shacks covering its hillsides in 1849 into a sprawling center of trade, finance, transportation, and manufacturing. Other cities with 10,000 or more inhabitants—Sacramento, Oakland, Stockton, San Jose, and Los Angeles—raised to 34 percent the share of California's urban population.[11]

The growth of California's cities suggests the scale and character of social change. The transformation of mining, which declined in importance as urban enterprise grew, illustrates the processes at work. By no later than the mid-1850s, the surface deposits of the Sierra Nevada goldfields had been exhausted; as a result, those mining centers that remained into the 1860s and 1870s bore a very different aspect from the camps of 1849. Gold and silver mining became increasingly an industrial enterprise, foreshadowing (on a small scale) later developments in Nevada. Replacing the small groups and individuals who lived in the mining camps of the early 1850s were hired gangs who washed entire mountains hydraulically or worked for mining companies that pioneered deep-rock "quartz" mining. The blasting, tunneling, hoist and cable works, and processing mills that hard-rock mining required transformed the industry from an individualized, small-scale, labor-intensive enterprise into one restricted to companies that could marshall the capital to purchase sophisticated equipment and hire engineers, metallurgists, and skilled laborers.[12]

As the character of mining altered and the industry, relatively speaking, declined, urban-based enterprise grew. In San Francisco and elsewhere, heavy and light manufacturing, finance, retail, and other areas of trade and commerce became dominant. Profits from mining and, later, accumulated in trade during the Civil War years provided the critical impetus. Although between 1850 and 1860 the California economy was marked by an erratic business cycle, the cumulative effects of these years carried the state far beyond the gold rush (as well as beyond the remnants of the earlier Hispanic regimes, which by the 1880s had become the subject of romanticized historical chronicles along the lines of Hubert

Howe Bancroft's *California Pastoral*.)[13] Over the ten years following 1849 a continuous stream of fortune seekers and the expansion of the early mining economy created instant (if uncertain) markets, initiating the development of market agriculture, finance, light manufacturing, and commercial services. Merchants in San Francisco, Sacramento, and Stockton, along with smaller-fry peddlers in the mines, alternately bulled and beared the local market for food, clothing, tools, supplies, and other goods imported from outside the state. While the immediate effect was boom and bust, by 1861–1862, when the effects of the Civil War became apparent, the foundation had been set for a decade of sustained growth.[14]

In the 1860s the economic preeminence of California in the Far West was reaffirmed through growth and diversification. Capital invested in industry increased tenfold, the work force twentyfold and the value of manufactured goods by 400 percent.[15] San Francisco entered the short list of American cities whose regional significance made them genuine metropolitan centers. According to Bryce, it "dwarf[ed]" the other towns of the Pacific Coast and was "more powerful over them than is any Eastern city over its neighbourhood. It is a New York which has got no Boston on one side of it, and no shrewd and orderly rural population on the other."[16]

The foremost source of the growth and prosperity of the 1860s was unanticipated: the Civil War. Disrupting eastern production, the war cut off the supply of imported goods on which Californians depended and thus created a vast new market, one that Pacific Coast (above all San Francisco) entrepreneurs made the most of. The local production of shoes, woolens, clothing, cigars, and other light industrial goods flourished, filling the vacuum. At the same time, the discovery and development of the Comstock Lode brought a boom to California exchanges, enhanced the market for consumer goods, and pushed to new heights the demand for heavy equipment—engines, cables, pipe, and milling machinery—which new San Francisco foundries hastened to provide.[17] Moreover, with manufacturing booming and immigration reduced by the war, labor was at a premium, particularly in San Francisco. There, wages for skilled craft workers exceeded pay in New York and Pennsylvania by 40 percent, reinforcing (and reshaping) memories of the early 1850s as a time when "labor was king."[18]

The Civil War years also saw far-reaching developments in California agriculture, notably the growth of large-scale ranching and industrially organized grain production for export to the Atlantic Coast and England.[19] Between 1861 and the mid-1870s California agriculture became a big business, dependent on international markets and credit and dominated by large landowners who, by a variety of means (not the least of which was the manipulation of the courts and the state and federal land offices), came into possession of massive parcels of agricultural land.

The "factories in the fields" that first appeared in the California countryside in the 1860s continued, in a new key, the patterns of concentrated landownership that had begun under the mission fathers and persisted through the Californio regime. After statehood another shift in
control (but not layout) of the land occurred as control passed from the
Hispanic elite of the 1840s to a new class of Anglo-American land lawyers, speculators, and large-scale agricultural combinations. Three interrelated factors accounted for this shift: litigation over Mexican titles, the
operation of various federal land laws, and the building of the railroad.[20]

Protracted litigation over Mexican land grant titles followed Congress's creation of a commission in 1851 to review and, as needed, patent
or repudiate grants made by the Spanish, Mexican, and California governments prior to 1846.[21] The commission received 813 requests for deliberation in the 1850s. Although a majority (604, or 74 percent) were
eventually secured, the amount of time the review process took—an
average of seventeen years—brought insuperable difficulties to the original claimants.[22] The value of their land dissolved while they waited for
the commission to take up their claim; then for the U.S. District and, in
many cases, Supreme courts to review the commission's action; then—if
successful—for the U.S. Land Office to survey the property; and finally,
for the delivery of a new patent. During the interim period, too, landholders were plagued by squatters who defied their ownership of unimproved tracts that were part of disputed grants. In addition, high property taxes, years of drought (1856, 1863–1864) interspersed with years
of excessive rainfall (1861–1862), and a cycle of boom and bust in the
market for Southern California cattle further strapped landholders of
the Californio regime. Lacking clear title, they could neither sell their
property nor mortgage it except at significant discount; and without the
funds to pay their legal costs, many were forced to sign over undivided
portions of their land, again at discount, to attorneys who specialized in
land title cases. By the end of the 1860s, although on paper many of the
princely Californio domains remained intact, ownership had passed to
lawyers in lieu of fees, or to speculators who foreclosed mortgages they
had extended to desperate claimants.[23]

Also contributing to the persistence of concentrated land ownership,
if in a new guise, was the very operation of the state and federal land
offices that oversaw the distribution of public lands under federal legislation enacted in the 1860s and thereafter. By the end of the Civil War
decade almost 9 million acres of the public domain had passed into private hands through preemption, sale, and grants made under the homestead, swampland, and other federal land acts. Because these programs
were meant to populate the countryside with farming families, parcels
were limited to 160 acres per grantee. In practice, however, the quickly
and crudely devised procedures for distributing the public domain lands

provided manifold opportunities for fraud and abuse, and served in the end only to magnify the concentration of land ownership in California.[24] Artful speculators employed a variety of means to avoid the letter of the law. In hastily organized exchanges they bought land warrants and war script distributed to veterans in recognition of their service.[25] Some paid sailors and unemployed laborers to make dummy entries under the Homestead Act. Others colluded with private surveyors hired by the state to mark off available lands and bribed land office officials to make off-auction purchases. By the 1870s the consequences were apparent. Instead of supporting fifty thousand farming families, the 8.7 million acres of distributed public lands had become the sparsely populated site of cattle ranches and bonanza wheat farms. Noted land barons such as William S. Chapman, Henry Miller, and Charles Lux possessed estates that encompassed hundreds of thousands of acres, while more modestly endowed landlords held parcels measured in tens of thousands of acres.[26]

Motivating such speculators was the Southern Pacific Railroad, a major landowner in its own right. Completed in the 1870s, the Southern Pacific linked the Central Valley of California to the Atlantic Coast and the world via the transcontinental railroad and the ports of San Francisco, Los Angeles, and, eventually, Portland. Construction of the Southern Pacific coincided with the opening of a vast market for wheat in industrializing England. Each step in the line's construction provided new opportunities for "bonanza farmers" with ties to Liverpool merchants, who in turn extended credit to Californians for purchase of the land and machinery necessary for industrially organized agriculture. This symbiotic relationship linking the railroad, foreign capital, and large-scale agriculture pushed land prices beyond the means of small farmers; as a result, many left the state, and those who remained sunk into debt to large landlords.[27]

In addition to giving this new form of agriculture its impetus, construction of the railroad made the Southern Pacific Company the state's largest landowner in its own right. Through land subsidies from local, state, and federal governments the company came into possession of more than eleven million acres, much of it in California's Central Valley heartland.[28] The Southern Pacific transportation and real estate empire actually extended throughout the Far West, for its major officers were the same men who, in the 1860s, had built the Central Pacific Railroad, the western portion of the nation's first transcontinental line.[29] At the head of this combination were the infamous "Big Four": Leland Stanford, Collis Huntington, Mark Hopkins, and Charles Crocker. Through their control of east-west and later north-south railroad communications—the lifeline of California's merchants, manufacturers, and farmers—as well as vast amounts of land, these men became the dominant political and economic force in the state.[30] Unabashedly pursuing a policy of monopoly control, the Big Four drove out competitors by means of price cutting, combinations, and outright intimidation.[31] Their control over transportation, their dominant presence on the land, and their commonality of interest with rural land barons produced a storm of protest in the 1870s—resentment immortalized by Frank Norris in his classic of literary naturalism, *The Octopus*.[32]

Even before its completion the Southern Pacific system came to symbolize a new age of industrialism. In the 1850s Californians had avidly supported construction of a transcontinental link between the coasts, and as the Central Pacific–Union Pacific line approached completion in the late 1860s all expected that it would only enhance the decade's prosperity. However, far from extending the booming economy of the war years, the railroad's completion in 1869 magnified for Californians the national depression of the 1870s. The transcontinental link, coming as it did directly after the Civil War, upended California's economy. For those manufacturers who produced light consumer goods for the local market, the new ease of communication with the Mississippi Valley proved disastrous. The renewal of eastern manufacturing, along with aggressive marketing on the part of Chicago wholesale merchants, brought a flood of products to the Far West. Thrown into a competitive national market, local manufacturers watched as prices declined and their command over California markets dissolved. The consequences were evident as early as 1870. Business and manufacturing concerns faced failure; many went under. Unemployment rose, and market demand fell even further. With their profits shrinking, employers cut wages and—ominously—turned to the Chinese as a source of labor.[33] An explosive issue was born.

The Chinese population in California, which increased from 25,000 in the mid-1850s to 50,000 in 1870 and more than 75,000 in 1880, had long been a target of white violence and prejudice. But not until the late 1860s, when Chinese employment on railroad construction crews ended and they moved in large numbers to San Francisco, did they begin to compete with white laborers. Although only a small proportion of the white labor force, in semi- and unskilled occupations, was affected, the "Chinese issue" suddenly came alive.[34] During the first generation of statehood, calls for Chinese exclusion became the rallying point for California's labor movement and, no less, politicians in the state's political parties. In the campaign preceding the 1879 constitutional convention both radical workingmen and more conventional party figures linked Chinese labor to the railroad and other "monopolies," in the process making Chinese exclusion the centerpiece of California's second effort at constitution writing.

Between 1849 and 1879, politics followed life in California. Even before the delegates to the first constitutional convention left Monterey, maneuvering for office began. Following adjournment, the constitution writers met with interested onlookers and named a slate of candidates for statewide office. Coveting a Senate seat, and looking forward to a Democratic organization he might control, William Gwin apparently played the key role in naming the ticket.[35] For the most part events went according to his plan. He and other delegates desiring office canvassed the heavily populated mining districts in the weeks preceding the November 1849 election. The voters overwhelmingly endorsed the proposed constitution, and the constitution writers who ran for office did well. Although Peter Burnett, Morton McCarver's erstwhile Oregon friend, won the governorship, ten of the constitution writers gained seats in the first state legislature, one became lieutenant governor, and another was elected to Congress.[36]

In the first legislature, veterans of the convention held four of thirty-six seats in the assembly and six of sixteen in the senate.[37] Meeting in San Jose, the legislature had as its first order of business the selection of two senators to present the case for statehood. John Frémont, son-in-law of Missouri's influential senator Thomas Hart Benton and a military figure of heroic stature to Anglo-American immigrants who remembered the conquest, was chosen on the first ballot. Prominent in the list of candidates for the second seat were Gwin and Halleck, as well as President Taylor's emissary, T. Butler King. Gwin's electioneering in the legislative canvass apparently made the difference: a day after Frémont's election, he gained the post he so desired.[38] In order to keep his date with Stephen Douglas, he then hurried to San Francisco and departed for Washington, D.C., with the two congressmen-elect, Edward Gilbert and Sacramentan George Wright.

In the nation's capital, the Californians found the president, Senate, and House struggling over the disposition of slavery in the territory won from Mexico. Sharp differences between the president and Congress, and within Congress, between the parties as well as the sections, delayed for nine months final action on California's bid for statehood. The complexities of this struggle, which resulted in the Compromise of 1850, are well known.[39] What deserves notice here is how the 1850 debates in Washington reprised those that had occurred in the California constitution writers' dispute over the state's boundary.

In the many-sided Congressional conflict that followed the war with Mexico, partisans of President Taylor hoped to forestall a congressional impasse by encouraging residents in the newly acquired territories to create new, free-soil states. Northern antislavery congressmen countered by demanding adherence to the Wilmot Proviso. Still others proposed that Congress follow the doctrine of popular sovereignty, leaving to local residents the disposition of slavery. Among southerners who rejected all of the above, some, like Jefferson Davis, called for the extension of the 1820 Missouri Compromise line—and thereby the area of slavery—to

the Pacific, while allies of John Calhoun insisted that the federal government protect slave property everywhere in the new territories of the
Far West.

Out of the conflict between these positions Congress ultimately fashioned the nation's last great compromise between freedom and slavery.
At its heart was a series of resolutions, originated by Henry Clay and
then refashioned by Stephen Douglas, that placated sectional differences without resolving the larger question of slavery's place in the western territories. In the debates on the issue, the California constitution
played no small role. Despite the desire of the constitution writers to
avoid congressional opposition, their free-soil charter inevitably became
a sticking point, foreclosing as it did any southern demand for slavery's
protection in what was considered the most valuable part of the ceded
Mexican territory. By presenting Congress with a fait accompli, though,
the California constitution had the effect of encouraging southern compromise, and in turn northern acquiescence, on points such as the disposition of slavery in the remainder of the Mexican cession and the
fugitive slave law.[40] On September 7, 1850, its energies exhausted, the
House of Representatives concurred in the Senate bill admitting California. The compromise was complete, and the senators and representatives of the new state quickly took their seats.

Over the decade that followed the admission of California, the Democratic party, as in Oregon, became the dominant political organization in
the state. Like Oregon as well, California politics swirled about a Democratic majority troubled more by internal conflict than by an organized
anti-Democratic adversary. Only once did an anti-Democratic challenge
succeed on the statewide level. In 1855, the Know-Nothing candidate for
governor, J. Neely Johnson (whom we have encountered during his
years in Nevada), won the executive office and went to Sacramento with
his party in control of the legislative lower house. The Know-Nothing
victory was shortly overturned, however, by the crisis surrounding the
organization of the San Francisco vigilance committee. Far from marking the beginning of a substantial challenge to Democratic domination,
the importance of the Know-Nothing interlude rested above all in its
illumination of the brewing conflicts that beset the California Democracy
throughout the 1850s, conflicts that were the product of local jealousies
and individual ambitions, ethnic animosities, and—connecting state to
national politics—competing sectional loyalties.

Behind the Know-Nothing victory at the polls in 1855 was the defection of thousands of Democratic voters allegiant to one of two competing
wings of the California party. The schism in party ranks had appeared
within two years of statehood and would persist until the California De-

mocracy collapsed in 1860–1861. It paralleled (although imperfectly) the intraparty conflict that beset Democrats in the Oregon Country, who, in the 1850s, divided their loyalty between Joseph Lane and Asahel Bush. In California, the foremost antagonists were William Gwin and David Broderick. Drawing, respectively, on national and local patronage powers, the two built political machines that were at odds throughout the decade. Gwin (like Joseph Lane, but more openly and with greater effect owing to his senatorial position) utilized to the fullest his position in the nation's capital. There he closely watched the federal patronage, rewarding faithful followers and denying the disloyal. Within a year of his election to the Senate he had created a political organization overseen at home by allies at every level of the appointive system, from U.S. district judge to local postmaster. Known as the "Chivalry," the name of Gwin's organization reflected the prominence of transplanted southerners in it, as well as its leader's alignment in the Senate with his party's southern wing.[41]

Set against Gwin and the Chivalry was another Democratic organization, coined "Tammany" and directed by Broderick, a former New York stonecutter and saloon keeper who arrived in California in early 1850.[42] (In New York he had been a minor functionary in the city's Democratic organization—thus the label applied to his organization in California.) To his new home Broderick carried a form of workingman's Democracy that differed sharply in style and substance from Gwin's Chivalry. Urban, working-class, and northern in background, Broderick drew a sharp line between his conception of Democratic doctrine and that of Gwin, exploiting wherever he could the latter's patrician pretenses and gravitation to old southern friends in the Senate. The challenge that Broderick presented—his open appeal to class, ethnic, and sectional interests—had a symbiotic effect on Gwin, encouraging, if not forcing, the latter to move even closer to the southern wing of the national party (despite his personal ambivalence toward slavery) and to sharpen the line between his Democratic friends and enemies via the lever of patronage. In turn, Broderick became a magnet for Democrats jealous of Gwin's power and suspicious of his southern background.

By the mid-1850s the schism was complete and seemingly irremediable, as Broderick grew ever more prominent in state politics, offering a powerful counterpoint to Senator Gwin. Broderick's rise, moreover, was rapid. In 1851 he was elected to represent San Francisco in the state senate. There he was elected president (pro tem) of the upper house and, when Burnett resigned from the governorship in January 1851, became acting lieutenant governor as well. From this position he quickly built a political organization that on the state level soon paralleled—and challenged—Gwin's.

While Gwin secured his hold on the federal patronage, Broderick

concentrated on the largess he could dispense from city and state cof-
fers. To do so, he and his partisans organized volunteer fire companies
in San Francisco's largely Irish-Catholic workingmen's districts, which
became the nuclei of his political organization in the city. Re-creating the
system of favors, jobs, and political loyalty he had learned in New York,
Broderick's machine (disparaged as the "Shovelry" by its adversaries) became quickly entrenched in San Francisco. He then moved to extend his
power throughout the state. In 1851 he convinced the state Democratic
convention to apportion its membership according to population, which
made his San Francisco delegation the foremost voice in the selection of
candidates for statewide office. Broderick soon dominated the Democratic State Committee, which oversaw party affairs between conventions, and in 1854 he became the party's state chairman. Drawing on this
post's influence, he arranged an alliance with another ambitious Democrat jealous of William Gwin, Governor John Bigler. Together, Broderick
and Bigler attracted a statewide following by appealing to Democrats
fearful of the Chivalry's southern orientation and holding out state patronage appointments to party men whom Gwin passed over. By the
mid-1850s their machine rivaled Gwin's organization everywhere.

Loyalty and hatred—held with equal intensity—underscored the intraparty contest between Gwin and Broderick in the 1850s. Such passions stemmed from ideological differences and, no less, the two men's
common style of party organization. In the Senate, Gwin took every opportunity to secure his position at home. In his first term he obtained
appropriations for a mint in San Francisco, as well as for numerous harbor improvements, coastal aids to navigation, and military installations.
He was a prominent spokesman for the construction of the transcontinental railroad, although his support for a southern route gave his actions a sectional cast. He also devised the controversial legislation that
created the commission to review Mexican land grants. The public works
bills put at his command scores of appointments and millions of dollars
in public money; the land commission, based on the presumption that
Mexican titles were imperfect, appealed to arriving Anglo-Americans
who hungrily eyed, and in many cases squatted on, the land of the
Californios.[43]

Yet at the same time that this legislation drew supporters to Gwin, it
drove others away. Delays, influence peddling, and sweetheart deals (no-
toriously in the contracts for the San Francisco mint) fed partisan attacks
on the senior senator. So did the manifest injustice afforded native Californians by the land commission legislation. His support for a transcontinental link between the South and California demonstrated to many
his adherence to the cause of slavery. As a result, when Gwin returned to
California in 1855 to stand for reelection, he found himself in political
trouble. Broderick, portraying Gwin as a corrupt dispenser of privilege,

enemy of the worker, and far western agent of a conspiratorial "slave power," blocked the senator's reelection.[44] For two years a legislative deadlock between Gwin and Broderick men continued, leaving empty Gwin's seat in the Senate.

Broderick, too, was a controversial figure. Presenting himself as the champion of the workingman against Gwin's personal party, he waged constant political war against not only fellow Democrats, but also San Francisco employers and merchants, anti-Democrats on the whole, who identified their political problems with Broderick and the economic difficulties they faced as the uncertain economy cycled through booms and busts in rapid succession. Twice in the 1850s merchant frustration led to popular uprisings: the vigilance committees of 1851 and 1856. In both instances, what Robert Senkewicz and Roger Lotchin have described, respectively, as merchant frustration with an uncertain economy and bourgeois fears of the political power of foreign workers (living in highly segregated and largely male enclaves) erupted in movements that defied the established authorities and took control of the city. While the ostensible objective of both vigilance committees was to purge alleged criminals in command of the municipal government and courts, their proximate target was David Broderick's Tammany organization. To merchant vigilantes, his Democratic machine—and its Irish, Catholic, working-class adherents—embodied a portentous alliance between an alien Roman dogma and the forces of urban disorder.[45]

Whereas the vigilante uprising of 1851 was short-lived (in the space of one month the participants hanged four suspected criminals, banished fourteen others, and then disbanded), the eight-thousand-member Committee of 1856 had lasting force. Led by the city's large merchants, who confronted at the time the worst depression of the 1850s, it gave voice to the same anti-Democratic (above all anti-Broderick), anti-Catholic, and anti-Irish sentiments that, the preceding fall, had contributed to a statewide victory for the Know-Nothing party.[46]

The travail of Governor Johnson in dealing with the vigilance committee and the simultaneous collapse of the Know-Nothing movement have been recounted above.[47] Here it will suffice to note the ironic reversals that marked the political season of 1855–1856 in California. The twelve months that followed the fall 1855 election began with the stirring Know-Nothing victory at the polls, followed shortly by vigilantes claiming sovereignty over San Francisco through force of arms. However, any common ground that might have existed between the anti-Democratic Know-Nothings and the similarly anti-Democratic vigilantes was undercut by the fact that the nativists' electoral victory stemmed not from an attraction to Know-Nothingism per se, but largely from the support of Chivalry Democrats who defected to destroy Broderick and defeat his friends in the state legislature. Furthermore, Johnson's confused response to the insurgents in San Francisco and his failure to find a political resolution to the crisis quickly drove a wedge between the Know-Nothings' nominal leader and the San Francisco movement. The resulting debacle led to the undoing of the governor and, more generally, of the Know-Nothing party.

In San Francisco, in contrast, the political effects of the vigilante movement were enduring. Although the committee disbanded within six months of its formation (after hanging four men and banishing dozens of others), its principals, calling themselves the "Committee of Twenty-one," announced a ticket for the municipal election of 1856 drawn from Whigs, nativists, and independents who were long-standing opponents of the Broderick machine.[48] Running under the banner of the "People's party," the vigilantes swept into control. The new merchant-led party dominated San Francisco politics until the late 1860s, when a rehabilitated Democratic party returned to power.

In the meantime, the vigilantes' proximate target, David Broderick, stayed out of harm's way by leaving San Francisco. In the face of the attempt by the vigilance committee to dismantle his San Francisco organization, he directed his energies instead to shoring up support elsewhere throughout the state. The effort paid off. His statewide, if not San Francisco, organization remained intact; in the fall 1856 election, Democrats, most of them Broderick partisans, wrested control of the legislature from the party of J. Neely Johnson.[49]

The legislative session that followed the urban uprising and simultaneous political convolutions had as its first duty the selection of two U.S. senators. Gwin was aware that Broderick had maintained, and perhaps even increased, his ability to block Gwin in a reelection bid; to reclaim his still-vacant seat, therefore, he publicly agreed that his nemesis deserved one of the vacant Senate seats and, furthermore, that he, Gwin, would relinquish his control of the federal patronage in return for Broderick's support. Broderick sealed the deal, and the two adversaries became Senate colleagues. Although the bargain seemed to give Broderick the upper hand, in Washington President Buchanan, prompted by Gwin and in any case wary of Broderick's preference for the Douglas side of the party, refused to acknowledge the arrangement and ignored the junior senator. Thus, in yet another reversal, Gwin's power was renewed, though at the cost of becoming ever more closely tied, indeed beholden, to a president increasingly identified as prosouthern. Gwin, once again in control of the patronage, now rebuilt his California organization, freezing out Broderick's friends wherever possible. His return to the Senate, as well as the collapse of the Know-Nothings, reinvigorated the Chivalry and produced resounding victories for its adherents in the 1858 election.[50] The timing was important, for at the same moment, Gwin, Broderick, and other California Democrats—precisely because of the link between local animosities and local organizations to Democratic divisions in Washington, D.C.—found themselves drawn into a controversy that joined the fate of the state party to that of the nation.

This controversy stemmed from the Kansas-Nebraska Act of 1854, which reopened the question of slavery's expansion into the territory of the Louisiana Purchase.[51] According to the bill's "popular sovereignty" provisions, the territory's residents were given the responsibility of determining the status of slavery when they wrote their state constitution. In Kansas, pro- and antislavery forces turned constitution writing into a veritable battlefield. Antislavery Kansans boycotted both the constitutional convention held in the town of Lecompton and the subsequent vote on that convention's constitution. Consequently, Congress was forced to decide whether the proslavery charter was a genuine expression of the popular will. President Buchanan, speaking as the party's leader, said yes, and William Gwin followed him. Hesitantly, Stephen Douglas, the architect of Kansas-Nebraska and the foremost spokesman for popular sovereignty, said no. So did David Broderick. Indeed, his opposition to Lecompton came even more quickly, fired no doubt by his outrage at Buchanan's refusal to honor his agreement with Gwin over the patronage.[52]

In the Senate, neither Californian played a decisive role in the congressional crises that unfolded in the late 1850s over "Bleeding Kansas" and the Lecompton constitution, but in California politics turned on their conflicting positions. While Gwin requested and received the local party's endorsement of his stand behind Buchanan, Broderick joined and then moved beyond Douglas toward an alliance with the new Republican party. Declaring slavery "old, decrepit, and consumptive; freedom . . . young, strong, and vigorous," he became a Democratic renegade.[53] In the state election of 1859 the conflict reached a boil. Broderick engineered a fusion of Douglas Democrats and Republicans, which nominated candidates for statewide office and many legislative posts. During the month preceding the vote, Broderick and Gwin separately visited the towns of northern California, verbally abusing each other along the way. Although many Democrats were put off by Gwin's increasingly strident prosouthernism, Broderick's alliance with the "Black Republican" adversary was unacceptable to far more, and the fusion tickets (one of them containing future Nevadan Charles E. De Long) met defeat almost everywhere.

Nonetheless, the Chivalry's 1859 victory quickly proved a prelude to disaster. The day after the election, one David S. Terry challenged Broderick to a duel on a matter of personal honor. Terry was a prominent member of the Chivalry who had served a term as judge of the state supreme court. In a manner evincing the crooked path of California politics in the mid-1850s, he had been elected to the court as a Know-

Nothing; by 1857, however, he was back in the Democratic fold. At the party convention two years later, he roundly denounced those men— above all, by implication, Broderick—who opposed congressional endorsement of the Lecompton constitution. In response, Broderick declared Terry a blackguard. One thing led to another, and on September 13, 1859, the two squared off in a field south of San Francisco. Broderick fired first, missing Terry completely. Terry's shot found the senator's heart; three days later he died. The effect was sensational.[54]

Broderick became a martyr, transformed by his dying words into a symbol of Republican resistance to the slave power. "They have killed me," he reportedly gasped, "because I was opposed to the extension of slavery, and a corrupt administration." To his friends, he sent a message: "Protect my honor. I die for a principle."[55] At a public assembly of mourning in San Francisco thousands heard (and wept at) the eulogy of Broderick given by Republican stalwart E. D. Baker, the lifelong friend of Abraham Lincoln whose career in the Far West intersected so often with the Californians, Oregonians, and Nevadans treated here. Through Baker the duel became the opening act of the 1860 presidential election. Placing responsibility for Broderick's "assassination" on Chivalry Democrats, his speech, heralded in the local press, doomed William Gwin. Gwin left San Francisco quickly, in the hearing of cries and in the sight of banners demanding that "the murderers of David C. Broderick never return to California."[56]

In the 1860 election the Democracy of California collapsed into parts that displayed how long-standing local divisions had become joined to the sectional breakup of American politics. The conflict between Gwin and Broderick—between the Chivalry and the Shovelry—provided the template through which Democrats divided between Breckenridge and Douglas, between the South and the North. The upshot of the Democratic division was a slim plurality for Lincoln—a slim plurality that marked as well the end of a political era.

The national crisis that followed the South's secession carried California's Democrats and Republicans alike into the wartime Union party. This organization, however, was more than a transitory haven for those loyal to the northern cause; it was also a workshop in which a new generation built the political and economic institutions of post–Civil War California. Foremost within this group were young Republicans such as Leland Stanford, who in the 1860s was both president of the Central Pacific Railroad and first Republican governor of the state. For him and others the war provided a tangible lesson in politics and economics, insofar as the mission to preserve the Union affirmed federal supremacy over the states and, more generally, tied the principle of centralized action to the realization of moral ends of the highest order. In this respect, wartime domestic legislation such as the Homestead Act and Morrill Land Grant Program exemplified the material benefits achievable by co-ordinated undertakings that were national in scope. More powerful in effect, and closer at hand for Californians, was the transcontinental rail-road, an enterprise often described in military metaphors redolent with the imagery of the Civil War. A national project analogous in scale to the war for the union, and one that promised material rewards similarly analogous to the moral returns of that great conflict, the building of the railroad suggested a new ideological equation between politics and eco-nomics—essentially, a redefinition of American society in light of an emerging, if not yet fully evident, corporate order.

Over the last third of the nineteenth century, the increasing signifi-cance of large-scale manufacturing, integrated systems of production and distribution, nationally oriented corporations, and the spread of wage labor called old understandings into question.[57] The postwar re-construction of party politics saw a subtle yet far-reaching revision of basic terms. While partisan lines were everywhere uncertain and shift-ing, the modern Republican party did not prosper solely because of its identification with the preservation of the Union. Alongside this moral bond between party and electorate was an alteration in the language of progress inherited from the past. Increasingly, the older view of a so-ciety of individuals acting independently in small communities was being rejected, in favor of a vision of the transformative powers of corpora-tions, whose financial force and managerial prowess, it was promised, would push the aggregated commonwealth to new heights. In postwar California, the signs of this new age in both city and country—under-scored at every turn by the presence and power of the railroad—sharp-ened the GOP's identity as the party of capital.

The postwar rehabilitation of California's Democratic party followed a related path. Directed by new men who could not be implicated in the party's disaster before the war, the revived Democracy had at its heart an alliance with a nascent trade union movement that grew in tandem with California's industrial development. On the surface, Democratic par-tisans drew on the same appeals and imagery that had animated work-ingmen's adherence to the antebellum party, but again the connotations of language and symbol had changed. Behind the old defense of the rights of workingmen had been a particular set of images grounded in the independent-producer ethic of artisans who controlled a productive system of apprentices, journeymen, and masters. After the war, how-ever, the increase in machine-based manufacturing and the correlative transformation of craftsmen into wage workers focused Democratic ener-gies on the rights of employees within the wage system. In so doing the party presented itself not so much as an opponent of the emerging corporate-industrial order, but rather as the advocate of labor's—above all, skilled craft labor's—claim to a maximum share of that order's productive returns.

In California the platforms of the revived, postwar Democracy emphasized the eight-hour day, a rising standard of living for workers, government restrictions on land and financial monopolies, and, above all, the exclusion of Chinese laborers from the state.[58] In calling for Chinese exclusion, as Alexander Saxton has shown, Democratic leaders, allied with leaders of San Francisco's anticoolie clubs and trade unionists, updated antebellum convictions about the racial limits to American society in a way that avoided, as overt appeals to Negrophobia could not, the "bloody shirt" and charges of disloyalty.[59] In terms that resonated historically, Democratic aspirants characterized the Chinese as a degraded race whose willingness to work at starvation wages promised to reduce white workers to a similarly mean and desperate level. According to this argument, the birthright of a just return to labor was rapidly disintegrating; rather, the forces of monopolistic privilege were encouraging competition between white and Chinese labor in order to impose wholesale wage slavery.

The effectiveness of this appeal became apparent in 1867 when Democrats captured the state legislature and governor's office.[60] In that election, Democrats painted their opponents' political strategy as based on enfranchising dependent nonwhite laborers, Negroes in the South and Chinese in the West, whose pliability at the polls would hasten the destruction of white labor's fragile claim to liberty. "Take away the Chinese, negro-suffrage, and negro-brotherhood planks from their [Union-Republican] platform," the Democratic *San Francisco Examiner* charged in a characteristic attack, "and they simply become a plunder league, banded together to rob the Government and use its powers for the aggrandizement of special interests and favored classes."[61]

The protracted depression that struck California two years after the Democratic victory of 1867 magnified all the more the power of this symbolic amalgamation of railroads, monopolies, and Chinese labor. Behind the depression were many factors: the rapid growth of the 1860s, the undercutting of local business by eastern manufacturers and Chicago merchants, the spreading effects of the national downturn that began with the panic of 1873.[62] But over and above these was a series of specific events that produced in California a longer and more severe depression than elsewhere. The result was a widespread sense of crisis, captured in the phrase "the terrible seventies."[63]

Most spectacular in this respect was the collapse of the Pacific Coast's premier financial institution, the Bank of California, whose Comstock Lode speculations could not withstand a sudden drop in stock prices in 1875. Although the bank reorganized and returned to business, its unexpected failure vivified the recurring personal disaster that struck scores of small speculators in Comstock Lode stocks. More generally, in the 1870s business failures became commonplace. Before the decade was out almost three thousand incorporated firms had gone bankrupt, thus swelling the ranks of the un- and underemployed in the state. In San Francisco alone, an estimated fifteen thousand men were without work in 1877.[64] And beyond the cities, a persistent drought beginning in 1875 destroyed crops and cattle for two years in succession, producing rural refugees who added all the more to the number and desperation of the jobless in the state.[65]

In the short run, Democratic success in tying the plight of white laborers to the Chinese and Republican monopolies effectively diverted attention from the party's complicity in the Civil War, but over the longer term the logic of such tactics proved difficult to contain. Democratic control of state government eventually carried with it a measure of responsibility for the depression, which reduced the effect of partisan attacks on Republicans. Continuing the call for bold (and usually unconstitutional) measures to rid the state of the Chinese also became more problematic; in the end, party figures had no choice but to emphasize the need for federal, as opposed to state, action on the Chinese question. At the same time, Republicans slowly but surely embraced the cause of Chinese exclusion. By the mid-1870s it was difficult to distinguish between the parties' anti-Chinese planks: both favored exclusion and passed the buck to Washington, D.C.[66]

This political consensus, however, had little appeal to white laborers who had been taught for a decade that Chinese labor was the source of their personal, day-to-day travail and that the Democratic party would do something about it.[67] Ineluctably, the more modest aims of the parties encouraged a workingmen's insurgency demanding direct action. The catalyst was an enigmatic San Franciscan, Denis Kearney, who emerged at the head of the newly organized Workingmen's party in early 1878, just months before the election of delegates to California's second constitutional convention. Kearney's rise followed a summer of violence in San Francisco, when crowds attacked Chinese neighborhoods and the property of the foreigners' alleged protectors, the railroads. Murders, incendiary fires, and battles between police and rioters ensued. In response, Democratic authorities in the city and state governments, assisted by the Republican administration in Washington, D.C., mobilized their forces. Allied with them was a hastily assembled "pick-handle brigade," a vigilante-style organization devised and led by prominent businessmen (foremost among them William Coleman, a veteran of the 1856 uprising). Together, this bipartisan combination between the established parties and San Francisco commerce quelled the disorder.[68] No sooner had quiet returned, however, than Kearney began to channel the energies of violent dissent into a political force. By pushing the antimonopoly and Chinese exclusion arguments of Democrats and trade unionists beyond the bounds of establishment politics, he became a force to reckon with.

Kearney's political program was based on an appeal to the politically unorganized as well as to workingmen aligned with the Democratic party.[69] His venue was not the working-class wards but emotionally charged public gatherings, held in the sandlots that faced the city hall then under construction. There he harangued eager crowds with attacks on the state's political establishment—Democratic and Republican—tying them to the twin evils of railroad monopoly and Chinese labor. "Are you ready," he asked on one occasion, "to march down to the wharf and stop the leprous Chinaman from landing?" To another gathering: "I will give the Central Pacific just three months to discharge their Chinamen, and if that is not done, Stanford and his crowd will have to take the consequences." To still another: "The dignity of labor must be sustained, even if we have to kill every wretch that opposes it."[70]

For his remarks Kearney was jailed again and again; each time his following grew. By the time of the Workingmen's first convention in January 1878, it was clear that the party included not only marginal workers but also significant numbers of skilled laborers who normally voted Democratic. Furthermore, that winter and spring the new organization demonstrated its ability to win at the polls. Suddenly, six months before the election of delegates to the state's second constitutional convention, Democrats and Republicans faced the prospect—widely predicted in the press—of a constitutional convention dominated by "communist" Kearneyites.[71] Against this threat the established parties responded by agreeing to a "nonpartisan," or, as William Issel and Robert Cherny have better put it, "bipartisan and anti WPC," fusion. The tactic was successful: the nonpartisans carried the vote by a two-to-one margin, capturing roughly two-thirds of the convention seats against one-third for the Workingmen.[72]

The second constitutional convention is commonly described as a confrontation between radical Workingmen and conservative nonpartisans; such were the terms used at the time in the press and by advocates of the nonpartisan fusion. Yet to characterize the division in the modern terms of class conflict distorts as much as it reveals. The nonpartisan fusion was an uneasy alliance at best. Significantly, it included a rural, "granger" bloc of approximately twenty-five delegates who were willing to ally with the Workingmen on questions relating to land concentration, taxation, and railroad regulation. From time to time, though inconsistently, this group was able to tip the balance of power in favor of constitutional reforms favored by the Workingmen delegates.

Contrary to fears voiced in the California press, rural delegates and other nonpartisans aligned with the Workingmen because the latter's agenda for the new constitution—in contrast to Kearney's political rhetoric—was *not* radical. Workingmen in office were not interested in revolutionizing California. They did not oppose private property, or the market economy, or even corporations. Their energies were directed, rather, toward reform. As delegate Clitus Barbour observed, the party had "no desire to root out the foundation of society or throw down the social structure, or to impair any of the well known interests of our country"; its purpose, rather, was to "reconstruct the fabric which has been eaten into." Added his colleague Charles Beerstecher: "We can see that corporations have rights, and we are willing to give them their rights, but we also desire to have the rights of the people recognized."[73]

In practice, the Workingmen's program merged the liberal vision of a society of equal men pursuing their self-interest in the market with a sense that individual autonomy and opportunity were being destroyed in California because of the insuperable power of corporate combinations over individuals—both the individual wage worker and a dwindling band of rural and urban proprietors, each of which confronted the market power of corporate competitors.[74] In this respect, most of the Workingmen reforms were, simply, more starkly phrased versions of Democratic and Republican measures; beyond the posturing of the different sides there was significant, if in the end vague, agreement. The new charter had to counter the concentration of landed wealth, revise inequitable tax systems, curtail railroad domination, and—the ever-present issue—exclude Chinese laborers. The 1879 constitution of California was thus an effort to make sense of a modernizing corporate order by preserving freedom for the individual proprietor while at the same time accepting the presence, even the dominant presence, of supra-individual combinations. In a sense, with this document the delegates, Workingmen and nonpartisan alike, were anticipating the regulatory state that would be established by Progressive reformers a generation hence.[75] They intended to widen government's role as the guarantor of individual liberty, giving it the responsibility to limit and control, but also assist, the pursuit of private advantage.

This intent was most evident in the Workingmen's agenda, but it is important to note that Democratic and Republican newspapers readily admitted that there was little in the Workingmen's proposals to offend more conservative tastes. The San Francisco *Daily Evening Bulletin*, for example, observed that "the Workingmen's platform is such as any party might incorporate in its declaration of principles"; the *Marysville Daily Appeal* concurred, asking, "Who [could] want a better platform to stand upon?"[76] Underneath the rhetoric exchanged by Workingmen and their nonpartisan adversaries rested a broad area of agreement in which an older political tradition was redefined in light of the emerging corporate order.

In enunciating their position in platforms and pronouncements, the California Workingmen of 1879 were quick to draw upon republican symbols. In their first declaration, for example, party adherents put the case as follows: "The republic must and shall be preserved. . . . Our shoddy aristocrats want an emperor and a standing army to shoot down the people. We propose to wrest the government from the rich and place it in the hands of the people, where it properly belongs." These thoughts were amplified in the party's constitution:

> The rights of the people, their comfort and happiness, are wholly ignored, and the vested rights of capital are alone considered and regarded, both in the states and the nation; the land is fast passing into the hands of the rich few; great money monopolies control Congress, purchase the state legislature, rule the courts, influence all public offices, and have *perverted the great republic of our fathers into a den of dishonest manipulators*. This concentration and control of wealth has impoverished the people, producing crime and discontent, and retarded the settlement and civilization of the country. In California, a slave labor [i.e., the Chinese] has been introduced, to still further aggrandize the rich and degrade the poor, and the whole tendency of this class of legislation is to undermine the foundation of the republic and pave the way to anarchy and misrule.

Finally, in resolutions endorsed just prior to the constitutional convention the same points were reaffirmed: "The duty of making the laws of our country," Workingmen declared in appealing for electoral support,

> has hitherto been confined to the non-producing elements of society, who have failed to secure us in our inalienable rights, utterly ignoring the welfare of the producers, upon whose labor individual and national prosperity depends; reducing our farmers and wage laborers to a state of dependence, compelling them to compete with a degraded class of Mongolian laborers imported from abroad, and whose presence is demoralizing as well as dangerous to the preservation of our liberties . . . our legislative halls, national, state, and municipal, have become infested by thieves who do not scruple to take bribes, until our national forum has become a byword of reproach among nations . . . our courts have become corrupt, the equal rights of the people violated until the administration of justice has become a mockery and a farce.[77]

The symbols emphasized in these appeals are striking: the "republic" and its betrayal; " producers" and their "inalienable rights"; the corruption of government and the increasing "dependence" of those "upon whose labor individual and national prosperity depends."

The republic whose betrayal California Workingmen feared, however, differed significantly from the republic conceived, and worried over, by Oregonians to the north. For the Californians the heart of the republic rested in access to market opportunities by individuals—opportunities, as they saw it, threatened by a force they identified simply (and so failed to examine systematically) as "monopoly." Their desire to restore a betrayed republic thus pushed them toward the outlines of an activist state that, to the end of proscribing "monopoly," was empowered to regulate industrial capitalism so as to preserve a place for the individual within the liberal order. "The line of demarcation is now drawn," Workingman Clitus Barbour proclaimed, "and we draw it between monopoly on the one hand and anti-monopoly on the other." [78]

Opposition to monopoly, viewed thus, did not countenance the destruction of private property, or the corporate form of enterprise, or social class distinctions; nor did it suggest the confiscation of accumulated wealth. Rather, "monopoly" and "antimonopoly" contrasted the right to possess property with the monopolization of land through illegitimate means; the right to accumulate wealth with the amassing of wealth through corruption of government agencies and the courts; and the natural occurrence of class distinctions due to differing capacities with the creation of dependent classes through manipulation of the economy and polity.

According to the logic of capitalism, of course, these are minute, perhaps irrelevant, distinctions. But in the context of the 1870s they were self-evident to most delegates, nonpartisan and Workingmen alike. Constitutional revision afforded, or so it seemed, an opportunity to draw a precise line between monopoly and antimonopoly, and in such a way that respected the rights of property while curtailing the abusive tendencies of wealth. To the convention the Workingmen carried detailed plans to do just this, most of which found their way into the constitution. Among them was an elected railroad commission to oversee transportation rates and other company practices; jury trials to protect small landowners in cases of eminent domain; a prohibition of thirty-three different varieties of special legislation; and a ban on the public sale of harbor frontages, tidewaters, or navigable streams. Furthermore, the constitution made lobbying a felony; empowered the legislature to establish an income tax; divided property taxes proportionately between mortgagors and mortgagees; and, in a weak echo of Henry George's single tax, provided for the taxation of farmland irrespective of improvements.

With regard to labor, the constitution was similarly precise. It included a mechanics' lien provision and required an eight-hour day on all public works. Convict labor was restricted in order to avoid competition with free laborers. The constitution also contained a series of anti-Chinese measures, although they stopped far short of the immediate exclusion demanded by Kearney in his sandlot harangues. Following the well-worn line of Democrat and Republican officeholders, the delegates petitioned Congress for federal legislation excluding Chinese. In addi-

tion, the constitution prohibited Chinese employment on public works
and charged the legislature with passing laws allowing towns and cities to
remove Chinese from their limits.

The long and emotion-packed convention was followed by a bitter
campaign in which the new constitution was, more often than not, denounced for its length, statutory character, and cumbersome, poorly devised measures. In a memorable phrase Henry George dismissed the
document as a "mixture of constitution, code, stump speech, and man-
damus."[79] Despite the attacks, Californians endorsed the new charter,
demonstrating their conviction that new laws were needed to meet a new
age. However, any hope that the constitution would remedy concentrated
landownership, curtail the power of the railroad, assist debt-ridden
small farmers, or ameliorate the plight of labor was quickly disabused.
Measures intended to draw a line between monopoly and antimonopoly
failed in the face of outright bribery, courts sympathetic to corporate interests, and the Southern Pacific's corruption of elections. Above all, they
failed because they glossed over a dilemma central to liberal society. As
twentieth-century Progressives would discover, it is extraordinarily difficult to identify the point at which the pursuit of self-interest—to the end
of accumulating wealth and power—becomes illegitimate.

The contrast between this confrontation over constitution writing—
the issues, leaders, and electorate—and its antecedent of 1849 could
hardly have been sharper. From the vantage point of 1879 the postconquest–early gold rush era retained little overt relevance to the politics of
a society in which changes ordinarily associated with centuries had been
compacted into three decades. The *Alta California*'s obscure reference to
the constitution writers of 1849—its halfhearted suggestion that they be
consulted about revising the state's charter—testified implicitly to the
obscurity that time had brought to the founding fathers of the state. Yet
in the individual stories of these men's historical obscurity one finds the
spinning out of the antebellum traits that carried them to California in
the 1840s, that informed their writing of the state's first constitution,
and—most importantly, if more visibly in the lives of other Californians—that underscored the development of the state, as Bryce put it,
into "the most striking in the whole Union."[80]

Between 1849 and the 1880s California's founding fathers continued
to be motivated by the same mixture of closely calculated ambition, imperial vision, and assiduous attention to the main chance that marked
their early lives. This continuity was fully evident in the six leading men
we have followed to 1849: James McHall Jones, Morton McCarver,
Henry Halleck, Lansford Hastings, William Gwin, and Charles Botts.

For many reasons, none attained the goal they sought; miscalculations, early death, immodest ambition forestalled their capture of fame. But each did gain a measure of notoriety, carrying forward—if at the margins of a world passing them by—the culture of the California gold rush.

Of the six, the first to die was James McHall Jones, who succumbed to tuberculosis at the age of twenty-six, two years after the convention. The failure of Jones's health came quickly, accelerating with brutal speed after his mother's death from the same disease in the spring of 1851.[81] Jones died a wealthy man, having made a fortune in property speculation, above all in lands to which he gained title as attorney for Hispanic land grant holders. He also enjoyed a measure of political success, despite his Whig loyalties in a state dominated by the Democracy. William Gwin (after 1850, Senator Gwin) remembered his fellow southerner by arranging his appointment as U.S. district judge for Southern California. Jones's closest friend and law partner was another prominent Democrat, John Weller—former congressman, noted member of the California Chivalry, and later U.S. senator. What all this might have meant cannot be said, for Jones's death came just as his law practice was taking off and he was preparing to begin his judgeship.[82]

Although Jones's shortened life tells little about what the second half of the nineteenth century held for California's founding fathers, this was not the case with the other leading men of the California constitutional convention. All five lived beyond the Civil War, Gwin and Botts into the 1880s. In their lives—their successes as well as failures—one finds a final measure of California's first generation of public men.

After leaving the convention, Morton McCarver fell back into the prior patterns of his life. Between 1850 and his death in 1875 he continued his wandering ways, moving between different parts of the Far West, searching for the main chance much as he had as a young man in the border, southern, and plains states. In mid-1850, having lost his holdings in Sacramento real estate to floods and fires, he left California and returned to Oregon.[83] Near Oregon City he set up a farm, which remained his base of operations, if not home, for much of the next decade. There McCarver briefly farmed, invested in a variety of enterprises, and all the while kept his eye out for an opportunity at public office. During the Oregon Indian Wars of the mid-1850s he enlisted in the territorial militia and served as its commissary general. In 1856 he traveled to Washington, D.C., to seek congressional funding for the territorial scrip he had distributed to finance military expeditions. While in the nation's capital he tried to enlist the support of his Kentucky friend Senator John Breckenridge in securing an appointment as Oregon's territorial governor. His effort, which was ridiculed by Oregon men, came to naught, for reasons curiously similar to those that had hampered this headstrong man in the 1849 California convention. There he had been tagged the "delegate from Oregon," a label applied facetiously but pointedly insofar as it identified McCarver as a man out of his element and not to be taken seriously on political matters in California. In an analogous way, to the Oregonians with whom he reunited after the California convention he was an outsider as well, this time a politician from California, a figure without enduring bonds to place, a man too obviously out for himself and thus offensive to the subtleties and nuances central to the culture of the Oregon Democracy.[84] Thus, undone by ill-concealed ambition, Mc-Carver eventually concluded (as he had in 1848) that greater opportunities lay beyond the ingrown American colony of the Willamette Valley.

In 1857–1858 McCarver followed the mining rush to the Fraser River in British Columbia, and in 1862 he moved to the mining camp at Bannock City, Idaho, where he worked for a while as a merchant. From Idaho he briefly relocated to New York City, promoting—without success—stock in Idaho gold-mining companies. When fire destroyed his Idaho mercantile house and eastern speculators failed to hearken to the lure of his frontier promotions, he returned to Oregon, settling this time in Portland. From there he moved on in 1868, embarking on his last enterprise in town (now "city") building, on the Puget Sound in Washington Territory. There McCarver organized (as he had in Iowa, Oregon, California, and Idaho over a span of twenty-five years) another urban promotion, first called "Commencement City," then "Tacoma." His scheme was a grand one: a city to serve as the western terminus of the Northern Pacific Railroad recently chartered by Congress. For five years he remained in clammy quarters by Commencement Bay, overseeing the platting of his city, the sale of house lots, and the construction of roads and accommodations.

In 1873, now aged sixty-five, McCarver received the welcome news that the Northern Pacific had selected Tacoma as its western headquarters. His elation soon dissolved, however, when he learned that the railroad's terminal and yards were to be constructed some distance from his property, thus shifting the course of city growth (and the immediate opportunity for profit) away from his holdings. Once again, so close but yet so far: McCarver's final attempt to "see the Elephant," like his previous ones, came to less than he thought his due. Two years later he died. An almost "Jacksonian man"—frontier town builder, itinerant merchant, promoter and speculator, constitution writer, Negro hater, and Indian fighter—McCarver never attained the fortune or renown he sought across the western half of the American continent. Yet his lifetime of constant movement, full of small triumphs and larger defeats, nonetheless displayed, albeit through a prism of disappointment and failure, the inner life of an American type heralded in his time and after.

In a different way, the life of Henry Wager Halleck after 1849 was also marked by a combination of grand ambition and poignant failure. In Halleck's case, triumph and failure followed a steeper trajectory that carried him, if fleetingly, to wealth and prominence in gold rush California, battlefield honor during the Civil War, and finally scorn, failure, and (worst of all) obscurity.

At the close of the constitutional convention Halleck turned down those who promoted his candidacy for the U.S. Senate or governorship of the new state. He remained in the army for four years, then resigned to give his attention to the practice of law. In San Francisco he became senior partner in the firm Halleck, Peachy, and Billings, by the mid-1850s the premier land title practice in California. Drawing on his knowledge of Mexican land law gained in the 1840s while military secretary of state, he became an extremely wealthy man.[85] Although he had interests in quicksilver mining and railroad promotions, the foremost source of his fortune was Mexican land titles. In engaging in such speculation, Halleck belied to many the self-image he had curried while an official of the military government and member of the 1849 constitutional convention. By the mid-1850s even those unsympathetic to the travail of Hispanic landholders found his manipulation of the beleaguered Californios too crass, too self-interested. As one observer noted in 1857,

> Halleck . . . professes now to be a lawyer, but in fact is a speculator in Mexican land grants and city real estate, and has been more extensively and intimately associated with the confirmation of Mexican grants than any other individual in California. It is said he now has an interest in a greater number of grants than any other one man in the state. . . . He is cold, austere, aristocratic, *pertinaciously* selfish, and is his own best friend all the time.[86]

With the outbreak of the Civil War, Halleck's life took a turn. He was called back to the army and, on the recommendation of Winfield Scott, appointed to the rank of major-general. In quick succession he commanded the Department of the Missouri (1861), the Army of the West (1862), and, after the Battle of Corinth (1862), the Union forces in their entirety, with the impressive title general-in-chief of the United States Army. For Halleck it was a luckless appointment. Disdained by other Union officers for his pedantic approach to the battlefield (he was known as "Old Brains") and incapable of working with the president or his cabinet, he soon fell out of favor and found himself shunted off to what were, essentially, clerical duties.[87] Despite his learned treatises on the art of warfare and an inflated sense of his own genius, Halleck spent the remainder of the war isolated from power, overshadowed by men such as U. S. Grant and William T. Sherman who better understood the imperatives of total war. By the time of the Confederacy's capitulation to Grant (a man Halleck once commanded and never trusted), his name was in disrepute. At the end of the war he found himself without influence and in failing health. Shuffled from obscure post to obscure post, he landed finally in Louisville, Kentucky, in 1869. There, three years later, he died unexpectedly, apparently of alcoholism.[88] Notices of his death in the California papers weakly defended his wartime command, but of greater interest to San Francisco readers, it appeared, was the value of his estate.[89]

The Civil War was the undoing of Lansford Hastings as well. After the convention he returned to merchandising, an itinerant law practice in the mines, and a failed attempt to promote a trading town, "Sutterville," which he intended to carry gold rush commerce away from Sacramento. The failure of this speculation bankrupted Hastings, and to escape his creditors he fled California, luckily enough with a federal appointment (arranged, perhaps, by William Gwin) as postmaster of Arizona City, New Mexico (later Yuma, Arizona). There he opened a law practice, became a territorial judge, and gained a measure of local notoriety by leading a movement for the creation of a separate territory out of the small settlements of western New Mexico.

With the Civil War Hastings, an outspoken Democrat and southern sympathizer, was removed from his judgeship, and he returned with his family to California. When his wife died unexpectedly (whereupon he placed his daughter in a Catholic convent), he set out on a remarkable journey that recapitulated—in the context of the Civil War—his filibustering expeditions to the Far West in the 1840s. Making his way through Arizona and Mexico to Louisiana, he conferred with Confederate generals John B. Magruder and E. Kirby Smith and then continued on to Richmond. In the capital of the Confederacy he presented to Secretary of State James A. Sedden a bold plan to bring the southwestern territories, and with them California, into the war on the side of the South. By using the "blind" of a mining company, Hastings proposed to assemble in California a force of one thousand to five thousand "sterling Southern men" with whom he would seize the U.S. arsenal in Yuma, Arizona, "establish[ing there] . . . [a] Confederate Territorial Government, hold[ing] permanent possession of the Territory, keep[ing] the thoroughfare [to the Pacific] open, [and] maintain[ing] an unbroken intercourse between the Confederate States and California."[90] Confederate generals were skeptical of the project, but Jefferson Davis (perhaps simply to get rid of him) issued Hastings letters of marque and reprisal,[91] and by the end of 1863 "Judge" Hastings was back in California. There, according to a suspicious writer for the *Los Angeles Star*, he was engaged in arranging a mining expedition to the "Colorado River area . . . financed by San Francisco capitalists."[92]

Nothing came of either the rumored mining expedition or Hastings's grandiose scheme to win the Southwest and California for the South. Indeed, once he left Richmond Confederate officials did nothing to encourage him further. With the war's end, however, the proposal became public knowledge in California, and Hastings became persona non grata on the Pacific Coast. In 1866 he turned up in Alabama promoting an emigration/colonization scheme that recalled his filibustering two decades earlier. This time his efforts were directed toward creating a Brazilian haven for ex-Confederates left hopeless by the Union victory. In Mobile he published another "emigrants' guide," describing the virtues of the Brazilian interior for southern agriculturists and implying an opportunity to rebuild the world that planters had lost in war. In 1867 and 1868 he tried three times to lead to Brazil the few who responded to his bizarre scheme for a Dixie colony deep in the Amazon jungle, five hundred miles from the Atlantic. Plagued by disinterest, lack of money, breakdowns, disease, and shipwrecks, none of the expeditions reached the intended destination.[93] During the third and final attempt, the Confederate adventurers' ship was forced into St. Thomas. There the forty-eight-year-old trail guide, filibusterer, and soldier-of-fortune, suffering from yellow fever, died.[94]

William Gwin's political career—if not life—also ended with a bizarre wartime scheme. For one who had gained a place near the center of national power in the 1850s, the public repudiation that followed the death of David Broderick and the secession of the South was a heavy blow. Shortly after Lincoln's inauguration Gwin left Washington, D.C., on what turned out to be a decade-long odyssey. His first stop was Mississippi, where he inspected the plantations he had owned since the 1830s. Then, in quick succession, he traveled to Washington, D.C., California, and New York, consolidating his property in preparation for the worst. Fearful of imprisonment (twice in 1861 he was jailed briefly on suspicion of treason), he collected his family in 1862 and set sail for Paris. There, with the backing of Napoleon III, he hatched a scheme more remarkable and mysterious than that of Hastings.

Playing to Napoleon III's desire for a French foothold in the Americas, Gwin convinced him that with sufficient financial and military support he could induce tens of thousands of southerners and Californians to colonize the Sonora and Chihuahua provinces of Mexico for the French. To carry out his scheme Gwin asked only that Napoleon order his Mexican puppet, "Emperor" Maximilian, to guarantee the American colonists military protection from natives and the right to claim and mine silver in the northern regions. Napoleon embraced the plan, seeing it in terms of *la grande pensée de l'empereur,* his vision of a French empire in America.[95] The benefits that Gwin foresaw in the project are more difficult to discern. The appeal may well have been leadership of a wealthy province inhabited by Americans that, like California, would quickly become a natural addition to the American union. Such a scenario was Maximilian's fear: "What will happen," he inquired of Napoleon, "when a compact Anglo-Saxon group is established on the frontier? They will become rich and will they follow our rule or want to be independent?"[96]

Maximilian's suspicions and, more importantly, the unraveling of his regime (and with it the French design for a Mexican empire) doomed Gwin's bold enterprise. By the fall of 1865 he concluded correctly that Maximilian was about to fall and that his program to colonize northern Mexico had no chance of success. From Mexico he fled to Texas and then, shortly after the Confederacy fell, to Louisiana. There he was captured and imprisoned by federal forces. For eight months he was kept incommunicado while his jailers sought instructions from Washington, D.C. Gwin's spirits flagged, and to his jailer he made a remarkable (though possibly apocryphal) confession. In a long conversation with Colonel S. G. Hamblen he told the story of his French-Mexican scheme, insisting that with French protection he could easily "have had three hundred thousand miners there in two years." Hamblen, playing to Gwin's vanity, agreed, and then spun out the conclusion implied by what his prisoner did *not* say. "You would have had your miners," Hamblen observed, "enough for a small nation—or a large state—all American citizens, in a region adjoining the United States. What would they have done? Submit to the doubtful chance of Mexican control? Or turn to the United States and add another star to the Stars and Stripes?" To Hamblen the ex-senator's intention was obvious: "W. M. Gwin would have been the first senator from the state of Sonora, all the same."[97] Gwin did not disagree.

Shortly thereafter, without explanation, Gwin was released. He departed immediately for Paris, where he reunited with his family. They remained in the French capital for two years, joining the city's large community of Confederate expatriates. All along, however, he looked for a way to return to California free of harassment. An opportunity, he concluded, came in 1867 with the return of the Democratic party to power in the state, and early the following year the Gwins came back to San Francisco. He sold off what remained of his properties in California and Mississippi, investing the returns in quartz mines. The mines paid well and once again Gwin was a wealthy man, though this time as a capitalist, not an absentee plantation owner.[98]

Although Gwin failed to recover the political standing he had possessed in the 1850s, he never gave up his hope of returning to power,
and remained active in Democratic circles from 1870 to his death in
1885. In 1876 and 1880 he served in the California delegation to the
Democratic national convention. At the time of his death he was earnestly seeking a variety of appointments from the newly installed Democratic administration in Washington, D.C.[99] But, tainted by a reputation
for ruthlessness, his prosouthern sympathies, and, even more, an identity as a consummate and wily schemer, he was never taken seriously in
his desire for a substantive role in the affairs of the party. According to
one biographer, "To the new generation he seemed like a survivor from
an antediluvian period, an age that already had become legendary."[100]

By virtue of his past (as a Jacksonian and a senator sympathetic to the
South), his wealth, and his patrician bearing, Gwin was ill suited for
leadership in a Democratic party inhabited increasingly by wage workers.
His world in the 1870s centered on the polite society of San Francisco's
nouveaux riches; politically as well as socially, he was more at home in
the drawing rooms of Nob Hill than in the city's working-class wards.[101]
Within his party he gravitated toward a small but influential band of conservatives who regarded the party's antirailroad, antimonopoly, and
even anti-Chinese planks as "communistic and agrarian."[102] Within this
circle Gwin reshaped his Jacksonianism to fit the new, postbellum world.
He did so in telling ways, ways testified to in part by the praise he received from Republicans.

In 1875, for example, the Republican *Alta California* praised "California's great old Democratic law-giver" for his willingness to tour the South
and "call around him . . . his old-time confreres in Congress in behalf of
a sound metallic basis for business and commercial prosperity." Gwin
made the trip "in the Directors' [of the Southern Pacific] Special Car"
at the behest of former (Republican) governor Leland Stanford and in
the company of Southern Pacific officer Charles Crocker. An added
benefit of his trip, the *Alta* reported, was the support he would engender
among southerners for the Southern Pacific's proposed transcontinental
extension.[103]

Gwin's opposition to paper money in this instance was unexceptional
in light of his lifelong insistence on the virtues of a metallic currency, not
to mention the state of public opinion in California in the 1870s. Yet the
argument against a paper currency had shifted since the 1840s. Instead
of being a threat to the independence of farmers, artisans, and mechanics, it had become an inflationary device that, while perhaps benefiting
debtors, threatened the "national credit" and "business and commercial
prosperity"—that is, the national system of finance, manufacturing, and
distribution.[104]

Most suggestive of Gwin's Democratic response to the post–Civil War
United States, however, was his support of the presidential ambitions of

Supreme Court justice Stephen J. Field. A Democrat appointed to the high court by Lincoln, Field served as a judicial bridge of sorts between ante- and postbellum eras. Far from being "'cut from the same bolt of cloth' as William G. Sumner's Social Darwinism," Field sought, via principles learned as an antebellum Jacksonian, to find "government's legitimate role in American life" by devising legal rules "to separate the public and private sectors into fixed and inviolable sectors."[105] Although Field was not, as often portrayed, the undiscriminating judicial friend of the new corporate-industrial elite, his disdain for the postwar labor movement made him anathema to the rank and file of his own party. When, in 1880 and 1884, he was mentioned as a possible presidential candidate, it was not because of a groundswell in California. Nonetheless, he was the man for Gwin. In 1880, the ex-senator, while preparing for the national Democratic convention, contrived an intricate scenario to give the judge the party nomination. His reasoning, however, did not convince even the otherwise sympathetic *Alta California.* "We give Dr. Gwin the credit of possessing great political sagacity," the editor remarked, "but doubt very much whether his prophetic political vision will prove true."[106] The *Alta*'s prediction was in the end correct. Field's chances were doomed by the instruction of the state Democratic convention to its delegates: oppose his nomination at all costs.

Denied the role of kingmaker, and now well into his seventies, Gwin faded from view. As his eightieth birthday approached in 1885 he made his last trip to Washington, D.C., where he unsuccessfully sought appointment as U.S. minister to Japan. He then went on to West Point and New York. En route he was stricken with dysentery, and a week later, in a New York hotel, he died.[107]

Although Gwin was in California during the state's second constitutional convention, there is no record of his views on the charter or the men who wrote it. The only veteran of the first constitutional convention who played any role whatsoever in the events of 1879 was Gwin's nemesis from thirty years before, Charles T. Botts. In thus participating he ended a long retirement from public affairs that had been brought on by his disgrace during the Civil War.

Before 1861–1862, Botts had been well known as a stalwart Democrat. In the first state election he ran for attorney general, losing by a single vote. He then moved from Monterey to the more promising legal territory of San Francisco, where he became known as a ruthless, and very successful, attorney. Originally a Democrat with Whig inclinations (witness his banking proposals in the constitutional convention), after statehood he allied himself with the Gwin-led Chivalry, and his partisanship grew as the party schism widened in the mid-1850s. In 1857 (the year of the Chivalry's revival after the defeats of 1855), he was appointed district judge, in which position he proved a loyal operative. At the close of his term he took on the party's Broderick-Douglas wing directly, editing a pro-Chivalry political paper, the *Democratic Standard*. In the election of 1859 he benefited from the Chivalry's statewide sweep, becoming the state printer, but shortly thereafter the Democratic crisis of 1859–1860—the death of Broderick, Lincoln's election, and the South's secession—swept him from office.

In the 1860 presidential campaign Botts devoted his energies to the Breckenridge-Lane ticket, insisting that a Republican victory meant the dissolution of the Union.[108] The election of Lincoln, he declared, would require "a convention with a view to the establishment of a separate and independent Republic upon the Pacific Coast."[109] This appeal, however, fell on deaf ears; a week after he printed it, his paper ceased publication. Even without the paper, however, Botts remained outspoken in his opposition to the Union party. During the war he published a pamphlet, "Secession and Coercion: The Relation Between the State and Federal Governments," that continued his call for an independent Pacific republic, and declared before the state legislature his "sympathy with [the] Confederacy, with all my heart and with all my soul." In the midst of the war, these sympathies made Botts persona non grata, and in 1862 the *Alta California* reported that he had left California for "the Sonora silver mines."[110]

Botts's absence was short-lived. Soon he was back in San Francisco, followed (along with reports that he had departed for Brazil) by an interlude in Virginia at the end of the war, apparently to salvage what he could of his family's property. The postwar South, however, did not hold his attention, and by the end of the 1860s he had reappeared in California and resumed his law practice.[111] His disillusionment with Republican domination of politics and the postwar gilded age was palpable. Despite the wealth he gained as a ruthless "black letter" lawyer, Botts roundly scored the materialism of postwar California. "Everything," he complained to a friend from the 1850s, "is sacrificed to the acquisition of material wealth. We bow down before the golden calf and he who attempts to overthrow the popular idol, is very like[ly] to be crucified."[112]

Only once before his death in 1884 did Botts again participate in public affairs, in response to a request to evaluate the proposed 1879 constitution before it went to a vote of the people. His response was revealing. In an essay for the *San Francisco Daily Bulletin* he compared the original and proposed constitutions, declaring the latter a "mass of crudities and absurdities . . . a retrogression in political science and a great calamity to the community." His disquisition, which covered the front page of the *Bulletin*, condemned the new charter for its length, complexity, internal contradictions, loopholes, and confusion. For each major section he predicted that the ends sought—railroad regulation, equitable taxation, protection of labor against the power of capital, the exclusion of Chinese laborers—would not be realized by the document's ratification. This was so, in his view, only partly because of the complexity of the various prohibitions and requirements contained in the new charter; more important, he averred, was the fact that "no mortal convention" could ever right the wrongs that Californians perceived around them. That "the existing state of things was deplorable" he readily granted. "The country," he admitted, "was full of stock gamblers . . . the body politic was festering with corruption . . . wealth aggregated in the hands of individuals and powerful corporations controlled the halls of legislation." The consequences were foreboding: "The rich [are] getting richer and the poor poorer . . . we [are] drifting from a Republic into an aristocracy of wealth." [113]

This said, to Botts's mind there was no alternative. In so concluding he drew on themes—indeed, a theory of history and society—that serve as an appropriate coda to the lives of the California founding fathers. His thoughts, in a way he did not realize, tied 1879 back to 1849 and in the process indicated the historical fate of the liberal individualism that had carried men to gold rush California. With the days of '49 fully in mind, Botts declared that stopping the juggernaut of accumulated wealth was impossible:

> It has pleased the Creator, for some inscrutable purpose, to make a world of universal warfare. From man to the humblest plant that springs from the bosom of the earth, it is one universal struggle for life, and the result is the survival of the strongest. By an inexorable law of his nature, man is compelled to seek his own happiness and to prefer that happiness to the happiness of another. Hence we have competition and strife. Hence we have the government and the governed. The weak are, have been and always will be hewers of wood and drawers of water to the strong. Much as we may regret this state of things, we can no more escape from it than we can escape from death itself. . . . The unequal distribution of wealth under the existing social system . . . [is] God's distribution, and no mortal convention could better it. [114]

EIGHT

Crisis and Renewal:
Oregon, 1857–1890

To many visitors in the 1860s, 1870s, and 1880s Oregon was an odd place. For those who came through California, the border crossing seemed to mark a passage to a world incomparable to the one immortalized by Lord Bryce—and lamented by Charles Botts. In contrast to the enterprise and speculation, the political passion and cultural energy, the vast (and vulgar) displays of wealth alongside poverty and deprivation that impressed and repulsed observers of California scenes, life in Oregon seemed staid to a fault, lacking the vital edge that even eastern cosmopolites appreciated in a place like San Francisco.[1] J. H. Beadle, writing in 1873 for the *Cincinnati Commercial*, was struck by what he found:

> There is a distinctively Oregonian look about all the natives and old residents which is hard to describe. Certainly they are not an enterprising people. . . . They left Missouri and Illinois—most of them—because those states were even then "too crowded" for them and they wanted to get away where "they was plenty o' game" and have a good easy life. . . . They acknowledge their own laziness and talk about it so good humoredly that one is compelled to sympathize with them.[2]

Oregonians, of course, were quick to give the lie to disparaging comments like Beadle's, but the fact remains that contrasts rather than similarities struck outsiders—this despite forces at work in the generation after statehood, which drew the state into the sinews of a national economy, society, and political system. In the Pacific Northwest as in California, the secession crisis initiated a political realignment that contributed to the formation of the modern Republican-Democratic party system. Oregonians, too, experienced their own peculiar "railroad era" and, if subtly, confrontation with the excesses of the gilded age. From the 1860s through the 1880s the state witnessed modest population growth and signs of "modern" economic development, central to which was the emergence of Portland as the premier city in the state. A center of banking and finance, light industry and commerce, it was by 1890 the second city of the Pacific Coast after San Francisco.

And yet, if the usual measures of post–Civil War U.S. history are applied to the region, significant features of the Oregon Country in the later nineteenth century are obscured. Change here occurred at a cadence different from that of its southern neighbor. Except in a small way, Oregon lacked the mineral wealth that, transformed into capital, shaped California long after the mines played out. Pacific Northwesterners remained wedded to farming, and as farmers their embrace of market agriculture was subdued even after the isolation of the early decades ended. Although commercial farming increased in the 1870s, 1880s, and 1890s—most importantly east of the Cascade mountain range—the older mixture of subsistence and market family farming in the Willamette Valley continued long after the 1850s. This was the case to no small degree because of the persistence of the early comers to the state. With the exception of those who briefly sojourned in Oregon during its mining rushes in the 1860s, life there was marked, if not dominated numerically, by those who stayed behind.[3]

The social authority of these early settlers persisted as well, particularly in their commitment to a way of life tied to the soil. Market ambition and the appeal of speculation and accumulation in service to material improvement and industrial "progress" were muted in Oregon, counterbalanced by modest material horizons and the goal of property ownership. These traits were evident in the cities as well as the countryside, among urban capitalists as well as rural folk. Cautious to an unusual degree, the early merchant capitalists of Oregon ran their businesses with an eye more to the present advantage than to risky, if potentially lucrative, future prospects. They were marked, Kimbark MacColl has pointed out, by "conservative financial practices which eschewed credit for cash [and] the pursuit of sound investment instead of risky speculation."[4] Less prosaically, Joaquin Miller observed in 1872 that Portland's "bankers and merchants—mostly home-made, or 'valley-tan'—still show traces of their weak pin-feathers, and decline to take any great flights in speculation or outside commerce."[5]

Contributing to the persistence of the political and material culture of the early settlers was the very timing of change in Oregon. Rail transportation and the transformative effects of regular links to national and world markets did not arrive until the middle 1880s, more than fifteen years later than in California. Until then, the state remained relatively isolated. This isolation, by limiting the scope of opportunity available to nascent manufacturers and merchants, entrenched the first-comers, those who in the 1840s and 1850s claimed land under the Donation Land Act, bought Portland and other town properties at low prices, and established their command over local markets. Early possession of the limited array of tangible assets in this slow-changing region, augmented by the persistence of the pioneer generation, produced a provincial society that, long after other parts of the United States had entered an industrial age, still remembered, even honored, convictions that contemporaries outside the state thought more appropriate to a prior age.

The modest pace of change in Oregon over the generation that followed statehood made it a place in which its founding fathers thrived, notwithstanding the larger political crisis of the nation. The contrast with California in this regard is stunning. Thirty years after California entered the union the men who wrote its first constitution were little remembered and even less honored. Just the opposite was the case in Oregon. The constitution writers of 1857 remained not only in the state but also, to an impressive degree, in the thick of its public life. Few of them left the state after statehood; indeed, most remained Oregonians to their death, a fact that reflects the widespread ownership of land that marked them as a group and the predominance of agricultural occupations among them. Of the sixty delegates, fifty can be traced to their deaths; of these, forty-four (88 percent) died in Oregon. Moreover, again in contrast to the Californians, the Oregon constitution writers were long-lived. Of the fifty whose full lives we can follow, only four died before 1870, and twenty-eight (56 percent of those traced) lived past 1885. Eleven lived to see Oregon enter the twentieth century.[6]

Attached to place and favored with good health and long lives, these men left an indelible mark on the politics of their state in the 1860s and 1870s. Despite the crisis that confronted the Democratic faithful in the decade after 1859, they remained active at the local, state, and national levels, and played a central role in the reconstruction of political institutions and ideas during and after the Civil War. Of the convention delegates, at least thirty-five held office after 1857. For nine, tenure was limited to local posts—mayor (four became mayor of Portland), city councilmen, county judges and commissioners, and the like. Twenty-three held state offices: two became governor, fifteen sat in the state legislature, four became members of the state supreme court, and the remainder held a variety of executive posts. Seven went on to national office: four became U.S. senators, among them Delazon Smith, George Williams, and La Fayette Grover (the fourth was James Kerr Kelly, who in 1870 succeeded Williams); two were elected congressional representatives; and one, Matthew Deady, remained on the bench of the U.S. district court until his death in the 1890s. Nor was these founding fathers' participation in the public life of state and nation limited to a few years after statehood. Collectively, they held forty-one offices in the 1860s, fif-

teen in the 1870s, and seven in the 1880s. The last of them elected to
office, George Williams, became mayor of Portland in 1902.

That so many of the Oregonians managed to maintain positions of
power and authority in the postbellum era testified to the residential
persistence and continuing authority of Oregon's first-comers, as well as
to the perduring bonds between friends and neighbors in small communities, an important source of political power even despite the destruction of the party system in the secession crisis of 1859–1861. But their
perseverance in office also required that they come to grips with the unraveling of the political ideas and institutions they had learned in their
youth and carried as immigrants to the Far West. In response to the Civil
War, and no less to the currents of economic change that began to en-
velop Oregon in the closing decades of the century, they had to make
sense, to themselves as well as their constituents, of what at first glance
seemed a revolutionary break with the past. The facility with which they
mastered the crisis of their age—particularly the Democratic kingpins
we have followed through the 1850s—affirmed their abilities as political
men. Of more interest, in their careers we can see how Americans who
came of age in the antebellum era crossed the chasm of Civil War and
industrialization. By no later than the mid-1860s the boldest among
these state makers had been born again politically. Their conversions
were played out publicly. And they were permanent.

The successes enjoyed by these constitution writers over the first generation of statehood underscore the continuing isolation of Oregon
from the nation and the world. Until the mid-1880s, potential settlers
still faced an arduous overland journey, with immigration to Oregon following from much the same logic that had drawn the first pioneers.
Newcomers were largely farming families from the Midwest who were
attracted by the Pacific Northwest's healthy climate, good farming conditions, and the prospect of guaranteeing family self-sufficiency free of the
struggles known in other agricultural regions. Those who arrived in the
1860s and 1870s magnified the persistence of older ways, thereby emphasizing Oregon's identity as a last frontier in ways that went beyond its
physical isolation in the northwest corner of the continent. From 1860
until the mid-1880s, population growth and the signs of agricultural and
industrial change were steady but modest—modest in comparison to the
industrial transformation under way in other rural regions (outside the
South) and, more importantly, in comparison to Oregon itself after 1885.

Neither 1860 nor 1870 nor even 1880 marked a turning point of any
significance. Growth occurred, but always along familiar lines. The
population of the state grew from 52,160 in 1860 to 174,763 in 1880,
a more than twofold increase. Throughout, Oregon retained (with one

notable exception) the social, ethnic, and racial homogeneity that had marked it from the beginnings of Anglo-American settlement. In 1880, as in 1850, rural emigrants from the Ohio and Mississippi River valleys predominated.[7] Recent or old arrivals, they remained tied to the land and devoted to the mix of subsistence and market agriculture that had marked Oregon since the 1840s. Over the twenty years from 1860 to 1880, improved agricultural acreage increased at a rate (145 percent) substantially below the growth of population, while capital investment in agriculture grew by 236 percent. In contrast, the value of the state's agricultural products increased by only 86 percent—testifying to the persistence of household habits and poor access to external markets (as well as the deflationary trend in staple prices that beset commercial agriculture everywhere). At the same time, the number of manufacturing establishments in the state increased in step with population (250 percent), as did the value of manufacturing products (267 percent). Capital invested in manufacturing did grow at a faster rate (372 percent), although not dramatically so, reflecting the virtual zero point from which it began.[8] Steady and modest, these figures attest more to a process of quantitative growth than a qualitative shift in the nature of the local economy—to more of the same rather than fundamental change.

In 1880, moreover, as in 1855, 1860, and 1870, the majority of Oregonians remained concentrated in the Willamette Valley. Even by the understated standards of the Bureau of the Census, 85 percent of the population in that year was fixed to rural residence.[9] Oregon's largest city, Portland, had only 17,577 residents; Salem, the state's second "metropolis," had fewer than half that number; and Astoria, the next largest, under 3,000. Manufacturing played a minor role in the productive lives of Oregonians, eclipsed everywhere by a form of agriculture that mixed the selling of surplus crops with the essential business of providing for families' immediate needs.[10] As of 1880, excepting the area around Portland, the value of agricultural goods in the state was almost double that of manufactured products.

The almost-inhibited growth that marked Oregon over the twenty-five years after statehood is all the more evident when contrasted to the changes that *did* occur after the mid-1880s. At the heart of this transformation was the completion, after a twenty-year, Byzantine struggle, of regular rail links with California, the nation, and the world. The delay in the railroad's coming to Oregon had many facets. Despite the passage in 1864 of the Northern Pacific Act to encourage a line from the Great Lakes to the Pacific Northwest, the small population in the region made any such a venture risky and less attractive than a line to California. In addition, Oregonians themselves, despite public pronouncements to the contrary, remained at best passive participants in railroad promotions. Oregonians, Joaquin Miller remarked bluntly, were "at war with the railroad. Men, whose land has been trebled in value by the location of [the] line . . . [fight] every foot of its advance."[11] Indeed, river transportation magnates—Oregon's "biggest businessmen" in the 1860s and 1870s and thereby the obvious local promoters—actually constituted the foremost barrier to railway construction in the state.

Consequently, the men who brought the railroad to Oregon were outsiders. They, not resident capitalists, came to control transportation lines to and from the state and also the profits accruing from the sale of hundreds of thousands of acres distributed to them by the national government as a bounty for constructing the lines. In contrast to California, which became home to the far-flung Southern Pacific "Octopus," Oregon became a tributary state to a series of foreign railroad syndicates, not the least of which was the Southern Pacific.

By the turn of the century the Southern Pacific line through Oregon's Willamette Valley had become an important part of the overall Southern Pacific system. Yet the infamous "Big Four" of California, masterminds of that line, played no role in the original financing or construction of any Oregon railroad. Rather, the key figure in bringing rail transport to the state was a German émigré, Henry Villard. Between 1879 and 1883 Villard was instrumental in the eventual construction of three different transcontinental routes into Oregon. One was the Oregon and California line, which he took over from the ill-starred California promoter Ben Holladay and later lost to the Southern Pacific. The centerpiece, however, was the Oregon Railway and Navigation Company (later incorporated into the Northern Pacific Railroad Company), which he created in 1879, shortly after taking over the O & C. Villard built the Oregon Railway and Navigation Company on an existing company, the Oregon Steam and Navigation Company, which Portlanders had established in 1860 to carry goods and passengers between Portland and points along the Columbia River. Serendipitously, within a year of that company's formation the first mining rushes to eastern Oregon and Washington, Idaho, and Montana began. Well placed to take advantage of the demand for transport to the mines, the OS & N quickly captured monopoly control of river transportation and the vital portages on the Columbia. Within five years of its founding it had become the largest business enterprise in the state. By the end of the 1860s its transportation empire extended well beyond Oregon—across Idaho to Montana and north to Canada; its system of water and land routes linked not only the inland mining regions but also prospective farming areas by stage, express, and steamer to the oceangoing port at Portland. As the company's business grew, so did the financial authority and social status of its officers in Portland. In the 1860s and 1870s, the company and its founders underwrote much of the new business in the city.[12]

In the 1870s, the men of the OS & N stood at the pinnacle of Oregon's economy. There, moreover, they gave ample testimony to the restrained ambitions and modest market horizons characteristic of their society. Although wealthy and able to command the attention of capital markets in Oregon and elsewhere, they shied away from augmenting their local transportation empire with a railroad system connected to a transcontinental. Indeed, satisfied with what they had, they did what they could to block any such plan. Their actions in this regard followed interest narrowly conceived: they feared the competitive threat to their water transport company posed by a railroad along the Columbia. Yet, as observers have long since pointed out, their reasoning held only if—as was apparently the case for the OS & N men—they were content with the wealth and local position they enjoyed and unprepared to risk all in a railroad gamble, despite the prospect of a magnificent return.[13]

The likelihood that the Portland owners of the OS & N thought along these lines is strongly suggested by their willingness to sell their company to Villard, who saw the steamship company as the perfect vehicle for putting together a railroad empire. With the stroke of his pen on a new article of incorporation prepared as soon as his purchase was complete, Villard transformed the Oregon *Steam* and Navigation Company into the Oregon *Railway* and Navigation Company. Under his direction, the renamed company by 1882 had built more than five hundred miles of track stretching from Portland into eastern Oregon and Washington, thus opening this territory to the development of large-scale, capital-intensive wheat farming imitative of the Central Valley of California. Villard's ambition, moreover, did not stop at the plains. Buoyed by the success of his Oregon enterprise, he put together a financial scheme that brought him control of the Northern Pacific Railroad, whose progress west of the Great Lakes had been stalled at Bismarck, North Dakota, since the company's collapse in 1873.[14] Within two years of becoming president of the Northern Pacific, Villard helped drive the last spike in a line connecting Portland (and the Puget Sound) with the Midwest and, from there, the rest of the nation.

Villard's success, however, was short-lived. In completing the Northern Pacific he overextended himself financially. Soon after the line was finished he defaulted on bonds and lost control of the Northern Pacific, the Oregon Railway and Navigation Company, and the still-unfinished Oregon and California line.[15] In the ensuing reorganization, control of both the Northern Pacific and Oregon Railway and Navigation companies went to capitalists in Boston and New York. California's Big Four purchased the O & C and added it to their Southern Pacific "octopus," which then, in 1887, completed the final gap in the line from Sacramento to Portland.

Although late in coming, the effects of the struggles over the building of the railroad to Oregon were manifold. The rail systems completed in the mid-1880s connected the state to markets that before had been beyond the pale. They also opened Oregon to goods from abroad on a scale previously unknown. Immigration began in a new key as the Northwest became accessible via a relatively simple railroad trip as opposed to a perilous journey overland or by sea. The railroad companies, moreover, had every incentive to encourage immigration, for not only did they profit from the sale of land to newcomers; immigration also increased the pool of customers of their road.

The combined effect of new markets, imported goods, and immigration, though short of revolutionary, was apparent well before the end of the century. Between 1880 and 1900, the population of Oregon increased to more than 400,000, an eightfold increase from the 50,000 living there in 1860. More significantly, while Portland grew from 2,852 in 1860 to 17,552 in 1880, by the turn of the century its population approached 100,000 inhabitants (and double that by 1910), a testament to the recent development of finance, shipping, and entrepôt manufacturing serving the Oregon hinterland. In 1880, the value of agricultural goods produced in the state had been almost twice that of manufactures; ten years later precisely the opposite was the case. Whereas in 1882 only one national bank was chartered in the state, by 1886 eighteen were.[16] The capital invested in manufacturing facilities, which grew by 372 percent between 1860 and 1880, when measured from 1860 to 1900 increased 2,400 percent. The labor force in manufacturing, 978 in 1860 and 3,500 in 1880, exceeded 17,000 at the century's end, with three groups unknown in the earlier years now included in its ranks: women, children, and Chinese.[17]

Related to the emergence of Portland after 1880 as a Pacific Coast center of transport, finance, and manufacturing was the transformation of the Oregon countryside. After 1880 the predominance of the Willamette Valley declined in terms of both population and agricultural production. Population spread west to the coast and east to the high plains beyond the Cascade mountain range. In 1860, only 3,120 people lived in these two regions, but by 1900 more than 138,000 were found there, accounting for almost half (44 percent) of the population in the state. With the exception of Portland, the decennial increase in the population of coastal and eastern Oregon was the greatest in all of Oregon.

The spread of population from the Willamette Valley was the direct result of railroad and ocean links to markets for wheat, fish, and timber. Once these links were established, the wheat fields of central and eastern Oregon quickly became the site of intensive, market-oriented agriculture. The rate of growth in these commercial farming centers was stunning, eclipsing the heartland counties in the Willamette Valley. In 1860, for example, the eastern counties accounted for less than 5 percent of agricultural production in the state, the Willamette Valley and neighboring southern counties, more than 80 percent. Thirty years later eastern Oregon produced over 40 percent of the agricultural goods in the state, equal to the combined output of the valley and southern Oregon counties. In less dramatic fashion, the towns on the Oregon coast, tiny and isolated in the 1850s and 1860s, also became centers of fish canning and timber exporting by the 1890s. As late as 1880, the capital invested in coastal manufacturing facilities was a mere $358,800, less than 6 percent of all such investment in the state; by the end of the century, however, it had increased by 1,261 percent, to approach $5,000,000. At the same time, both the number and scale of these coastal "manufacturing establishments" grew: in 1880, 61 shops employed 156 workers, an average of 2.6 workers per establishment, while in 1900, 272 establishments employed 1,953 workers, or 7.2 each.

The arrival and elaboration of railroad transportation, the growth and spread of population east and west of the Willamette Valley, the development of Portland, and the new importance of capital-intensive wheat farming, timber processing, and fish canning all point to the mid-1880s as a turning point in Oregon history. These years also witnessed the climax of another trend (though a short-term one) away from the homogeneity and provincialism of pioneer Oregon: Chinese immigration. To no small degree, the growth of population in eastern and coastal Oregon was a consequence of Chinese immigration, most of it from California.[18] Although Chinese miners had migrated to southern Oregon during the 1850s (providing the inspiration for the constitutional proscription of Chinese property ownership and voting discussed in chapter 5), the number of so-called celestials in Oregon was small until the mid-1860s, when thousands of Chinese miners arrived from California in search of treasure and refuge from discrimination. Although the mines of eastern Oregon quickly played out, the Chinese remained. There, as elsewhere on the mining frontier, they worked the tailings abandoned by white miners or turned to other sources of work from which they were not proscribed—railroad construction gangs, woolen mills, canneries, domestic service, restaurants, laundries. In 1880 the ten thousand or so Chinese in the state (7 percent of the population) were without question the most visible people of color in Oregon. They stood out starkly in an otherwise homogeneous population, particularly given the concentration of their numbers in but three areas: eastern Oregon, Portland, and Astoria. In the eastern counties one in ten inhabitants was Chinese; in Portland, one in fourteen; and along the coast near the canneries of Astoria, one in three.

Oregon, however, offered no real refuge for a people everywhere the victims of legal discrimination and violence. In 1886, in the wake of the San Francisco sandlot riots, the National Exclusion Act of 1882, and more recent riots in Seattle, white laboring men in Portland took to the streets to demand the immediate eviction of all Chinese from the city. Although forced departures like those taking place in Washington State did not occur in Oregon, the warning implicit in labor's public protest had effect. After reaching a peak of 10,000 in the middle 1880s—in Portland, perhaps as many as 7,500, or 20–25 percent of the city's population—the Chinese population steadily declined. By 1920, only 3,000 remained.[19]

In Oregon, the events of the last fifteen years of the nineteenth century replicated—at a later date and on a decidedly smaller scale—the transformation of city and country in California during the 1860s and 1870s. Yet in contrast to the neighboring state, Oregon's relatively late participation in these modernizing trends, its physical isolation, and the persistence of its early settlers all contributed to the pioneer generation's retention of public place and political authority, through the Civil War and beyond. Although statehood drew Oregon's founding fathers into the political convulsions of the 1860s, their involvement was at arm's length. Similarly, while the great engine of the nation's second industrial revolution, the railroad, was present as an issue from 1860 forward, it did not become a force in the state for another twenty-five years. The tardiness of these developments provided a certain insulation from the transformative effects of the Civil War, Reconstruction, and industrialization. But even so, the state's founding fathers could not escape the force of political change that was sweeping the nation; in the end they had to deal with their own peculiar version of the political crisis of secession and civil war. Initially, the crisis turned on old divisions carried over from the territorial period. Once caught in the swirl of national events leading to the South's secession, however, its proportions, and its stakes, were magnified dramatically.

The unraveling—and reraveling—of Oregon politics between 1858 and 1865 proceeded via a series of small convulsions whose cumulative effects were profound, if utterly unanticipated. The first portents of trouble dawned slowly, after a statehood election in November 1857 that came off as expected.[20] When the vote was taken—viva voce, in full public view—it became apparent that the electorate held the same antislavery, anti–free Negro, free-soil sentiments that had dominated the constitutional convention. Oregonians endorsed the constitution by a large margin (69 percent to 31 percent). In a stunning display of the conviction that free soil and free labor meant white soil and white labor, they also prohibited slavery *and* the immigration of free Negroes by respective majorities of 75 percent and 89 percent.[21]

On its face the ratification election seemed to uphold the course of the regular, Salem, Democracy. Members of the Bush regime, in the saddle,

looked forward with confidence to congressional ratification of the constitution. This task was in the hands of Delegate Lane, and as matters
turned out, it proved far more difficult than expected, for reasons
having to do with the continuing imbroglio in Washington, D.C., over
Kansas statehood, Lane's embrace of President Buchanan's course with
respect to that issue, and the very provisions in the Oregon constitution
on slavery and free Negro immigration. In Congress, southerners opposed admitting Oregon because of the prohibition of slavery; at the
same time, some Republicans united to block it because of the treatment
afforded free Negroes and the Chinese. Lane, full of presidential ambitions of his own and outspoken in his support of Buchanan's position
on the Lecompton constitution of Kansas, was unable to break the impasse. If anything, his partisanship only encouraged further Republican
resistance.[22]

While matters stewed in Washington during the congressional session
of 1858, the fragility inherent in the Oregon Democracy became increasingly apparent. Contrary to Bush and his circle's hope that statehood
would provide an opportunity to jettison Lane and place reliable, regular men in the Senate and House of Representatives, the opposite occurred. The first state election under the constitution, scheduled for the
spring of 1858, witnessed the organization of the so-called National
Democrats ("softs" to Bush) in defiance of the Salem Clique. Embold-
ened by the prospect of statehood, they held a separate convention and
nominated candidates for Congress, the governorship, and the legislature. In this local clash between competing Democratic organizations,
both sides claimed Lane's support. For his part, Lane refused to endorse
either side, thus infuriating Bush who charged in letters to friends
(though not yet publicly) that the delegate was privately assisting the insurgency to further personal ambitions. The results of the first state election, which took place despite the absence of congressional ratification of
the constitution, did nothing to resolve the Democratic division. Although the regular Democratic candidates for governor (John Whit-
taker) and Congress (La Fayette Grover) defeated their national challengers, the legislative elections were inconclusive, sending to the state
house and senate a mixture of regulars and nationals, "hards" and
"softs." Bush despaired. The legislative division made impossible any
challenge to Lane's claim to a seat in the Senate, which was carried by
acclamation. The editor's only consolation—brief consolation, it turned
out—came when Delazon Smith was elected to the other Senate seat.[23]

Although this first state election brought the long-standing division
within Democratic ranks to the surface of local politics, its destructive
effects were not apparent until another year had passed—until, at long
last, Congress ratified the constitution (in February 1859, fifteen months
after its endorsement by the voters of Oregon) and a second state elec-

tion was at hand. During this spring campaign the existing fault lines within the Oregon Democracy cracked open, producing a party emergency that prefigured the Civil War political realignment. At the center of this crisis was Senator Lane's attempt to take control of the state party machinery in anticipation of the 1860 presidential nominating convention. The resulting conflict, although initiated in the context of local animosities, became the vehicle by which the national Democratic division between President Buchanan and Senator Douglas—between the South and the North—was carried to Oregon. By the fall of 1859, the old hard/soft rift within the Oregon Democracy was overlain by the sectional clash splitting the country. Once let loose, its splintering effect could not be restrained.

Curiously enough, the immediate catalyst to the collapse of the Oregon Democracy was Asahel Bush's longtime ally Delazon Smith, who, cooling his heels as a senator-to-be in Washington, D.C., was drawn into the camp of Joseph Lane. Impressed by his colleague's high standing in the Buchanan administration and caught up in the talk of a Lane presidency, Smith moved to Lane's side in the struggle for control of the state party. He thereby changed the tenor of Democratic politics in Oregon, and after Congress ratified Oregon statehood in early 1859, the consequences quickly broke. Upon qualifying as a senator, Smith drew by lot the short term, which ended in a matter of weeks. This confronted him with the immediate necessity of gaining renomination and reelection by a divided party. Desperate to retain his seat, he devised with Lane a two-pronged strategy to capture the Oregon Democracy from the Salem Clique.[24]

While Smith hurried home, Lane took steps in Washington. Drawing on the goodwill of President Buchanan, he had Bush Democrats with patronage appointments replaced with men sympathetic to his cause. Concurrently, he instructed loyalists in Oregon to prepare, in league with Smith's friends, a slate of delegates to the next state Democratic convention that would insure Smith's renomination and place allies of the two senators in control of the state party. The plan was successful, and, to Bush's horror, the party convention, which met in April 1859, came off as Lane and Smith hoped. Caught off guard and outnumbered, Bush loyalists, led by La Fayette Grover, walked out. The remaining "soft" (Lane) men proceeded to renominate Smith for the Senate and another of Lane's friends, Lansing Stout, for the House. As importantly, they removed all Salem Democrats from the state central committee, thereby gaining control over the selection of delegates to (and perforce the composition of) the following year's convention. For the first time, moreover, the Oregon Democracy took sides in the Buchanan-Douglas dispute, ratifying a platform that upheld the Dred Scott decision and the course of the Buchanan administration in the matter of Kansas.[25]

From this point onward, until the Oregon Democracy collapsed in the spring of 1861, the two sides of the party were constantly at odds. Following the 1859 convention, Bush threw off the cautious note of neutrality that had marked the *Statesman's* coverage of the conflict between Buchanan and Douglas and became outspoken in his support of popular sovereignty, openly attacking Lane and Smith as heretics. Bush also redoubled his forces to block Smith's reelection, in which he succeeded. By prearrangement, "regular" Democrats walked out of the legislature when matters turned to the election of a senator: they left the legislature without a quorum and, consequently, Smith without his Senate seat.[26]

The next month's general election, in which the voters were to name a successor to Congressman Grover, was another matter. The nominee of the Lane-Smith convention, Lansing Stout, faced only Republican opposition. The Republicans, previously a minor factor in Oregon politics, found themselves suddenly empowered by the fracturing of Democratic ranks. Now, confronted with the possibility of winning an election, anti-Democrats like Thomas Dryer and David Logan, who had previously disparaged the new party, rushed to its side, increasing its numbers dramatically. In a testament to the power of prospective electoral triumph over principle, the Republicans nominated as their candidate none other than Logan, his long-standing denunciation of "black Republicanism" momentarily forgotten. Similarly, they fashioned a platform calculated to appeal to Bush Democrats, emphasizing popular sovereignty as Republican principle and repudiating any sympathy for abolition.

The response of the regular, Bush, Democrats—now openly identified as Douglas Democrats—to the currying of their favor by Republicans was a clear indication of things to come. Officially, the *Statesman* endorsed Stout; but to any reader of Bush's paper, it was apparent that the editor preferred his old enemy Logan over the heretic Stout. Throughout the campaign Bush left Logan alone while heaping scorn on Lane's speeches for Stout, disparaging his "vulgar witticisms," "shocking profanity," and "coarse personal abuse."[27] The outcome of the election was remarkably close, and no doubt crushing for Logan: he lost by a mere sixteen votes, out of more than eleven thousand cast.[28] Over and above Logan's defeat, the distribution of the vote displayed the speed with which the realignment of the electorate was taking place. Logan's best showings came in former strongholds of the Salem Clique. In Marion County, where Salem was located, he won over 80 percent of the vote.[29]

Between this election and 1861, when the Civil War suppressed party competition and carried through the realignment of parties in Oregon, the implications of the informal fusion of Whigs-Americans-Republicans and Bush-Douglas Democrats in the Stout-Logan campaign were played out. The next step occurred in the election of June 1860, when the voters filled both Smith's still-empty and Lane's senatorial seats. In

preparation, Republicans and Douglas Democrats quietly arranged informal combinations in county after county. In Marion, for example,
Republicans held back from nominating anyone, offering instead to support the choices of Douglas Democrats; in Polk County, a variation on
this theme occurred when Republicans and Douglas Democrats fused to
nominate an "opposition" slate of candidates. The alliance was effective:
the resulting state legislature was divided among nineteen Lane men,
eighteen Douglas Democrats, and thirteen Republicans. That the balance of power rested in a fusion of the latter two blocs became apparent
over the course of a long and complicated session that denied reelection
to both Smith and Lane.[30] For both men the defeat was a bitter one, but
for Lane it was an extreme embarrassment—he had just been named the
vice-presidential running mate of John Breckenridge at the splinter convention of Southern Democrats in Baltimore.

Aware of—indeed, roused by—the damage they were doing to Lane's
national stature, the legislative combination of Republicans and Douglas
Democrats replaced Smith and Lane with Edward Dickinson Baker, a
Republican, and James Nesmith, a longtime Democratic crony of Asahel
Bush. Remarkably enough, Baker was not even an Oregonian. This former Illinoisan—friend of Abraham Lincoln, commanding officer of the
regiment in which David Logan had served during the Mexican War,
and for a time law partner of Logan's father—had only recently come to
Oregon from California. There he had gained local fame for putting together an alliance of Republicans (such as Thomas Fitch) and Douglas
Democrats (such as Charles De Long) to check the "Chivalry" of William
Gwin. But even more to the point, Baker had become nationally famous
for his spellbinding antislavery oratory, above all his eulogy for the martyred David Broderick.[31]

In late 1859, a delegation of Oregon Republicans led by Thomas
Dryer traveled to San Francisco to enlist Baker's aid in the cause of defeating Joseph Lane. Although they did not recruit Baker as a senatorial
candidate, over the course of the maneuvering in the 1860 legislature he
emerged as the only Republican acceptable to Douglas Democrats.[32] The
immediate significance of the legislative fusion—over and above defeating the Smith-Lane wing of the Oregon Democracy—stopped short of
turning Douglas Democrats into Republicans. To the contrary, it hardened the Democratic division between Douglas-Bush and Breckenridge-
Lane adherents and in so doing created the conditions that led to Republican victory in an overwhelmingly Democratic state.

In the fall of 1860, Lincoln carried Oregon by the narrowest of plu-
ralities. His 37 percent of the vote sufficed only because Democrats divided closely between Breckenridge (35 percent) and Douglas (28 percent): out of 14,549 votes cast, Lincoln defeated Breckenridge by a mere
270 votes and Douglas by barely 1,200.[33] Oregonians remained Demo-

crats, although Democrats at odds with one another. The final breaking of their loyalties was still to come. It awaited the crisis of political faith that accompanied the Civil War.

In Oregon, the war had profound political effects. After it began, politics in the state narrowed to a single question: loyalty or disloyalty? On this score the electorate spoke as one. Former Democrats—adherents of Breckenridge and Lane as well as Douglas—moved alongside Republicans into the ranks of the Union party. In that this organization, dominant by 1862, had grown out of Union Clubs established county by county to express loyalty to the Union after the declaration of war in 1861, its organizers eschewed all issues but the restoration of the Union against insurrection.[34] Yet the very length of the war made it impossible to maintain a nonpartisan front. Over the long term, membership in the Union party had unstated, even unrecognized, consequences for the political men of Oregon. For many Democrats, what began in 1861 as a narrowly defined affirmation of the Union slowly broadened, between 1861 and 1865, into an embrace of the broader causes of the Republican party. This wartime migration—the routinization of Republicanism, so to speak—gave the postwar Republican party a decidedly old-Democratic cast. When two-party politics revived in the late 1860s it did so, ironically, under the auspices, on both sides, of men who only a few years before had been allies in the "party of repudiation." To no small degree Oregon politics, during and after the war, was nothing but antebellum Democratic politics carried out under a new name.

Over the decade of political crisis that followed statehood, Oregon's founding fathers faced the dual problem of revitalizing both the body politic and their individual places within it. Measured simply in terms of their persistence in political office, they succeeded as often as not—particularly in contrast to their California counterparts. How they did so, however, was neither simple nor neat. For example, Thomas Dryer and David Logan never managed to profit from the rise of the Republican party in Oregon—not for want of trying, but for reasons having to do with the Democratic cast of the Oregon GOP and, no less, the persistent strains of Whiggish antipartyism in both men. Yet the person who in 1860 and 1861 seemed least likely to survive the political perils of war, Matthew Deady, became by the end of his life in 1893 as near a "great man" as any of his generation of Oregonians. A federal judge for thirty-four years, he remained close to the center of political affairs in the state. Notably, he did so as neither a Democrat nor a Republican but as a "Federalist"—a political identity he defined with illuminating precision. Delazon Smith was the only other adherent to Lane and Breckenridge among the leading Democrats whose lives we followed to the constitutional convention; but alas, he died, suddenly and forlornly, a few days after the 1860 presidential election. The cases of George Williams and La Fayette Grover, both of whom took the side of Douglas (and Bush) in that campaign, offer a study in contrasts. Williams, a Douglas Democrat in 1860—and predictably so, given the views he articulated in his free-state letter of 1857—astonished all in the 1860s by embracing not just the Republican cause but the cause of its radical wing. Grover, a Unionist in the first years of the war, reaffirmed his Democratic identity as soon as peace was at hand. He, more than any other man, was responsible for reconstructing the Oregon Democracy. Using tactics learned earlier at the side of Asahel Bush, he knit together a new Democratic majority in the late 1860s by enunciating old Democratic issues in a new key, one fashioned out of the experience of war and the foil of Republicanism.

Outside the ranks of the constitution writers, two overpowering Democratic figures in antebellum Oregon, Joseph Lane and Asahel Bush, offer an illuminating counterpoint to the political persistence of the founding fathers. Although they remained Oregonians to their deaths (Lane in 1881, Bush in 1913), both departed from politics shortly after the war began. Lane, humiliated by electoral defeat, secession, and public repudiation, retired to the solitude of Roseburg in southern Oregon, where he lived out his years quietly in the midst of a large extended family.[35] Bush—political *primus inter pares* during the territorial period—sold the *Statesman* and retired from public affairs soon after the organization of the Union party and, more importantly, the unexpected death of his wife. He spent the remainder of his life tending to more personal matters. Ironically for such a staunch antebellum Democrat, he devoted the years after 1863 to his avocation of the 1850s: banking. During the territorial years Bush had developed a network of personal creditors among both political friends and adversaries (including Joseph Lane's son). In 1868 he formalized and expanded these relationships through a private banking partnership with William Ladd, an early settler in Portland and cofounder of the Oregon Steam and Navigation Company. The Ladd and Bush Bank turned Asahel Bush the political operative into Mr. Bush the conservative man of business and finance. In 1882 he bought out Ladd and, to the end of his life, directed what was known in the Willamette Valley as "Mr. Bush's bank." To its proprietor, the foremost criteria of creditworthiness were an applicant's landholdings, length of residence, and reputation. Thus his bank, like his newspaper before, served to perpetuate the power of and confer first-citizen status on early settlers and their descendants. To no small degree the central Willamette Valley became his financial domain in the last third of the nineteenth century, a domain he governed with methods devised as a political leader in the 1850s.[36]

Personal tragedy and political fatigue over the Democratic collapse in the late 1850s carried Bush away from public life. No small part of his fatigue was the result of the all-consuming vendetta he and Delazon Smith waged against each other in the eighteen months preceding the election of 1860. The rift was anticipated by no one and, for that very reason, was all the more furious. To both men its source was found in a combination of personal and political betrayal. Played out in the con-text—indeed, the vortex—of the Oregon Democracy's splintering into Lane (southern) and Bush (northern) factions, the conflict between the two men captured the intensity of the party's internal crisis in the months prior to its collapse.

Smith's election as senator in 1858 marked the final attempt by the two sides of the Oregon Democracy to get along. "Hard" Democrats in Bush's circle promoted Smith's election in the hope that he would serve as a counterweight to the ambitious and untrustworthy Joseph Lane. Anti-Bush Democrats accepted him in the hope of dampening intra-party conflict—at least until the state's admission was secured.[37] Neither side's desire, however, was borne out, owing to the symbiotic effect of three factors: the delay over Oregon's admission, Bush's growing (almost paranoid) distrust of Lane, and, in turn, Lane's decision (for partisan and ideological reasons) to end the pretense of Democratic solidarity. Smith's position vis-à-vis the two rivals—ally of the first and senatorial colleague of the second—demanded an emotional balance he did not possess. Once he took sides, what had begun as a petty contest between two men who would be king of the Oregon Democracy quickly devolved into a hopeless split. Although at first Smith stood by Lane only as a point of honor, once committed he was carried away not only from old friendships but also from the principles regarding slavery and popular sovereignty that he had articulated throughout the territorial years.

The struggle between Asahel Bush and Joseph Lane for the alle-giance of Oregon Democrats, a struggle in the beginning unrelated to ideology, unleashed forces that sealed the doom of the party. What is remarkable is how innocuously it all began. For reasons having less to do with facts than with the simple opportunity to undercut a rival, Bush in 1858 began to speculate—first in private, then in the *Statesman*—about what was causing the delay in Oregon's admission to the union.[38] His tar-get was Lane, whom he charged with encouraging the delay in order to secure his salary and travel expenses as territorial delegate until assured of election as senator. Smith, before he left to join Lane in Washington, D.C., did not discourage such speculation;[39] but upon his arrival in the nation's capital his transformation took place quickly, if painfully. "*You, my dear friend*," he wrote to Bush after meeting with Lane, President Buchanan, and others, "cannot doubt my personal friendship." But, he continued, "a true friend and an honest man will not deceive. . . . You want me to tell the truth, and communicate my honest convictions. This I will now do." The "truth," Smith realized, would not please Bush, for

> notwithstanding the unpleasant, tart, criminating and recriminating correspondence that has passed between you . . . Gen. Lane is a faithful and zealous representative of the people of Oregon. . . . The *truth* is simply this: —if I had possessed a disposition to break and quarrel with Gen. Lane, it would have been, and would still be, madness to have done so. . . . And the *truth* is that there is no man at the Federal Capital who stands higher with the President, heads of Departments, and with Senators and representatives from North, South, East and West than does the Delegate from Oregon. And the *truth* is that there is no man in the nation more talked of in private circles than is Gen. Lane for either the Presidency or Vice Presidency in 1860.[40]

In this letter of late 1858 Smith's desire to resolve the party division was palpable, as was the fact that in the national split between Buchanan and Douglas he still took the side of the latter. Quickly, however, matters turned upside down. Bush's reply was scolding, and Smith's response—the last communication between the two—defensive and condescending. Smith sent it to Bush a few weeks before Oregon's admission, responding point by point to the editor's criticism of him for "yielding to Lane's supreme control," "excessive praise of Gen. Lane," of having forged an "alliance" with him, of insisting that the *Statesman* had "become a medium of mere praise, cant and humbug concerning Gen. Lane." Against each accusation Smith stood on "truth"—known immediately (as only it could be to one, like Smith, imbued with the principles of faculty psychology): "*Truth* will do its office-work sooner or later," he lectured his former patron, "and he who leans upon anything else will find that he leans upon a reed that will break and pierce his hand! . . . When a man is convinced of the truth he ought to follow it—when he is in error to abandon it." The facts—which were self-evident to Smith in Washington, D.C.—demonstrated not only Lane's innocence of Bush's charges; they also proved that on most matters Lane was in the right. The upshot for Smith was simple: "If what I have frankly written . . . shall have the effect to alienate your friendship, I have only to say, that whilst I shall regret it, I cannot help it. I am responsible for what *I* write and for that only."[41]

Whether Bush responded to this letter we do not know, but within two months—specifically, when the divisive 1859 state Democratic convention took place—the break was complete. The legislative refusal to reelect him enraged Smith. In response he returned to journalism, inaugurating the *Oregon Democrat* in his hometown of Albany—to vindicate his name, promote his chances a year hence, and expose Asahel Bush's treachery. In light of his disaffection from Bush, there was nothing remarkable about the calumny of the *Oregon Democrat* against "the defection and ill-disguised treason of the Statesman," Bush's "defiance to the party which has given him all the importance he possesses," his arrogant attempt "to transfer, the Democratic party, bodily into the camp of the enemy . . . from motives of personal selfishness, ambition, revenge, and hate! . . . his wanton assaults upon, and vile abuse of, those Democrats who are supporting the party, advocating its principles, and urging the election of its standard-bearers!"[42]

More striking (if less noticeable) was the political course that Smith set for the paper, for in it the political effects of the local feud between Lane and Bush were evident: Smith, in a word, took the side of the southern Democracy. Stephen Douglas and popular sovereignty were replaced in his Democratic canon by Buchanan, Lane, and Dred Scott. The latter became a newfound touchstone of regularity, the "authoritative, correct, just, and final exposition of the Constitution." The *Oregon Democrat*, he announced, "will contend for and advocate the equal rights of all the States of the Union, both in and out of the Territories."[43]

Smith's campaign in the *Oregon Democrat* did him no good. Indeed, his public standing declined in proportion to the intensity of his attacks on Bush, Douglas, and other renegade Democratic stalking horses for "black Republicanism."[44] After the Douglas Democratic–Republican fusion of 1860 once again blocked his reelection, he took on the cause of Breckenridge and Lane with almost maniacal fervor. Named an elector for the ticket of his new patron, he canvassed the state before the November vote. (With him went Thomas Dryer, as an elector for Lincoln and Hamlin.) The very closeness of the Republican victory over Breckenridge and Lane, according to contemporaries, broke Smith's health and spirit. Recalled John McBride: "Within a few days after the election which made Abraham Lincoln President, he was taken seriously ill at the home of a friend, and embittered by the defeat and the dismal prospect of the future, he died more from a broken heart than physical illness."[45]

The course of Delazon Smith's life after the Oregon constitutional convention—full of ironic twists and turns—displayed the intertwining of personality and ideology in the close-knit political culture of early Oregon. Carried to the side of Joseph Lane for reasons that stemmed initially from his sense of honor and his ambition (and encouraged by his understanding of truth as immediately present to common sense), he soon discovered that his course had unavoidable political and ideological implications that catalyzed the breaking of the Oregon Democratic party, and eventually the spirit of the man. Because Smith died early, we cannot know how he would have dealt with the crisis that subsequently unfolded. However, given the intensity and personal nature of his break with old friends and allies in the Bush wing of the party, it is unlikely that he would have recovered, as they did with such apparent ease. Ironically, among the Oregon founding fathers for whom the realignment of the 1860s was most disappointing were those who had, much earlier than Delazon Smith, identified the Democratic regime of Asahel Bush as the embodiment of political perfidy. Even though both Thomas Dryer and David Logan made their peace with the Republican party in the last years of the 1850s, and even though both for a time enjoyed a place in its inner councils, that party's rise in the state brought neither the recognition nor the rewards they thought their due.

Twenty years after Oregon's admission as a state Thomas Dryer died penniless and alone in Portland, abandoned by friends and, reports imply, family alike.[46] Disaster did not strike him quickly or all at once. He remained editor of the *Oregonian* until 1861 and between the constitutional convention and that time figured in the affairs of the state. Ironically, his fall from grace originated in his greatest personal and political success: appointment by President Lincoln in recognition of his service to the party in Oregon. Although not as notably as Delazon Smith, Dryer also followed a circuitous path from 1857 through 1860, one that saw him soften (if not abandon) his war of words with his old nemesis Asahel Bush. As the split in the Oregon Democracy widened and the fusion of anti-Democrats and Bush partisans became ever more evident, Dryer went along, encouraging combinations where they occurred and, when possible, taking a hand in them. In 1859 he helped recruit E. D. Baker to Oregon and promoted his senatorial ambitions. By 1860 the *Oregonian* had become a Republican paper, though one that emphasized (appropriately enough) not so much the party as the need for nonpartisan unity among popular-sovereignty men.[47]

Identified as an ally of Baker, Dryer was named a Lincoln elector by the 1860 party convention. During the campaign he toured the state for the ticket, at the side, as was customary, of a spokesman for the opposition, Delazon Smith.[48] After the vote was taken, Dryer, confident that his days as an editor were over, sold the *Oregonian* and departed for Washington, D.C., with the official returns. There, along with scores of other Republicans (among them, James Nye of Nevada), he sought a share in the spoils of Republican victory. Dryer's reward was neither a coveted national appointment nor, for that matter, a position of power in his home state. But it was sufficient: minister to the Kingdom of the Sandwich Islands. From Washington Dryer went directly to Hawaii.[49] But if Dryer believed he had forever escaped Oregon for a life of service to great causes, he was mistaken. His tenure in Hawaii was short. Disparaged as a loudmouthed buffoon by the expatriate English and American residents, and constantly drunk (at least according to the *Statesman*), he was recalled from his post in 1863.[50] In Lincoln's papers is found the follow-

ing doggerel, which a friend of the president enclosed in a letter urging
Dryer's removal:

> Like some might Ajax, wielding his battle-axe,
> Behold how he strides along,
> Not to bloody the nose of his country's foes,
> But to avenge his personal wrong.
> Now the Knight of the Quill, shall catch his fill
>   From this chief of *a-sassy-nation*,
> And the disciple of Faust, shall learn to his cost
>   This new *type* of civilization,
> Who carrying a knife, to protect his dear life,
> Draws it out for intimidation.[51]

Dryer, recalled within a year of his arrival in Honolulu, returned to
the United States via Washington, D.C., whether to plead for another
chance before the president cannot be said. Slowly he and his family
worked their way back across the United States, arriving in Portland in
1865. He returned, according to one report, "broken down and dispirited," and thereafter took "no active part in public affairs."[52] For the
remaining years of his life, his fortunes declined steadily. He did not return to journalism but, rather, depended on a small income that came
his way as a justice of the peace and coroner—mere remnants of patronage for a man once famous in the city and state. When he died in 1879
his old paper, the *Oregonian*, remembered him briefly as a figure of some
note during the 1850s, relegating the notice of his burial to the back
pages.[53]

In a somewhat different key, David Logan's disappointments after the
constitutional convention were as complete as those of Thomas Dryer.
Before his death in 1874 Logan failed three times to be elected to Congress. His defeat in 1859 as the fusion candidate of Republican and
Douglas Democrats was replayed a year later when he was once again
narrowly outpolled by the candidate of the Lane-Smith Democracy.[54]
For Logan, the second race was particularly dispiriting, following as it
did the elevation of E. D. Baker to the U.S. Senate. The two men knew
each other well from Springfield, Illinois, and to Logan's eternal distress
the public (and likely his father's) measure of the honor and brilliance of
the two was always in Baker's favor. Reportedly, Logan was among those
who encouraged Baker to come to Oregon. If so, there is no doubt that
for Logan the invitation did not involve the U.S. Senate, for Baker's election enraged him. After Baker left Oregon for Washington (and a martyr's death), Logan made his hatred known in the petulant tones of a boy
too often relegated to the shadows of an older, smarter, and more attractive brother. Among those to whom he complained was his old law

teacher, Abraham Lincoln. He wrote to the president in the fall of 1861, warning that Baker was using his friendship with Lincoln to further a conspiracy against Oregon Republicans who would not acquiesce in his rule of the party. Declaring that Baker had made it impossible for him to remain in Oregon, Logan beseeched Lincoln for an appointment as district judge of Southern California. "I had determined," he wrote, "that I would not trouble the administration for any appointment either for myself or for any of my friends—but owing to the peculiar situation of parties and political combinations in this state—I make this request on my own behalf." Lincoln owed him the post, he implied, for the president, in agreeing to Baker's recommendations for patronage, had effectively, if unwittingly, assisted in the campaign to destroy his public and private standing in the state. "Every man that this administration has appointed to office in Oregon," Logan averred, "are favorites of Col. Baker, and they have instituted against me, politically & personally publically & in my private affairs a system of most annoying warfare, hoping since I have done the work for the party to work me out and have the coast clear for them." [55]

If Logan thought the president would take his side or offer consolation he was sadly mistaken. For reasons never broached but likely related to old wounds, Lincoln refused to do anything for the son of his former partner and lifelong friend. Even while refusing Logan any patronage, however, Lincoln did let him know through intermediaries that he wished, "fervently," that he succeed on his own account in his quest for office. Lincoln in 1860, like Stephen Logan in 1849, apparently awaited the younger man's redemption—and demanded that he accomplish it on his own.

That Lincoln so viewed Logan is implied by the letter of another former Illinois "Junto" man, Simeon Francis, who in 1859 moved from Springfield to Oregon. Shortly after his arrival he assayed the local situation for Lincoln, and in his remarks David Logan figured prominently. Francis told his friend of Logan's close defeat in the congressional election, complimented the younger man for (honorably) not contesting the outcome, and then concluded by stating—suggestively, if vaguely—"I am glad to say that I hear good reports of Logan. Nobody here doubts that as a legal man, he leads the bar here; and that he is now right on all other points and has been ever since he was a candidate for Congress and some time before. I think he has passed the crisis and hereafter will be all his friends desire." [56] If the "crisis" to which Francis referred was Logan's alcoholism, it had not passed. Until his death in 1874 his reputation as a drunk persisted. [57] But so did his courtroom brilliance and the steady stream of clients seeking his services. The income from his practice, along with investments in Portland real estate, gave him a modest fortune, and during the last years of the Civil War, thanks to his standing as a Republican and his prominence in legal and business circles, he was elected mayor of the city.

This position marked Logan's only successful election after statehood; yet the honor of the post in no way matched his ambition. To the end of his life he remained intent on gaining a place in Congress, and his defeats in 1859 and 1860 only intensified the quest. At every Republican convention during the 1860s his name appeared among the nominees. Each time he was passed over—until 1868, when he carried the Republican standard in the congressional campaign once again. As it turned out, though, he had little prospect of winning. Not only did he face a Democratic party revitalized by the end of the war and the migration of California miners to eastern Oregon, but his nomination by the Republican party itself occurred under less than auspicious circumstances.

In 1868 the party was beset by factionalism arising from two sources: regional jealousies between northern and southern Oregonians, and resentments between those who favored or opposed Ben Holladay's railroad promotions. Tying these disparate factors together was a common animosity toward the senior Oregon senator, (Republican) George Williams. Williams, by carrying Holladay's application for a federal subsidy through Congress, had raised the ire of opponents of the Californian throughout the state. Complementing this group's desire to remove Williams from the Senate was that of southern Oregonians, who wished to see a local man take the seat. To both groups, Logan's candidacy promised to assist a larger aim: southern Oregonians saw the election of Logan, a northerner himself, as a means of insuring the rotation of Williams's seat to the south in 1870; anti-Holladay Republicans, reasoning similarly, looked forward to making an anti-Holladay man senator in 1870. These views coalesced in the 1868 convention, and the everambitious Logan received what turned out to be his last chance at the national office he had sought for twenty years.[58]

Once again, however, Logan was disappointed by a narrow defeat. This time, his response was an act of desperation. In a bizarre move to win the elusive prize he had sought so long, he turned to the Democratic party. According to a series of exposés in the *Oregonian*, Logan agreed to work for the election of a Democratic majority in the 1870 legislature in exchange for the Democrats' promise to make him U.S. senator. To the Republican paper, the intrigue was incredible in both a political and a personal sense. Not only, reported the *Oregonian*, had Logan "joined the enemies of the party he has professed heretofore to belong to," he had willingly become the "tool" of men, William S. Ladd and James Nesmith, who were longtime associates of his most vicious enemies. Ladd, among other things, was the business partner of Asahel Bush; Nesmith was the (former) editor's oldest friend. Republicans, dumbfounded by the reports, concluded simply that the old doubts about Logan's character were correct. He was, the *Oregonian* judged, a man "who would sacrifice all the political principles he ever professed to gratify a personal dislike. . . . The Republican party is now fully done with him."[59]

Logan's final gambit (more than the *Oregonian* recognized) contained a final political truth about the man. In addition to showing the depths and desperation of his ambition, the hapless intrigue displayed the peculiar logic of his antipartyism. He betrayed the Republican party because he saw his ambition slipping away; but he betrayed the party also because, simply, it was a party. Having done so, Logan had nowhere to turn. Shortly thereafter he left Portland, settling with his wife on a farm in Yamhill County. He still followed the courts (and he still did well), but as far as politics were concerned he had become a nonperson. In 1874 he died. In a final bitter irony, he was buried in Salem, in a grave near that of Asahel Bush's wife (and later of the old nemesis himself). The small band who paid their respects included a larger contingent of Logan's old Democratic enemies—among them Matthew Deady—than of Republicans. To them Logan had long since ceased to be a threat; he was now little more than an odd figure from the old days. Among Republicans in Oregon, Illinois, and Washington, D.C.—those whose approval he had sought so long—his death passed without notice.[60]

The public failures and private disappointments that marked the poststatehood lives of Thomas Dryer and David Logan stemmed in no small degree from personal traits that made both men unsuited for political success in Oregon. But in addition, the silence that met their deaths testified to the consequences of their antipartyism, the logic of which they worked out individually over the twenty years divided by civil war. Neither man's conversion to Republicanism was complete or comfortable, precisely because this new organization was a party, organized and operated in much the same manner as the Democracy they had so long abhorred. Indeed, the relationship between the antebellum Democracy and the Republican party in Oregon during its first generation of existence went beyond functional similarities. In practice, as it turned out, it was as much the creation of old Democrats as of newcomers or, for that matter, old anti-Democratic partisans.

A hint of the mixed genesis of Republicanism in this state is found in the language employed by the (Republican) *Oregonian* in its denunciation of Logan. There the political syntax characteristic of Asahel Bush remained evident: in the *Oregonian* of 1870, as in the *Statesman* of 1855, *party* was a collective noun. As for Bush the Democracy "are," so for the *Oregonian* the Republican party "have."[61] The point is a small one, but its implications were displayed in the roles that former Democratic enemies of Dryer and Logan played in Oregon's Republican party. As striking as the failures that enveloped the latter men was the continued prominence and power of antebellum Democrats after the Civil War—in Republican as often as Democratic guises.

Although the full story is a complex one, its main outlines are found in the careers of George Williams, La Fayette Grover, and Matthew Deady. Each lived a long life. Each died an Oregonian. In contrast to Dryer and Logan, their deaths (Deady in 1893, Williams in 1910, and Grover in 1911) were neither ignored nor left to the back pages of local papers. At the time of their deaths Senator and (U.S.) Attorney General Williams, Governor and Senator Grover, and (U.S. District) Judge Deady were still men who mattered, if in different ways. After 1857 these three old Democrats followed distinctive, often hostile, paths that testified both to persistence and change in their older beliefs and to the range of conclusions men could draw out of the political and material transformation of their place in time.

When David Logan made his last desperate attempt for office in 1870, the man whom he wanted to replace as U.S. senator was George Williams. For ten years the two had been political allies, though never congenial ones. No doubt reinforcing Logan's desire to defeat the incumbent in 1870 was the fact that Williams at the time was among the most prominent Republicans in Oregon, one whose prior Democratic allegiance seemed to matter little to Republicans in either Oregon or Washington, D.C. Indeed, for Williams the transition from Pierce Democrat in 1852 to Douglas Democrat in 1860 to Lincoln Republican in 1864 had been painless. By no later than 1863 he had become a leading Republican in Oregon. A year later he gained the Senate seat denied him as a Democrat in 1858, 1859, and 1860. Reborn as a Republican in 1864, Williams thereafter moved ever closer to the center of national politics, first as a radical Republican in the U.S. Senate, then as attorney general in the cabinet of U. S. Grant. By 1870, Oregon papers (if no one else) were connecting his name to the presidency.[62]

Williams's political conversion during the Civil War did not occur suddenly. Long before he began his Republican ascent, he displayed the logic that linked his actions as a Democratic constitution writer to his radical, then gilded-age, Republicanism. It was indicated clearly, for example, in an otherwise obscure speech he delivered (as a Douglas Democrat) to the Agricultural Society of Multnomah County in the summer of 1860. Before the assembled farmers, he blended classical republican imagery and the staples of antebellum Democratic oratory into a vision that soon became his Republican gospel. The address opened with references unremarkable to an audience of rural Democrats of the old school. "'Let kings to farmers make a bow,'" he opined, for "kings are more dependent on farmer than farmers upon kings. . . . All other pursuits derive their vitality from it. Learning would starve, ships would rot in their ports, grass would grow in the marts of commerce, and art produce nothing but the rude instruments of warfare, or the chase, if there was no Agriculture. It is the foundation and indispensable support of all kinds of business." From this premise Williams drew out two related conclusions. First, based on the authority of a Jefferson he painted in the classical hues of country party ideas, was the moral indispensability of farmers to "good government." That great Democrat, he reminded his audience,

> said that great cities were great sores on the body politic. Politically and morally this is true. Corruption and crime love city life. They love its dazzling temptations—its constant opportunities, and hiding places. But they find no congenial abode in the country. Industry, temperance, and pure association are their enemies. The town is false, impure and imperfect, but the country is true, pure and beautiful. The home of the farmer is in the country. Patriotism and public virtue spring up and grow under the shelter of that home.[63]

Having set the stage with these paeans to the country life and the civic virtues incident to rural residence, Williams turned to the second topic on his mind: "Progress." Reducing it to its essentials, he defined the progress of civilization as a matter of commerce. In turn, he identified the fulcrum of commerce as trade in the productions of farmers. Agriculture, in his telling, drew forth the "love," implanted in man by nature, "to be more, and a dislike to be less, than others." Through the ages, the effects of this competitive instinct on science and innovation—handmaidens of agriculture—had been fundamental. The upshot for Williams, vis-à-vis both the progress of civilization and the preservation of republican society, was the necessity of developing and extending the great modern instrument of agricultural commerce: the railroad. Opening up new markets, the railroad spurred the competitive, improving, instinct in farmers. Thus enabled, they would increase their individual production and profit and thereby the wealth of society. This self-sustaining process, grounded and sustained in rural enterprise, promised in turn to protect republican society from decay by insuring the growth and vitality of the countryside. "I make this prediction," he remarked in closing,

> that in less than ten years, the iron horse, with the breath of the Mississippi valley in his nostrils, will waken the echoes from our mountain crags and startle the deer in our grassy vales. This road is the master enterprise of the age. When the energies of this mighty nation are concentrated upon the work, it will appear across the continent, comparatively speaking, like the rainbow athwart a summer's cloud. . . . Have faith and hope. They will remove mountains. Go on increasing the stores of your knowledge, and extending your improvements, and you may ere long see the day when

among all in our Union who cultivate the soil, the wealthiest, healthiest, and happiest, will be the farmers of Oregon.[64]

During the Civil War Williams carried into the Republican party this vision of a commercial republic with ever-expanding horizons, markets without limits, competition without pain. The example of the war and his experiences in the Senate, however, expanded his vision in new ways. The war made him think nationally. The business of the Senate shifted his conceptual point of departure from a republic of individuals striving in rural communities to an interdependent "union" coordinated and carried forward by the helping hand of the national government. What remained constant in Williams's view was his image of the farmer as quintessential republican citizen and his conception of the instrument of progress. That instrument remained the railroad, envisaged now as the ligaments of a system of agricultural production and trade that was continental, indeed international, in scope.

As a freshman senator during the last months of the Civil War and the Reconstruction years, Williams played no small role in congressional history. His name appeared as a coauthor of the Civil Rights Act of 1865, the fourteenth amendment, the Military Reconstruction Act, and the Tenure of Office Act. He was an outspoken senatorial critic of Andrew Johnson. But there was more to Williams the senator than the radical Republicanism for which he is known. Although underplayed in the few studies that have been done, his constant efforts in behalf of government subsidies for western railroads provide as apt a measure of his politics. In these efforts he elaborated the political-economic convictions he articulated in the Oregon constitutional convention, and to which he testified in his 1860 address to the farmers of Multnomah County. Attached to the Republican party's mission of preserving the Union in the crucible of war, Senator Williams's advocacy of the cause of the Northern Pacific Railroad, and in Oregon, of Ben Holladay, expressed his belief that railroad enterprises were "necessary to the development of the country and to the commercial interests of the entire world."[65] Second only to the winning of the war, this project possessed for him a moral as well as political-economic imperative. "Blood has been spilled upon a hundred battle-fields to create and continue the Federal Union," he noted in a characteristic speech, "but now the age of steam and iron has come, with its powerful and peaceful agencies, to secure and confirm the sacrifices and triumphs of patriotism."[66]

To many contemporaries, Williams's promotion of railroad land grants, loan guarantees, and bounties tagged him as a corrupt spoilsman; indeed, by any measure he was a remarkably imperfect man. Yet his motives, while never pure, were not simple, either. Williams taken whole presents a conundrum. In politics—as a senator, Grant's attorney general, nominee for chief justice, and, at the end of his life, mayor of Portland—he remained a respected, even honored figure despite the charges of corruption that swirled about him. Driven from the Senate in 1870, he returned to Oregon to become its "Grand Old Man." Allegiant to the party of laissez-faire capitalism from 1863 to his death, he defined himself, when asked, in anticapitalist terms drawn from the language of classical republicanism. A corporate lawyer, he lent his support (albeit modestly) to the anticorporate insurgence of the 1890s that presaged the "Oregon system" that Progressive reformers put in motion in the early twentieth century.

In the end, Williams remained a respected and powerful figure in Oregon for three reasons. First was his, and his pioneer counterparts', sheer longevity, which insured his entrée to the circles of power in Oregon until his death. Second was his contemporaries' evaluation of him as a weak rather than venal man, one who failed to recognize or resist more powerful personalities around him. On these grounds Williams's pioneer peers eventually forgave (if not forgot) the charges that dogged his career in Washington, D.C.[67] Reinforcing this judgment, finally, was the fact that Williams's gilded-age Republicanism was always tempered by strains of classical republicanism recognized and honored in the political culture of his state. As such, in the last years of the nineteenth century he became a local icon, the "Grand Old Man of Oregon": a pioneer in a society where pioneers remained close to power; a carrier of the republican political culture brought to the Pacific Northwest by its first settlers; a true Oregonian despite his flaws.

Williams's eventual exoneration and political resurrection, judged by his record in office, was just sort of remarkable, for his years in Washington did not suggest the life of a republican statesman. As a senator, his alliance with Ben Holladay in the late 1860s divided his party at home and doomed his prospects for reelection. Furthermore, it contributed to the Democratic resurgence of 1870 by making the Republican party the party of corporate monopoly—a powerful foil that Democrats exploited to the hilt. Despite these troubles, however, Williams was saved from retirement through the good offices of Ulysses S. Grant, who appointed him to the Alabama Claims Commission and, in 1871, to his cabinet as attorney general. His time at the Department of Justice in the early 1870s turned out to be as troubling as his last years in the Senate. Connected (though only as an acquiescent figure on the periphery) to the scandals of the Grant presidency, he earned no one's praise. Thus the surprise was universal when, in 1873, Grant nominated him to succeed Salmon Chase as chief justice of the Supreme Court. Outside Oregon the nomination was denounced. Eventually Grant withdrew it—for reasons having to do as much with the offenses of Williams's wife against Washington society as with charges of corruption against the nominee himself.[68] Even then, Williams stayed on as attorney general until, fifteen months later, the scandals of the Grant administration made his continuation impossible.

After leaving the Grant cabinet, Williams remained in Washington, and there he accumulated a modest fortune as a lawyer before the Supreme Court. In 1881 he returned to Portland. Renewing old acquaintances and establishing new ones, he quickly took his place in the legal and commercial life of the growing city. As Portland achieved metropolitan status, he invested in urban real estate near the city's eastside railroad yards and, with their development in the 1880s and 1890s, became a wealthy man. Recruited (along with other pioneers) to the boards of numerous banks incorporated in the boom years that followed his return, he helped to institutionalize the conservative financial practices—focused on the exploitation for export of Oregon's natural resources rather than the development of manufacturing and industry—that marked the state in his time and thereafter.[69] With the passage of time old political animosities dissolved, and Williams once again became a presence in Republican party affairs, honored as a founding father who brought the wisdom of Oregon's pioneer generation to bear on the dilemmas of a changing world.

In the twenty-five years that preceded his death Williams played this role time and again. As a power broker in the Republican party and as a speaker at political conventions, civic celebrations, and business, fraternal, and social organizations, he spoke both as a contemporary and as a pioneer. In doing so he displayed the persistence of his generation and of the political culture they had created in the 1850s. Nowhere was this fact more evident than in 1889, when he appeared at the closing ceremonies of a grand two-day celebration in Portland to commemorate the centennial of Washington's inauguration. The festivities included militia demonstrations, parades of workingmen, fraternal societies, and schoolchildren. Religious leaders, Protestant, Catholic, and Jewish, presided over ecumenical displays of patriotic solidarity. Capping the ceremonies were speeches by great men, among them George Williams.[70]

Williams's speech, in part jeremiad and in part apologia, addressed Oregonians in the language of classical republicanism. The enduring significance of the first president, Williams averred, was simple and profound: it was found in the moral force of his character. Embodying the disinterestedness of the ancient republican, Washington insured the young nation's survival because his example was so pure, his virtues so complete, his republican vision so pristine. Father of the nation, patriarch to his own and subsequent generations, he provided a constant reminder of the nation's first principles. In this regard, Williams argued, the centennial celebration was of more than ritual significance. It demanded a stock-taking of the intervening century, and it called on

Americans to take vital measure of themselves in light of the example of their republican father.

On both scores, Williams was less than sanguine. The century that followed Washington's inauguration, he held, had not only seen wondrous strides in the growth of the republic—continental expansion, innovation and improvement, and command over nature; it also displayed the signs of republican decay well known to all students of history. To make the point, Williams turned his audience's attention to the "school of nations," the ancient Greek and Roman republics, and the source of their early republican greatness. This he located in "the education and habits of her people . . . [and] the development, cultivation and discipline of the individual." During the golden age of each, he argued, "simplicity of life and fewness of wants were the national virtues." [71]

From this virtuous state, Williams continued, both civilizations declined and then collapsed. The reasons he gave, while they would have made an eighteenth-century republican moralist proud, were full of foreboding for 1889. "Ambition looked abroad for dominion. Faction and the lust of power made their appearance. Great riches were accumulated by the few, while the multitude struggled in abject poverty. Luxurious habits supervened; indolence, effeminacy and vice followed, and [these] once glorious land[s] of philosophers, poets, and heroes sank into obscure imbecility." After reciting the cycles of republican growth and decay, Williams turned back to the present and drew out the moral. The examples of Greece and Rome, he averred, were not to be taken lightly. The bribery so prevalent in recent elections proved that the social decay that destroyed the ancient republics was not peculiar to them. On the contrary, the same corruption threatened the American republic in the present. "The fact is," he insisted,

> that the greed for gold and great riches absorb, to a great degree, the aspirations and activities of our people. Associated wealth and corporate power have enthroned themselves in the vital energies of our country. Our trust is that God will protect and preserve us as a nation; but the beacon lights of history show that the descent is easy from wealth to luxury, from luxury to ease, from ease to effeminacy, and finally to destruction. [72]

For a figure so often suspected (if absolved) of bribery and "greed for gold," the speech at first glance seems contrived. Yet it is perhaps better read as the apologia of an imperfect man, as well as a jeremiad calculated to touch a nerve among a population for whom republicanism was not yet an alien tongue. In this respect Williams's closing contained a suggestive play on a familiar revolutionary phrase, one that suggests the personal as well as political purpose of his thoughts: "Eternal vigilance is the price," he declared, not of liberty, but "of moral character." [73]

Williams lived twenty-one years past 1889. In that time, he gave voice to the meaning, personal and public, contained in his Washington centennial address and, as ever, to his inability to measure up to the "eternal vigilance" that "moral character" required. In 1902, at the age of seventy-nine, he ran for, and won, the post of mayor of Portland. His term, characteristically, was marred by charges of corruption and once again resulted in his failure to win reelection. But by the same token, his election as mayor turned on his identification with measures that became the centerpieces of twentieth-century Progressivism: the "Oregon system" of initiative, referendum, and recall; women's suffrage; and professionalism as opposed to patronage in the management of municipal affairs. Williams ran for mayor as a Roosevelt Republican devoted to the purification of politics and the necessity of trust busting.[74] He claimed the mantle of Roosevelt proudly and with reason. While running for mayor, he was also president of the Direct Legislation League in Oregon—which had launched the movement to amend the state constitution to include initiative, referendum, and recall. As president of the league, and as a candidate for mayor, he called on Oregonians in 1902 to amend their constitution as a means of removing the "evil" that "combinations of capital" had introduced into politics.[75] The amendments passed, and Williams rejoiced. To his mind, the measures served republican purposes by helping to protect the state from the fate of the ancients.

Elections and amendments aside, however, a reform mayor Williams was not. Confronted by a city growing rapidly and confronting fiscal crisis, he took the advice of friends and advisers (again the weak man following the line of least resistance) and allowed gambling and prostitution rings to flourish, by his own admission in order to collect revenue in the form of fines. His acquiescence made him the target of social welfare leagues and clean government organizations.[76] In 1905, his bid for reelection was soundly defeated by a new generation of Oregon reformers who, in their own way, furthered the republican language Williams had enunciated, if not lived by, as a young as well as "Grand Old" Oregonian.

Five years later, Williams died. Ignoring the controversies that had enveloped his public career, newspapers hailed him as the carrier of a pioneer creed that remained relevant. Twelve months later followed the death of another veteran of the 1857 constitutional convention, La Fayette Grover. In the years since 1857, Grover, like Williams, had mastered the political challenge of the Civil War, gone on to represent Oregon in the U.S. Senate, and then returned to Portland, where he too accumulated a modest fortune in real estate and took a hand in founding the city's modern financial corporations. Yet, similarities aside, Grover's passage to this end contrasted significantly with that of Williams.

In 1870, the year of Williams's defeat for reelection to the Senate,

La Fayette Grover became governor of Oregon. At the time, he and the Republican senator were avowed political enemies—a striking development, given their friendship as Salem neighbors in the 1850s, collaboration in founding the Willamette Woolen Mills, and common political course before the Civil War. In the constitutional convention they had seen eye to eye on most issues, and in the ensuing crisis of the Oregon Democracy they had grown even closer, upholding Bush against Lane and, when national issues intervened, Douglas and popular sovereignty against Lane, Smith, and Dred Scott. In the presidential election of 1860 both supported the Illinois Democrat, and when war broke out, both took a hand in the organization of the Union party.[77]

The Civil War and the ascension of the Republican party, however, had wholly different effects on Grover than on Williams. Grover's Democratic loyalties were enduring, and his adherence to the Union never approached an embrace of Republicanism. In 1864 he supported McClellan's "Peace Democrat" presidential candidacy; according to rumors, he was active as well in secretive copperhead organizations.[78] But for the most part he bided his political time during the war, focusing instead on the milling establishment he and Williams had established with others in 1857. In 1860 Grover became the largest single stockholder in the Willamette Wollen Mills; three years later he, with friends, seized complete control of the enterprise. After four years of expansion, which saw the addition of a flouring mill to the complex, Grover became the day-to-day manager of a modest manufacturing empire that exemplified the kind of local industry George Williams defined as the natural and necessary accompaniment to the agricultural republic.[79]

Grover's wartime business success, however, failed to satisfy his ambition, and once peace was at hand he quickly made his move back into politics—as a Democrat. In 1866, he attended the party's first state convention in six years. The reassembled Democracy chose him as presiding officer of the meeting and then made him chairman of the state central committee. As head of the party, he turned his considerable energies to the work of Democratic revitalization, reestablishing old political contacts throughout the state and adding new ones among arriving immigrants. In 1868 the result of his efforts became apparent in the election of his law and business partner, Joseph Smith, to Congress over David Logan.[80] Grover then set his sights on 1870, devising an appeal and tactics that produced a stunning Democratic victory. In that year he became governor, and a Democratic legislature replaced Senator George Williams with one of their own (another veteran, as it happened, of the 1857 constitutional convention, James Kerr Kelly). Behind the Democratic success was candidate Grover's updating of antebellum symbols for postwar audiences. In stump speeches delivered across the state he appealed to racial phobias and the specter of a slave power conspiracy against free labor and free soil that had played so prominent a role in prewar politics. In doing so, however, he did not simply restate antebellum rhetoric; rather, substituting the Chinese for Negroes and "corporate monopolists" for slave owners, he placed old fears into a new and powerful context, one insulated from Republicans waving the bloody shirt.

As the standard-bearer of his party, Grover crossed the state in 1870, declaring that the forces of monopoly, in the form of (Republican) railroad capitalists like Ben Holladay and their bribed tools in office like George Williams, had taken control of the government under the guise of defending the union. They intended, he charged, to impoverish the producing classes in state and nation, reducing them to wage slavery by placing them in competition with the Chinese laborer, stimulating "the absorbing and leaching process of his work among us."[81] Central to the Republican conspiracy, he insisted, was the Burlingame Treaty of 1868. By extending to China most-favored-nation status, this Republican measure encouraged Chinese laborers to "swarm in upon us like locusts."

The implications were frightening: "Their coming will unhinge labor, degrade industry, demoralize the country, and by claiming and receiving the ballot . . . upturn our system of government altogether."[82] That Republicans intended to enfranchise the Chinese, Grover cautioned, was beyond doubt. "The present policy of the General [Republican] Government [is] to enfranchise all inferior and servile races, and to encourage their immigration to the United States." Witness, he continued, the fifteenth (as well as fourteenth) amendment, which had deprived Oregonians of "the first element of [their] Constitution, guaranteed by her admission to the Union, the right to regulate suffrage." The reconstruction amendments, he charged, had planted in the Constitution "the essential elements of tyranny"; they had destroyed a basic principle of the founders, "local self government in the states." The remedy, he concluded (on the authority of Washington's farewell address), was removal of Republican officeholders and a national convention to reestablish constitutional balance between the general and state governments, a balance shattered by Republican radicalism.

Grover's anti-Chinese appeal was drawn from rhetoric intended in California for workingmen, but it resonated in the historical memory of rural Oregonians as well, striking a chord of fear concerned not with jobs lost or wages degraded but, perhaps more powerfully, with an image of Oregon transformed. In Grover's telling, continued Republican rule would destroy the state as home to a homogeneous and like-minded populace by encouraging and protecting the immigration—the "swarming"—of dependent, alien nonwhites fit for nothing but menial labor in manufacturing. The danger thus rested not in the Chinese per se but in what they portended: the degradation of white Oregonians to dependence, socially, economically, and politically.

That locals understood Grover in these terms a Portland association known as the Labor Exchange testified to directly. The exchange was not a workingmen's association but, rather, a Portland business group devoted to stimulating immigration. They had sent their congratulations to the new governor, along with an explanation of their purpose—which Grover considered important enough to append to his inaugural remarks on the Chinese. In this communication, the officers of the exchange went out of their way to affirm that they in no way countenanced Chinese immigration. The purpose of the exchange, they reported, was to court immigrants of a congenial social and ethnic type: white farming families indistinguishable from the existing stock of old Oregonians. "We need population," they wrote the Governor, but

> not of traders, professional men, or mere laborers, for a large influx of those classes, without a corresponding accession of producers, would be a positive detriment. . . . We want a farming population, especially of that class that requires land in small tracts for permanent homes, and devotes itself to the cultivation of a variety of products; for our country and climate are adapted to their pursuits.[83]

By "demagoguing" (in the words of Matthew Deady) on the Chinese issue, painting the Republican party as the party of monopoly, race mixture, and a corporate conspiracy against rural virtues, Grover led his party's return to power. Once in office, he put the Chinese issue aside (except for ceremonial occasions) and turned his attention to bringing partisan order to state government. Reinvigorating old alliances, he recreated the system of party patronage he had known in the 1850s. Drawing on funds from the sale of federal lands, he directed the building of public works and state institutions throughout Oregon—aids to river navigation, harbor improvements, fisheries, common schools, the university and agricultural college, the state capitol, an insane asylum, and a penitentiary, among others. Through the contracts and jobs these required he built a statewide machine that eclipsed—while recalling—the old Bush organization. (Republican critics did not miss the similarity, dubbing Grover's machine the Salem clique from time to time.) The machine made Grover a powerful man—at least for the moment. It secured his reelection as governor in 1874 and, in the summer of 1876, made him U.S. senator.

Grover's election to the Senate testified to his command of politics in Oregon, but it also set in motion the collapse of his Democratic organization. His refusal either to resign or to finish his governorship before seeking a Senate seat nettled even loyal Democrats, as did his insistence on naming his successor as governor (yet another delegate to the 1857 constitutional convention). Clouding his election were widespread charges that he had openly bought the votes of wavering men. Grover, ever more arrogant, ignored the rumbling around him and pressed his partisan advantage. Looking forward, no doubt, to a hero's welcome from Democrats in the U.S. Senate, he attempted in December 1876 to win the presidency for Samuel Tilden by delivering one of Oregon's three electoral votes to the Democrat—notwithstanding Hayes's victory in the popular vote. To this end he disqualified Hayes elector John W. Watts (an old anti-Democrat who had also served in the constitutional convention) on the grounds that Watts, a U.S. postmaster, was ineligible to hold two offices concurrently. Republicans were prepared for the disqualification but expected the other Republican electors to name Watts's replacement. Neither they, nor most Democrats, were prepared for Grover's certification of a Tilden elector in Watts's place.

Grover's ruling, had it stood, would have made Tilden president. But the uproar that met it, both in Oregon and across the nation, assured the opposite result. Suddenly notorious, Grover was condemned for political larceny. Worse for him, he was dismissed, as the *New York Times* put it, as "the ready, but somewhat ignorant, tool of smarter people."[84] The congressional commission that devised the compromise of 1877 repudiated his action, and Grover, instead of arriving in Washington, D.C., as a Democrat of national stature, became a pariah. To his chagrin, the (Republican) Senate refused to seat him and opened an investigation into his senatorial election. After hearings that included direct testimony about suddenly enriched Oregon legislators he was allowed to take his place, but the prospect that he would play a role of substance in the Senate was nil.

Slapped down by the majority and shunned by his own party, Grover spent his six years in the Senate as a frustrated backbencher. To make matters worse, he confronted daily the unraveling of the partisan tactics he had devised to rebuild the Oregon Democracy. As senator-elect he had promised Oregonians that he would work for repeal of the Burlingame Treaty with China and, more generally, oppose the conspiracy of Republicans and the railroads to foist their monopolistic designs on the nation. To this end he joined the debates that led to the 1882 Chinese Exclusion Act, even entering his 1870 inaugural remarks into the *Congressional Record*. But on the floor of the Senate he found himself upstaged at every point by Oregon's senior senator, John Mitchell. For Grover, the irony of the situation must have been bitter.

Mitchell was a railroad lawyer, George Williams's friend, and leading light of the Grand Old Party in Oregon during the last quarter of the nineteenth century.[85] By 1877, Grover's charge that Republicans were the party of Chinese labor had lost much of its credence, for now men like Mitchell (correctly described by Mary Roberts Coolidge as a venomous racist) had adopted as their own the rhetoric of race pioneered by reconstruction Democrats.[86] Finding his favorite issue appropriated by the opposition, Grover was forced to content himself with a leisurely term in office, promoting, among other things, federal railroad subsidies on behalf of Henry Villard's Northern Pacific Company.[87]

Grover returned to Oregon in 1884 to find his political standing destroyed. A resurgent Republican party had turned him into a symbol of Democratic corruption and ruthlessness and, as such, an effective campaign foil. The end of his political career became apparent when he moved from Salem, his home and base of political power for better than thirty years, to Portland. Although Grover continued to appear from time to time at Democratic functions, his influence was at an end. Whether he expected to return to power eventually cannot be said. Resolutely he turned his attention to more personal undertakings, as he had during the 1860s, and with some success. Like George Williams, he became a prominent figure in the business affairs of Portland. He renewed his practice of the law, speculated modestly in residential real estate, and served on the boards of banks, corporations, and civic organizations.

Behind the turn in Grover's life in 1884 was his recognition of political defeat and, also, a lesson he apparently had learned in Washington, D.C.: to wit, that the future was to be played out in cities. To this conclusion he testified shortly after his return, in a Fourth of July oration that proved to be his last as a political figure. His remarks began with a congratulatory look back on the role he had played in "originating the movement for the restriction of Chinese immigration to the America." It was, he observed, a "great movement . . . vital to the good character of our future development." But, he continued, Chinese exclusion was only the prelude to another, broader and more indispensable reform: "the restriction of the influx of paupers, infected persons, and contract labor from Europe." Bars on wide-ranging immigration, he averred, were needed in order to preserve the homogeneous racial stock of the state and nation in the face of "coming great changes in our condition."[88]

The great changes Grover foresaw were to his mind unprecedented. Added to the terrors of an "influx of paupers" was the imminent closing of the frontier. "The next ten years," he observed, will bring to an end "the work of two hundred and fifty years. [They] will close the last chapter of the great European exodus to the west in quest of the new and the wild, and the movements of our own people, seeking out the surest lands of promise, and planting their homes in new places." Unlike the man who came of age in 1820 or 1850, the youth of 1885 would not have the opportunity to take as his own "the new lands of the public domain, whose virgin soil has heretofore been a never failing resource for the enterprising. . . . He must content himself with other prospects."[89]

The "other prospects" that Grover identified (without great enthusiasm) were urban. Although he sought a role in the growth of Portland, as both a lawyer and a cautious and conservative director of banks and manufactories he, like Williams, embraced the urban epoch timidly and with misgiving. In the final analysis, Grover's valedictory warning to the people of his state best captured this charter settler of the Oregon country. Imploring his fellow citizens to guard their borders, stem the tide, preserve their material as well as racial homogeneity, he gave voice to the persistence of anxieties and desires carried to the Oregon country a generation before.

In Grover the classical republican vocabulary evident in George Williams was largely absent. At best it existed as an undercurrent expressed through his adherence to antebellum Democratic customs and usages. A tactician and organizer above all, he drew upon the customs of his party to exploit racial fears—still salient echoes of old agrarian beliefs—that persevered in this provincial society. The contrast between Grover and Williams in this regard underscored the antiseptic quality of the classical republican themes to which the latter turned at moments of personal crisis. But it was in the poststatehood career of Matthew Deady, more than anywhere else, that the salience of eighteenth-century discourse to the political culture of nineteenth-century Oregon was substantiated.

Of all the constitutional convention delegates, none measured his life by ideas as closely as Deady or left behind as complete and complex a record of his measurement—in his legal reasoning as a judge from 1859 to 1893, orations at commencements and patriotic ceremonies, and his private journal, where, like Pepys and Boswell, he recorded the details of his world and his course through it. All display Deady as a man troubled by his times, as one who found guidance not in the political conventions and understandings of industrializing America but, rather, in the eighteenth century. Before the Civil War, he had found his touchstone in country-party ideas that he attributed to Jefferson, but these doctrines he repudiated, quickly and completely, after the South's secession. Nominally, he became a Unionist and then Republican; by his own reckoning—a reckoning more to the point—he became a Federalist.

In the immediate aftermath of the constitutional convention there was no inkling of the shift, from self-styled Jeffersonian to self-styled Federalist, that occurred in Deady's views. In the November 1857 statehood election he openly advocated a proslavery vote. Eight months later, in the first state election, he won a seat on the state supreme court. He never took the office, however, for on the recommendation of Senator Joseph Lane, President Buchanan, in appreciation of Deady's support of his position on Kansas, appointed him to the U.S. district court, at which post he remained until his death. From his appointment until 1860, in the local contests between Bush and Lane Democrats, Deady took the latter's side; once national issues were attached to these local disputes, he supported the Buchanan—southern—Democracy. He embraced Dred Scott as constitutional doctrine on the grounds that property was property, be it in man or otherwise. Douglas and popular sovereignty—"squatter sovereignty," to his mind—he denounced, as late at the summer of 1860, as "the essence of anarchy lawlessness and mob rule."[90] As that year's presidential election approached, his identification with the Lane wing of the Oregon Democracy and the southern wing of the national party seemed unalterable. The Lane-dominated party convention chose him as a delegate to the Charleston convention. In the election, he attached his personal and official prestige to the cause of Breckenridge and Lane.

Deady's loyalty to the southern Democracy, indeed the Democracy in any shape, proved short-lived. In the spring of 1861 he made an unexpected (to onlookers remarkable) exit from the party that he identified, with praise before 1861 and scorn thereafter, with the historical figure of Thomas Jefferson. Behind Deady's departure was an idiosyncratic, as well as biographically illuminating, attempt to make sense of the South's secession. This he did by seeing secession in 1861 through the eyes of Federalists fearful of Jeffersonian sedition in 1798. From 1861 to the end of his life he interpreted both instances as symptomatic of the same Jeffersonian malady: idealization of the popular will and majority rule and a conflation of self-interest with the common good.[91] In this regard he came to appreciate and defend John Adams for his republican vigilance and, by the same token, denounce Jefferson for his "seductive . . . humbugs about every man being his own government." Shortly after the firing on Fort Sumter, Deady testified to the logic and depth of his conversion in a letter reminding an old Democratic friend that it was Jefferson (the "Coryphaeus of the sect") who "overthrew the Federal govt as well as the Federal party with his resolutions of /98, and to day we are reaping the consequences. He has been the model for every disturber of the public peace ever since, and his resolutions and declaration of Independence contain enough of revolution nullification secession and anarchy to set the four corners of the world by the ears."[92]

After 1861, Deady's reconception of Jefferson and his party never wavered. The Democracy remained for him the party of demagogues who manipulated the "Polloi" with the "Sans Culottes" doctrine of "might makes right." His prior identification with this party he explained as an "accident of birth" and error of youth.[93] When charged with disloyalty and threatened with removal from the federal bench, he explained to Republican friends (who intervened in his behalf with Attorney General Bates)[94] that

in the hey-day of what the host calls "sweet two and twenty" it was natural that under the generous but unthinking impulses of that age, I should continue to believe that mere numbers made right, that the boy was as wise as the man, the *vox populi vox Dei;* but time and experience have dimmed these youthful fancies, so that . . . now, I might and may be considered more of a Federalist of the Washington and Hamilton school, than a disciple of the Sans Culottes philosophy of Jefferson.[95]

There were two sides to Deady's political crisis and renewal during the Civil War, one negative, the other positive. First was his renunciation of the Democracy as the "Sans Culottes" party, and second his affirmation of "Federalism," the identity he maintained to the end of his life. Over the years he explored and deepened what he meant by it in his judicial career, journal entries, and, most explicitly, constant round of public addresses—commencement speeches, Fourth of July discourses, and, last but not least, his oration (alongside George Williams) at the 1889 centennial celebration of Washington's inauguration. As a Federalist he positioned himself outside and above the political mainstream of the industrializing nation—outside both parties and above what he denigrated as the two narrow alternatives provided by "modern political economy": the social Darwinism of gilded-age Republicans and the insurgent doctrines of the masses, working class and otherwise. Against both he affirmed republican principles that he attributed to Jefferson's eighteenth-century nemesis, Alexander Hamilton.

In the 1870s and 1880s Deady displayed the logic of his Federalist republicanism most conspicuously in public addresses he delivered (at the drop of a hat, it seems) around the state. In them he stated his alienation from the social Darwinian views of a nouveau riche capitalist class and countervailing mass movements, both of which he denounced as narrow and degraded ideologies of selfishness and private interest. Although arrayed against each other, they shared the shortsighted premise that "the conflict of private interests will produce economic order and right." As such, he argued, "the modern political economy reduced the relation between capital and labor to the mere matter of supply and demand, and limits the duty and obligation of the one to the other, to the payment of minimum wages for the maximum labor on the one hand, and getting of the maximum of wages for the minimum of labor on the other."[96]

Based on instincts of self-interest, capitalist and working-class politics (often correlated by Deady with Republicans and Democrats) threatened the republic's survival. But despite his conscious self-positioning outside the political currents of the day, his antipathy was not apportioned equally between the political alternatives he identified. Deady's greatest enmity was directed toward working-class movements. Although in rural Oregon the labor movement was small and insurgence infrequent, on one occasion it came to the fore, and Deady's opposition to it was immediate, outspoken, and startling to contemporaries. That exception, of course, was the anti-Chinese movement, which Grover incited and to which both parties thereafter pandered. In the 1870s and 1880s Deady, as judge and citizen, opposed anti-Chinese agitators of every stripe, surprising all who remembered his proslavery views in the 1850s and, more precisely, his 1857 advocacy of a constitution dedicated to the "pure white race." The racial proscriptions in the constitution (which he had helped write) he came to dismiss as mere sops to the mobocracy. The anti-Negro and anti-Chinese provisions, he declared in 1876 (with no little legerdemain), have "always been a dead letter. . . . At the time of the formation of the Constitution," he noted, both "were generally regarded as a mere piece of *brutum fulmen*, intended to quiet the fears and placate the prejudices of a certain class of voters who were supposed to stand in dread of being overslaughed by an influx of these black and yellow people."[97] The "certain class" to which Deady here referred was the Jeffersonian "rabble," and when they came before his court to ask enforcement of the constitution's anti-Chinese provisions, he condemned them.[98] Outside his courtroom he similarly denounced the popular crowds that organized in the 1880s to drive the Chinese from Oregon, and advised the governor to bring the full force of the law down upon them.[99]

This shift in racial views Ralph James Mooney has attributed to Deady's lifelong aristocratic pretensions, shaped in the postbellum era by his identification with Portland elites who employed Chinese and wished to protect them as a cheap supply of labor.[100] This interpretation illuminates Deady in important ways, although to it needs be added an understanding of how his aristocratic views were fostered by his peculiar metamorphosis during the Civil War—that is, his renunciation of Jeffersonianism and embrace of Federalism. Symbiotically, these shaped the aristocratic tenor of his thought and, in turn, his evaluation of the anti-Chinese movement. Just as importantly, Deady's *eighteenth*-century politics insured that his identification with *nineteenth*-century merchant and financial elites was never complete.

The driving force behind Deady's defense of the Chinese was his animosity toward their enemies. The anti-Chinese movement, in his rendering, was the modern—Democratic and working-class—incarnation of Jeffersonian doctrines, a contemporary instance of the same principles of "revolution nullification secession and anarchy" he placed within his political genealogy of the American "Sans Culottes" party, from the sedition crisis of 1798 through nullification to secession. In 1886, anti-Chinese crowds mobilized in Oregon City and Portland to force the immediate expulsion of the Chinese from Oregon. Against them Deady called a grand jury, to which he declared:

> An evil spirit is abroad in the land, not only here but everywhere. It tramples down the law of the country and fosters riot and anarchy. . . . Lawless and irresponsible associations of persons are forming all over the country,

claiming the right to impose their opinions on others. . . . The dominant motive of the movement is some form of selfishness, and its tendency is backward to barbarism—the rule of the strongest, guided by no other or better precept than this: Might makes right.[101]

In reaction to the crowds and their precept of "might makes right," Deady did align himself with the financial, merchant, and manufacturing elite of Portland. That he shared much with these men (on matters over and above the Chinese issue) goes without saying: they were his neighbors, fellow members of the bar and congregants in Portland's foremost Episcopalian church, and frequent dining companions. Above all, they were old friends, men whose acquaintance he had first made in the 1850s. But although Judge Deady traveled in and around the higher circles of Oregon society in the postbellum period, his ties to them were always marginal. His income as a judge (paid in depreciated currency through much of his career) imposed upon him a comparative, and nettling, poverty. To keep up even modest appearances, he found himself from time to time forced to accept financial favors, which he recognized, with ill-concealed chagrin, as a form of middle-class charity. In the final analysis, Deady's attitude toward his superiors in wealth was ambivalent. He appreciated their industry and praised their contributions to religious, cultural, and educational institutions (while never thinking them generous enough); but to the extent that they took pride in their riches and equated their personal interests with right, he denounced them as certainly as those he saw as the modern representatives of the Jeffersonian rabble. The grounds on which he denigrated the higher orders were eminently Hamiltonian: they failed his test of public virtue. They lacked the manners and morals of a republican gentry, mistaking the accumulation of personal wealth for adherence to the common wealth.

On the acquisitiveness of the late-nineteenth-century elites, Deady always cast a jaundiced eye. While as a newborn Hamiltonian he overcame his antebellum distrust of commerce, manufacturing, and corporations, the peace he made with the contemporary embodiment of the new order, the industrial corporation, was neither complete nor comfortable. As a judge he accepted the legal view of the corporation as an individual protected by the law (and, more precisely, the fourteenth amendment), but his decisions in such matters ring with indifference. For example, in a case brought by an injured worker against the Northern Pacific Railroad, he ordered the jury to consider the antagonists as they would "any two ordinary individuals. . . . The corporation," he advised, "stands before you as any other individual. It is nothing more than a collection of individuals who have associated themselves together for a lawful purpose, and they are not liable, and ought not to be made to pay any damages at your hands, unless any other collection of individuals would be required to do so under the like circumstances." And yet, to these in-

structions Deady added that he "suppose[d]" it was "proper," in "considering this case upon its general merits . . . to consider that the plaintiff is
a poor man, probably without means and without resources to make his
case [and] that the defendant is wealthy."[102]

Deady's ambiguity was even more evident in a subsequent case (1884),
in which an injured workingman brought suit for damages against a railroad corporation. In *Gilmore v. Northern Pacific Railroad Co.*, Deady made
law. Departing from the fellow servant rule (the rule that a laborer could
not hold his employer accountable for injuries on the job brought about
by the negligence of a fellow worker), he noted that in the "progress of
society . . . ideal and invisible masters and employers" (corporations)
had replaced "the actual and visible one of former times." This shift, he
judged in a ruling cited thereafter in other courts, required mitigation of
the fellow servant rule and a holding of corporate employers to "a due
and just share of the responsibility for the lives and limbs of the persons
in [their] employ."[103]

As a judge, Deady's stance toward the emerging corporate-industrial
order was cautious and understated, shaped (if not hedged) by his rever-
ence for legal precedent and the traditions of the common law—America's great inheritance from England, he pointed out at every opportunity (and in Hamiltonian terms). But here, Deady the judge must be
placed beside Deady the civic exhorter, who in speeches to Fourth of
July celebrators and graduating classes (composed, needless to say, of
the rising gentry) most clearly affirmed, in classical republican terms, his
"Federalism."

In these addresses—delivered at the same time he was denouncing
the Jeffersonian rabble—Deady engaged in prolonged lamentations on
the social Darwinian doctrines of gilded-age capitalists. The "gilded juggernaut," as he put it, held out only

> vulgar extravagance, fast living, and garish display[.] [B]eing accepted as
> evidence of distinctions and high social position, the giddy, vain, and aspir-
> ing poor, soon endeavor to vie with the diamond-decked nabobs and mil-
> lionaires in everything, and then comes peculation, theft, bribery, and all
> the gross and dishonest practices and devices which of late years had cor-
> rupted and debased the United States.

The outcome of luxury, extravagance, and display, Deady insisted, was
well known historically—the history to which he referred being, as in
George Williams's case, that of the ancient republics. "The Censors of
Rome," he advised audiences on numerous occasions, "referring to the
decline of Roman morals and manners consequent upon the contact
with the corrupt and lascivious people of Antioch, were wont to exclaim:
'The waters of the Orontes have muddied the Tiber!' . . . So," he went
on, drawing out the contemporary moral of his republican tale, "in view

of the events which have transpired within the last few years in the city bearing the honored name of the father of his country, may not we with equal reason exclaim: 'The waters of the Hudson have muddied the Potomac.'"[104]

Against the "gilded juggernaut," on the one hand, and the "Sans Culottes" politics of the working class, on the other, Deady called for a return to the first principles of the founders—more precisely, the Federalist founders, Washington and Hamilton. In a speech he repeated numerous times in the 1870s and 1880s, Deady paid homage to these men, calling upon his listeners to

> preserv[e] and improv[e] this heritage . . . by promoting and encouraging that individual integrity and intelligence, without which civic virtue is impossible. . . . Any form of government in which the People have any considerable voice or power imperatively requires a corresponding amount of individual integrity and intelligence. The decay and downfall of popular governments have always arisen from and always will be the result of a lack of public virtue—a failure on the part of the majority of the people entrusted with power and influence, to exercise the same for the highest public good.[105]

The alternative, as Deady enunciated it, was decay and collapse. "The decay and downfall of popular governments," he averred, "has always arisen from and always will be the result of a lack of public virtue." What he meant by "public virtue" was clear: it was

> that love of country which puts the common-weal before self, the people before the individual—that lofty and disinterested sentiment which led Curtius and Decius to devote themselves to certain death for the safety of Rome; that moved—
>
> > "The patriot Tell; the Bruce of Bannockburn;"
>
> And that impelled Arnold Winkelried to impale his body upon the hostile spears of the Austrian invaders and thus "make way for liberty."[106]

As he grew older Deady's republicanism grew stronger, reinforced, to no small degree, by his social and professional position in Portland. Struggling financially while his pioneer friends prospered, he was constantly reminded of the relative poverty his republican calling as a judge had brought him. In this light, his laments about the venality of his times, the power of "faction and personal gain" in public life, the corresponding absence of public virtue, and his disparaging of those who had "suddenly amassed . . . colossal fortunes . . . without the . . . experience, training or culture needed to fit them for the proper discharge of the duties . . . of such a trust" all contained an element of rationalization and righteous self-congratulation.[107]

Yet Deady was not a man without honor in his state; his anachronistic conception of his political self resonated in the political culture of Oregon. In his declamations on republican responsibility and in his actions as a judge, he expressed an alternative to the doctrines of "modern political economy" that struck a chord. In this respect, one final element—ironically, less Hamiltonian or Federalist than Jeffersonian—to Deady's political views bears notice. In 1887 he recorded in his journal: "Have been reading at odd hours Montesquieu and am getting quite interested. I have often said that it requires more virtue to run a republic or a democratic form of government, but did not know that he had anticipated me in the opinion."[108] Discounting his philosophical impertinence, we must acknowledge an important truth to his recognition of the similarities between his and the French thinker's views. Since the 1870s (unaware of Montesquieu) Deady had held that "the seed plot of the civic virtues is the home government—the government of the neighborhood—the State." The nurturing of civic virtue could occur, he insisted, only within "a limited and well defined locality—one having a marked natural boundary and identity or long established separate existence." As ever, he underscored his point with classical references:

> When the city of Rome made itself mistress of the civilized world and extended the boasted privilege of Roman citizenship to all the nations of the earth, the identity and individuality of the city was proportionally destroyed. The sentiment of patriotism diffused over so large and ill-defined a surface as the empire, became too attenuated and indistinct, to be of any avail as a motive power or incentive to noble and disinterested action.

"So," he concluded, "however powerful and extended this American Union may yet become . . . its beneficent duration must primarily rest on and depend on the character of local communities and governments out of which it is constituted."[109]

The local community and government that Deady had in mind, of course, was Oregon, a state that in 1893, the year of his death, was as much a backwater as it had been in 1849, the year of his arrival. Deady alternately celebrated and feared for Oregonians' resistance to the political economy of modernity, but, judging by his popularity as a speaker, he always found in Oregon an environment receptive to his atavistic views. Honored upon his death as the state's "first citizen," remembered thereafter as "Oregon's Justinian" (a reference he doubtless would have appreciated), commemorated for his encouragement of public education and culture, Deady reflected the extent to which Oregon retained at the nineteenth century's close the marks of its founding generation and, as well, its limited embrace of the modern world.

NINE

Industry and Exodus:
Nevada, 1864–1885

In August 1865, one year after the Nevada constitutional convention adjourned, *Harper's New Monthly Magazine* carried an article describing the people, economy, and politics of the new state. The author, Thomas Fitch, described the place and its history in unhesitatingly modern terms. He began with a description of the visual wonders of Nevada's barren terrain, and then recalled the "vivifying power," glittering promise, and "busy era of adventure, enterprise, and toil" that followed the 1859 discovery of the Comstock Lode. This said, he went on to emphasize the artificial, indeed dangerous, character of these early years, when "speculation ran riot, and the Territory of Nevada was converted into one vast swindling stock exchange. . . . What wonder," he exclaimed, that in the year of statehood "the bubble burst" and the ensuing depression brought "distrust and disgust . . . as widespread as the [economic] disaster" itself. For Fitch, the source of the "disaster" was readily apparent: "Of every hundred who invested in mining stock ninety-nine never saw, or intended to see, or designed to work [a] mine. To seek out, to speculate, to gamble was the object of all."[1]

Far from bemoaning the collapse of the wildcat hopes and small-scale speculations of the early days, Fitch saw salutary consequences in the mining depression. Above all, he hailed the departure of the "refuse ruffianism of California," which had streamed across the Sierra Nevada between 1860 and 1863. "The hard times that succeeded the financial crash of the spring of 1864," he explained, had driven "this undesirable class of citizens to 'fresh fields and pastures new.'" With relief he predicted that their leaving would end the speculative frenzy of the early years. Ever the booster, Fitch closed his essay with a promise of prosperity to settlers who brought to Nevada "either a small capital in money, or the wealth of honest industry contained in a pair of strong, willing arms."[2]

Notwithstanding these paeans to the small producer, the weight of Fitch's words pointed in another direction, to the immigration of capital and labor of a very different kind. From the perspective of 1865 Fitch already saw "the outlines of a glowing picture" and signs of "civilizing tendencies," evident, above all, in a "new system of procuring capital." Fitch's prophecy of a bright future for Nevada turned on two beliefs shared widely in 1864 and 1865. First was the conviction that the bullion locked beneath the Nevada desert was virtually limitless, that "unlike California, unlike any gold bearing country in the world, silver mines are inexhaustible, and, as a rule grow richer as they descend into the earth."[3] Second was the conclusion, seldom challenged since the depression began, that the discovery and recovery of this treasure required a new system of mining that drew together large-scale corporate enterprise, scientific and mechanical innovation, and railroad links to the outer world.

In so framing his thoughts Fitch offered a prescient, if incomplete, sketch of Nevada's future, for the years following 1864 did bring remarkable changes to this state. If not exactly as he hoped, this era saw the emergence of the corporate-industrial order implied in his 1865 piece. Nevada became a stark antithesis to the "old California" celebrated in the brief interval between the discovery of the Comstock Lode and the constitutional convention. The depression that began in the spring of 1864 did not end quickly, and when conditions improved later in the decade they did so under the auspices of a series of corporate combinations—the Bank of California, the Central Pacific Railroad, the Nevada Mine and Milling Company, and the famed "Bonanza firm"—that from 1865 to the turn of the century vied for dominion over the state and its people. In Nevada, more so than any other place in the late-nineteenth-century United States, the term *monopoly* seemed to capture reality. No longer a magnet for "old Californians" or their latter-day equivalents, the state increasingly was home to managers of mining corporations and wage laborers recruited for their skill as "deep-rock" miners, their discipline to the clock, and their habituation to the cadence of the machine. Simultaneous with the rise of this new regime, as Fitch perceived in 1865, was an exodus of the first-comers to Washoe—the self-styled old Californians—for whom the emerging corporate order had little appeal.

These features of the poststatehood era in Nevada were displayed fully in the lives of its constitution writers. Here, even more quickly than in California (and in stark contrast to Oregon), the charter group disappeared from the scene, some within months, all but a handful within a decade. Of the thirty-five men who served in the 1864 constitutional convention, only fourteen still resided in Nevada in 1870; six years later, only five.[4] Their departure testified to the first settlers' dedication to an individualist ethos and the pursuit of private interest. Many of the constitution writers, alongside their neighbors, set out for new mining areas in the Great Basin, Rocky Mountain region, and Pacific Northwest. Others returned to California. In many cases their migration to "fresh pastures and fields new" continued to the end of their lives. Just as they had joined in the exodus from California to Nevada in the late 1850s and early 1860s, so did they leave the state they created in 1864 once the promise it had held out to individuals evaporated. In this respect their lives after statehood reflected the currents of historical change that swept over Nevada from 1860 to 1900. The speed of their exodus, and the reasons for it, testified to the hold of the beliefs that had carried them to Washoe in the early 1860s. At the same time, their departure offered quiet but suggestive testimony about the transformation of this mining country in the post–Civil War years.

The pace of change in Nevada from 1864 forward was stunning. The campaign over ratification that fall and the simultaneous experience of Judge John North showed just how quickly new political-economic beliefs had taken hold. Despite the disillusionment that marked the closing days of the constitutional convention, the opposition to statehood hinted at by J. Neely Johnson and others never materialized. On the contrary, most of the constitution writers joined in the general call for statehood on the grounds that the new charter and new institutions of government were vital to ending the dull times that plagued the territory. "Public opinion," reported the *Sacramento Daily Union* shortly after the convention adjourned, "is changing rapidly in Nevada Territory in favor of adopting the State Constitution." According to California observers and Nevadans on the scene, the reason for this change was apparent. Announced the (Virginia City) *Territorial Enterprise:*

> The only hope we have of effecting a speedy and absolute cure of our crushing ills is in the adoption of a State Government. It is an imperative necessity, and as such we accept it. . . . Better to pay even double taxes, if by doing so we can make our property ten times more productively valuable, than to pay even less and let property continue to depreciate. It is for the interest of all—and particularly the miner—that work shall speedily as possible be resumed in the temporarily abandoned mines. If we should have flush times again, we must vote for the State Constitution.[5]

Three weeks later, upward of 90 percent of the voters endorsed this line of reasoning, making Nevada, "battle born," the newest member of the union.[6]

At the time no one remarked on the rather dramatic shift in public opinion that had taken place since the aborted statehood movement eight months earlier. That those days were out of sight and mind the experience of Judge John North confirmed. During the summer, while

the constitutional convention was in session, William Stewart renewed
his charge of corruption against the judge. This time, in contrast to the
prior winter, the charges stuck. North resigned from the bench even before statehood abolished his office.

In the final analysis, however, the judge's travail had little to do with
the substance of Stewart's attack. More important was a fundamental
shift in public opinion about North's stand on the issue that had dominated territorial politics in the winter of 1863–1864, the one- versus
many-ledge theories of the Comstock Lode. In the aftermath of the
spring depression (as the debates of the constitutional convention attested) a substantial majority of Nevadans had come to attach recovery
and prosperity with outside capital and corporate development, not
small-scale mining. Once this occurred, the many-ledge theory (and
North's judicial affirmation of it) lost its political and economic significance. Rather, attention now shifted to the courts as a contributor, if not
prime cause, of the depression.

As the conviction that the courts were the central impediment to recovery strengthened, North's old adversaries renewed the charge of judicial corruption raised by Stewart the winter before. Although North
again went on the offensive, this time the attacks did not mobilize a
movement against Stewart or alleged monopoly interests.[7] Quite the
contrary. Somewhat sheepishly—but effectively—former defenders of
the judge joined the chorus of criticism. Late in the summer of 1864, for
example, a speaker before a recently established "miners' league" in
Storey County offered that "a most potential cause of the present depression of mining industry, is the universal distrust of our judiciary."
Over the following weeks, members of the league circulated a petition
throughout Virginia City and Gold Hill demanding dismissal of the entire territorial court. By mid-August more than 3,500 voters—mine
owners, merchants, workingmen—had signed it, displaying their acceptance of the view that identified the territorial courts as a prime cause of
the depression.[8] As the *Nevada Transcript* put it:

> It is possible—barely possible—that [the territorial judiciary] may be above
> reproach. But enough has been brought to light to destroy all confidence
> in their integrity. [Nevada] never can prosper while the judiciary is sus-
> pected. Capital will refuse to go there for investment unless at heavy pre-
> mium for risk, and men of families will decline to make a spot for their
> homes where vice instead of virtue reigns.[9]

By the end of August, North had had enough. Perhaps convinced that
he and his colleagues could no longer function, or perhaps worried over
his health (his ostensible reason), he resigned.[10] Ironically, North's last
judicial decision brought the controversy over the one- and many-ledge
theories to an end. Acting on the report of a court referee he had earlier

appointed to reexamine the question, North ruled in favor of the company that argued that the Comstock Lode consisted of a single ledge of ore. The irony of North's decision did not lie in the ruling itself, for he had always ruled in favor of the many-ledge theory on empirical grounds, and in his last decision he did exactly the same, concluding that the referee's "long, anxious, and laborious examination" supported the opposite of what had previously seemed to be the case.[11] The irony, rather, lay in the public response to it. There was no outcry, no wail of indignation from the little interests, no charge of judicial capitulation to monopolists. The one- versus many-ledge controversy had lost its power to inflame Nevadans. It no longer seemed to matter to the future of the territory.

The shift in public sentiment over the Comstock Lode theories, as striking as it appears in hindsight, went unnoticed at the time. The editors of the *Virginia Daily Union,* unrelenting in their opposition to the one-ledge theory in the winter campaign against statehood, calmly reviewed and accepted the legal settlement of the question. "We have read the published decision of John Nugent, Esq., referee in this case," the *Union* reported.

> It is very carefully and elaborately prepared, and presents the whole case, very fairly, we should judge. It is especially important as a complete and extended showing of all the facts and arguments in support of the one ledge theory; and, we think, presents a strong case in its support. . . . We would suggest that as the one ledge claimants have now got the advantage, and are generally wealthy, they buy up the opposing titles and stop the litigation which is retarding our progress so much. This can now be done, we believe, cheaper than to continue the litigation, from the fact that the decision will depress the value of all opposing titles.[12]

Although the connection went unnoticed at the time, other developments of even greater significance coincided with the electoral ratification of statehood, the fall of John North, and the shift in opinion toward the composition of the Comstock Lode. In the spring of 1864, financier William Ralston organized the Bank of California in San Francisco. He immediately established a branch in Virginia City, to which he dispatched as cashier (manager) William Sharon, a gold rush merchant and real estate speculator who, in the 1850s, had made and lost a number of fortunes through mining investments. Nevada newspapers, reflecting the new desire to encourage imported capital, hailed the arrival of the new bank and its agent, reasoning that it promised "a speedy release of cash capital."[13] No one foresaw the radical effect this institution would have on Nevada—that within two or three years it would usher in a very different political, economic, and social order on the Comstock Lode.

Indeed, with the coming of the Bank of California began an era of concentrated corporate control and rapid industrialization that shaped the state to the end of the nineteenth century.

William Sharon arrived in Nevada just before the constitutional convention began its work. Without delay, he put into effect a program that quickly created what nineteenth-century historian Charles Shinn described as the "infamous, fortified monopoly system" of the Bank of California.[14] Offering loans to struggling mine and mill owners at half the prevailing rate of interest, Sharon acquired a growing portfolio of notes. Because of the depression, the stock in these companies was undervalued; thus their value to the bank as collateral was (at least potentially) inflated. Furthermore, the mortgagors' ability to repay their loans, as long as the depression persisted, was questionable. Sharon gambled that both conditions would turn to his advantage, providing the Bank of California with the opportunity to gain a stranglehold over Comstock Lode mining.

He judged correctly. When the depression persisted into 1865 and many failed to meet their payments, the bank foreclosed, gaining possession of a multitude of Comstock mines and mills. In the spring of 1867, Ralston, Sharon, and other Bank of California officers—now known as the "Bank Crowd"—consolidated these into a single holding company, the Union Mine and Milling Company. Through it Sharon and his associates put together a vertical and horizontal combination of Comstock properties. In addition to its mine and mills, in 1867 and 1868 the bank crowd incorporated the Virginia and Truckee Railroad to run from Virginia City to Carson City and Reno (connecting there to the transcontinental Central Pacific line). Displaying the political dimensions of their economic command, they extracted $500,000 in bonds from Storey and Ormsby counties as well as $700,000 from mining companies on the Comstock Lode to underwrite its construction. The railroad was completed in 1872, "fortifying" the bank's monopoly over transportation to and from the Comstock Lode. Wood and water followed. Sharon and his associates bought the timber reserves in the Tahoe Basin, constructed their own fluming company to deliver the wood, and, finally, through the Virginia City and Gold Hill Water Company captured control of the scarce water resources essential to life as well as the operation of the Comstock mines and mills.[15]

Although Sharon's manipulation of the money market established what at the time appeared to be an insurmountable monopoly of Comstock properties, the Bank Crowd's control did not survive. Illustrating Gabriel Kolko's thesis that, *ceteris paribus*, industrial and financial concentration encourages rather than dampens economic competition, challengers to the Bank Crowd (emulating Sharon's strategies) soon appeared.[16] In 1870, John P. Jones, superintendent of one of the bank's mines, Crown Point, quietly began to buy up its stock. At the time Crown Point was producing only low-grade ore, and the price of its stock was depressed. According to expert opinion, the mine was worked out, and there was little likelihood that more bullion lay within its bounds deeper in the earth. Jones knew better. In league with his brother-in-law, Alvinza Hayward (who was also one of the original organizers of the Bank of California), he sought a corner on Crown Point stock. Before Sharon realized what his employee and erstwhile associate were up to, the two gained a controlling interest in the mine. Shortly thereafter the new owners announced a major discovery. As the mine produced more paying ore and the value of its stock increased, Jones and Hayward parlayed their profits into their own corporate combination, the Nevada Mine and Milling Company, independent of the "fortified" system of the Bank of California.[17]

At virtually the same time another group of old California miners, allied to San Francisco financiers in competition with the Bank Crowd, opened another offensive against the fortified monopoly. These were the famed "bonanza kings": John Mackay, James Fair, James Flood, and William O'Brien. Their tactics were the same as Jones and Hayward's but played more boldly. This third ring began by buying stock in the Hale and Norcross Mine, which, like Crown Point, was depressed and considered worthless. Its superintendent, James Fair, like Jones before him, knew otherwise. Once Fair and his partners confirmed their financial control, they announced another bonanza. On that basis they speculated in other claims, without success until the mid-1870s, when their gambles paid off. In 1872, the ring acquired the Consolidated Virginia Company, which different companies had worked without profit for almost a decade. According to the conventional wisdom, its boundaries were outside the major Comstock ledge, but the conventional wisdom was wrong. Two years later their workers made the biggest strike in Comstock Lode history, the famed "Big Bonanza." With it the most productive era in Nevada mining began. From 1873 to 1882 deep-rock miners in the employ of the Bonanza firm extracted an estimated $100 million in bullion. Drawing on the example of the combinations that preceded them, Mackay, Fair, and company established their own integrated system of mines, mills, timber, and water companies, failing to crack only the Bank Crowd's command over transportation.[18]

The discovery of the Big Bonanza was accompanied by reveries that rivaled those of the early 1860s. Observers announced that flush times were back—indeed, that an era of limitless prosperity had opened on the Comstock Lode. The tale of the Big Bonanza, at the time and thereafter, became part of a seamless social history of the Comstock Lode, in which the principals of the Bonanza firm enjoyed the central, heroic, roles.[19] Through their lives, their early struggles and late triumphs, the

Comstock Lode of the early 1860s was imaginatively tied to the new order of the 1870s and 1880s. The logic of the tale was biographical, for each of these men was a gold rush veteran who had come to California as a poor youth, prospering only in a small way in the placer fields and early quartz mines. With the discovery of the Comstock Lode they had joined other old Californians who crossed the Sierra Nevada in pursuit of the fading promise of the early 1850s. In 1876, the Comstock Lode journalist William Wright (writing as Dan De Quille) emphasized this feature of the story in his classic account of the great strike, *The Big Bonanza*. He dedicated his book to "John Mackay, Esq., Prince of Miners," affirming Mackay's heroic stature—as a hardy individualist, not pioneer of corporate industrial innovation. Later in the century Charles Shinn portrayed these men in much the same way. Mackay and Fair, he emphasized, were respectively a "Dublin born youth" and "Tyrone lad" who, taken by the "California gold fever, had come to the far west in the 1850s." Poor workingmen, first in the California placers and then in the quartz mines, they "deserved large success as far as constant labour and study and steady habits may be said to deserve it." According to Wright and Shinn—and more generally to the individualist ethos to which western mining gave voice—they embodied "the splendid and fortunate element that one likes to think of as belonging to every mining district."[20]

Yet the story of the bonanza kings (and their counterparts) involved more than the success of hardworking, clever, and lucky individuals. Understandably lost in the richly textured details of their personal quests, and their combat with one another for control of Nevada capital, was the fact that their individual triumphs signaled the denouement of the individualist ethos that had drawn ambitious self-seeking men to California in 1849 and, with the exhaustion of the gold rush placers, to other mining centers of the Far West. Their lives and their contests with one another were part and parcel of the individualist culture of the early mining frontier; but they also marked the beginning of a new, vastly different historical period dominated by industrial corporations. Representative figures of the short-lived but legendary era that glorified a society of every man for himself and defined the common good as the natural outcome of a collective pursuit of self-interest, these men spun out the logic of their individualist beliefs, ushering in—without contradiction—a world that suppressed mortal individuals in favor of the artificial being of the corporation.

The contours of this new order are fully apparent only through consideration of another, complementary, side to the entrepreneurial contests of the 1860s and 1870s: the development of an industrial, wage-labor, working class on the Comstock Lode. Between 1864 and 1875, as depression gave way to corporate combinations, the character of the miner's labor, indeed the composition of the Comstock region population, changed quickly and dramatically. Gone was the early, raucous society of individual miners who worked for a wage only as a last resort, desiring instead to seek out their own bonanza or speculate in will-o'-the-wisp hopes for a quick killing in the market for mining stocks. Replacing these sojourners, figuratively and substantively, were "armies" of skilled deep-rock miners operating hydraulic drills and other complex machinery in what Shinn aptly called "the city underground," the labyrinthine mining factories that snaked thousands of feet in every direction beneath Virginia City and Gold Hill.[21] Along with these laborers came mining engineers, salaried superintendents of corporate properties, foremen hired on for their expertise, and bankers sent to monitor the investments of San Francisco, New York, and London financiers. Machinery and complex organization unprecedented in scale dominated work and life. Writing in 1883, geologist Eliot Lord could only wonder at the mechanical magnificence of the Comstock mines:

> Ten boilers at the Yellow Jacket Mine works, 16 feet in length and 54 inches in diameter, resting upon a grate surface of 250 square feet, supply steam to engines whose aggregate horse-power is 2,941. The two hoisting-engines at the working compartments of the shaft are 1,000 horse-power each . . . and the pump compartment hoisting engine is of 500 horse-power. . . . At the Union shaft . . . the hoisting-engine for the working compartment is of 1,200 horse-power, and the pump compartment hoisting-engine of 400 horse-power. The twelve boilers, with a grate surface of 270 square feet, consume thirty-three cords of wood every twenty-four hours. The main hoisting-engine at the C. & C. shaft, double cylinder, horizontal, direct-acting, with brake fly-wheels, is of 2,000 horsepower. This great engine raises an iron cage with three car-loads of ore or waste rock, weighing 12,400 pounds, a distance of 2,500 feet with perfect ease, lowering a cage filled with men or empty at the same time.

To contemporary chroniclers of the Comstock Lode, these signs of mechanical genius were breathtaking. The works of the Yellow Jacket Mine in 1881 alone, Lord pointed out, nearly doubled in horsepower the combined power of all the Comstock mines in 1866.[22]

With the industrialization and complex mechanization of mining, the daily routine of the Nevada miner changed. As early as 1866, the *Gold Hill Evening News* described the opening of the miner's day in terms that displayed how quickly the industrial regime appeared. "The operatives," reported the *News*, "were collected in a large room connected with the engine-room, waiting for the roll-call, which took place at 5 o'clock." A new and all-encompassing emphasis on punctuality, precise accounting of time below, and a division of labor and authority were apparent: "Each man answer[ed] to his name as the same was called by the timekeeper, and immediately after starting to his place—and as the last name was called, those that had been at work passed out, each one giving his name as he passed, which was checked by the time-keeper. By this means no mistake is made, and punctuality is secured which otherwise could not be done."[23] Lord marveled at the daily routine of the Comstock miner, spent for the most part deep inside the earth. "View their work!" he implored his readers.

> Descending from the surface in the shaft-cages, they enter narrow galleries where the air is scarce respirable. By the dim light of their lanterns a dingy rock surface, braced by rotting props, is visible. The stenches of decaying vegetable matter, hot foul water, and human excretions intensify the effects of the heat. The men throw off their clothes at once. . . . Yet, though naked, they can only work at some stopes for a few moments at a time, dipping their heads repeatedly under water showers from conduit pipes, frequently filling their lungs with fresh air at the open ends of blower-tubes.[24]

Fifteen years later, at the close of the Comstock era in the 1890s, Shinn celebrated the perfection of bureaucratic routines and the mechanization of laboring men initiated in the mid-1860s. At the beginning of each shift, he observed, the workers of the Comstock Lode "form in line in the hoisting works and march into the cages. They leave the mines in the same way. Three shifts of eight hours each make the day of twenty-four hours. 'Morning shift' is from 7 a.m. to 3 p.m.; 'afternoon shift' is from 3 to 11 p.m.; and 'night shift' till 7 again." The hierarchy of authority and the division between management of the firm and management of its men were highly developed. Each level of the mine, Shinn continued, had three shift bosses.

> The clerk who acts as timekeeper has an office in the hoisting works and registers every man's ingoing and outcoming with the regularity of a machine. The shift bosses report men missing or sick, also accidents, or anything else of importance. They tally loads of ore and waste rock, filling up a printed blank. The superintendent thus knows how much work each shift has accomplished. Each level has a foreman. The mine has also a general underground foreman, and an assistant to take his place at night.

Finally, precise gradations of skill and task defined the miners' work underground. "As regards the workmen," Shinn pointed out, "there is complete classification. The timber men attend to the supports of the various workings; the miners, drill men, and drifters hew and cut passages and extract the ore; the pump men and engineers see to their respective duties. Watchmen make regular rounds, messengers carry orders, take the men water or tools, and gather up dulled picks and crowbars to send them to the forges."[25]

Over the 1860s and 1870s, the men who rode the giant hoisting works thousands of feet into the earth to construct the tunnels, drove the hydraulic drills, ran the underground railroad systems, and operated the ventilator shafts required to fend off quick suffocation gave the Comstock Lode a new human face. On the surface, the raucous, male-dominated saloon life that so struck visitors to Nevada throughout the nineteenth century seemed constant. In 1896, Shinn felt compelled to describe Virginia City in terms that echoed J. Ross Browne's portraits from the 1860s: "The social order of this masterful, masculine commu-nity," he averred, composed "heroic fellowship at its best."[26] Below the surface, however—actually as well as figuratively—by the 1870s the char-acteristic Nevadan, in background, skill, and temperament, was a very different type, no longer a "miner," simply put, but a "deep-rock miner," the era's term for the skilled laborer working in the mines for a wage.

Some of those who made up this new working class were figures from the old days, remade by necessity into wage workingmen. Increasingly prevalent, however, were workers whom the managers of the new Com-stock combinations had recruited from California and abroad precisely for their industrial skills and discipline to the regimen of clock, shop whistle, weekly check, and company store. By the 1870s Cornish and Irish miners, who migrated to Nevada from California as well as directly from the British Isles, accounted for two-thirds of the Comstock work force.[27] More so than their Washoe predecessors, these men were accus-tomed to the industrial regime: the Irish by virtue of experience in the early quartz mines of California, the Cornish from work in the tin, lead, and copper mines of Cornwall. They were, as John Rowe has put it,

> prepared to go and "work for wages"—a thing that did not come easy to individualist pioneers. The latter class, indeed, now took themselves off to newer fields in Arizona and Colorado, just as a similar development of capitalism and of wage-earning had made Californian pioneers ready to go to Washoe when the news of the first discoveries in 1858 and 1859 reached the western side of the Sierra Nevada.

The "Cousin Jacks" of Cornwall, in particular, brought "old country skills of hard-rock mining—drilling, blasting, tunnelling, and shaft-sink-ing." English firms with interests in Nevada mines often recruited and transported these workers directly. Although, like the early itinerant miners, many of these foreign-born deep-rock miners were "birds-of-passage," their migratory habits turned to a different master. Their quest was not the individual one for fortune that drew earlier prospec-tors and speculators; rather, they were lured by like-minded coun-trymen and the promise of steady, high wages to carry home.[28]

With this shift in the nature of mining and in the makeup of the miner, the hazy and indeterminate lines between miner and mine owner, laborer and entrepreneur, that had marked the first years of settlement hardened into clear lines between capital and labor. By 1870 these distinctions had been institutionalized, on the one hand by the primacy of the mining corporation, on the other by miners' unions. As Richard Lingenfelter has observed,

> Industrialization and unionization of the western mines developed together in the later half of the nineteenth century. . . . The best interest of the corporation was not necessarily the best for the miner, and disputes inevitably arose over wages, working hours, use of dynamite, employment of the Chinese, hospital fees, and a long list of other issues. All of these problems grew more acute as labor forces grew larger and labor-management relations became less personal with the growing industrialization, capitalization, and absentee ownership of the western mines. With these problems grew the hardrock miner's need for collective action through industrial unions.[29]

The history of union building from 1863 to 1870 provides a complementary perspective on the corporate-industrial transformation evident in the changes of mind toward statehood and John North in 1864, and the rise of the bank crowd, Jones-Hayward, and Bonanza firm combinations. The very names of the organizations that constitute the genealogy of the Nevada unions reflect the crooked, yet certain, path that Comstock laborers followed to working-class consciousness. Preceding the establishment of the rightly famed "union" of Comstock Lode workingmen in 1866 were two short-lived organizations. The first, calling itself the Miners' Protective Association, appeared in 1863 when more than three hundred men assembled in Virginia City and endorsed the following resolutions: first, "the securance to practical miners of a good remuneration for their toil"; second, "the providing of aid and comfort for them in times of sickness and adversity"; and, third, "the exposure and defeat of speculative plans affecting their interests injuriously."[30]

Shortly after this mass meeting, the protective association disappeared, likely because of the ambiguity of its enunciated purposes. While the first two resolutions echoed characteristic wage and fraternal aims of antebellum workingmen, the last displayed the extent to which the early miners of Nevada did not identify themselves solely, or for that matter primarily, as wage laborers. With equal measures of hope and worry they participated in the wildcat speculation that marked the years before 1864. The third resolution—indeed, the very definition of the organization as a *protective association*, part union, fraternal organization, and business association—testified to a measure of confusion among those who joined it. Was the association to speak for the thousands of small-scale miners and individual investors who worried over manipulation of mining stocks by San Francisco financiers? Or was it an organization of the wage working class? Unable to define itself or identify its constituency, the Miners' Protective Association dissolved quietly. Given the nature of life on the Comstock Lode in 1863, this is not surprising. No clearly defined working class existed, nor did any one overpowering adversary face the ambitious immigrant. Where mine ownership was spread far and wide, the identity of wage worker loosely fixed, and the laboring class made up of men who floated in and out of the wage work force, the "nabob in fancy"—or so many were convinced—"might yet be a nabob in fact." [31]

Shortly after the disappearance of the protective association, depression struck, changing the situation for the "little interests" in the mines in every respect. At the very time the Nevada constitution writers were at work in Carson City, trying in their own way to devise a constitutional resolution to dull times, the superintendents of a number of Comstock mines announced wage cuts on orders from San Francisco. In response, the miners of Gold Hill struck, proclaiming that they would close the mines down before accepting a wage below four dollars per day. After successfully stopping work in the mines at their corner of the Comstock Lode, they marched to Virginia City to the accompaniment of the Gold Hill Brass and String Band playing "all the defiant airs in their scorebooks."

Along the way the strikers shouted their demand: "Four dollars a day!" "No reduction of wages!" [32] This wildcat organization, calling itself the Miners' League of Storey County, distinguished itself from its predecessor by limiting its demands to the "sole purpose" of "keeping wages at a standard of Four Dollars per day" and the imposition of a closed shop in the underground mines. For a brief time, the Miners' League forced owners to accede to its demands. But its ability to maintain its ranks proved, in the end, as incomplete as its predecessor's. As the league's involvement in the movement for statehood and against the territorial judiciary attested, its members retained much of the ambiguity of purpose that had marked the protective association. More importantly, the league was unable to maintain, much less increase, its membership as the depression in the mines continued into 1865 and 1866 and its corporate adversaries organized a so-called Citizens' Protective Association. This organization, despite its name, was an alliance of mine owners and their superintendents dedicated to breaking the Miners' League. To this end its members coordinated the firing and blackballing of league men, replacing them with scabs (imported where necessary from outside of Nevada) who were willing to defy the nascent union. Prominent among these were Cornish immigrants—"aliens," according to the Miners' League, "who come here only to hoard their gains in order to carry them back to their native land." [33]

In the fall of 1864 the miners' league disappeared, and for more than two years the mine owners kept unionization at bay. In late 1866, how-

ever, workingmen on the Comstock Lode organized once again, this
time with enduring success. Their new organization, the Miners Union
of the Town of Gold Hill, neither dissolved for want of clear purpose,
nor was it broken by corporate antagonists. Indeed, it became the model
for organizing deep-rock mine workers throughout the West and the
foundation of what in 1893 became the Western Federation of Miners.[34]
In moving from "protective association," to "league," to "union," the
workingmen of the Comstock Lode crossed, in ideological terms, a fundamental divide.

Behind the success and endurance of the union were three factors.
First, in the form of William Sharon and the Bank Crowd, was the presence of a tangible and mighty adversary, a combination of capital whose
control of the mines, mills, and associated enterprises—and perforce the
wages of workers—was apparent to all. Ironically, the very structure of
the fortified monopoly served the union well. Because of the failure, in
1865, 1866, and 1867, to find a new bonanza, the Bank Crowd's Union
Mining and Milling Company was able to show a profit only by keeping
its mills and transportation companies in constant operation. This required that the mining companies controlled by the combination continue to extract ore, even at a loss. The difference between the value of
the bullion taken from the mines and the companies' operating expenses
(that is, the cost of transporting and milling the ore) was made up
through "assessments" to stockholders. Because a work stoppage in the
mines would threaten the profitable portions of the Union Mine and
Milling Company, the Bank Crowd, unable to endure a strike, had no
choice but to deal with the union if they were to keep their combination
intact. As Eliot Lord described the situation, "If the Union Milling and
Mining Company and the Virginia and Truckee Railroad Company had
not been formed, it is most probable that the union of miners would
have melted away in 1870, as the league, its predecessor, had dissolved in
1865, and so, if the miners had been clear-sighted, they would have wel-
comed a dreaded combination, as in truth a champion even if *malgré
lui.*"[35]

Second, the presence of a single overwhelming adversary in the form
of the Bank Crowd had the effect of forcing Comstock miners to put
aside the ethnic animosities among native-born, Irish, and Cornish
miners that the mine owners' Citizens' Protective Association had exploited so effectively in 1864 and 1865. In contrast, the 1866 union celebrated the solidarity of workingmen (*white* workingmen), no matter what
their origin. This newly defined identity of interests among Comstock
Lode miners was readily apparent in the union's founding meeting,
which was held in December 1866 at McCluskey's Theater Hall in Gold
Hill. There, presiding over a crowd of three to four hundred miners,
was a forty-seven-year-old Cornish miner, John G. White. The partici-

pants—native born, Irish, and "Cousin Jack"—displayed a militance and working-class consciousness absent by comparison in the previous attempts to organize Comstock miners. In contrast to their predecessors, the founders of the miners' union emphasized the inevitability of conflict between labor and capital. The interests of wage laborers they defined narrowly: a closed shop and maintenance of a four-dollar daily wage for underground workers. Highlighting the distinction between capital and labor, the new union successfully mobilized deep-rock miners who worked for the dominant combinations of the Comstock Lode. "In view of the existing evils which the Miners have to endure from the tyrannical oppressive power of Capital," its constitution declared,

> it has become necessary to protest, and to elevate our social condition and maintain a position in society, and that we should cultivate an acquaintance with our fellows in order that we may be the better enabled to form an undivided opposition to acts of "tyranny" —Therefore,
>
> We the Miners of Gold Hill have resolved to form an association for the promotion and protection of our common interests, and to adopt a constitution for its guidance, for without Union we are powerless, with it we are powerful; —and there is no power that can be wielded by Capital or position but which we may boldly defy, —For united we possess strength; let us then act justly and fear not.[36]

The third factor that helped close the ranks of the Comstock Lode workingmen was the alleged threat of Chinese labor. With the completion of the Central Pacific rail line across the Great Basin in 1869, Chinese construction crews found themselves suddenly out of work. In search of employment they moved to towns throughout the Far West. In the mining centers of Nevada, as in San Francisco and elsewhere, they became the immediate target of organizing white workers. To the recently unionized miners of the Comstock Lode, the Chinese appeared in a particularly threatening guise: as a reserve army that the capitalists of the fortified monopoly stood ready to use to break the newly organized ranks of labor. When the first such "threat" appeared, the miners' union acted immediately. In 1869, William Sharon hired a Chinese crew to grade the road bed of the Virginia and Truckee line from Virginia City to Carson. With their appearance, Shinn recounts,

> a committee of three hundred and fifty-nine miners from the Union went out, four abreast, like a military company, in two battalions, and descended on the Chinese. The sheriff of the county ordered them to disperse and return home. One man replied that they would do so as soon as they were through, and advised the official to sit down and watch the proceedings. He halted them and read the Riot Act, to which they listened with grave attention until he had finished that impressive document. Then they roared sealike applause, gave three cheers for the "United States of America," and marched on with loud Homeric laughter. As they went along the

course of the railroad construction the Chinese deserted pick and shovel and fled into the gulches. Not a shot was fired. The "Committee" returned to report progress, and for eight days not a Chinaman dared to do a stroke a work, while the lordly Sharon was supplicating the Unions to permit the resumption of railroad grading. Finally he signed an agreement by which he removed the Chinese from the districts of Virginia City and Gold Hill.[37]

To the deep-rock miners of Nevada the Chinese were first and foremost a threat to the power of the union against the bosses. Given the pace of industrialization on the Comstock Lode and the newly forged solidarity among its deep-rock workingmen, the arrival of Chinese laborers was galvanizing. Conceived as the tools of corporate monopolists, the Chinese stood before white laboring men, in and outside the mines, native born and not, as a threat to an always fragile balance of power between capital and labor. Here as elsewhere in the Far West between 1865 and 1890, the Chinese provided a powerful symbol through which workers, by closing their shops to people of color, fortified the house of labor.[38]

With the strikes of the late 1860s and early 1870s and the appearance of new corporate combinations on the Comstock Lode, the unions controlled who could work in the mines. By 1870 they effectively excluded Chinese laborers from employment. By no later than 1875 the closed shop was a reality for underground workers. Neither corporate agents nor nonunion laborers dared defy the pronouncement that "no man, except superintendents and foremen of the mines, will be permitted to go underground unless he can exhibit his card of regular membership of the Union to which he belongs or may wish to belong." To the end of the century, the Comstock mines remained, in the words of their historian, "the bastion of unionism in the western mines."[39]

By the same token, the success of the Comstock unions testified to the dimensions of the transformation of economy and society since the early 1860s. This transformation was a puzzle of many pieces: the constitution writers' resolution of the mining tax issue, the travail of John Wesley North, the arrival of the Bank of California "crowd" and subsequent Jones-Hayward and bonanza king combinations, and the division of society between the corporations and the unions. Although no one at the time put these pieces together, it is apparent in hindsight that their interlocking marked the closing of a brief historical moment in which Washoe spoke to still fresh, and deeply embedded, male dreams of a social order where individuals sought and achieved self-realization through the pursuit of self-interest. By the end of the 1870s this dream had dissolved in the face of a new order divided between men in control of capital and men in control, solely, of their labor power. Workingmen in Nevada enjoyed high wages and (in striking contrast to the implicit proscription and outright violence that marked late-nineteenth-century labor history elsewhere) the acquiescence of mine owners to their fundamental demands.

This new world, however, had little appeal to many of the old Californians who had migrated to Nevada between 1859 and 1863, and their response was exodus. Their departure, as Thomas Fitch observed, began in 1864 and continued until most were gone, whether back to California or off to other (smaller but to individual prospectors more enticing) mining districts in Nevada, Idaho, Montana, Colorado, and Arizona. Not least among the exiles were the founding fathers of the state.

The contours of Nevada politics from the late 1860s to the end of the century reflected the modus vivendi of capital and labor worked out in the decade following statehood. The result was a division of political life into class domains. At the local level in those areas where unions prevailed, officeholding turned to the tune of labor. On the Comstock Lode most markedly, but in other districts as well, sheriffs, justices of the peace, and county commissioners often came directly from the ranks of workingmen; if not, they served insofar as they followed the dictates of labor, particularly on matters related to strikes and the enforcement of union regulations. In contrast, state and national offices became for all intents and purposes the property of corporate interests—the Bank Crowd, the Jones-Hayward combination, the Bonanza firm, and the Central Pacific Railroad.[40] Sometimes in league with one another, sometimes in competition, the major industrial combinations in the state protected their interests through bald purchase of legislators, congressmen, and senators.

The political domains of labor and capital coexisted effectively, if uneasily, throughout the generation following statehood. While workingmen gained control over the affairs of their immediate locale, the men who served in the statehouse and the state's congressional delegation failed to follow the cues of corporate patrons only at their peril. By the early 1870s a system of corporate politics was well developed in Nevada. The pivotal figures in each biennial election became the so-called sack bearers, agents of one ring or another who dispensed large amounts of money to promote—or undermine—candidates for the legislature and other state offices. The labors of the sack bearers were successful as often as not and remarkably open to public view. Witness Henry Yerington, who for more than thirty years doubled as general manager of the Virginia and Truckee Railroad and local political manager for the rail line's owner, the Bank of California. In an 1879 letter to his counterpart at the Central Pacific company, Yerington minced no words in pointing out that

> during every Nevada legislature since 1869 bills have been introduced to regulate freight and fares, and many other matters connected with the working of railroads in this state, most of them have been of a blackmailing character requiring *Coin* to prevent them from being introduced or to get

them out of the road after introduction. This Co. has put up the Coin in large sums every session and the result has been not one bill inimical to railroads has been passed during all these years.[41]

Yerington wrote to chide the Central Pacific for not contributing its proper (in his view) share of the cost of controlling the state legislature. His requests for assistance, however, never brought the response he desired, for the larger company remained content to let the trunk line tend to matters within the state while it focused its attention, and largess, on the men who represented Nevada in Congress. Its success, although far from complete (it had, after all, to compete in this arena with the similarly ambitious mining moguls), was nonetheless impressive. The result was a senatorial delegation that, from 1865 to the end of the century, was intimately tied to (according to many observers, the bribed tool of) the railroad or one of the dominant mining combinations in the state. Over these years only five men represented Nevada in the U.S. Senate; together, they held office for fourteen terms. Only one, former territorial governor James Nye, was neither a principal in nor the hand-picked agent of a California or Nevada corporation.[42] The other four, who represented Nevada in the Senate for all but eight of the years from 1865 to 1900, were in every case identified with the Central Pacific, a mining corporation, or both. These men were William M. Stewart, the "Great Lawyer" of the early Comstock Lode; William Sharon, mastermind of the "fortified monopoly"; James G. Fair of the Bonanza firm; and John P. Jones, whose Pacific Mining and Milling Company had challenged Sharon's combination in the late 1860s. Sharon and Fair held office for only one term each; both, it seems, sought the senatorship out of vanity as much as anything. Stewart, whose service was interrupted by the consecutive terms of Sharon and Fair, served for a total of twenty-eight years (1865–1875 and 1887–1905). And Jones returned to Washington, D.C., for the thirty years between 1873 and 1903.[43]

Stewart, aptly described by his biographer Russell Elliott as a "servant of power," refined the Nevada system of corporate politics with remarkable skill. Elected senator by the first state legislature, his relationship with the Central Pacific Railroad was, as Elliott recounts, "originally cemented when Charles Crocker presented him with two hundred shares of railroad stock in 1866."[44] Three years later Collis Huntington, the principal manager of the rail company, attested to Stewart's loyalty in a letter to Crocker in which he implored the latter to "let him into some good things in and about San Francisco and Oakland. He has always stood by us."[45] Yet despite his good service to the railroad and, after 1870, the Bank of California, Stewart's senatorial career was interrupted abruptly in 1875.[46] William Sharon, whose senatorial ambitions were well known, withdrew from Stewart the funds and sack bearers at his command and pressured the railroad to do so as well. Recognizing the writing on the wall, Stewart took himself out of the race, citing (with more truth than he intended) his need, for financial reasons, to return to private life. In turn, six years later, Sharon's own attempt at reelection was checked by the ambitions of James Fair, his longtime mining adversary from the Bonanza Ring, who expended an estimated $350,000 to take the seat. In 1886, the tables turned once again: to defeat Fair, the Central Pacific leagued with the incumbent's former associate in the Bonanza firm, John Mackay, and, in a battle of the sack bearers, returned Stewart to Washington, D.C. There he remained until 1905.[47]

During his last three terms, Stewart was best known for his work toward the remonetization of silver and, all along, his efforts in behalf of Collis Huntington and the Central Pacific Railroad.[48] Less obviously, but of equal significance, he pioneered a system of political apprenticeship and patronage that endured long after his death. Recruiting young men from various Nevada locales, he arranged for their legal education while employed on his senatorial staff. After they had joined the bar, completed their tutelage in the system of patronage linking officeholder to corporate patron, and made evident their loyalty to the system, he dispatched them back to Nevada with a federal appointment or the promise of "assistance" in a run for state office. The resulting political machine, which created and then tied prominent young men at the grass (or sagebrush) roots to one or another interested corporation, via William Stewart, underlined the Great Lawyer's long career in office. It provided, as well, a model of machine politics that was drawn upon, and after a fashion perfected, by Stewart's successors, above all Pat McCarran, whose long tenure in the Senate and resulting power in the twentieth-century seniority system helped identify Nevada as America's "great rotten borough."[49]

～

William Stewart, master of machine politics in service to the powers that appeared in Nevada after statehood, stood out from his generation by virtue of his success in finding a place in the new regime. The corresponding record of his old adversaries from the territorial period was one of persistent failure, as the experience of the state constitution writers illustrates. Of the thirty-five men who served in the constitutional convention, not one attained the office or public standing they sought and, for that matter, considered their due. Their failure was not for want of trying; indeed, it came in spite of persistent effort. The careers of these men after statehood illuminates the extent of the changes that occurred in Nevada after 1864 and, more generally, the fate of men who still embraced the individualist ethos of antebellum America in the dawning of the modern age.

In one respect, the fate of the Nevada constitution writers after statehood was similar to that of the Californians. Testifying to the physical rigor of life on the mining frontier, a good number, despite the youth that marked them as a group, died shortly after the constitutional convention. James Banks, a former forty-niner from the Humboldt region in eastern Nevada, died suddenly in 1867, as did Cornelius Brosnan of Virginia City, who at the time was serving on the state supreme court. George Hudson, like Banks a delegate from an outlying mining district (in Lyon County), died a year later, followed in 1871 by Nathaniel Ball, a Virginia City banker who had represented Storey County in the convention. The following year, the number of survivors declined by two with the deaths of Francis Kennedy, a Lyon County colleague of Hudson, and the man who had presided over the convention, J. Neely Johnson.

The ranks of the constitution writers were also thinned by the general exodus that began in the very year of statehood. By 1876 only five of the constitution writers remained Nevadans, and notably, four of those lived in "cow counties" outside the mining regions. Two, a lumberman and a farmer, were tied to the land and thus less susceptible to the "jackpot mentality" that governed the early mining population; the others were merchants in Carson City and similarly isolated from the changes occurring on the Comstock Lode. All four had settled in Nevada because of opportunities secondary to mining itself, and they stayed because local markets for their wares flourished. Relative to their mining-region colleagues, they were affected but little by the transformation that overtook Nevada in the late 1860s and 1870s. Politically they displayed only modest ambitions in the years after statehood, content with a place in the public life of their locales, outside both the industrial metropolises in the state and the high-wager political contests between corporate antagonists.[50]

The handful of cow county men who stayed behind makes all the more striking the exodus of the remaining Nevada constitution writers. Few took part in the emigration that Fitch noted approvingly in 1865. Rather, their departures began in the late 1860s and accelerated after 1870—at the very time the power of new corporate combinations became apparent. In the interim, over the first few years after statehood, a sizable number of the constitution writers prospered in the public life of the state. In the first state election, for example, local voters sent nine of them back to Carson City as state legislators. E. F. Dunne was elected to the state district court, George Nourse to the position of lieutenant governor, and Cornelius Brosnan, as noted, to the supreme court. Yet by 1870, with the exception of Thomas Fitch and J. Neely Johnson, none remained in office, and when the latter two left office (in 1871 and 1872, respectively) the political careers of the Nevada founding fathers, for all intents and purposes, came to an end.[51] For some, no doubt, ambition pulled in nonpolitical directions. But more than a few did seek a place in Nevada politics, drawing on old acquaintanceships with the newly powerful men in state affairs—men like the Big Four of the Central Pacific Railroad, mining barons such as Sharon, Jones, Mackay and Fair, and, not least, William Stewart. Their failures, not their attempts, are surprising, for doggedness and more than a modicum of success had marked their careers before statehood. Moreover, with perhaps the exception of Johnson, none displayed any reticence about working with, indeed for, the men who headed the new controlling combinations, whose lives, like their own, had been shaped in gold rush California and the wildcat days of the Comstock Lode. Likely Stewart's success had something to do with their failures, for the Great Lawyer had a long memory, and many of the Nevada constitution writers had won that office on the strength of opposition to him in the first statehood campaign.[52] In addition, their lives suggest another factor, though one that cannot be confirmed: an indomitable sense of self, a headstrong individualism that led those who controlled the political money to suspect their reliability.

Whatever the reason, the disappearance of these founding fathers, from Nevada if not in every case from the historical record, is striking. The lives of those who can be followed beyond 1864 testify to the persistence of their quest for the main chance, a quest that began in the 1850s and in some cases continued to the century's end. For a few, such as Fitch and E. F. Dunne, it took the form of an odyssey from one end of the continent to the other in search of private success and public honor.[53] For others the transformation of Nevada after 1864, foreclosing opportunity as they understood the term, occasioned a move back to California and the more diverse collection of market opportunities it offered. For still others—perhaps the largest number—newer mining regions in Arizona, Colorado, Idaho, and Montana held out one more chance for the self-styled "old Californian."

The later lives of the four men followed to the 1864 constitutional convention in chapter 6 tell no single story but, rather, four variations on a common theme. In contrast to the Oregonians, who remained neighbors, allies, and adversaries through the postbellum decades, the paths of J. Neely Johnson, Charles De Long, Thomas Fitch, and John Collins seldom crossed after statehood. Each, after his own fashion, displayed the persistence of his youthful individualist convictions. Each (with the exception of Johnson, who died in 1872) left in the record of his life testimony as to how, through lenses shaped by antebellum America, he tried to make sense of the modern industrial age.

It is difficult to make much of J. Neely Johnson's short life after statehood. This former Know-Nothing governor of California had regained during Nevada's wildcat era of the early 1860s much of the public standing destroyed in his confrontation with the San Francisco vigilantes. Johnson's election as president of the 1864 convention testified to his rehabilitation, and his high standing continued after statehood despite his

"cow county" residence and his well-known opposition to the constitution's mining-tax provision. For the first two years after statehood
Johnson tended quietly to his Carson City law practice. Upon the death
of Cornelius Brosnan in 1866, he was appointed interim judge of the
state supreme court, and in 1868 he was elected to the court in his own
right. As a judge Johnson once again took up the cause he had lost in the
writing of the state constitution. On the tax cases that came before the
high court he opined—forgetting the majority (if not unanimous) intent
of the constitution writers—that the state constitution required that
taxes on the proceeds of mines be levied at the same rate as the general
property tax.

So holding, as Romanzo Adams has shown, involved no little legal legerdemain, for Johnson knew as well as anyone in Nevada that the winning side in the constitutional convention had sought, and succeeded, in
disconnecting the taxation of the mines from the taxation of property in
general. Moved, as Adams puts it, "not by strict technical considerations,
but by broad considerations of justice," believing that discrimination in
favor of mining property was "atrociously unjust," Johnson held his
ground. At the same time, he further undermined whatever standing he
may have regained by taking on the Bank Crowd's Virginia and Truckee
Railroad. In a dissenting opinion (one consequently without any force),
he declared that Ormsby County had no legal obligation to subsidize
William Sharon's road.[54] Having thus gone out of his way to make his
dislike of the new regime clear, Johnson became persona non grata
among those whose opinion—and money—counted in the state. At the
close of his term in 1871 he did not stand for reelection. Rather, he left
for Salt Lake City in search of surroundings that offered, once again, a
chance to restore his standing. His exact intentions are unclear, although
his move to the Mormon colony coincided with a statehood movement
there—a movement managed by Thomas Fitch, like Johnson a veteran
of the Nevada constitutional convention disappointed by the new political order in Nevada. But whether Johnson went to Utah with Fitch to
remake a political career stalled in Nevada remains unknown. Shortly
after he arrived, he died, suddenly and alone.[55]

Although Johnson's last years remain obscure, he, like so many of his
counterparts, ended his life beyond the borders of the state he helped
make in 1864. In a different way, Charles De Long's later life also testified to the force of ambition rather than the hold of place. De Long lived
four years longer than "the representative man of the cow counties" and
over that time gave voice to larger ambitions and more deeply felt disappointments. Despite the fact that he was ever eager (like Stewart) to serve
the California mining combinations present in Nevada, in contrast to

Stewart he lacked the temperament of a "servant of power" and never gained the support so necessary to winning the senatorial office he coveted. He personally knew the principals in the Bank Crowd, Bonanza firm, and Central Pacific and outwardly embraced their interests as his own, but there was something about him—a headstrong independence and seemingly unrestrained ambition—that made those who controlled the patronage wary of him. Seeing himself as the equal, not subordinate, of gilded-age kingpins, he followed his own instincts—seeking, for example, the political favor of striking workers while in the pay of companies targeted by strikers—and so closed off access to the avenues of power.[56]

Between 1864 and 1876 De Long came close to gaining high elected office, but try as he might he never succeeded. Against former territorial governor James Nye he ran for U.S. senator in 1864 and 1867. Nye won both times in bitter campaigns that turned on an alliance with Stewart and the insinuation, which Nye and friends exploited with great effect, that De Long's Republicanism was late in coming and his loyalty to the union incomplete.[57]

After failing in 1864 and 1867 and finding as well that the best business in Virginia City was going to other lawyers, De Long moved to an outlying mining district (Aurora), where signs of the wildcat days were still in evidence. He found the place more to his liking and did well, professionally and politically. Bolstered by support from districts outside the Comstock Lode, he turned his sights on the Senate once again in 1868. To prepare for the canvass, he affirmed his status as a Republican stalwart through service in the Nevada delegation to the 1868 national party convention. There he attached himself to friends of war hero U. S. Grant, following their cues as a member of the platform committee. From the Chicago convention he returned to Nevada wrapped in the banner of nominee Grant, thereby giving the lie (or so he thought) to the complaints of jealous opponents such as James Nye. Upon his arrival he announced his candidacy for the Senate, this time against William Stewart, like Nye in 1867 an incumbent bent on reelection. To everyone's surprise, however, De Long took himself out of the race before the nominating convention met to name its choice. Orchestrated praise from party men followed his withdrawal, hailing his "patriotic self-denial so noble in its character, and so gratifying to the people of Nevada."[58] But more than a concern for Republican solidarity or respect for Stewart's senatorial qualities had taken De Long out of the race. Stewart had made him an offer (attended, apparently, by threats should he refuse it) he could not turn down: a presidential appointment to high diplomatic office.

In early 1869 President Grant named De Long minister resident to Japan. He accepted the call without hesitation. As he had done when

first elected to the California legislature eleven years before, he took the
time to record his personal progress and rising fame since coming to the
Far West. "This is," he noted with self-conscious attention to posterity,
"the anniversary of my landing in California 19 years ago . . . today [I]
took the oath of office as *Minister Resident to Japan. . . .* Retrospect. 19
years ago today a boy alone and penniless I reached these shores.
Through the vicissitudes of a pioneer's life I have achieved a fair professional standing, am a Foreign Minister and chiefly blest with a loving
wife and two sweet children. Reader," he asked in closing the entry,
"what is your verdict upon the result of my last 19 years?"[59]

Despite the pride that De Long took in the appointment, his ministry
was just short of disastrous. His manner put off not only his hosts, but
the American and English in Japan as well. To the latter he was a crude
frontiersman wholly unsuited to diplomacy by virtue of upbringing,
temperament, and appearance. Remarked the *London Mail* archly:
"Having passed many years in a wild part of America, where men sit
down to table in full suits of bowie knives and revolvers, with bullet but-
tons and gunpowder cuffs and collars, he talks of acts of violence as
lightly as women sip tea."[60] In addition, De Long failed the protocol demands of the Department of State. He habitually (and cavalierly) went
over the head of Secretary of State Fish—a mistake of the first order—to
communicate directly with his sponsor, Senator Stewart, or even the
president himself.[61]

Although his ministry occasioned a milestone in Japanese foreign relations—the Iwakura mission to the United States and Europe in 1872—
De Long's role in the mission, for that matter his entire tenure in Japan,
was overshadowed by a major embarrassment he caused his government
the same year. In keeping with an existing arrangement among the
United States, Japan, and Peru, De Long represented the latter nation's
affairs in Japan as they arose. The arrangement placed him in the
middle of a diplomatic firestorm when, during his absence in the United
States with the Iwakura mission, the Japanese government seized the
human cargo of a Peruvian coolie ship, the *Maria Luz,* whereupon De
Long's replacement refused "protection and assistance" to the captain of
the ship on the grounds that U.S. law prohibited the coolie trade. After
De Long returned, however, he reversed this decision, bringing the
wrath of both the Japanese government and the State Department down
upon him. Notwithstanding his insistence that he abhorred the coolie
trade and acted only because of his responsibility to represent Peru, his
handling of the affair gave credence to the charge of American protection of coolie merchants and confirmed to his detractors that he was unfit for the post of minister.[62] To the chagrin of Secretary Fish, Grant did
not remove De Long as minister immediately (thus displaying the same
loyalty he was simultaneously showing George Williams). However,

there were limits to the president's forbearance, and after his inauguration in 1873 he requested, to De Long's great surprise, that he resign.[63]
Although some observers at home, among them the editors of the *New
York Times,* gave De Long high marks for his diplomatic accomplish-
ments, the prevailing opinion was quite the contrary.[64] Payson Treat,
writing sixty years later, concurred with the general damnation of De
Long in his time, concluding that "no other American Minister to Japan
received censure so frequently and praise so seldom as this shirt-sleeves
diplomat, and it would be surprising if the records showed any comparable record of a Minister who was permitted to serve a full term. . . .
His temperament was lacking in the first requisites of diplomacy, and he
commenced his career by bullying the Japanese and ended it by quarrel-
ing with his countrymen."[65]

Late in 1873, De Long returned to the United States. Leaving his wife
and children in Oakland, California, he went on to Nevada and there set
out, instinctively it seems, to win the political prizes that had eluded him
in the 1860s. He opened a law office in Virginia City and plunged into
Republican politics. Once again he declared his candidacy for the U.S.
Senate, this time against John P. Jones. When his run came to naught he
complained bitterly (and in seeming ignorance of the new political system in the state) that the Central Pacific Railroad had leagued against
him for refusing ten years before to support its interests in the constitutional convention.[66] Undaunted, he remained a regular participant in
party conventions and the Nevada-California political circuit. It became
clear, however, that time and circumstances had passed him by. In 1876
his announced candidacy for district attorney of Storey County was met
with derision, in spite of his offer to give away half his salary. His attempt
for the Republican congressional nomination the same year met a similar response.[67]

That fall, De Long embarked on his last campaign tour, speaking for
the Hayes presidential ticket through California and Nevada. Despite his
recent disappointments, he was greeted with enthusiasm; he could, he
discovered, still move an audience. At town after town he turned the
crowds to his side, no doubt revitalizing his sense of personal destiny.
Waving the bloody shirt, he reminded audiences (and himself) that "the
Democratic party of today [is] no longer the Democratic party of the
past." In addition—giving no recognition of the personal irony—he
ridiculed Democrats who tied the Republican party to Chinese immigration and "coolie labor."[68] Late in the campaign, however, he contracted
typhoid. In October he died. He was forty-four years old.

To the end of his life De Long remained, despite his outward embrace
of the gilded age, much the antebellum youth who had set out in 1850 to
seek his fortune and fame in the California gold rush. This elusive quest
remained his touchstone. In 1870 he testified to his brother on the hold

that gold rush images had on him. "I most entirely approve of your . . . getting up and getting out of that old nook in the world where we all happened to be born," he wrote. "There is no margin in such a Country as that for a man's purse or mind ever to find enlargement. . . . In the great west a man finds a chance to do something on every side of him. Poverty there is neither a sin nor a crime."[69]

Although he had attempted to ingratiate himself among men of the new order, for De Long the West remained to the end "old California." After the Civil War he became—though not for want of trying, and not without small successes—an outsider to the political doings of Nevada and California. His response was consistent and revealing. He never questioned his belief that he was destined for political greatness. Even when he suffered disastrous losses in the stock market—precisely because he was not privy to the financial maneuvering of the new capitalist class—his spirit was untouched. "Business trials and disappointments," he wrote his brother, did not concern him. "Do not infer," he wrote in the midst of political and financial defeat,

> that I am crushed or that I have lost my spirit and hope. I have fought gallantly in the battle of life and I mean when I fall to die with my harness on. —I am working like a trojan; trying to gather up the wreck of my shattered fortunes and build up a practice and a business in my profession. . . . When fortune again smiles upon me *as I will make her smile* (for she is the bond slave of effort) I will again assist you.[70]

Only once did De Long drop the veil of his individualist self-confidence in these last years. In a letter to his wife discussing their losses in the stock market, his characterization of the new order of things in the Far West was simple. "Damn these monied aristocrats," he wrote, "they have no hearts[,] no gallantry."[71]

De Long died in Nevada, but it is apparent that his life was tied less to this particular place than to the "great [far] west" generally, where, as he put it to his brother, "a man finds a chance to do something on every side of him." Although a minor figure in the larger scheme of things, in thought and deed he exemplified the predominant place of self and the subdued sense of community that was so prevalent among the charter settlers of Nevada. Indeed, his life displayed the paradox of the state's first settlers: their defining mark was that they were *not* Nevadans. This feature was even more true in the case of De Long's convention colleague Thomas Fitch. Over a long life (Fitch died in 1923 at the age of eighty-five), he lived in virtually every state and territory west of the Rockies, as well as Washington, D.C., Chicago, New York City, and Hawaii. Although, like De Long, he never gained the public renown and high office he thought his due, Fitch, as a celebrity and entertainer (if not a statesman) enjoyed a local following in each place he resided.[72] He was well known through regular appearances on the campaign stump— sometimes for, sometimes against the Republican party—where he showed a talent for bending to the winds of gilded-age opinion. He was a master of the bloody-shirt declamation, alternately defender and denouncer of corporate combinations, and outspoken proponent of Chinese exclusion and repression of Indians resisting removal.[73] At the same time, audiences throughout the West knew him as an actor, playwright, and lecturer. In the 1890s he (with his wife) flirted with fame through their literary construction of a fictional utopia.[74]

Even more so than Charles De Long, Fitch tried to ingratiate himself with the new industrialists of the Far West. His sole reward was a single term in Congress from 1869 to 1871. While there, he became known as the hired hand of the Bank Crowd and Central Pacific Railroad. Not above threatening other members of Congress when they failed to follow his advice on railroad matters, he proved an embarrassment to his patrons. Among those who felt his ill-timed and indiscreet wrath was Oregon senator George Williams: for blocking Fitch's effort to have Congress affirm an extension of the Central Pacific line from Nevada to Oregon, he received a political death sentence from the younger congressman. In Oregon, although Williams's opponents made much of his labors against the railroad, Fitch's attacks pleased no one. Remarked the *Oregonian:*

> So much for the excellent Mr. Fitch of Nevada, the tool of the Central Pacific railroad company. In 1868 it elected [him] . . . to Congress to do its work. It bought votes for him with its coin, and he, in turn, does the bidding of the corporation whose instrument he is. We speak of Fitch in this way because we noticed that a letter of his has gotten into print, in which he says he is going to "punish" an Oregon Senator for having done a thing that the Central Pacific company don't like.

Fitch, advised the Oregon paper, "as the paid agent of the great company which controls [his] state, may as well confine himself to affairs at home."[75]

Fitch's sponsors apparently agreed, and when he returned in 1870 to run for reelection he found he had been abandoned. Repudiated by men whose support he had curried since the early 1860s, he looked elsewhere. From Nevada he moved to Salt Lake City, where he practiced law and promoted mines and, most importantly, won the favor of a new political sponsor, Brigham Young. With Young's blessing he became the official (albeit gentile) lobbyist for Utah statehood, receiving in return a guarantee that he would be chosen the first senator of the state. In behalf of the Mormon colony, Fitch lectured throughout the nation, praising the mainstream character of Mormon theology and counseling patience with what he described as the dying institution of polygamy.[76] In

1872, he ushered a version of the Nevada constitution through the constitutional convention of the state of Deseret, and after its ratification the legislature of the prospective state chose him as its first senator.[77] Fitch carried the charter to Washington, D.C., where he urged its acceptance by the Congress he hoped to rejoin. He was unable, however, to convince the House and Senate that the Mormons had embraced American habits and customs, and the application for statehood failed.[78] Embittered (in his reminiscences written a quarter-century later he made no mention of his time in Utah), he briefly turned his back on the Republican party, taking to the stump for Horace Greeley and the short-lived Liberal Republican insurgence of 1872.[79]

Fitch then embarked on an odyssey that continued for more than thirty years, moving first to San Francisco and, from there, to Arizona, Oregon and Washington, San Diego, Reno, New York, Salt Lake, and Hawaii; finally, by now in his seventies, he settled to stay in Southern California.[80] Although the Republican party he had joined in the 1850s remained his touchstone, Fitch's politics turned more to the tune of immediate personal advantage than partisan loyalty. A few short years after the defeat of Utah statehood and his dalliance with the Greeley campaign, for example, he reappeared briefly in Nevada as a hired speaker for the Bank of California, defending the Bank Crowd combination as the salvation of "hardy prospectors and miners."[81] Nothing came of this service to power, and in 1876 (like De Long) he was back in California, where he reaffirmed his Republican regularity in the Hayes campaign.[82] Shortly thereafter, when Californians divided over the revised constitution, he moved beyond his party, campaigning against the railroads and warning Republicans to disentangle themselves from the "Triumvirate of Tyrants."[83] In the 1890s Fitch briefly became a silverite and Populist, but after Bryan's 1896 defeat he returned, again, to the Republican party.

Throughout his meandering across the political landscape, high office was never far from his mind. He considered running for Congress at almost every election and tested the political waters (after Utah always tepid) whenever an opening—in California, Nevada, Arizona, and elsewhere—appeared.[84] Beginning in the late 1880s, he opened a correspondence with the graying eminence of Nevada, Senator William Stewart. Time and again over a span of fifteen years Fitch tried, without success, to put aside old quarrels, beseeching his fellow pioneer to arrange a federal appointment for him. In 1906, after Stewart had left the Senate and shortly before he departed Washington, D.C., Fitch made a final, desperate plea "for the sake of auld lang syne." Stewart put him off.[85]

Along with this restless man's movement from place to place, cause to cause, and patron to patron was a more cerebral and, in the final analy-

sis, representative enterprise. As an essayist, lecturer on science, philosophy, and religion, and, lastly, novelist, he tried to make sense of the
changing world around him. His efforts in this vein were well displayed
in a popular lecture he gave before various audiences in the 1870s and
1880s. In it he paid homage to what he called the "moral police," by
which he meant the inner principle of evolution. Interpreting Darwin
and Spencer to his audiences, he "reasserted the doctrine of evolution as
a truth." Evolution, in his metaphysical rendering, was a law of continuous progress—social, economic, political, moral—governed by what he
defined as the principle of "compensation, or retribution, for the good
or evil which men do in this life." Through its continuous operation, he
held, the world cumulatively and continuously moved toward an ever
finer state of perfection. "The perfection of the precedent," Fitch
offered, was "the groundwork and plane for evolution to start anew
from—for the subsequent form to build on and aggregate around. . . .
Science," he boldly summarized, "proves evolution, nature demonstrates
it, the Bible affirms it."[86]

In 1891 Fitch and his wife sought to give substance to this obtuse dialectic in a novel addressed to popular audiences but designed, consciously, to educate as well as entertain. Their express goal was to explain how evolution, and the "principle of compensation" within it,
might unfold in the contemporary world. The book (one of the scores of
utopian novels that appeared in the 1880s and 1890s) presents industrializing America as a stage in historical evolution, a stage that heralded
a genuine transformation in social relations and political economy.
Against current fears of the command of mechanization over people's
lives, the Fitches attempted, as Alan Trachtenberg has more generally
observed, to cover "all signs of trauma with expressions of confidence."
This they did by fusing, in the figure of a Christ-like frontier millionaire,
evolutionary notions to a belief in progress, and the industrial regime to
hopes for individual independence.[87] During the nineteenth century,
the Fitches held, society had evolved from an order of individual proprietors to one of industrial entrepreneurs; now it was poised before a
new age of domestic cooperation, international comity, and material
abundance. Common to the first two stages—and ultimately, the means
of their transcendence—was the same figure: the free, self-determined
individual. In *Better Days, or a Millionaire of Tomorrow*, Fitch and his wife
projected a revolutionary role for this figure.

At the time of its publication some reviewers compared *Better Days*
with Bellamy's *Looking Backward*, although the Fitches' utopian sketch
differed on fundamental points from its famous contemporary.[88] *Better
Days* was dedicated to "the eight thousand millionaires of America," its
objective being to "point out to [the nabobs of the gilded age] some way
to use their millions for the benefit of the world outside of the beaten

track of endowing educational institutions."[89] As one reviewer put it, the book offered an antidote to "the socialistic ideas" of Bellamy, although "its general purpose is the same."

> [*Better Days*] advocates the amelioration of the condition of the human family—but it teaches the lesson that great wealth may be a blessing instead of a curse; that all things may be accomplished by individual effort properly directed; that the possession of a large fortune connotes the possession of superior ability which should be employed for the benefit of humanity, and that the power of money, usually deemed so base and acrid, has been misunderstood, because it has been so generally abused.

Drawing upon—indeed, projecting outward from—personal experience, the Fitches' story tells the life of the aptly named "David Morning," a young speculator who discovered in Arizona a gold and copper mine inexhaustible in its treasure.[90] Instead of using the treasure to sate his personal greed, the hero determines to resolve the issues of his age: the "conflict of labor and capital, railroad transportation, homes for the people, reforms in the system of jurisprudence, the currency question and the cessation of war, through a congress of nations." To these ends Morning uses his wealth to save the U.S. Treasury from the nefarious designs of Wall Street bankers, build cooperative and profit-sharing enterprises, and endow a national loan program for small farmers. On Manhattan Island, he constructs a new community consisting of "model dwelling houses for men of moderate means and another series of dwellings for poorer people." Furthermore (here evincing Fitch's desire to get back at the railroad barons who had abandoned him in the 1870s), he uses his wealth to frustrate railroad plutocrats, sending them to prison where they belong and in the process creating an efficient and fairly operated transcontinental system that releases, not oppresses, the private energies of individual proprietors. Finally, aided by his invention of a new explosive—"potentite," which has the capacity to destroy cities "in the twinkling of an eye"—and his ownership of a fleet of airships and submarine torpedo boats, Morning induces world leaders to establish an international court of arbitration. The court, possessing the secret of potentite, ushers in an age of global peace which nicely complements the domestic tranquility that Morning's philanthropy—quickly emulated by other advanced millionaires—produces in the United States.

The Fitches' novel was neither insightful nor prescient, expressing as it does (crudely) a type of reform evolutionism not uncommon in the last decades of the century.[91] To Fitch and his wife, as to others, the era's great private accumulations of wealth did not contradict the antebellum vision of a society of independent proprietors and free laborers; rather, they represented the next, but not final, stage in that society's evolution.

Gilded-age capitalism, the consequence of the survival of the fittest, confirmed "the doctrine of evolution as a truth": it was "the groundwork and plane for evolution to start from anew." Through the exploits of David Morning, then, the Fitches speculated as to the course of evolution and testified to their hope that individuals of destiny like Morning would bring the amelioration, not aggravation, of the hard edges of industrial civilization. Heroic "millionaires of tomorrow," accordingly, were the fulfillment of God's evolutionary design by serving as altruistic guides to a higher, humane form of industrial society. As Fitch had earlier declared, "Evolution has always been in motion, is now in motion, and always will be in motion [toward] . . . higher forms of existence." [92]

Better Days never caught the fancy of a reading public hungry for imaginative, hopeful explanations of the modern age. Tinged with gratuitous anti-Semitism and vicious depictions of Indians rightly put down for their savagery, unconvincing in its portrayal of a hero who (as any reader could see) possessed the power to oppress and destroy as well as liberate and reform, the novel was, in the end, largely the product of a man disappointed by life's treatment yet still full of a belief in his destiny. On the surface, *Better Days* attempted to counter contemporary critics— labor, socialist, and agrarian—who charged that concentrated private wealth bespoke the need for a redistribution of property and power. But it also reflected the persistence (revised to fit the age) of convictions Fitch had expressed thirty years before. In 1862, Fitch had begun his eulogy of E. D. Baker by reflecting on "the character of the Infinite," giving it much the same qualities he ascribed in the 1880s and 1890s to the "moral police" of evolution. Similarly, the fictional script for David Morning depended, like the apotheosis of Baker, on divine appointment. "Circumstances, accident, or industry," Fitch said in the 1860s and still believed in the 1890s, "never made a great man. They often develop latent genius, but God Almighty enjoys a monopoly of the creation." [93]

Neither circumstance, accident, nor industry (nor God) made Thomas Fitch a great man. He died in relative obscurity, remembered, if at all, as a frontier character who displayed, if never mastered, the openness of the "great west." In a different key, the much more obscure life of John Collins attested to the same. Like Fitch, after statehood Collins searched for a role in, and an intellectual understanding of, the postbellum world of industry, mechanization, and combination in the Far West. Like Fitch as well, he was drawn to utopian speculation. The utopian destination that Collins reached, however, was different indeed.

After 1864 Collins's life witnessed a return of the repressed in ideological terms. Gone by 1870 was the "brazen-faced businessman" who, to the dismay of abolitionists and socialists, had parted from friends and truth in moving to California in 1849. To the contrary, the focus of his life from 1870 to his death in 1890 was once again on reform, from a stance that combined earlier enthusiasms with lessons learned from the Civil War and industrial revolution. In contrast to the modicum of prominence he enjoyed in the 1840s, however, his postbellum career was spent at the margins of far western reform movements. To no small degree this was because of the same headstrong and patronizing tendencies that had served him so poorly as an abolitionist and socialist, and the fact that these traits could no longer be explained away as youthful impatience. Rather, they made Collins at best a comical, but more commonly an unlikable, even pathetic, figure within reform circles. As one old acquaintance reported in the early 1870s, "He settled in San Francisco for the purpose of taking a prominent part in all matters of reform. He has been at all times prepared to accept the chairmanship of almost any association, but modest enough to assume the humbler function of treasurer. But we regret to say that his services seem to have been but rarely required in either capacity. . . . He has been defeated for office; when nominated for chairman of political meetings he has almost invariably been voted down." [94] Although these remarks referred to Collins's disappointments in the early 1870s, as time proved, they described his later life as a whole.

Like his fellow constitution writers and, more generally, the old Californians who first settled Washoe, Collins remained a Nevadan for only a few years after statehood. He stayed in Virginia City until 1868, running his hotel and saloon, practicing law, and—under a growing cloud of suspicion—superintending the county school system. Charged with financial "irregularities" in the school fund he controlled, Collins resigned his post and took his leave from the state, returning to San Francisco, his home until his death. [95] There, living off the income of a small law practice, he gave his attention to various reform and radical movements that flourished in the 1870s and 1880s. Collins first appeared in his new radical-reformist guise in 1869–1870, as a participant in meetings to found a women's suffrage society for the Far West. A vice-president of the society's first convention, he was there elected a member of its Board of Control. In the early years he was a featured speaker for the cause and helped carry the suffrage message to the state legislature. In 1871, he served as president of the Pacific Slope Female Suffrage Convention. From time to time, too, Collins and his wife hosted visits by the Oregon suffragist Abigail Scott Duniway. [96]

The effects of these activities, however, did not redound to Collins's credit. In the end he made a mockery of himself and—to those opposed to the movement—suffragism as well. With each appearance resentment toward his imperious ways grew. The antisuffrage San Francisco *Call* reported (gleefully) in 1871 that his presiding over the suffrage convention of that year had almost certainly ruined the movement. Two years later the *Territorial Enterprise* confirmed through intelligence from San Francisco that most attributed the (then) moribund state of the suffrage movement in California to his presence.[97] The reason was simple: Collins's patronizing attitude toward women and his heavy-handed plotting for power drove people away. He was, according to reports, unwilling to take a backseat in the movement "to which he has been clinging for the past three or four years with a last desperate possibility of political advancement." In a battle for control with Emily Pitt-Stevens (a friend of Elizabeth Cady Stanton), "the dignity of the Colonel," explained the *Territorial Enterprise,* "would not allow him to yield." Although he

> was not a member of the convention, and had no right, of course, to participate in the deliberations of that body . . . step by step, speaking and seconding motions . . . he crowded his way through the body of the convention, and the third day we found him contesting the presidency of the body with Mrs. Emily Pitt-Stevens. So much for a little perseverance. He was beaten by Mrs. Stevens, but he became a power in the organization at once. The members of the present convention attribute the decline of interest in the movement to the mismanagement of the Colonel. They declare that his course has disgusted the members as well as the public.[98]

Pitt-Stevens ultimately forced Collins out of the suffrage movement. According to old friends in Nevada (who commiserated with a cocked eye), his defeat came at the hands of those who wanted the movement "run by women exclusively" and, thus, unfairly denounced "Collins as an old rooster scratching after worms for the hens and looking for one for himself now and then." With obvious pleasure, the *Territorial Enterprise* advised: "Let them attempt to 'run the convention by women exclusively,' . . . and we will next hear of him taking a seat in the convention with a close shave and in petticoats, and with credentials from Mud Springs."[99]

After a few years of relative inactivity Collins resurfaced in the late 1870s, as a participant in various causes associated with Henry George. Echoing his earlier abolitionism, he joined George on the rostrum of public meetings to denounce the anti-Chinese demagoguery of Kearneyites in San Francisco. Because of these activities—and after a silence of thirty years—he reconciled with William Lloyd Garrison when the latter lent his name and prestige to opponents of anti-Chinese violence in California.[100] Collins also participated in the movement against the second California constitution, for reasons (like George) that had nothing to do with the hue and cry raised by conservative opponents (the likes of Charles Botts). To Collins, the new constitution offered only a patchwork of reforms, not the wholesale—and to his mind necessary—restructuring of society that the times required.

Three years after the new constitution was ratified, when its reformist promise had been proved false, Collins drew out the implications of his critique in a plan for social reformation, which he presented to San Francisco audiences. In it he combined lessons learned from the Civil War, the administrative example of the postbellum corporation (perceived from experience in Nevada and California), and the (Henry) George-ian critique of monopoly property. Collins's utopian sketch reflected both his understanding of the changes the years since 1860 had brought to the Far West—his perception of the passing of this frontier—and the persistence of his youthful perfectionism. Most striking is how the thirty years that followed his immigration to California, while ultimately revitalizing his radical spirit, had altered his conception of what a perfected America would be like. No longer did he call for the creation of small, autonomous communities to serve as examples to the larger society. Rather, for the later Collins the lessons of nineteenth-century history and the corporate example of the industrial age pointed toward a socialist order organized and perfected through the bureaucracies of a vastly expanded federal government.

Collins presented his program for social revitalization at San Francisco's Dashaway Hall in the winter of 1882. Drawing on George-ian phrases, he entitled the lectures "Plenty, Poverty, and Public Danger" and "Unification of Conflicting Interests."[101] In the first, displaying his persistent lack of faith in religious solutions to social problems, he diagnosed the ills of contemporary society. "Notwithstanding the benign influences of religion," he declared, "all species of pauperism and crime are increasing in our midst," their source being

> combinations of men and consolidations of wealth. Money is power and money dominates the mechanical giants that today are the controlling factors of production which must always be beyond the reach of the masses. Under the present system the masses are the slaves and appendages of machines, and machines are controlled by associated capital. We have outgrown the physical force system and punish the man who robs on the highway; but today a more terrible force is working in our midst—the force of concentrated intelligence, energy, and wealth over the weak and ignorant.

"We are living in peace," he granted, but it "is [only] an armed peace, preserved by soldiers and police," masking signs of an impending cataclysm.

Collins insisted that his views were neither "communistic or agrarian" but, rather, intended to "create reform by morality and the power of love." Yet when he turned from diagnosis to treatment in his second lec-

ture, it was clear that he had more in mind than an appeal to good instincts. He began from the premise that a "desirable condition of things"
required a bold extension of the principle of centralized public action
legitimated by the Civil War. "Reform," he argued, "ought to emanate
from, and be under the patronage of, the Federal Government. . . .
Government," he continued, "has subsidized commerce, manufactures,
etc.; let it now subsidize a plan that will better the condition of its
people."

The objective of his plan was the transformation of the existing capitalist system of private property and corporate combination into a single,
national cooperative that, as he portrayed it, mixed memories of an
older, intimate, world of individual producers with elements of the
postbellum industrial order. Evincing (if crudely) George's critique of
private property in land, he advocated the outright abolition of all real
property ownership. At the same time, he called for discouraging
(though *not* outlawing) "the invention of mechanical substitutes for hand
labor . . . as having a tendency to degrade and cheapen labor." To put
his plan into effect Collins proposed a constitutional amendment that
would allow the Department of the Interior to purchase, and thereafter
hold as trustee, the nation's productive capital. Out of this property Collins foresaw the creation of a grand national cooperative, industrial and
agricultural, organized by family and household, each possessing an
equal share. In place of the "armed peace" of a private economy dominated by and redounding to the benefit of a few private parties, his system would have Interior officials in Washington, D.C., running an integrated, humane, and wasteless system of production and distribution. In
place of competition for wages and the private banking system, he suggested an elaborate system of productivity accounting, based, it seems,
on the labor theory of value. Accordingly, experts in the government
were to tally up the output of each household and, after an accounting
of each year's aggregate production, distribute back to them cooperative
dividends to meet their needs for the coming year.

This sketch of a new "system . . . [to] bring about a desirable condition
of things" was Collins's last testament to a life that encompassed a remarkable collection of nineteenth-century American enthusiasms. Before coming to Nevada he had moved from Calvinism to the perfectionism of New England and the "burned over district" of New York,
and from there to the individualist order of gold rush California. After
his interlude as an entrepreneur on the Comstock Lode he retraced his
steps—literally back to California, figuratively back to concerns that revealed the young man persisting within the old. The socialism that Collins espoused in the 1880s both recalled and differed from his utopian

vision for Community Place in the 1840s. The program for social reconstruction he proposed as an old man testified to his memory of earlier times and lessons learned as a witness to the transformation of California and Nevada during the Gilded Age. Although the notices of Collins's death in 1890 made little of the time he had spent in Washoe, his persistent restlessness, ambition, and dissatisfaction with things as they are made him—like Johnson, De Long, and Fitch—the quintessential Nevadan.

EPILOGUE

When, in the 1880s, John Collins presented his bureaucratic program for the socialist "Unification of Conflicting Interests," he was not talking about the Far West, much less Nevada. He spoke, rather, about the incorporated nation, and he offered, however crudely, a vision of how a central institution of the Gilded Age, the industrial combination, provided a model for the revitalization of America. When Thomas Fitch and his wife constructed their fictional program for renewal through the genius of enlightened industrial entrepreneurs like David Morning, they, too, took as their framework a national society in crisis. By the same token, when Matthew Deady mused on the pertinence of Montesquieu, and when he directed the attention of Oregon youth to republican precepts, his concern was with the "gilded juggernaut" that to his mind was overtaking the nation, "muddying the waters of the Potomac" as in ancient Rome the Orontes had muddied the Tiber. George Williams's intonation of classical republicanism at the 1889 centennial celebration, similarly, targeted "the associated wealth and corporate power [that] have enthroned themselves in the vital energies of our country." It was thus, finally, for Charles Botts as well, when in Darwinian terms he described the inevitable failure of attempts to repair "a country . . . full of stock gamblers," a body politic "festering with corruption," a nation in which "wealth aggregated in the hands of individuals and powerful corporations controlled the halls of legislation."

Each of these men—Nevadans, Oregonians, and Californians, respectively—affirmed their common awareness of the Gilded Age, and in doing so attested to the broader incorporation of the Far West into the "changed, more tightly structured [national] society" that was apparent by the century's close. As such they gave ample evidence of the influence that succeeding waves of immigrants, the spread of national markets, institutions, and standards, and the shrinking effect of new communication and transportation technologies had had on the idiosyncracies of the early years of American settlement in the Far West. Although one finds among the constitution writers no thinker of Emersonian proportions, and although the efforts of Collins, Fitch, Deady, Williams, and Botts went unnoticed in the metropolitan corridors of gilded-age culture, their testimony was of a piece with the intellectual life of a nation struggling to come to terms with modern corporate capitalism.

And yet, the sense these men made of the new incorporated order was clearly refracted through their experience of it in California, Oregon, and Nevada. In Botts, the natural-law individualism of the gold rush persisted in a new key that captured, through its implicit contrast of Darwinian despair with Lockean exuberance, the "progress and poverty" of California during the 1860s and 1870s. The classical republican vocabulary of Deady and Williams similarly bore the imprint of the early Oregon Country and the persistence of the world of its charter settlers across a generation of crisis and renewal. Finally, in the warmed-over utopianism of Collins and Fitch lingered traces of the hopes and expectations that carried old Californians across the Sierra Nevada to Washoe in 1859 and 1860, in forms altered by these mens' and their fellow charter settlers' confrontation with the industrial transformation of the Comstock Lode and exodus to other, often chimerical, places of opportunity.

While each of these men took as his subject the United States, neither their understanding of the incorporated nation nor their prescriptions for its reform were simply derivative of the greater thoughts of thinkers in greater places. In the final musings of these old far westerners—and, more generally, in their lives and the lives of their fellow constitution writers—local and national history coalesced. Their peculiar responses to the Gilded Age testified in equal measures to the revolutionary pressures of modernity and the persistence of habits, customs, and understandings that had marked the charter societies of the Far West. The ideas they drew upon and the courses of action—or inaction—they followed in meeting the new age were embedded in the politics and society of charter settlers who, a generation before, had carried out the conquest and American founding of California, Oregon, and Nevada.

The lives of the charter settlers we have followed attest to both the continuity and the changes that marked California, Oregon, and Nevada from midcentury to the 1880s. In addition, they testify to the complex relationship between local history and the making of the modern United States. In the founding of charter societies in the Far West and in the incorporation of the resulting states into the modern nation, we discover the paradoxical origins of modernity in the narrow particularities of individual lives. In the final analysis the founding of the Far West offers proof of the maxim that people make their own history—although not exactly as they might have liked—and that in the process they leave a mark on history that is both persistent and difficult to discern. The traces of the Far West's founders are with us yet.

Appendixes

APPENDIX 1A.　California Constitutional Convention Delegates, 1849

Name	Birthdate (Age in 1849)	Birthplace	Interim Residence
Joseph Aram	1811 (39)	New York	Illinois
Charles Tyler Botts	1809 (40)	Virginia	Virginia
Elam Brown	1793 (56)	New York	Missouri
José Antonio Carrillo	1796 (53)	California	California
José M. Covarrubias	1809 (40)	France	France
Elisha Oscar Crosby	1815 (34)	New York	New York
Lewis Dent	1823 (26)	Missouri	Missouri
Kimball Dimmick	1815 (34)	New York	New York
Manuel Domínguez	1800 (49)	California	California
Alfred J. Ellis	1816 (33)	New York	New York
Stephen D. Foster	1821 (28)	Maine	Missouri
Edward Gilbert	1822 (27)	New York	New York
Pablo de la Guerra	1813 (36)	California	California
William M. Gwin	1805 (44)	Tennessee	Louisiana
Henry Wager Halleck	1817 (32)	New York	New York
Julian Hanks	1810 (39)	Connecticut	Connecticut
Lansford Hastings	1819 (30)	Ohio	Ohio
Henry Hill	1816 (33)	Virginia	Virginia
Joseph Hobson	1810 (39)	Maryland	Maryland
John Hollingsworth	1824 (25)	Maryland	New York
Jacob Hoppe	1814 (35)	Maryland	Missouri
James McHall Jones	1824 (25)	Kentucky	Louisiana
Thomas Larkin	1802 (47)	Massachusetts	Massachusetts
Benjamin Lippincott	1815 (34)	New York	New Jersey
Francis Lippitt	1812 (37)	Rhode Island	New York
Morton M. McCarver	1807 (42)	Kentucky	Iowa-Oregon
John McDougal	1817 (32)	Ohio	Indiana
Benjamin F. Moore	1820 (29)	Florida	Texas
Myron Norton	1822 (27)	Vermont	New York
Pacificus Ord	1815 (34)	Maryland	Louisiana
Miguel de Pedrorena	1808 (41)	Spain	Spain
Antonio Pico	1809 (40)	California	California
Rodman Price	1819 (30)	New Jersey	New York
Hugo Reid	1811 (38)	Scotland	Mexico
Jacinto Rodríguez	1813 (36)	California	California
Pedro Sansevaine	1818 (31)	France	France
Robert Semple	1807 (42)	Kentucky	Missouri
William Shannon	1822 (27)	England	New York
Winfield Sherwood	1817 (32)	New York	New York
Jacob Snyder	1815 (34)	Pennsylvania	Missouri
Abel Stearns	1798 (51)	Massachusetts	Mexico
William M. Steuart	1800 (49)	Maryland	Maryland

District (Years in California)	Occupation	Political Party	Death (Departure)
San Jose (3)	Agriculture	Unknown	1898
Monterey (1)	Lawyer	Democrat	1884
San Jose (2)	Agriculture	Whig	1889
Los Angeles (53)	Rancher	Democrat	1862
San Luis Obispo (15)	Rancher	Democrat	1870
Sacramento (1)	Lawyer	Whig	1895 (1860)
Monterey (3)	Lawyer	Democrat	1874 (1855)
San Francisco (3)	Lawyer	Unknown	1861 (1850)
Los Angeles (49)	Banker	Unknown	1882
San Francisco (3)	Merchant	Whig	1883
Los Angeles (3)	Agriculture	Democrat	1898
San Francisco (3)	Printer	Democrat	1852
Santa Barbara (36)	Unknown	Whig (after 1850)	1874
San Francisco (1)	Agriculture	Democrat	1885
Monterey (3)	Military	Democrat	1872 (1861)
San Jose (10)	Agriculture	Unknown	1867
Sacramento (6)	Lawyer	Democrat	1867 (1857)
Monterey (1)	Military	Democrat	1866 (1850)
San Francisco (1)	Merchant	Unknown	1897
San Joaquin (3)	Military	Unknown	1889 (1849)
San Jose (3)	Merchant	Whig	1853
San Joaquin (1)	Lawyer	Whig	1851
Monterey (16)	Merchant	Whig	1858 (1850)
San Joaquin (4)	Merchant	Democrat	1870
San Francisco (3)	Lawyer	Whig	1902 (1861)
Sacramento (1)	Agriculture	Democrat	1875 (1850)
Sacramento (1)	Merchant	Democrat	1866
San Joaquin (1)	Elegant Leisure	Whig	1866
San Francisco (1)	Lawyer	Democrat	1886
Monterey (1)	Lawyer	Democrat	1900 (1865)
San Diego (12)	Merchant	Unknown	1850
San Jose (40)	Agriculture	Unknown	1869
San Francisco (4)	Military	Democrat	1894 (1850)
Los Angeles (16)	Lawyer	Unknown	1852
Monterey (11)	Agriculture	Unknown	1878
San Jose (11)	Lawyer	Whig (after 1850)	1904 (1876)
Sonoma (5)	Printer	Democrat	1854
Sacramento (3)	Lawyer	Whig	1850
Sacramento (1)	Lawyer	Democrat	1870
Sacramento (4)	Surveyor	Democrat	1878
Los Angeles (20)	Lawyer	Whig (after 1850)	1871
San Francisco (1)	Lawyer	Whig	Unknown (1850)

APPENDIX 1A.   *(continued)*

Name	Birthdate (Age in 1849)	Birthplace	Interim Residence
John B. Sutter	1802 (47)	Switzerland	Missouri
Henry A. Tefft	1823 (26)	New York	Wisconsin
Mariano Vallejo	1807 (42)	California	California
Thomas L. Vermuele	1814 (35)	New Jersey	New York
Joel P. Walker	1797 (52)	Virginia	Missouri-Oregon
Oliver M. Wozencraft	1815 (34)	Ohio	Texas

SOURCE: "Members of the Convention of California," in J. Ross Browne, *Report of the Debates in the Convention of California on the Formation of the State Constitution in September and October, 1849* (Washington, D.C.: John T. Towers, 1850), 478–479; with additions and corrections.

District (Years in California)	Occupation	Political Party	Death (Departure)
Sacramento (10)	Agriculture	Democrat	1880 (1865)
San Luis Obispo (1)	Lawyer	Unknown	1852
Sonoma (42)	Military	Whig (after 1850)	1890
San Joaquin (3)	Lawyer	Democrat	1856
Sonoma (1)	Agriculture	Democrat	1879
San Joaquin (1)	Physician	Whig	1887

APPENDIX 1B.　Oregon Constitutional Convention Delegates, 1857

Name	Birthdate (Age)	Birthplace	Previous Residence
Levi Anderson	1818 (39)	Kentucky	Iowa
Jesse Applegate	1810 (47)	Kentucky	Missouri
A. D. Babcock	1818 (39)	New York	Indiana
Reuben P. Boise	1819 (38)	Massachusetts	Massachusetts
J. H. Brattrain	1813 (44)	Ohio	Iowa
Paul Brattrain	1801 (56)	North Carolina	Iowa
W. W. Bristow	1826 (31)	Kentucky	Illinois
B. F. Burch	1825 (32)	Missouri	Missouri
A. J. Campbell	1828 (29)	Indiana	Iowa
Hector Campbell	1794 (63)	Massachusetts	Massachusetts
Stephen Chadwick	1825 (32)	Connecticut	New York
Jesse Cox	1821 (36)	Missouri	Missouri
Joseph Cox	1811 (46)	Ohio	Missouri
Reuben Coyle	1821 (36)	Kentucky	Illinois
John T. Crooks	1807 (50)	Virginia	Illinois
Matthew Deady	1824 (33)	Maryland	Ohio
Thomas Dryer	1810 (47)	New York	California
L.J.C. Duncan	1818 (39)	Tennessee	California
Luther Elkins	1809 (48)	Maine	Ohio
William H. Farrar	1826 (31)	New Hampshire	Massachusetts
Solomon Fitzhugh	1804 (53)	Kentucky	Missouri
La Fayette Grover	1826 (31)	Maine	Pennsylvania
S. B. Hendershott	1832 (25)	Illinois	Iowa
Enoch Hoult	1820 (37)	Virginia	Illinois
James Kelly	1819 (38)	Pennsylvania	California
John Kelsay	1819 (38)	Kentucky	Missouri
Robert Kinney	1813 (44)	Illinois	Iowa
Haman Lewis	1803 (54)	New York	Missouri
David Logan	1826 (31)	North Carolina	Illinois
Asa Lovejoy	1811 (46)	Massachusetts	Missouri
John McBride	1832 (25)	Missouri	Missouri
Stephen McCormick	1828 (29)	Ireland	New York
Perry Marple	1819 (38)	Virginia	Missouri
William Matzger	1819 (38)	Germany	Illinois
Charles Meigs	1830 (27)	Connecticut	Ohio
Richard Miller	1802 (55)	Pennsylvania	Missouri
Isaac Moores	1796 (61)	Illinois	California
Daniel Newcomb	1800 (57)	Virginia	Illinois
H. B. Nichols	1821 (36)	Connecticut	Iowa

County (Years in Oregon)	Occupation	Farm Acreage	Political Party	Death (Place)
Washington (5)	Farmer	160	Anti-Democrat	1889 (Oregon)
Umpqua (14)	Farmer	642	Anti-Democrat	1888 (Oregon)
Polk and Tillamook (5)	Lawyer	159	Democrat	1879 (Oregon)
Polk (7)	Lawyer	640	Democrat	1907 (Oregon)
Linn (11)	Farmer	640	Democrat	1859 (Oregon)
Lane (5)	Farmer	160	Democrat	1883 (Oregon)
Lane (11)	Farmer	640	Democrat	1874 (Oregon)
Polk (12)	Farmer	640	Democrat	1893 (Oregon)
Lane (4)	Mechanic	309	Democrat	1870 (Oregon)
Clackamas (8)	Farmer	640	Democrat	1873 (Oregon)
Douglas (6)	Lawyer	160	Democrat	1895 (Oregon)
Lane (6)	Farmer	320	Democrat	Unknown
Marion (10)	Farmer	640	Democrat	1876 (Oregon)
Linn (10)	Farmer	640	Democrat	Unknown
Linn (9)	Farmer	640	Democrat	1896 (Oregon)
Douglas (8)	Lawyer	320	Democrat	1893 (Oregon)
Mult./Wash. (7)	Editor	None	Anti-Democrat	1879 (Oregon)
Jackson (7)	Miner	Unknown	Democrat	Unknown
Linn (5)	Farmer	320	Democrat	1887 (Oregon)
Multnomah (4)	Lawyer	320	Democrat	1873 (Washington, D.C.)
Douglas (7)	Farmer	640	Democrat	1884 (Oregon)
Marion (6)	Lawyer	None	Democrat	1911 (Oregon)
Josephine (4)	Miner	None	Democrat	Unknown
Lane (4)	Farmer	320	Democrat	1884 (Oregon)
Clackamas (6)	Lawyer	Unknown	Democrat	1903 (Washington, D.C.)
Benton (4)	Farmer	Unknown	Democrat	1899 (Oregon)
Yamhill (10)	Farmer	Unknown	Anti-Democrat	1875 (Oregon)
Benton (12)	Farmer	640	Democrat	1889 (Oregon)
Multnomah (8)	Lawyer	Unknown	Anti-Democrat	1874 (Oregon)
Clackamas (14)	Lawyer	Unknown	Democrat	1882 (Oregon)
Yamhill (11)	Lawyer	323	Anti-Democrat	1904 (Washington state)
Multnomah (6)	Printer	None	Democrat	1891 (California)
Coos (6)	Farmer	Unknown	Democrat	1862 (Oregon)
Benton (10)	Mechanic	640	Anti-Democrat	Unknown
Wasco (2)	Lawyer	Unknown	Democrat	Unknown
Marion (10)	Farmer	578	Democrat	1890 (Oregon)
Lane (5)	Surveyor	320	Democrat	1861 (Oregon)
Jackson (4)	Farmer	320	Democrat	Unknown
Benton (5)	Farmer	320	Anti-Democrat	1907 (Oregon)

APPENDIX 1B. *(continued)*

Name	Birthdate (Age)	Birthplace	Previous Residence
Martin Olds	1799 (58)	Massachusetts	Michigan
Cyrus Olney	1815 (42)	New York	Iowa
William Packwood	1832 (25)	Illinois	Illinois
J. C. Peebles	1826 (31)	Pennsylvania	Indiana
Paine Page Prim	1822 (35)	Tennessee	Ohio
J. H. Reed	1824 (33)	Pennsylvania	Missouri
Nathaniel Robbins	1793 (64)	Virginia	Indiana
Levi Scott	1797 (60)	Illinois	Iowa
Davis Shannon	1815 (42)	Missouri	Indiana
Erasmus Shattuck	1824 (33)	Vermont	New York
James Shields	1811 (46)	Illinois	Missouri
Robert V. Short	1823 (34)	Pennsylvania	Illinois
Nicholas Shrum	1803 (54)	Tennessee	Missouri
Delazon Smith	1816 (41)	New York	Iowa
William Starkweather	1822 (35)	Connecticut	California
William H. Watkins	1827 (30)	New York	New York
John W. Watts	1830 (27)	Missouri	Missouri
Frederick Waymire	1807 (50)	Missouri	Missouri
John S. White	1828 (29)	Tennessee	Illinois
Thomas Whitted	1832 (25)	Ohio	Indiana
George Williams	1823 (34)	New York	Iowa

SOURCE: George H. Himes, comp., "Constitutional Convention of Oregon," *Oregon Historical Society Quarterly* 15 (September 1914): 217–218; with additions and corrections.

County (Years in Oregon)	Occupation	Farm Acreage	Political Party	Death (Place)
Yamhill (6)	Farmer	324	Anti-Democrat	1877 (Oregon)
Clatsop (6)	Lawyer	321	Democrat	1870 (Oregon)
Curry (8)	Miner	Unknown	Anti-Democrat	1917 (Oregon)
Marion (7)	Farmer	399	Democrat	1897 (Oregon)
Jackson (6)	Lawyer	None	Democrat	1899 (California)
Jackson (2)	Lawyer	Unknown	Democrat	1884 (Washington state)
Clackamas (5)	Farmer	326	Democrat	Unknown
Umpqua (13)	Farmer	321	Anti-Democrat	1890 (Oregon)
Marion (13)	Farmer	626	Democrat	1889 (Oregon)
Washington (4)	Lawyer	Unknown	Anti-Democrat	1900 (Oregon)
Linn (5)	Farmer	320	Democrat	1879 (Oregon)
Yamhill (10)	Surveyor	640	Democrat	1908 (Oregon)
Marion (11)	Farmer	645	Democrat	Unknown
Linn (5)	Lawyer	318	Democrat	1860 (Oregon)
Clackamas (7)	Farmer	161	Democrat	1905 (Oregon)
Josephine (5)	Physician	160	Anti-Democrat	1888 (Oregon)
Columbia (5)	Physician	640	Anti-Democrat	1901 (Oregon)
Polk (12)	Mechanic	644	Democrat	1873 (Oregon)
Washington (12)	Farmer	634	Anti-Democrat	1886 (Oregon)
Douglas (7)	Farmer	321	Democrat	Unknown
Marion (4)	Lawyer	None	Democrat	1910 (Oregon)

APPENDIX 1C.   Nevada Constitutional Convention Delegates, 1864

Name	Birthdate (Age)	Birthplace	Interim Residences
Nathaniel A. H. Ball	1827 (37)	New Hampshire	Massachusetts California
James Banks	1828 (36)	Pennsylvania	New York California
W. W. Belden	1834 (30)	Vermont	Wisconsin
Henry B. Brady	1836 (28)	Connecticut	California
Cornelius Brosnan	1815 (49)	Ireland	Vermont New York California
Samuel Chapin	1812 (52)	Massachusetts	Illinois Michigan California
John A. Collins	1814 (50)	Vermont	Massachusetts New York California
Israel Crawford	1822 (42)	New York	California
John S. Crosman	1820 (44)	New York	California
Charles F. De Long	1832 (32)	New York	California
E. F. Dunne	1836 (28)	New York	Ohio California
Josiah Earl	1822 (42)	Ohio	Indiana Alabama California
Thomas Fitch	1835 (29)	New York	Illinois Wisconsin California
Lloyd Frizell	1824 (40)	Ohio	Illinois California
Gilman Folson	1829 (35)	Maine	California
George Gibson	1824 (40)	Maine	Massachusetts California
J. W. Haines	1825 (39)	Canada	Ohio California
Albert T. Hawley	1831 (33)	Kentucky	Tennessee California
Almon Hovey	1819 (45)	New York	California
George Hudson	1810 (54)	Massachusetts	Pennsylvania California
J. Neely Johnson	1826 (38)	Indiana	Iowa California
Thomas Kennedy	1839 (25)	Pennsylvania	California

County (Years in Nevada)	Occupation	Presidential Vote, 1860	Death (Place)
Storey (2)	Banker	Douglas	1870 (California)
Humboldt (1)	Mining Superintendent	Lincoln	1867 (California)
Washoe (5)	Lumber Dealer	Lincoln	Missing 1870[a]
Washoe (2)	Mechanic	Lincoln	Missing 1870
Storey (1)	Lawyer	Douglas	1867 (Nevada)
Storey (4)	Miner	Lincoln	1890 (California)
Storey (4)	Miner	Lincoln	1890 (California)
Ormsby (1)	Editor	Lincoln	Missing 1870
Lyon (1)	Miner	Douglas	Missing 1870
Storey (1)	Lawyer	Douglas	1876 (Nevada)
Humboldt (1)	Lawyer	Douglas	Missing 1870
Storey (1)	Lumber Dealer	Douglas	1884 (Australia)
Storey (1)	Lawyer	Lincoln	1923 (California)
Storey (5)	Lawyer	Douglas	1877 (California)
Washoe (3)	Lumber Dealer	Lincoln	1917 (Nevada)
Ormsby (5)	Merchant	Breckenridge	After 1880
Douglas (5)	Agriculture	Breckenridge	After 1890 (Nevada)
Douglas (3)	Lawyer	Bell	Missing 1870
Storey (5)	Merchant	Douglas	Missing 1870
Lyon (3)	Mill Owner	Lincoln	1868 (California)
Ormsby (4)	Lawyer	Breckenridge	1872 (Utah)
Lyon (4)	Lawyer	Breckenridge	1871 (Nevada)

APPENDIX 1C. (*continued*)

Name	Birthdate (Age)	Birthplace	Interim Residences
John H. Kinkhead	1827 (37)	Pennsylvania	Ohio Missouri Utah California
A. J. Lockwood	1834 (30)	New York	Ohio California
John G. McClinton	1838 (26)	Illinois	California
B. S. Mason	1818 (46)	New York	Illinois California
Nelson Murdock	1800 (64)	New York	California
George Nourse	1825 (39)	Maine	Massachusetts Minnesota
H. G. Parker	1829 (35)	Vermont	California
Francis Proctor	1828 (36)	Kentucky	California
James H. Sturtevant	1836 (36)	New York	California
Francis Tagliabue	1833 (31)	England	California
C. W. Tozer	1832 (32)	New York	Michigan California
James H. Warwick	1826 (38)	Connecticut	New York California
William W. Wetherell	1820 (44)	Pennsylvania	New Jersey California

[a]"Missing 1870" indicates that the delegate was not listed as a Nevada resident in the 1870 *Federal Manuscript Census*.

[b]"Missing 1875, 1880" indicates that the delegate was not listed as a Nevada resident in the 1875 *State Census* or 1880 *Federal Manuscript Census*.

SOURCE: "Homographic Chart of the Convention," in Andrew J. Marsh, *Official Report of the Debates and Proceedings in the Constitutional Convention of the State of Nevada, Assembled at Carson City, July 4th, 1864, to Form a Constitution and State Government* (San Francisco: Frank Eastman, 1866), xvi; with additions and corrections.

County (Years in Nevada)	Occupation	Presidential Vote, 1860	Death (Place)
Ormsby (4)	Merchant	Breckenridge	1904 (Nevada)
Ormsby (4)	Mechanic	Douglas	After 1880
Esmeralda (3)	Editor	Lincoln	Missing 1875, 1880[b]
Esmeralda (4)	Physician	Douglas	Missing 1870
Churchill (4)	Mill Owner	Douglas	Missing 1870
Washoe (1)	Lawyer	Lincoln	1901 (California)
Lyon (1)	Mining Superintendent	Douglas	Missing 1875, 1880
Nye (6)	Lawyer	Breckenridge	Missing 1875, 1880
Washoe (7)	Agriculture	Douglas	1899 (California)
Nye (5)	Surveyor	Lincoln	Missing 1875, 1880
Storey (4)	Miner	Bell	Missing 1870
Lander (1)	Lawyer	Lincoln	Missing 1870
Esmeralda (3)	Miner	Breckenridge	Missing 1870

APPENDIX 2A. The Leading Men

The analysis of power in legislative bodies is the subject of a large literature. Although I have calculated various "power indices" for the delegates to each of the far western constitutional conventions, my choice of the leaders in the three conventions is principally based on my reading of the debates and proceedings, and my evaluation of whose speeches and proposals—whose sheer presence—had the greatest impact, whether negative or positive.

In a precise statistical sense, therefore, I chose these leaders arbitrarily. Nonetheless, the extent of their activities in the conventions does reinforce my point that these individuals were particularly influential in the convention deliberations and the politics of state making. Although the men I have identified as leaders composed only 12.5 percent, 10 percent, and 11 percent, respectively, of the California, Oregon, and Nevada constitutional conventions, their activities in the conventions were in most categories far out of proportion to their number, as the accompanying table illustrates. For example, the six Oregonians held almost half the committee chairmanships in their convention and were responsible for between 39 percent and 49 percent of the remarks made in the meeting. The corresponding percentages for the Nevadans and Californians are similarly high, with the exception of committee chairmanships in the California convention—where membership on most committees (save one, the Select Committee on the Constitution, chaired by William Gwin) was largely ceremonial.

In the following table, the number of remarks on the Proceedings of the conventions and on the content of the constitutions varies significantly because of the nature of the extant records of the debates and proceedings in the three states. Of the three, only the Andrew Marsh report of the Nevada constitutional convention provides a full verbatim account. J. Ross Browne's report of the California constitutional convention intermixed paraphrased summaries of delegate remarks with verbatim reports. From time to time Browne simply listed the names of delegates who remarked on a particular question. (For the purpose of tallying the number of convention and constitutional remarks made by each delegate, the latter remarks—which Browne noted but did not record—were included.) It is possible, though not certain, that Browne also failed to report delegates' remarks on any number of occasions. In the case of the Oregon constitutional convention, the situation is even more complex, for the territorial government made no provision for an official report of the convention debates. The Charles Carey volume is a compilation of reports published in the Portland *Oregonian* and Salem *Oregon Statesman*. Although both newspapers kept a complete record of roll call voting in the convention, neither provided a comprehensive report of the debates. Rather, the Democratic *Oregon Statesman* emphasized the remarks of Democratic delegates; the *Oregonian* those of anti-Democrats. The unintentional result of this partisan reporting is a relatively balanced record, even though both papers omitted many remarks from their reports and paraphrased others. Consequently, for California and, especially, Oregon, the aggregate count of remarks must be taken as a rough estimate only. In the case of the Oregon reports, given that the biases inherent in the *Oregon Statesman* and *Oregonian* reports tend to offset one another, the relative percentages reported in the following table are, I think, credible measures of the general balance of remarks within this convention.

Convention Activities of the Leading Figures
California, Oregon, and Nevada Constitutional Conventions

State	Percent of Convention	Chair of the Committee of the Whole	Committee Chairmanships	Remarks on the Proceedings of the Convention	Remarks on the Content of the Constitution	Roll Call Motions
California (entire convention)	100%	30	17	549	1154	167
Botts Gwin Halleck Hastings Jones McCarver	12.5%	7 (23%)	3 (18%)	248 (45%)	502 (44%)	75 (45%)
Oregon (entire convention)	100%	38	20	344	671	343
Deady Dryer Grover Logan Smith Williams	10%	17 (45%)	9 (45%)	169 (49%)	265 (39%)	127 (37%)
Nevada (entire convention)	100%	87	24	1238	3050	330
Collins De Long Fitch Johnson	11%	41 (47%)	8 (33%)	287 (23%)	1132 (37%)	68 (21%)

SOURCE: Compiled from J. Ross Browne, *Report of the Debates in the Convention of California on the Formation of the State Constitution in September and October, 1849* (Washington, D.C.: John T. Towers, 1850); Charles Henry Carey, ed., *The Oregon Constitution and Proceedings and Debates of the Constitutional Convention of 1857* (Salem, Oreg.: State Printing Department, 1926); Andrew J. Marsh, *Official Report of the Debates and Proceedings in the Constitutional Convention of the State of Nevada, Assembled at Carson City, July 4th, 1864, to Form a Constitution and State Government* (San Francisco: Frank Eastman, 1866).

Other approaches to the identification of power in legislative settings are found in R. Duncan Luce and Arnold A. Rogow, "A Game-theoretic Analysis of Congressional Power Distribution for a Stable Two-Party System," *Behavioral Science* 1 (April 1956): 83–95; Robert A. Dahl, "The Concept of Power," *Behavioral Science* 2 (July 1957): 201–215; William H. Riker, "A Test of the Adequacy of the Power Index," *Behavioral Science* 4 (April 1959): 120–131; and Allan Bogue, "Some Dimensions of Power in the Thirty-seventh Senate," in *The Dimensions of Quantitative Research in History,* ed. William O. Aydelotte, Allan G. Bogue, and Robert William Fogel (Princeton: Princeton University Press, 1972), 285–318. A model application of these (and other) techniques of legislative analysis is Allan Bogue, *The Earnest Men: Republicans of the Civil War Senate* (Ithaca: Cornell University Press, 1981).

APPENDIX 2B.   Factor Analysis, California Constitutional Convention
Roll Call Votes

The following table includes information about roll call voting in the California
constitutional convention. Column 3 gives the Riker Index of "significance" for
each roll call vote. This index provides one measure of the division over a given
issue, taking into account both the difference between yea and nay votes, and the
number of delegates who cast a vote (as opposed to abstaining). In addition, the
table includes an illustrative portion of the results from an "R-Technique" factor
analysis of the California convention roll calls. Shown in the table are the first
four and the tenth rotated factor "loadings," a coefficient that statistically represents patterns existing in the correlation matrix of roll call votes. (The fifth
through the ninth coefficients yielded patterns similar to those for the tenth and
subsequent factors, and thus were omitted.) Roll calls that have significantly high
loadings (0.500 or greater) are highlighted. In general, high factor loadings—
for example, those for roll calls 32, 42, 44 through 47, 49, 51, and 52—identify
voting based upon a similar alignment of delegates.

Roll Call	Issue	Riker Index	Rotated Factor Loadings				
			1	2	3	4	10
1	Convention—state or territory	.40	0.104	0.290	0.173	−0.182	0.053
2	Committee appointments	.35	0.056	0.073	−0.031	−0.008	0.161
3	Delegate compensation	.54	0.212	0.167	0.159	0.245	0.016
4	Record of debates	.34	−0.110	−0.049	0.131	0.116	0.168
5	Seating of delegates	.32	−0.202	−0.018	−0.034	0.143	0.124
6	Delegate compensation	.38	−0.038	0.093	0.108	**−0.566**	0.354
7	Delegate compensation	.55	−0.069	−0.105	−0.088	**−0.735**	−0.003
8	Delegate compensation	.66	0.087	−0.075	−0.125	**0.848**	0.109
9	President's salary	.55	0.032	−0.225	0.151	**0.597**	0.213
10	Appoint Law Commission	.45	−0.155	−0.080	−0.188	−0.035	−0.132
11	Appoint Law Commission	.80	−0.241	0.055	−0.009	−0.394	−0.103
12	Suffrage, Indians	.69	0.140	0.468	0.064	0.027	−0.203
13	Suffrage, Indians	.86	−0.274	−0.268	−0.067	−0.164	0.151
14	Term, State Senators	.37	0.257	−0.105	−0.055	0.286	0.076
15	Residency Requirement	.29	−0.289	0.071	0.364	−0.290	0.109
16	Customs Revenues	.68	0.221	0.049	−0.443	0.107	−0.163
17	Customs Revenues	.38	−0.017	0.233	−0.074	−0.102	−0.067
18	Port Revenues	.34	−0.093	−0.082	**−0.692**	0.071	0.142
19	Corporations	.32	0.067	−0.087	0.025	−0.050	0.133
20	Corporations	.26	−0.153	0.060	−0.010	0.311	−0.119
21	Banking Restrictions	.23	0.140	0.122	0.106	−0.019	−0.047
22	Banking Restrictions	.43	−0.052	0.072	**−0.847**	−0.078	−0.113
23	Banking Restrictions	.66	0.048	0.158	−0.069	0.003	−0.061
24	Banking Restrictions	.77	−0.104	−0.057	**0.522**	−0.111	−0.124
25	Free Black Prohibition	.52	−0.019	**0.801**	0.049	0.087	−0.079
26	Free Black Prohibition	.43	0.135	**0.672**	−0.139	0.057	−0.226
27	Free Black Prohibition	.46	0.122	**0.771**	0.170	−0.184	−0.030

Roll Call	Issue	Riker Index	Rotated Factor Loadings				
			1	2	3	4	10
28	Free Black Prohibition	.29	0.238	**0.696**	−0.198	0.060	0.163
29	Gubernatorial Term	.46	0.045	−0.015	0.231	0.230	0.330
30	School Lands	.32	−0.389	0.253	−0.008	0.047	0.358
31	School Fund	.43	−0.206	−0.026	0.429	0.064	0.151
32	School Fund	.40	**0.625**	−0.038	0.126	−0.121	−0.240
33	Amendments	.62	0.306	**0.582**	0.108	−0.104	0.139
34	Amendments	.69	0.222	**0.739**	−0.119	−0.127	0.142
35	Amendments	.69	0.236	0.449	0.088	0.016	0.338
36	Amendments	.60	0.446	0.429	0.001	−0.027	0.199
37	State capital	.77	0.066	0.132	0.163	0.003	−0.097
38	Duelling Prohibition	.66	0.318	0.076	0.059	0.008	0.077
39	Duelling Prohibition	.77	0.108	0.132	0.032	0.060	−0.002
40	Jurisdiction of state	.48	−0.010	−0.082	0.050	0.113	−0.121
41	Jurisdiction of state	.43	−0.400	−0.126	0.040	0.199	0.160
42	Boundary	.88	**0.869**	−0.049	−0.053	0.013	−0.004
43	Boundary	.63	−0.235	−0.257	−0.293	−0.157	−0.227
44	Boundary	.77	**0.867**	0.093	0.165	0.153	0.123
45	Boundary	.83	**0.830**	0.151	−0.017	0.105	0.073
46	Boundary	.94	**0.930**	0.154	−0.029	0.036	0.106
47	Boundary	.94	**−0.930**	−0.154	0.029	−0.036	−0.106
48	Boundary	.66	−0.164	−0.085	0.011	−0.042	−0.054
49	Boundary	.94	**0.501**	0.094	0.166	0.101	**0.517**
50	Boundary	.86	0.470	−0.012	−0.037	0.121	**0.759**
51	Boundary	.77	**−0.888**	−0.140	0.084	−0.009	−0.055
52	Boundary	.40	**0.573**	0.077	0.155	−0.057	−0.291
53	Use of Mineral lands	.68	0.067	0.342	0.144	0.158	0.028
54	Adjourn	.20	−0.179	−0.092	0.176	0.098	0.023
	% Total Variance:		13.993	8.374	4.891	5.351	4.004

The table illustrates two aspects of the California convention discussed in chapter 4. First, factor 1 displays the significance of the boundary issue (roll calls 42–52). The roll call votes on this question were marked by both high factor loadings *and* high Riker Index scores. (Appendix 2C presents a cluster analysis of the boundary votes.) Second, other than those pertaining to the votes on McCarver's free Negro prohibition (roll calls 25–28, which have relatively low Riker indices), the other factor loadings illustrate the transitory character of alignments in the convention.

The formal equation for the Riker Index (and a good discussion of its value and shortcomings) can be found in Lee F. Anderson, Meredith W. Watts, Jr., and Allen R. Wilcox, *Legislative Roll-Call Analysis* (Evanston, Ill.: Northwestern University Press, 1966), 81–87. The application of factor analysis to roll call voting is discussed in chapter 7 of the same. An illuminating example of the latter method of analysis is Peter Smith, "The Making of the Mexican Constitution," in *The History of Parliamentary Behavior*, ed. William O. Aydelotte (Princeton: Princeton University Press, 1977), 186–224.

APPENDIX 2C.   Cluster Analysis, California Constitutional
Convention Boundary Roll Calls

The following cluster analysis illustrates the clustering of roll call votes on the boundary issue in the California constitutional convention (roll calls 42–52). The chart identifies, in stages, groups of delegates who voted alike (those bracketed together near the left margin) and those groups who opposed one another (identified by brackets that approach the right margin).

Several features of the chart deserve mention. First, the delegates in the top half voted in favor of the Gwin-Halleck extended boundary (see map 3, p. 132); those below opposed it. Second, the cluster analysis identifies the swing bloc of Californio delegates: Carrillo, Pedrorena, Foster, Dominguez, and Vallejo. After initially helping to pass the Gwin-Halleck extended boundary (roll call 47), these men resolved the issue by switching their votes (on roll calls 49 and 50) to the Sierra Nevada compromise. The pandemonium that followed the passage of the Gwin-Halleck boundary is reflected in the low factor loading of roll call 48 (which adjourned the convention for the day; see, above, pp. 136–137).

Third, the chart identifies delegate Francis Lippitt as falling between the two major clusters. This occurred because Lippitt missed most of the boundary votes. Some forty years later Lippitt claimed to have saved the Sierra Nevada boundary by leaving his sickbed in time for the final crucial vote. (See Francis Lippitt, "The California Boundary Question in 1849," *Century Magazine* [September 1890]: 794–795.) Finally, delegate Julian Hanks fell outside all clusters: his pattern of votes on the boundary issue did not correlate with that of any other group of delegates. In other words, it was the most "dissimilar" pattern in the convention.

INCREASING DISSIMILARITY ⟶

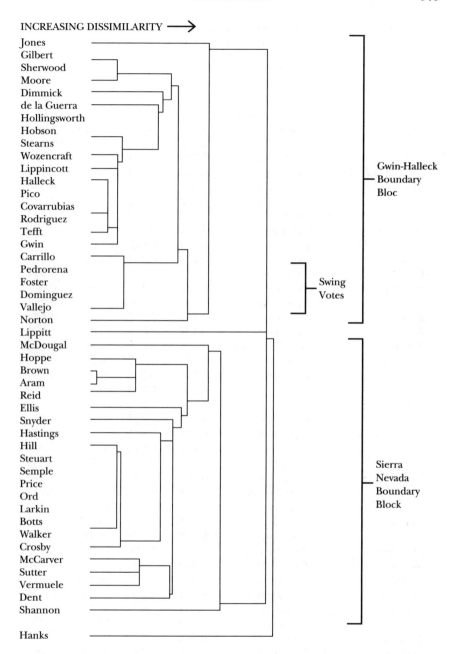

APPENDIX 2D. Factor Analysis, Oregon Contitutional Convention
Roll Call Votes

Name	Party		Rotated Factor Loadings
		1	2	3	8
Anderson	Anti-Democrat	0.047	**0.605**	−0.179	−0.065
Applegate	Anti-Democrat	−0.054	0.242	0.047	−0.061
Babcock	Democrat	**0.643**	−0.171	0.291	−0.083
Boise	Democrat	**0.706**	−0.118	0.318	−0.138
Brattrain, J. H.	Democrat	**0.728**	0.040	0.090	−0.159
Brattrain, Paul	Democrat	0.486	0.230	0.186	−0.088
Bristow	Democrat	**0.522**	0.072	−0.016	0.083
Burch	Democrat	**0.681**	0.163	0.143	0.169
Campbell, A. J.	Democrat	0.328	−0.002	0.087	0.046
Campbell, Hector	Democrat	**0.704**	0.028	0.080	−0.008
Chadwick	Democrat	**0.581**	−0.212	0.449	0.219
Cox, Jesse	Democrat	0.426	−0.055	0.138	**0.554**
Cox, Joseph	Democrat	**0.713**	−0.176	−0.021	0.025
Coyle	Democrat	**0.644**	0.086	−0.340	0.267
Crooks	Democrat	**0.751**	0.034	0.082	0.123
Deady	Democrat	0.404	−0.331	0.427	0.125
Dryer	Anti-Democrat	−0.204	0.056	−0.047	−0.100
Duncan	Democrat	0.373	−0.107	**0.731**	0.139
Elkins	Democrat	**0.716**	−0.106	0.031	0.284
Farrar	Democrat	−0.152	**0.798**	0.031	0.119
Fitzhugh	Democrat	**0.697**	−0.209	0.279	0.288
Grover	Democrat	**0.754**	−0.123	0.144	0.215
Hendershott	Democrat	0.192	0.095	−0.135	0.184
Hoult	Democrat	**0.614**	0.014	0.143	0.082
Kelly	Democrat	0.301	−0.061	0.155	0.305
Kelsay	Democrat	0.327	0.116	0.203	**0.674**
Kinney	Anti-Democrat	0.068	0.458	−0.052	0.254
Lewis	Democrat	0.053	0.327	−0.081	0.033
Logan	Anti-Democrat	−0.168	**0.790**	−0.065	−0.085
Lovejoy	Democrat	**0.700**	−0.048	0.241	−0.030
McBride	Anti-Democrat	−0.118	**0.500**	0.057	−0.036
McCormick	Democrat	**0.569**	0.142	0.078	0.108
Marple	Democrat	0.018	0.117	0.172	−0.010
Matzger	Anti-Democrat	0.171	0.167	−0.058	0.146
Meigs	Democrat	0.337	−0.020	0.144	0.118
Miller	Democrat	**0.580**	−0.144	−0.024	0.305
Moores	Democrat	**0.549**	0.160	0.043	0.082
Newcomb	Democrat	0.355	−0.027	**0.603**	0.091
Nichols	Anti-Democrat	0.139	0.405	0.058	0.022
Olds	Anti-Democrat	−0.105	**0.803**	−0.050	−0.041
Olney	Democrat	0.366	−0.082	0.003	−0.016
Packwood	Anti-Democrat	0.113	0.411	−0.052	0.182

APPENDIX 2D.   (*continued*)

Name	Party	Rotated Factor Loadings			
		1	*2*	*3*	*8*
Peebles	Democrat	**0.678**	−0.235	0.143	0.080
Prim	Democrat	0.380	−0.058	0.395	0.124
Reed	Democrat	0.278	−0.111	0.113	−0.136
Robbins	Democrat	**0.643**	−0.021	−0.145	0.041
Scott	Anti-Democrat	0.110	**0.682**	0.064	0.054
Shannon	Democrat	**0.536**	−0.385	0.050	0.202
Shattuck	Anti-Democrat	−0.027	0.159	0.018	0.014
Shields	Democrat	**0.764**	−0.008	−0.007	0.216
Short	Democrat	0.038	**0.743**	−0.132	0.077
Shrum	Democrat	0.302	−0.085	−0.077	0.141
Smith	Democrat	**0.779**	−0.016	0.100	0.065
Starkweather	Democrat	0.428	0.168	0.075	0.045
Watkins	Anti-Democrat	−0.132	0.310	0.040	0.190
Watts	Anti-Democrat	0.068	0.416	0.014	**0.558**
Waymire	Democrat	**0.683**	0.098	0.110	−0.065
White	Anti-Democrat	−0.028	**0.702**	−0.086	0.131
Whitted	Democrat	0.460	−0.338	0.405	0.205
Williams	Democrat	**0.564**	−0.243	0.027	0.169
	% Total Variance:	22.342	10.046	4.193	3.789

In contrast to Appendix 2B, this table represents the results of a "Q-Technique" factor analysis of the Oregon constitutional convention roll call voting. Here, the factors measure the strength or weakness of partisan alignments in the convention (whereas the R-Technique measures the relationships between issues). Factor 1 of the Oregon Q-Technique analysis displays the general, though far from complete, solidarity of the Democratic delegates in this convention. Factors 2 through 8 (4 to 7, omitted in the table, are similar to factor 3 in that only two or three delegates have high factor loadings on them) illustrate the splintered character of the anti-Democrats, as well as the presence of small groups of anti-Salem Democrats.

APPENDIX 2E.   Factor Analysis, Nevada Constitutional Convention Roll Call Votes

Roll Call	Issue	Riker Index	Unrotated Component 1	Rotated Factor Loadings			
				1	2	3	4
1	Elect Convention Secretary	.68	−0.252	**−0.646**	0.007	0.038	−0.260
2	Adjourn *sine Die*	.64	0.106	−0.034	0.039	0.111	−0.100
6	Declaration of Rights	.48	−0.190	−0.079	−0.087	−0.217	0.087
11	Adjourn *sine Die*	.48	0.242	−0.020	0.004	0.243	−0.368
12	Women's Rights, Sole Traders	.49	0.049	0.191	0.199	0.242	0.104
13	State Franchises	.72	0.248	0.145	−0.079	−0.037	0.040
15	Railroad Bonds	.68	0.451	0.161	−0.054	0.067	−0.136
16	Mining Tax	.49	0.335	0.281	−0.072	0.015	−0.131
17	Mining Tax	.61	**0.515**	0.049	**−0.644**	0.208	−0.528
18	Mining Tax	.46	0.377	0.245	−0.093	0.168	0.094
19	Mining Tax	.65	0.334	0.029	−0.173	0.047	−0.053
20	Mining Tax	.88	**−0.770**	**−0.843**	0.129	−0.071	0.165
21	Adjourn (Mining Tax)	.92	0.435	**0.578**	0.129	0.097	−0.369
22	Mining Tax	.84	**0.677**	**0.803**	−0.071	0.078	−0.200
23	Adjourn	.57	0.229	0.217	−0.002	−0.002	0.004
24	Appeal Decision of Chair	.32	**−0.921**	**−0.530**	0.383	−0.043	**0.588**
25	Mining Tax	.42	−0.459	−0.258	0.106	−0.211	0.288
26	Mining Tax	.88	**0.779**	**0.803**	−0.167	0.081	−0.297
27	Mining Tax	.65	**−0.728**	−0.375	0.256	0.099	**0.592**
28	Mining Tax	.69	**0.942**	**0.556**	−0.370	0.116	**−0.586**
29	Mining Tax	.61	**0.834**	**0.519**	−0.386	0.012	−0.439
31	Loyalty Oath	.76	**−0.666**	−0.131	0.339	−0.200	**0.738**
32	Loyalty Oath	.60	**0.535**	0.185	−0.026	0.062	**−0.858**
33	Loyalty Oath	.68	**0.537**	0.136	−0.027	0.093	**−0.886**
35	Railroad Bonds	.52	**−0.591**	−0.399	0.253	−0.334	0.157
36	Railroad Bonds	.45	0.147	0.233	0.182	0.252	0.059
39	Mining Tax	.52	**−0.658**	**−0.535**	0.199	−0.021	0.293
40	Mining Tax	.80	**−0.841**	**−0.771**	0.293	0.060	0.331
41	Mining Tax	.64	**0.866**	**0.593**	−0.259	0.225	−0.467
46	Impeachment	.51	**−0.685**	−0.106	**0.867**	−0.121	0.204
47	Impeachment	.52	**−0.569**	−0.186	**0.940**	−0.037	0.041
48	Impeachment	.60	**−0.659**	−0.090	**0.895**	−0.124	0.184
49	Impeachment	.52	**−0.569**	−0.186	**0.940**	−0.037	0.041
50	Salaries	.40	0.176	0.345	−0.011	−0.210	0.090
52	Misc. Provisions	.55	−0.139	−0.066	0.134	−0.024	0.027
53	Misc. Provisions	.44	−0.108	0.003	0.245	0.053	0.027
54	Judiciary	.32	−0.460	**−0.638**	0.034	−0.337	−0.074

Roll Call	Issue	Riker Index	Unrotated Compo- nent 1	Rotated Factor Loadings			
				1	2	3	4
57	Schedule	.36	0.484	0.151	−0.200	**0.897**	−0.111
58	Schedule	.36	0.484	0.151	−0.200	**0.897**	−0.111
60	Adjourn	.39	−0.411	−0.425	0.120	0.301	0.214
61	Chaplain	.31	−0.256	0.002	0.190	−0.326	−0.005
63	Schedule	.39	0.270	0.194	−0.036	0.139	0.078
64	Schedule	.32	−0.240	0.164	−0.068	**−0.727**	0.261
	% Total Variance:		28.904	15.169	11.706	7.407	11.422

In this R-Technique factor analysis of the Nevada convention the first *unrotated* component loading is included (along with the rotated factor coefficients) to underscore the centrality of the mining tax issue in this convention and the fact that a similar, though not identical, alignment marked much of the convention. This general alignment turned on a group of mining county delegates who voted initially with the cow county delegates, but, for reasons discussed in chapter 6, sided (after roll call 27) with the antitax mining county delegates. The unrotated component loadings illustrate the common dimension that marked roll calls 17 to 50. The more precise rotated factor loadings delineate the shifts that occurred over the course of the convention. Because of the large number of unanimous (or near unanimous) votes in the Nevada convention—for the most part votes to re-pass sections of the defeated 1863 constitution—only roll calls with a Riker Index greater than .30 have been included in the analysis.

APPENDIX 2F.   Cluster Analysis, Nevada Constitutional Convention
Roll Calls (Riker Index > .30)

This cluster analysis of the roll calls with high coefficients on the unrotated component and on rotated factors 1 through 4, given in Appendix 2E, illustrates the voting patterns of individual delegates, revealing the basic mining county / cow county division in the Nevada convention. In addition, the cluster labeled "swing bloc" identifies those delegates who, beginning with the "Kennedy compromise" over the mining tax, switched their votes—and the balance of power in the convention—from the cow county to the mining county delegates.

INCREASING
DISSIMILARITY ———▶

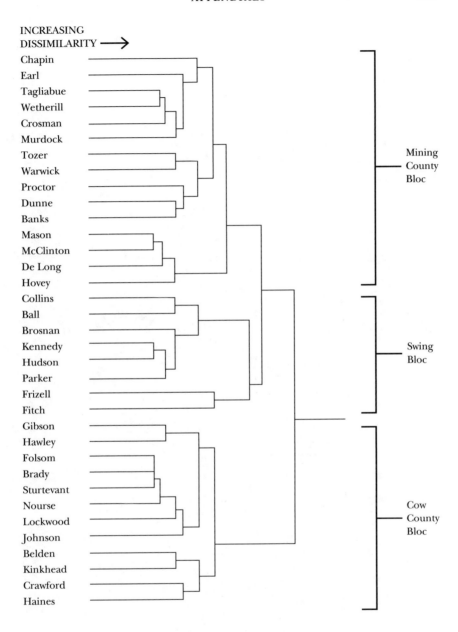

NOTES

PREFACE

1. Gordon Wood, *Creation of the American Republic, 1776–1787* (New York: W. W. Norton, 1972), 606–615. Since the publication of Wood's book, and largely because of questions it raised, historians have uncovered Americans espousing classical republican doctrines well into the nineteenth century. See, for example, the symposium on Wood's *Creation of the American Republic, William and Mary Quarterly* 44 (July 1987). Generally, see Dorothy Ross, "The Liberal Tradition Revisited and the Republican Tradition Addressed," in *New Directions in American Intellectual History,* ed. John Higham and Paul Conkin (Baltimore: Johns Hopkins University Press, 1979), 116–131. On classical republicanism and nineteenth-century American politics, see Stephen Watts, *The Republic Reborn: War and the Making of Liberal America, 1780–1820* (Baltimore: Johns Hopkins University Press, 1987); and Harry Watson, *Liberty and Power: The Politics of Jacksonian America* (New York: Noonday Press, 1990).

2. See Kenneth D. Owens, "Government and Politics in the Nineteenth-Century West," in *Historians and the American West,* ed. Michael Malone and Rodman Paul (Lincoln: University of Nebraska Press, 1983), 148–176. Although the Oregon Territory existed for ten years (1849 to 1859), California had no territorial stage, and Nevada's lasted only a short while. Furthermore, as Howard Lamar has pointed out, after the Civil War—following the statehood of California, Oregon, and Nevada—the territorial system "assumed a permanency and importance which it had never had before" (*Dakota Territory, 1861–1889: A Study of Frontier Politics* [New Haven: Yale University Press, 1956], 18). The very operation of the post–Civil War territorial system—which delayed the admission of further western states—underlined the peculiar experience of the three states considered in this book.

The literature on the territorial system of the United States from the eighteenth to the twentieth century is voluminous. Among the most significant works are Earl Pomeroy, *The Territories and the United States, 1861–1890: Studies in Colonial Administration* (1947; reprint, Seattle: University of Washington Press, 1970);

Lamar, *Dakota Territory;* Howard Lamar, *The Far Southwest, 1846–1912: A Territorial History* (New Haven: Yale University Press, 1966); Lewis Gould, *Wyoming: A Political History, 1868–1896* (New Haven: Yale University Press, 1968); Clark Spence, *Territorial Government and Politics in Montana, 1864–1889* (Urbana: University of Illinois Press, 1975); Jack Eblen, *The First and Second United States Empires: Governors and Territorial Government* (Pittsburgh: University of Pittsburgh Press, 1968); Robert W. Larson, *New Mexico's Quest for Statehood, 1846–1912* (Albuquerque: University of New Mexico Press, 1968); Jay J. Wagoner, *Arizona Territory, 1863–1912: A Political History* (Tucson: University of Arizona Press, 1970); Thomas Alexander, *A Clash of Interests: Interior Department and Mountain West, 1863–1896* (Provo: Brigham Young University Press, 1977). Two important works on the politics of the Oregon territory are Robert W. Johannsen, *Frontier Politics and the Sectional Crisis: The Pacific Northwest on the Eve of the Civil War* (Seattle: University of Washington Press, 1955); and James E. Hendrickson, *Joe Lane of Oregon: Machine Politics and the Sectional Crisis, 1849–1861* (New Haven: Yale University Press, 1967). There are few specialized studies of Nevada territorial affairs; noteworthy (and also concerned with Oregon) is Kent D. Richards, "Growth and Development of Government in the Far West: The Oregon Provisional Government, Jefferson Territory; Provisional and Territorial Nevada (Ph.D. diss., University of Minnesota, 1966).

In addition to the article cited above, Kenneth Owens has theorized with great insight about territorial politics in "Pattern and Structure in Western Territorial Politics," *Western Historical Quarterly* 1 (October 1970): 373–392. Older essays by Earl Pomeroy and W. Turrentine Jackson remain influential: see Pomeroy, "The Territory as a Frontier Institution," *The Historian* 7 (Autumn 1944): 29–41; and Jackson, "Montana Politics During the Meagher Regime, 1865–1867," *Pacific Historical Review* 12 (June 1943): 139–156; "Indian Affairs and Politics in Idaho Territory, 1863–1870," *Pacific Historical Review* 14 (September 1945): 311–325; and "The Wyoming Stock Growers' Association: Political Power in Wyoming Territory, 1873–1890," *Mississippi Valley Historical Review* 33 (March 1947): 571–594.

INTRODUCTION

1. The United States from which the subjects of this book emigrated is the topic of a vast historical literature. Different, but equally ambitious, syntheses of the period are found in Robert Wiebe, *The Opening of American Society: From the Constitution to the Eve of Disunion* (New York: Alfred A. Knopf, 1984); and William L. Barney, *The Passage of the Republic: An Interdisciplinary History of Nineteenth-Century America* (Lexington, Mass.: D. C. Heath, 1987). Recent works I have used include, for politics, Stephen Watts, *The Republic Reborn: War and the Making of Liberal America, 1780–1820* (Baltimore: Johns Hopkins University Press, 1987); Harry Watson, *Liberty and Power: The Politics of Jacksonian America* (New York: Noonday Press, 1990); Edward Pessen, *Jacksonian America: Society, Personality, and Politics* (Homewood, Ill.: Dorsey Press, 1978); John Ashworth, *'Agrarians' and 'Aristocrats': Party Political Ideology in the United States, 1837–1846* (Cambridge: Cambridge University Press, 1983); Richard P. McCormick, *The*

Second Party System: Party Formation in the Jacksonian Era (New York: W. W. Norton, 1973); Ronald Formisano, *The Transformation of Political Culture: Massachusetts Parties, 1790s–1840s* (New York: Oxford University Press, 1983); Joel Silbey, *The Partisan Imperative: The Dynamics of American Politics Before the Civil War* (New York: Oxford University Press, 1985); Marvin Meyers, *The Jacksonian Persuasion* (Stanford: Stanford University Press, 1957); Daniel Walker Howe, *The Political Culture of the American Whigs* (Chicago: University of Chicago Press, 1979); Eric Foner, *Free Soil, Free Labor, Free Men: The Ideology of the Republican Party Before the Civil War* (New York: Oxford University Press, 1970); Jean H. Baker, *Affairs of Party: The Political Culture of Northern Democrats in the Mid–Nineteenth Century* (Ithaca: Cornell University Press, 1983); and Michael Holt, *The Political Crisis of the 1850s* (New York: John Wiley, 1978). "Metropolitan industrialization" and its social and political consequences are the subject of Sean Wilentz, *Chants Democratic: New York City and the Rise of the American Working Class, 1788–1850* (New York: Oxford University Press, 1984); Cynthia J. Shelton, *The Mills of Manayunk: Industrialization and Social Conflict in the Philadelphia Region, 1787–1837* (Baltimore: Johns Hopkins University Press, 1986); and Christine Stansell, *City of Women: Sex and Class in New York, 1789–1860* (Urbana: University of Illinois Press, 1987). The social and political order of new manufacturing towns is treated in Jonathan Prude, *The Coming of Industrial Order: Town and Factory Life in Rural Massachusetts, 1810–1860* (New York: Cambridge University Press, 1983); Mary P. Ryan, *Cradle of the Middle Class: The Family in Oneida County, New York, 1790–1865* (New York: Cambridge University Press, 1981); Paul Johnson, *A Shopkeeper's Millennium: Society and Revivals in Rochester, New York, 1815–1837* (New York: Hill & Wang, 1978); Anthony F. C. Wallace, *Rockdale: The Growth of an American Village in the Early Industrial Revolution* (New York: Alfred A. Knopf, 1978); and Thomas Dublin, *Women at Work: The Transformation of Work and Community in Lowell, Massachusetts, 1826–1860* (New York: Columbia University Press, 1978). Antebellum culture is covered superbly in Daniel Walker Howe, ed., *Victorian America* (Philadelphia: University of Pennsylvania Press, 1976); Ann Douglas, *The Feminization of American Culture* (New York: Alfred A. Knopf, 1977); John Kasson, *Civilizing the Machine: Technology and Republican Values in America, 1776–1900* (New York: Penguin Books, 1979); and Rush Welter, *The Mind of America, 1830–1860* (New York: Columbia University Press, 1975). Society and economy in rural America are examined in John Mack Faragher, *Sugar Creek: Life on the Illinois Prairie* (New Haven: Yale University Press, 1986); Malcolm Rohrbough, *The Trans-Appalachian Frontier* (New York: Oxford University Press, 1978); Steven Hahn, *The Roots of Southern Populism: Yeoman Farmers and the Transformation of the Georgia Upcountry, 1850–1900* (New York: Oxford University Press, 1983); Clarence Danhof, *Change in Agriculture: The Northern United States, 1820–1870* (Cambridge, Mass.: Harvard University Press, 1969); Hal Barron, *Those Who Stayed Behind: Rural Society in Nineteenth-Century New England* (New York: Cambridge University Press, 1984); and the essays in Steven Hahn and Jonathan Prude, eds., *The Countryside in the Age of Capitalist Transformation: Essays in the Social History of Rural America* (Chapel Hill: University of North Carolina Press, 1985).

   2. Patricia Nelson Limerick, *The Legacy of Conquest: The Unbroken Past of the American West* (New York: W. W. Norton, 1987), 27.

3. Alan Trachtenberg, *The Incorporation of America: Culture and Society in the Gilded Age* (New York: Hill & Wang, 1982), 3–4.

4. Robert Wiebe, *The Seach for Order, 1877–1920* (New York: Hill & Wang, 1967), chap. 2.

5. T. H. Breen, "Creative Adaptations: Peoples and Cultures," in *Colonial British America: Essays in the New History of the Early Modern Era*, ed. Jack P. Greene and J. R. Pole (Baltimore: Johns Hopkins University Press, 1984), 204. Breen draws the concept of "charter group" from John A. Porter, *The Vertical Mosaic: An Analysis of Social Class and Power in Canada* (Toronto: University of Toronto Press, 1965), chap. 3. Cultural geographer Wilbur Zelinsky similarly describes the "Doctrine of First Effective Settlement" as "roughly analogous to the psychological principle of imprinting in very young animals. Whenever an empty territory undergoes settlement, or an earlier population is dislodged by invaders, the specific characteristics of the first group able to effect a viable, self-perpetuating society are of crucial significance for the later and social and cultural geography of the area, no matter how tiny the initial band of settlers may have been" (Zelinsky, *The Cultural Geography of the United States* [Englewood Cliffs, N.J.: Prentice-Hall, 1973], 13).

6. This point is drawn from my reading of the debate carried on by historians of the American West since the beginning of the twentieth century. From this—but more importantly, out of my confrontation with the political history of the United States—I have been impressed by, and drawn to, the continuities between the history of California, Oregon, and Nevada and larger themes of U.S. history, as well as with the ways the idiosyncratic features of local history shaped those larger themes.

A convenient introduction to the debate about western history, as it stood in the 1950s, is George Rogers Taylor, ed., *The Turner Thesis Concerning the Role of the Frontier in American History*, rev. ed. (Boston: D. C. Heath, 1956). In an important 1955 essay, "Toward a Reorientation of Western History: Continuity and Environment," *Mississippi Valley Historical Review* 41 (March 1955): 579–600, Earl Pomeroy took issue with the reigning assumption, Turnerian in origin, of western "exceptionalism." More recently William Robbins has similarly, and persuasively, evaluated western historiography and recommended its reorientation along neo-Marxian lines, in "Western History: A Dialectic on the Modern Condition," *Western Historical Quarterly* 20 (November 1989): 429–449. Robbins's essay is part of an exciting and reinvigorating discussion of the western United States that is appearing in the pages of the *Western Historical Quarterly*, *Pacific Historical Review*, and topical anthologies on western history, as well as in the work of scholars such as Patricia Nelson Limerick, Donald Wooster, William Cronon, and Richard White, in which the longstanding controversy over western exceptionalism—as opposed to its continuity with national (and, for that matter, international) experience—has been illuminated from perspectives drawn from the broad body of social, economic, cultural, environmental, and political history. Important guides to this discussion include Richard White, "American Environmental History: The Development of a New Historical Field," *Pacific Historical Review* 54 (August 1985): 297–335; William G. Robbins, "The 'Plundered Province' Thesis and the Recent Historiography of the American West," *Pacific Historical Review* 55 (November 1986): 577–597; Richard Maxwell Brown, "Rainfall and History: Perspectives on the Pacific Northwest," in *Experiences in a Promised Land: Essays in Pacific Northwest History*, ed. G. Thomas Edwards and Carlos Schwantes (Seattle: University of Washington Press, 1986), 13–27; Donald Wooster, "New West, True West: Interpreting the Region's History," *Western Historical Quarterly* 18 (April 1987): 141–156; William Cronon, "Revisiting the Vanishing Frontier: The Legacy of Frederick Jackson Turner," *Western Historical Quarterly* 18 (April 1987): 157–175; and Walter Nugent, "Frontiers and Empires in the Late Nineteenth Century," *Western Historical Quarterly* 20 (November 1989): 393–408. A mark of the importance of Limerick's *Legacy of Conquest* is seen in the symposium discussion of it by Donald Wooster, Susan Armitage, Michael Malone, David Weber, and Patricia Nelson Limerick, published in *Western Historical Quarterly* 20 (November 1989): 393–408.

7. California, Oregon, and Nevada were the only states west of Kansas (and Texas) to enter the union before the Civil War. In what Earl Pomeroy has identified as the Pacific slope, Washington (in 1889) was the next state created, followed by Idaho (1890), Utah (1896), and Arizona (1912). Broadening the Far West to include Colorado, Montana, Wyoming, and New Mexico, the respective dates are 1876, 1889, 1890, and 1912. See Pomeroy, *The Pacific Slope: A History of California, Oregon, Washington, Idaho, Utah, and Nevada* (Seattle: University of Washington Press, 1973).

8. On the earlier frontier, see Malcolm J. Rohrbough, *The Trans-Appalachian Frontier* (New York: Oxford University Press, 1978).

9. This approach has an important place in numerous studies of the English settlement of North America. See, in addition to Breen, "Creative Adaptations," Sumner Chilton Powell, *Puritan Village: The Formation of a New England Town* (Middleton, Conn.: Wesleyan University Press, 1963); David Grayson Allen, *In English Ways: The Movement of Societies and the Transferal of English Local Law and Custom to Massachusetts Bay in the Seventeenth Century* (New York: W. W. Norton, 1982); and, most recently, David Hackett Fischer's fascinating exploration *Albion's Seed: Four British Folkways in America* (New York: Oxford University Press, 1989). The concept of a "fragment society" is usually associated with Louis Hartz; see his *The Liberal Tradition in America* (New York: Harcourt, Brace & World, 1955); and *The Founding of New Societies: Studies in the History of the United States, Latin America, South Africa, Canada, and Australia* (New York: Harcourt, Brace & World, 1964).

10. See the insightful discussion in Morton Keller, "Reflections on Politics and Generations in America," *Daedalus* 107 (Fall 1978): 123–135, which also includes a good introduction to the social science literature on the concept of political generations. In American history the work of Arthur Schlesinger, Sr., and Arthur Schlesinger, Jr., has been particularly influential and deserves special mention; see Schlesinger, Sr., "The Tides of National Politics," in *Paths to the Present* (New York: Macmillan, 1949); and Schlesinger, Jr., *The Cycles of American History* (Boston: Houghton Mifflin, 1986). A number of important studies, which illuminate this point by departing variously from it, have sharpened my sense of the far westerners' place in time. Of particular significance to what follows are George Frederickson, *The Inner Civil War: Northern Intellectuals and the Crisis of the Civil War* (New York: Harper & Row, 1965); Morton Keller, *Affairs of State: Public Life in Late-Nineteenth-Century America* (Cambridge, Mass.: Harvard University

Press, 1977), esp. chaps. 1–7; Charles W. McCurdy, "Justice Field and the Juris-prudence of Government-Business Relations: Some Parameters of Laissez-Faire Constitutionalism, 1863–1897," in *American Law and the Constitutional Order: His-torical Perspectives*, ed. Lawrence M. Friedman and Harry N. Scheiber (Cam-bridge, Mass.: Harvard University Press, 1978), 246–265; and Hal S. Barron, *Those Who Stayed Behind: Rural Society in Nineteenth-Century New England* (New York: Cambridge University Press, 1984). Along the same lines, see the discus-sion of Baker in *Affairs of Party*, 19–24 and pt. 3, passim.

11. Lawrence Stone's essay "Prosopography," in *Historical Studies Today*, ed. Felix Gilbert and Stephen Graubard (Ithaca: Cornell University Press, 1971), 107–140, describes the origins and development, as well as the value and peril, of collective biography. A more recent and equally important, if briefer, discus-sion is in Allan Bogue, "The New Political History in the 1970s," in *The Past Be-fore Us: Contemporary Historical Writing in America*, ed. Michael Kammen (Ithaca: Cornell University Press, 1980), esp. 243–244.

12. The derivative character of nineteenth-century state constitutions is dis-cussed in Lawrence M. Friedman, *A History of American Law* (New York: Simon & Schuster, Touchstone Books, 1973), 108 and passim; Gordon Morris Bakken, *Rocky Mountain Constitution Making, 1850–1912* (Westport, Conn.: Greenwood Press, 1987), 11 and passim; Morton Keller, "The Politics of State Constitutional Revision, 1820–1930," in *The Constitutional Convention as an Amending Device*, ed. Kermit Hall, Harold M. Hyman, and Leon V. Sigal (Washington, D.C.: American Historical Association, 1981), 70–72, 75–78. The derivative character of civil law is detailed in the important book of John Phillip Reid, *Law for the Elephant: Property and Social Behavior on the Overland Trail* (San Marino, Calif.: Huntington Library, 1980).

13. Dealing with men who seldom thought or wrote systematically about poli-tics has impressed on me the care one must take in making terms like *ideology* and *political culture* carry precise definitions. I consequently use them descriptively and heuristically in order to identify the central features of my subjects' (individ-ual) political ideas and (common) partisan activities, as these persisted and changed over time. In this regard, while mindful of the influential essays of Clifford Geertz (above all "Ideology as a Cultural System," in *Interpretation of Cul-tures* [New York: Basic Books, 1973], 193–233), I have been guided above all by the theoretical essays of George Lichtheim, "The Concept of Ideology," *History and Theory* 4 (1965): 164–195; and Joyce Appleby, "Value and Society," in Greene and Pole (eds.), *Colonial British America*, 290–316. Other writings that I have found helpful in arriving at a working definition of terms are Gabriel Almond and Sidney Verba, *Civic Culture: Political Attitudes and Democracy in Five Nations* (Boston: Little, Brown, 1965), 1–44; Joyce Appleby, "Republicanism in Old and New Contexts," *William and Mary Quarterly* 43 (January 1986): 20–34; Baker, *Affairs of Party*, 11–12 and pt. 1, passim; and Howe, *Political Culture of the American Whigs*, 1–10.

14. J. Willard Hurst, *Law and the Conditions of Freedom in the Nineteenth-Century United States* (Madison: University of Wisconsin Press, 1956), 10. Hurst's insights have been applied to western constitution writing in Bakken, *Rocky Mountain Constitution Making*. For a contrasting interpretation of nineteenth-century Amer-ican law, see Morton J. Horwitz, *The Transformation of American Law* (Cambridge, Mass.: Harvard University Press, 1977).

15. A recent restatement of the "liberal interpretation" of American history is John P. Diggins, *The Lost Soul of American Politics: Virtue, Self Interest, and the Foundations of Liberalism* (New York: Basic Books, 1984). "Lockean liberalism," of course, is conventionally associated with Louis Hartz's *Liberal Tradition in America.*

16. See Allan Bogue, *From Prairie to Cornbelt: Farming on the Illinois and Iowa Prairie in the Nineteenth Century* (Chicago: University of Chicago Press, 1963); Faragher, *Sugar Creek;* and Rohrbough, *Trans-Appalachian Frontier.*

17. Dorothy Johansen, "A Working Hypothesis for the Study of Migrations," in Edwards and Schwantes (eds.), *Experiences in a Promised Land,* 41. Johansen attributes the anecdote to the 1850s but does not cite a source for it.

18. The desire for a "middle landscape" was not, of course, peculiar to nineteenth-century Oregonians; see Leo Marx, *The Machine in the Garden: Technology and the Pastoral Ideal in America* (New York: Oxford University Press, 1964); and, along different lines, David Shi's splendid book *The Simple Life: Plain Living and High Thinking in American Culture* (New York: Oxford University Press, 1985).

19. See, for example, William A. Bowen, *The Willamette Valley: Migration and Settlement on the Oregon Frontier* (Seattle: University of Washington Press, 1978), 18–21.

20. The provisions of the 1844 land law enacted by the Oregon provisional government, as well as the 1850 congressional "donation" act, are recounted in ibid., 69–72. In addition, see Harlow Head, "The Oregon Donation Claims and Their Patterns" (Ph.D. diss., University of Oregon, 1971). Peter Boag, *Environment and Experience: Settlement Culture in Nineteenth-Century Oregon* (Berkeley and Los Angeles: University of California Press, 1992), offers a detailed analysis of the Calapooian settlements.

21. Ashworth, '*Agrarians' and 'Aristocrats,'* 21–34, 87–110.

22. Although otherwise full of praise, reviewers of '*Agrarians' and 'Aristocrats'* have correctly pointed out that Ashworth did not adequately relate the party ideologies of the Jacksonian era to the republican debate of the founding and early national periods; see, for example, the reviews by Harry L. Watson, *Journal of Southern History* 53 (May 1987): 330–331; and Major Wilson, *American Historical Review* 93 (October 1988): 1115–1116.

The literature on classical republicanism in its eighteenth-century American setting is voluminous. Essential early studies that have provoked and guided students for a generation are Caroline Robbins, *The Eighteenth-Century Commonwealthmen: Studies in the Transmission, Development, and Circumstances of English Liberal Thought from the Restoration of Charles II Until the War with the Thirteen Colonies* (Cambridge, Mass.: Harvard University Press, 1959); Bernard Bailyn, *The Origins of American Politics* (New York: Vintage Books, 1965); and Bailyn, *The Ideological Origins of the American Revolution* (Cambridge, Mass.: Harvard University Press, 1967). Three other studies are similarly invaluable: Gordon Wood, *The Creation of the American Republic* (New York: W. W. Norton, 1969); J. G. A. Pocock, *The Machiavellian Moment: Florentine Political Thought and the Atlantic Republican Tradition* (Princeton: Princeton University Press, 1975); and Joyce Appleby, *Capitalism and a New Social Order: The Republican Vision of the 1790s* (New York: New York University Press, 1984). For an informed and provocative critique, see Thomas Pangle, *The Spirit of Modern Republicanism: The Moral Vision of the American Founders and the Philosophy of Locke* (Chicago: University of Chicago Press,

1988). Recent writings that illustrate the importance and limitations of the concept are Appleby, "Value and Society"; and Isaac Kramnick, "The Great National Discussion: The Discourse of Politics in 1787," *William and Mary Quarterly* 45 (January 1988): 3–32. Useful guides to the literature are Robert E. Shalhope, "Republicanism and Early American Historiography," *William and Mary Quarterly* 39 (April 1982): 334–356; Shalhope's earlier "Toward a Republican Synthesis: The Emergence of an Understanding of Republicanism in American Historiography," *William and Mary Quarterly* 29 (January 1972): 49–80; and, most recently, Peter Onuf, "Reflections on the Founding: Constitutional Historiography in Bicentennial Perspective," *William and Mary Quarterly* 46 (April 1989): 341–375. Two (companion) essays that bring out the major points of difference between the "classical republican" and "liberal" syntheses are Lance Banning, "Jeffersonian Ideology Revisited: Liberal and Classical Ideas in the New American Republic," *William and Mary Quarterly* 43 (January 1986): 3–19; and Appleby, "Republicanism in Old and New Contexts." The discussion of republicanism begun by historians of the revolutionary and founding periods has been carried into the nineteenth century in, among others, Watts, *The Republic Reborn;* and Watson, *Liberty and Power;* and Barney, *Passage of the Republic.* More generally, see Dorothy Ross, "The Liberal Tradition Revisited and the Republican Traditions Addressed," in *New Directions in American Intellectual History,* ed. John Higham and Paul Conkin (Baltimore: Johns Hopkins University Press, 1979), 116–131.

23. See, among others, Michael Merrill, "Cash Is Good to Eat: Self-Sufficiency and Exchange in the Rural Economy of the United States," *Radical History Review* 4 (Winter 1977): 42–71; James Henretta, "Families and Farms: *Mentalité* in Pre-Industrial America," *William and Mary Quarterly* 35 (January 1978): 3–32; James T. Lemon, "Comment on James A. Henretta's 'Families and Farms: *Mentalité* in Pre-Industrial America,'" and Henretta's reply, *William and Mary Quarterly* 37 (October 1980): 688–696, 696–700; Lemon, "Early Americans and Their Social Environment," *Journal of Historical Geography* 6 (April 1980): 115–131; Henretta, "Wealth and Social Structure," in Greene and Pole (eds.), *Colonial British America,* 262–279 (read with Gary Nash, "Social Development," ibid., 233–261); Christopher Clark, "Household Economy, Market Exchange, and the Rise of Capitalism in the Connecticut Valley, 1800–1860," *Journal of Social History* 13 (Winter 1979): 169–189; John Mack Faragher, *Women and Men on the Overland Trail* (New Haven: Yale University Press, 1979); Faragher, *Sugar Creek;* and, generally, the essays in Hahn and Prude (eds.), *The Countryside in the Age of Capitalist Transformation.* Of particular importance, empirically as well as theoretically, is the model study by Hal Barron, *Those Who Stayed Behind.*

24. A recent study of change in the mining regions of California (from which the charter settlers of Nevada came) is Ralph Mann, *After the Gold Rush: Society in Grass Valley and Nevada City, California, 1849–1870* (Stanford: Stanford University Press, 1982).

25. *Gold Hill Evening News* (Gold Hill, Nevada), October 31, 1862.

CHAPTER ONE: POLITICS IN A DIVIDED WORLD

1. Two recent books are the starting point for any discussion of the European conquest and colonization of California: Albert Hurtado, *Indian Survival on the*

California Borderland Frontier, 1819–60 (New Haven: Yale University Press, 1988), esp. 14–25; and Douglas Monroy, *Thrown Among Strangers: The Making of Mexican Culture in Frontier California* (Berkeley and Los Angeles: University of California Press, 1990), esp. 21–23. See also Charles E. Chapman, *A History of California: The Spanish Period* (New York: Macmillan, 1921), 455–472; Hubert Howe Bancroft, *History of California*, 7 vols. (San Francisco: History Company, 1884–1890), 2:112–119. An influential discussion of the Spanish mission is Herbert Eugene Bolton, "The Mission as a Frontier Institution in the Spanish-American Colonies," *American Historical Review* 23 (October 1917): 42–61.

 2. Monroy, *Thrown Among Strangers*, chaps. 1 and 2; Sherburne F. Cook, *The Conflict Between the California Indian and White Civilization* (Berkeley and Los Angeles: University of California Press, 1976), pt. 1; George H. Phillips, "Indians and the Breakdown of the Spanish Mission System in California," *Ethnohistory* 21 (1974): 291–302. Recently, in part because of the proposed canonization of Junipero Serra, a vigorous debate has swirled around the work of Cook and those who follow him. See, on the one hand, Francis F. Guest, O.F.M., "An Examination of the Thesis of S. F. Cook on the Forced Conversion of Indians in the California Missions," *Southern California Quarterly* 61 (Spring 1979): 1–77; Guest, "Cultural Perspectives on California Mission Life," *Southern California Quarterly* 65 (Spring 1983): 1–65; Guest, "Junipero Serra and His Approach to the Indian," *Southern California Quarterly* 67 (Fall 1985): 223–261; and Clement W. Merghan, "Indians and California Missions," *Southern California Quarterly* 69 (Fall 1987): 187–201; and on the other, Rupert Costo and Jeannette Henry Costo, eds., *The Missions of California: A Legacy of Genocide* (San Francisco: Indian Historian Press, 1987).

 3. Rev. Gerald J. Geary, A.M., *The Secularization of the California Missions (1810–1840)* (Washington, D.C.: Catholic University of America, 1934), 16–17, argues, contrary to most authorities, that no time limit was placed on the missionaries. See also Chapman, *History of California*, 153; and Irving Berdine Richman, *California Under Spain and Mexico* (Boston: Houghton Mifflin, 1911), 40, 62–68.

 4. Monroy, *Thrown Among Strangers*, 260–269, discusses the myth of "California Pastoral." See also Fr. Zephyrin Engelhardt, O.F.M., *The Missions and Missionaries of Upper California*, 4 vols. (San Francisco: James H. Barry, 1908–1915), 2:599, which refers to the first decade of the nineteenth century as the "Golden Age of the California Missions"; and chapter 31 of Chapman, *History of California*, which is entitled "The Romantic Period, 1782–1810," as well as ibid., 370–375, 381–382, 386–387.

 5. Cook, *Conflict Between the California Indian and White Civilization*, 403–406, 446; James J. Rawls, *Indians of California: The Changing Image* (Norman: University of Oklahoma Press, 1984), 13–21 and passim; Bancroft, *History of California* 1:575–599; Chapman, *History of California*, 373–374; Engelhardt, *Missions and Missionaries* 2:490–491, 535–539. For additional information on the physical transformation of the missions, see Engelhardt's volumes on individual missions, for example *San Diego Mission* (San Francisco: James H. Barry, 1920), 146–147, 151; *San Luis Rey Mission* (San Francisco: James H. Barry, 1921), 35; *San Juan Capistrano Mission* (Los Angeles: n.p., 1922), 26–28; *Santa Barbara Mission* (San Francisco: James H. Barry, 1923), 60–63.

 6. C. Alan Hutchinson, "The Mexican Government and the Mission Indians

of Upper California, 1821–1835," *Americas* 21 (April 1965): 338–342; Hurtado, *Indian Survival*, 36–37; Bancroft, *History of California* 2 : 399–400.

7. See, for example, "El Interrogatoria del Año de 1812," in Francis Flores McCarthy, *The History of Mission San José California, 1797–1835* (Fresno, Calif.: Academy Library Guild, 1958), 268–276; more generally, see Monroy, *Thrown Among Strangers*, 47–49; and Hutchinson, "Mexican Government and the Mission Indians," 340–342.

8. Monroy, *Thrown Among Strangers*, 117–118. [*Dr. George Heinrich von*] *Langsdorf's Narrative of the Rezanov Voyage to Nueva California in 1806* . . . , trans. Thomas C. Russell (San Francisco: privately published, 1927), 50–54, describes Mission Santa Clara de Asís. Secondary accounts with respect to this question include Engelhardt, *Missions and Missionaries of Upper California* 3 : 77–78, which details mission production as of 1819. Theodore H. Hittell, *History of California*, 4 vols. (San Francisco: N. J. Stone, 1885–1898), 2 : 514–528, evaluates the "character of the missionaries" through an examination of the eighteenth- and nineteenth-century accounts of La Perousse (1786), Vancouver (1792–1794), Galiano (1792), Valdez (1792), Robinson (1829), Dana (1840), and Du Mofras (1841). Richman, *California Under Spain and Mexico*, chap. 9 passim (also 466 n.34), discusses related topics: rising Indian resistance to missionization (219–222); missionary opposition to secularization (222); and charges that missionaries abrogated their vows of poverty (222–224). In 1806, for example, Guardian José Gasol wrote to California missionaries: "The office that you exercise does not excuse you from the extreme poverty that we profess. Consequently the use of silver watches and other valuable jewelry is prohibited. . . . I advise that those who have silver watches, or other jewelry of value for personal use, send them immediately to the Father President [for sale]" (ibid., 222–223). Similarly, in 1817 Prefect Sarría wrote: "You should realize that it is edifying for a missionary to appear in the greatest simplicity, and so the world is caused to understand that the interest we take in things of the Mission is not personal, but that of our savior Jesus Christ in the poverty-stricken, as are the neo-fites. It sounded ill to me, as to others, to hear that carriages had arrived . . . , and I wish you would abstain absolutely from taking them. I might go into detail concerning fine hats, costly chests, *etc.*, but enough" (ibid., 223). Geary, *Secularization of the California Missions*, 63, counters charges that Franciscan missionaries became reluctant to lose the material rewards of their posts. A general discussion of the path to secularization is in Manuel P. Servín, "The Secularization of the California Missions: A Reappraisal," *Southern California Quarterly* 47 (June 1965): 133–149.

9. The demography of the California Indians is examined in detail in Cook, *Conflict Between the California Indian and White Civilization*, pt. 1. Rawls, *Indians of California*, 18, estimates the decline of the Indian population in the areas affected by the missions at 75 percent. See also Monroy, *Thrown Among Strangers*, 79–91; Engelhardt, *Missions and Missionaries of Upper California* 2 : 608–610, for evidence of missionaries' concern over the Indian death rate as early as 1804. An important discussion of the controversy over Cook's estimates is in Hurtado, *Indian Survival*, 2–4.

10. Cook, *Conflict Between the California Indian and White Civilization*, 11–12, 400–446.

11. Ibid., 220–250, 425–426; Monroy, *Thrown Among Strangers*, 86–90; Hurtado, *Indian Survival*, 31–39; *Langsdorf's Narrative*, 47–49, 66–67; Richman, *California Under Spain and Mexico*, 177. Engelhardt, *Missions and Missionaries of Upper California* 2:490–491 and passim, describes missionary "exploring expedition[s]" in search of "savages not yet brought under the influence of the Cross." Desertions from the missions rose from 1,263 between 1796 and 1805, to 1,927 between 1806 and 1815, 2,954 between 1816 and 1825, and almost 9,000 between 1826 and 1834.

12. Monroy, *Thrown Among Strangers*, 121–127; Rawls, *Indians of California*, 19–20; Richman, *California Under Spain and Mexico*, chaps. 12–14; Chapman, *History of California*, 466–472.

13. Monroy, *Thrown Among Strangers*, 169–173. The classic Anglo-American account of this trade is Richard Henry Dana, *Two Years Before the Mast* (1840; reprint, New York: Penguin Books, 1981). See also William Dane Phelps, *Alta California, 1840–1842: The Journal and Observations of William Dane Phelps, Master of the Ship Alert*, ed. Briton Cooper Busch (Glendale, Calif.: Arthur H. Clark, 1983), 19–27; and Bancroft, *History of California* 3:116–140, 363–381; 4:79–106, 206–211.

14. Monroy, *Thrown Among Strangers*, 121–127, 135–136; Leonard Pitt, *The Decline of the Californios: A Social History of the Spanish-speaking Californians, 1846–1890* (Berkeley and Los Angeles: University of California Press, 1971), 7–11; Albert Camarillo, *Chicanos in a Changing Society: From Mexican Pueblos to American Barrios in Santa Barbara and Southern California, 1848–1930* (Cambridge, Mass.: Harvard University Press, 1979), 10–14; Richman, *California Under Spain and Mexico*, chaps. 12–14. An important episode in this conflict is covered in C. Alan Hutchinson, *Frontier Settlement in Mexican California* (New Haven: Yale University Press, 1969).

15. Politics of provincial California are covered in Bancroft, *History of California*, vols. 3, chaps. 2, 3, 7, 8, 9, 10, 15–20; and 4, chaps. 1, 4, 7, 11, 14, 17, 20–22. Hutchinson, *Frontier Settlement in California*, 142–180, covers the conflict between ambitious locals and the Hijar-Padres colonists from Mexico. More generally, Richard Griswold del Castillo, *The Los Angeles Barrio, 1850–1890: A Social History* (Berkeley and Los Angeles: University of California Press, 1979), 19–20, emphasizes the function of social-political conflict in affirming communal life in Mexican California, as does Monroy, *Thrown Among Strangers*, 175–177. Other discussions of provincial politics are in Pitt, *Decline of the Californios*, 7–11; Richman, *California Under Spain and Mexico*, 229; and Chapman, *History of California*, 455–477.

16. Chapman, *History of California*, 473–484; Richman, *California Under Spain and Mexico*, 257; Hittell, *History of California* 2:228–235.

17. Geary, *Secularization of the California Missions*, chap. 5; Rawls, *Indians of California*, 19–21; Bancroft, *History of California* 3:339–356; Hittell, *History of California* 2:295–306, 379–383.

18. David Hornbeck, "Land Tenure and Rancho Expansion in Alta California, 1784–1846," *Journal of Historical Geography* 4 (1978): 371–390; Richman, *California Under Spain and Mexico*, 346–349.

19. Monroy, *Thrown Among Strangers*, 134–154, convincingly portrays the social order constructed during the Californio regime as a "seigneurial society."

See also Pitt, *Decline of the Californios*, 1–25; Camarillo, *Chicanos in a Changing Society*, 6–13; and Griswold del Castillo, *Los Angeles Barrio*, 7–25.

20. American interest in California, along with the reports that encouraged it, is discussed in Norman A. Graebner, *Empire on the Pacific: A Study in Continental Expansion* (New York: Ronald Press, 1955), 51–64, 83–89.

21. Hurtado, *Indian Survival*, 72–77. For contemporary examples, see Dana, *Two Years Before the Mast*, 171–177; George Simpson, *Narrative of a Voyage to California Ports in 1841–42* (San Francisco: T. C. Russell, 1930), 75; Zenas Leonard, *Narrative of the Adventures of Zenas Leonard* (Clearfield, Penn.: D. W. Moore, 1839), 48–50; John Charles Frémont, *Report of the Exploring Expedition to the Rocky Mountains in the Year 1842, and to Oregon and California in the Years 1843–45* (Buffalo, N.Y.: Derby, 1851). Between 1843 and 1845, Thomas Larkin "became a one man chamber of correspondence for California" in letters to the *New York Herald* and *Journal of Commerce* (Graebner, *Empire on the Pacific*, 51–52). The vast majority of overland migrants before 1849 had Oregon, not California, as their destination; according to John D. Unruh, Jr., *The Plains Across: The Overland Emigrants and the Trans-Mississippi West, 1840–1860* (Urbana: University of Illinois Press, 1979), 119, of the 5,397 people who emigrated to the Pacific Coast between 1840 and 1846, only 1,885 (23 percent) went to California.

22. Bancroft, *History of California* 5:524; Woodrow James Hansen, *The Search for Authority in California* (Oakland, Calif.: Biobooks, 1960), 54.

23. Griswold del Castillo, *Los Angeles Barrio*, 22–23; Pitt, *Decline of the Californios*, 18–19; Bancroft, *History of California* 4:115–116; Hornbeck, "Land Tenure and Rancho Expansion," 388.

24. Hittell, *History of California* 2:275–284. Richman, *California Under Spain and Mexico*, chap. 14, divides the Anglo-Americans into "loyal" and "disloyal" classes. In 1840, Hispanic Californians' suspicion of Anglo-Americans filtering into the province resulted in the "Graham Affair." Trapper Isaac Graham, a shadowy figure who had briefly allied himself with Alvarado during the latter's intrigue against the Mexican governor, was arrested, charged with plotting insurrection, and shipped to Mexico to stand trial. Under pressure from the United States, he was eventually released and returned to California. See Hittell, *History of California* 2:267–274.

25. Monroy, *Thrown Among Strangers*, 163, 165; see also the commentary in Thomas Larkin, *The Larkin Papers*, ed. George P. Hammond, 11 vols. (Berkeley and Los Angeles: University of California Press, 1951–1968), 4:322–334.

26. Pitt, *Decline of the Californios*, 19.

27. Griswold del Castillo, *Los Angeles Barrio*, 23–24, makes a similar comparison between American settlers in the Hispanic communities and those in the interior.

28. The following account of military affairs surrounding the American conquest of California is based on Neal Harlow, *California Conquered: War and Peace on the Pacific, 1846–1850* (Berkeley and Los Angeles: University of California Press, 1982), which updates and supersedes much of the material in Bancroft, *History of California*, vol. 5, chaps. 4–19. See also (on Frémont) William Goetzmann, *Exploration and Empire: The Explorer and the Scientist in the Winning of the American West* (New York: Random House, 1966), 240–250; and Richman, *California Under Spain and Mexico*, 305–310.

29. Harlow, *California Conquered*, 78, 82–85, examines Frémont's claims about instructions from Buchanan. The Bear Flag affair is covered in ibid., 95–114; and John A. Hawgood, "John C. Frémont and the Bear Flag Revolution: A Reappraisal," *Southern California Quarterly* 49 (June 1962): 67–96. On the nominal leader of the Bear Flag filibusterers, see Simeon Ide, *A Biographical Sketch of the Life of William B. Ide . . .* (Claremont, N.H.: Simeon Ide, 1880).

30. Harlow, *California Conquered*, 137–232.

31. Theodore Grivas, *Military Governments in California, 1846–1850* (Glendale, Calif.: Arthur H. Clark, 1963), 79–120.

32. Pitt, *Decline of the Californios*, 38. The majority of gubernatorial appointments (47 of 68, or 78 percent) made by American military governors from Stockton to Riley went to non-Hispanics. There was, however, a regional pattern to the appointments. In the southern districts, Hispanics received ten of nineteen appointments, or 53 percent. These figures are compiled from the appointments listed in the "Letter Books of the Governor and Secretary of State of California," March 1, 1847, to March 9, 1848; March 10, 1848, to August 1, 1848; and August 1, 1848, to September 23, 1848; microfilm, Record Group 94, Records of the Adjutant General's Office, National Archives, Washington, D.C.

33. Donald C. Biggs, *Conquer and Colonize: Stevenson's Regiment and California* (San Rafael, Calif.: Presidio Press, 1977), 29–30; Bancroft, *History of California* 5:524–530, 554–557. The estimate of overland migrants is from Unruh, *Plains Across*, 119.

34. *California Star* (Monterey), March 27, 1847.

35. Ibid., January 22, 1848.

36. Grivas, *Military Governments in California*, 151–157; Hittell, *History of California* 2:656–657.

37. *Californian* (San Francisco), July 17, 1847.

38. *California Star*, January 23, 1847.

39. Walter Colton, *Three Years in California* (1850; reprint, Stanford: Stanford University Press, 1949), 55.

40. On the controversial nature of this proclamation, and its repeal, see Grivas, *Military Governments in California*, 170–185; *Memoirs of General W. T. Sherman, Written by Himself*, vol. 1 (New York: D. Appleton, 1875), 30, 34, 37; Hittell, *History of California* 2:657–661.

41. See, for example, Mason to General R. Jones, August 19, 1848, in U.S. President (Zachary Taylor), *Message Transmitting Information in Answer to a Resolution from the House, December 31, 1849, on the Subject of California and New Mexico*, 31st Cong., 1st sess., House Executive Document 17 (Washington, D.C.: Government Printing Office, 1850), 597 (hereafter cited as *California Message and Correspondence*).

42. Mason to Jones, November 24, 1848, in ibid., 649.

43. Mason to Jones, August 17, 1848, in ibid., 533.

44. Roger Lotchin, *San Francisco, 1846–1856: From Hamlet to City* (New York: Oxford University Press, 1974), 100–102. The term *instant city* is taken from Gunther Barth, *Instant Cities: Urbanization and the Rise of San Francisco and Denver* (New York: Oxford University Press, 1975).

45. Quoted in Lotchin, *San Francisco*, xix.

46. *Daily Picayune* (New Orleans), October 6, 1849.

47. Peter Decker, *Fortunes and Failures: White-Collar Social Mobility in Nineteenth-Century San Francisco* (Cambridge, Mass.: Harvard University Press, 1978), 28–31.

48. Rodman Paul, *Mining Frontiers of the Far West* (New York: Holt, Rinehart & Winston, 1963), 22–27; Charles Shinn, *Mining Camps: A Study in American Frontier Government* (1884; reprint, Gloucester, Mass.: Peter Smith, 1965), 110–122 and passim; David A. Johnson, "Vigilance and the Law: The Moral Authority of Popular Justice in the Far West," *American Quarterly* 33 (Winter 1981): 558–586.

49. Bayard Taylor, *Eldorado, or Adventures in the Path of Empire* (1850; reprint, New York: Alfred A. Knopf, 1949), 76.

50. *Daily Picayune*, August 5, 1849.

51. Quoted in Louis Wright, *Life on the American Frontier* (New York: Harper & Row, 1971), 177–178. See also "Sacramento City," *Placer Times* (Sacramento), May 5, 1849, 2; and *Daily Picayune*, October 9, 1849. A description of Sacramento in the *Alta California* (San Francisco), November 8, 1849, remarked at its growth: "This city of Sacramento, next to San Francisco, is the greatest specimen of the advance of California, I have yet seen. Less than one year ago on the very site where I write, I pitched my tent and cooked my food a la Robinson Crusoe. Now there are large hotels, restaurants, iron and wooden warehouses, great piles of provisions and merchandise, pack animals and trains of loaded wagons to be seen in every direction; and away out among the trees, where hunters used to kill deer and rabbits, you can see the long lines of buildings which mark the different streets. The whole town is like a vast hive, alive and crowded with an active, enterprising and industrious population."

52. Peter H. Burnett, *An Old California Pioneer* (Oakland, Calif.: Biobooks, 1946), 175.

53. *Alta California*, January 25, 1849.

54. *California Star and Californian* (San Francisco), December 23, 1848.

55. *Alta California*, March 29, 1849; Bancroft, *History of California* 6:210–212; Hubert Howe Bancroft, *Popular Tribunals*, 2 vols. (San Francisco: History Company, 1887), 1:76–102; Hittell, *History of California* 2:724–727.

56. J. Ross Browne, *Report of the Debates in the Convention of California on the Formation of the State Constitution in September and October, 1849* (Washington, D.C.: John T. Towers, 1850), app. xvi.

57. *Alta California*, January 4, 1849.

58. On the Sonoma district legislature, see *Alta California*, February 15 and March 1, 1849; on that of Sacramento, *Placer Times*, May 5, 1949; and on that of San Francisco, *Alta California*, February 15, 22, 1849, and passim.

59. Quoted in *Alta California*, April 9, 1849; see also the issues of June 20 and July 12, 26, 1849.

60. *California Star and Californian*, December 2, 1848. See also *Alta California*, January 4, 25; February 1, 22; March 1, 22; April 24, 26; May 3; and June 14, 1849; Bancroft, *History of California* 6:268–274.

61. See, for example, *Alta California*, June 14, 1849.

62. Ibid., March 15, 1849.

63. Riley explained his action in a June 30, 1849, letter to General R. Jones,

Adjutant and General of the Army, in *California Message and Correspondence,* 748–750.

64. Ibid., 777–778.

65. *Alta California,* June 14, 1849.

66. Ibid.

67. Ibid., June 20, 1849.

68. In addition to the six native Californians, I have included in this tally three men—José Maria Covarrubias, Miguel de Pedrorena, and Pedro Sansevaine—who, although foreign born, considered themselves Californios (see appendix 1A). Regarding San Diego, the convention investigated charges that the military had rigged the district's election; its delegation consisted of Henry Hill (a military officer who listed his address as Monterey) and Miguel de Pedrorena, a ranchero. See the report of Henry Tefft on the San Diego delegation, Working Papers of the California Constitutional Convention, 1849, California State Archives, Sacramento, California.

69. "Stephen Clark Foster's Ride to the Convention," in Henry D. Barrows, *A Memorial and Biographical History of the Coast Counties of Central California* (Chicago: Lewis, 1893), 4; typescript in the collection of Colton Hall Museum, Monterey, California.

70. *Alta California,* August 16, 1849.

71. Hansen, *Search for Authority in California,* 98–99; see also Myrtle M. McKittrick, *Vallejo, Son of California* (Portland: Binford & Mort, 1944), 289–290; and *Alta California,* February 15, 1849.

72. *Alta California,* August 2, 1849.

73. See the reports of Durivage and Freaner in the *Daily Picayune,* September 18, 22, 1849.

74. Quoted in *Alta California,* July 2, 1849.

75. Ibid.

76. See, for example, ibid., February 2, 15, 22 and March 22, 1849.

77. James McHall Jones to his mother, August 26, 1849; T. W. Norris Collection, Bancroft Library, Berkeley, California.

78. Ibid., October 1, 1849.

79. *Daily Picayune,* October 13, 1849.

80. E. Gould Buffum, *Six Months in the Gold Mines* (Philadelphia: Lea & Blanchard, 1850), 139–141.

81. Colton, *Three Years in California,* 41–48, 75–76, 195–197, 234–237, 249–250.

82. Sherman, *Memoirs,* 29; William Robert Garner, *Letters from California from Our Special Correspondent, William Robert Garner,* ed. Donald Munro Craig (Berkeley and Los Angeles: University of California Press, 1970), 179–180, 202–203.

83. Craig (ed.), *Letters from California,* 193.

84. John Frost, *History of the State of California . . .* (Auburn, N.Y.: Derby & Miller, 1850), 104.

85. Craig (ed.), *Letters from California,* 179–180.

86. The following discussion of Monterey in 1836 is based on "Padron general que manifiesta el numero de havitantes que ecsisten en la municipalidad de Monterrey, 1836" (ms., Bancroft Library, University of California, Berkeley;

diacritics lacking in the original). I am indebted to Professor David Hornbeck of California State University, Northridge, for providing me with a photocopy of this document.

87. The following description of Monterey at the time of the constitutional convention is drawn from the *Seventh Manuscript Federal Census, 1850*, Schedule of Population, California, Monterey County (National Archives microfilm #35); Mary Tucey and David Hornbeck, "Anglo Immigration and the Hispanic Town: A Study of Urban Change in Monterey, California, 1835–1850," *Social Science Journal* 13 (April 1976): 1–7; and David Hornbeck and Mary Tucey, "The Submergence of a People: Migration and Occupational Structure in California, 1850," *Pacific Historical Review* 46 (1977): 471–484.

88. Tucey and Hornbeck, "Anglo Immigration and the Hispanic Town," 6–7.

89. For California generally, see Camarillo, *Chicanos in a Changing Society*, esp. chaps. 1–5; and Hornbeck and Tucey, "Submergence of a People," 471–484.

90. Frost, *History of the State of California*, 104.

91. *Daily Picayune*, October 13, 1849.

92. Taylor, *Eldorado*, 102.

93. Frost, *History of the State of California*, 105.

94. Taylor, *Eldorado*, 103–104.

95. Augusta Fink, *Monterey County: The Dramatic Story of Its Past* (Santa Cruz, Calif.: Western Tanager Press, 1982), 114–117. See also (delegate) Henry Tefft to Guillermo Dana, September 7, 1849; copy in the collection of Colton Hall Museum, Monterey, California.

96. Elisha Oscar Crosby, "Address to the Alameda Parlor of the Native Sons of the Golden West," July 11, 1887; typescript, California Historical Society, San Francisco.

97. Fink, *Monterey County*, 118. There is some question as to whether the Frémonts were in Monterey at the time of the convention. Elisha Crosby, in his reminiscences, declares emphatically that they were not. Jessie Frémont, in *A Year of American Travel* (New York: Harper & Bros., 1878), 140–151, claimed to have played a role in the convention's decision to outlaw slavery, which apparently led to Crosby's denunciation of her and his declaration that neither she nor her husband was in the town during the convention. Crosby's claim is accepted by Charles Albro Barker, the editor of Crosby's memoirs; see *Memoirs of Elisha Oscar Crosby: Reminiscences of California and Guatemala from 1849 to 1864*, ed. Charles Albro Barker (San Marino, Calif.: Huntington Library, 1945), 35–36 and n. 20. However, the Frémonts' departure from San Francisco for Monterey is mentioned in a June 20, 1849, letter quoted in John Francis McDermott, "Two Fourgeaud Letters," *California Historical Society Quarterly* 20 (June 1941): 123. Moreover, John Durivage, who reported on the convention to readers in the New Orleans *Daily Picayune*, noted the Frémonts' presence in Monterey (*Daily Picayune*, September 28, 1849); as did Lottie Wescott, who wrote her sister from Monterey during the convention; see Miriam Drury, "The Jeffers-Willey Wedding," *California Historical Society Quarterly* 35 (March 1956): 11–21.

98. *Daily Picayune*, November 13, 1849.

99. James McHall Jones to his mother, October 1, 1849.

100. Barker (ed.), *Memoirs of Elisha Oscar Crosby*, 40.

101. Ibid., 41.

102. Browne, *Report of the Debates*, 18.

CHAPTER TWO: FARMING AND POLITICS

1. The familial character of the overland migration to the Oregon Country is covered in William A. Bowen, *The Willamette Valley: Migration and Settlement on the Oregon Frontier* (Seattle: University of Washington, 1978), chaps. 1 and 2; and John Faragher, *Women and Men on the Overland Trail* (New Haven: Yale University Press, 1979), 18–20 and passim.

2. Delegates George Williams, Matthew Deady, and Cyrus Olney sat on the territorial supreme court. Reuben Boise received his commission as a justice of the same court shortly after the close of the convention. Boise, Hector Campbell, John Crooks, Thomas Dryer, Luther Elkins, La Fayette Grover, Isaac Moores, J. C. Peebles, Levi Scott, Robert Short, Delazon Smith, William Starkweather, and Frederick Waymire had served in the territorial legislature. William Farrar was the U.S. district attorney; Stephen Chadwick, the assistant U.S. district attorney; Paine Page Prim was prosecuting attorney for southern Oregon; John Watts, receiver for the Public Land Office in Oregon City; Erasmus Shattuck, probate judge for Multnomah County; La Fayette Grover had been the territorial district attorney and U.S. auditor for claims made during the Indian wars of 1855–1856. Jesse Applegate had played an important role in the establishment of Oregon's provisional government in 1843. Lists of local, territorial, and national officers are found in Hubert Howe Bancroft, *History of Oregon*, 2 vols. (San Francisco: History Company, 1888), vols. 1 and 2, passim; Howard McKinley Corning, *Dictionary of Oregon History* (Portland: Binford & Mort, 1956); Charles Henry Carey, *The Oregon Constitution and Proceedings and Debates of the Constitutional Convention of 1857* (Salem, Oreg.: State Printing Department, 1926). In addition, see the sources cited in chapter 5 below.

3. *Sacramento Daily Union*, August 27, 1857.

4. In 1841 Captain John Wilkes estimated the white population of Oregon at 700 to 800, about 150 of whom were Americans; see Samuel N. Dicken and Emily F. Dicken, *The Making of Oregon: A Study in Historical Geography* (Portland: Oregon Historical Society, 1979), 65. The provisional government census of 1845 placed the population at 2,110; and territorial censuses for 1849 and 1850 placed it, respectively, at 8,770, and 13,294; see Bowen, *Willamette Valley*, 14, 55.

5. Bowen, *Willamette Valley*, 69–71. The inspiration for the land laws of the provisional government is generally considered to be the Oregon donation land bills introduced by Missouri senator Lewis F. Linn, which (although they did not pass Congress) would similarly have allowed settlers to claim a section of land. Roy M. Robbins, *Our Landed Heritage: The Public Domain, 1776–1970*, 2d ed. (Lincoln: University of Nebraska Press, 1976), 72–91 (describing preemption), 153–154 (background to the Oregon land laws).

6. Ibid., 18.

7. Quoted in Dorothy O. Johansen, "The Land Base of Oregon's Economy," *Genealogical Material in Oregon Donation Land Claims*, vol. 2 (Portland: Genealogical Forum of Portland, Oregon, 1959), 1. The full historical significance of the

Donation Land Law has yet to be fully evaluated. An introduction to the law and the claims is Harlow Z. Head, "The Oregon Donation Claims and Their Patterns" (Ph.D. diss., University of Oregon, 1971).

8. Ruth Rockwood, ed., "Diary of Rev. George H. Atkinson, D.D., 1847–58, Pt. 4," *Oregon Historical Society Quarterly* 60 (December 1939): 361.

9. Bowen, *Willamette Valley*, 14.

10. Arthur L. Throckmorton, *Oregon Argonauts: Merchant Adventurers on the Western Frontier* (Portland: Oregon Historical Society, 1961), 88.

11. The Oregon merchants, according to Throckmorton (ibid., 115), sought "a competence" and "preferred a location in an agricultural area."

12. George Abernethy, quoted in ibid., 101. See, generally, ibid., 87–106; and James Henry Gilbert, *Trade and Currency in Early Oregon: A Study in the Commercial and Monetary History of the Pacific Northwest* (1907; reprint, New York: AMS Press, 1967), 73–77.

13. Gilbert, *Trade and Currency in Early Oregon*, 91–94; Throckmorton, *Oregon Argonauts*, 107–123.

14. Bowen, *Willamette Valley*, 73–94. Well into the 1850s, Throckmorton (*Oregon Argonauts*, 161) observes, "wheat farming in Oregon . . . was still handicapped by the laborious use of scythe and cradle."

15. Quoted in Throckmorton, *Oregon Argonauts*, 161. In 1865, E. L. Applegate, the surveyor-general for Oregon (and himself a recipient of a donation land claim), decried the effects on the industry of farmers and, in turn, Oregon as a whole: "A heavy proportion of the articles necessary to his [the farmer's] comfort or taste have not been manufactured or produced in the country, because the interests of the farm have been neglected; and instead of applying his means to its improvement and the increase of its productions, supplying the demands of home consumption, furnishing a surplus for other markets and offering a guarantee of such supplies to the manufacturer to come to the country and keep its wealth here and build it up, the farmer, when opportunity has offered, has too often pursued the unwise policy of still further extending his already too expansive acres. Thus a man deprives the country of a dozen valuable farmers, and the hundred villagers whom they would supply for their handiwork. . . . And having so many hundred acres more than he can cultivate, he comparatively cultivates none; hence it is no evidence to the world of natural poverty, that Oregon has permitted California to sell hay, flour, and other produce in the streets of her chief emporium." Another commentator in the 1860s, John Mullen, reached similar conclusions after traveling through the Willamette Valley: "In passing through this rich and exuberant country," he reported, "I could not but regret that the donation law that first opened homes to the first settlers of Oregon was as generous as it was in the largeness of its grant—six hundred and forty acres, in other words, was too large a grant for the full and truly healthy growth of any new country . . . [and] I verily believe that one half the grant would have brought as many settlers as double the amount has done. The true index, doubtless, of the prosperity of a country might be regarded the ration of its population to the square mile; but when we find only one settler to the square mile, the country, from necessity, must be sparsely populated; and this condition must hold for so long a period that detriment in a large scale must be felt" (both

quotations are from Head, "Oregon Donation Claims and Their Patterns," 162–163).

16. Quoted in Throckmorton, *Oregon Argonauts*, 211. Elsewhere (160), Throckmorton describes as "strange" the failure of Oregon farmers in 1851 and 1852 to produce more flour than they did, given the high prices paid for it in San Francisco. In 1853, flour, ham, butter, beans, and pork were imported into the territory (ibid., 167).

17. [Samuel Thurston], "Oregon, Its Climate, Soil, Productions, etc.," *Stryker's American Register* 4 (July 1850): 210, 214–215, 222.

18. Earl Pomeroy, "Carpet-Baggers in the Territories, 1861–1890," *The Historian* 2 (November 1939): 53–64.

19. James E. Hendrickson, *Joe Lane of Oregon: Machine Politics and the Sectional Crisis, 1849–1861* (New Haven: Yale University Press, 1967), 2. William E. Wilson, *Indiana, a History* (Bloomington: Indiana University Press, 1966), 132, notes that the men he led in the Mexican War knew him as "Old Rough and Ready No. 2."

20. Lane's message to the territorial legislature is found in the *Oregon Spectator* (Oregon City), October 4, 1849. His role in the execution of the Indian scapegoats for the deaths of the Whitmans and the effects of the Indian execution within the settler population are covered in Hendrickson, *Joe Lane*, 12, 14–17.

21. Lane's margin was 2,375 to 543 (*Oregon Statesman*, July 4, 1851). The *Oregon Statesman's* place of publication moved with the territorial capital throughout the 1850s. From March 28, 1851, to June 4, 1852, Asahel Bush published the paper in Oregon City; on June 11, 1852, he moved it to Salem; on April 14, 1855, to Corvallis; and on December 15, 1855, back to Salem.

22. Bancroft, *History of Oregon* 1 : 155–156.

23. The standard biography of Lee is Cornelius J. Brosnan, *Jason Lee: Prophet of Oregon* (New York: Macmillan, 1932); the following account of the Lee mission is derived from Robert J. Loewenberg, *Equality on the Oregon Frontier: Jason Lee and the Methodist Mission, 1834–1843* (Seattle: University of Washington Press, 1976), esp. chaps. 3, 6, and 7.

24. On the Hudson's Bay Company, see John S. Galbraith, *The Hudson's Bay Company as an Imperial Factor, 1821–1869* (Berkeley and Los Angeles: University of California Press, 1957). Its role in the settlement of the Oregon Country is covered from different perspectives in Hubert Howe Bancroft, *History of the Northwest Coast*, 2 vols. (San Francisco: History Company, 1884), vol. 2, chaps. 14, 18, 20, and 22; Throckmorton, *Oregon Argonauts*, 3–13; Gordon B. Dodds, *Oregon, a History* (New York: W. W. Norton, 1977), 48–89 and passim; Loewenberg, *Equality on the Oregon Frontier*, 14–35; and Kent D. Richards, "Growth and Development of Government in the Far West: The Oregon Provisional Government, Jefferson Territory, Provisional and Territorial Nevada" (Ph.D. diss., University of Wisconsin, 1966), 30–32.

According to Robert Loewenberg's careful reconstruction of Lee's politics, two early events galvanized Lee's opposition to the Hudson's Bay Company: the first concerned Lee's failure (and McLoughlin's success) in stopping the construction of a distillery in the Willamette Valley; the second was the arrival, with

McLoughlin's blessing, of Catholic missionaries in 1838; see Loewenberg, *Equality on the Oregon Frontier*, 96–98, 146–152, 169–177. On the latter topic, see also Sister Letitia Mary Lyons, *Norbert Blanchet and the Founding of the Oregon Missions (1838–1848)* (Washington, D.C.: Catholic University of America Press, 1940).

25. Priscilla Knuth, "Nativism in Oregon" (B.A. thesis, Reed College, 1945), chap. 2; Loewenberg, *Equality on the Oregon Frontier*, 77, 180, 188–192.

26. Loewenberg, *Equality on the Oregon Frontier*, 192, 204–205.

27. For different views on the creation of Oregon's provisional government, see Robert J. Loewenberg, "Creating a Provisional Government in Oregon: A Revision," *Pacific Northwest Quarterly* 68 (January 1977): 13–24; and Loewenberg, *Equality on the Oregon Frontier*, 140–168, 195–228; contrast with Richards, "Growth and Development of Government in the Far West," 38–41, 56–64.

28. Brosnan, *Jason Lee*, 228–275, esp. 246–268; Richards, "Growth and Development of Government in the Far West," 79–80.

29. Lewis Hubbell Judson, "Sketches of Salem . . . ," *Marion County Historical Society* 2 (June 1956): 47 (reprinted from J. Henry Browne, *1871 Salem Directory*); Richards, "Growth and Development of Government in the Far West," 80–81; Bancroft, *History of Oregon* 1:221–224; Throckmorton, *Oregon Argonauts*, 50.

30. Loewenberg (*Equality on the Oregon Frontier*, 155n) prefers "Methodist party," noting that the period of Methodist participation in provincial politics antedated the death of Lee and the closing of the Oregon mission.

31. Quoted in Richards, "Growth and Development of Government in the Far West," 82. See, more generally, ibid., 82–85; *Oregon Spectator*, June 25, 1846.

32. Knuth, "Nativism in Oregon," 34–37, 40–44.

33. Gilbert, *Trade and Currency in Early Oregon*, 88–89.

34. Exactly who nominated Willson, and why, is not known. The only surviving notice of his candidacy is a one-sentence report that "citizens of Marion County" had nominated him; *Oregon Spectator*, May 22, 1851.

35. Biographical details on Willson's life are fragmentary; see Malcolm Clark, *Eden Seekers: The Settlement of Oregon, 1818–1862* (Boston: Houghton Mifflin, 1981), 240; Knuth, "Nativism in Oregon," 53–54; Caroline C. Dobbs, *Men of Champoeg: A Record of the Lives of the Pioneers Who Founded the Oregon Government* (Portland: Metropolitan Press, 1932), 56–59. Willson was nominated for the territorial council by the Marion County Temperance Convention in 1854 (*Oregon Spectator*, May 12, 1854), and his signature on the "Subscribers Pledge" of the Washingtonian Society is found in MS. 932, Oregon Historical Society, Portland, Oregon.

36. *Oregon Statesman*, June 13, 1851.

37. Thurston's role in the founding of the *Oregon Statesman* is evident in his letters to Asahel Bush, a typescript copy of which is held by the Bush House Museum, Salem, Oregon; see the letters of July 27 and 28, August 11, September 3, November 30, 1850; January 27, February 9 and 10, 1851.

38. Despite an excellent manuscript collection detailing his activities, Bush's biography is yet to be written; see George S. Turnbull, *History of Oregon Newspapers* (Portland: Binford & Mort, 1939), 74–81; Sidney Teiser, "Reuben P. Boise, Last Associate Justice of the Oregon Territory Supreme Court," *Oregon*

Historical Quarterly 66 (March 1965): 1; James O'Meara, "Constitutional Convention," *Oregonian* (Portland), November 2, 1890; John McBride, "Annual Address," *Transactions of the Oregon Pioneer Association* (Portland: Oregon Pioneer Association, 1897); Hendrickson, *Joe Lane*, 27–28.

39. To bolster his position, Gaines sought and received opinions in support of his veto from the appointed (Whig) majority in the territorial supreme court and from (Whig) U.S. Attorney General John J. Crittenden. Far from ending the matter, however, this show of support from Whigs in Oregon and Washington, D.C., only gave the capital question an increasingly partisan cast. See Walter Carleton Woodward, "Rise and Early History of Political Parties in Oregon, Pt. 2," *Oregon Historical Society Quarterly* 12 (March 1911): 38; Bancroft, *History of Oregon* 2 : 147.

40. Quoted in Charles Henry Carey, *A General History of Oregon* (Portland: Metropolitan Press, 1935), 498.

41. See, for example, *Oregon Statesman*, June 13, August 5, 1851.

42. Woodward, "Rise and Early History of Political Parties in Oregon, Pt. 2," 44–46.

43. *Oregonian*, December 4, 1850; see also the *Oregon Statesman*, April 4, 1851. The title of the *Oregonian* newspaper in Portland changed a number of times in the 1850s and 1860s. At its inauguration on December 4, 1850, it was known as the *Oregonian;* beginning February 4, 1854, the name shifted to the *Weekly Oregonian.* On February 4, 1861, it became a daily paper called the *Morning Oregonian.* Editorially these were the same newspaper, and for the sake of simplicity I refer throughout to the *Oregonian.*

44. *Oregonian*, August 9, 1851.

45. Ibid., December 20, 1851.

46. *Treason, Stratagems, and Spoils* was published in the February 7, 14, and 21 and March 6 and 13, 1851, issues of the *Oregonian;* in April 1852 it was reissued in pamphlet form. The following citations are from William L. Adams, *A Melodrama Entitled "Treason, Stratagems, and Spoils,"* ed. George N. Belknap, (New Haven, Conn.: Archon Books, 1968).

47. This is the dominant theme of act 2; see ibid., 29–30, 69–87.

48. Ibid., 59.

49. An evaluation of *TS&S* is in ibid., 1–47. On the "Oregon style" of journalism, see Turnbull, *History of Oregon Newspapers*, 81–85.

50. Bush-favored candidates, called "regular Democrats" in the *Oregon Statesman,* swept the farming counties of the mid–Willamette Valley, giving the clique a two-to-one margin in the legislature. In the trading centers near the newly discovered mines in southern Oregon, along the coast, and surrounding Portland, fusion tickets composed of Whigs and disaffected, or "independent," Democrats prevailed. For the voting results, see the *Oregonian*, June 12, 1852.

51. *Oregon Statesman*, February 24, 1852; O'Meara, "Constitutional Convention."

52. Dryer first used the label in the *Oregonian*, March 13, 1852.

53. The figures are from *Eighth Census of the United States, 1860*, 3 vols. (Washington, D.C., 1864–1865): Population, 400–405; Agriculture, 120–121; Manufactures, 490–492. These counties held 55 percent of the state population, 79 percent of the improved acreage, 64 percent of total farm land valuation,

67 percent of the value of agricultural equipment and machinery, 62 percent of the stock valuation, 60 percent of real property valuation, and 56 percent of personal property valuation. Their share of manufacturing establishments and value of manufactures was, respectively, 42 percent and 43 percent, which indicates the prominence, in this regard, of Multnomah (Portland) and Clackamas (Oregon City) counties.

54. Michael Holt, *The Political Crisis of the 1850s* (New York: John Wiley, 1978), 33.

55. Three historians who have traced classical republican traditions into nineteenth-century politics are John Ashworth, *'Agrarians' and 'Aristocrats': Party Political Ideology in the United States, 1837–1846* (Cambridge: Cambridge University Press, 1983); Harry Watson, *Liberty and Power: The Politics of Jacksonian America* (New York: Noonday Press, 1990); and Jean Baker, *Affairs of Party: The Political Culture of Northern Democrats in the Mid–Nineteenth Century* (Ithaca: Cornell University Press, 1983).

56. *Oregon Statesman*, June 27, 1851.

57. See, for example, *Oregonian*, June 26, August 28, September 25, 1852; October 7, 1854.

58. I have drawn this portrait of the Oregon Democracy from Jean Baker's portrait of George Bancroft and his "transitional" idea of the party. See her brilliant discussion in *Affairs of Party*, 119–125, esp. 122–124, and passim.

59. Jean Baker, "From Belief into Culture: Republicanism in the Antebellum North," *American Quarterly* 37 (Fall 1985): 545–546.

60. Adams, *Treason, Stratagems, and Spoils*, 59. Fifty years later, a Democratic participant in territorial politics reminisced that Whigs were "impatient of [party] control" (Woodward, "Rise and Early History of Political Parties in Oregon, Pt. 2," 85).

61. Using ecological regression techniques I have estimated the percentage of Democratic (and anti-Democratic) voters who voted for the same party in the congressional delegate elections of 1853, 1855, and 1857. The procedure produced estimates of the percentage of Democrats who remained loyal to their party across elections at 76 percent (between the elections of 1853 and 1855), 76 percent (between the elections of 1855 and 1857), and 73 percent (between the elections of 1853 and 1857). The corresponding percentages for anti-Democratic voters are 77 percent (between 1853 and 1855), 67 percent (between 1855 and 1857), and 62 percent (between 1853 and 1857).

The population estimates used in this analysis were derived from *Seventh Census of the United States, 1850* (Washington, D.C.: Government Printing Office, 1853); *Eighth Census of the United States, 1860*, Population; and the territorial censuses in the *Papers of the Provisional and Territorial Governments of Oregon, 1841–1859* (microfilm, Oregon Historical Society, Portland); the voting returns were compiled from the *Oregon Statesman* and the *Oregonian*, 1853–1858.

The method used to estimate the percentages described above (formally, the "transition probabilities") is described in J. Morgan Kousser, "Ecological Regression and the Analysis of Past Politics," *Journal of Interdisciplinary History* 4 (Autumn 1973): 237–262; Dale Baum, "Know-Nothingism and the Republican Majority in Massachusetts: The Political Realignment of the 1850s," *Journal of American History* 64 (March 1978): 959–986, and *The Civil War Party System: The*

Case of Massachusetts, 1848–1876 (Chapel Hill: University of North Carolina Press, 1984); E. Terence Jones, "Ecological Inference and Electoral Analysis," *Journal of Interdisciplinary History* 2 (Winter 1972): 249–272, and "Using Ecological Regression," *Journal of Interdisciplinary History* 4 (Spring 1974): 593–596. Paul F. Bourke and Donald A. Debats have examined voting patterns in Washington County, Oregon, in "Identifiable Voting in Nineteenth Century America: Toward a Comparison of Britain and the United States Before the Secret Ballot," *Perspectives in American History* 11 (1977–1978): 259–288; "Individuals and Aggregates: A Note on Historical Data and Assumptions," *Social Science History* 4 (Spring 1980): 229–250; and "The Structures of Political Involvement in the Nineteenth Century: A Frontier Case" (unpublished paper in the author's possession).

62. *Oregon Spectator,* April 17, 1851; February 3, March 2, 1852; May 12 and 19, July 21, October 7, 1854; see also Knuth, "Nativism in Oregon," 49–52.

63. *Pacific Christian Advocate* (Salem), September 22, 1855, quoted in Knuth, "Nativism in Oregon," 54. In addition, see ibid., 55–56; Bancroft, *History of Oregon* 2 : 356–357 n.23.

64. *Oregonian,* June 18, 1853; Woodward, "Rise and Early History of Political Parties in Oregon, Pt. 2," 56.

65. The phrase is Ronald Formisano's; see his *The Birth of Mass Political Parties: Michigan, 1827–1861* (Princeton: Princeton University Press, 1971), 58.

66. This is contained in his announcement of his American party candidacy for delegate to the constitutional convention; *Oregonian,* May 30, 1857. Dryer's involvement in Oregon temperance circles (despite Bush's constant charges that Dryer was a drunk) began soon after his arrival in Oregon; see the *Oregon Spectator,* May 22, 1851.

67. Adams, *Treason, Stratagems, and Spoils,* 32–38; Woodward, "Rise and Early History of Political Parties in Oregon, Pt. 2," 70–71.

68. On Adams's complementary attention to temperance and nativism in the *Argus,* see Knuth, "Nativism in Oregon," 55, 63–74. On Adams's attacks on Bush, see, for example, *Oregon Argus* (Oregon City), August 1, 1857. A characteristic Czapkay advertisement is in the *Oregonian,* August 29, 1857. Bush gladly returned the abuse in kind, calling Adams "Parson Billy" and his paper the "Air-Goose"; a characteristic retort is in the *Oregon Statesman,* November 17, 1855.

69. Samuel Thurston and William H. Willson, for example, were both Democrats; see Woodward, "Rise and Early History of Political Parties in Oregon, Pt. 2," 36, 39–40; Hendrickson, *Joe Lane,* 29.

70. *Oregon Statesman,* December 12, 1854.

71. On other state Democratic parties, see Holt, *Political Crisis of the 1850s,* 140 and passim.

72. The system had material benefits for Bush. As early as 1852 Democratic legislators recognized their political indebtedness by awarding Bush the territorial printing contract, a patronage plum worth five thousand dollars a year that he held without interruption throughout the 1850s.

73. Bush's political correspondents in the 1850s numbered well over fifty individuals, who wrote him with political information from across the territory— over one hundred Oregon addresses. These figures, which derive from an examination of the partial transcription of his correspondence done by the WPA

Arts Project in the 1930s and from the Oregon Historical Society microfilm copy of the original letters, represent a conservative estimate of his entire correspondence. The WPA fully transcribed Bush's correspondence with twenty-two men—his closest friends and political associates; in addition, the project completed transcripts of thirteen miscellaneous correspondents whose surnames ended with *A*, but did not complete the *B*'s through *Z*'s.

74. A fine analysis of the break points in territorial Oregon politics is Robert S. Elliott, "Oregon Territorial Politics: An Illustration of National Political Development" (B.A. thesis, Reed College, 1949), 86–128. See also Hendrickson, *Joe Lane*, 109–134, 146–153; Robert Johannsen, *Frontier Politics and the Sectional Crisis* (Seattle: University of Washington Press, 1955), 55–62.

75. Deady to James Nesmith, April 18, 1855; quoted in Hendrickson, *Joe Lane*, 111.

76. Bush's designation of the insurgents as "softs," as opposed to regular "hard" party members, is an adoption of language used in New York State in the early 1850s by the Barnburner and Hunker factions of the Democratic party. "Soft" refers to disloyal members of the party who nonetheless claim a voice in its affairs. See Holt, *Political Crisis of the 1850s*, 141–142.

77. Johannsen, *Frontier Politics and the Sectional Conflict*, 54–58; Hendrickson, *Joe Lane*, 69.

78. *Oregon Statesman*, December 23, 1856.

79. Ibid., January 13, 1857.

80. Ibid., April 21, 1857.

81. Ibid.

82. See Dryer's rebuttal of the Democratic charges in the *Oregonian*, August 15, 1857.

83. Ibid.; *Oregon Argus*, September 5, 1857. In response to one attack that he was an abolitionist, Dryer declared: "While we oppose slavery, we deny being an abolitionist in the modern sense. We claim to be a 'free white man over the age of 21 years,' and therefore entitled by the constitution of our country, to all the rights and privileges of a *freeman*" (*Oregonian*, June 27, 1857).

84. See the *Oregon Argus*, April 18, 1857, and passim. On August 22, 1857, the *Argus*, which Adams edited, published a five-part essay (apparently written by Adams), "For the *Argus*," entitled "Slave Labor and Free Labor," which presented the free-soil/labor argument against slavery in great detail.

85. This argument is detailed in the *Oregon Argus*, September 19, 1857.

86. In the first Republican address to the people of Oregon, published in the *Oregonian*, April 18, 1857, the party's position against the expansion of slavery is presented in great length. The author of this "Address" was William Lysander Adams.

87. On this surmise, see Holt, *Political Crisis of the 1850s*, 106–109.

88. See, for example, *Oregon Spectator*, May 19, 1854; *Oregonian*, May 13, 1854; May 24, 1856.

89. *Democratic Standard* (Portland), December 4, 1856.

90. *Oregonian*, November 8, 1856. Elsewhere Dryer claimed that the plan of the "Salem *banditti*" was to establish slavery in Oregon in order that the slave states "obtain the political preponderance in the Senate of the United States" (ibid., July 18, 1857).

91. The vote was 7,617 in favor of the convention, 1,629 opposed; ibid., July 7, 1857.

92. Ibid., April 18, 25; May 9, 23; June 6, 13, 20, 1857; *Oregon Statesman,* June 9, 16, 30, 1857.

93. *Oregon Statesman,* June 9, 1857.

94. Dryer's attack on Bush's favor of a free Negro exclusion is in the *Oregonian,* August 8, 1857.

95. River travel was subject to adequate draft and usually was halted during the late summer months. Patrick Malone, traveling to Salem for the convention, noted that steamship service had been suspended (*Sacramento Daily Union,* August 27, 1857). An overview of transportation in the Pacific Northwest may be found in Oscar Osburn Winther, *The Old Oregon Country: A History of Frontier Trade, Transportation, and Travel* (1950; reprint, Lincoln: University of Nebraska Press, 1969), 124–125, 139–140, 150–152, 157–161. See also Lloyd D. Black, "Middle Willamette Valley Population Growth," *Oregon Historical Society Quarterly* 43 (March 1942): 45; Ben Maxwell, "Salem in 1859," *Marion County History* 5 (June 1959): 10.

96. *Sacramento Daily Union,* August 27, 1857.

97. Judson, "Sketches of Salem," 47, 49.

98. Judson, "Sketches of Salem," 52–54; Reuben P. Boise, "History of Salem" and "Recollections of Salem" (n.d.), typescript, Special Collections, University of Oregon Library.

99. The following statistical characteristics of Salem's population were derived from the *Eighth Manuscript Federal Census, 1860,* Schedule of Population, Oregon, Marion County (National Archives microfilm #1056).

100. John Mack Faragher, *Women and Men on the Overland Trail,* 33–36.

101. Testifying to the market in wives engendered by the land law of the provisional government was an act of 1844 declaring "that all males of the age of sixteen years and upwards, and all females of the age of twelve years and upwards, shall be deemed competent to enter into the contract of marriage" (quoted in Philip Henry Overmeyer, "The Oregon Justinian: A Life of Matthew Paul Deady" [M.A. thesis, University of Oregon, 1935], 56).

102. At least two constitutional convention delegates were closely involved in the Willamette Woolen Mill: George Williams was president of the corporation, La Fayette Grover a member of the board of directors. See Alfred L. Lomax, *Pioneer Woolen Mills in Oregon: History of Wool and the Woolen Textile Industry in Oregon, 1811–1875* (Portland: Binford & Mort, 1941), 97–117. See, also, the *Alta California,* October 19, 1857.

103. *Oregon Statesman,* June 4, 1853. The *Statesman's* first offices were at the corner of Front and Trade streets; Judson, "Sketches of Salem," 19.

104. *Oregon Journal* (Portland), April 13, 1941.

105. *Oregon Statesman,* May 19, June 23, July 28, August 4, and September 5, 8, 22, 29, 1857. In a letter dated September 3, 1857, a correspondent of the San Francisco newspaper *Alta California* reported: "The town is crowded with theatrical companies. There is the Sager troop of infant prodigies, giving light farces, comedies, etc. The Chapman family, including Mr. and Mrs. George Chapman, who are making a tour. . . . There is also Risley, D'Evani, and Rosseter, performing under a tri-colored tent. They all expect to reap

golden luck, but this is very doubtful, as there is very little money spent here. They are waiting (the Convention) for some of the rich Californians to come up here, and distribute some of their change" (*Alta California,* September 11, 1857).

106. *Oregon Statesman,* August 25, 1857.

107. *Sacramento Daily Union,* September 22, 1857.

108. Quoted in Carey, *Oregon Constitution,* 33.

CHAPTER THREE: "THE LAND FOR THE OLD CALIFORNIAN"

1. Ralph Mann, *After the Gold Rush* (Stanford: Stanford University Press, 1982), chap. 3.

2. Russell R. Elliott, "Nevada's First Trading Post: A Study in Historiography," *Nevada Historical Society Quarterly* 13 (Winter 1970): 3–11.

3. Russell R. Elliott, *History of Nevada* (Lincoln: University of Nebraska Press, 1973), 50–56; Hubert Howe Bancroft, *History of Nevada, Colorado, and Wyoming* (San Francisco: History Company, 1890), 66–80. The phrase *Great Basin kingdom* is taken from Leonard Arrington's book of the same name, *Great Basin Kingdom: Economic History of the Latter-Day Saints, 1830–1900* (1958; reprint, Lincoln: University of Nebraska Press, 1966).

4. Arrington, *Great Basin Kingdom,* 71–76, 84–86.

5. In response to the first petition, the government of Utah affirmed its control over the western Great Basin by establishing Carson County and appointing a judge to oversee legal matters there. In the second instance, the California legislature acted favorably, sending to Congress a resolution requesting that the state's borders be enlarged to take in the eastern slope settlements. Congress, however, denied the request. Elliott, *History of Nevada,* 52–58.

6. Arrington, *Great Basin Kingdom,* 170–174.

7. Ibid., 177.

8. The Mormons received approximately fifty thousand dollars for property that, with the Comstock Lode strike two years later, became immensely valuable; ibid., 178.

9. Elliott, *History of Nevada,* 57–59.

10. The petition is reprinted in Myron Angel, *History of Nevada* (1881; reprint, Berkeley, Calif.: Howell-North Books, 1958), 63.

11. The records of the provisional convention are preserved in ibid., 68–72. See also *Sacramento Daily Union,* September 18, 1859; Bancroft, *Nevada, Colorado, and Wyoming,* 87.

12. Angel, *History of Nevada,* 65–66. See also Elliott, *History of Nevada,* 60–61.

13. Eliot Lord, *Comstock Mining and Miners* (1883; reprint, Berkeley, Calif.: Howell-North Books, 1959), 63. The rush to the Comstock Lode is placed in its larger context in Rodman Paul, *The Far West and the Great Plains in Transition, 1859–1900* (New York: Harper & Row, 1988).

14. On Virginia City, see Lord, *Comstock Mining and Miners,* 93–94. Twenty three hundred people (94 percent male) inhabited Virginia City within a year of its establishment. See also Marion S. Goldman, *Gold Diggers and Silver Miners* (Ann Arbor: University of Michigan Press, 1981).

15. The 1860 federal census places the population of Nevada at 6,857. Eighty-nine percent (6,137) were male; 73 percent (4,988) were males between the ages of twenty and forty. Fifty-two percent (3,660) percent lived in Gold Hill, Virginia City, or Silver City, the Comstock Lode mining towns. See *Eighth Census of the United States, 1860*, 3 vols. (Washington, D.C.: Government Printing Office, 1864–1865), Population, 562–565. The territorial census of 1861 claimed 16,374 residents; Elliott, *History of Nevada*, 70. According to the 1870 federal census, Nevada's population was 42,491; *Ninth Census of the United States, 1870*, 3 vols. (Washington, D.C.: Government Printing Office, 1872), Population, 632.

16. *Congressional Globe*, 38 Cong., 1st sess., 788.

17. See Alexander Saxton, *The Indispensable Enemy: Labor and the Anti-Chinese Movement in California* (Berkeley and Los Angeles: University of California Press, 1971), 46–52 and passim.

18. John Hittell, "Mining Excitements of California," *Overland Monthly* 2 (1869): 415.

19. J. Ross Browne, "A Peep at Washoe," *Harper's New Monthly Magazine* 22 (December 1860): 10. See also *Virginia Daily Union* (Virginia City), January 11, 1864.

20. On Nevada's early development, see Rodman Paul, *Mining Frontiers of the Far West, 1848–1900* (1963; reprint, Albuquerque: University of New Mexico Press, 1974), chaps. 4 and 5; Robert B. Merrifield, "Nevada, 1849–1881: The Impact of an Advanced Technological Society upon a Frontier Area" (Ph.D. diss., University of Chicago, 1959), chaps. 4 and 5; Lord, *Comstock Mining and Miners*, chaps. 9–11; Richard Lingenfelter, *The Hard Rock Miner: A History of the Mining Labor Movements in the American West, 1863–1893* (Berkeley and Los Angeles: University of California Press, 1974), chaps. 1–3.

21. Grant Smith, *History of the Comstock Lode, 1850–1920*, Geology and Mining Series no. 37, *University of Nevada Bulletin* (July 1943): 25, 31–32; *Humboldt Register* (Unionville, Nevada), November 12, 1864.

22. Lord, *Comstock Mining and Miners*, 126.

23. *Gold Hill Evening News*, October 31, 1862.

24. *New York Herald*, March 2, 1861; quoted in Harry J. Carman and Reinhard H. Luthin, *Lincoln and the Patronage* (New York: Columbia University Press, 1943), 109. Nye was Lincoln's second choice for the post, after Rufus King; see Lincoln's "Memorandum on Appointments to Territories, March 20–27, 1861," reproduced in *Nevada: The Centennial of Statehood—An Exhibition in the Library of Congress* (Washington, D.C.: Library of Congress, 1965), 2.

25. Samuel Clemens, *Roughing It* (1872; reprint, New York: New American Library, 1962), 47.

26. The first site of the legislature's sessions was a stone building two miles east of the town, in the Warm Springs Hotel, which the legislature later transformed into the territorial prison; *Letters from Nevada Territory 1861–1862, by Andrew J. Marsh*, ed. William C. Miller, Russell W. McDonald, and Ann Rollins (Carson City: Legislative Counsel Bureau, State of Nevada, 1972), 2 (hereafter cited as *Marsh's Letters*).

27. Kenneth N. Owens, "Pattern and Structure in Western Territorial Politics," in *The American Territorial System*, ed. John Porter Bloom (Athens: Ohio University Press, 1973), 163–166.

28. The *Gold Hill Evening News*, December 12, 1863, for example, discussed the rumors about "copperhead" influence in territorial politics but dismissed them as "too inconsiderable to be of any moment." A similar point is made in the *Virginia Daily Union*, January 21 and May 27, 1864. However, the *Gold Hill Evening News*, January 15, 1864, also declared (without naming names) that copperheads were behind the opposition to the first Nevada constitution; see also the *Sacramento Daily Union*, June 6, 1864. Governor Nye, in addition, discussed the dangers posed by southern sympathizers at great length in his correspondence with the State Department; see Nye to Seward, March 25, 1864, in State Department Territorial Papers, Nevada Ser., vol. 1, May 13, 1861–October 31, 1864 (microfilm, National Archives, Washington, D.C., 1942). Nye discussed disloyal sentiment in the territory in the *Virginia Daily Union*, May 27, 1864.

29. *Marsh's Letters*, 94.

30. Ibid., 63.

31. The bill's fate in the first session of the territorial legislature is traced in ibid., 50, 63–64, 94, 109, 177, 183–186, 366, 376, 393. Its progress in the second session can be followed in ibid., 454, 589, 595–600, 605–608, 613–620.

32. The editors of Andrew Marsh's letters surmise that the Third House was a nickelodeon or music hall act; ibid., 671–672n.56. Marsh himself wrote that "the 'Third House' is a peculiar institution of Carson, designed as a burlesque upon the legitimate Legislature. . . . This august body meets every evening in a rear building, as Mrs. Malaprop would say, 'contagious to' a drinking saloon" (ibid., 457). Samuel Clemens, apparently, was the mastermind behind the Third House; see the *Virginia Daily Union*, January 30, 1864.

33. *Marsh's Letters*, 613.

34. Ibid., 626, 623. The Corporation Bill was invalidated by Congress; see the *Sacramento Daily Union*, March 9, 1863.

35. *Marsh's Letters*, 565–566.

36. Ibid., 659–660.

37. Dr. Charles Anderson to his wife, December 21, 1862; Bancroft Library, University of California, Berkeley.

38. Nye traveled to Washington, D.C., in the spring of 1863 to lobby for an enabling act. The effort failed in the House. The bill passed by the territorial legislature may have been the governor's doing, although there is no evidence one way or the other. See Elliott, *History of Nevada*, 78.

39. Andrew J. Marsh, Samuel L. Clemens, and Amos Bowman, *Reports of the 1863 Constitutional Convention of the Territory of Nevada*, ed. William C. Miller and Eleanore Bushnell (Carson City: Legislative Counsel Bureau, State of Nevada, 1972), 225 (hereafter cited as *Reports of the 1863 Constitutional Convention*). These reports were compiled from fragments of the *Territorial Enterprise* (Virginia City) and *Virginia Daily Union* that survive in the Orion Clemens Scrapbook, Bancroft Library, University of California, Berkeley.

40. Stewart's career is covered in Russell R. Elliott, *Servant of Power: A Political Biography of Senator William M. Stewart* (Reno: University of Nevada Press, 1983).

41. Lord, *Comstock Mining and Miners*, 131–180; Smith, *History of the Comstock Lode*, 69.

42. *Reports of the 1863 Constitutional Convention*, 245.

43. Ibid., 226, 276.

44. Angel, *History of Nevada*, 82–84.

45. *Reports of the 1863 Constitutional Convention*, 228.

46. Ibid., 276.

47. Ibid., 413–415.

48. Angel, *History of Nevada*, 82–84.

49. See, for example, the *Gold Hill Evening News*, January 4, 1864; *Virginia Daily Union*, January 6, 8, 9, 1864.

50. This discussion is drawn from my "Industry and the Individual: A Case Study of Politics and Social Change in Early Nevada," *Pacific Historical Review* 51 (August 1982): 247–249. See also Lord, *Comstock Mining and Miners*, 151–161; Smith, *History of the Comstock Lode*, 64–74; Merlin Stonehouse, *John Wesley North and the Reform Frontier* (Minneapolis: University of Minnesota Press, 1965), 159–161. For contemporary comments, see the *Gold Hill Evening News*, November 4, 1863, and March 26, 1864; and J. Ross Browne, "Washoe Revisited," *Harper's New Monthly Magazine* 31 (July 1865): 154–156.

51. Lord, *Comstock Mining and Miners*, 165–171; Smith, *History of the Comstock Lode*, 74.

52. *Virginia Daily Union*, January 19, 1864; *Sacramento Daily Union*, December 31, 1864; *Gold Hill Evening News*, January 4, March 26, 1864.

53. *Gold Hill Evening News*, November 4, 1863; *Sacramento Daily Union*, December 31, 1863; Stonehouse, *John Wesley North*, 156–177. One of North's rulings against the one-ledge theory is reprinted in Lord, *Comstock Mining and Miners*, 144.

54. *Sacramento Daily Union*, December 31, 1863. John North's understanding of the contest is found in his February 7, 1864, letter to George Loomis; North Papers, Huntington Library, San Marino, California.

55. *Virginia Daily Union*, January 1, 1864.

56. See, for example, the *Gold Hill Evening News*, January 11, 1864.

57. *Virginia Daily Union*, January 15, 1864 (reprinted from the *Carson Independent*).

58. Ibid., January 10, 1864.

59. *Sacramento Daily Union*, December 31, 1863.

60. *Virginia Daily Union*, January 13, 1864.

61. Ibid., January 9, 1864.

62. Ibid., January 15, 1864 (reprinted from the *Carson Independent*).

63. *Humboldt Register*, January 16, 1864; see, also, the *Virginia Daily Union*, January 15, 1864.

64. *Virginia Daily Union*, January 19, 1864.

65. See the *Virginia Evening Bulletin* (Virginia City), January 11, 12, 18, 25, 27, 1864; *Virginia Daily Union*, January 17, 19, 24, 27, 1864; and *Sacramento Daily Union*, January 19, 1864.

66. Stewart called the meeting to respond to charges made against him by the judge's supporters. (Unidentified individuals had referred to Stewart as a "dirt-eating individual"; *Virginia Daily Union*, January 17, 1864.) See also the *Virginia Evening Bulletin*, January 18, 1864.

67. *Reese River Reveille*, January 18, 1864; quoted in the *Virginia Daily Union*, January 19, 1864, where Stewart is also referred to as "the Satan of Nevada" in a reprint of a *Carson Independent* article.

68. Quoted in the *Sacramento Daily Union*, January 26, 1864.

69. *Virginia Daily Union*, January 22, 1864.

70. *Virginia Daily Union*, January 21, 1864.

71. Earl Pomeroy thoroughly discusses the considerations that led to the enabling legislation for the second Nevada constitutional convention in "Lincoln, the Thirteenth Amendment, and the Admission of Nevada," *Pacific Historical Review* 12 (December 1943): 362–368. Pomeroy's interpretation revises that of F. Lauriston Bullard, "Abraham Lincoln and the Statehood of Nevada," *American Bar Association Journal* 26 (March–April 1940): 210–213, 236, 313–317.

72. *Gold Hill Evening News*, January 18, 1864.

73. Both men are quoted in Pomeroy, "Lincoln, the Thirteenth Amendment, and the Admission of Nevada," 367–368.

74. The Enabling Act—which did away with not only the customary territorial referendum to test local sentiment for statehood but also Congress's review of the proposed constitution—was introduced in the Senate on February 8 and passed on February 24. The House concurred on March 17, and Lincoln signed the legislation on March 22. See the *Congressional Globe*, 38 Cong., 1st sess., 596, 789, 1166, 1228.

75. *Humboldt Register*, July 23, 1864.

76. Paul, *Mining Frontiers of the Far West*, 74–75; Lord, *Comstock Mining and Miners*, 181–182; Smith, *History of the Comstock Lode*, 48–49.

77. *Sacramento Daily Union*, July 16, 1864. See also *Virginia Daily Union*, June 10, 1864.

78. See, for example, *Humboldt Register*, October 1, 1864; *Gold Hill Evening News*, June 4, 10, 1864.

79. *Gold Hill Evening News*, May 7, 1864.

80. Ibid., October 31, 1863.

81. *Humboldt Register*, September 17, 1864. See also *Gold Hill Evening News*, June 24, September 17, 1864; *Sacramento Daily Union*, August 5, 10, 30, 1864.

82. *Humboldt Register*, September 17, 1864.

83. *Gold Hill Evening News*, May 7, 1864.

84. *Sacramento Daily Union*, August 5, 1864.

85. *Humboldt Register*, September 17, 1864.

86. *Esmeralda Star*, June 8, 1864. This fragment is in Nevada Newspaper Miscellany, 1 : 1, Bancroft Library, University of California, Berkeley. See also the *Carson Independent*, June 7, 1864, quoted in the *Virginia Daily Union*, June 8, 1864; the *Gold Hill Evening News*, June 7, 1864; and the *Daily Message* (Gold Hill), June 9, 1864. The last item is in the Orion Clemens Scrapbook, Bancroft Library, University of California, Berkeley.

87. The ten were N.A.H. Ball (Storey), Cornelius Brosnan (Storey), Samuel Chapin (Storey), John Collins (Storey), George Gibson (Ormsby), James Haines (Douglas), George Hudson (Lyon), J. Neely Johnson (Ormsby), Frank Kennedy (Lyon), and John Kinkead (Ormsby). Samuel Chapin had voted against the mining tax article. See *Reports of the 1863 Constitutional Convention*, app. C.

88. Delegates Thomas Fitch, Charles DeLong, Almon Hovey, Lloyd Frizzell, and Cornelius Brosnan were apparently among the eight or nine "bolters from the Storey County convention"; see the *Virginia Daily Union*, January 1, 6, 18, 1864; *Gold Hill Evening News*, December 28, 29, 31, 1863; January 2, 14 and Feb-

ruary 2, 1864. In addition, Charles DeLong, Thomas Fitch, John A. Collins, and Lloyd Frizzell were listed as members of the "People's Committee" to oppose the constitution in Storey County; *Virginia Daily Union*, January 6, 9, 19, 1864.

89. *Virginia Daily Union*, June 10, 1864.

90. "Carson City," *Pacific Monthly* 2 (August 1864): 1.

91. *San Francisco Daily Herald*, January 6, 1860, describes agricultural activities in Ormsby County. Quartz mills were also built in the vicinity of Carson, although they did not rival the Comstock-area mills; Sam Davis, *History of Nevada* (Reno, Nev.: Elm, 1913), 980–981.

92. Davis, *History of Nevada*, 973–996. Angel, *History of Nevada*, 550.

93. Carson City's plat is preserved in maps in the collection of the Nevada Historical Society, Reno. See also the sketch in Henry DeGroot, *Sketches of the Washoe Silver Mines . . .* (San Francisco: Hutchings & Rosenfield, 1860), 12.

94. *Nevada Tribune*, July 1876; quoted in Angel, *History of Nevada*, 550.

95. *The Nevada Directory for 1868–69 . . .* (San Francisco: M. D. Carr, 1868), 131.

96. DeGroot, *Sketches of the Washoe Silver Mines*, 12. These figures are from the 1860 U.S. census and 1861 territorial census, summarized in *First Directory of Nevada Territory . . .*, intro. Richard Lingenfelter (1862; reprint, Los Gatos, Calif.: Talisman Press, 1962), v.

97. *The Journals of Alfred Doten*, ed. Walter Van Tilburg Clark, 3 vols. (Reno: University of Nevada Press, 1973), 1:713; "Carson City," 1. These estimates are undoubtedly too high: 1,500 to 2,500, given the number of taxpayers in the town, is probably more accurate.

98. Susan Mitchell Hall, "The Diary of a Trip from Ione to Nevada in 1859," *California Historical Society Quarterly* 17 (March 1938): 76.

99. Anderson to his wife, September 6, 1862; *First Directory of Nevada Territory*, 66.

100. J. Ross Browne, "A Peep at Washoe," *Harper's New Monthly Magazine* 22 (January 1861): 150.

101. *Territorial Enterprise*, September 17, 1859; quoted in Angel, *History of Nevada*, 553. The *Territorial Enterprise* was published in three Nevada towns during its lifetime. From its inauguration in 1858 to November 5, 1859, it was published in Genoa; on November 12, 1859, publication shifted to Carson City; and on November 3, 1860, to Virginia City.

102. Angel, *History of Nevada*, 555; Bancroft, *Nevada, Colorado, and Wyoming*, 169–70.

103. *Silver Age* (Carson City), October 2, 1862; *Carson Independent*, June 17, 1864. Dr. Charles Anderson described the White House Hotel as follows: "It is the *aristocratic* House of the place. No liquor saloon there, about the only House without one" (Anderson to his wife, September 17, 1862).

104. *First Directory of Nevada Territory*, 67–92; *Second Directory of Nevada Territory . . .* (Virginia City, Nev.: Valentine, 1863), 95–117; Davis, *History of Nevada*, 985; *Virginia Daily Union*, January 21, 1863; *Daily Evening Bulletin* (San Francisco), February 22, 1864; Angel, *History of Nevada*, 555.

105. *Placerville Observer*, June 26, 1859, quoted in Angel, *History of Nevada*, 553; Jacob Klein, "Founders of Carson City," ms., Bancroft Library, University of California, Berkeley, 3.

106. *Gold Hill Evening News,* October 14, 1863.

107. Anderson to his wife, February 11, 1863.

108. Elizabeth Williams, "Among the Sierras," *Hesperian* 10 (October 1863): 256, notes the absence of churches in Carson City, as well as a cemetery: "On the hill side, scattered here and there, without line or bound to mark a limit, sleep the remains of those who have passed from busy life in this valley." See also *Gold Hill Evening News,* October 14, 1863.

109. In 1870, 1880, 1890, and 1900, the male proportion of Ormsby County's population was, respectively, 76 percent, 64 percent, 65 percent, and 51 percent. These figures are based on the entire county, which took in surrounding rural settlements, and thus likely understate the predominance of males in Carson City. See *Ninth Census of the United States, 1870,* Population, 648; *Twelfth Census of the United States, 1900,* 10 vols. (Washington, D.C.: Government Printing Office, 1901–1902), Population (2 vols.), 1:512. The statistics on Carson City's population were derived from the *Eighth Manuscript Federal Census, 1860,* Schedule of Population, Utah Territory, Carson County (National Archives microfilm #1314); *First Directory of Nevada Territory; Second Directory of Nevada Territory;* Ormsby County Tax Rolls, 1863–1865 (Nevada State Archives microfilm).

110. The advertisement for the "french hair dresser" appeared in Carson's *Daily Morning Star* (n.d.); in Nevada Newspaper Miscellany, 1:91, Bancroft Library, University of California, Berkeley.

111. Looked at a bit differently, only 28 percent of the individuals listed in the 1862 *Directory* were present in the 1863 *Directory*.

112. *Nevada Directory for 1868–69,* 130.

113. Kenneth Lynn, *Mark Twain and South Western Humor* (1960; reprint, Westport, Conn.: Greenwood Press, 1972), 142.

114. Andrew Marsh, *Official Report of the Debates and Proceedings in the Constitutional Convention of the State of Nevada, Assembled at Carson City, July 4th, 1864* (San Francisco: Frank Eastman, 1866), 3, 128.

115. Marsh, *Official Report,* 5.

CHAPTER FOUR: A NEW REGIME

1. M. M. McCarver to Francis Voris, September 19, 1849; California Historical Society, San Francisco.

2. J. Ross Browne, *Report of the Debates in the Convention of California on the Formation of the State Constitution in September and October, 1849* (Washington, D.C.: John T. Towers, 1850), 24, 27 (hereafter cited as *Report of the Debates*). Among the convention working papers (California State Archives, Sacramento) is an annotated copy of the Iowa constitution, on which an unidentified delegate kept a tally of the sections adopted by the convention.

3. *Report of the Debates,* 27–29, 379–380; Merrill Burlingame, "The Contribution of Iowa to the Formation of the State Government of California in 1849," *Iowa Journal of History and Politics* 30 (April 1932): 189–191.

4. Marvin Meyers, *The Jacksonian Persuasion* (Stanford: Stanford University Press, 1957), 267 and, more generally, 253–275. See also Bray Hammond, *Banks and Politics in America, From the Revolution to the Civil War* (New York: Columbia University Press, 1957), 614–615.

5. Michael F. Holt, *Political Crisis of the 1850s* (New York: John Wiley, 1978), chap. 5.

6. Roy Nichols, *The Disruption of the American Democracy* (New York: Collier Books, 1948).

7. Voting patterns in the California constitutional convention are discussed in appendix 2B.

8. Appendix 1A contains a prosopographical table describing the delegates to the convention.

9. Richard Hofstadter, *The American Political Tradition and the Men Who Made It* (New York: Vintage Books, 1948), 56–59. Similar discussions of Jacksonian-era male character are in Meyers, *Jacksonian Persuasion*, 36–56; and William Goetzmann, *Exploration and Empire: The Explorer and the Scientist in the Winning of the American West* (New York: Vintage Books, 1966), 106–109.

10. See Joseph Kett, *Rites of Passage: Adolescence in America from 1790 to the Present* (New York: Basic Books, 1977), 14–31.

11. The traders who migrated directly to California were A. J. Ellis, Julian Hanks, Joseph Hobson, and Abel Stearns; the soldiers were Kimball Dimmick, Edward Gilbert, John McHenry Hollingsworth, Francis Lippitt, Benjamin S. Lippincott, Myron Norton, William Shannon, Thomas Vermeule, Lewis Dent, Rodman Price, and William Steuart.

12. As counted here, a "move" understates the geographical mobility of the delegates. I have included only instances in which a delegate established a new residence outside the *region* in which he previously resided, the regions being New England, Middle Atlantic, Southeast, Southwest, Border, Northwest, Plains, Europe, and Mexico.

13. Two men—Thomas Larkin and Julian Hanks, both New England merchants who had arrived in California during the 1830s—do not fit precisely into the three regional groupings. In the convention debates and voting they gravitated to the side of the midwesterners.

14. Josiah Royce, *California, from the Conquest in 1846 to the Second Vigilance Committee in San Francisco: A Study in American Character* (Boston: Houghton Mifflin, 1886), 261.

15. Sutter, of course, was a German-born Swiss; however, to the convention reporter J. Ross Browne he identified his prior residence as Missouri, and in the convention voting he most often allied with the "old settler" group dominated by midwesterners.

16. Of the thirteen delegates who had migrated to California from New York or New Jersey, ten (77 percent) arrived with the military; seven of these had arrived with Stevenson's New York Volunteers: Kimball Dimmick, Edward Gilbert, John McHenry Hollingsworth, Francis Lippitt, Myron Norton, William Shannon, and Thomas Vermeule. The other New Yorkers who arrived with the military were Henry Halleck, military secretary of state; Benjamin Lippincott, a member of Frémont's battalion; and Rodman Price, purser to Commodore Sloat. On the convention delegates who arrived with the New York Volunteers, see Donald C. Biggs, *Conquer and Colonize: Stevenson's Regiment in California* (San Rafael, Calif.: Presidio Press, 1977), 177–196 and passim.

17. For more on Gilbert, see *Biographical Directory of the American Congress* (Washington, D.C.: Government Printing Office, 1950), 1208; Frank Soule, *The Annals of San Francisco* (New York: D. Appleton, 1855), 773–778.

18. See James McHall Jones to his mother, August 26, 1849; T. W. Norris Collection, Bancroft Library, University of California, Berkeley.

19. The four European-born delegates were Frenchmen José María Covarrubias (San Luis Obispo) and Pedro Sansevaine (San Jose); Spaniard Miguel Pedrorena (San Diego); and Scot Hugo Reid (Los Angeles). All together they had lived in California an average of thirteen years (15, 11, 11, 15, respectively). The three Anglo-Americans tied by marriage to the old regime were Abel Stearns (Los Angeles), Stephen Foster (Los Angeles), and Henry Tefft (San Luis Obispo). The last two had arrived in California within a year of the convention and quickly married into prominent California families.

20. Douglas Monroy, *Thrown Among Strangers: The Making of Mexican Culture in Frontier California* (Berkeley and Los Angeles: University of California Press, 1990), 135–136; Albert Camarillo, *Chicanos in a Changing Society: From Mexican Pueblos to American Barrios in Santa Barbara and Southern California, 1848–1930* (Berkeley and Los Angeles: University of California Press, 1979), 10–11; Leonard Pitt, *The Decline of the Californios: A Social History of the Spanish-speaking Californians, 1846–1890* (Berkeley and Los Angeles: University of California Press, 1971), 6–7.

21. The Californio delegates' landholdings (that is, grants in which they held full or partial title) can be traced in Amado González, *Act of Possession,* published as Rose Hollenbaugh Avina, *Spanish and Mexican Land Grants in California* (New York: Arno Press, 1976). Their holdings were as follows: Delegate Carrillo, 110,000 acres (nos. 99, 282, 406); Covarrubias, 57,000 (nos. 292, 399); Domínguez, 25,000 (no. 3; see p. 38); Foster (lands obtained through wife), 30,000 (no. 8); de la Guerra, 57,000 (no. 337); Pedrorena, 97,000 (nos. 410, 397); Pico, 84,000 (nos. 132, 295); Reid, 13,000 (no. 379); Rodríguez, 35,000 (no. 339); Sansevaine, 6,000 (no. 271); Stearns, 28,000 (nos. 121, 129); Tefft (through father-in-law), 38,000 (no. 93); and Vallejo, 67,000 (no. 285)—for a total of 647,000 acres.

22. Generally, see Woodrow James Hansen, *The Search for Authority in California* (Oakland, Calif.: Biobooks, 1960), 98–99, 186 n.16; Pitt, *Decline of the Californios,* 43. In addition, on de la Guerra, see Mayo Hayes O'Donnell, "A Letter About Old Monterey," copy in the collection of Colton Hall Museum, Monterey, California. On Pedrorena, *Representative and Leading Men of the Pacific,* ed. Oscar T. Shuck (San Francisco: Beacon, 1870), 362; and Neal Harlow, *California Conquered: War and Peace on the Pacific, 1846–1850* (Berkeley and Los Angeles: University of California Press, 1982), 208. On Vallejo, Myrtle M. McKittrick, *Vallejo, Son of California* (Portland: Binford & Mort, 1944), 255–290; and Madie Brown Emparan, *The Vallejos of California* (San Francisco: Gleeson Library, University of San Francisco, 1968), 12–44. On Stearns, Doris Marion Wright, *A Yankee in Mexican California: Abel Stearns, 1798–1848* (Santa Barbara, Calif.: Wallace Hebberd, 1977).

23. See appendix 2A.

24. *Memoirs of Elisha Oscar Crosby: Reminiscences of California and Guatemala from 1849 to 1864,* ed. Charles Albro Barker (San Marino, Calif.: Huntington Library, 1945), 39–40.

25. McCarver to Voris, September 19, 1849.

26. Thomas W. Prosch, *McCarver of Tacoma* (Seattle: Lowman & Hanford,

1906), 5, 40–41; Michael B. Husband, "Morton M. McCarver: An Iowa Entrepreneur in the Far West," *Annals of Iowa* 40 (Spring 1970): 242.

27. Leon Litwack, *North of Slavery* (Chicago: University of Chicago Press, 1961), esp. chap. 3; Eugene H. Berwanger, *The Frontier Against Slavery: Western Anti-Negro Prejudice and the Slavery Expansion Controversy* (Urbana: University of Illinois Press, 1967), 30–59.

28. Prosch, *McCarver of Tacoma*, 5.

29. Ibid., 9–13; Husband, "Morton M. McCarver," 242–244.

30. Husband, "Morton M. McCarver," 245.

31. Ibid., 246–249; Prosch, *McCarver of Tacoma*, 37–38; Kent D. Richards, "Growth and Development of Government in the Far West: The Oregon Provisional Government, Jefferson Territory, Provisional and Territorial Nevada" (Ph.D. diss., University of Wisconsin, 1966), 73, 96, 119–122.

32. Husband, "Morton M. McCarver," 249–250; Prosch, *McCarver of Tacoma*, 52–56.

33. Prosch, *McCarver of Tacoma*, 57–58; *Placer Times*, May 5, 1849.

34. Information on Hastings's life prior to the California constitutional convention is fragmentary. The following discussion is based on the notes of Carl Hayden (Colton Hall Museum, Monterey, California). Hastings's career is discussed in Thomas Andrews, "The Ambitions of Lansford W. Hastings: A Study in Western Myth-Making," *Pacific Historical Review* 39 (November 1970): 473–491; and Thomas Andrews, "The Controversial Hastings Overland Guide," *Pacific Historical Review* 37 (February 1968): 21–34. See also Charles H. Carey, ed., *The Emigrants' Guide to Oregon and California* (Princeton: Princeton University Press, 1932), vii–xiv; J. Roderic Korns, ed., *West from Fort Bridger: The Pioneering of the Immigrant Trails Across Utah, 1846–1850* (Salt Lake City: Utah State Historical Society, 1951), 23–28, 43–50, 108–117; and Dale Morgan, ed., *Overland in 1846: Diaries and Letters of the California Trail*, 2 vols. (Georgetown, Calif.: Talisman Press, 1963), 1:21–43, 93–95.

35. Andrews, "Ambitions of Lansford W. Hastings," 484; Robert J. Loewenberg, *Equality on the Oregon Frontier: Jason Lee and the Methodist Mission, 1834–1843* (Seattle: University of Washington Press, 1976), 166, 191.

36. Richards, "Growth and Development of Government in the Far West," 77; Loewenberg, *Equality on the Oregon Frontier*, 166, 180, 186, 199. Andrews, "Ambitions of Lansford W. Hastings," 477–480, 483–484, 486–487, 490–491, reviews and refutes the charge that Hastings sought to create a Pacific republic.

37. The quotations are from Andrews, "Ambitions of Lansford W. Hastings," 482. A letter in the *Oregon Spectator* of June 25, 1846 (signed in the presence of two witnesses), charges that Hastings described to emigrants Sutter's and his plan to "revolutionize" California.

38. Andrews, "Ambitions of Lansford W. Hastings," 476n.10.

39. Hubert Howe Bancroft, *History of California*, 7 vols. (San Francisco: History Company, 1886–1890), 4:585–586. Robert Semple, later president of the California convention, was in this party.

40. Lansford W. Hastings to John Marsh, March 16, 1846; John Marsh Collection, California State Library, Sacramento.

41. Bancroft, *History of California* 5:526–530; Andrews, "Controversial Hastings Overland Guide," 21–34.

42. Hayden, Notes on Lansford W. Hastings, 4–5; Bancroft, *History of California* 5:579, 645, 678, 681.

43. Hayden, Notes on Lansford W. Hastings, 6.

44. Samuel S. Willey, "Recollections of General Halleck," *Overland Monthly* 9 (July 1872): 9. Halleck's activities on the Pacific Coast prior to his appointment as secretary of state are discussed in John D. Yates, "Insurgents on the Baja Peninsula: Henry Halleck's Journal of the War in Lower California," *California Historical Society Quarterly* 54 (Fall 1975): 221–244.

45. Halleck's early life is covered briefly in Stephen E. Ambrose, *Halleck: Lincoln's Chief of Staff* (Baton Rouge: Louisiana State University Press, 1962), 3–10; Judge T. W. Freelon, "Henry Wager Halleck," in Shuck (ed.), *Representative and Leading Men of the Pacific*, 375–377; Henry W. Halleck, "Autobiography in His Own Hand" (1861), ms., Huntington Library, San Marino, California; Willey, "Recollections of General Halleck," 9–17; Allen Johnson and Dumas Malone, eds., *Dictionary of American Biography*, 20 vols. (New York: Charles Scribner, 1946–1958), 8:150–151.

46. Pitt, *Decline of the Californios*, 38.

47. Willey, "Recollections of General Halleck," 15.

48. Halleck, "Autobiography," 4–5.

49. Botts's activities in Monterey can be followed in Thomas Larkin, *The Larkin Papers*, ed. George P. Hammond, 11 vols. (Berkeley and Los Angeles: University of California Press, 1951–1968), 7:205–209, 261, 310, 352; 8:ix, 1, 30–34, 40, 41, 80, 86, 129, 130, 149, 152–155, 182, 193, 224, 242; and Walter Colton, *Three Years in California* (1850; reprint, Stanford: Stanford University Press, 1949), 257–264.

50. Johnson and Malone (eds.), *Dictionary of American Biography*, 1:472.

51. Ibid.

52. See Botts's remarks in *Report of the Debates*, 178.

53. Reprinted in the *Southern Planter*, January 1940 (Centennial Issue), 3.

54. *Report of the Debates*, 178–179.

55. George Cosgrove, "James McHall Jones: The Judge That Never Presided," *California Historical Society Quarterly* 20 (June 1941): 97. On Jones's relationship with his mother, see, in particular, his letters of September 28, 1845; and May 10, 1851.

56. Jones to his mother, October 10, 1845; January 1, 1846.

57. Ibid., September 19 and 28, October 10 and 12, November 5 and [?], 1845; January 1, 1846; December 1, 1850; May 10, 1851.

58. The ship that Jones took from the Isthmus of Panama to San Francisco cannot be determined. Cosgrove ("James McHall Jones," 100) concludes that he did not travel to California on the *Panama;* however, from Monterey he wrote his mother about his friendship with these government figures. At the time of the convention he and Weller had begun a law partnership, and shortly thereafter Gwin arranged Jones's appointment to the federal bench.

59. This is suggested in Cosgrove, "James McHall Jones," 100; and Jones to his mother, August 26, 1849.

60. Jones to his mother, August 26, 1849.

61. Ibid., October 1, 1849.

62. The duel, with Henry Tefft of San Luis Obispo, was averted through the intercession of Gwin and others; *Report of the Debates,* 57–61; Jones to his mother, October 1, 1849.

63. Jones's compromise proposal on the boundary resolved the convention's thorniest issue; see *Report of the Debates,* 441–459; and discussion, pp. 130–137, this volume.

64. "Memoirs of Hon. William M. Gwin," ed. William Henry Ellison, *California Historical Society Quarterly* 19 (March 1940): 1; Lately Thomas, *Between Two Empires: The Life Story of California's First Senator, William McKendree Gwin* (Boston: Houghton Mifflin, 1969), 3–4. A contemporary account of Gwin's senatorial ambition is in an August 1849 letter by J. Ross Browne to his wife; see *J. Ross Browne: His Letters, Journals, and Writing,* ed. Lina Fergusson Browne (Albuquerque: University of New Mexico Press, 1969), 121.

65. James O'Meara, *Broderick and Gwin* (San Francisco: Bacon, 1881), 34. On Gwin and Jackson, see Thomas, *Between Two Empires,* 6–14.

66. Thomas, *Between Two Empires,* 16; Alonzo Phelps, *Contemporary Biography of California's Representative Men* (San Francisco: Bancroft, 1881), 239.

67. Edwin A. Miles, "Andrew Jackson and Senator George Poindexter," *Journal of Southern History* 24 (February 1958): 51–66.

68. Quoted in ibid., 63–64.

69. Thomas, *Between Two Empires,* 11–12.

70. Ibid., 14–16.

71. "Memoirs of Hon. William M. Gwin," 2.

72. Thomas, *Between Two Empires,* 22.

73. "Memoirs of Hon. William M. Gwin," 1–2.

74. Ibid., 2–3. The passage ends: "Eleven months thereafter, Mr. Gwin handed his credentials to Judge Douglas, who presented them to the Senate."

75. Ibid., 4.

76. Ibid.

77. Throughout chapters 4, 5, and 6 I distinguish between different branches of the constitutional conventions as follows: the "convention," the "committee of the whole," and specific "committees" (in California, the Select Committee on the Constitution; in Oregon and Nevada, committees with specific responsibilities—to draft the article on the judiciary, for example). These three subdivisions of the constitutional conventions embodied practically the process of constitution writing.

This process began with the presiding officer of the "convention" formally appointing committees to draft the articles that made up the constitution. In California a single Select Committee on the Constitution was given this entire task. In Oregon and Nevada, a series of committees (on the bill of rights, judiciary, executive, suffrage, and so forth) were appointed specific parts of the overall constitution.

Once these committees completed a draft of an article, they "reported" it back to the convention. The convention then went into the "committee of the whole" (meeting, that is, as a committee made up of the whole membership of the convention). In the committee of the whole, the delegates discussed the proposed article, (likely) amended it, and then passed it *as a committee.* The article as amended by the committee of the whole was "reported" back to the convention, which as a body then voted formally to pass or reject it.

In this way legislative procedure separated the work of constitution writing into three separate components: (1) drafting articles (the work of committees); (2) debate over and amendment of the draft articles (the work of a committee consisting of the "whole membership"); and (3) the passage or rejection, in the convention, of the article as best finished as the committee of the whole could make it.

78. An excellent survey of the legal and organizational history of corporations—particularly useful in that it is set in the context of Nevada and California history—is Maureen Ann Bloomquist Jung, "The Comstock and the California Mining Economy, 1848–1900: The Stock Market and the Modern Corporation" (Ph.D. diss., University of California, Santa Barbara, 1988), chap. 1.

79. James Willard Hurst, *The Legitimacy of the Business Corporation in the Law of the United States, 1780–1970* (Charlottesville: University of Virginia Press, 1970), 30–47; Rush Welter, *The Mind of America, 1820–1860* (New York: Columbia University Press, 1975), 79–82, 113–115.

80. See William Stanton, *The Leopard's Spots: Scientific Attitudes Toward Race in America, 1815–1859* (Chicago: University of Chicago Press, 1960); and, more generally, George Frederickson, *The Black Image in the White Mind: The Debate on Afro-American Character and Destiny, 1817–1914* (New York: Harper & Row, 1971), chaps. 3–5.

81. See appendix 2C. This conclusion differs from that of Donald E. Hargis, "Native Californians in the Constitutional Convention of 1849," *Historical Society of Southern California Quarterly* 36 (March 1954): 3–13.

82. *Report of the Debates,* 20–23.

83. Ibid., 136. The constitution's individual liability clause is discussed in Ira Cross, *Financing an Empire: History of Banking in California,* 4 vols. (Chicago: S. J. Clarke, 1927), 1:113. More generally, see Hurst, *Legitimacy of the Business Corporation,* 26–29.

84. *Report of the Debates,* 112.

85. Ibid., 112, 118.

86. Ibid., 125, 324.

87. Ibid., 116. Gwin twice referred to the lessons of the 1830s about banks and paper money: ibid., 117, 132.

88. Ibid., 108. This is from art. 7, sec. 1, of the 1846 Iowa constitution; Francis Newton Thorpe, *The Federal and State Constitutions . . . ,* 11 vols. (Washington, D.C.: Government Printing Office, 1909), 2:1132.

89. *Report of the Debates,* 325–326.

90. Ibid., app., vi.

91. Ibid., 326. Jones took the same position; see ibid., 131.

92. See ibid., app., vi. The first prohibition is found in the first clause of art. 4, sec. 34; the second in art. 4, sec. 35. Regarding the latter, James McHall Jones commented that "the Committee [of the Whole] has at length got itself into the predicament of having prohibited the Legislature from granting any charter for banking purposes; and, at the same time, tacitly allowing any person or persons, associations or companies, except those particular associations named in the article just passed, to exercise any of the privileges of banking" (ibid., 135).

93. Banking in nineteenth-century California (and the irrelevance of the constitutional prohibitions to it) is covered in Cross, *Financing an Empire,* vol. 1; and Leroy Amstrong and J. O. Denny, *Financial California* (San Francisco: Coast Banker, 1916), 16–25.

94. At the time of the convention this limitation was in effect in twenty-three of thirty states. The exceptions were Maine, New Hampshire, Vermont, Massachusetts, Rhode Island, New York, and New Jersey; in each of these states, property qualifications limited the franchise, and in New York a property qualification specific to free Negroes was in effect. The relevant documents are found in Thorpe, *Federal and State Constitutions,* passim.

95. *Report of the Debates,* 63.

96. Ibid., 61–63.

97. Ibid., 64–65.

98. Ibid., 306. Similarly, delegate Jacob Hoppe argued: "There was not a *rancho* where you would not find fifty or a hundred buck Indians, and the owner could run these *freemen* up to the polls, and carry any measure he might desire" (ibid.).

99. Henry Tefft declared his support for the exclusion of "Mexican Peons," as well as "Negroes . . . or any class of that kind" (ibid., 143).

100. Ibid., 305. On Domínguez, see Anne Loftis, *California—Where the Twain Did Meet* (New York: Macmillan, 1973), 65.

101. The proviso was moved by Thomas Vermuele; *Report of the Debates,* 341. The debate over this provision is examined in detail in Hansen, *The Search for Authority in California,* 121–122, 153–154.

102. Loftis, *California,* 65.

103. *Report of the Debates,* 137. McCarver earlier (ibid., 44) proposed the section as part of the bill of rights, but withdrew it in favor of proposing a separate section of the legislative article.

104. Ibid., 137.

105. Ibid., 138.

106. Ibid., 142, 144.

107. Ibid., 332, 336.

108. Shannon's position was a shifting one. Following his plea against McCarver's exclusion on the grounds that the services provided by free Negroes were "necessary to the comfort and convenience of domestic life" (ibid., 139), he declared that he could not countenance McCarver's proposal because, as a citizen of New York, he knew many free men of color who were the "most respectable of citizens; they are men of wealth, intelligence, and business capacity" (143). Yet at the same time, he favored a proposal to ban the immigration of ex-slaves brought to California "under bonds of indenture or servitude" (143).

109. Ibid., 141, 145.

110. Ibid., 150.

111. McCarver to Voris, September 19, 1849. The measure's passage is found in *Report of the Debates,* 152.

112. Ibid., 340.

113. Ibid., 338.

114. Ibid.

115. Ibid., 167. See also Glen Leonard, "Southwestern Boundaries and the

Principles of Statemaking," *Western Historical Quarterly* 8 (January 1977): 39–53.

116. *Report of the Debates*, 169.

117. Ibid., 194.

118. This characterization oversimplifies the tangle of congressional politics, which actually divided four ways: for the proviso, for extension of the Missouri Compromise line, for popular sovereignty, and for protection of slave property throughout the western territories. See David Potter, *The Impending Crisis, 1848–1861*, completed and edited by Don E. Fehrenbacher (New York: Harper & Row, 1976), 63–89.

119. These missions are described in Michael Holt, *The Political Crisis of the 1850s* (New York: John Wiley, 1978), 77–78; Dale L. Morgan, "The State of Deseret," *Utah Historical Quarterly* 8 (April–October 1940): 92–95; Hubert Howe Bancroft, *History of Arizona and New Mexico* (San Francisco: History Company, 1889), 446–447n.11.

120. *Alta California*, June 14, 1849; King's activities can be traced in *Memoirs of Elisha Oscar Crosby*, 30–32; Bancroft, *History of California* 6 : 281–283; William Henry Ellison, *A Self-governing dominion: California, 1849–1860* (Berkeley and Los Angeles: University of California Press, 1950), 24–25; Harlow, *California Conquered*, 328–329.

121. *Report of the Debates*, 184, 190, 436–437.

122. Halleck, "Autobiography," 4–5. Compare the comment in his biography with his remarks in *Report of the Debates*, 436–437.

123. *Report of the Debates*, 175.

124. Ibid., 169, 197, 198.

125. Californians were aware of Douglas's efforts. On March 22, 1849, the *Alta California* reprinted a version of his California bill and reported (incorrectly) that its passage was likely. Douglas's bill went through various incarnations in 1849. He first moved that the entire Mexican cession be made a single state. Then he limited the proposed state boundaries to the area west of the Sierra Nevada. Then he favored the territory, excepting New Mexico, that extended from the Pacific to the Rockies. The latter—which was Gwin's proposal as well—Douglas (like Gwin) justified by reference to the Preuss map of 1848, which indicated that under Mexican rule this region composed California. Furthermore, Douglas (again like Gwin) also emphasized the precedents of Virginia, Kentucky, and Tennessee. See 30 Cong., 2d sess., 21, 190–196, 262, 381, 685; *Report of the Debates*, 194–198.

126. *Report of the Debates*, 197.

127. See appendix 2C.

128. Gwin's remark is found in *Report of the Debates*, 196. Two weeks later, after the Californios' support for Gwin and Halleck dissolved, Miguel Pedrorena and José Antonio Carrillo denied that they had voted for the extended boundary in order to separate southern from northern California; ibid., 446.

129. The vote in favor of the Gwin-Halleck proposal was nineteen to four; report does not give individual votes. See ibid., 200.

130. A different view of the boundary dispute is in Leonard, "Southwestern Boundaries," although the principle of "appropriateness" he describes (40 and passim) is relevant to the following discussion.

131. Potter, *The Impending Crisis*, 70–72.

132. *Report of the Debates*, 422, 447, 173.

133. Ibid., 185.

134. Ibid., 187.

135. Ibid., 173. Analogies between the Gwin-Halleck proposal and the Wilmot proviso are found in ibid., 181 (Winfield Sherwood), 184 (Morton Mc-Carver), 191 (William Shannon), 440 (Charles Botts), and 448 (Francis Lippitt).

136. Ibid., 441.

137. See appendix 2C, which describes the boundary voting alignments.

138. *Report of the Debates*, 442.

139. Ibid., 442.

140. Ibid., 449–450.

141. See the discussion that followed in ibid., 450–458.

CHAPTER FIVE: A LIBERAL COMMONWEALTH

1. Jean Baker, "From Belief into Culture: Republicanism in the Antebellum North," *American Quarterly* 37 (Fall 1985): 544 and passim.

2. The original report appeared in the *New York Tribune*, October 6, 1857. It is reprinted, along with *Oregon Statesman* editor Asahel Bush's commentary, in the *Oregon Statesman*, November 17 and 24, 1857.

3. Ibid., November 17, 1857.

4. Charles H. Carey, ed., *The Oregon Constitution and Proceedings and Debates of the Constitutional Convention of 1857* (Salem, Oreg.: State Printing Department, 1926), 74 (hereafter cited as Carey, *Oregon Constitution*).

5. Ibid., 73.

6. Ibid.

7. *Sacramento Daily Union*, August 28, 1857.

8. Ibid., September 28, 1857. In addition, see Carey, *Oregon Constitution*, app. (a), 468–482; Helen Leonard Seagraves, "Oregon's 1857 Constitution," *Reed College Bulletin* 30 (1952): 9.

9. Carey, *Oregon Constitution*, 101.

10. These features of state constitutions revised in the 1830s and 1840s are generally interpreted as expressing a Jacksonian desire to assist the "release of private energies" by forestalling legislative corruption through restrictions on legislative authority to grant special corporate charters and enlarged gubernatorial (checking) powers. Although this view is certainly correct, it should be recognized that this context, to varying degrees in different places, also encouraged constitutional reformers to think in terms of an older, classical republican discourse. To some, the concern of these new constitutions with privilege, corruption, and the degrading effects of commercialism echoed classical republican fears as well as celebrated the market freedom of the individual. Expansion of the range of elected officers similarly evinced, in both republican and Jacksonian terms, a desire to check the sway of the "money power." See the valuable discussions in Morton Keller, "The Politics of State Constitutional Revision, 1820–1930," in *The Constitutional Convention as an Amending Device*, ed. Kermit L. Hall, Harold M. Hyman, and Leon W. Sigal (Washington, D.C.: American Historical Association and American Political Science Association, 1981), 71–73, 88–89, and passim; and Kermit L. Hall, *The Magic Mirror: Law in American History* (New York: Oxford University Press, 1989), 94–105, esp. 103–105. The works of J.

Willard Hurst are of crucial importance in this regard; see *The Growth of American Law: The Law Makers* (Boston: Little, Brown, 1950), 241–242 and, more generally, 1–19, 199–246; *Law and the Conditions of Freedom in the Nineteenth-Century United States* (Madison: University of Wisconsin Press, 1956), passim; and *Law and Social Order in the United States* (Ithaca: Cornell University Press, 1977), 42–65.

11. William G. Shade, *Banks or No Banks: The Money Issue in Western Politics, 1832–1865* (Detroit: Wayne State University Press, 1972), 113–123, 138–141; James Roger Sharp, *The Jacksonians versus the Banks: Politics in the State After the Panic of 1837* (New York: Columbia University Press, 1970), 207–208.

12. See appendix 1B. Of the forty-five donation land claims held by the convention delegates, six were for 160 acres, nineteen for 320 acres, and twenty for 640 acres; the average holding was 411 acres (figures compiled from *Genealogical Materials in Oregon Donation Land Claims*, 5 vols. [Portland: Genealogical Forum of Portland, Oregon, 1957–1975]; *Genealogical Materials in Oregon Provisional Land Claims* [Portland: Genealogical Forum of Portland, Oregon, 1982]).

13. Of the seventeen delegates who were lawyers, eight also possessed donation land claims of sizes from 160 to 640 acres: A. D. Babcock, Reuben Boise, Stephen Chadwick, Matthew Deady, James Kerr Kelly, John McBride, Cyrus Olney, and Delazon Smith (*Genealogical Materials in Oregon Donation Land Claims* and *Oregon Provisional Land Claims*).

14. Most notably Joseph Lane, Asahel Bush, James Nesmith, George Curry, and William Lysander Adams.

15. The delegation from Clackamas County, south of Multnomah (Portland) and north of the central Willamette Valley counties, contained a mixture of men, including prominent "National" Democrats such as James Kerr Kelly, as well as loyalists to the Salem organization.

16. On my selection of the leading delegates, see appendix 2A. In addition, two contemporary evaluations are germane: *Sacramento Daily Union*, August 22 and September 11, 22, and 28, 1857; *Alta California* (San Francisco), September 13 and 24, 1857.

17. Deady to Bush, May 12, 1854; Bush Papers, Bush House Museum, Salem, Oregon; and Bush to Deady, November 2, 1856, Deady Papers, Oregon Historical Society, Portland. Unless otherwise noted, all letters between Deady and Bush are, respectively, from these collections.

18. Grover to Thurston, December 14, 1850; Thurston Papers, Oregon Historical Society.

19. Ibid.; [La Fayette Grover], *Biographical Sketch of La Fayette Grover of Oregon* (privately published, n.d.), 3–4.

20. Alfred L. Lomax, *Pioneer Woolen Mills in Oregon: History of Wool and the Woolen Textile Industry in Oregon, 1811–1875* (Portland: Binford & Mort, 1941), 97–106.

21. Grover received 743 votes in Marion County. The lowest number of votes necessary for election was 626 (received by Richard Miller). *Oregonian*, June 20, 1857.

22. Quoted in the *Sacramento Daily Union*, September 25, 1857 (Dryer's comments are dated by the *Union* as of September 9).

23. T. W. Davenport, "Recollections of an Indian Agent, Pt. 3," *Oregon Historical Society Quarterly* 8 (September 1907): 249.

24. *Gold Hill [Nevada] Evening News*, September 30, 1864.

25. *Oregon Statesman*, July 26, 1853; I am indebted to Caroline Stoel for bringing Williams's written opinion to my attention. On the Holmes case, see Malcolm Clark, *Eden Seekers: The Settlement of Oregon, 1818–1862* (Boston: Houghton Mifflin, 1981), 259–261; and Oscar C. Christensen, "The Grand Old Man of Oregon: The Life of George H. Williams (M.A. thesis, University of Oregon, 1939), 6–7.

26. *Oregon Statesman*, July 28, 1857; reprinted in "The Free-State Letter of Judge George H. Williams," *Oregon Historical Society Quarterly* 9 (September 1908): 254–273. See also Walter C. Woodward, "Rise and Early History of Political Parties in Oregon, Pt. 3," *Oregon Historical Society Quarterly* 12 (June 1911): 151–153.

27. "Free-State Letter of Judge George H. Williams," 259.

28. Ibid., 260–261, 265–266.

29. Ibid., 260–261, 268–269, 272. See also Williams's support of such restrictions in the constitutional convention, in Carey, *Oregon Constitution*, 234–236.

30. Malcolm Clark, ed., *Pharisee Among the Philistines: The Diary of Judge Matthew P. Deady, 1871–1892* (Portland: Oregon Historical Society, 1975), xxxii–xxxiii.

31. Philip Henry Overmeyer, "The Oregon Justinian: A Life of Matthew Paul Deady" (M.A. thesis, University of Oregon, 1935), 19–21. The influence of Kennon on Deady was great. In 1881, shortly after his teacher's death, Deady revisited the town in which he had studied with the judge and went to Kennon's grave in order "to acknowledge my indebtedness to the precepts and example of my old preceptor" (quoted in ibid. 19n.23).

32. Hubert Howe Bancroft, *Chronicles of the Builders of the Commonwealth* (San Francisco: History Company, 1892), 609; see also Sidney Teiser, "A Pioneer Judge of Oregon," *Oregon Historical Society Quarterly* 44 (1943): 72.

33. Clark, *Pharisee Among the Philistines*, xxxiv; Overmeyer, "Oregon Justinian," 56–59.

34. Clark, *Eden Seekers*, 244.

35. Amory Holbrook, the appointed (Whig) territorial attorney, was the foremost opponent of removing the capital to Salem; see Bush to Deady, August 5 and 19, 1851.

36. In Deady to Bush, September 25, 1851, he wrote that "the com. on the location question was written in reply to your invitation."

37. Deady to Lane, January 21, 1853; this letter is in the Bush Papers.

38. James E. Hendrickson, *Joe Lane of Oregon: Machine Politics and the Sectional Crisis, 1849–1861* (New Haven: Yale University Press, 1967), 68–70. In addition, see Deady to Lane, December 28, 1852 (in the Deady Papers); and Deady to Bush, February 10, 1853, in which he declares that "many young men who are Whigs say publicly that they will vote for me for delegate against any other man." See also Bush to Deady, April 4, 1853.

39. Although Lane arranged Deady's appointment to the court, what appears to have been an innocent error in the preparation of his commission produced suspicion between him and Lane. In the commission, Deady's name was misspelled as *Mordecai;* thus initially his claim to the post appeared invalid. Although Lane was blameless, Deady interpreted the mistake as a personal as well as political affront and never forgot it. He remained outwardly cordial toward

Lane, but his trust was broken and remained so until, following the constitutional convention, the political crisis over secession drew them together once again. The most extensive treatment of this affair is in Overmeyer, "Oregon Justinian," 151–158; it is also covered (from slightly different angles) in Hendricksen, *Joe Lane*, 74–75, 82–85; and Clark, *Eden Seekers*, 257–258, 265–266.

40. During the territorial period, Deady spent at least six months of every year on the circuit of his court; Overmeyer, "Oregon Justinian," 83. To James Nesmith, Deady wrote in the winter of 1853, as he worked to establish his farm: "If I ever help break in another new country, it will be because I can't help it" (quoted in ibid.).

41. Deady explained his decision to run for delegate in a letter of April 21, 1857, to Bush: "I believe that I have consented to receive the nomination to the constitutional convention. The nomination comes off next Saturday. When I get there I may change my mind if I think there will be a fight for it" (quoted in ibid., 116n.59). In 1858, Deady did stand for election to the state supreme court, but in that race he refused to canvass; see Deady to Bush, March 7, 1858.

42. *Oregon Statesman*, June 23, 1857. The leading vote getter for delegate from Douglas County was Democrat Solomon Fitzhugh, who received 397 votes, 43 percent more than Deady, who received 279; the returns are reported in the *Oregonian*, June 20, 1857.

43. Deady's views were best expressed in a letter (in the Deady Papers) to Benjamin Simpson, from which I have taken the following passages. It was written, ironically, on the day Williams's letter appeared in the *Statesman*, July 28, 1857.

44. Benjamin Simpson to Deady, June 22, 1857. See also James M. Pyle to Deady, August 4, 1857.

45. Deady to Simpson, July 28, 1857.

46. *Alta California*, September 24, October 21, 1857.

47. John McBride, "The Oregon Constitutional Convention of 1857," in Carey, *Oregon Constitution*, 490.

48. The material on Smith's life is scant and based for the most part on a single source, "Hon. Delazon Smith, Senator in Congress from the State of Oregon," *United States Magazine and Democratic Review* 43 (1859): 79–86.

49. Joseph Kett, *Rites of Passage: Adolescence in America, 1790 to the Present* (New York: Basic Books, 1977), 14–37.

50. R. Carlyle Buley, *The Old Northwest: Pioneer Period, 1815–1840*, vol. 2 (Bloomington: Indiana University Press, 1951), 2:405–406.

51. McBride, "Oregon Constitutional Convention," 489.

52. "Hon. Delazon Smith," 85.

53. Delazon Smith to his brother, January 1, 1858, and July 12, 1857; Oregon Collection, University of Oregon.

54. Smith to Bush, July 27, 1856; Bush Papers, Bush House Museum, Salem, Oregon.

55. Ibid., March 15, 24, 1855.

56. The eulogy may be found in the *Oregon Statesman*, April 23, 1853; the following quotations are from this source.

57. Smith to Bush, July 12, 1853.

58. *Oregon Statesman*, December 19, 1854.

59. See the discussion in Baker, "From Belief into Culture," 548.

60. Smith to Bush, July 12, 1853.

61. Ibid., July 27, 1856. See also ibid., May 25, 1853, and March 15, 20, 1855.

62. Ibid., July 11, 1857.

63. Applegate considered the *implicit* agreement, embraced by almost all the delegates except himself and McBride, to avoid discussion of slavery cowardly. His charge of cowardice did not, however, stem from a desire to air the issue; rather, he objected to the delegates' refusal to declare *explicitly* that they would not debate the issue. When a majority defeated his resolution prohibiting any discussion of slavery (which they did despite the general agreement in both the convention and the party caucus that in fact they would not discuss the question), Applegate took his leave. See Carey, *Oregon Constitution,* 79–80, 86, 88, 215–217. McBride, reminiscing forty-five years later, emphasized the refusal of the Whigs in the convention to support his call for an airing of the slavery issue; see McBride, "Oregon Constitutional Convention," 493.

64. Quoted in the *Oregon Spectator,* August 8, 1850.

65. Ibid.

66. Ibid., April 17, 1851.

67. Deady, for example, wrote to Bush on August 9, 1852: "I see Dryer is down on King and Deady for raising the price of that useful commodity—*whiskey.* I hope the change in the market has not found him with short rations. If so that accounts for his chagrin. The damned old sot! Where I have drank a pint he has drank his gallons."

68. In 1853 Dryer was suspended from his Masonic lodge for drinking; E. Kimbark MacColl, *Merchants, Money, and Power: The Portland Establishment, 1843–1913* (Portland: Georgian Press, 1988), 54.

69. *Oregonian,* May 5, 1855.

70. Ibid., July 5, 1856.

71. Ibid.

72. Responding editorially to Republican organization in 1856 Dryer wrote: "We have always supposed we were a Republican, we think so still. . . . If our republicanism don't suit you gentlemen, your republicanism won't suit us, and we shall not endorse it" (ibid., November 8, 1856).

73. Dryer ran for a seat in the convention as joint delegate from Multnomah and Washington counties. In Multnomah County, he ran as an "Independent"; in Washington County, as an "American." See ibid., June 6, 13, 1857.

74. Ibid., July 18, 1857.

75. This is the assessment of John J. Duff, *A. Lincoln: Prairie Lawyer* (New York: Rinehart, 1960), 94–95.

76. On Stephen Logan, see Stephen B. Oates, *With Malice Toward None: The Life of Abraham Lincoln* (New York: New American Library, 1977), 64.

77. Ibid., 78.

78. "Stephen T. Logan Talks About Lincoln," *Lincoln Centennial Association Bulletin,* no. 12 (September 1, 1928): 5. Logan made his comments in 1875.

79. His departure may also have been prompted by the death of his "sweetheart," Jane Jones. Logan pined for her; as he wrote to his sister upon his arrival: "I am isolated and alone so I expect to live so to die. My hopes of all else now slumber in the silence of the grave[.] [M]y wants and desires are few & easily

satisfied, the means easily obtained, one desire I have to visit once more the Tomb of my beloved Jane[.] [T]his gratified I have nothing more to ask." In 1862, at the age of thirty-seven, Logan married Mary Waldo, daughter of a noted anti-Democrat in Portland, after a decade-long courtship. Logan wrote his sister in 1853 that "perhaps I shall be married before long," and again in 1859 that "it has been put off from time to time, until the present." See "22 Letters of David Logan, Pioneer Oregon Lawyer," ed. Harry E. Pratt, *Oregon Historical Society Quarterly* 44 (September 1943): 260 and n. 11 (January 3, 1851), 266 (September 2, 1853), 279 (September 7, 1859).

80. Ibid., 270 (January 27, 1856), 272 (September 10, 1856).

81. Ibid., 258 (November 20, 1850), 260 (January 3, 1851).

82. Ibid., 263 (June 20, 1852).

83. Chapman was a proprietor of Portland and founder of the *Oregonian;* Chinn died in 1856 but in the early 1850s was a prominent Portland Whig often featured in the pages of the *Oregonian;* Shattuck was a nativist and temperance advocate (and a delegate to the constitutional convention). On Chinn, see Walter C. Woodward, "Rise and Early History of Political Parties in Oregon, Pt. 2," *Oregon Historical Society Quarterly* 12 (March 1911): 67–69; on Chapman, see Maccoll, *Merchants, Money, and Power,* 15–17 and passim; and on Shattuck, see Rev. Harvey K. Hines, *An Illustrated History of Oregon* (Chicago: Lewis, 1913), 241–242.

84. George Williams, "Political History of Oregon, 1853–1865," in Carey, *Oregon Constitution,* 505.

85. Deady to Bush, May 23, 1851. See also "22 Letters of David Logan," 257n.7, 259, 260, 263.

86. Clark, *Eden Seekers,* 250. Deady won the election by a vote of 168 to 106. The story about his getting Logan to drink became somewhat legendary. In 1868, James Nesmith wrote to Deady to say, "Many of your old Democratic friends express the hope that you would be back in time to get him [David Logan] drunk before the close of the Canvass, *as you did when he ran against you for the Council in Yam Hill*" (Nesmith to Deady, March 27, 1868; quoted in Overmeyer, "Oregon Justinian," 95).

87. In November 1854, Deady sent a detailed account to James Nesmith: "Some weeks since a friend of mine sent to Leland a certificate more than sustaining the Budget correspondence [in the *Democratic Standard* regarding the rape]. I now know there is no mistake about it from eyewitnesses. The statement of the facts as I ascertain them are these. At noon on the eighth of August, Logan was seen on the open ground at the end of one of the Main Streets of the town in full view of a large number of persons male and female. A squaw came along . . . Logan took after her and caught her by the blanket, the blanket pulled off and she escaped. He held on to the blanket[;] she came back after it and he then caught her and threw her down unbuttoning his pantaloons and went through the motions. After he was through and up, she having been screaming all the time, he gave her some money and went off to the creek nearby and washed himself" (Deady to Nesmith, November 2, 1854; Nesmith Letters, Oregon Historical Society).

88. Deady to Bush, November 24, 1854.

89. The epithet "Mingo Chief" was drawn from the well-known story in Jefferson's *Notes on the State of Virginia* about the Mingo (Indian) Chief Logan,

whose family was massacred by whites in 1774, precipitating Lord Dunsmore's War. According to Malcolm Clark, David Logan was called the Mingo Chief "because of a bent toward high oratory and low boozing shared with that other Logan, the Indian leader celebrated in Jefferson's *Notes on the State of Virginia*" (Clark, *Eden Seekers: The Settlement of Oregon, 1818–1862* [Boston: Houghton Mifflin, 1982]: 270). While Clark's characterization of the eighteenth-century "Chief Logan" is undoubtedly incorrect, it may well capture the partisan mythology of nineteenth-century Oregon Democrats who used the story to ridicule David Logan. Convenient discussions of Jefferson and the controversy over Chief Logan are found in Merrill D. Peterson, *Thomas Jefferson and the New Nation: A Biography* (New York: Oxford University Press, 1970): 581–586; and Dumas Malone, *Jefferson the Virginian* (Boston: Little, Brown, 1948): 385–387. The relevant passage in Jefferson's *Notes on the State of Virginia* can be consulted in *The Portable Thomas Jefferson,* ed. Merrill D. Peterson (New York: Penguin Books, 1977): 99–100.

90. Quoted in McBride, "Oregon Constitutional Convention," 493.

91. Carey, *Oregon Constitution,* 319.

92. "22 Letters of David Logan," 272, 277 (September 10, 1856, and September 7, 1859).

93. Carey, *Oregon Constitution,* 199.

94. Ibid., 204–205.

95. Appendix 2D describes the voting alignments in the Oregon convention.

96. Carey, *Oregon Constitution,* 187–188.

97. Ibid., 188.

98. Ibid., 181–182. At question was whether one of the proprietors of the town (Democrat Thomas Lownsdale) or the "public" owned the riverfront. Arrayed against Lownsdale's claim were the Whig illuminati of Portland, including Thomas Dryer and his patrons, Steven Coffin and W. W. Chapman. Lownsdale, in the face of (some but not all) town council instructions as well as various court decisions, sold property along the river throughout the 1850s and otherwise managed to treat the town's waterfront as his own. All the while, by appealing territorial court decisions to the U.S. Supreme Court and relying on contradictory edicts from the city council—a city council on which men beholden to him sat—he was able to resist efforts to halt his development of the waterfront. By 1857 the levee was dotted by warehouses, mills, and private wharfs constructed by associates of Lownsdale, many of them prominent Democrats. The conflict over the Willamette River levee is discussed in Jeffrey G. Carter, "A History of the Portland Waterfront Between Southwest Clay and Washington Streets, Its Land Use and Legal Problems," (M.A. thesis, Portland State University, 1981); see also MacColl, *Merchants, Money, and Power,* 12–17, 49–61.

99. According to Dryer, "the municipal court should be a court of record, so that an appeal could be taken from their decision" (Carey, *Oregon Constitution,* 192).

100. Ibid., 181.

101. Compare sec. 19 of the Indiana Bill of Rights to sec. 19 of the draft report submitted to the Oregon convention, in Francis Newton Thorpe, *The Federal and State Constitutions . . . ,* 11 vols. (Washington, D.C.: Government Printing Office, 1909), 2:1075; and Carey, *Oregon Constitution,* 120.

102. Carey, *Oregon Constitution*, 311.

103. Ibid., 314.

104. Ibid., 311–312.

105. Ibid., 314.

106. Ibid., 311.

107. Ibid., 313.

108. Ibid., 314. In its final form, the section (art. 1, sec. 16) read: "the jury shall have the right to determine the law, and the facts under the direction of the Court as to the law . . ." (ibid., 402).

109. Morton J. Horwitz has traced this shift through the case law of the antebellum period. See Horwitz, *The Transformation of American Law, 1780–1860* (Cambridge, Mass.: Harvard University Press, 1977), 28–29, 142–143.

110. The passage from the Indiana constitution is in Thorpe, *Federal and State Constitutions* 2 : 1073–1076; the Oregon preamble reported by the committee is in Carey, *Oregon Constitution*, 119.

111. Carey, *Oregon Constitution*, 305.

112. Ibid.

113. Ibid., 304.

114. Ibid., 120. This is sec. 34 of the draft bill of rights.

115. Ibid., 320.

116. The Indiana provision is found in Thorpe, *Federal and State Constitutions* 2 : 1076; cf. Carey, *Oregon Constitution*, 173.

117. Carey, *Oregon Constitution*, 320.

118. Ibid., 318–320. In this discussion Logan disagreed with other anti-Democrats. Although admitting that he "had been slightly burned with Know Nothingism," he opposed restrictions on the grounds that as a new state Oregon would necessarily find that its "population will, in all probability, be made up of many foreigners" (ibid., 322).

119. Ibid., 324.

120. Ibid., 361–362.

121. Ibid., 369, and art. 15 (Miscellaneous Provisions), sec. 8 (ibid., 427). At the same time—in unintended testimony to their conception of the margins of citizenship—the delegates briefly debated a provision reported by the Committee on Miscellaneous Provisions to secure the property rights of married women. Williams moved to strike the section, holding that "in this age of woman's rights and insane theories, our legislation should be such as to unite the family circle, and make husband and wife what they should be—bone of one bone, and flesh of one flesh. . . . If we established this provision, we must provide laws by which the husband and wife can sue each other." With respect to Williams's proposal, party lines did not seem to matter. Smith and Bush crony Frederick Waymire, for example, joined Dryer and Logan in opposing the motion. Smith observed that he "did not think it would contribute to the harmony of the family circle. . . . He was for woman's rights, and was not afraid of her having too many. She had been too long denied her just rights. He would protect her property from dissipated or mercenary wretches." The motion lost. See ibid., 368–369.

122. Art. 11, sec. 1; ibid., 423.

123. Ibid., 242.

124. Ibid., 246–247.

125. Ibid., 248.

126. Ibid., 248–249.

127. Ibid., 250.

128. Ibid., 250–251.

129. Ibid., 250–252.

130. Ibid., 274.

131. Ibid., 255.

132. Ibid., 234–235.

133. Ibid., 241.

134. Ibid., 235–236.

135. Ibid., 261, 262, 265.

136. Ibid., 242–243.

137. Waymire's amendment is at ibid., 275; see also his comments about corporations, 237.

138. Ibid., 388, 394. Smith's speech is at 386–397.

139. Ibid., 381, 382, 383. Dryer's entire speech is at 381–384.

CHAPTER SIX: BETWEEN GOLDEN AND GILDED AGES

1. Andrew J. Marsh, *Official Report of the Debates and Proceedings in the Constitutional Convention of the State of Nevada, Assembled at Carson City, July 4, 1864, to Form a Constitution and State Government* (San Francisco: Frank Eastman, 1866), 7–10.

2. Ibid., 274.

3. See appendix 1C. Of the thirty-five delegates, fourteen had voted for Lincoln in 1860, thirteen for Douglas, six for Bell, and two for Breckenridge. All but one, Democrat Francis Proctor of Nye County, listed their current political affiliation as Union (ibid., xvi). In the convention, Thomas Fitch argued that it was the delegates' duty to provide a precedent for the "denationaliz[ation] of the whole southern country" (ibid., 103). See also the remarks of E. F. Dunne and B. F. Mason; ibid., 137–138, 460.

4. Ibid., 621.

5. Ibid., 824.

6. The prosopographical table in appendix 1C contains further information on the Nevada constitution writers.

7. On the selection of the leading delegates, see appendix 2A.

8. Oliver Johnson, *W. L. Garrison and His Times* (1881; reprint, Miami: Mnemosyne, 1969), 300. Johnson was an abolitionist friend of Collins.

9. Louis Filler, *Crusade Against Slavery* (Algonac, Mich.: Reference Publications, 1986), 165. Generally, see Russell Nye, *William Lloyd Garrison and the Humanitarian Reformers* (Boston: Little, Brown, 1955), 107–110. J. Earl Thompson discusses Andover and antislavery in "Abolitionism and Theological Education at Andover," *New England Quarterly* 47 (June 1974): 238–261. "The faculty [of Andover]," he notes, "supported only gradual, peaceful, and non-controversial reform organizations for which there was a high probability of extensive evangelical Protestant backing on a national scale. Colonization barely qualified in this category but not immediatism" (260).

10. Garrison to George W. Benson; quoted in *A House Divided Against Itself: The*

Letters of William Lloyd Garrison, ed. Walter M. Merrill and Louis Rucharme, 6 vols. (Cambridge, Mass.: Harvard University Press, Belknap Press, 1971–1981), 3 : 40.

11. While in England Collins wrote a polemical account of American controversies entitled *Right and Wrong Amongst Abolitionists in the United States* (Glasgow, 1841); see Filler, *Crusade Against Slavery,* 165n.56.

12. Quincy to Garrison, January 29, 1843; in *William Lloyd Garrison: The Story of His Life, Told by His Children,* 4 vols. (New York: Century, 1885–1889), 3 : 89. Before his departure from Garrison's movement in 1843 Collins organized the "One Hundred Conventions" in the West and oversaw for Garrison the first public appearances of Frederick Douglass on behalf of the society. Douglass disliked Collins's heavy-handed treatment; see Nathan Irvin Huggins, *Slave and Citizen: The Life of Frederick Douglass* (Boston: Little, Brown, 1980), 2, 17–20. The most important discussion of Collins is John Thomas, "Antislavery and Utopia," in *The Antislavery Vanguard: New Essays on the Abolitionists,* ed. Martin Duberman (Princeton: Princeton University Press, 1965), 254–259.

13. Quoted in Thomas, "Antislavery and Utopia," 256.

14. Garrison to Henry G. Wright, April 1, 1843; in Merrill and Rucharme, (eds.), *Letters of William Lloyd Garrison* 3 : 145.

15. Ibid.

16. Collins outlined his conception of the experiment in *A Bird's Eye View of Society As It Is, and As It Should Be* (Boston: J. P. Madison, 1844). On Community Place, see also Thomas, "Antislavery and Utopia," 256–259; Mark Holloway, *Heavens on Earth: Utopian Communities in America, 1680–1880* (London: Turnstile Press, 1951), 124–125; John Humphrey Noyes, *History of American Socialisms* (1870; reprint, New York: Hillary House, 1961), 161–180; Edmund Norman Leslie, *Skaneateles: History of Its Earliest Settlement and Reminiscences of Later Times* (New York: Andrew H. Kellogg, 1902), 175–177.

17. Arthur Bestor, *Backwoods Utopias: The Sectarian and Owenite Phases of Communitarian Socialism in America, 1663–1829* (Philadelphia: University of Pennsylvania Press, 1950), 50.

18. Noyes, *History of American Socialisms,* 180.

19. Ibid., 167.

20. Thomas, "Antislavery and Utopia," 257.

21. Noyes, *History of American Socialisms,* 171; Holloway, *Heavens on Earth,* 125.

22. Quoted in Whitney Cross, *The Burned Over District: The Social and Intellectual History of Enthusiastic Religion in Western New York* (New York: Harper & Row, 1965), 332–333.

23. Samuel J. May to Richard D. Webb, July 12, 1864; quoted in Filler, *Crusade Against Slavery,* 141n. Collins left Boston by ship in March 1849 and arrived in June; see Charles Warren Haskins, *The Argonauts of California, Being the Reminiscences of Scenes and Incidents That Occurred in California in Early Mining Days* (New York: Fords, Howard, & Hulbert, 1890), 459.

24. In 1851 another New England immigrant wrote: "I heard of John A. Collins as being in the city, but did not see him. It is said that he has acquired considerable property during the short time he has been in the country" (quoted in John W. Caughey, ed., "Life in California in 1849: As Described in the 'Journal' of George F. Kent," *California Historical Society Quarterly* 20 (March 1941): 31,

45n.11. Later in the 1850s Collins was a co-owner of the Grass Valley Mining Company (from 1851 to 1857; see Harry Laurens Wells, ed., *History of Nevada County, California* . . . [Oakland, Calif.: Thompson & West, 1880], 193) and also involved in organizing the Pacific Mining Company at Gold Bluffs near the Klamath River, a notorious fraud. According to Frank Soule in the *Annals of San Francisco* . . . (New York: D. Appleton, 1855), 311–314, "Mr. Collins measured a patch of gold and sand, and estimates it will yield to *each* member of the company the snug little sum of $43,000,000." This goldfield, as it turned out, was "salted." John S. Hittell, in *A History of the City of San Francisco* . . . (San Francisco: A. L. Bancroft, 1878), 273, concludes that Collins was himself an innocent dupe of other men. In 1859, Collins was listed in the San Francisco city directory as an importer and dealer of "bedding, spring mattresses, etc." I am indebted to Robert Chandler for citations on Collins.

25. Collins to "General" Jonathan Wilson, July 6, 28, 1851, Bancroft Library, University of California, Berkeley.

26. *San Francisco Evening Press*, August 8, 1851.

27. Collins to Wilson, July 28, 1851.

28. Ralph Mann, *After the Gold Rush: Society in Grass Valley and Nevada City, California, 1849–1870* (Stanford: Stanford University Press, 1982), 28.

29. The *Virginia Evening Bulletin* reported (July 9, 1863) that Mark Twain and Thomas Fitch appeared at the opening festivities of the Collins House. On Collins's activities in Virginia City, see the *Territorial Enterprise*, April 3; July 7, 8, 9, 27; August 8, 11, 20, 1863.

30. At an "Anti-Monopoly—Grand Ratification Meeting, of The People's Ticket," held by antistatehood advocates, Collins spoke along with John North, Governor Nye, and others; *Virginia Daily Union*, January 9, 1864. In the race for delegate, Collins ran third out of twenty candidates, receiving 1,192 votes in the county (the top candidate, C. W. Tozer, received 1,227; the lowest number required for election as a delegate was 593, received by Thomas Fitch); ibid., June 8, 1864.

31. Material on Johnson's life is difficult to find. The following is drawn from Howard Brett Melendy, *The Governors of California* (Georgetown, Calif.: Talisman Press, 1965), 66–79, and sources listed below.

32. Winfield J. Davis, *History of Political Conventions in California, 1849–1892,* Publications of the California State Library, no. 1 (Sacramento: CSL, 1893), 43. Among the candidates Johnson defeated for the nomination was John Collins's friend "General" Jonathan Wilson.

33. Payton Hurt, "The Rise and Fall of the 'Know Nothings' in California," *California Historical Society Quarterly* 9 (March–June 1930): 16–49, 99–128.

34. On King and the 1856 vigilance committee, see Roger Lotchin, *San Francisco, 1846–1856: From Hamlet to City* (New York: Oxford University Press, 1974), 245–275.

35. My discussion of the 1856 vigilance committee of San Francisco follows Robert M. Senkewicz, S.J., in *Vigilantes in Gold Rush San Francisco* (Stanford: Stanford University Press, 1985). Lotchin, *San Francisco*, 245–275, correctly emphasizes that, in addition to partisan concerns, the vigilance committee mobilized the growing "bourgeois" (middle-class business and Victorian) sector of the San Francisco population. An important contemporary source on the San Francisco

vigilance committee is volume two of Hubert Howe Bancroft, *Popular Tribunals* (San Francisco: History Company, 1887), which is devoted to the 1856 uprising.

36. Senkewicz, *Vigilantes in Gold Rush San Francisco*, 258n.33.

37. Ibid., 171–172. Johnson's actions toward the San Francisco committee can be followed in Herbert G. Florken, ed., "The Law and Order View of the San Francisco Vigilance Committee of 1856: Taken from the Correspondence of Governor J. Neely Johnson," *California Historical Society Quarterly* 14 (1935): 350–374; 15 (1935): 70–87, 143–162, 247–265.

38. Senkewicz, *Vigilantes in Gold Rush San Francisco*, 175.

39. Quoted in Melendy, *Governors of California*, 72–73.

40. Senkewicz, *Vigilantes in Gold Rush San Francisco*, 183–188. In addition to the four men hanged and thirty deported, partisans of the vigilance committee estimated that hundreds of other desperate characters left the city.

41. On Johnson and the Union party, see the *Gold Hill News*, January 4, 1864; January 3, 1865. His law practice is noted in the *Daily Silver Age*, August 26, 1861. On his openhandedness, see the announcement in the *Territorial Enterprise*, January 10, 1863, of the "grand ball" he put on at Steamboat Springs.

42. *Virginia Daily Union*, June 8, 1864.

43. Thomas Fitch, *Address on the Life and Character of Col. Edward D. Baker* (Placerville, Calif.: *Placerville Republican*, 1862), 1. Fitch delivered this speech at Placerville on February 6, 1862.

44. Quoted in *Western Carpetbagger: The Extraordinary Memoirs of "Senator" Thomas Fitch*, ed. Eric N. Moody (Reno: University of Nevada Press, 1978), 18–19.

45. Ibid., 19.

46. Ibid., 21. *Marysville Daily Appeal*, August 31, November 2, 1860; *Alta California*, November 14, 1860. I am indebted to Robert Chandler for bringing these newspaper reports to my attention.

47. Quoted in the *Sacramento Daily Union*, August 16, 1861. See also the *Mountain Democrat* (Placerville), October 19, 1861.

48. *Alta California*, December 11, 1860; *Marysville Daily Appeal*, August 31, November 2, 1860; Moody, *Western Carpetbagger*, 21.

49. His appointment was announced in the *Daily Evening Bulletin*, June 10, 1861; and his resignation reported in ibid., July 10, 1861, effective July 22. On his firings and hirings at the mint, see the *Sacramento Bee*, November 22, 1861; April 8, 1863.

50. *Daily Evening Bulletin*, July 16, 1861.

51. Ibid.; *Sacramento Bee*, October 23, 1861.

52. On this campaign, see the *Sacramento Daily Union*, August 2, 1862; and the *Mountain Messenger* (Downieville, California), September 13, 1862.

53. On the mining tax, Fitch hedged his bets, declaring while a candidate for delegate that "I am in favor of re-enacting as much of the late Constitution as says, 'Property of all kinds shall be equally taxed,' and of striking out, as unnecessary, the words, 'including mines and mining property,' leaving it to future State legislatures to decide upon, and future State Courts to construe, the question of mining taxation" (*Virginia Daily Union*, May 31, 1864).

54. Fitch's participation in the insurgence is made evident in the *Virginia Daily Union*, January 1, 9, 1864. See also ibid., December 31, 1863; January 6, 19, 1864; *Gold Hill Evening News*, December 31, 1863; January 2, 14, 1864.

55. Fitch published a card a week before the election in which he defended his position in favor of greenbacks and declared his intention to remain a candidate for delegate to the convention; *Virginia Daily Union*, May 31, 1864. Five days earlier, an opponent in the race had been named (by whom is unclear); see ibid., May 25, 1864; and *Gold Hill Evening News*, June 4, 1864. The election returns are found in the *Gold Hill Evening News*, June 7, 1864; and *Virginia Daily Union*, June 8, 1864. Fitch received 593 votes; the top candidate, C. W. Tozer, 1,227.

56. The primary (and invaluable) source on De Long is "California's Bantam Cock: The Journals of Charles E. De Long, 1854–1863," ed. Carl I. Wheat, *California Historical Society Quarterly* 8 (1929): 193–204; 9 (1930): 50–80, 128–181, 243–287, 345–397; 10 (1931): 40–78, 165–201, 245–297, 355–395; 11 (1932): 47–64 (my citations to De Long's journal are by volume and page). Wheat prefaces the journal with an introductory outline of De Long's life (8:193–198) and includes at the end (11:47–64) an "Appendix: Outline of De Long's Career after December 11, 1862," which includes an overview of his activities and a selection of letters. The quoted verse is from 8:197.

57. De Long's manner of getting by in the mines is captured in his early journal; see, in particular, ibid., 8:199–208. His public activities become more apparent in the mid-1850s; see ibid., 8:337–364 and 9:50–80, 129–181, covering the years 1855–1857. See also De Long to James R. De Long (his brother), February 12, 1853; December 1854; August 21, September 16, 1855; quoted ibid., 11:54–55.

58. Quoted in Oscar Shuck, *Representative and Leading Men of the Pacific* (San Francisco: Bacon, 1870), 220.

59. See, for example, Wheat (ed.), "Journal of De Long," 9:132.

60. Quoted in ibid., 9:171.

61. California politics in the 1850s is treated in greater detail below, in chapter 7.

62. On De Long's reelection, see Wheat (ed.), "Journal of De Long," 9:356–357, 387n.109; on his defeat in 1859, 10:173.

63. References to Collins, Fitch, Nye, and Stewart (among others with whom De Long served in the convention) are found in ibid., 10:61, 165, 166, 170, 173, 174, 180, 187, 189, 254, 256, 359, 360, 361, and 377.

64. Ibid., 10:384.

65. Ibid., 11:60.

66. De Long to James R. De Long, September 2, 1863; quoted in ibid., 61.

67. *Virginia Daily Union*, January 9, 1864.

68. Marsh, *Official Report*, 764. See also the views of J. H. Warwick at 761.

69. Ibid., 17–18 (and generally, 14–24).

70. See, for example, Collins's remarks, in ibid., 19–20.

71. Ibid., 5. On the plan to nominate Collins as president and remove the convention to Virginia City, see the *Daily Evening Washoe Herald*, July 2, 1864; in the Nevada Newspaper Miscellany, Bancroft Library, University of California, Berkeley.

72. The "cow counties" were Washoe, Ormsby, and Douglas; the "mining counties," Storey, Humboldt, Lyon, Douglas, Esmeralda, Churchill, Nye, and Lander.

73. Marsh, *Official Report*, 5.

74. Ibid., 41.

75. Ibid.

76. See, for example, De Long's September 2, 1863, letter to James R. De Long, quoted in Wheat (ed.), "Journal of De Long," 11:61: "Brother do you know I have come near joining the army several times? Nothing but my family prevents it but I assure you I feel very much ashamed at times to think that I am lying idle at this hour of our country's peril, but so it is, and the time will come when I know that I shall regret my present inaction. But I now think that it will not be long before the worst of it will be over with. . . . We of the Pacific watch and praise you. In your misfortunes we sorrow[;] in your successes we rejoice."

77. Marsh, *Official Report,* 42.

78. Ibid., 43.

79. Ibid., 73.

80. Ibid., 256–257. The debate concerned an amendment to the original section offered by E. F. Dunne, to the effect that all voters, on registering, would be given an oath by the registrar of voters.

81. Ibid., 255–256.

82. Ibid., 257, 258.

83. Ibid., 260.

84. Ibid., 263.

85. Ibid., 264.

86. Ibid., 186.

87. Ibid., 180.

88. Ibid., 192.

89. Ibid., 189.

90. Limited liability was adopted without discussion; ibid., 163.

91. Ibid., 164–165; cf. art. 7, sec. 6, at 844.

92. Ibid., 164. Nourse described himself politically at 47.

93. Ibid., 452. See also the comments of James Banks at 453.

94. De Long proposed the measure in consultation with Fitch. Final passage by the convention, as in the case of the loyalty oath, came later in the session, after resolution of the tax issue. See ibid., 211–212.

95. The text of the original article (10, sec. 1) is in William C. Miller and Eleanore Bushnell, eds., *Reports of the 1863 Constitutional Convention of the Territory of Nevada* . . . (Carson City: Legislative Counsel Bureau, State of Nevada, 1972), 429.

96. Marsh, *Official Report,* 318–322 and passim. Johnson's amendment was defeated (383), but later in the day it was revived by George Nourse (406) in slightly different form (using the words *possessory rights*), and passed the convention (429). In the text I refer to it as Johnson's proposal.

97. Ibid., 429. On the measure as a compromise, see Collins's comments (with which Fitch concurred) at 444.

98. According to Kennedy, "After the heated discussion which we had last evening upon this question, there seemed to be such a conflict almost in the views of members as to render it impossible to come to any conclusion in regards to this matter, but during the hours of last night and this morning I have conversed with a number of gentlemen in regard to it, and this amendment seems to meet their views" (ibid., 436).

99. Ibid., 476.

100. Ibid., 436–437.

101. Ibid., 437–439. According to delegate J. G. McClinton, who wrote a brief report about the convention to his hometown newspaper, "the ungenerous action of the cow county delegates has driven [the] conservatives over to the anti-mining tax side of the house" (*Esmeralda Union* [Aurora, Nevada], July 20, 1864, in the Beinecke Library, Yale University).

102. Marsh, *Official Report*, 443–444.

103. Ibid., 356–357. The voting alignments on the taxation issue are discussed in appendix 2E.

104. Ibid., 373.

105. Ibid., 368–369.

106. See, for example, ibid., 376, 377, 421, 422.

107. Ibid., 376.

108. Ibid., 327.

109. Ibid., 170.

110. See Fitch's explanation of his switch as perfectly consistent in ibid., 439–440. Fitch's and Collins's depiction of the Kennedy measure as a compromise is in ibid., 444. Fitch's desire to have *some* constitution, no matter what, in order to have Nevada congressmen in place should the presidential election go to the House of Representatives, is clear in ibid., 309.

111. Ibid., 463.

112. Ibid., 495. See also De Long's earlier comments at 458.

113. Ibid., 494–499.

114. Ibid., 478.

115. Ibid., 264.

116. Ibid., 478.

117. Ibid., 483–484.

118. Ibid., 487.

119. Ibid., 491.

120. Ibid., 493.

121. Ibid., 558–559; see, generally, 541–565.

122. Ibid., 829.

CHAPTER SEVEN: PROGRESS AND POVERTY

1. James Bryce, *The American Commonwealth*, 2 vols. (London: Macmillan, 1889), 2:372.

2. Ibid., 373.

3. Ibid., 373.

4. Ibid., 374.

5. At an 1874 pioneer reunion, William Gwin contrasted the San Francisco he encountered in 1849 with the city twenty-five years later. "When we landed here," he remarked, "the permanent population of San Francisco did not exceed one thousand; now it is over two hundred thousand. The ground beneath us was a shapeless mound of sandy desert. Diagonally across from where we are sitting is a strip of ground, covered with almost worthless buildings, that sold the other day, as an investment, for $300,000. The 100-vara lot, of which that strip was a

small portion, cost, at the date of our arrival, $16, just the fee for issuing the alcalde's title" (quoted in William Issel and Robert Cherny, *San Francisco, 1865–1932: Politics, Power, and Urban Development* (Berkeley and Los Angeles: University of California Press, 1986), 7.

6. *Alta California,* April 30, 1878. The delegates that the *Alta* incorrectly listed as deceased were Joseph Aram (d. 1898), Stephen Foster (d. 1898), and Myron Norton (d. 1886). Those incorrectly identified as living were José Antonio Carrillo (d. 1862), Kimball Dimmick (d. 1861), Lansford Hastings (d. 1867), Henry Hill (d. 1866), James McHall Jones (d. 1851), Morton McCarver (d. 1875), Miguel Pedrorena (d. 1850), Hugo Reid (d. 1852), and Thomas Vermuele (d. 1856).

7. These figures are drawn from appendix 1A.

8. On Price's checkered career after 1849, see the *Dictionary of American Biography,* 20 vols., ed. Allen Johnson and Dumas Malone (New York: Charles Scribner, 1946–1958), 15:214–215; Duane Lockard, *The New Jersey Governor: A Study in Political Power* (Princeton: Princeton University Press, 1964), 62; Charles Merriam Knapp, *New Jersey Politics During the Period of the Civil War and Reconstruction* (Geneva, N.Y.: W. F. Humphrey, 1924), 52–55; *Biographical Directory of the American Congress, 1774–1949* (Washington, D.C.: Government Printing Office, 1950), 1482; *Alta California,* January 17, 1880; O. C. Wheeler, *First Steamship Pioneers* (San Francisco: H. S. Crooker, 1874), 355–360; Record Book no. 1, Society of California Pioneers (n.p., n.d.) (the last two in the biographical files of the Colton Hall Museum, Monterey, California). On Gwin, see the discussion that follows below and, more generally, Lately Thomas, *Between Two Empires: The Life Story of California's First Senator, William McKendree Gwin* (Boston: Houghton Mifflin, 1969).

9. Peter Decker, *Fortunes and Failures: White-Collar Mobility in Nineteenth-Century San Francisco* (Cambridge, Mass.: Harvard University Press, 1978), ix and chap. 7, similarly observes that in San Francisco a new generation of merchants and manufacturers emerged in the 1860s, eclipsing the pioneers of the 1850s. See also Rodman Paul, "After the Gold Rush: San Francisco and Portland," *Pacific Historical Review* 51 (1982): 1–21.

10. Henry George, *Progress and Poverty* (1879; reprint, Garden City, N.Y.: Doubleday, Page, 1914), 12.

11. Doris M. Wright, "The Making of Cosmopolitan California: An Analysis of Immigration, 1848–1870," *California Historical Society Quarterly* 19 (December 1940): 323–343; Commonwealth Club of San Francisco, *The Population of California* (San Francisco: Parker Printing, 1946), 7.

12. Rodman Paul, *The Mining Frontiers of the Far West* (Albuquerque: University of New Mexico Press, 1974), 28–36; Richard Lingenfelter, *The Hard Rock Miner: A History of the Mining Labor Movement in the American West, 1863–1893* (Berkeley and Los Angeles: University of California Press, 1974), 3–30; Mark Wyman, *Hard-Rock Epic: Western Miners and the Industrial Revolution, 1860–1910* (Berkeley and Los Angeles: University of California Press, 1979), 3–31. See also John Rowe, *The Hard Rock Men: Cornish Immigrants and the North American Mining Frontier* (New York: Barnes & Noble Books, 1974), 108–126.

13. Hubert Howe Bancroft, *California Pastoral* (San Francisco: History Company, 1888).

14. Decker, *Fortunes and Failures,* 34–44.

15. Issel and Cherny, *San Francisco*, 22.

16. Bryce, *American Commonwealth* 2 : 375.

17. Alexander Saxton, *The Indispensable Enemy: Labor and the Anti-Chinese Movement in California* (Berkeley and Los Angeles: University of California Press, 1971), 68–71; Ira Cross, *Financing an Empire: History of Banking in California*, 4 vols. (Chicago: S. J. Clarke, 1927), 1 : 240–241; Decker, *Fortunes and Failures*, 147–148. Hubert Howe Bancroft, *History of California*, 7 vols. (San Francisco: History Company, 1886–1890), 7 : 73–75, 94–97, 99–101, catalogues, without analysis, manufacturing in the state between 1850 and 1890.

18. Decker, *Fortunes and Failures*, 166. Prices in San Francisco, it needs to be noted, rose at a faster rate than wages in the 1860s; see Saxton, *Indispensable Enemy*, 68.

19. Rodman Paul, "The Beginnings of Agriculture in California: Innovation Versus Continuity," in *Essays and Assays: California History Reappraised*, ed. George H. Knoles (San Francisco: California Historical Society, 1973), 27–34, esp. 31–34; Bancroft, *History of California* 7 : 4–8, 26; John S. Hittell, *The Resources of California* . . . (San Francisco: A. Roman, 1863), 151–237; cf. ibid., 6th ed. (1877), 148–215; Lawrence J. Jellinek, *Harvest Empire: A History of California Agriculture* (San Francisco: Boyd & Frazier, 1979), 33–44.

20. An influential critique of concentrated property ownership, based on California, is Henry George, *Our Land Policy, National and State* (1871; New York: Doubleday & McClure, 1901).

21. W. W. Robinson, *Land in California* (1948; reprint, Berkeley and Los Angeles: University of California Press, 1979), 99–100, discusses the proposals of Frémont, Benton, and Gwin with respect to the Mexican grants. Paul Gates, *The Farmer's Age: Agriculture, 1815–1860* (New York: Harper & Row, 1960), 388–389, defends the act as in keeping with prior experience. See also the Gates essays listed in notes 23–25 below.

22. Robinson, *Land in California*, 106–109. Gates, *Farmer's Age*, 390, notes that by 1860, 88 patents had been issued; by 1870, 320; by 1875, 465; and by 1880, 517, leaving 87 that were issued more than thirty years after statehood.

23. A detailed discussion of the crisis of the Californios is in Leonard Pitt, *The Decline of the Californios: A Social History of the Spanish-speaking Californians, 1846–1890* (Berkeley and Los Angeles: University of California Press, 1971), 83–110; according to Pitt, between 25 and 40 percent of the rancheros' land went to their lawyers. Gates, *Farmer's Age*, 389, estimates an interest rate as high as 8 percent per month. See also Douglas Monroy, *Thrown Among Strangers: The Making of Mexican Culture in Frontier California* (Berkeley and Los Angeles: University of California Press, 1990), 222–232, 272–277; Albert Camarillo, *Chicanos in a Changing Society: From Mexican Pueblos to American Barrios in Santa Barbara and Southern California, 1848–1930* (Berkeley and Los Angeles: University of California Press, 1979), 113–116; Robinson, *Land in California*, 106. *Memoirs of Elisha Oscar Crosby: Reminiscences of California and Guatemala from 1849–1864*, ed. Charles Albro Barker (San Marino, Calif.: Huntington Library, 1945), 65–74, offers a participant's indictment of U.S. policy. In an important series of essays, Paul Gates has argued that the land commission operated equitably and did not impose undue hardship on landholders; see his "Adjudication of Spanish-Mexican Land Claims in California," *Huntington Library Quarterly* 21 (May 1958):

213–236; "California's Embattled Settlers," *California Historical Society Quarterly* 41 (June 1962): 99–130; "Pre–Henry George Land Warfare in California," *California Historical Society Quarterly* 46 (June 1967): 121–148; "The Suscol Principle, Preemption, and California Latifundia," *Pacific Historical Review* 39 (November 1970): 453–472; "The California Land Act of 1851," *California Historical Society Quarterly* 50 (December 1971): 395–430; and "California Land Policy and Its Historical Context: The Henry George Era," in *Four Persistent Issues: California's Land Ownership Concentration, Water Deficits, Sub-State Regionalism, Congressional Leadership* (Berkeley, Calif.: Institute of Governmental Studies, 1978), 3–13.

24. Gates, *Farmer's Age*, 391–392; Paul Gates, "The Homestead Law in an Incongruous Land System," in *The Public Lands*, ed. Vernon Carstensen (Madison: University of Wisconsin Press, 1968), 328–329; Gates, "California Land Policy," 13–14; Gerald Nash, *State Government and Economic Development: A History of Administrative Policies in California, 1840– 1933* (Berkeley, Calif.: Institute of Governmental Studies, 1964), 124–136.

25. Robinson, *Land in California*, 168–173; Paul W. Gates, "California's Agricultural College Lands," *Pacific Historical Review* 30 (May 1961): 103–122; Gates, "California Land Policy," 13–15.

26. Paul W. Gates, "Public Land Disposal in California," *Agricultural History* 49 (January 1975): 158–178; Jellinek, *Harvest Empire*, 28–32.

27. Jellinek, *Harvest Empire*, 34–43.

28. Robinson, *Land in California*, 157.

29. Stuart Daggett, *Chapters in the History of the Southern Pacific* (New York: Ronald Press, 1922), 122–123.

30. Ibid., 140–153. A popular treatment of the line's founders is Oscar Lewis, *The Big Four* (New York: Alfred A. Knopf, 1938).

31. Daggett, *Chapters in the History of the Southern Pacific*, 104–118, 222–236; Nash, *State Government and Economic Development*, 159–164.

32. Frank Norris, *The Octopus* (New York: Doubleday, Page, 1901). Henry George's skepticism was exceptional; see "What the Railroad Will Bring Us," *Overland Monthly* 1 (October 1868): 297–306.

33. Decker, *Fortunes and Failures*, 159–163; Saxton, *Indispensable Enemy*, 71.

34. Saxton, *Indispensable Enemy*, 5–6. Recently, Sucheng Chan, in *Bittersweet Soil: The Chinese in California Agriculture, 1860–1910* (Berkeley and Los Angeles: University of California Press, 1986), published the first in a series of books that reshape the history of Asians in California. Older but useful works on anti-Chinese actions before the 1860s are Rodman Paul, "The Origin of the Chinese Issue in California," *Mississippi Valley Historical Review* 25 (September 1938): 181–196; Gunther Barth, *Bitter Strength: A History of the Chinese in the United States* (Cambridge, Mass.: Harvard University Press, 1964), 129–156.

35. Francis Lippitt, *Reminiscences, Written for his Family, His Near Relatives, and Intimate Friends* (Providence, R.I.: Preston & Rounds, 1902), 81.

36. The constitution was endorsed by a 12,064-to-811 margin. Burnett's vote in the governor's race was 6,783, which easily bested former delegates Winfield Sherwood (3,220), John Sutter (2,201), and William M. Steuart (619). John McDougal, an ally of Gwin throughout the 1850s, was elected lieutenant governor; delegate Edward Gilbert became Congressman. See the *Alta California*, December 29, 1849.

37. The delegates elected to the Legislative Assembly were Joseph Aram and Elam Brown (San Jose), José María Covarrubias (Santa Barbara), and Benjamin Moore (San Joaquin); to the Senate, Elisha Crosby (Sacramento), Pablo de la Guerra (Santa Barbara), Benjamin Lippincott (San Joaquin), William Shannon (Sacramento), Mariano Vallejo (Sonoma), and Thomas Vermuele (San Francisco). Ibid., December 15, 1849.

38. Ibid., December 24, 1849.

39. On the Compromise of 1850, see, among others, Michael Holt, *The Political Crisis of the 1850s* (New York: John Wiley, 1978), chap. 4; Holman Hamilton, *Prologue to Conflict: The Crisis and Compromise of 1850* (New York: W. W. Norton, 1966); David Potter, *The Impending Crisis, 1848–1861,* completed and edited by Don E. Fehrenbacher (New York: Harper & Row, 1976), 90–120.

40. The effect was implicit; see Holt, *Political Crisis of the 1850s,* 83; Hamilton, *Prologue to Conflict,* 53–83; Potter, *Impending Crisis,* 99–100.

41. Thomas, *Between Two Empires,* 84, 92; Thomas's material on the 1850s is drawn extensively from James O'Meara, *Broderick and Gwin* (San Francisco: Bacon, 1881). See also David A. Williams, *David C. Broderick: A Political Portrait* (San Marino, Calif.: Huntington Library, 1969), 74–75.

42. What follows is drawn from Williams, *Broderick,* chaps. 1–6; and William Henry Ellison, *A Self-governing Dominion* (Berkeley and Los Angeles: University of California Press, 1950), 279–306.

43. Robinson, *Land in California,* 99–100; a defense of Gwin is in Thomas, *Between Two Empires,* 123–128.

44. Williams, *Broderick,* 80–89; Thomas, *Between Two Empires,* 110–112.

45. Williams, *Broderick,* 128–133; Decker, *Fortunes and Failures,* 125–143; Robert M. Senkewicz, S.J., *Vigilantes in Gold Rush San Francisco* (Stanford: Stanford University Press, 1985), 126–154; Robert A. Burchell, *The San Francisco Irish, 1848–1880* (Berkeley and Los Angeles: University of California Press, 1980), 125–133; Richard Maxwell Brown, *Strain of Violence: Historical Studies of American Violence and Vigilantism* (New York: Oxford University Press, 1975), 134–143; and Roger Lotchin, *San Francisco, 1846–1856: From Hamlet to City* (New York: Oxford University Press, 1974), 245–275.

46. Peyton Hurt, *The Rise and Fall of the Know Nothing Party in California* (San Francisco: California Historical Society, 1930).

47. See also Theodore H. Hittell, *History of California,* 4 vols. (San Francisco: N. J. Stone, 1885–1897), 3:497–507, 531–532.

48. Senkewicz, *Vigilantes in Gold Rush San Francisco,* 185–202; Lotchin, *San Francisco,* 265–275.

49. Williams, *Broderick,* 134, 142–144; Hittell, *History of California* 4:194.

50. Williams, *Broderick,* 159–170.

51. See Potter, *Impending Crisis,* 199–246; Holt, *Political Crisis,* 144–149 and passim.

52. The positions of Gwin and Broderick on Lecompton and the resulting division in California are discussed in Thomas, *Between Two Empires,* 166–178, and Williams, *Broderick,* 171–188.

53. Quoted in Thomas, *Between Two Empires,* 169.

54. Williams, *Broderick,* chap. 13.

55. Quoted in O'Meara, *Broderick and Gwin,* 253.

56. Quoted in Thomas, *Between Two Empires*, 191.

57. According to Peter Decker, *Fortunes and Failures*, 151, in California corporations and joint stock companies had, by the mid-1860s, become the "preferred form of business arrangement."

58. Hittell, *History of California* 4:411–412; Bancroft, *History of California* 6:364.

59. Saxton, *Indispensable Enemy*, 259–260; on the early trade union movement, see also Bancroft, *History of California* 7:333–335, 349–350.

60. Bancroft, *History of California* 7:325–327.

61. Quoted in Saxton, *Indispensable Enemy*, 81; see also Hittell, *History of California* 4:410–411.

62. Bancroft, *History of California* 7:325–327.

63. The phrase first appeared in Gertrude Atherton, *California, An Intimate History* (New York: Harper & Bros., 1914).

64. Hittell, *History of California* 4:352.

65. See, for example, Rodman Paul, *The Far West and the Great Plains in Transition, 1859–1900* (New York: Harper & Row, 1988), 211–213.

66. Hittell, *History of California* 4:343–344, describes the bipartisan action in Congress against the Chinese in the 1870s: the explicit exclusion of "Mongolians" from naturalization; the prohibition of importing Chinese women for "illicit acts"; the prohibition of importing laborers under contract; and agitation for unilateral abrogation of the Burlingame Treaty.

67. Ibid., 344, makes this point.

68. Ibid., 594–599.

69. Bancroft, *History of California* 7:354.

70. Quoted in Saxton, *Indispensable Enemy*, 118. See also Bancroft, *History of California* 7:355–362; Hittell, *History of California* 4:602.

71. See, for example, *Marysville Daily Appeal*, May 2, 11; June 14, 1878; *Daily Evening Bulletin*, May 23, June 11, 1878; *Alta California*, June 19, 1878; Carl Brent Swisher, *Motivation and Political Technique in the California Constitutional Convention, 1878–1879* (1930; reprint, New York: DaCapo Press, 1969), 17–24.

72. Issel and Cherny, *San Francisco*, 127. The actual count of delegates' partisan attachments is confused by a number of resignations and deaths. Elected were fifty-one workingmen (one of whom died and one of whom resigned), seventy-eight nonpartisans (two of whom died), eleven Republicans, ten Democrats, and two Independents. The Republicans, Democrats, and Independents are generally considered to have sided with the nonpartisans. A list of the delegates is found in Winfield J. Davis, *History of Political Conventions in California, 1849–1892*, Publications of the California State Library, no. 1 (Sacramento: CSL, 1893), 390–392.

73. E. B. Willis and P. K. Stockton, official stenographers, *Debates and Proceedings of the Constitutional Convention of the State of California . . .* , 3 vols. (Sacramento: J. B. Young, 1880–1881), 1:18.

74. As one observer put it, "The real strength of the Workingmen's, Greenback, or National organizations lies with those of their members who are capitalists in a small way at least" (*Marysville Daily Appeal*, May 19, 1878).

75. California Progressivism is treated from complementary perspectives in Spencer Olin, *California's Prodigal Sons: Hiram Johnson and the Progressives, 1911–*

1917 (Berkeley and Los Angeles: University of California Press, 1968); George Mowry, *The California Progressives* (Chicago: Quadrangle Books, 1963); and Mansel Blackford, *The Politics of Business in California, 1890–1920* (Columbus: Ohio State University Press, 1977).

76. *Daily Evening Bulletin,* May 18, 1878; *Marysville Daily Appeal,* June 5, 1878. See also ibid., May 16; June 8, 14, 15, 1878; *Daily Evening Bulletin,* June 14, 1878; *Alta California,* May 12, 17; June 13, 1878.

77. Davis, *History of Political Conventions,* 366–367, 379, 384.

78. Willis and Stockton, *Debates and Proceedings* 1 : 18. The most forceful statement of the "line" between monopoly and antimonopoly is found in the convention debate over the minority report from the Committee on Land and Homestead Exemption. Written by three workingmen delegates (James O'Sullivan, John P. West, and Hamlet Davis), it called for strict limitations on land ownership and inheritance. The limitation, declared O'Sullivan, was justified as follows: "Land monopoly is regarded as unjust by all men of fair minds, who are not biased by selfish interest; it is condemned by the verdict of mankind; . . . it is destructive of the general interest and injurious to the State; it is un-American, anti-Republican, and can only maintain its existence under the iron hand of despotism. . . . Of all the States of this Union, California is the most afflicted by this curse; it is keeping out population, retarding our prosperity. In all the older States small farms is [*sic*] the rule, and large ones a rare exception. There we see general prosperity prevailing, at least among the rural population; there we see an independent yeomanry planted, who are the pride and the mainstay of the Republic—its wealth producers in peace, its defenders in war. If we desire to transmit the liberty which we enjoy, unimpaired, to future generations; if we desire that our posterity shall be a free, contented, happy, people, we must rid ourselves of this imported feudalism, and provide means for a general ownership of land in small farms. There can be no prosperity, no contentment, no happiness, otherwise in this land. As the poet has aptly said of another country where this blighting curse still exists: 'Ill fares the land, to hast'ning ills a prey, Where wealth accumulates, and men decay; Princes and lords may flourish, or may fade; A Breath can make them, as a breath has made; But a bold yeomanry, their country's pride, When once destroyed, can never be supplied'" (ibid., 738 [the minority report], 1139–1140 [the final quote]; I am indebted to Sarah Sharp for bringing this passage to my attention).

79. Henry George, "The Kearney Agitation in California," *Popular Science Monthly* 17 (August 1880): 445–446.

80. Bryce, *American Commonwealth* 2 : 372.

81. Her death, he wrote his stepfather, left him "now [able to] part from the world with but little pain besides that which we naturally feel for ourselves" (James McHall Jones to his [step]father, May 10, 1851; T. W. Norris Collection, Bancroft Library, University of California, Berkeley).

82. George Cosgrave, "James McHall Jones: The Judge That Never Presided," *California Historical Society Quarterly* 20 (June 1941): 107–113.

83. Michael B. Husband, "Morton M. McCarver: An Iowa Entrepreneur in the Far West," *Annals of Iowa* 40 (Spring 1970): 250.

84. The *Oregonian,* July 25, 1857, recounts McCarver's claims to the office of governor: "He knew the Vice President's mother, and prophesied to her that *her*

son would be President of the United States. He has *blown,* gassed, and made a fool of himself long enough. He has been to the States, delivered lectures, set all things right, was offered the *governorship of Utah,* but modestly declined; cause why, he says, 'I can stand Indians, but not Mormons. I have other business of more importance to attend to.' WHEW! Wat [*sic*] is it?"

85. Halleck prepared the first English report on the Mexican titles, a report that served an important documentary purpose in the land grant litigation; see Henry Wager Halleck, "Report on California Land Grants," 31st Cong., 1st sess., H. Ex. Doc. 17 (Washington, D.C., 1850), 112–133.

86. *Daily Evening Bulletin,* August 17, 1857. Leonard Pitt, *Decline of the Californios,* 91–94, defends Halleck as one of a handful of honest, "worthy counsels," who forthrightly defended the property rights of Californio landowners.

87. Stephen Ambrose, *Halleck: Lincoln's Chief of Staff* (Baton Rouge: Louisiana State University Press, 1962); and T. Harry Williams, *Lincoln and His Generals* (New York: Alfred A. Knopf, 1952), 59–61, 70, 84–86, 134–143, 153–157, 301–302, 334–335.

88. *Sacramento Daily Union,* January 11, 1872, described the cause of his death as "congestion of the brain superinduced by liver disease to which he has been subject for some time."

89. *Alta California,* April 24, 1873.

90. Carl Hayden, "Tentative Sketch of the Life of Lansford Warren Hastings," 15; typescript in Colton Hall Museum, Monterey, California. See also William J. Hunsaker, "Lansford W. Hastings' Project for the Invasion and Conquest of Arizona and New Mexico for the Southern Confederacy," *Arizona Historical Review* 4 (July 1931): 5–12.

91. *Official Records of the Rebellion,* 1st ser., vol. 50, pt. 2, 621. I am indebted to Robert Chandler for providing this citation.

92. *Los Angeles Star,* November 28, 1863.

93. Lawrence F. Hill, "The Confederate Exodus to Latin America," *Southwestern Historical Quarterly* 39 (October 1935): 130.

94. Blanche Henry Clark Weaver, "Confederate Emigration to Brazil," *Journal of Southern History* 27 (February 1961): 43.

95. See Kathryn Abbey Hanna, "The Roles of the South in the French Intervention in Mexico," *Journal of Southern History* 20 (February 1954): 3–21. The diplomatic context is discussed in Arnold Blumberg, "The Diplomacy of the Mexican Empire, 1863–1867," *Transactions of the American Philosophical Society,* n.s., 61, no. 8 (1971): 11, 76–78.

96. Hanna, "Roles of the South in the French Intervention," 18.

97. This exchange, taken from the unpublished memoirs of Hamblen, is in Thomas, *Between Two Empires,* 357–358.

98. According to a letter of 1871, Gwin owned "one of the most extensive gold mining estates on [the] coast," an industrial mining company at which "eighty stalwart men" operated "forty-six stamps to crush eighty tons of quartz daily." See Gwin to the family of Samuel G. Hamblen, July 19, 1871, quoted in ibid., 374.

99. See the *Call* (San Francisco), September 5, 1885. According to the *New York Times,* December 7, 1876, Gwin—"the evil genius of TILDEN"—was the mastermind of Oregon governor La Fayette Grover's attempt to steal the presidential election for the Democratic party; see also chapter 8, below.

100. Thomas *Between Two Empires,* 375.

101. The Gwins were fixtures in the (largely Republican) social life of San Francisco's elite in the 1870s; ibid., 370–371.

102. The phrase is Stephen J. Field's, quoted in R. Hal Williams, *The Democratic Party and California Politics, 1880–1896* (Stanford: Stanford University Press, 1973), 21.

103. *Alta California,* October 26, 1875.

104. Ibid.

105. Charles W. McCurdy, "Justice Field and the Jurisprudence of Government-Business Relations: Some Parameters of Laissez Faire Constitutionalism, 1863–1897," in *American Law and the Constitutional Order,* ed. Lawrence Friedman and Harry Scheiber (Cambridge, Mass.: Harvard University Press, 1978), 247–248.

106. *Alta California,* June 17, 1884.

107. *Call,* September 5, 1885.

108. *Alta California,* October 14, 1860.

109. *Democratic Standard* (Sacramento), November 11, 1860.

110. *Sacramento Daily Union,* January 25, February 4, May 1, 1861; Appendix, California Legislature, *Journals of the Senate and Assembly* (1862), no. 37, 183–184; *Alta California,* November 16, 1862. I am indebted to Robert Chandler for providing information on Botts.

111. His wandering through the 1860s can be traced in the *Alta California,* November 16, 1862; August 24, 1863; *Viginia Daily Union* (Virginia City, Nevada), September 27, 1864; the *Butte Record* (Oroville), November 17, 1866; and the *Dispatch and Vanguard* (San Francisco), March 28, 1868.

112. Botts was described as the "best black letter lawyer in the state" in the obituary carried on his death in the *Daily Evening Bulletin,* October 6, 1884. The quotation is from Botts to Henry Haight, March 30, 1870, Bancroft Library, University of California, Berkeley.

113. *Daily Evening Bulletin,* April 25, 1879.

114. Ibid.

CHAPTER EIGHT: CRISIS AND RENEWAL

1. See Kevin Starr, *Americans and the California Dream* (New York: Oxford University Press, 1973), esp. chap. 13, for a twentieth-century evocation of the same idea.

2. J. H. Beadle, correspondent for the *Cincinnati Commercial,* 1873; quoted in Dorothy Johansen, "A Working Hypothesis for the Study of Migrations" (1967) in *Experiences in a Promised Land: Essays in Pacific Northwest History,* ed. Thomas Edwards and Carlos Schwantes (Seattle: University of Washington Press, 1986). Along the same lines, Joaquin Miller wrote in 1872: "A well known, but not popular writer, as far as the will of Oregon goes, once wrote, when on the tour of the Pacific, that California ended and Oregon began where white sugar failed, and a brown, Kanaka article was substituted. This is, perhaps, fiction; but it is safe to say that even the Chinese wall does not divide two more distinct peoples than did the Siskiyou Mountains, until within a very few years. And, even now, after the infusion of the new life, the original Chinook or Cayuse Oregonian—a

transplanted cross of Pike and Posey County—remains, as uninformed and un-affected as the Chinaman, after twenty years contact with the Yankee" ("A Ride Through Oregon," *Overland Monthly* 8 [April 1872]: 303).

3. Preliminary results of a study on the population of Marion County, Ore-gon, sustains this point; David A. Johnson, "Migration, Settlement, and the Making of Oregon's Political Culture," (paper presented at the 1990 convention of the Western Historical Association, Reno, Nevada). Of the more than eight hundred donation land claim settlers in the county, better than 70 percent still lived in the county as of 1880—a generation after their arrival in the 1840s and 1850s—or had died there in the intervening years. Furthermore, three-quarters of the men who held county office (legislator, judge, assessor, surveyor, and the like) between 1846 and 1878 came from the ranks of the donation law claimants. These figures are derived from *Genealogical Material in Oregon Donation Land Claims, Abstracted from Applications,* 6 vols. (Portland: Genealogical Forum of Oregon, 1957–1987). County officeholders are recorded in *Historical Atlas Map of Marion and Linn Counties, Oregon* (San Francisco: Edgar Williams, 1878), 98. The donation land claimants were traced through the 1850–1880 manuscript censuses.

4. E. Kimbark MacColl, *The Shaping of a City: Business and Politics in Portland, Oregon 1885–1915* (Portland: Georgian Press, 1976), 5.

5. Miller, "Ride Through Oregon," 307.

6. See appendix 1B.

7. The homogeneity of the Oregon population is attested to by the continu-ing importance of immigrants from the Ohio and Mississippi River valleys. In 1860, 1870, 1880, and 1890, respectively, individuals from the border, Old Northwest, and Plains states accounted for 41.2, 45.5, 27.7, and 29.4 percent of the state's population. When these individuals are combined with the Oregon-born population, the corresponding percentages become 73.0, 77.9, 66.6, and 65.5. Compiled from *Eighth Census of the United States, 1860,* 3 vols. (Washington, D.C., 1864–1865), Population, 616–623; *Ninth Census of the United States, 1870,* 3 vols. (Washington, D.C., 1872), Population, 328–342; *Tenth Census of the United States, 1880,* 22 vols. (Washington, D.C., 1883–1888), Population (17 vols.), 1: 481–495, 525; *Eleventh Census of the United States, 1890,* 25 vols. (Washington, D.C., 1892–1897), Population (4 vols.), 1: 560–581, 606–609, 652.

8. Derived from *Eighth Census of the United States, 1860,* Agriculture, 120–121; Manufactures, 490–492; *Tenth Census of the United States, 1880,* Agriculture (2 vols.), 1: 130; *Tenth Census of the United States, 1880,* Manufactures (2 vols.), 1: 165.

9. The census definition of urban residence included all inhabitants of incor-porated towns and cities with a population exceeding 2,500 people. In the nation as a whole, then, in 1870, 26 percent and 1880, 28 percent of the population was designated "urban." In Oregon, the figures for 1870 and 1880 are, respectively, 8,000 (7 percent) and 26,000 (14 percent) (of the latter figure, 16,000 lived in Portland). See *Historical Statistics of the United States* (Washington, D.C.: U.S. De-partment of Commerce, Bureau of the Census, 1975), 2–3, 12, 33.

10. The ratio of the value of agricultural to manufactured goods (a measure of the relative weight of agriculture in the state's economy) for all of Oregon is as follows for 1860, 1870, 1880, 1890, and 1900, respectively: 2.39, 1.03, 1.21, 0.47,

0.75; for the state less Portland and environs (i.e., less Multnomah, Clackamas, Washington, and Columbia counties) the figures are 2.88, 1.77, 1.77, 1.51, and 1.71. Derived from *Eighth Census of the United States, 1860*, Agriculture, 120–121; Manufactures, 490–492; *Ninth Census of the United States, 1870*, Agriculture, 230–231; Manufactures, 560–561; *Tenth Census of the United States, 1880*, Agriculture, 1:130; Manufactures, 1:165; *Eleventh Census of the United States, 1890*, Agriculture (2 vols.), 1:224–225; *Eleventh Census of the United States, 1890*, Manufactures (3 vols.), 1:560–565; *Twelfth Census of the United States, 1900*, 10 vols. (Washington, D.C.: Government Printing Office, 1901–1902), Agriculture (2 vols.), 1:294; Manufactures (4 vols.), 2:732–743.

11. Miller, "Ride Through Oregon," 306. See also James Blaine Hedges, *Henry Villard and the Railways of the Northwest* (New York: Russell & Russell, 1930), 54–55. Oscar Osburn Winther attributes the resistance to fear among Portlanders of losing the trade of southern Oregon to Californians; see Winther, *The Old Oregon Country* (Stanford: Stanford University Press, 1950), 295.

12. Winther, *Old Oregon Country*, 139.

13. This was the contemporary evaluation of the *Oregonian*'s editor, Harvey Scott; see, for example, his remarks in the *Oregonian* on June 5, 1870.

14. Hedges, *Villard*, 56–86; E. Kimbark MacColl, *Merchants, Money, and Power: The Portland Establishment, 1843–1913* (Portland: Georgian Press, 1988), 209–213.

15. MacColl, *Merchants, Money, and Power*, 223–226.

16. Ibid., 313.

17. These, and following statistics, are derived from *Eighth Census of the United States, 1860*, Population, 400–405; Agriculture, 120–121; *Eleventh Census of the United States, 1890*, Agriculture, 1:224–225; *Twelfth Census of the United States, 1900*, Population, 1:517–518; Manufactures, 2:732–743.

18. Gordon B. Dodds, *The American Northwest: A History of Oregon and Washington* (Arlington Heights, Ill.: Forum Books, 1986), 79–80.

19. Ibid., 118–121. The U.S. census figures for the Chinese population of Portland in 1880 are 1,678 (9.5 percent of the total population) and, in 1890, 4,539 (8.8 percent). See *Tenth Census of the United States, 1880*, Population, 1:753; *Eleventh Census of the United States, 1890*, Population, 1:652. These figures apparently obscure the fact that during the 1880s, because of the arrival of laborers from China (more than 5,000 in 1882), railroad construction crews, and Chinese driven out of Seattle and Tacoma (and, to a lesser extent, neighboring Oregon towns), the number and proportion of Chinese in Portland burgeoned briefly— to perhaps as high as 25 percent of the city population. By the same token, from the mid-1880s to the twentieth century the number of Chinese in Portland (and Oregon) declined consistently. The reasons for this decline (in the city and the state) are poorly understood. It was not—in contrast to Washington, for example—the consequence of mob violence and pogroms. Rather, it seems to have originated in attitudes and practices that were at once more subtle, persistent, *and* effective than anti-Chinese movements elsewhere. On this point, in addition to the discussion in Dodds cited above, see Malcolm Clark, Jr., "The Bigot Disclosed: 90 Years of Nativism," *Oregon Historical Society Quarterly* 75 (1974): 122– 131, where Clark estimates (131) that the Chinese composed 25 percent of the Portland population in 1885; Hugh Clark, *Portland's Chinese: The Early Years*

(Portland: Center for Urban Education, 1978); Nelson Chia-chi Ho, *Portland's Chinatown: The History of an Urban Ethnic District* (Portland: Bureau of Planning, 1978); Carlos Schwantes, "Unemployment, Disinheritance, and the Origin of Labor Militancy in the Pacific Northwest, 1885–1886," in Edwards and Schwantes (eds.), *Experiences in a Promised Land*, 179–194; Catherine Biancaccio, "Old Portland Today" (1974), Pamphlet File, Oregon Historical Society.

20. This was the case despite Thomas Dryer's fears that the proposed charter was a stalking horse for the Slave Power—a fear encouraged by the appearance of proslavery newspapers during the ratification campaign.

21. *Oregon Statesman*, December 22, 1857.

22. In terms of the development of a Republican position on the rights of free Negroes, Eric Foner has emphasized the importance of the protracted congressional debate over the admission of Oregon; see Foner, *Free Soil, Free Labor, Free Men: The Ideology of the Republican Party Before the Civil War* (New York: Oxford University Press, 1970), 288–290. See also Henry H. Simms, "The Controversy over the Admission of the State of Oregon," *Mississippi Valley Historical Review* 32 (December 1945): 355–374.

23. James E. Hendrickson, *Joe Lane of Oregon: Machine Politics and the Sectional Crisis, 1849–1861* (New Haven: Yale University Press, 1967), 183–188.

24. By the time Smith learned that his term was about to end, time was of the essence, insofar as reelection was concerned. The state convention to name a nominee for his Senate seat was scheduled to meet in April, followed in May by a special legislative session to select the senator.

25. Robert W. Johannsen, *Frontier Politics on the Eve of the Civil War* (Seattle: University of Washington Press, 1955), 72–75; Hendickson, *Joe Lane*, 208–209.

26. Hendrickson, *Joe Lane*, 210–211.

27. Ibid., 211.

28. Republican suspicions of vote fraud in this (and the following year's) election were ill concealed. See, for example, the *Oregonian*, July 2, 23, 1859; Simeon Francis to Abraham Lincoln, December 26, 1859, in the Lincoln Papers, ser. 1, no. 2178 (microfilm, Library of Congress, Washington, D.C., 1959). Logan wrote his sister: "A great many people wished me to contest Stout's election. Persons in California, in the States, & in Oregon have said & written much to me on the subject" ("22 Letters of David Logan, Pioneer Oregon Lawyer," ed. Harry E. Pratt, *Oregon Historical Society Quarterly* 44 [September 1943]: 281).

29. In Marion the vote for Logan was 1,062, against 296 for Stout; Hendrickson, *Joe Lane*, 211.

30. The planning that preceded this convention is indicated in John McBride's comment to David Craig before the balloting for senator: "Nesmith and Baker will be elected—*but keep it still*" (quoted in Johannsen, *Frontier Politics*, 124n.143.

31. The text of Baker's eulogy is in the *Pacific Steamer Times* (San Francisco), September 20, 1859. It, along with Baker's career in California, is discussed in David A. Williams, *David C. Broderick: A Political Portrait* (San Marino, Calif.: Huntington Library, 1969), 189–192, 245–248.

32. Johannsen, *Frontier Politics*, 116–126; Hendrickson, *Joe Lane*, 234–236.

33. Walter C. Woodward, "The Rise and Early History of Political Parties in Oregon, Pt. 5," *Oregon Historical Society Quarterly* 12 (December 1911): 324. The vote for Lincoln was 5,344; for Breckenridge, 5,074; and for Douglas, 4,131.

34. George H. Williams, "Political History of Oregon from 1853 to 1865," in *The Oregon Constitution, and Proceedings and Debates of the Constitutional Convention of 1857*, ed. Charles Henry Carey (Salem, Oreg.: State Printing Department, 1926), 508–509.

35. Hendrickson, *Joe Lane*, 249–262.

36. Bush's informal banking in the 1850s and early 1860s is displayed in his correspondence with Portland merchant John McCracken (Bush Papers, Bush House Museum, Salem, Oregon). Bush's "career" as a banker is recounted in O. K. Burrell, *Gold in the Wood Pile: An Informal History of Banking in Oregon* (Eugene: University of Oregon Books, 1967), 47–48, 279–300; Claude Singer, *U.S. National Bank of Oregon and U.S. Bancorp, 1891–1984* (Portland: U.S. Bancorp, 1984), 47–48.

37. According to Robert Johannsen, *Frontier Politics*, 65n.53, Lane preferred Smith over other Salem men for the second Senate seat, believing (correctly, it turned out) that Smith's loyalties could be turned.

38. *Oregon Statesman*, December 21, 1858.

39. See Smith to Bush, July 31, 1858; this and all subsequent references to the correspondence of Asahel Bush are taken from the Bush Papers, Bush House Museum, Salem, Oregon.

40. Ibid., November 30, 1858.

41. Ibid., February 2, 1859.

42. Delazon Smith, "A Circular and Prospectus of the *Oregon Democrat*," July 18, 1859 (original in the Oregon Historical Society). According to the *Oregonian*, during the 1860 canvass Smith, in an Oregon City speech, "denounced 'popular sovereignty,' and said 'he had rather be a decent man's nigger at the south than a white laborer at the north.' Mr. Holbrook was called out to reply and he scarcely left enough of Smith to make a grease spot. He proved that one year ago he professed himself the friend of the white laborer and the champion of popular sovereignty" (*Oregonian*, June 2, 1860).

43. Ibid.

44. A representative column of the *Oregon Democrat* reads as follows: "Assohell Bush who runs the Salem smut machine, the club-footed loafer Beggs and Nesmith, the vilest and most loathsome creature that wears the human form on the Pacific Coast, are asserting that *We* are politically dead! Dead!! Never! Never!! No, Never!!! Let these cut-throats, assassins, murderers and their bastard vagabond allies in this county put that in their pipes and smoke it!!!!" (quoted in Woodward, "Political Parties in Oregon," 308).

45. John R. McBride, "The Oregon Constitutional Convention, 1857," in Carey (ed.), *Oregon Constitution*, 490.

46. In the 1870 manuscript census, Dryer listed no property. *Ninth Manuscript Federal Census, 1870*, Schedule of Population, Oregon, Multnomah County (National Archives microfilm #1287).

47. See, for example, Dryer's characterization of Republican doctrine in the *Oregonian*, August 6, 1859. As late as the spring of 1858 he still insisted that Whiggery, as a persuasion if no longer a party, remained vital and alive: "Let the names of Clay and Webster remain forever at the head of our muster roll," he wrote. "We have," he admitted, "no Whig organization . . . What shall we do?" His advice was characteristic: "Be patient: try the candidates, hear their merits and demerits; examine carefully their principles; keep your powder dry; be

ready for the fight; when it is to be made on principle, preserve unbroken the ranks of the remnant of the 'old guard,' and when we strike let it be for our country and our principles. The day may yet come, and the ere long, when it will be necessary to rally the 'old guard' to the rescue of the Union. When that time comes, be ready. When the roll is called let not 'deserted' be written against the name of any old line Whig in Oregon" (*Oregonian*, April 10, 1858).

48. T. W. Davenport, "Slavery Question in Oregon, Pt. 2," *Oregon Historical Society Quarterly* 9 (December 1908): 358–359.

49. To afford the trip to Washington, D.C., Dryer had borrowed money, leaving as collateral various Portland properties that he did not in fact own. To James Nesmith, Deady wrote in 1861: "Dryer did not return to this place. He has left for the Cannibal Islands. His creditors would like to dispose of the powder they bought to celebrate his return to specie payments. If he had come up here he would have been arrested for obtaining money under false pretenses. When he went east last fall, he borrowed $800 of Knott. Hoyt went his security. To secure H- D- gave him a deed of some lots in town, with a request that the transaction should remain secret and he would send the money here to pay the debt as soon as he drew the milage [*sic*] at Wash. No money came. H- was not appointed Col. at Astoria. D- did not come from San Fran, and H- became alarmed and concluded he would put his deed on record, But when he came to examine the matter another 'Bugger' owned the lots and D- had no interest in them" (Deady to Nesmith, May 26, 1861; Nesmith Papers, Oregon Historical Society).

50. See, for example, the *Oregon Statesman* of December 10, 1860; April 15; May 6, 20; December 30, 1861; March 16, 31, 1862; and February 16, March 9, July 6, 1863.

51. Included in a letter from D. L. Gregg to Lincoln, April 15, 1861 (Lincoln Papers, ser. 1, no. 9110, Library of Congress).

52. *Sacramento Daily Union*, April 12, 1879.

53. *Oregonian*, March 31, April 2, 1879.

54. The margin was 108 votes; *Oregonian*, June 30, 1860.

55. Logan to Lincoln, September 15, 1861 (Huntington Library, San Marino, California). In 1860, Logan openly opposed Baker's election as senator; see Johannsen, *Frontier Politics*, 123, 125.

56. Francis to Lincoln, December 26, 1859 (Lincoln Papers, ser. 1, no. 2178, Library of Congress).

57. See, for example, Matthew Deady's diary notations of Logan's drinking in *Pharisee Among the Philistines: The Diary of Judge Matthew P. Deady, 1871–1892*, ed. Malcolm Clark (Portland: Oregon Historical Society, 1975), 7, 19, 34.

58. This interpretation is drawn from the correspondence between John Kelly and George Williams in March and April 1868 and December 1869; Kelly Papers, University of Oregon Special Collections.

59. *Oregonian*, June 30, 1870. Earlier (June 2, 1870), the paper had remarked indignantly, "There is no man in Oregon by whom the Republican Party have stood by more closely than by David Logan. They have done their best to advance him, and if they have failed, it has been his fault more than theirs. . . . They have stood by him through all vicissitudes; though it is but truth to say that he has not always pursued such a course as to justify their devotion to him. He is a man who is governed entirely by his resentments and animosities." On went the

denunciation, ending with a final flourish: "For what the Republican party had done for Mr. Logan, . . . he now recompenses it by uniting with its enemies in schemes to secure its defeat . . . simply because he is not this year placed at [the party's] head, and because he hates some of those who are."

60. Deady recorded his attendance at the funeral, "a rather dreary pagan affair," in his diary; see Clark (ed.), *Pharisee Among the Philistines,* 44.

61. See, for example, the description of the "party" in reference to Logan in the *Oregonian,* June 2, 30, 1870.

62. The only extended treatment of Williams's political career is Oscar C. Christensen, "The Grand Old Man of Oregon: The Life of George H. Williams" (M.A. thesis, University of Oregon, 1939); reference to Williams as a possible presidential candidate is in the *Oregon State Journal,* June 11, 1870 (cited in ibid., 30).

63. George H. Williams, "Address, Delivered Before the Multnomah County Agricultural Society at the Second Semi-annual Meeting, Held July 7, 1860," *Oregon Farmer* 2 (July 21, 1860): 194.

64. Ibid.

65. *Congressional Globe,* 39 Cong., 1st sess., 3834.

66. "The Oregon and California Railroad," in George H. Williams, *Occasional Addresses* (Portland: F. W. Baltes, 1895), 129.

67. Clark (ed.), *Pharisee Among the Philistines,* 17; MacColl, *Merchants, Money, and Power,* 373.

68. Williams's ill-starred career as attorney general and the controversy that surounded his nomination as chief justice are recounted in Sidney Teiser, "Life of George Williams, Almost Chief Justice, Pt. 2," *Oregon Historical Society Quarterly* 47 (December 1946): 417–440. In addition to the generally low regard in which he was held because of his direction of the Department of Justice, two particular factors are generally believed to have destroyed his chances for confirmation. First was the uproar that met Williams's suppression of an investigation into an elections bribery case in Oregon, in which he fired the U.S. attorney who was about to indict Republican senator John H. Mitchell for buying the legislative votes necessary to his election. Second (more importantly, according to contemporaries) was the attempt of Williams's wife to force Senate confirmation through a war of rumors against well-placed senators and their wives. In addition to Teiser, see Clark (ed.), *Pharisee Among the Philistines,* 142–158; Allan Nevins, *Hamilton Fish: The Inner History of the Grant Administration,* rev. ed. (New York: Frederick Ungar, 1957), 661 and passim; and William S. McFeely, *Grant: A Biography* (New York: W. W. Norton, 1981), 389–391.

69. Williams held directorships in the following Portland financial institutions: the Commercial National Bank (1886), the Northwest Loan and Trust (1887), and the Oregon National Bank (1887). See Teiser, "Life of George Williams," 435; James H. Gilbert, "The Development of Banking in Oregon," *University of Oregon Bulletin* 9 (September 1911): 22–28.

70. The celebration is described in the *Oregonian,* May 1, 1889.

71. "George Washington," in Williams, *Occasional Addresses,* 38–39.

72. Ibid., 39–40.

73. Ibid., 42.

74. See, for example, the *Oregonian,* May 30, 31; June 1, 2, 3, 1902. Curi-

ously, the *Oregonian* made much (May 27, 1902) of an endorsement of Williams by John Minto, an even older pioneer who had first cast a vote in an Oregon election in 1845.

75. *Oregonian*, May 27, 1902. Speaking of the initiative, referendum, and recall, Williams exaggerated wildly in remarking: "I was a member of the convention chosen to frame the constitution of the State of Oregon, and I was then of [the] opinion that the people should have the right to have all such important acts as affect their rights referred to them by the Legislative Assembly. I proposed a provision in the constitution to that effect, but in those days it was a novel proposition, and, of course, was not adopted." See also the *Oregonian's* characterization of him as a reformer in his race for mayor; ibid., May 30, 31; June 1, 1902.

76. MacColl, *Merchants, Money, and Power*, 366–369, 372–373.

77. *Oregon Statesman*, May 20, 1861.

78. Ibid., April 11, 1864, reported that Grover figured prominently in a "copperhead convention" held in Albany to nominate candidates for the upcoming election; the charges persisted, even beyond the end of the war. See ibid., October 17, 1864; May 28, 1866.

79. Alfred L. Lomax, *Pioneer Woolen Mills in Oregon: History of Wool and the Woolen Textile Industry in Oregon, 1811–1875* (Portland: Binford & Mort, 1941), 134–135; Rev. H. K. Hines, *Illustrated History of the State of Oregon* (Chicago: Lewis, 1893), 304–305.

80. Grover described the race in a 1901 interview with the *Oregonian*. See Scrapbook no. 41, Oregon Historical Society, p. 186 ("Lawyers of Oregon Fifty Years Ago; Personal Recollections of Hon. L. F. Grover, Ex-Governor and Ex–United States Senator").

81. *Inaugural Address of Governor L. F. Grover, Delivered to the Legislative Assembly, September 14, 1870* (Salem, Oreg.: T. Patterson, 1870), 6.

82. *Oregonian*, September 15, 1870.

83. "Communication from the Labor Exchange, Portland," in *Inaugural Address of Governor L. F. Grover*, app., 6.

84. Phillip Kennedy, "Oregon and the Disputed Election of 1876," *Pacific Northwest Quarterly* 60 (July 1969): 135–144; William D. Fenton, "Political History of Oregon, from 1865 to 1876, Pt. 2," *Oregon Historical Society Quarterly* 3 (March 1902): 54–56; M. C. George, "Political History of Oregon, 1876–1895, Inclusive," *Oregon Historical Society Quarterly* 3 (June 1902): 107–109. According to the *New York Times*, December 7, 8, 9, 15, 1876, Grover's disqualification of the Hayes elector was taken at the command of none other than William Gwin of California: "Grover has always had the reputation of being an unscrupulous partisan, and his extraordinary conduct in the conspiracy carried out yesterday shows that fame has not misrepresented him. [Oregon senator] Kelly had promised Gwin, the evil genius of Tilden, that Oregon should be delivered to Tilden on election day. He failed to execute the contract, and Gwin telegraphed his reproof, with its sinister order to spare no expense or pains to secure the State, notwithstanding the result of the election. Grover appears to have been the ready, but somewhat ignorant tool of smarter people." The *Times's* Oregon correspondent also charged that Grover had arranged bribes to assure the appointment of Stephen Chadwick (yet another veteran of the 1857 constitutional con-

vention) to the governorship upon his resignation; ibid., July 23, 1877. A different version of the electoral college affair in Oregon, as full of charges of scheming and bribery, is in Clark (ed.), *Pharisee Among the Philistines*, 225–227.

85. MacColl, *Shaping of a City*, 61–64.

86. *Congressional Record*, 45th Cong., 3d sess., 1267. The assessment of Mitchell is from Mary Roberts Coolidge, *Chinese Immigration* (New York: Henry Holt, 1909), 132, 217.

87. *Congressional Record*, 46th Cong., 1st sess., 128; ibid., 47th Cong., 2d sess., 1090.

88. *Oregonian*, July 5, 1884.

89. Ibid.

90. Deady to [ ] Cole, July 31, 1860; Deady Papers, Oregon Historical Society.

91. *Oregonian*, November 16, 1861, included the following report: "The *Advertiser* furnishes us with a chapter on the sedition laws of John Adams. It says that the law was aimed to destroy democratic newspapers. It is a long time since that law was passed and repealed, probably both took place before the *Advertiser* man was born. We have heard that the law was intended to prevent 'sedition,' another name for treason and rebellion. We were interested not long since in learning that the expediency of repeal of that law was doubted by a gentleman so well qualified to judge, as Judge Deady of this State—we speak with all respect— who had given the law a serious examination. We learn further, that he expressed himself in this wise, that had the law been continued, after repealing an objectionable provision, it would have enabled the government to put down, without difficulty the present rebellion. It covered those cases of unrepentant treason, such, as we suppose, have been frequently presented in the publication of this Portland *Advertiser*. Such being the case we have reasons for the hostility so often exhibited toward the long dead and buried 'sedition law.' It is fair to say that Governor Curry's opinion is entirely opposed to that of Judge Deady, and public opinion will readily settle the matter which is the more worthy of respect."

92. Deady to Nesmith, May 16, 1861; Nesmith Papers, Oregon Historical Society. The description of Jefferson as the "Coryphaeus of the sect" is in Deady to Applegate, November 12, 1861; Deady Papers, Oregon Historical Society (unless otherwise specified, subsequent references to Deady's correspondence can be found in the Deady Papers).

93. See, for example, Deady to Applegate, November 8, 1862; Philip Henry Overmeyer, "The Oregon Justinian: A Life of Matthew Paul Deady" (Ph.D. diss., University of Minnesota, 1935), 173. In an 1862 letter Deady had the following to say about the Democratic party: "The Republicans are in the possession of the government and the country and the government and country are engaged in a war with the South to maintain the authority over that people and country which the laws and constitution give them. Whatever may be the issue of it, while it lasts, no party can exist in opposition to it on this question, and accomplish any practical good to the country. Those who oppose the government on that question at the polls and on the stump, will be necessarily regarded as more or less influenced by the same feelings as those who oppose it in the field with arms. Besides no party can or ought to exist on a mere negation. . . . In short, you cannot, with propriety, and without forever destroying your future usefulness, organize a party in opposition to the war, and to do so in opposition to the Republi-

cans simply because they are Republicans is merely a scramble [over] who shall have the offices.

"Like many other great parties and even nations, the Dem party has run its course. It belongs to the past. It has gone to the tomb, and no power that I know can resurrect it, unless it be him who called to life the son of the widow of rain, and between you and me I don't think he will" (Deady to Joseph Watts, January 20, 1862).

94. Applegate's intervention in behalf of Deady with his friend (Attorney General Bates) is discussed in Overmeyer, "Oregon Justinian," 196.

95. Deady to Applegate, November 8, 1862.

96. Quoted in Overmeyer, "Oregon Justinian," 173.

97. Deady's comment is found in his decision of *Chapman v. Toy Long,* 5 F. Cas. 497 (C.C.D. Or. 1876) (No. 2,610); quoted in Ralph James Mooney, "Matthew Deady and the Federal Judicial Response to Racism in the Early West," *Oregon Law Review* 63 (1989): 589n.117.

98. As Mooney points out (ibid., 589), Deady did not rule on the Oregon constitution; he only pointed out that the Burlingame Treaty of 1868 likely voided the measure in the Oregon constitution. In the case in which this came up (*Chapman v. Toy Long,* 5 F. Cas. 497 [C.C.D. Or. 1876] [No. 2,610]), the constitutional issue was not relevant.

99. Against the crowds, Deady recorded in his journal, he advised the governor "to issue a proclamation . . . stating the rights of the Chinese here and warning all persons against undertaking to carry out the direction of the [anti-Chinese] Congress and the penalty they would incur if they did" (quoted in Overmeyer, "Oregon Justinian," 172).

100. Mooney's illuminating discussion of Deady's racial views (part of an extended treatment of Deady's judicial decisions relating to race) is in "Matthew Deady and the Federal Judicial Response to Racism," 627–637.

101. Quoted in Overmeyer, "Oregon Justinian," 173.

102. *Daub v. Northern Pacific Railway Co.,* 18 Fed. Rep. 626 (C.C.D. Or. 1884).

103. *Gilmore v. Northern Pacific Railroad Co.,* 18 Fed. Rep. 866 (C.C.D. Or. 1884). The significance of this decision is suggested by Lawrence Friedman's citation of it (as precedent) in *A History of the American Law* (New York: Touchstone Books, 1973), 422.

104. Matthew Deady, *An Address to the Graduating Class of Wallamet [sic] University* (June 1, 1876) (Portland: George H. Himes, 1876), 8, 21.

105. Matthew Deady, *Oration Delivered at Roseburg* (July 4, 1877) (Portland: George H. Himes, 1877), 19; see also *Oration Delivered at Portland* (July 4, 1885) (Portland: George H. Himes, 1885).

106. Deady, *Address to the Graduate Class of Wallamet University,* 20.

107. Ibid.

108. Clark (ed.), *Pharisee Among the Philistines,* 521 (August 13, 1887).

109. Deady, *Oration Delivered at Roseburg,* 19; *Oration Delivered at Portland.*

CHAPTER NINE: INDUSTRY AND EXODUS

1. Thomas Fitch, "Nevada," *Harper's New Monthly Magazine* 31 (August 1865): 318–319.

2. Ibid., 321–322.

3. Ibid., 322–323.

4. See appendix 1C.

5. Quoted in the *Sacramento Daily Union*, August 19, 1864.

6. The vote was 10,375 (89 percent) for ratification, 1,284 (11 percent) opposed; Russell Elliott, *History of Nevada* (Lincoln: University of Nebraska Press, 1973), 86.

7. See Russell Elliott, *Servant of Power: A Political Biography of Senator William M. Stewart* (Reno: University of Nevada Press, 1983), 43–45. North ultimately received partial vindication by court-appointed referees who, while they did not award North the damages he sought, did hold that Stewart's charges were slanderous. See also the *Virginia Daily Union*, August 24, 1864.

8. *Gold Hill Evening News*, August 14, 1864.

9. Quoted in ibid., August 11, 1864.

10. In 1865 North joined the exodus from Nevada, first pursuing his interests as a carpetbagger in Tennessee. In 1870 he returned to the Far West, helping to found a cooperative colony in Riverside, California. See Merlin Stonehouse, *John Wesley North and the Reform Frontier* (Minneapolis: University of Minnesota Press, 1965), 176 and passim; Tom Patterson, *A Colony for California: Riverside's First Hundred Years* (Riverside: Press-Enterprise, 1971).

11. Eliot Lord, *Comstock Mining and Miners* (1883; reprint, Berkeley, Calif.: Howell-North Books, 1959), 171; the referee's report is discussed at 165–171 and passim.

12. *Virginia Daily Union*, August 24, 1864. Two days later the editors backpedaled a bit, insisting that "we did not express any opinion approving the one ledge theory." The communication concluded, however: "The interests of the community are suffering very much from this contest between the two theories, which is in fact the most fruitful source of litigation we have, and it is very desirable to put an end to it. Many of our citizens must suffer from the final decision when it comes, whichever way it is decided. It would be better for either party to compromise now than continue the litigation. The moral atmosphere of this region would be purified by such a course" (ibid., August 26, 1864.)

13. *Gold Hill Evening News*, June 17, 1864.

14. Charles H. Shinn, *The Story of the Mine, as Illustrated by the Great Comstock Lode of Nevada* (1896; reprint, Reno: University of Nevada Press, 1980), 163.

15. On the creation of the "fortified monopoly," see ibid., 167; Lord, *Comstock Mining and Miners*, 249–256; Elliott, *History of Nevada*, 128.

16. Gabriel Kolko, *Main Currents in Modern American History* (New York: Pantheon Books, 1984), chap. 1.

17. As Elliott, *History of Nevada*, 128–129, points out, Sharon reached an understanding with Jones and Hayward, in which he affirmed the latter's control of the Crown Point Mine by exchanging his stock in it for theirs in the Belcher Mine. This later provided the margin that preserved the bank's properties on the Comstock Lode.

18. Lord, *Comstock Mining and Miners*, chap. 16; Elliott, *History of Nevada*, 132–137; Grant Smith, *The History of the Comstock Lode, 1850–1920*, Geology and Mining Series no. 37, *University of Nevada Bulletin* (July 1943), chaps. 13 and 17.

19. Popular treatments include George Lyman, *Ralston's Ring: California*

Plunders the Comstock Lode (New York: Charles Scribner, 1937); Oscar Lewis, *Silver Kings: The Lives and Times of Mackay, Fair, Flood, and O'Brien—Lords of the Nevada Comstock Lode* (New York: Alfred A. Knopf, 1947); Ethel Van Vick Tomes, *Rocket of the Comstock: The Story of John William Mackay* (New York: Ballantine Books, 1973).

20. Shinn, *Story of the Mine*, 175–177; Dan De Quille [William Wright], *The Big Bonanza: An American Classic—The Story of the Discovery and Development of Nevada's Comstock Lode*, intro. Oscar Lewis (1876; reprint, New York: Alfred A. Knopf, 1947), 399–408.

21. Shinn, *Story of the Mine*, chap. 19.

22. Lord, *Comstock Mining and Miners*, 347.

23. *Gold Hill News*, January 9, 1866, quoted in Mark Wyman, *Hard-Rock Epic: Western Miners and the Industrial Revolution, 1860–1910* (Berkeley and Los Angeles: University of California Press, 1979), 10.

24. Lord, *Comstock Mining and Miners*, 389.

25. Shinn, *Story of the Mine*, 226.

26. Ibid., 241.

27. Richard Lingenfelter, *Hard Rock Miners: A History of the Mining Labor Movement in the American West, 1863–1893* (Berkeley and Los Angeles: University of California Press, 1974), 7.

28. John Rowe, *The Hard-Rock Men: Cornish Immigrants and the North American Mining Frontier* (New York: Barnes & Noble Books, 1974), 185–191.

29. Lingenfelter, *Hard Rock Miners*, 30.

30. Quoted in ibid., 33.

31. Lord, *Comstock Mining and Miners*, 126.

32. Lingenfelter, *Hard Rock Miners*, 34.

33. Ibid., 37, 39–40.

34. Ibid., 132.

35. Lord, *Comstock Mining and Miners*, 266. See also Lingenfelter, *Hard Rock Miners*, 64.

36. Quoted in Lingenfelter, *Hard Rock Miners*, 43.

37. Shinn, *Story of the Mine*, 251.

38. Alexander Saxton, *The Indispensable Enemy: Labor and the Anti-Chinese Movement in California* (Berkeley and Los Angeles: University of California Press, 1971).

39. Lingenfelter, *Hard Rock Miners*, 60, 63.

40. Ibid., 54–58, observes that the miners' unions were able to veto unfriendly legislation but for the most part were unsuccessful in getting the state legislature to pass laws specifically in their interest.

41. Yerington to A. N. Towne, January 11, 1879; quoted in Elliott, *History of Nevada*, 160.

42. Ibid., 162. The exception was James Nye, governor during the territorial period and U.S. senator from 1865 to 1873. Nye never gained the trust nor support of a corporate patron. When at the end of his term he returned to Nevada to make a try for reelection his bid was ignored.

43. Russell Elliott has pointed out that both Sharon and Fair were largely absent from the Senate during their terms and displayed little interest in the work of the legislature; ibid., 163–166, 394; and Elliott, *Servant of Power*, 91.

44. Elliott, *Servant of Power,* 64.

45. Ibid., 65.

46. During his first two terms in the Senate, Stewart was best known for his authorship of the national mining law of 1866, which gave statutory authority to the mining regulations, drawn from the makeshift arrangements in the California mining camps during the gold rush, through which the right to claim and work land in the public domain without fee was institutionalized in federal law— defeating proposals that the federal government sell mineral lands on the public domain as a means of reducing the national debt swollen by the Civil War. In addition, in service to the Central Pacific, Stewart opposed aid to that company's adversary, the Union Pacific. For the Bank of California, he blocked Senate action on a bill to assist Adolph Sutro, whose scheme to build a ventilating and transportation tunnel into the Comstock Lode mines threatened to break the control over water and transportation possessed by the Union Mine and Milling Company. See ibid., 47–55, 66–82.

47. This material is covered in ibid., 80–100.

48. Ibid., chaps. 7–11.

49. The system pioneered by Stewart is dealt with in Jerome E. Edwards, *Pat McCarran: Political Boss of Nevada* (Reno: University of Nevada Press, 1982), 130 and, generally, chap. 7. Nevada as a "rotten borough" is the subject of Gilman Ostrander, *Nevada: The Great Rotten Borough, 1859–1964* (New York: Alfred A. Knopf, 1966).

50. See appendix 1. I have traced the delegates in 1870, 1875, and 1880 through three sources: the index to the 1870 U.S. census for Nevada at the Nevada Historical Society; *Census of the Inhabitants of the State of Nevada, 1875,* 2 vols. (Carson City: John J. Hill, 1875); and Ronald Vern Jackson, ed., *Nevada 1880 State Census* (Salt Lake City: Accelerated Index Systems, 1979). The five men mentioned in the text are Gilman Folsom, a lumberman from Washoe County, who died in 1917 in Carson City; George Gibson of Ormsby County, a newspaper editor in 1860 who was still listed in the 1880 census as a resident of Carson City (though with no occupation); J. W. Haines, a farmer and merchant from Genoa (Douglas Co.) who died there after 1900; A. J. Lockwood, who is listed in the 1880 census as a carpenter in Empire City, Ormsby County; and J. G. McClinton, of Virginia City, the only mining region delegate still in Nevada as of 1875 (according to the state census), though he was missing from the 1880 federal census. In the late 1880s and 1890s Haines became a part of Stewart's machine, as his lengthy correspondence with the senator reveals. See especially Stewart to Haines, April 25, 1888; February 7, July 8, 1889; January 31, 1891; January 4, May 25, June 21, August 5, 1892; April 18, 1893; December 27, 1894; February 18, 1897; and Haines to Stewart, September 18, December 19, 1896; Stewart Papers, Nevada Historical Society, Reno. The many moves of John H. Kinkhead, who ultimately died in Nevada, are described in note 51, below.

51. The exception is John H. Kinkhead (or Kinkead). Kinkhead settled in Carson City in 1859, where he operated a branch of a merchant house owned with his father-in-law and headquartered in Marysville. Nye appointed him territorial treasurer in 1862, and he served in both constitutional conventions. In 1867, Kinkhead left Nevada for Alaska upon its purchase by the United States. He remained there until 1871, then returning to Nevada, where he established

another mercantile business in Unionville, a short-lived mining town in Humboldt County. In 1879 he was elected governor of the state. After the close of his term he was appointed territorial governor of Alaska. When Cleveland did not renew his appointment in 1888, Kinkhead returned to Nevada, settling in Carson City, where he remained a businessman until his death in 1904. See J. H. Kinkhead, "In Nevada and Alaska," Dictation to H. H. Bancroft, Bancroft Library, University of California, Berkeley; Myrtle Myles, *Nevada's Governors, from Territorial Days to the Present* (Sparks, Nev.: Western Printing and Publishing, 1972), 25–29.

52. For example, when Stewart renewed his charges against North in the summer of 1864, cards in defense of the judge signed by local attorneys appeared in the local newspapers. Among those who took a public stand for North, and against Stewart, were John Collins, Charles De Long, and Thomas Fitch. See the *Virginia Daily Union*, August 24, 1864.

53. I have found only tantalizing hints about Dunne's later career. In 1874 he left Nevada with an appointment as chief justice of the Arizona territorial supreme court (while George Williams was attorney general). There he raised a storm by opposing secular education and advocating public support for parochial schools. Among others, the *Alta California* (November 3, 1875) called for his dismissal, which came within a year of his appointment. (See also John S. Goff, "The Appointment, Tenure, and Removal of Territorial Judges: Arizona—A Case Study," *American Journal of Legal History* 12 [1968]: 216, 226.) From Arizona Dunne apparently moved first to New Mexico, then Utah, and then Chicago, where he was a railroad lawyer. By the early 1880s he was in Florida, "at the head of the San Antonio colony." On February 27, 1884, the *New Mexico Review* reported that "Pope Leo XIII has conferred on Edmund Dunne, formerly Chief Justice of Arizona . . . title of count, with the reversion to his male descendants." In the late 1890s, while still residing in Florida, he renewed his acquaintance with William Stewart, whom he tried to get to support his appointment to the U.S. Supreme Court, citing references from Cardinal Gibbons, Archbishop Chappella, and Monsignor Blenk, "all of whom," he advised Stewart, "know me and express great desire that I should be honored with this appointment." Stewart's response, if any, is not known. See E. F. Dunne to William Stewart, December 2, 1898; January 13, April 11, 1900; Stewart Papers, Nevada Historical Society.

54. Romanzo Adams, *Taxation in Nevada: A History* (Carson City: Nevada State Printing Office, 1918), 76–78 and passim. The case mentioned in the text is *Gibson v. Mason, Treasurer of Ormsby County* (5 Nev. 257–260). Curiously enough, George Gibson—who questioned the subsidy in the courts (the respondent in the appeal before the supreme court)—was a "cow county" ally of Johnson in the 1864 constitutional convention.

55. Howard Brett Melendy, *The Governors of California* (Georgetown, Calif.: Talisman Press, 1965), 77–78.

56. See Lingenfelter, *Hard Rock Miners*, 35, 37, 47.

57. Nye's election as senator was surrounded by charges that he won only after promising Stewart control of the patronage; see Elliott, *History of Nevada*, 89.

58. Quoted in "California's Bantam Cock: The Journals of Charles E. De

Long, 1854–1863; (Appendix): Outline of De Long's Career after December 11, 1862," ed. Carl I. Wheat, *California Historical Society Quarterly* 11 (1932), 50n.

59. Ibid.

60. Quoted in the *Alta California*, May 15, 1870.

61. Payson J. Treat, *Diplomatic Relations Between the United States and Japan, 1853–1895*, 3 vols. (1938; reprint, Gloucester, Mass.: Peter Smith, 1963), I: 524.

62. De Long's insistence that he opposed the coolie trade is found in dispatches quoted in ibid., 460; generally, see 450–493, esp. 488–493. De Long, who also represented the Kingdom of Hawaii during his time in Yokohama, narrowly avoided involvement in another controversy over the transportation of bound laborers—this time indentured Japanese laborers headed for the island kingdom; see Hilary Conroy, *The Japanese Frontier in Hawaii, 1868–1898* (Berkeley and Los Angeles: University of California Press, 1953), 44–47.

63. De Long did not leave his post for many months after his forced resignation, as his, and his successor's, instructions were lost or delayed; see Treat, *Diplomatic Relations* 1: 520–525.

64. See, for example, the *New York Times*, April 27, May 3, 1873; April 10, 1874.

65. Treat, *Diplomatic Relations* 1:524.

66. See the *Territorial Enterprise* (Virginia City), June 13–October 20, 1874. De Long also blamed his defeat on unnamed mining corporations that, according to his reckoning, disliked his support in the constitutional convention of taxation of mining property.

67. *Territorial Enterprise*, February 8, 1876. De Long offered to give half his salary to the widow of the recently deceased district attorney. His run for Congress is noted in Wheat (ed.), "California's Bantam Cock; Appendix," 51.

68. See, for example, the *Alta California*, September 16, 1876.

69. Charles E. De Long to James R. De Long, March 8, 1870; quoted in Wheat (ed.), "California's Bantam Cock; Appendix," 63–64.

70. Ibid., 64.

71. Ibid.

72. Fitch's career can be reconstructed from *Western Carpetbagger: The Extraordinary Memoirs of "Senator" Thomas Fitch*, ed. Eric N. Moody (Reno: University of Nevada Press, 1978); *Biographical Directory of the American Congress, 1774–1949* (Washington, D.C.: Government Printing Office, 1950), 1160. On his life in California and Nevada in the early 1860s, see Moody (ed.), *Western Carpetbagger*, chap. 5; Myron Angel, ed., *History of Nevada* (Oakland, Calif.: Thompson & West, 1881), 89–90.

73. See, for example, the *Territorial Enterprise*, August 20, September 6, 8, 1868; June 9; July 1, 20; August 19; October 6, 1870; *Alta California*, June 13, 1870; June 26, September 29, 1876; *Sacramento Daily Union*, October 21, 1876; December 31, 1895; *Call* (San Francisco), October 29, 1908.

74. On Fitch's involvement in the theater, see Margaret G. Watson, *Silver Theatre: Amusements of the Mining Frontier in Early Nevada, 1850–1864* (Glendale, Calif.: Arthur H. Clark, 1964), 143–144; Lewis, *Silver Kings*, 26; George E. Packham, "Reminiscences of an Active Life," *Nevada Historical Society Papers* 2 (1917–1920): 15–16. These and other sources are summarized by Rosemary Gipson, who covers Fitch's theater activities in Arizona after 1879 in "Tom Fitch's Other

Side," *Journal of Arizona History* 16 (Autumn 1975): 287–300. Fitch's play "Old Titles" was panned in the *Alta California*, November 12, 1876. On his utopian novel, *Better Days*, see pp. 341–343.

75. Williams opposed the Central Pacific on the grounds that its proposed line, which was to enter Oregon from the east and reach the Willamette Valley at a point near Eugene, bypassed southern Oregon and thereby cut it off from any rail connections. See the *Oregonian*, June 1, 5, 1870; and *Territorial Enterprise*, May 5, 10, 1870. Fitch's activities in behalf of the Central Pacific while congressman are noted by Howard Lamar in *The Far Southwest: A Territorial History* (New York: W. W. Norton, 1970), 460, 461n.7.

76. See, for example, the *New York Times*, November 30, 1871.

77. See Gordon Bakken, *Rocky Mountain Constitution Making, 1850–1912* (Westport, Conn.: Greenwood Press, 1987), 11.

78. Thomas Fitch, "Statement," Bancroft Library, University of California, Berkeley; Dale Morgan et al., "The State of Deseret," *Utah Historical Quarterly* 8 (April, July, and October, 1940): 119–153; Howard Lamar, "Carpetbaggers Full of Dreams: A Functional View of the Arizona Pioneer Politician," *Arizona and the West* 7 (Autumn 1965): 201.

79. See the *Pioche [Nevada] Weekly Record*, September 24, 1872, which reported that during the campaign Fitch praised Greeley's call for universal amnesty and universal suffrage while damning Grant's Reconstruction policy for the "destruction wrought on the South by carpetbaggers—'subalterns' [of Grant sent to] feast upon their [southern] misfortunes."

80. Fitch's moves from place to place are charted in Gipson, "Tom Fitch's Other Side," 293–296; and Moody (ed.), *Western Carpetbagger*, chap. 7 and passim.

81. *Alta California*, October 26, 1874.

82. See ibid., September 29, 1876.

83. *New York Times*, September 18, 1882.

84. In 1879 Fitch was elected to the Arizona territorial legislature, and served as speaker of the lower house. During the Arizona governorship of John Frémont, moreover, he was known as "a veritable Richelieu behind the chair of Gov. Fremont" (quoted in Gipson, "Tom Fitch's Other Side," 290). He was involved with Frémont in a notorious lottery scheme (ibid.) and for a time was Wyatt Earp's attorney (see *I Married Wyatt Earp: The Recollections of Josephine Sarah Marcus Earp*, ed. Glenn C. Boyer [Tucson: University of Arizona Press, 1981], 75n.16, 100). As Howard Lamar points out, however, Fitch's "exact role in Arizona remains ill defined" (Lamar, *Far Southwest*, 469n.38).

85. See Fitch to Stewart, March 20, 1906; Stewart Papers, Nevada Historical Society. In this instance Fitch desired appointment as chief justice of the Hawaiian territorial supreme court. Stewart refused to recommend him.

86. Fitch presented his understanding of evolutionary doctrine in "The Invisible Police," a lecture he delivered many times in the 1880s; *Call*, September 4, 1882. In addition, see his comments on Robert Ingersoll and on Christianity, in Moody (ed.), *Western Carpetbagger*, 247–256, 257–272, respectively.

87. Alan Trachtenberg, *The Incorporation of America: Culture and Society in the Gilded Age* (New York: Hill & Wang, 1982), 39 and passim. See also John Kasson, *Civilizing the Machine: Technology and Republican Values in America, 1776–1900* (New York: Penguin Books, 1977), 189 and passim.

88. The book was originally published in 1891 by the Fitches' "Better Days Publishing Company" of San Francisco; a revised edition appeared in 1892, published by F. J. Schulte in Chicago.

89. All the quotations regarding *Better Days* are from two uncited and undated reviews of the book in the Biographical Information File, California State Library, Sacramento.

90. As Rosemary Gipson, "Tom Fitch's Other Side," 296, observes, "The central character . . . is what Tom Fitch would like to have been, or what he thought he would like to have been, had he become fabulously rich in his mining ventures."

91. See, for example, Lewis Perry, *Intellectual Life in America: A History* (New York: Franklin Watts, 1984), 291–294.

92. *Call*, September 4, 1882.

93. *Address on the Life and Character of Col. Edward D. Baker* (Placerville, Calif.: Office of the *Placerville Republican*, 1862), 1.

94. *Territorial Enterprise*, April 11, 1873.

95. *Gold Hill News*, May 29, 1865; January 5, 1866; *Virginia Evening Bulletin*, January 25, 1869; *Territorial Enterprise*, March 11, 1868.

96. See Elizabeth Cady Stanton, Susan B. Anthony, and Matilda Joslyn Gage, eds., *History of Women's Suffrage* (Rochester, N.Y.: Charles Mann, 1887), 3:752–757; Ruth Barnes Moynihan, *Rebel for Rights: Abigail Scott Duniway* (New Haven: Yale University Press, 1983), 85.

97. *Call*, May 20, 1871; *Territorial Enterprise*, April 11, 1873.

98. *Territorial Enterprise*, April 11, May 17, 1871.

99. Ibid., April 11, 1873.

100. *William Lloyd Garrison, 1805–1879: The Story of His Life, Told by His Children*, 4 vols. (New York: Century, 1885–1889), 4:301; *Daily Evening Bulletin*, May 2, 1879.

101. The following quotes are from the *Call*, February 1, 3, 1882.

INDEX

Abernethy, George, 59
Abrego, José, 39
Adams, John, 306
Adams, Romanzo, 334
Adams, William Lysander, 64; author of *Treason, Stratagems, and Spoils*, 55–56; antipartyism of, 60
Agriculture: in California, 235, 239–241; in Oregon, 2, 42, 26–48, 273, 275–277; in Nevada, 79
Alabama Claims Commission, 296
Alcalde: office of, 24–25; revolts against, 28–29
Alvarado, Juan (California governor), 19, 36, 107
American Bible Society, 52–53, 165
American party. *See* Know-Nothing (American) party
"American school" of ethnology, 121–122
American Tract Society, 165
Anderson, Charles: quoted, 93, 94
Anti-Democrats, Oregon: and temperance, 58; sabbatarianism of, 58; nativism of, 58, 59, 60; weakness of partisan organizations, 58–61; on slavery, 64; and statehood, 65; political culture of, 140; in Oregon Constitutional Convention, 162; and charge of faction, 174–175; on corporations, 182–183, 187
Applegate, E. L.; on donation land claims, 398n.15
Applegate, Jesse (delegate, Oregon Constitutional Convention), 162, 172; with-

drawal from Constitutional Convention, 425n.63
Ashley, Congressman James (Ohio): promotes Nevada statehood, 88
Ashworth, John, 9
Atkinson, George: quoted, 44

Baker, Edward Dickinson, 148, 168, 169, 203, 205, 209, 343; eulogy for David Broderick, 250; elected to Senate from Oregon, 282, 283, 288; and David Logan, 289–290
Baker, Jean: quoted, 58, 139–140
Ball, Nathaniel (delegate, Nevada Constitutional Convention), 332
Bank Crowd. *See* Bank of California
Bank of California: failure of, 252; in Nevada, 314, 317, 318, 329, 334, 335, 339, 340; "fortified monopoly" of, 317–319, 326, 327
Banks: debate in 1849 California Constitutional Convention, 122–125, 418n.92; debate in Oregon Constitutional Convention, 181–182; debate in 1864 Nevada Constitutional Convention, 220–221; in Oregon, 276
Banks, James (delegate, Nevada Constitutional Convention), 332; on loyalty oath, 215–216
Bates, U.S. Attorney General Edward, 306
Beadle, J. H.: quoted, 269
Bear Flag insurgence, 22, 107
Beerstecher, Charles: quoted, 255

461

INDEX

471

holder liability; Suffrage; Women's
property rights
Oregon Railway and Navigation Company,
274, 275
Oregon Steamship Navigation Company,
274, 275

Pacific railroad, 71; as symbol of Union,
219–220; as remedy for economic de-
pression in Nevada, 220; as image in
Republican politics, 251
Pedrorena, Miguel de (delegate, California
Constitutional Convention), 107, 372
Pico, Antonio (delegate, California Consti-
tutional Convention), 32
Pierce, Franklin, 149
Pitt-Stevens, Emily, 345
Poindexter, George, 118
Political culture, 6, 386n.13
Pomeroy, Earl: quoted, 48
Popular sovereignty, 161, 172, 249, 306
Portland, 270, 276; levee of, in debate on
judiciary article, 176, 427n.98
Price, Rodman (delegate, California Con-
stitutional Convention), 106, 237
Prim, Paine Page (delegate, Oregon Con-
stitutional Convention): on Chinese re-
striction, 181
Progressivism, 255, 258, 299

Quincy, Edmund: quoted, 196

Railroad subsidy: Debate in 1864 Nevada
Constitutional Convention, 191, 213,
214, 218–221, 226–228
Ralston, William, 317, 318
Reese, John, 73
Religion: in debate of Oregon Constitu-
tional Convention, 178
Reno, 318
Republican party, 166, 171, 202; in Cali-
fornia, 204; fusion in California with
Douglas Democrats, 249; and ideology
of corporate capitalism, 251; promotes
Chinese exclusion, 252, 253; position
on corporations in 1879 California
Constitutional Convention, 255; fusion
in Oregon with Douglas Democrats,
281, 282; in Oregon, 283; migration of
Democrats into, 292–293
Richardson, William, 200

Riley, Bennett C. (military governor of
California), 30–31, 34, 106, 114, 138
Rohrbough, Malcolm, 8
Roosevelt, Theodore, 298
Rowe, John, 323
Royce, Josiah: quoted, 105

Sacramento, 27, 28, 72, 238, 239, 394n.51;
election of delegates to California Constitutional Convention, 33
Salem, Oregon, 5, 53, 66–69, 147; compared to Monterey, 67; population, 67;
family and household structure, 67; occupational structure, 67–68
Salem Clique, 55, 56, 60, 65, 176
Salt Lake City, 73
San Francisco, 26, 28, 106, 238, 239, 269,
270, 435–436n.5; movement against
military rule, 31; election of convention
delegates, 32–33
San Joaquin district: election of convention
delegates, 33
San Jose, 238; election of convention dele-
gates, 32
Saxton, Alexander, 252
Seattle, 277
Semple, Robert (delegate, California Con-
stitutional Convention), 24, 105, 107,
123; president of California Constitu-
tional Convention, 40; on free Negro
prohibition, 127
Senkewicz, Robert, 247
Serra, Junípero, 16, 17
Seward, William M., 77
Shannon, Davis (delegate, Oregon Consti-
tutional Convention): on free Negro
prohibition, 419n.108
Shannon, William (delegate, California
Constitutional Convention): on free
Negro prohibition, 128–129
Sharon, William, 330, 332; engineers Bank
of California monopoly of Comstock
Lode, 317–318
Shattuck, Erasmus (delegate, Oregon Con-
stitutional Convention), 170; on corpo-
rations, 183
Sherman, William Tecumseh, 201, 262
Sherwood, Winfield (delegate, California
Constitutional Convention), 106; on
race and citizenship, 126
Shinn, Charles: on Comstock Lode, 318,
320, 321, 322, 323

Compositor: G&S Typesetters, Inc.
Text: 10/12 Baskerville
Display: Baskerville
Printer: Braun-Brumfield, Inc.
Binder: Braun-Brumfield, Inc.